# The ASTD E-Learning Handbook

## Other books of interest from McGraw-Hill:

*The 2002 ASTD Training and Performance Yearbook*
   Edited by John A. Woods and James W. Cortada

*The 2001/2002 ASTD Distance Learning Yearbook*
   Edited by Karen Mantyla and John A. Woods

# The ASTD E-Learning Handbook

**Allison Rossett**

**McGraw-Hill**

New York   Chicago   San Francisco   Lisbon   London   Madrid
Mexico City   Milan   New Delhi   San Juan
Seoul   Singapore   Sydney   Toronto

# McGraw-Hill

*A Division of The **McGraw·Hill** Companies*

Copyright © 2002 by The McGraw-Hill Companies, Inc. All rights reserved. Printed in the United States of America. Except as permitted under the United States Copyright Act of 1976, no part of this publication may be reproduced or distributed in any form or by any means or stored in a data base or retrieval system, without the prior written permission of the publisher.

2 3 4 5 6 7 8 9 0 AGM/AGM 0 9 8 7 6 5 4 3 2

ISBN: 0-07-138796-X

The sponsoring editor for this book is Richard Narramore. Maureen Harper was the manufacturing supervisor. Tama Harris was the editing supervisor. Editorial, design, and production services were provided by CWL Publishing Enterprises, Madison, WI, www.cwlpub.com.

Printed and bound by Quebecor World Martinsburg.

This publication is designed to provide accurate and authoritative information in regard to the subject matter covered. It is sold with the understanding that the publisher is not engaged in rendering legal, accounting, or other professional service. If legal advice or other expert assistance is required, the services of a competent professional person should be sought.
>    —*From a declaration of principles adopted by a committee of the American Bar Association and a committee of publishers*

All McGraw-Hill books are available at special quantity discounts to use as premiums and sales promotions, or for use in corporate training programs. For more information, please write to the Director of Special Sales, Professional Publishing, McGraw-Hill, Two Penn Plaza, New York, NY 10121. Or contact your local bookstore.

 This book is printed on recycled, acid-free paper containing a minimum of 50% recycled de-inked fiber.

# Contents

# Foreword

## Tina Sung
## President and CEO, ASTD

During this year of dot.com boom and bust, I've come to expect technology to surprise me on a regular basis, and so far it hasn't let me down. At the ASTD International Conference in Orlando I heard some talk about the peer-to-peer exchange of learning through Napster-like networks of PCs. So I typed "learnster.com" into a search engine, and sure enough, a Canadian site materialized, although it was still under construction.

Soon I began to encounter more and more predictions that peer-to-peer computing was not just the next wave for the Internet, but the next wave for e-learning. I read that Napster had no users in 1997 and 40 million users in 2000 and I quickly imagined a network of learners spontaneously sharing knowledge through their PCs or more likely through some wireless form of distributed computing. After all, computer developers are already looking beyond the desktop to a new generation of software that will augment human activity and intelligence.

I believe that a worldwide learning network will arise because there is more possibility for such new forms of learning than there has ever been in the history of this profession. And that has presented us with a paradox: Our profession is experiencing change at stunning speed but still feeling the need to reinforce and build upon the fundamentals. We want to capture the remarkable power of technology, yet hold true to the traditional values we've nurtured over the years.

We are a community of practice, but also a community of learners, trying to keep ahead of the waves of change. Whether you are wading eagerly into the e-learning ocean for a bracing swim, or pacing the shore looking for the lifeguard, you cannot ignore the impact of e-learning. It is the transformational event of our professional lives.

As the collection of articles in this yearbook makes clear, the profession is rethinking its role in an e-learning world. So I encourage you to think of this book as two things: a peer to peer exchange among a community of learners, and a handbook for this year's stage of the e-learning revolution.

*Tina Sung is the President and CEO of ASTD based in Alexandria, Va. Sung is recognized as an award-winning leader and expert in the Quality movement, having served as the Director of the Federal Quality Consulting Group, a team that provides consulting services to executive level government leaders. She is a founding member and former vice chair of the Asian American Government Executives Network, a member of the Society for Organizational Learning, the Alliance for Business Excellence, the American Society of Association Executives, the American Society for Quality, the Service Leadership Forum, and the Senior Executives Association.*

# Preface

As little as one year ago, this would have been a different book. Most authors would have gushed with enthusiasm. That handbook would have sung the praises of e-learning, touting the benefits, and encouraging participation in this great and inspiring adventure. Indeed this one does this and appropriately so.

But it also has a more muted tone. While many authors remain ecstatic about e-learning, myself included, we are cautiously so. We admit the challenges and describe strategies to increase odds for success. We attend to the nitty-gritty details associated with topics like converting classroom training to the Web, collaborating with IT, standards, objects, framing questions for online communities, games that teach, fertilizing the culture, and expanding the definition of e-learning to include knowledge management.

My purpose here is to support people who have begun to move beyond their e-learning honeymoons. No longer besotted with the e-learning concept and technology, readers and writers are ready for the negotiations, associations and evaluations that come next. Here you will find perspectives, guidance and tools for those who are ready to do the heavy lifting involved in translating e-learning promises into performance.

What's a learning professional to do? What do we know about what constitutes effective e-learning? Where do e-learning investments go awry? How do we align organizations around e-learning? What's next? How do we take advantage of so many new opportunities without being swept under?

Enter *The ASTD E-Learning Handbook*. This book gathers the best ideas, strategies, research and examples together in one place, with the promise of a new collection following in the near future. Designed to save professionals the trouble of reading dozens of trade periodicals, this handbook provides current, cutting-edge thinking, approaches and cases. Here we've gathered recent print and online articles and white papers, and added fresh commentary and ideas from leading sources in the industry. Note the resource directory intended to lure professionals into further study on their own.

What will you find in *The ASTD E-Learning Handbook*?

- **A focus on your questions.** The book is for you if you've been wondering: What is e-learning and why all the excitement? What are others doing? How is the role of the training and development professional changed and changing? What do I need to know and do? Where can I go to continue my education? Where can I go for references and examples? Are there new ways to think about e-learning, ways that take me beyond a classroom metaphor? What does e-learning have to do with e-commerce? What is blended learning? Is anybody in my industry doing anything like this?

- **A focus on what might keep you up at night.** The gap between what is promised and delivered can be daunting. At best, the authors in the handbook will help you sleep through the night. At the least, they'll give you a heads-up on the vexing challenges to come. How do I execute on the promises associated with e-learning? How can I measure return on investment from e-learning? How can I create online questions and enhance online community? How do I pick effective software? What are the myths surrounding e-learning and how do I work around them?

- **A comprehensive e-learning sourcebook.** The handbook is divided into six parts. The first part tours the current state of e-learning, including articles that paint pictures about involvement, persistence and satisfaction. Part Two is all about developing great e-learning, including guidance for vendors attempting to create learning software, and for internal professionals who must make decisions about which software to choose. Part Three focuses on management and implementation. Recognizing the challenges, authors describe what it takes to implement e-learning systems and technologies in real and complex organizations. In Part Four we ask a pivotal question: Is e-learning too good to be true? Part Five tends to our seed corn by providing new directions and resources for the professional development of the e-learning professional. The last part, Part Six, serves up many case studies in organizations as diverse as technology companies, higher education and government. The handbook concludes with a resource section and index.

- **Many renowned experts.** Marc Rosenberg, Elliott Masie, Jack Phillips, Brandon Hall, William Horton, Gloria Gery, and Wayne Hodgins have written original or revised pieces for the handbook. I'm thrilled to have their newest thinking on topics like standards, games and e-learning, return on investment, blended learning and the culture and communications essential to successful implementation.

- **Many familiar authors.** When I set out to find recent articles that would add value to the book, recognizable and worthy sources popped up. You'll find

Patricia Galagan, Sarah Fister Gale, Zane Berge, James Moshinskie, Tom Barron, Albert Ingram, Patti Shank, Karl Albrecht, Rob Foshay, Dean Spitzer and Gary Dickelman. You've read their work in *Training and Development, Performance Improvement, Knowledge Management*, and others; you'll see some of the best recent efforts reprinted here.

- **Many new voices.** Meet Warren Longmire, Rebecca Vaughan Frazee, Chris Völkl, Nory Jones, David Wiley, and Bob Hoffman. I made a concerted effort to invite recent graduates and emerging professionals into the project.

- **Many diverse cases.** The handbook includes stories about Cisco, Oracle, the University of Virgina, the U.S. government, and Prudential Insurance, to name just a few. You'll also find sales training via technology, e-learning for orientation, project management training online through the use of an object-oriented approach, and the shift of soft skills training to a more blended and technology inclusive approach.

- **A tool for professional development.** The handbook is designed to encourage dialogue, reflection, planning and action surrounding e-learning. Rich resources will help orient and educate practitioners and executives about e-learning.

- **American, but with some international flavor.** Most authors are Americans, but not all. There is an article, for example, that describes e-learning in Europe. I favored articles that included global perspectives, and sought examples and cases from organizations that do their business across the world. The topics covered here, from e-learning persistence to online games to collaboration to cognitive distribution to knowledge management, are as important to a German or British training professional as to a North American.

The handbook is meant to inform, coach, entice, caution, and encourage. Articles were chosen and crafted to help professionals cope with vendors that promise vast multiples of improved cognition via e-learning, OR quotes like Roger Schank's "Right now e-learning is a disaster. All you're getting is somebody's classroom notes on the Web." We acknowledge the hype on both sides of the e-learning coin, from those who promise that e-learning will cure all that ails your organization, to those who see a devil trying to take away classroom training. This handbook attempts to help you move towards that fruitful, productive middle ground.

If this compilation prompts you to sharpen your e-learning efforts, we've all succeeded.

Allison Rossett
San Diego, California
October, 2001

e

# Acknowledgements

When I set out to create the Yearbook, I was determined that it would go beyond beating the drum for e-learning. I wanted to produce a compendium of articles that would encourage reasoned, practical, and thoughtful conversation and action about e-learning. Thanks to all the wonderful people whose views, ideas, successes and lessons are included here.

Of course, thanks to Sue, always Sue. And then there's smart colleagues and students in Educational Technology at San Diego State University. Their fresh ideas and lack of complacency continuously help me look down the road and around the bend.

Thank you also to Rebecca Vaughan Frazee, my assistant. She was and is a strong, wise and systematic force for excellence on this project. I shudder to think how many good works might have slipped away, if she wasn't there to help keep it all together.

I also want to thank McGraw Hill's Richard Narramore and John Woods of CWL Publishing Enterprises for encouraging the project and for assisting in its final execution. I know we're all glad we did what had to be done.

Finally, thanks to Tina Sung for writing our foreword. We need her and ASTD to contribute mightily to the e-learning venture.

*Allison Rossett is a Professor of Educational Technology at San Diego State University and the year 2000 inductee into* Training *magazine's HRD Hall of Fame. She is the co-author of* Beyond the Podium: Delivering Training and Performance to a Digital World *and the author of* First Things Fast: A Handbook for Performance Analysis. *Free online tools and resources are available at www.jbp.com/rossett.html. You can contact her at arossett@mail.sdsu.edu.*

# Welcome to Part One: The State of E-Learning

**W**here are we today? What is the current status of e-learning? How can we characterize a venture that is attracting billions of dollars in Wall Street investments, near rabid enthusiasm from executives, and some hesitation from employees?

There's no end to the words surrounding e-learning. "Revolution," "evolution," "hope," and "hype" are just a few of them. At this moment in time, perhaps a short phrase would provide the most accurate picture: "mixed bag."

In Part One we take on e-learning today. Allison Rossett reminds us of what's so great about e-learning today. Dave Simmons and Rossett review some of the numbers associated with participation, satisfaction, and persistence, and Sarah Fister Gale directs attention to copyright issues.

Gloria Gery and Rossett also note the challenges that training people face in converting e-learning hype into strategic results. And Christian Völkl and Folkert Castelein bring e-business and e-learning together as they focus on Europe. Wayne Hodgins gives us a look at the future in his piece on "learnativity," and Eliot Masie mixes past and present techniques in discussing blended learning.

Simultaneous with describing the tasty possibilities associated with e-learning, Part One also makes a case for new roles, responsibilities, measurements, and partnerships. After reading the articles in this part, you'll know why we should be cautiously optimistic and continuously humble about e-learning. In Parts Two and Three, authors describe how to move forward with e-learning.

# Waking in the Night and Thinking About E-Learning

**Allison Rossett**

*The good and the bad about e-learning—and there's definitely more good than bad, as documented in this article by the editor of this yearbook. E-learning has lots of promise, but it takes commitment and resources for an organization to see its potential realized. So you think e-learning is the answer to your training problem? It may be, but you've got to do it right. Learn more here.*

I've been having these two parallel dreams about e-learning. One is rosy and rich with possibilities. The other isn't quite a nightmare, but it has people running down corridors and bumping into walls.

In that first happy dream, an executive is extolling the virtues of e-learning, eyes lit up by the promise of reduced costs, standardized messages, and instantaneous updates. This executive is responding to promises like the one offered online by Accenture's e-learning venture, Indeliq: our approach can accelerate learning up to three times and improve cognition and retention up to 15 times, over traditional, lecture-based classes.

Who wouldn't be exuberant?

But in that second dream, the mood is anxious. Many employees hesitate to sign up for e-learning, and when they do, their participation is spotty. So is persistence. Materials that go online languish there, suffering from a lack of maintenance and relevance. Students long for the good old days, when instructors cared about them and entertained them with war stories.

Who, then, wouldn't worry that exuberance about e-learning is unwarranted, even irrational?

If I'd edited this handbook 18 months ago, that first glorious vision would dominate. I would have commenced by pointing to the executives who are mandating the transfer of substantial chunks of education and training to e-learning. Even GE's Jack Welch did it; in fact, he will keynote Elliott Masie's e-learning conference in October 2001. I would have crowed about the fact that W.R. Hambrecht & Co. (www.wrhambrecht.com) has commenced coverage of e-learning in ways that are parallel to their investment reviews of electronics, finance and health. I would have noted how much money is expected to pour into the enterprise, such as IDC's (www.idc.com) prediction that e-learning will be a $14 billion dollar business by 2004.

I would have added to the hopes and fanned the hype.

But now, as reality bites, I take a more measured approach. There is good news and some momentum. At the same time, at recent ASTD (Orlando) and Training 2001 (Atlanta) conferences, the expos were big, but didn't seem as big, with a more muted tone from attendees and vendors. Software innovator Pensare and live e-learning provider Caliber Learning Network aren't around anymore.

My own e-learning experiences could best be described as mixed (see Rossett, 2000 and Rossett and Sheldon, 2001), with reasons for hope, yet causes for concern. Some of my favorite sources, such as Rosenberg (2001) and Lguide (www.Lguide.com), admit to the magnitude of the challenges involved in putting technology to good use in learning, support and knowledge management.

Here, in this chapter and in the yearbook, let's look at both sides of the enterprise.

## E-Learning Now

Up, up, and away? Not exactly. ASTD's *2001 State of the Industry Report* (Van Buren, 2001) reported data suggesting that executives in 1998 were smitten with e-learning. The executives predicted that as much as 23% of their training would be delivered via technology in 2000. It hasn't happened. The technology-based portion of the training enterprise hovers in the 8%-9% range, reflecting little of the leap in participation that was anticipated. At the same time, participation in instructor-led training experiences has increased slightly over three years.

This Van Buren report (2001) does not judge e-learning as a disappointment or failure. Not yet. ASTD characterizes what's happening as a "breather," suggesting that resources are now being devoted to enhancing technology platforms. Another possibility, in my view, is that prior glitches have forced attention to essential heavy lifting associated with e-learning, such as the development of strategy, outcome measures, and alliances across the organization and with outsources. Even though student numbers have not risen dramatically, strategy and technology infrastructure are being established.

In Spring 2001, the Masie Center and ASTD collaborated to release yet another study, *E-Learning: If We Build It, Will They Come?* It examined participation in 30 courses at 16 companies in the United States. The focus was on learners' views of their technology-based learning experiences, as manifested in start rates, motivation, and satisfaction. One of the great benefits of e-learning is that it empowers individuals, enabling employees to study when and where they elect. The flip side of that benefit, of course, highlights the relevance of the ASTD/Masie (2001) effort. The individual who chooses to study online can also choose not to (Rossett, 2000). The freedom to learn at will thus extends to the freedom to not bother to sign up or to persist in the effort.

ASTD/Masie (2001) found that start rates varied, not surprisingly, by the nature of the course: 69% commenced classes that were mandatory; only 32% started voluntary classes. These numbers are grim. Only 69% chose to start their *mandatory* e-learning classes? Are such numbers acceptable for placebound classes? Why would we consider 69% a good showing for e-learning? And if 69% commence a mandatory class, I shudder to think what percentage will complete, given the notoriously low persistence in online education. Was it the topics? (Consider how employees feel about telephone and diversity classes.) Was it e-learning as a modality? Was it technology platform hassles? Did they long for instructor-led training? Was it a lack of organizational support and marketing?

According to the recent ASTD/Masie study, the answer to the question "If we build it, will they come?" is inclining more toward *no* than toward *yes*. E-learning success, it appears, is by no means automatic.

## A Sunnier Picture

Skillsoft commissioned Taylor Nelson Sofres (2001) to conduct a benchmark study of Canadian and United States businesses and their involvement in e-learning. They queried HR and training leaders from 300 private and public organizations.

TNS found a climate of awareness and enthusiasm, with 43% reporting some implementation of e-learning, 85% intending to increase usage in the next year, and 33% more planning to get involved with e-learning in the next three years.

While ASTD's *State of the Industry Report* suggested recent, scaled-down expectations for e-learning penetration, Sofres found an optimistic, upward trend. TNS reported that e-learning was the most rapidly growing segment of the training enterprise, and that technology was being used not just for information technology skills development, but also for management and professional domains.

The Taylor Nelson Sofres (2001) and ASTD/Masie (2001) studies highlighted the importance of the participant's first e-learning experience. Both studies support user optimism about e-learning for subsequent content areas. Most striking of all was that nearly every respondent in the TNS benchmarking study said that current e-learning initiatives had met or exceeded anticipated business benefits.

## Which Is It, Then?

It's both, I think. Good things are happening; many are enthusiastic about the benefits of technology for training, support, and knowledge management, especially those in leadership roles. At the same time, harsh realities emerge. Online seats go unfilled, persistence is iffy, technology platforms languish, and student satisfaction lags executive and vendor enthusiasm.

It's entirely possible for an organization or an individual to be both taken with the possibilities and cognizant of the pitfalls. The wise leader is humbled by all that's involved in converting e-learning promises into programs that deliver.

Pat Weger, Vice President of Learning and Organizational Development for AT&T Broadband, holds both views about e-learning. Pat is optimistic, cautious, and game. With a career that has included leadership stints at Digital Equipment Corporation and Fidelity Investments, Pat now finds herself needing to simultaneously develop the workforce *and* conserve its financial resources.

Pat teed off on e-learning at first. "It's a bandwagon now, with everybody urging everybody to move everything to the Web. I worry that it's just another tech fad that could turn out the way of the other fads, with lots of excitement but very little results. There's all this hurry to move employees to e-learning so they won't be away from their jobs, but then you have to have the right e-learning for them."

She lamented the quality of the online training she was reviewing. "Much of it is bad, worse than the late 1970s page-turning CBT." She reminded me about the population she serves at AT&T Broadband, where most of the customer-facing employees are not college-educated. "That's a bad match with most e-learning. My folks are typically not readers! Recently, a vendor visited and said that they could take all our documentation, manuals, and instructor-led materials and put them online. They just about promised to wave a wand over the materials and convert them, presto, into e-learning. Imagine how wordy and dense those programs would have been. Could that be effective for our people? It's doubtful."

Pat was also keen on the positive side of e-learning. "Oh, you need to know that there is much about technology and learning that is great. I'm excited about update and revision, standardized messages, and scalability. We can reach out across the country and bring Michael Armstrong's [chair and CEO of AT&T] message to 40,000 immediately and at low cost."

She offered an example of a budding e-learning success. Pat has many employees eager for very technical training, on topics such as maintenance of Cisco routers. Her organization established a relationship with Smartforce (www.smartforce.com) that commenced with 1,500 seats for the line. Those seats sold out and initial feedback has been positive. "E-learning is helping me narrowcast to a population that is dying to know more about how to do their work. We used technology to meet that need and at a reasonable cost."

Pat expressed pleasure that exempt employees have begun to pursue higher education online. Through Jones International University (www.jonesinternational.edu), for example, employees are taking classes and achieving milestones that surprise and delight. She sees degree studies for busy adults as a growing benefit of e-learning.

We circled back to the sobering issues involved in e-learning. I pressed Pat about the changing roles for people in the learning business. She said, "The changes here are about making good decisions about blended solutions, about how to fit e-learning into all the ways that we prepare and support employees. When do we use technology? When don't we? When should we bring our people into classrooms with instructors? How do we get supervisors involved? That last question isn't so new, is it?"

## Enthusing About E-Learning

While skepticism is appropriate—and humility essential—I don't want to sour anyone on e-learning. Instead, my purpose is to focus energy and commitment for the effort it takes to convert the hype into substantive results.

### The Big Tent of E-Learning

E-learning, especially a big tent view of it, has much to commend it. That big-tent view incorporates at least five functions:

**Learning.** Current views support a definition of learning that revolves around a change in the brain, in what we can remember and use, when needed. You could say that we've learned when we "get it." Typically, that takes some effort, some thought, some mental manipulation, such as working on a problem and comparing what you've done with an expert, or looking at what someone else has done and attempting to identify errors. Through examination, actions, and feedback, repeated over time, people learn. There's an investment involved in learning because we are changing what we know about safety, running a meeting, leading employees, or troubleshooting a local area network.

**Information support and coaching.** While learning is directed at enhancing individual capacity, information support and coaching focus on building an external resource into which the individual dips at the moment of need. Want to install a new motherboard? Want to change the message on your answering machine? Want to mix a margarita? Want to figure out which dog breed to buy? Want to bone up on the products of a pesky competitor? Want to compare WebCT and Blackboard as online course delivery systems prior to a purchase decision? Want to know what to do when the control panel in the nuclear plant suggests a festering problem? All these topics matter, *when you need to know*. Perhaps you don't want to rely on your memory or elect to invest in memorizing the information. Or perhaps it's so critical that you don't dare make a false move. When these circumstances are in effect, the topics become candidates for online help systems, technology-based coaching, or a nifty online support tool, such as how-to-pick-a-dog-breed at www.purina.com.

**Knowledge management.** When information grows into a full-blown system that reaches out to capture, organize, and stir organizational brainpower, knowledge management (KM) is happening. KM is an attempt to maximize the "smarts" that exist within people and organizations. A famous quote about Hewlett Packard pinpoints the need: "If HP only knew what HP knows...." Research conducted by Szulanski (1996) for the American Productivity & Quality Center (APQC) revealed that successful practices linger in a company for years, unrecognized and unshared. When recognized, it took more than two years before other entities within a company began to actively adopt best practices, if at all. KM is represented by large and small efforts to collect documents, practices, and lessons learned in a way that facilitates wide distribution. Getting a grip on this knowledge, nurturing it, making it accessible, encouraging conversation about it, and updating it are at the heart of KM.

**Interaction and collaboration.** Even though classroom instruction is often remembered for its interactive moment, technology too can be used to engage, stir, and foment. It can bring people together for many purposes, such as one-to-one development and coaching, online communities of practice, pre- and post-class listservs, and individual engagement with complex simulations and examples. One pharmaceutical creates interdisciplinary and global teams to work on pressing problems; a telecommunications company creates a collaborative online workspace to manage and push their product launch; and a group of graduate students rely on a database of rubrics (edweb.sdsu.edu/webquest/rubrics/weblessons.htm) to help them develop, assess, and improve papers and reports. Interactive? I think so. Collaborative? Definitely.

**Guidance and tracking.** New technology enables more and better guidance, assessment, tracking, and information. Individual contributors can look at themselves in light of standards and test their mettle on scenarios that reflect organizational trends and emerging priorities. Best of all, systems can guide individuals towards critical skills. Managers can enjoy a better view of employee skills and knowledge, with more insight into what has been studied and completed, what information is sought, where people return for more information, and what is contributed to knowledge bases. Executives too can capture a view of organizational skills and needs, looking at what people elect to study, where they don't, where they search and what they find, and how they participate in online communities of practice. In addition, leaders can comfort themselves with technology-based information about compliance and risk avoidance. They'll know who has taken the safety or sexual harassment classes, for example, and whether performance requirements have been satisfied.

Under this big tent of e-learning, the functions are enmeshed, so that users experience few hiccups between taking an online class, consulting an online coaching tool, or referring to a knowledge base.

Consider a salesperson charged with selling a new customer on a complex and expensive technology system. The salesperson reviews other proposals that have been submitted to the knowledge base on the topic from all over the world. She reads commentary from proposal authors, noting what worked and what didn't. As part of the sales community listserv, she exchanges messages with others selling that product line. She realizes that she's not quite ready to write yet and that she needs to get smarter about the antecedents for the product and methods for implementation. She decides to take two related short courses available online. That 75-minute commitment fits into her career development plans, is applauded by her supervisor, and, once she's taken a short post-test, is recorded in her personnel record. Most important of all, she now feels ready to tackle writing that proposal, with tools, templates, and boilerplate at her side.

That's the individual experience of the big tent of e-learning. The organizational experience is one that repurposes materials to add value as components of classes, knowledge bases, online tools, and tracking systems. A sales proposal, for example, might be used as an in-class example. The budget is picked apart by the instructor and groups of students. The executive summary is rewritten and compared to an online quality rubric or checklist. Research on local geography and industry conditions happens during class to establish habits for use after class is over. Then that same proposal, author comments, customer reaction and results, and expert opinion reside in the knowledge base with other proposals, so salespeople can search by product, customer, problem, strategy, or even component of the proposal.

## Rational Exuberance About the Benefits

The delicious e-learning honeymoon appears to be over. In Table 1, I present e-learning benefits in the left-hand column, then add a cautionary voice to the right.

In Table 2, I catalog some aspects of the enterprise that are keeping people up at night. I then provide some hope in response to these concerns.

| Benefits | Discussion |
|---|---|
| E-learning saves money. | E-learning has the potential to save money, if many have reason to use the online resources. Seek out opportunities with high value and high user numbers associated with them. This benefit has that ring of truth to it, especially when you consider travel expenses, but ... remember that development and implementation costs often surprise. |
| E-learning distributes a standard message. | This is a tasty aspect of e-learning. Note, however, that a standard distributed message isn't necessarily the right message. Effort must be invested in what the message is and then in maintaining the information. Currency is key. |
| E-learning provides our people with access to experts we can't afford to bring into our organization. | This is true, but must be considered with caution. Recently, I reviewed some how-to-communicate and sexual harassment e-learning software from two vendors. While expert authors were featured, the programs were lame. What an expert can "sell" in a classroom does not necessarily transfer online. Look hard at what you're buying. |
| E-learning provides our people with world-class learning experiences from vendors. | We can hope so. Note that vendors such as NetG, Skillsoft, Element K, and Digitalthink are having a large say in what *your* employees learn. The dilemma is that organizations can only buy what vendors have created, materials not typically customized for individual settings. This represents a worrisome shift away from customized, tailored training and towards a generic "one size fits all." Encourage vendors to tailor. Will you invest in it? |
| E-learning is readily updated and distributed to everybody. | E-learning can be readily updated, but will it be? Remember how difficult it is to engineer main-tenance on any classes and materials? Update and distribution are critical e-learning benefits, but they will not happen without commitment from the line. |
| E-learning is convenient and contextualized. | That's the promise–that training, information support, online coaching, and knowledge bases can be where the work and workers are. Wireless technologies create even more possibilities. My experiences suggest that most organizations are not yet there, with platforms that are undependable and far from speedy. |
| E-learning is human and interactive. | It can be. Examples from Quisic and Element K come to mind. Are programs peppered with authentic scenarios? Do characters respond in compelling and familiar ways? Do you get a chance to try your hand at realistic problems? Can you compare your view to others, to experts? Can you self-assess on challenges that look and feel like what happens at work? Note that the ASTD/Masie study (2001) reported that roughly 58% of respondents said they did not participate in sufficient interaction during online instruction. |

**Table 1.** Benefits of e-learning

| Benefits | Discussion |
|---|---|
| E-learning enables the organization to make better use of its resources. | Very true and in three ways: (1) stirs, captures, and spreads organizational smarts; (2) holds onto intel-lectual capital, even if the person leaves; (3) allows the reuse of work across the organization, so that best practices and products can be found and used. |
| E-learning makes sense as one component in a larger, integrated performance system. | Sure does. The potential is huge. But questions linger. Technology when? Instructors in rooms with students when? What happens online before? After? How do we decide? What are the attributes of effective blended systems? What role for supervisors? Linked to larger strategy how? Why, when systems have foiled HR and training professionals for many moons, do we expect to execute here? There remains a strong preference for silver bullets. |
| E-learning enables the presentation and consideration of multiple perspectives. | This is a definite plus. Consider the sales example above. The saleswoman can look at many proposals, not just the ones she or her supervisor or an instructor have created. E-learning also allows for access to many relevant views on a problem. A favorite medical ethics training program presents the views of doctors, ethicists, lawyers, psychologists, and patients. |

**Table 1.** Benefits of e-learning (continued)

| Concerns | Discussion |
|---|---|
| E-learners drop out. | The numbers are grim, but they do improve when classes are part of a larger system, with assessment, tracking, syndication, incentives, and record keeping. Our online courses in educational technology at SDSU suffer no more dropouts than our campus courses. And consider new ways of thinking about the issue. If we let go of conventional views of classes with beginnings and endings, then we can see the online materials as resources to which participants continuously return. Finishing, then, might not be the best thing. How do we keep them coming back to look at new examples, references, and tools? |
| I'm not sure my people are keen on e-learning. They seem to be less enthusiastic than executives and vendors. | Some are, some aren't. Wheeler (2000) talks about this problem. Higher education (pegasus. cc.ucf.edu/~rite/ ImpactEvaluation.html) is finding that campus students are willing and eager to diversify into e-learning. In other settings, it's less certain. Taylor Sofres Nelson (2001) found a satisfied response. Recent work for a government agency suggested that employees are lagging behind their leaders in their willingness to embrace e-learning. Make certain that maiden experiences are pleasant and valuable: critical impressions are being formed. |

**Table 2.** Concerns about e-learning

| Concerns | Discussion |
|---|---|
| I'm not sure my people know how to learn online, or that they'll be good at using support systems and knowledge bases. | This is a reasonable concern, and one expressed by Pat Weger above. Are your people good at learning independently? Are they comfortable with technology? Are they curious about the topic, and eager for development and answers to questions? You want affirmative answers to these questions. This is also an opportunity to "blend," for example, incorporating e-learning resources (such as communities of practice, assessments, and knowledge bases) into orientation and classes. Create habits. |
| E-learning classes aren't particularly good. | Some are, some aren't. E-learning is so new that there is little agreement as to which systems, software, platforms and vendors are best. The result is that some prefer Softskills classes, while others like Playback Media, Unext, and still others prefer Element K products or Netg. What do your people prefer? Negotiate contracts that enable you to gather data on satisfaction and performance. Ask supervisors what they like and why. Then make selections. |
| Big-tent e-learning breaks content and classes into little pieces. What if the pieces lose meaning and importance? | That's a good point. As we move to small objects that are selected by individuals at the moment of need, it makes sense to worry about synthesis and application. Here's an expanding role for professionals who will 'syndicate' objects so that they acquire meaning. |
| | That rich library of 'objects' could confuse and overwhelm. Provide guidance and recommended combinations. Demonstrate context. |
| E-learning enables vendors to decide what our people will learn instead of us. | The dilemma is that organizations can only buy what vendors have created, materials not typically tailored for individual settings. This is a shift away from customized, tailored training and towards a generic, "one size fits all." The next wave for portal companies will be to add substantial customization and implementation services. The need is certainly there. |
| E-learners get hooked on short answers and don't seem to want to bother with learning, with reflecting. Some say, "Just give me the answers, no need for a class." | The Web encourages the human tendency to favor a quick fix over the effort involved in understanding the subject. Model a commitment to taking classes online and in rooms for students. Make certain that executives do it and talk about it. And most important, make certain that online learning options are useful and targeted. A powerful and personable instructor might get away with a flabby class. Not so for an online experience. |
| | How will your organization honor development? How will you encourage employees to set longer term developmental goals, a special challenge when employees are typically measured in speed and quantity? Create recognition programs that honor study, reference and persistence. |

**Table 2.** Concerns about e-learning (continued)

| Concerns | Discussion |
|---|---|
| Everyone looks like an expert online. Aren't some of the programs wrong, inaccurate? | The WWW is democratic, with opinions having the appearance of being equally accurate. What is your organization going to do to encourage employees toward the best classes and online materials? How will you collect and distribute feedback? How will supervisors share scuttlebutt and kudos? These are efforts worth making. |
| To do e-learning right, I'll need all kinds of involvement from the line. That doesn't happen as often as I'd like. | It most definitely doesn't just happen. Make it a part of every program. Define a role for line leaders and supervisors from the get-go. Monitor their participation online. E-learning encourages individual agency; it transfers best, however, when the individual is encouraged by a manager and involved with peers. |
| To do e-learning right, we should hook it to our personnel management system. That's a big job. | Not only will employees benefit from more clarity regarding expectations and directions, the organization can link resources to those paths. |
| Will our culture be amenable to e-learning? Our people like classes. Our history is to offer lots of classes. Technology isn't our strongest suit. | Good question. See the sidebar, "Is Your Organization Ready for E-Learning?" Scrutinize your organization and improve its readiness. Don't take organizational support for e-learning for granted. |

**Table 2.** *Concerns about e-learning (concluded)*

# Facing Up to the Challenges

Much of the attraction surrounding e-learning involves access anywhere, anytime, including at the desktop. Davenport (2001) highlighted the problem with assumptions about the convergence of learning and work: "... the workplace is hardly a domain with plenty of slack attention lying around. The increasing speed and complexity of our business lives has become a ravenous user of our attention as well. Decades of global competition have produced lean organizations, very high customer expectations, short cycle times, and a need for just-in-time everything."

## E-Learning and the Camel's Nose

I dined with a friend who also does work in e-learning and organizational strategy. We fretted about an e-learning company we admire. Their programs are interactive, guided, and scenario-based. They teach online and also provide online coaching tools. A good word for their efforts would be vivid.

Our conversation focused on the response they were getting in the marketplace, which we knew to be tepid. The executives making purchasing decisions were not recognizing quality and, if they were, they were not electing to purchase it. We shared the perception that organizations preferred low costs first and foremost. Why? Does it sound a death knell for e-learning?

I don't think it does. Clayton Christensen's (1997) discussion of disruptive technology provides some explanation. New technologies—such as small Japanese cars, transistor radios, and PCs—gain entry and upward trajectory over established products (American cars and mainframes, for example) by being *cheap and accessible*. They enter at the low end. They don't win in the traditional ways that industrial giants expect, through customer focus, quality, and execution—*at least not at first*. Eventually, however, the disruptors perfect their processes, improve their innovations, and claim market share.

Might current e-learning be just such a disruptive innovation? Could the current grab bag of e-learning classes of variable quality be the camel's nose under the tent, hinting of the grand body to follow? Will we soon begin to see leaps in e-learning effectiveness and penetration? Will we see more robust standards for quality in e-learning products and in the implementation services that wrap around them? Will we get better and faster at producing programs that demonstrate a big-tent view of e-learning? If so, how do we begin to prepare for more and better e-learning products and services?

## Accentuating the Positive

I think we'll begin to enjoy more robust and consistent e-learning options in the near future. Market consolidation and partnering is occurring. Consider, for example, THINQ and Digitalthink. In the last week of June 2001, W.R. Hambrecht reported that Saba intends to acquire Ultris, a technology company that brings instant messaging to e-learning for the purposes of collaboration and mentoring during the learning process. Hambrecht noted that their technology also facilitates real-time access to relevant information, a feature that expands Saba's content management products. Standards are emergent, with continuous dialogue about quality, reach, authenticity, interactivity, scale, and reuse. E-commerce ideas are influencing e-learning as companies like MeansBusiness and LearningFramework make it possible to sell and track small and targeted knowledge morsels.

While the classroom can be a warm and nurturing place, it is also a black box. What instructor hasn't wondered whether participants are thinking about the course or a meal, if they'd choose to be in the room if they could find a way out the door? Web tracking and learning management systems can be helpful here, because they provide instantaneous insight into attention and performance. Employees can self-assess in light of career paths and expectations. Supervisors can scrutinize what employees select. Executives can examine start, completion, and persistence patterns. Customer satisfaction and error data, for example, can influence choices about what to improve, study, and research. Vendors, too, can get much smarter about how their products are used or ignored. So much transparency helps to target messages, coaching, and performance management systems.

Better programs, measurement, and transparency are welcome. However, they do not guarantee that e-learning will deliver on its promises. ASTD/Masie, 2001, Hall, 1997, Hartley, 2001, McGraw, 2001, Rosenberg, 2001, Rossett and Sheldon, 2001, and Rossett, 2001 point to the role of culture and communications in the successful implementation of e-learning programs. Who will serve as dependable champion, move supervisors into coaching roles, and ensure that marketing occurs and that e-learning and performance reviews are synchronous?

What of the professionals charged with learning and performance improvement? How will their work differ? What new priorities will they have? And how will they develop themselves for new roles that revolve around unfamiliar technologies, complex implementations, strategic contributions, and internal and external collaborations?

The new learning professional grapples with high-stakes questions. Is our organization ready for e-learning? Are our people ready to make independent decisions? Have we provided them with sufficient guidance, coaching, and clarity about expectations and career paths?

How will we define e-learning? How big a tent is right for us? Which functions will be included? On which topics will we concentrate? Can we teach soft skills online? Will programs from a developer based in Seattle and a portal in Chicago be successful in *my* company? How will we collaborate with HR and IT and make certain that the line is involved in maintenance and update? What do we do with our instructors?

Finally, which e-learning providers will give us the quality and services we need? Which will execute on their promises? While these are vital questions about *any* learning experiences or vendors, the flood of new providers and new technology formats makes decisions more vexing.

A chorus (McGraw, 2001, Rosenberg, 2001, Rossett and Sheldon, 2001, and Rossett, 2001) acknowledges an expanded and challenging role for professionals who must fertilize the organization for e-learning and knowledge management.

## Sleeping Through the Night

E-learning will reward those who proceed without irrational exuberance. How do you do that?

Assume that the organization is not yet sufficiently fertilized to capitalize on e-learning. Worry about individual readiness. Seek out programs that resonate with character, cases, and interactivity; eschew programs where legacy instructor-led and CBT have been "converted" to the Web. Define a role for managers and supervisors; use the intranet to ensure their participation. Measure everything. Create contracts with vendors and the line that allow you to do something with measurements. Link e-learning to performance reviews and strategic goals. Improve the technology infrastructure. Anticipate glitches, because they will surely come. Invest in keeping the glitches from becoming nightmares.

E-learning allows learning and performance professionals to do things we have always wanted to do: to deliver learning and information immediately; to deliver everywhere; to empower individuals; to coach; to collect and distribute best practices; to increase dialogue; to bust through the classroom walls; to increase community; and to know who is learning, referring to source materials, and contributing. While skepticism is essential to success with e-learning, there is much here to prompt us to wake up smiling.

---

## Is Your Organization Ready for E-Learning?

- Does your organization provide the infrastructure necessary to enable employees to access e-learning and knowledge bases? Bandwidth and access are issues that must be managed.

- Does the organization have an e-learning strategy and business case customized for it?

- Has the leadership allocated money to the effort?

- Are the resources allocated *over time*, with measures speckled throughout the effort, to enable data gathering and continuous improvement?

- Does the culture encourage learning, providing time and space for quiet study at the desktop? How will you protect employees when they are learning?

- Are managers and supervisors openly enthusiastic about online learning? Do they know the roles they must play? Are they ready to do so? Do they 'get' the business case for e-learning?

- Is a 'blended' strategy in place, one that makes defensible and rational decisions about when to use technology and when to involve instructors, coaches, and placebound experiences?

- What will the organization do to coordinate with external vendors? How will data be gathered and systems improved?

- How will programs be updated and maintained?

- Is something being done for employees for whom independent learning is a challenge? For employees who are less familiar with computers and keyboards?

- Is performance monitored and measured? Is performance linked to a larger individual and unit competency plan?

- Has the organization considered a big-tent view of training, one that encourages the collection, sharing, and stirring of resources in knowledge bases?

How does this larger view change the way you think about e-learning and what success looks like?

- How will the organization honor and reward persistence and involvement in e-learning? What is the carrot for completion? For participation and contribution to online communities and knowledge bases? How does it link to advancement and recognition?

- Are executives learning online? Are they referring to knowledge bases? Are they making contributions to the knowledge base?

## Notes

ASTD and The Masie Center, *E-Learning: If We Build It, Will They Come? Executive Summary* (Alexandria, VA: ASTD, 2001).

Christensen, Clayton M., *The Innovator's Dilemma: When New Technologies Cause Great Firms to Fail* (Boston: Harvard Business School Press, 1997).

Davenport, Thomas H., "E-Learning and the Attention Economy: Here, There and Everywhere?" Summer 2001, Linezine.com. www.linezine.com/5.2/articles. htm.

Hall, Brandon, *Web-Based Training Cookbook* (New York: John Wiley & Sons, 1997).

Hartley, Darin E., *On-Demand Learning: Training in the New Millennium* (Amherst, MA: HRD Press, 2000).

McGraw, Karen L., "E-Learning Strategy Equals Infrastructure," *Learning Circuits*, June 2001, www.learningcircuits.com/2001/jun2001/mcgraw.html.

Rosenberg, Marc J., *E-Learning: Strategies for Delivering Knowledge in the Digital Age* (New York: McGraw-Hill, 2001).

Rossett, Allison, "Confessions of a Web Dropout," *Training*, August 2000.

Rossett, Allison, "E-Trainer Evolution," *Learning Circuits*, June 2001, www.learning-circuits.org/2001/jun2001/rossett.html.

Rossett, Allison, and Sheldon, Kendra, *Beyond the Podium: Delivering Training and Performance to a Digital World* (San Francisco: Jossey-Bass/Pfeiffer, 2001).

Schank, Roger C., *Virtual Learning: A Revolutionary Approach to Building a Highly Skilled Workforce* (NewYork: McGraw-Hill, 1997).

Stewart, Thomas A., *Intellectual Capital: The New Wealth of Organizations* (New York: Doubleday, 1997).

Szulanski, Gabriel, "Exploring Internal Stickiness: Impediments to the Transfer of Best Practices Within the Firm," *Strategic Management Journal*, Winter 1996, pp. 27-43.

Taylor Nelson Sofres, "E-Learning in USA & Canada Benchmark Survey," www.skill-soft.com/resources/white_papers/whitepapers/tn_research.html.

Van Buren, Martin, *2001 State of the Industry Report* (Alexandria, VA: ASTD, 2001).

Wheeler, Kevin, "Why People Still Like the Classroom More than E-Learning," *e-learning Magazine,* July 2000, www.elearningmag.com/issues/july00/enterprise.asp.

*Dr. Allison Rossett, Professor of Educational Technology at San Diego State University, was the Year 2000 inductee into the* Training *magazine HRD Hall of Fame. She has authored three award-winning books:* First Things Fast: A Handbook for Performance Analysis *(1999),* Training Needs Assessment *(1989), and* A Handbook of Job Aids *(1991). In 2001, she co-authored* Beyond the Podium: Delivering Training and Performance to a Digital World. *Rossett has Web sites that provide tools associated with recent books and projects: www.jbp.com/rossett.html and edweb.sdsu.edu/people/ARossett/Arossett.html. Rossett is the editor of this yearbook and can be contacted at arossett@mail.sdsu.edu.*

# The Forum Report: E-Learning Adoption Rates and Barriers

**David E. Simmons**

*An increasing number of companies are adopting e-learning. But in their rush to take advantage of e-learning's benefits and promises, companies are finding that there are significant barriers to adoption, according to a Forum Corporation study of 144 U.S. companies.*

An increasing number of companies are responding to the promise of e-Learning by adopting advanced learning systems. While traditional workplace learning occurred in a classroom setting and was based on a face-to-face teacher-student model, it was, and is, often criticized for being expensive, time-consuming, and unresponsive to learners' immediate needs. By contrast, e-Learning promises lower costs of distribution, any time and anywhere access, and just-in-time learning that is responsive to learners' immediate needs.

Today's most insightful companies are adopting learning distribution models that incorporate the classroom as only one of several ways to deliver learning and development to their employees. Increasingly, companies are adopting collaborative and technologically enabled models. In doing so, they are responding to the demands of both their top executives and their employees, who are looking for learning that achieves both organizational and individual results. In addition, they are responding to the marketplace, which demands rapid responses to changing dynamics and rewards companies that are best able to apply new learning to key business issues.

## Key Findings

- The percentage of companies providing access to e-Learning for all employees is expected to more than double in two years.

- The number of companies providing learning communities that have collaboration technology is expected to grow 150 percent over the same time period, from 21 percent to 51 percent.

- More than 60 percent of companies expect to incorporate 10 of the 11 components of an e-Learning system within two years.

- Technology infrastructure is one of only seven major barriers to the adoption of e-Learning; other issues pose even more significant obstacles.

Forum's research indicates that companies are moving rapidly to meet the demand to make learning more relevant to their business priorities, their employees, and their customers. Figure 1 examines the current and future adoption of 11 aspects of an e-Learning system. (See the last page for research methodology.)

The survey indicates that respondents are aggressively pursuing an integrated, collaborative, and technologically enabled model of learning.

**Individualized Learning:** Respondents are adopting competency and skills assessments as well as individual learning plans to create learning and development that is relevant to the employee's individual needs.

**Knowledge Sharing:** The number of companies providing technologically enabled learning communities is expected to grow 150 percent, from 21 percent to 51 percent. In addition, respondents are investing in technology to capture relevant knowledge and to share individual knowledge.

**Technology:** Even if the projections in the research were reduced by half, we would still be in the midst of a learning revolution. Technologically enabled learning—in the form of online content delivery, tracking, enrollment, registration, and catalogue management—are projected to have nearly universal implementation within two years.

At the same time that companies are moving quickly to adopt e-Learning, they are encountering unexpected barriers that hamper their efforts. Respondents rated barriers to the implementation of an e-Learning system. Their responses, starting with the strongest barrier, were:

1. Time employees have available for training/learning
2. Cost versus value
3. Difficulty in measuring results
4. Quality of learning content

| Components | Current Usage | Expected Usage (in 2 yrs.) |
|---|---|---|
| Competency/skills assessment | 64% | 82% |
| Individual learning plans | 48% | 68% |
| Learning resources linked to organizational goals | 55% | 76% |
| Learning communities with collaboration technology | 21% | 51% |
| Process and technology to share individual knowledge | 46% | 66% |
| Technology to provide access to knowledge captured | 44% | 70% |
| Access to e-Learning by the entire organization | 34% | 71% |
| Learning/knowledge accessible through project or human resource management system | 35% | 65% |
| Online registration and administration of learning | 49% | 81% |
| Electronic catalogue of learning resources | 48% | 77% |
| Tracking and reporting of learning and knowledge | 48% | 75% |

**Figure 1.** Components of an advanced e-learning system

5. Perceived difficulty of using such a system
6. Technology infrastructure
7. Internal resistance to using technology instead of face-to-face learning

## Insight

How realistic are the respondents' projected adoption rates? In recent years, conventional wisdom has not accurately reflected the actual adoption rates for e-Learning. Research by The Forum Corporation and leading industry associations, such as the American Society for Training and Development, has shown that actual adoption rates are slower than expected. In fact, while expectations for the adoption of e-Learning have grown significantly over each of the last three years, the actual adoption rate has remained steady.

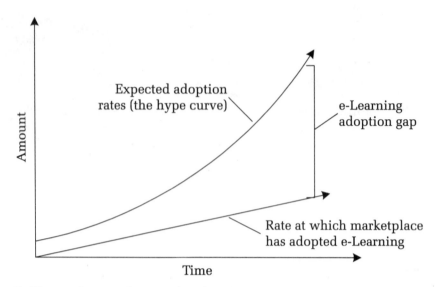

**Figure 2.** The gap between hype and reality (Dataquest: Worldwide Services Group, 1998)

The barriers to adoption identified by respondents reflect Forum's experience in developing and implementing e-Learning strategies for large, global companies. Technology issues, such as bandwidth and infrastructure, are critical to the success of e-Learning but are only the first hurdles to overcome.

The ability of the employee to find time for learning and the difficulties in measuring results represent the major barriers. In addition, learner resistance to e-Learning, while ranked by respondents as a relatively low barrier, should not be underestimated. A Harvard Business School Publishing study revealed a significant divergence of preference between learners and buyers for training delivery methods. When asked to choose from pairs of learning preferences, 87 percent of learners selected instructor-led training versus 12.7 percent who prefer to learn using a computer.

In-depth interviews with executives from eight companies at the vanguard of e-Learning reinforced the finding that technology is only one of several barriers companies encounter. "Technology is not a constraint. The assumption that [is] wrong is that people would be willing to use it at their desk … People are drowning in a sea of learning opportunity [and do not have the time]," said the senior vice president of human resources for a *Fortune* 500 network communications company, which has an advanced technological infrastructure.

## Implications

Clearly, the future holds tremendous opportunity for enhanced approaches to learning. To be effective, companies should pursue e-Learning with an informed approach that balances hope and hype, addresses the needs of the learner, and recognizes that e-Learning is one, albeit critical, part of an overall learning strategy.

Through our research into e-Learning, adult learning, and learning strategy, and through our work with our customers, Forum has identified four critical factors that influence companies' approach to e-Learning:

1. **Collaboration:** Technology should provide access to content *and* other people.
2. **Integration:** Learning solutions must be based on proven principles of adult learning that leverage multiple delivery media.
3. **Relevance:** Embedding learning into work processes results in significant and sustainable performance improvement for both the individual and the business.
4. **Fundamentals:** In their haste to adopt e-Learning, some companies lose sight of the fundamental principles of adult learning and focus more on the technology involved. Technology, or any other delivery medium, is a means to deliver effective learning and not an end in itself.

## Methodology

There were three stages to the study:

**Stage 1** Existing e-Learning research and literature were reviewed.

**Stage 2** Eight in-depth case studies were conducted of companies identified in stage 1 as leaders in e-Learning. Data was collected by Forum's research partner, Michael F. Corbett & Associates, through phone interviews with senior human resource and learning and development executives from each company. A survey protocol was developed from the findings of stages 1 and 2.

**Stage 3** A phone, fax, and web survey was conducted by Michael F. Corbett & Associates. Five hundred companies were targeted from seven industries identified in stages 1 and 2 as being advanced in the adoption of e-Learning: business services, consulting, financial services, healthcare, information technology, biotechnology, and a targeted population of high-technology manufacturing firms. Respondents were senior executives with representation from all organizational functions.

*David E. Simmons is director of market research for The Forum Corporation.*

# Performance Support—Driving Change

**Gloria Gery**

*As businesses turn more and more to performance support systems, what is the role of trainers and instructional designers? According to the author of this article, "It is our role and responsibility to take technology in hand, embrace it, and exploit it to address performance development."*

"I'm overwhelmed," said Marc, the sales rep. "Too much is going on ... too many products ... so many kinds of customers ... too many ways to think about configuring them to meet particular needs ... more objections than I can muster responses to."

"I agree," his colleague, Mary, responded. "And every time I turn around, there's another Web page I'm told about. What do I use, when, in what context, and for what purpose? When I talk with my manager, he throws up his hands too—and tells me to sort it out myself. Wish someone would simplify all of this for me. What we really need is someone to understand what it is we do and then connect the dots for us. What we need is an assistant who anticipates what we need—and then serves it up to us netted out. Just what we need ... in just the right form at the moment of need."

"Yeah ... but I asked for that," Marc lamented. "They told us at our regional meeting that the online learning that was just introduced is supposed to do that. I couldn't agree less! While that's great in that it keeps us from having to travel away from our territory for long courses, it's still too much and the content isn't accessible when I need it unless I know what module the stuff I need is in. Ironically, the more interactive it is, the less I can use it when I need it because I have to answer all those questions or go through all those exercises that are great when you're in a training program—but simply annoying barriers when I'm doing regular work."

"You know what I'd like, too," Mary exclaimed. "I'd love one of those wizards they have when you install new software. They ask you a bunch of questions and then make recommendations or, even better, do it for you. We need that kind of thing to help us in configuring products, doing proposals, troubleshooting problem sales situations, and other things. It's impossible to keep all the rules and relationships in my head. I'm always on the phone with the sales support hotline. Sometimes I even disguise my voice so they won't think I'm a pain in the neck. Do you think anyone is thinking about these kinds of things?"

"You're right, Mary. What we need for our work is something like the Intuit Turbo Tax program I use for my taxes!"

## What's Wrong with This Picture and How to Correct It

Today's employees are overwhelmed with resources. Ironically, the very reference, instruction, help systems, and Web sites we are madly creating to make life easier for them and to make them more successful are falling of their own weight. We in the performance development community need to step back and look at what we are creating and the impact of these resources on work and people. We need to evaluate whether doing more of the same—or even "better" versions of what we've been doing for the past 30 years—is appropriate. We must determine whether we need to reframe the problems we think we are addressing and examine alternatives—particularly the technological ones—to see if there isn't a better set of solutions.

## The Role of Training and Instructional Design, Now and in the Future

The *traditional* role of a training professional or instructional designer is to create formal, structured learning events (typically *courses or lessons*). These events are largely experienced outside of the work context and focus on *learning* rather than *doing*. While training programs sometimes include activities, tasks, and simulations designed to help learners *apply* the knowledge, more often than not these activities are limited and insufficient to truly achieve skill. In addition, since most instructional programs are single-threaded and address a specified and limited domain (e.g., software application, set of concepts, procedures, process, policy, law, marketplace, etc.), the applied exercises apply only to the domain. Job performance requires the integration of numerous domains—and training programs rarely integrate all of the domains or elements associated with doing real work. Unless there are rich, robust, and comprehensive simulations which weave all of the elements required for successful performance together, learners must spend significant time on the job and in courses to gain the knowledge and integrating experience necessary for competent performance.

The goal of this article is to focus on designing performance support systems—computer-mediated environments that are designed to generate immediate work performance, whether or not the individual performer has the knowledge or skill to perform the work independently *without the performance support system.* There are significant implications for trainers in both the short and long term. In fact, the implied objective of performance support system designers is to minimize or even eliminate the need for formal instruction. The underlying belief behind this effort is that learning and doing can be integrated so that learning can occur either *as a result of doing* or *at the moment of need.*

Of course, there will always be instruction—and learners need mental models and conceptual frameworks around which to incorporate or hang what they learn in incremental ways. But as has become clear in task-oriented commercial software and Web applications which structure performance of complex tasks such as making investment decisions, doing taxes, creating wills and trusts, and designing gardens, decks, or even houses, people are independently doing work previously performed by deep experts. This approach to designing performance support software has raised expectations for what is possible—and what is desirable.

This design approach requires a cross-functional project team composed of information systems professionals, knowledge engineers, content developers, and graphic artists.[1] Whether or not there is true *instruction* available to users of these systems—or whether they can learn while doing through presentation of relevant, powerfully represented content—will be a matter of design (and some disagreement).

Nevertheless, it is important that training professionals understand that their role will change dramatically—and quickly.[2] It is critical for us to understand these new performance support environments and to advocate, illustrate, participate, and influence them. In fact, we may have to subordinate or eliminate some of our historical goals.

How we will fit in is not precisely clear at this point. But we do know that unless those of us who understand learning and cognition are involved, these systems will be less than they could and must be to generate both learning and performance within our organizations.

## The Problem: Performance Development Is Not Viewed as a Process

There are many ways to view the problems and solutions facing our performers. We can think of them as training-, documentation-, or information-needs problems. Since the mid-1960's we've been throwing these solutions at people. We moved from analog versions, such as instructor-led courses and manuals, to e-learning and Web pages, online reference, and portals. Most of these solutions emerge from departments that are functional silos organized around the related outcomes.

In addition, our colleagues in information systems continue to program more and more applications software programs to help process the data so necessary to work today. They also implement more and more data-centric software—much of which is installed but unused (or partially used).

If we simply count the number and types of things people have to experience, use, or reference, there's hardly time to do any work. We're so busy learning about how to do it that we never get to the main event: performance on the job. Things are complicated further by the rate and volume of change, complexity, diversity of situations, and increasing differences in ability, knowledge skills, and motivation of the performers themselves.

Instructional programs that are experienced *out of context* are becoming too numerous and too long for employees or customers who are time-limited and urgent. They are increasingly withdrawing from participation out of sheer work pressure, if not frustration with the return on investment they experience as learners. We must step back and look at the role of instruction in developing performance and seriously evaluate how the learning and performance development process can be reconceptualized and transformed through technology and innovative thinking (see Exhibit 1).

In fact, we sit at our functional spinning wheels developing more and more *threads* about product, process, procedures, concepts, rules, requirements, marketplaces, tools, laws, contexts, etc. We then leave filtering, focusing, and integrating these threads to the performers. And often, these performers are not given the time or opportunity to experience or become comfortable with the content or knowledge that's embodied in the threads before they must apply it. In fact, performance is in the *weave* of these elements in relationship to the task or goal at hand.

To be brutally honest, we have failed to look at and reengineer the processes and actions that are applied to people—the most fundamental and expensive resource in our organizations. We pay more attention to the raw materials and processes in manufacturing, administration, and customer relationships than we do to our own performance development. We continue to throw *activities* and *resources* at the problem. It's time to stop and look at what it will take to truly achieve the goals of individual and organizational performance in support of expressed business objectives.

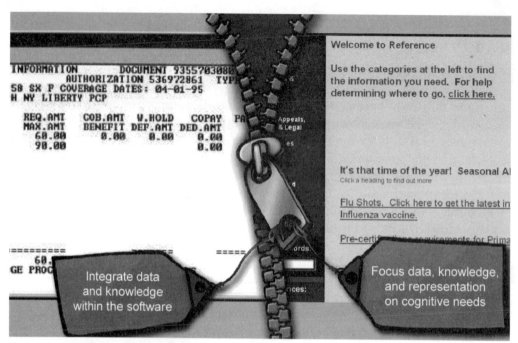

**Exhibit 1.** Integration is the key

Traditional resources reflect the focus of their developers. The left half of this illustration reflects a focus on data. The right half illustrates the content focus of technical writers and Web designers. Both are presented out of context to the user. We need to integrate data and content within a meaningful task context to make the resources useful to performers. (Courtesy of Ariel Performance Centered Systems)

## Directly Supporting Performance

In 1991, I wrote *Electronic Performance Support Systems*[3] to serve as a rallying call to examine whether a new alternative of providing direct support of work processing by technology would be a more powerful alternative to traditional training. Much has happened in the 10 years since the book appeared.[4] We've continued on our inexorable path toward providing electronic resources of increasing variety, but the fundamental defaults of training, providing reference resources, and periodic coaching for on-the-job learning have not shifted much in spite of all of the money spent on technology and things delivered by it.

Why hasn't there been more change? Some of the main reasons include the following, organized around the historical and powerful default approaches:

- Institutionalized organization structure, development methods
- Policy and practice (e.g., all employees must be trained, all software must have manuals or help systems)
- Staff skills and university programs developed and honed around the origi-

nal artifacts and associated development methods (e.g., Instructional Design, Software Development, and Technical Documentation)

- Business plans, objectives, measurement, and accountability around the artifacts (e.g., student days, number of Web sites, features and functions in software)
- Organizational politics that focus on control of historical and current turf, which is once again anchored in the historical artifacts
- Industry conferences and associations (such as the International Society for Performance Development, International Society for Performance Improvement, American Society for Training and Development, Society for Technical Communication, Training, etc.) focused on the historical artifacts
- Cultural values (e.g., good companies train; important people go to training; each department develops a Web site around its own function, product, service, etc.)
- Religious beliefs held by developers based on their education or functional viewpoint; inability or unwillingness to examine alternatives that violate their existing assumptions
- Vested interest in the status quo: organization, control, methodology, staffing levels, budget, professional memberships and certification

## Performance Support: An Integrating Viewpoint[5]

The performance support paradigm is a viewpoint advocated by those who are increasingly frustrated with the failure to achieve desired results associated with traditional activities—and who are able and willing to take the risks associated with new points of view, goals and processes. These advocates are now focusing on new and increasingly powerful models that technology affords—and they are moving beyond evangelism and prototypes to computer-mediated work and communication environments that have the explicit goal of generating immediate work performance without prior knowledge by the performer. In other words, they are creating work environments in which people who don't know what they are doing *can do it as if they did*—and, as appropriate, providing on-demand learning resources.

This perspective continues to gain acceptance and support, particularly by those with operational responsibility for getting work done. The professional literature is scattered through the various disciplines that are involved.[6]

To achieve integration, technology is required. As more and more work and communications are mediated by technology, we have the opportunity to achieve direct performance support designed to produce immediate, best-practice performance by all employees, customers, suppliers, and vendors to whom these tools are provided.

# The *Power* of Performance Support

The power of electronic performance support is a function of a number of variables and the way they are combined to result in a particular set of attributes,[7] the most significant of which are the following:

- the number of elements within the system
- how well these elements are integrated
- whether the resources are filtered and the basis on which they are filtered
- how well (i.e. clear, appropriate and powerful) the elements are represented
- the balance between structure and freedom provided to the performer
- the nature and degree of the task automation and deliverable creation provided within the application

Each of these variables will be explored in this chapter to provide an overall framework for trainers and instructional designers in considering and reconsidering their tasks, roles, methods, and organizational relationships.

## Integrating Resources in Powerful Ways

The types of resources to be integrated in performance support systems include the following:

- task structuring support
- knowledge
- data
- tools
- communications/collaboration support

Exhibit 2 summarizes those elements and related considerations.

The nature and degree of integration of these resources truly matter. For example, if an example is contained on the user interface or if instructions and messages are clear, much training can be avoided. If software developers viewed "system messages or dialogs" as instructional messages, rather than information about data validity or procedural sequences, people would be able to proceed further with their work more quickly. In fact, those of us in instruction should be participating in the user interface design to identify which knowledge resources should always appear, what should be linked, what should be layered, what should be automatically presented, and what should be invoked by performers. It's a new and critical role in designing computer-mediated workspaces.

## Filtering Is a Key Attribute of Good Performance Support

Performance support also advocates the filtering of resources to reflect the partic-

| Element | What It Is | Comments |
|---------|-----------|----------|
| **Task Structuring Support** | • Direct and conditional guidance through work process based on situational data and performer choices.<br>• Sometimes explicit on user interface, sometimes automated via underlying programming rules and data.<br>• Can be an alternative or the required and exclusive way of working. | Task structuring can be required or an option based on decisions about the degree of performer autonomy desired. Balancing structure and freedom should be a deliberate design decision based on performance requirements, culture, performer attributes, and other factors. |
| **Knowledge** | • Can include any or all types of content, including concepts, procedures, process, facts, rules, policy, relationships. Can be represented by any media type.<br>• Can be embedded in displays, expressed in underlying programming rules, presented by the software under certain conditions, or invoked by the performer as desired.<br>• Best when tightly coupled or fused with the workspace.<br>• Opportunities should be provided to capture new knowledge as generated or observed by performers. | Designers must overcome the tendency to dump and provide too much content. The goal is to identify precisely what is necessary given the condition, goal, and performer attributes—and to represent the content in the most powerful appropriate form. Content can be layered for optional use by those who want to learn more. Representation of knowledge becomes a main focus of those currently involved in software design. Can include the visual display of quantitative information, concepts, processes, etc. |
| **Data** | • Data about the problem, case, customer, condition, etc. may be provided from electronic data bases or entered/selected by the performer.<br>• Data will typically drive the task structuring.<br>• Knowledge can be filtered to relate to the specific data at hand.<br>• New types of data that support thinking and customer interaction must be identified to supplement the historical transaction or business data within business software applications. | Collaboration with information systems professionals is necessary. Knowledge and training developers are typically not familiar with the software and data used by performers, except when teaching or documenting software. Data is a primary filter and must be well understood by all performance support designers. New types of data requirements must be advocated and captured as appropriate. |

**Exhibit 2.** Elements of performance support systems (continued on next page)

| Element | What It Is | Comments |
|---------|-----------|----------|
| **Tools** | • Can include business software applications, utilities (such as word processors, spreadsheets, publishing programs, etc.), special purpose calculators. | Increasingly, software tools can automate creation of deliverables (e.g., reports, notes, presentations, communications, and incorporate relevant data). |
| **Communications/ Collaboration** | • Methods to support communications, both while actively working and once work is completed.<br>• Can be used for knowledge sharing, communications of results and requirements.<br>• May support joint work across time and space among two or more performers. | Deliverables are communications. Collaboration can be synchronous or asynchronous, interactive and dynamic or static.<br>Can involve document, data or image sharing using voice, text, graphics, video, etc.<br>May employ special-purpose collaboration tools supporting tasks such as document sharing, brainstorming, polling or voting, graphical display, group interaction, etc. |

**Exhibit 2.** Elements of performance support systems (continued)

ular requirements of the performer. Filtering applies to *all* of the elements of a performance support system, including knowledge, data, tools, task structuring, and communications. It requires designers to truly understand the context and to determine precisely what resources are appropriate and necessary to aid in performance and learning *from the performer's perspective.*

To successfully filter resources, designers must *anticipate* the performer's frame of reference and what is necessary to successfully perform the task. In addition, a determination must be made about how much content is appropriate to permit learning. The needs of *most* of the performers must be accommodated. Of course, some may want to learn more—and others less.

It is critical to remember that this is a *performance* context, rather than an *instructional* context, so extensive instructional resources are not appropriate from within a performance support system.

Instructional designers must be involved in determining which resources should appear, as well as how and when they should be presented or accessed. Filtering to eliminate inappropriate or unnecessary content—and determining ways to get performers to focus on what *is* presented—is a key role and responsibility for us in the future.

# Representation—Another Key to Successful Performance Support

Representation is essentially *the form and mechanisms for presenting information, data, and task.* Representation includes visualization and other types of media, use of metaphor, language, layout, etc. The designer's objective is to represent things in ways to create concrete and specific understanding *in the least possible time.* This means aiding in learning, analysis, interpretation, and action. Successfully representing data or knowledge results in rapid time to understanding. Again, it requires understanding the essence of the goals, data, task, and content and determining the appropriate mental models or metaphors to use. It also means understanding the natural language of the performer—and matching terminology to the way work is presented and how typical performers describe and discuss it.

Ironically, when developing instructional programs and software applications, instructional designers and software developers often call upon subject matter experts (SMEs) or business experts to aid in representing tasks, data, and content. These experts have deep understanding of the concepts and data and tools, but often have never done the work—or have not done it recently. They can barely remember how novices view the content or situation. They often use *shorthand* or technical terminology to express things—and these arcane representations do little to edify people trying to do good work.

Exhibit 3 illustrates the power of appropriate representation of data that uses powerful models to aid in interpretation. This data could have been shown as a detailed table of numbers, but such a chart would have been more work to review than it was worth and not at all memorable.

Exhibit 4 illustrates process representation which aids performers in understanding work flows and options—as well as providing rapid navigation to each task context via one click. This type of process representation is what we should achieve as we extract knowledge about *best practice* process during our task analysis. We should then work to design appropriate representations that aid in understanding.

Exhibit 5 illustrates a cascading menu which provides call center representatives with an easy mechanism to understand all call types in the way they are presented by callers. It also provides immediate and direct navigation to structured task support (through wizards) which guides performers through the appropriate steps to resolve the call.

## Method: Stop the *Madness*

Currently, each functional silo has its own analysis and development method. Instructional design, systems development, knowledge management, and techni-

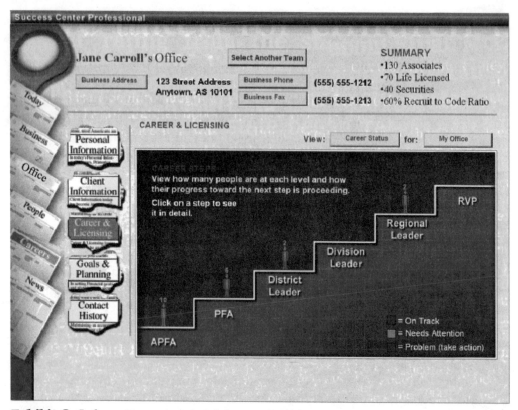

**Exhibit 3.** Information represented for easy interpretation and navigation to underlying detailed data

This stair-step metaphor reflects a mental model that a successful manager used in thinking about his recruits and their progress. Each step represents a key point in the certification and licensing process. The number of reps at each step is reflected by the "people figures" in different colors representing status: on target, caution, or at risk. Managers can quickly see where all their recruits are in the process and the summary of how they are doing. The user can click on the people figures to get the underlying detail about each representation in that step and achievement category. This display requires little or no interpretation by the user—and quickly and clearly illustrates current conditions. (Courtesy of Ariel Performance Centered Systems)

cal documentation methods have evolved to produce the known outcomes. If we overlay all of them, they are largely identical in process and steps. They differ in their focus. For example, information systems professionals focus on data—not content. Instructional designers and technical writers focus on task and content and disregard data, for the most part. Knowledge engineers focus on extracting best practice, rules, and content. And none of these methods requires those using them to integrate with the other functional groups.

In the future, instructional systems design methods—and all of the other analy-

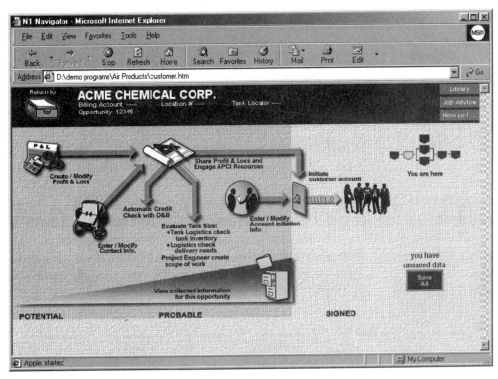

**Exhibit 4.** Sales process support: task flow for product sales

*Sales reps sell products they know—and products they know how to order, configure, and manage through the sales cycle. This display illustrates the best-practice sales process for a given type of product and provides direct and one-click navigation to related forms, data, and tools. It makes it inevitable that the salesperson handles things right—the first time! (Courtesy of Ariel Performance Centered Systems)*

sis, design, and development methods—will have to change to accommodate new outcomes and the merging roles. Many of the steps and activities will remain the same, but they will be applied to different deliverables. And many of the deliverables will be smaller than traditional programs. In fact, there may be *no* instruction in some cases. New methods must be forged as new, integrated thinking emerges.

## In Summary

The context is changing around us. We must adapt to it—and we must influence it. We must question our roles, methods, and deliverables and identify how our relationships and collaboration with other organizational groups must evolve. In fact, training professionals are probably the best suited to *advocating and reconceiving* how performance is developed in our organizations. Understanding and

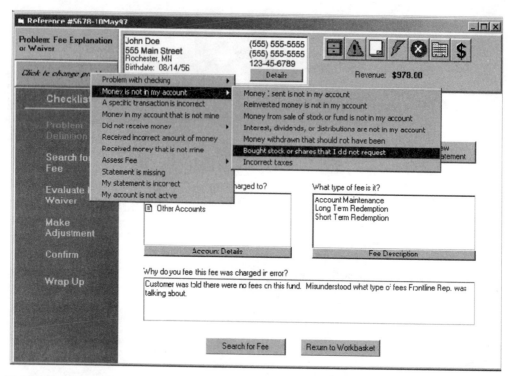

**Exhibit 5.** *Cascading menus with options: calls expressed in the voice of the customer*
*Typically, call center representatives listen to a caller's situation or help the caller express their situation. Experts understand the range of conditions and have mapped the required data, policy, tools, and process to the condition. Novices (most call center reps) can't do this. This display gives them a cascading menu of caller issues/conditions from which to choose. The menu can help the rep clarify the caller's situation. The language is that of callers, not deep experts; it's natural and clear. Clicking on a given situation leads reps to wizards which structure best-practice walk-throughs to problem resolution. These wizards progress conditionally, based on data provided by the caller. Novices perform as experts almost immediately. (Courtesy of Ariel Performance Centered Systems)*

motivation are unlikely to occur within groups focused on technology, data, and telecommunications.

It is our role and responsibility to take technology in hand, embrace it, and exploit it to address performance development. We must accelerate it. We must make it more efficient and more effective. We must add far more value than we do at present. And we must align performance development outcomes with business strategy. It is essential to our individual and organizational survival and prosperity.

## Notes

1. "Supporting Human Performance Across Disciplines: A Converging of Roles and Tools." Lorraine Sherry and Brent Wilson. *Performance Improvement Quarterly, 9* (4), 19-36 (1996). carbon.cudenver.edu/~lsherry/pubs/pss.html.

2. "Teaming Up for Performance Support: A Model of Roles, Skills, and Competencies." Burt Huber, Jenifer Lippincott, Cathie McMahon, and Catherine Witt. Edited by Gary J. Dickelman. *Performance Improvement Journal*, August 1999, *38* (7). www.pcd-innovations.com/pi_august_1999.htm.

3. *Electronic Performance Support Systems: How and Why to Remake the Workplace by the Strategic Application of Technology.* Gloria Gery, Gery Performance Press, Tolland, MA. (Originally published by Weingarten Publications and subsequently Ziff Communications.) Now available from the author at 413 258-4693 or Amazon.com.

4. "Performance Support in Internet Time: Discussion Between Gloria Gery, Stan Malcolm, Janet Cichelli, Hal Christensen, Barry Raybould, and Marc J. Rosenberg." Facilitated by Gary J. Dickelman. *Performance Improvement Quarterly*, Special Issue on Performance Support Perspectives and Practice, July 2000, *30* (6). www.pcd-innovations.com/pijuly2000/PSinInternetTime.pdf.

5. www.epssinfosite.com is a Web site dedicated to providing current and relevant resources, including articles, communications, examples, and discussions about performance support systems and their design, development, and implementation.

6. Special Issue: Performance Support Perspectives and Practice. Edited by Gary J. Dickelman. *Performance Improvement Quarterly*, July 2000, *30* (6). www.pcd-innovations.com/pi_july_2000.htm.

7. "Attributes and Behaviors of Performance Centered Systems." Gloria Gery. 1998. www.epssinfosite.com/gery%20attributes%20chart.htm.

**Acknowledgment:** I wish to thank Ariel Performance Centered Systems, Inc. for permission to illustrate some of the design ideas put forth in this chapter with examples of their fine work in performance-centered design. To learn more about Ariel, contact Matt Hummel, Senior Director of Business Development, at mhummel@arielpcs.com, call Ariel at 817 949-2215, or visit www.arielpcs.com.

*Gloria Gery is an independent consultant in Tolland, Massachusetts, specializing in e-learning and performance support systems. Gery was inducted into the HRD Hall of Fame in 1998 and in 1999 received the ASTD Distinguished Contribution Award. She is the author of* Electronic Performance Support Systems *(1991) and* Making CBT Happen *(1987). (Both are currently published by Gery Performance Press.) Gery is a frequent keynote speaker at training, knowledge management, and software conferences throughout the world. Her groundbreaking work in performance support is the basis for much new work in software design which integrates learning, support for work processing, knowledge, data, and tools. You can reach her at ggery@attglobal.net.*

# Learnativity: Into the Future

## Wayne Hodgins

*This article is an excerpt from a vision paper on the use of technology in adult learning. As the author notes, "This is all only a vision, only a dream, only a depiction of one possible scenario." He concludes, "The future is ours to imagine, ours to create."*

In February 2000, the American Society for Training and Development (ASTD) and the National Governors' Association Center for Best Practices (NGA) convened a Commission on Technology and Adult Learning that brought together governors and CEOs from business and post-secondary education to clarify and examine the most critical issues for public policy and practice raised by the changes in the economy and increasing use of information technology for adult learning. Supported by a task force of experts in learning and technology, corporate human resource development executives, and public policy representatives from federal and state agencies, the Commission brought together information and expert testimony and identified best practices, in order to make recommendations for public policy and private sector action. Some of the results of the Commission were published in the vision paper, *Into the Future*.

The purpose of this vision paper, *Into the Future*, is to provide a common platform from which to begin our discussion around the future of technology and learning, to draw on current work and developing trends, in order to create a vision of what the future could look like in terms of the use and impact of technology in adult learning. The vision paper can serve as either introduction to or reminder of the potential of the new world of learning "anytime anywhere" and of the education and training systems and practices now in place.

This paper is a demonstration not only of the new approaches to learning, but also of the new vocabulary, text formats, and ways of thinking that are part of that future. We know that technology's intersection with learning is not a simple trend of old approaches being replaced by new, but that new hybrid forms of learning and delivering content are emerging—with many combinations of traditional classes and teaching combined with technology-based methods for finding content and learning. In fact, a powerful argument has been made that the most effective technology-based delivery model is one that incorporates a heavy human component—professors, experts, tutors, mentors, and colleagues.

## Where We Are Now

The paper assumes awareness of the following:

- Technology is already widely used in adult learning. It is growing relatively "free form" and outside of the traditional social policy arena.
- There is a shift from "education and training" to "knowledge management."
- There have been leaps forward in the methods available to sort, retrieve, and reuse data and information through the application of "object-oriented" methods.
- The Internet and multimedia data and methods have already become a big part of adult learning.
- Separate technologies and organizations are merging to create multifaceted and multimedia delivery channels for content that enables learning.
- The wireless age and use of broadband cable are here, so that both individuals and institutions will have greatly expanded access to information at home, at work, at school—anywhere.
- Many teachers and technology experts are working together to launch a set of methods and standards that will enable easy reuse, recombination, and transfer of content among individuals, institutions, and countries.

### Issues for Public Policy and Private Practice

The Commission identified the following eight areas within public policy and private practice that are clearly affected by the possibilities of learning in the context of technology. These categories were included in the original proposal for this Commission.

**1. Equitable Access:** Aspects of this issue include: a) ensuring access to computers and the internet for all socio-economic groups (often described as the "digital divide"); b) overcoming barriers to learning using technology (including learning styles, basic skills); and c) developing and implementing common standards in the use of technology—such as interfaces, objects, platforms—that will enable reuse, communication, and the overall capability to access and use existing online or technology-based education and training resources.

**2. Accreditation and Licensure:** Issues here concern the need to revise existing systems for ensuring quality and excellence of curricula, developers, trainers, and educators. Existing systems are not easily applied to the methods, content, and flexibility of online learning.

**3. Assessment, Certification, and Acquiring Credentials:** The need is to define and establish appropriate systems and processes for assessing competency and knowledge and for formal assurance of the acquisition of knowledge that takes place outside of a traditional institutional structure or curriculum format. Individuals must be able to rely on credentials, which are portable and recognized in relevant professional or academic environments.

**4. Lifelong Learning:** There is growing realization that we can no longer define education and training in terms of traditional "blocks" and "silos." We need to move instead to a lifelong learning "pipeline" and to consider the role that online and other technology-based learning can play in an interdependent system beginning with pre-school and carrying on through ongoing workforce development and adult learning.

**5. Funding Sources and Funding Models:** Funding for adult education and training has been related primarily to institutions—post-secondary education institutions, private providers of training, formal training inside organizations, and others. Individual student aid is frequently restricted to particular hours or number of courses. We need to examine the processes and structures for funding, in order that they encompass the new realm of online education and training.

**6. State Investments for Economic Development:** The practical appeal of online learning has implications for state policies governing investments in education and training infrastructure to attract business and create jobs. The increasing importance of a workforce for the information technology and engineering sectors, as well as the necessity for all workers to use technology, requires the availability of online resources for skill development and retraining.

**7. Intellectual Property:** "Ownership" of content becomes more complex as open access to information expands. Traditional processes of copyright and "fair use" do not address online "learning objects" or the new ways content will be recombined and reused by teachers, trainers, and learners. As organizations develop new business models to support learning "anytime, anywhere," we need to take a new look at "rights management" for creators, authors, and publishers.

**8. Tax and Regulatory Policies:** Tax and regulatory policies governing not-for-profit and for-profit education and training providers may no longer be appropriate or optimal, as the process of learning "anytime, anywhere" blurs state and national boundaries with respect to location of providers and adult learners.

# Into the Future

> We can let the future happen or take the trouble to imagine it. We can imagine it dark or bright—and in the long run, that's how it will be.
>
> —David Gelertner, 2000

*Imagine ...*

- What we could do if we all shared a common vision of technology and adult learning.
- If our actions and decisions resulted in the reinvention of learning through the more effective application of available technology.
- What the future will be like if we choose to cultivate people with the skills needed to lead the technology that assists them in innovative problem solving.
- Reading in 2010 how this Commission was identified as one of the milestone catalysts at the takeoff point of the new learning economy.

Welcome to the future! In the space between this page and the last, time will be shifted forward five to ten years. Join us on a high-level flight over the new world of technology and adult learning that orbits around the unique learner in a knowledge-based universe. The rules of Newtonian physics have been superceded by those of learnativity, where the gravitational pull of creating new knowledge determines and shapes the actions of everything within. So suspend disbelief for the next little while, fasten your seat belts low and tight, make sure your tray table is in the locked and upright position, be open to the new world that is created by this shift, and remember that Einstein once said, "A change in perspective is worth at least 50 IQ points." Ready? Three ... two ... one ...

## Vision Paper Scope and Goals

This paper aims to help you envision the contributions of technology, adults, and learning to a bright and successful future society in which we would all want to live.

We will address these three areas:

- Adults, defined as individuals who are currently in or about to enter the work force
- Learning, as it relates to workforce development in a knowledge-based economy
- Technology, as it empowers and enables learning and the realization of the future.

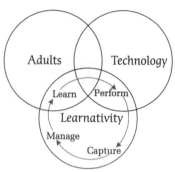

It is in the overlap of these areas that we find the questions and possibilities that need to be explored and addressed. We take a positive view of the future in this paper, but whether or not this future becomes reality will depend in large measure on the policies and practices that we and others begin to determine and put into place.

Our goals:

- Create a *shared vision* of a bright and achievable future for all working and learning adults.
- Identify the *common themes and forces* that shape the technology and adult learning environment of the future.
- Provide *new perspectives* and new ways of thinking about adults, learning, and technology.
- Foster *creative thinking and imaginative solutions.*

## Vision Paper Premise and Approach

The future isn't just happening to us any more; we make decisions every day that determine what decisions we will be able to make tomorrow. As we stand at the inflection point of a new learning economy, we realize that it will be shaped as we choose to shape it; it will be as rewarding and humane as we make it; the decisions we reach will determine what the world will be like for all of us.

The world of learning described in this paper does not rest easily within the public system of education and training that exists in this country today. Much of this system was put into place as a result of demand, and many of these demands of the time have changed dramatically or disappeared. The requirements for accreditation and assessment, the insistence on certification by accredited institutions, the establishment of public funding following the institution, the economic development policies of states in terms of funding educational establishments, the role of the public sector as a guarantor of access—these tenets of the system were put into place to ensure quality, value, marketability, equality of opportunity, and other goals of this society.

How must our public- and private-sector policies and practices change as we move into the new world of learning "anytime, anywhere"? Are these changes merely minor modifications of existing approaches to address new circumstances? Or are more fundamental changes needed in the principles, premises, and standards underlying our system? Will markets ensure access and quality in the new environment? As we realize that the individual is the new focus, locus, and customer, how do we protect and ensure the rights of the individual without creating barriers and intrusive authority?

The Commission on Technology and Adult Learning is being convened to look at the future of work and learning made possible through technology and identify policies and practices that make this future secure and available to all. In developing its policy recommendations, the Commission will be challenged to strike a balance between the new and the old, between the need to achieve results and the need to make sure that those results are achieved in a way that respects individual rights.

Thus, the task is not so much to see what no one yet has seen, but to think what nobody yet has thought about that which everybody sees.
—Arthur Schopenhauer (1788-1860)
*Essays and Aphorisms*

## The Power of a Shared Vision

We can only create what we can imagine. As Michelangelo reportedly remarked, sculpting a statue is easy—it's a matter of looking at a block of marble and taking away everything that doesn't belong there. More importantly, and what is often missed by many, is that Michelangelo worked with a group of 16 to paint the ceiling of the Sistine Chapel. Thus it was not the work of a single individual, however gifted, but the creation of a project team working with a shared vision.

## Great Groups

As they say, 'None of us is as smart as all of us.' That's good, because the problems we face are too complex to be solved by any one person or any one discipline. Our only chance is to bring people together from a variety of backgrounds and disciplines who can refract a problem through the prism of complementary minds allied in common purpose. I call such collections of talent Great Groups. The genius of Great Groups is that they get remarkable people—strong individual achievers—to work together to get results. But these groups serve a second and equally important function: they provide psychic support and personal fellowship. They help generate courage. Without a sounding board for outrageous ideas, without personal encouragement and perspective when we hit a roadblock, we'd all lose our way.
—Warren Bennis, 1997

We see this Commission on Technology and Adult Learning as a "Great Group," and this paper aspires to provide some clarity for a shared vision and hope that the future it describes is an achievable dream. Specifically, this Commission on Technology and Adult Learning will use the vision presented here to identify public policies and private sector practices that make this future secure and available to all. Creating the future dictates that, like Michelangelo, we have a vision of what we want things to be like, not in every particular, but sufficient to ensure that our multiple efforts have a unity of purpose and direction.

> There can be no innovation in the creation of strategy without a change in perspective.
>
> —Gary Hamel, 1996

## Future First: Plan Back

Alan Kay said, "The best way to predict the future is to invent it." This vision paper is based on the concept of inventing the future first and planning backwards from there to today. The first step is to think about what this future will look like.

## The Future Is a Knowledge-Based Economy

The term "new economy" refers to a set of qualitative and quantitative changes that, in the last 15 years, have transformed the structure, functioning, and rules of the world. Ideas and knowledge, rather than material resources, drive the new economy, and the keys to job creation and higher standards of living are innovation and technology embedded in services and manufactured products. In this economy, risk, uncertainty, and constant change are the rule, rather than the exception.

There is an infinite supply of knowledge, which means that knowledge-based economics are fundamentally different and poorly understood. Fundamental principles and laws that governed previous economics, such as the law of diminishing returns, are being flipped inside out. In this new, knowledge-based economy is a seemingly impossible reversal to the law of increasing returns. (See the quote by Kevin Kelly.) However, understanding this new reality is central to constructing a vision of tomorrow.

> The prime law of networking is known as the law of increasing returns. Value explodes with membership, and the value explosion sucks in more members, compounding the result. Industrial economies of scale stem from the Herculean efforts of a single organization. Networked increasing returns are created and shared by the entire network.
>
> —Kevin Kelly, 1997

## Putting Knowledge in Context: As Action

The future is about acquiring and acting on knowledge. Knowledge is not simply understanding and information; these are the raw resources of the new economy. Knowledge is the high value gained while providing services and creating products. When converged, learning, technology, and knowledge enable and empower individuals and teams to produce value for customers and competitive advantage for the team or organization.

The keys to success in the new economy are improving both individual performance and the productivity of teams and organizations. Both depend on under-standing what knowledge is and how it directly affects performance. Improvements in creating, managing, and transferring knowledge can lead to increased creativity, efficiency, productivity, and competitiveness for an individ-ual, a team, an organization, a country. This vision paper will illuminate this process as it is influenced by new technologies.

## Putting Learning in Context: Learnativity

Just as creating knowledge is the keystone of a knowledge-based economy, learning is an integral component of "learnativity." This is much more than just a word or a term. This is literally a new existence, a new way of living, a new way of being who we are. This is the state of the future.

As will be shown in more detail later, the learnativity model for creating knowledge is a continuous, spiraling conversion of tacit knowledge (such as know-how and experience) into explicit knowledge, which can be captured and turned into new tacit knowledge gained from learning by doing. In this context and in the knowledge-based economy, learning can be seen anew as an integral part of a knowledge creation spiral that involves

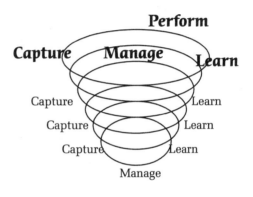

- Performing
- Capturing
- Managing
- Learning

An economic revolution changes how everyone does business, not just how a specific product is made. So the invention and production of the automobile, for example, is not a revolution. There were 200 or so auto manufacturers in the 1920s, and they eventually became just three, but business was conducted the same way. The steam engine, however, revo-lutionized how all work was done. Similarly, industrialization revolution-ized where and how all work was done. And in our time, computers, net-working, and the Internet are changing how all work is done. We're truly in a revolution.

—Dr. Lester Thurow, 1999

## A Bright Future Depends on Bright People

As we examine adults, technology, and learning, they all appear to be shaped by massive convergence, imploding to form a new common center of uniqueness. Roles and responsibilities that used to be divided nicely among different adults are now converged upon every individual. Technologies such as computers and telecommunications are converging, and learning is converging with performing, managing, and creating knowledge.

According to *Webster's New World Dictionary of the American Language*, College Edition, "quaquaversal" is defined as "directed from a common center toward all points of the compass; turning or dipping in all directions." We are entering upon a convergence of the inversed quaquaverse.

While this center of uniqueness is the inverse of what we have known, turning most of our perspectives and models inside out, it can also be seen as the nuclear center of quaquaversal motion—radiating out in every direction from the center—that is the nature of a bright new world and economy envisioned as the future of technology and adult learning.

The future will depend upon bright people using technology to cultivate their uniquely human skills. There is a significant difference, often overlooked, between machines that are able to perform so many functions that they usurp the roles of the people who use them and truly intelligent tools and technology. For example, self-serve gas station pumps and automated scanning devices at check-out counters have automated front-end sales so as to virtually eliminate the need for skilled labor, or for any person at all. This is in stark contrast to something such as 3D design technologies, which support their respective users but require higher-order thinking skills from the person using them.

When we automate an existing process we increase its efficiency, which increases the mechanical nature of the work that is required. However, intelligent tools and technology cause the opposite: an increase in effectiveness rather than efficiency, with more new and more skilled roles that also tend to pay higher salaries.

Higher-order cognitive skills are the key to ever more intelligent technology to extract and create the knowledge these technologies make available. The need for these skills is permeating literally all jobs, requiring everyone in the workforce to be bright, to be a knowledge-based worker and feed into the knowledge-based economy that increasingly predominates.

The choice is ours to make: we can choose to foster a workforce whose main function is to supplement the machines that do the work, or we can cultivate people so that they can acquire the skills necessary to lead the technology that assists them in innovative problem solving. In this vision paper, we choose the latter and offer you the option of the bright, personalized, knowledge-based future.

# Technology

*Imagine ...*

- Technology adapts itself to you and your environment, not vice versa.
- There is a pervasive, ubiquitous, and transparent technical infrastructure supporting all your learning and performance needs.
- Technology looks after all the details so you can stay focused on solving the real problems.
- You are part of the "infrastructure," a "node" connected to the system that is aware of who and where you are.

We finally have things in the right order, the horse before the cart. Technology is human-centric, designed to be intuitive and transparent. Just like oxygen, light, food, clothing, and shelter, we depend upon it to just be there. We expect it to actively and adaptively support our performance and productivity. Virtual and augmented reality, simulations, digital paper and ink, voice recognition and control, and biometric feedback are a few of the technologies that provide truly dynamic and adaptive support for learning and performing. Technology is so natural to use and so supportive of completing the right tasks well the first time, that the users are unconscious of the technology itself and focused instead on success.

Intelligent technology aids and abets our learning because of its own ability to learn through memory and pattern recognition. It learns about us as we use it, observes the surrounding conditions, notices the consequences and results, and is able to analyze what it learns to anticipate our future needs. We finally have truly just-in-time learning and performance support for achieving personal and group peak performance.

# Adults

*Imagine ...*

- We all know precisely what we need to know and learn at any given time.
- Every individual carries a detailed and continuously updated "inventory" of his or her skills and knowledge.
- For any given project, we can assemble the ideal team, based on skills, availability, costs, etc., and we know exactly what learning and support to provide for peak performance.
- Project teams learn as a single organism and get smarter as they work.

Adults (defined here as people who are in or about to enter the workforce) typically define themselves from several perspectives: as individuals, as professionals, as team players, as members of a community of practice, and as part of an organization.

| At a Glance |
| :--- |
| • Technology is disappearing much as electric motors did, embedded and invisibly working within virtually all appliances, clothing, even the soil and the air. |
| • Our own limitations for innovative thinking and application are the limits on the potential of technology. |
| • The most valued technology is not that which replaces reality or intelligence with artificial forms, but that which *augments* our own. |
| • Performance support and augmented intelligence technologies replace the need for *technology operators* and increase the demand for higher-order thinking skills of the know-why variety that are highly transferable. |
| • Technology will largely obviate the need for formal, classroom-type, event-based learning to produce know-what and know-how. |

| Today ⟶ | Tomorrow |
| :---: | :---: |
| Technology in the Foreground | Transparent, Embedded, Background |
| Smart | Intelligent (Learns in Use) |
| Virtual | Augmented |
| Artificial Intelligence | Augmented Intelligence |
| Generic | Task Specific |
| Good Guessing | Precision Predictablity |
| Pre-Programmed | Adaptive to User and Situation |
| Proprietary | Open Standards |

# Learnativity

*Imagine ...*

   • There is a new way of being that fuses learning, working, creativity, and knowledge creation into a single synchronous state.

## Convergence

Perhaps the most prevalent theme of the future is convergence. Technologies con-

| Points to Ponder |
|---|

**Work and Learning.** How will we cultivate the characteristics that let us use technology wisely, and how can we know what those characteristics are? How can we rapidly expand the use of technology for training and retraining the adult workforce?

**Individuals.** As technology advances at its exponential pace, and as technical limitations are resolved equally quickly, our ability to develop innovative and creative applications becomes the limitation on how quickly benefits advance. How do we accelerate the rate of *human* advance? What basic skills are needed to function effectively in the new world of technology-enhanced performance?

**Teams.** How can we create teams that have cohesive identities, yet enough flexibility to allow the useful participation of short-term consultants?

**Organizations.** How can organizations encourage the creation of technology that enables us and see that it reaches the marketplace?

**Policy and Practice.** What are public and private roles and responsibilities in developing intelligent technology supports for learning? How do we ensure that the necessary technology infrastructure for just-in-time access and delivery is available? What level of investment is required? What is the mix of public and private sector investment? The digital divide has its roots in more issues than the literal connections to technology. How do we ensure that all communities share the positive assumptions and expectations about the benefits of technology?

verge to create new technologies, and professional skills converge to create new professions. However, these convergences pale in comparison to the implosion of learning, working, capturing knowledge, and the management of their sum total. These previously disparate and relatively independent activities have converged to become one.

Just as in nuclear fusion, their intersection creates a previously unimagined new state producing equally unimaginable amounts of creativity, innovation, productivity, and performance. This fusion creates an infinite supply of the new energy source of the new economy: *knowledge.*

## Learnativity?

It is perhaps revealing that we do not have a word or a name for this new state. What do you call that which you and ever other person are doing every day as you solve problems, work, plan, communicate, and learn? When they used to stand still long enough, when they were independent activities, we simply called them by their own names. But when they happen all at once and all the time, fused

| Today ⟶ | Tomorrow |
|---|---|
| Corporation | Project Team |
| Technology Operator | Process Manager |
| Mass Certification | Skills and Knowledge Inventory |
| Managed | Motivated |
| Control | Responsibility |
| Diverse Masses | Unique Individuals |

## At a Glance

- Individuals, teams, and communities replace employers/workers/customers.
- Personalization is the key to enabling personal best performance.
- The motivation of the individual will be at the heart of knowledge creation, and the relationship between individuals and organizations will undergo profound changes as we uncover issues of ownership, intellectual property rights, authority and responsibility, etc.
- Working and learning will be the same thing.
- To be all that they can be, people become both in control of and personally responsible for their own development and learning.
- People primarily identify themselves through project teams and communities of practice.
- Teams and communities are enabled to create and grow their community knowledge.

## Points to Ponder

**Work and Learning.** Who controls and is responsible for work-related learning, if individuals control learning and are working predominantly in teams? When knowledge is created, who does it belong to? Who tracks the learning profile of adults and what issues related to privacy must be addressed through public policy?

**Individuals.** In the previous economy, ROI represents "return on investment." In the new knowledge-based economy, ROI represents "return on *individual*." How do you pay a person for inspiration? How do we balance individual rights and responsibilities in ways that offer some protection to the learner and guidance to the employer/organization?

**Teams.** As we increasingly understand teams as single organisms, how will we assign responsibility and compensate individual excellence? Project teams by definition exist for a finite time and then need to be dissolved. How do we deal effectively with the human resistance to breaking up such well-formed and bonded teams?

**Organizations.** How do organizations most effectively shift the focus of their capital investments to the new priority of the knowledge-based economy, human capital? How do they account for and value this? "Democratization" as a byproduct of technology-driven learning will mean that organizational success will depend upon a responsible, well-informed, and educated populace. What kind of cooperation and shared vision will be needed to produce this?

**Policy and Practice.** Who tracks the learning profiles of adults and what issues related to privacy must be addressed through public policy? What policy change, creation, and application are needed to match the completely new valuations of assets when most assets are intangible? What new systems of certification and credentialing of competencies are needed and what are the public and private responsibilities for creating and maintaining such systems? Is a learning profile as confidential as a medical record? How can individuals, organizations, and governments change the system while operating within it?

together into one single state of just being, what do we call it? For the purpose of this paper we will call it *learnativity*.

## Redefining Learning, Working, and Knowledge

Expertise used to demand constant improvement of one's ability to perform the tasks or skills of a profession or trade. However, as multiple professions converge and fuse, as tasks and skills are constantly replaced with new ones at an ever-increasing rate, expertise becomes a matter of steadily renewing one's knowledge base and extending it to new areas. Critical expertise has transformed into the con-

### At a Glance

- Learnativity, the nuclear fusion of capturing and managing knowledge, learning, and performing, releases the power of individuals and teams.
- Human attention is becoming our most scarce and most precious resource.
- Learning becomes a part of working and working becomes a part of learning.
- Learnativity creates an infinite supply of knowledge, the raw resource of the new knowledge-based economy.

tinuous creation and acquisition of knowledge and skills. This lifelong cycle of learning is the new foundation of personal self-worth and that of all teams and organizations. One's primary responsibility, and perhaps the only sustainable competitive advantage, is to improve one's ability to learn and apply the right things faster.

## Putting Learning (Back) into Context and Motion

A classic and historical problem with most approaches to education and training has been to see learning as an end in itself, an activity that is designed and studied independent of the learner and, most importantly, independent of the overall system within which it works. Learnativity is *not* a mechanical, static, linear process, nor one that can be understood by examining any of its components outside of its systemic context. It is a very human, dynamic, and complex flow that resembles an organic structure more than a mechanical one.

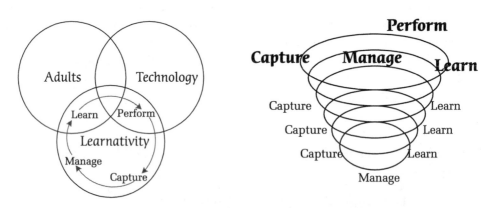

While this is obviously a complex model, we can use a simple example to illustrate. As the owner of a small business, you continuously learn what the customers like or dislike by walking around, asking questions, speaking with them and with the employees. You write down what you've learned or you invite your customers to fill out questionnaires and make suggestions. You share what you learn with your employees and invite them to suggest ways that the products and services you provide might be improved. Finally, you put these suggestions into action, incrementally improving your business and ensuring that your clientele remains loyal.

This all takes place on an ongoing basis within the context of this group of individuals and this company. It yields a sense of loyalty and value, a sense of purpose and accomplishment, for all those involved. This group bonding and learning produces yet more valuable knowledge, which can be subsequently utilized to bring more value to those being served, in the form of tangible services and goods.

Organizations that are successful in the creation and management of knowledge cannot mandate that knowledge will be created, nor can they automate the process. The organization can, however, provide conditions, an environment, that will foster, nurture and support this type continuous learning, which in turn results in peak performance.

It may seem that learning has been eliminated when in fact it has just faded from conscious awareness as it increasingly embeds itself into our products, services, tools, and technology. Learning takes its rightful place as a fundamental requirement of just being. It is no longer always an event, an activity that is divorced from the rest of our life and existence. Perhaps this is the ultimate form of the much-discussed convergence we see happening in most other areas, such as technology.

## Knowledge Creation in Action

Learnativity is knowledge in action, a continuous spiraling conversion of tacit knowledge (such as know-how and experience) into explicit knowledge that can be captured, shared with others, diffused within groups, and turned back into new tacit knowledge gained from learning by doing. Learnativity is a way of continuously creating new, actionable knowledge. The key is to see this as a single state, with the following four primary elements swirling within:

- **Performing.** Let's start where we want individuals, teams, and organizations to end: peak performance. Performing, as used in this paper, refers to the application of knowledge. We put knowledge to work, solving problems. Performing is the integration and application of knowledge in the activities, products, and services of the project team or organization. Explicit knowledge converts to tacit as successful performance achieves results and the workers move on.
- **Capturing.** Capturing knowledge means converting it from a tacit state into an explicit, comprehensible form—such as a video, a simulation, a model, or words and illustrations in a document—so that others can understand it.
- **Managing.** Management of information, learning, and performance is the conversion of explicit knowledge (formal and expressed) into complex and valuable combinations of ideas, insights, and experiences so they can be shared with others.
- **Learning.** Learning is the means by which tacit knowledge (informal and subjective) is exchanged between individuals and between the learner and the learning resources. It is therefore both social and personal in nature. It occurs in both formal and informal settings, and includes connections and direct interaction among people. Learning is also the personal transformation from explicit to tacit within the individual through reading, observation, and reflective thought.

# Back from the Future

Welcome back from the future!

Time is now restored to today. The future of working and learning is in the creation of knowledge, which is of course precisely what the Commission on Technology and Adult Learning has been created to do. Time is now, and time for the work and the learning that will be the Commission.

Never confuse a clear view of the future for a short distance.
—Paul Saffo, 1998

## Back to Reality

So now it is time to step out of this time machine and come back from the future. Let's get real. This is all *only* a vision, *only* a dream, *only* a depiction of one possible scenario. Clearly there are others. Many alternative scenarios range from less bright to depressingly black.

The word "democratization" is not used lightly within this paper. While never a certain outcome and always fraught with opportunities for sabotage and misdirection, it has proven to be the most powerful and enduring model for sustained change and prosperity. In any case, there would not appear to be a choice on this point; the individuals of the world are in increasing control and we will all cast our votes with our actions, our imagination, our commitment, or the lack thereof.

## The Broad and the Long View

Using the three words in the name of this Commission on *Technology* and *Adult Learning*, let's take a concluding look at each.

**Adults.** The challenge and the solution is a human one. We are seeing people at two extreme ends of a spectrum.

At one end, we see the accelerating momentum that is bringing control all the way down to the unit of one, the unique individual. This is not a reflection of selfishness but of empowerment, and along with control comes responsibility.

At the other end of the spectrum is the natural formation of these individuals into communities. In the context of adults, technology, and learning, there are two primary types of community:

- project teams, which form and dissolve with the projects themselves
- communities of practice, where people of like working and professional interests connect and collaborate with their peers

In both cases, they create and share "community knowledge." These communities, as systems of learning and performing, prove to be highly sustainable, scalable, transferable, and successful.

A bright future is dependent upon bright people. They are not simply the learned, who can memorize facts and figures; they are not just masters of their professions and crafts. They are instead those who are skilled at higher-order thinking, including analysis, planning, problem solving, creativity, and, perhaps most important, learning. These are skills that anyone can attain and develop. These are skills that are highly transferable, sustainable, and scalable. These are the skills that will lead to a bright future for individuals, project teams, communities, and countries worldwide.

**Technology.** Technology is attaining profound abilities to learn through analysis, deduction, and memory of the conditions and consequences of use. The future we want is very real, and technology should augment this reality and improve our ability to work effectively within it. Replacing real experiences with artificial substitutes, as in simulations, is often useful, but we are increasingly able to have the real thing as the first and lasting experience. Yet, while increasingly adaptive, technology is not alive. It does not change all by itself. We must demand these characteristics of those who can create the innovative technology solutions we seek. We should accept and expect no less.

The combined power that is created by connecting every person, every piece of information, and every object in our world, and enabling these connections to flow freely at the speed of innovative and creative human thought is the opportunity before us. The old boundaries of time, distance, status, and location, and even the confines of socio-economic, political, and racial status, are disappearing before our eyes. To be sure, new barriers and challenges are ahead. However, we are rapidly reaching the point where the technological capabilities and possibilities we have at our disposal are no longer the limits that contain us. The limiting factor is our ability to think boldly and differently enough to imagine and plan solutions and then form the resolve to execute those solutions.

Technology has perhaps had the least impact, relative to most other areas, upon learning. If we are prepared for the opportunities this presents, the results will be staggering. If not, we may miss or delay the greatest potential changes in learning, and subsequent empowerment of all people, that the world has witnessed.

*Guaranteed?* No!
*Probable?* Maybe
*Possible?* Absolutely!

**Learning.** The key to unlocking all this potential brings us back to bright people, people who have the sustained ability to learn and apply the right stuff faster. We refer to this capacity as "learnativity." This is not a technology, not an activity, not a resource. Learnativity involves a continuous, swirling set of experiences traveling through the domains of learning, capturing and creating information and knowledge, managing all these resources, and ultimately putting it all to work in solving problems. This all occurs in real time, all the time. As is the case with technology, learning in the future will fade from our conscious awareness, as it becomes embedded in every product, every service, and every facet of our lives. This will take place all the time, just in time, and just right for peak performance

In light of the complex, broad and daunting task before this Commission, surely Warren Bennis's phrase, "None of us is as smart as all of us," has never been more true. Thus the creation of this Commission, a *great group* of complementary minds with an eclectic mixture of experience and perspectives to take on this great challenge.

This will not be easy. This will not be fast. It will require innovative, out-of-the-box thinking. There will be the need to both suspend disbelief and abandon previously entrenched norms, customs, and habits of our economy and culture. If this Commission can find the collective and individual strength, the commitment and the solidarity to do so, there is no doubt that this vision will be realized.

There is an opportunity matched by a need.

The future is ours to imagine, ours to create.

## References

Bennis, Warren. (1997). *The Secret of Great Groups*. Available online: www.drucker-foundation.org/leaderbooks/L2L/winter97/bennis.html.

Bloom, B.S. (1984, June-July). The 2 Sigma Problem: The Search for Methods of Group Instruction as Effective as One-to-One Tutoring. *Educational Researcher*, 4-16.

Burke, James. (1995). *Connections*. New York: Little, Brown.

Chambers, John. (1999). Presentation at COMDEX '99. Available online: www.cisco.com.

Dede, Chris. (1995). Testimony to the U.S. Congress, House of Representatives Joint Hearing on Educational Technology in the 21st Century, Committee on Science and Committee on Economic and Educational Opportunities.

Gelertner, David. (2000, January). Conversation cited in "The Wired Diaries 2000." *Wired*, 69.

Gilder, George. (1999, October 4). The Brightest Star. *Forbes ASAP*, 29-34.

Hamel, Gary. (1996, July-August). *Harvard Business Review*.

IBM's "World Board." (2000, January). *Wired*, 60.

Kay, Alan. (1971). Meeting of the Palo Alto Research Center and Xerox Corporation planners.

Kelly, Kevin. (1997, September). *Wired*.

Mecklenburg, Steve. (1998). Knowledge Inc.: The Executive Report on Knowledge, Technology & Performance.

Nonaka, Ikujiro. (1991, November-December). The Knowledge-Creating Company. *Harvard Business Review*.

Model Tee: Golf instructor underwear. (2000, January). *Wired*, 64.

Parmentier, Michael A. (1999). A Vision of the Future Learning Environment. Brief presented at Advanced Distributed Learning Science & Technology workshop.

Saffo, Paul. Institute for the Future. Web site: www.startribune.com/digage/saffo.htm.

Schopenhauer, Arthur. (1976). *Essays and Aphorisms*. London: Penguin Books.

Shannon, Claude. (1995). Cited in Burke, James, *Connections*. New York: Little, Brown.

Solomon, Charlene Marmer. (1999). Global Search Engine. *Success*, 20-21.

Strassmann, Paul A. (1999). Information Production: Assessing the Information Management Costs of U.S. Companies. Information Economics Press.

Thurow, Lester. (1999). Ride the Wave. (Sidebar in article, The Wealth of Knowledge.) *CIO Magazine*. Available online: www.cio.com/archive/010100_book.html.

Zuboff, Shoshana. (1989). *In the Age of the Smart Machine: The Future of Work and Power*. New York: Basic Books.

*Wayne Hodgins, in his role as Director of Worldwide Learning Strategies at Autodesk, is the chief architect and strategic futurist responsible for increasing human performance (employees, partners, and customers) through what he calls "learnativity." Hodgins is currently the elected Chair of the IEEE P 1484 Standards Working Group for Learning Object Metadata and was most recently asked to be the Special Advisor and Strategic Futurist for the recently formed Commission on Technology and Adult Learning. To get a copy of the complete learnativity paper and/or contact Hodgins, visit www.learnativity.com.*

# Blended Learning: The Magic Is in the Mix

**Elliott Masie**

*The future of e-learning is in a return to the past, to the ways our ancestors learned. The success of e-learning systems is in what comes naturally, the ways we learn on our own. If you don't believe in blended learning, this article may well convince you.*

People are not single-method learners! When you or I learn something new, it is almost inevitable that we are using more than one method in the process. If I read a really insightful article, I will turn to my wife or nearest colleague for an instant conversation. That dialogue is a necessary part of the process of how adults learn. If I take an intriguing on-line lesson, I will often want to read something in print as part of process of mastering the new skill. And, if I am in a great classroom and the instructor tweaks my interest on a topic, a few hours (or minutes) later, I find myself at the computer checking out additional perspectives on the web.

I would argue that we are, as a species, *blended learners*. In classroom instruction, we have always known this, even if unconsciously. Good instructors have always combined great storytelling (an audio process), with print and whiteboard words and graphics (a reading process), with takeaway tools or even homework. And, then add the supplemental reading list. In my three decades as a classroom instructor, I have never done single-method learning.

## Single-Method Learning

Yet, in these early days of e-learning, there is a tendency for the marketplace and even internal training professionals to move toward *single-method* learning. This means that the learner is given a single, self-contained, method of mastering the materials. For example, a learner is provided with on-line reading on a key topic. This is only one method. If that is the whole package, several things will happen:

- The learner will be underwhelmed and may not participate or complete the learning activity.
- The learner *will* add a second or third method, either auditory, hands-on practice, or dialogue, except that it is all on the shoulders of the student to organize and access these methods.

Single-method learning may be cheaper and rolled into an easier-to-deliver package, but it may not even have a chance to work, if the learner is not engaged and motivated to participate.

On the other hand, blended learning adds significantly greater opportunity for the learner to master the material and move towards transfer and performance.

## Blended Learning

So, what do we mean by blended learning? In my world, it is the use of two or more distinct methods of training. This may include combinations such as:

- blending classroom instruction with on-line instruction
- blending on-line instruction with access to a coach or faculty member
- blending simulations with structured courses
- blending on-the-job training with brown bag informal sessions
- blending managerial coaching with e-learning activities

The format of blending learning that seems to have quietly taken hold in corporate cultures is the first one on my list, the combination of *classroom* and *e-learning*.

This format even comes in several blends and varieties:

- Learners take an on-line course prior to starting the classroom component. This on-line course can either be voluntary (in the form of digital pre-work) or mandatory, where the class registration does not happen until the learner participates in the e-learning offering and perhaps passes a competency exam.
- Learners are provided with a post-course e-learning set of activities, either synchronous or asynchronous, that extend the footprint of the class beyond the time limits of the course.

- Learners attend a face-to-face session at the beginning and at the end of a program, with the bulk of the content and learning activities occurring on-line in the middle of the training experience.
- Actual sessions of a multi-day class are offered synchronously or asynchronously, so that students who cannot attend all sessions can keep up with the flow of the course.
- On-line communities of practice that start at the beginning of a class and continue throughout and beyond, providing support and peer learning opportunities.

These combinations of classroom and e-learning modes have been well received by learners who are new to the changing training formats and provide a blend of the best of the face-to-face experience and the flexibility of the on-line experience.

## Effects of Blended Learning

Several things start to happen as organizations experiment with blended learning:

- In-person classes get shorter and fewer. The organization and the instructor feel less pressure to "cover the material" during the course, since they have a more elastic window of opportunity for knowledge transfer.
- The content during the classroom section of a blended learning experience shifts in format. We see fewer lectures and more interaction. There is less of a "sage on the stage" and more case studies, workgroups, and learner-driven content. In other words, the classroom is used for things that are best done in the classroom and pure information transfer is often shifted to on-line delivery.
- The intensity of the learning experience for the learner often increases. The MASIE Center has tracked increased levels of learner-to-trainer questions, increased levels of learner-to-learner interactions, and more total hours of learner attention than in pure on-line or pure classroom delivery.
- The work of the instructor often increases dramatically! Suddenly, the work-day does not end when the class leaves the room. Several colleagues have noted that they often work four to 10 times harder in delivering an blended learning course, until they develop better expectations and methods for handling learner demands.

The effectiveness and impact of these programs is dramatic. Several organizations, including IBM, have shifted management development for new managers to a blended learning model. In the case of IBM, the footprint for the total experience went from a two-week residential program to a year-long model that includes a trip to IBM headquarters in the middle of the year, after community, content mastery, simulation, and training activities have reached a key point.

In sales representative training, the blended learning model has been used to combine four dimensions:

- boot camp experiences
- on-line learning and assessment
- simulations and practice
- district manager coaching of new representatives

Even in the world of e-learning, a number of key vendors, including Digital Think and Smartforce, have extended their structured on-line offerings to include interactions with faculty, coaches, and community of peers.

## Challenges and Changes

Blended learning can present a challenge on the funding side, unless an organization is strategic in the application of learning resources. At first glance, it looks as though advocates of blended learning are advocating a dramatic increase in the resources per learning event. However, we see ways of using blended learning to deliver more learning for a lower cost or even to achieve overall cost containment:

- The e-learning elements of the program can be stable, long-lasting, asynchronous components. Once an instructor creates key pre- and post-classroom offerings, these can be delivered without additional development or instructional time expenditures.
- The faculty member does not have to be the coordinator of the blended learning activities. A call center model can be deployed where trained representatives launch and administer the progress of a learner, rather than a more expensive faculty member.
- Communities of learning and communities of practice can be nurtured to provide on-going support on a peer-to-peer basis.
- Explicit contracts with learners can be developed to create realistic expectations and demands for support.
- Classroom costs can be dropped by shortening the length of the face-to-face components of blended learning, lowering the instruction and lodging/travel expenses.

As blended learning grows in acceptance, there will be changes needed within the e-learning and training industry:

- Learning management systems (LMSs) must be adapted to track and invite the learner through various stages of a blended learning experience. For example, once a worker completes the pre-class content, a registration and invitation is triggered for the classroom component. The LMS needs to span the entire learning process, including the informal, reading, and on-the-job components!

- A needs analysis and instructional design model needs to take into consideration the various elements of a blended learning offering. This would include the technical ability of the learner to actually participate in a synchronous or asynchronous component of the course.
- Pricing models need to develop that will provide the resources to support the blended learning model. Currently, organizations do not often know what to charge for external blended learning and training organizations have the same confusion on the charge-back levels.
- We need a language to describe, as a category or even *brand*, what each variation of blended learning means. For example, if I hear that my wife is taking me to a dinner theater, I know that we will eat food and see something from a stage. Do learners know the same when they hear they are enrolled for a blended learning offering in the corporate university?
- Skills of instructors need to be expanded to include their changing roles as e-trainers and e-coaches and to help them mourn the potential loss of front-of-the-room presence.

If we push the envelope even further, we can imagine at least two future state variations of blended learning that are intriguing:

- **The course that never ends!** Why do we ever want to graduate or end a course, if we can provide ongoing digital learning and performance support for the learner? We predict that you will see a number of perpetual courses in the future!
- **Linking style preference/dominance to the blend!** If we know which styles of learning work best for a learner, we can start to provide blends that are appropriate on an individualized level. In the classroom, I know there are always a few learners who will stay after the end of class to have a more detailed dialogue with the trainer—and I know which ones will never approach me with a question. I alter my in-class training techniques to honor and engage both sets of learners. As we build blended learning, we should be able to either manually or automatically honor these style differences!

## Value and Power of Blended Learning

If I have not convinced you yet of the value and power of blended learning, do a personal inventory of your own approach to gaining new skills and knowledge. Answer a few of these questions:

- What are you doing in a several-hour class, other than just listening to the trainer talk?

- When you read a compelling article or book, what are you most likely to do?
- When you return from a great or confusing course, what role do your peers or managers play in processing that experience?
- When an on-line class gets confusing, what do you do to resolve your questions?
- When you are heading to an intensive class, what do you wish you could do to prepare for the program?
- When a class ends, what do you hope are your continuing resources as you start to transfer the learnings to the workplace?
- And, if you have a teenager, how does he or she do homework?

A colleague in China remarked that the power of e-learning was to return us to the blend of training that existed prior to the "industrialization" of the process. They saw the classroom as a recent, very industrial manifestation of how people are asked to learn. When they reflected on how their ancestors learned, it was a blended model. There was a mentor or master, lots of practice, peer learning, perhaps reading, and an expectation that learning happened over a longer period of time. They saw blended learning adding the incubation and patience dimensions to the training process.

In the next few years, you will see an explosion of blended learning. Personally, I hope the phrase "blended learning" does not catch on, just as I hope that the "e" in e-learning gets old as quickly as possible. Then, we can refer to training and learning as training and learning, as we find the magical in the mix of people and technology!

*Elliott Masie is the President of The MASIE Center. He is the editor of a free weekly e-letter,* TechLearn Trends, *and runs an active lab focused on how people, technology, and learning will fit together. Find out more at www.masie.com.*

# E-Learning in the Old World: A Reflection on the European E-Learning Situation

## Christian Völkl and Folkert Castelein

*As we come to realize the power of e-learning to cover great distances, we should be aware of how e-learning is developing in other areas of the world. This article provides an informative and interesting view of what's happening across the Atlantic.*

America, you've got it better! One could argue for hours over a glass of Italian wine, a French baguette, and Dutch cheese whether this claim still holds true since Goethe made it several hundred years ago. In terms of the economic situation at least, Western Europe is similar to the US when we think of the impact of the Internet and the related e-business revolution.

The challenges too are similar. Just like their US counterparts, European organizations face similar fast-paced change, a comparable shortage of corporate smarts, and an equally huge demand for human capital development, in order to enable all employees to be productive.

Does this also imply that European training managers and HR specialists have a comparable understanding of e-learning to their American counterparts? And do European companies approach e-learning in the same way as their US-based competitors?

It is our intention here to attempt to offer answers to these questions and to shed some light on the corporate e-learning situation in Western Europe. Let's begin by explaining that in Europe an e-learning definition has emerged that is broader than the typical technology-centric one. We will then discuss what organizations might want to consider if they want to be successful in the European e-learning arena and where we predict the market will be heading.

We wholeheartedly admit that we are offering anecdotal evidence coloured by our own points of view. Still, we are convinced that even in Internet times, the clocks tick a little differently in Europe, and in ways that will be of interest in North America.

## So Many Technologies, So Many Definitions: The E-Learning Babylon

How do we define e-learning in Europe? At first glance, this seems to be a simple question.

Let's have a look, for instance, at some definitions offered at the many e-learning conferences in Europe over the last couple of months: "A mix of traditional and technology-driven training" or "Every training delivery mechanism that uses the Web" or "A type of training that provides for an online exchange between learner and teacher during the learning process."

### An Infant Market

We quickly come to realize, however, that it is not easy to define e-learning. As a matter of fact, if you visit an e-learning summit in Europe these days, you will find from 50 to 100 exhibitors, some of them globally operating, some of them locally only, but all claiming to be 'the' professionals in e-learning. Some offer a catalog packed with Web-based learning modules. Others don't have any off-the-shelf content at all, but instead provide CD-ROM- or paper-based training solutions, in conjunction with an online instructor available for questions and guidance. Still others would like to sell you their authoring tool—compliant with all the standards in the world, of course. And finally, there might be a group of vendors promising consulting expertise in strategy development or implementing a learning management system (LMS).

What this tells us is that the e-learning market in Europe is highly fragmented and still in its infancy, with many parties offering all kinds of solutions, some of them complementing each other, some partnering with each other, and most competing with each other. As a logical consequence, the varying definitions of e-learning are less focused on customers and strategy and more based on the new or legacy products and solutions the companies are bringing to market.

## Enabling vs. Transforming Technologies

A quick look at the evolution of e-learning technologies, as described in Figure 1, explains why most of the previously mentioned technology-based or web-centric definitions do not sufficiently capture the essence of e-learning.

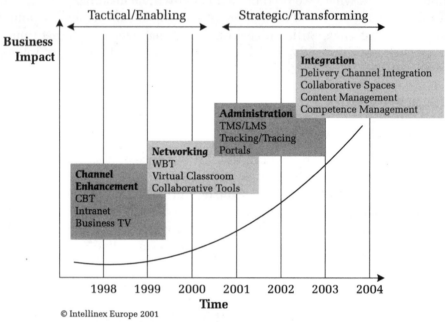

© Intellinex Europe 2001

**Figure 1.** Evolution of e-learning technologies in Europe

In the mid- to late '90s, e-learning in Europe was more or less synonymous with technology-based training and the focus was primarily on providing additional delivery channels for instructors or experts. At that time, the topic of e-earning came up only at specialized congresses and trade fairs, and the protagonists of these early stages were visionaries within the HR and training departments, who were lonely voices in their organizations. The intention was to reduce the costs of training delivery while simultaneously increasing the speed at which the learning materials could be provided.

The nature of the technologies deployed during these phases, however, was more *enabling* than *transforming*, and the focus was mostly tactical. As a consequence, the business impact was slight.

# Beyond Technology: A Definition of E-Learning

Many pilot projects later, companies are beginning to learn lessons. They have come to realize that placing many learning modules on the shelf and simply adding delivery channels doesn't guarantee good training or performance improvement. Now, people are starting to understand that one has to strategically integrate these offerings and to tie them to actual business goals in order to ensure effective human capital development.

## It's All About Integration

Figure 1 shows that in the past companies had to deal with many different and discrete solutions that were often not compatible with each other. Now, emerging standards and defined system interfaces make it possible to connect these e-learning solutions with other HR and workplace-related systems (as shown on the right side of Figure1).

Consequently, e-learning moves beyond the boundaries of the traditional training function. It becomes part of a firm's overall business-to-employee (B2E) efforts, as Dr. Michael Christ, leader of the e-HR practice at the German airline, Lufthansa, suggests. Wolfgang Rautenberg, Director of Training and Development with Deutsche Bank, has something similar in mind when he notes that learning must be fully integrated into the culture of an organization and its work processes. He calls this the shift from an HR planning economy to a free-enterprise economy with employees as individual agents at the core, each acting as a kind of "Me-Corporation" and being fully responsible for their own learning and development. This shift can also be described as the move from a push approach, where learning topics and modes are dictated to individuals, to a pull approach where individuals are responsible for identifying and accessing their own learning materials and means—a perspective offered by Simon Brown, Commercial Director of Bright Wave Limited, a British e-learning provider.

These more strategic goals articulated by Brown, Christ, and Rautenberg are echoed by business managers who are seeking end-to-end solutions for training and learning that match the entire HR value chain. Therefore we can say that the proliferation of e-business and its extension to HR and to training and development, respectively, is changing the learning landscape considerably. What becomes apparent is that professionals in the field are being asked by their senior management to transform traditional training and learning processes in a way similar to what e-business has done for general business processes. Table 1 lists examples of these changes.

## From E-Learning to E-Working

As you can see in Figure 1, we are just beginning to implement this "new breed" of e-learning technologies, so it would be premature to talk about the business impact of these installations as if it were a fact. For instance, one can compare the maturity of today's LMS solution providers to ERP companies such as SAP from

| | Past | Today |
|---|---|---|
| Training Department | • Tactical<br>• Stable processes<br><br>• Administration | • Strategic<br>• Continuously changing business requirements<br>• Service and delivery |
| Roles | • Administrator<br>• Trainer | • Consultants<br>• Coaches and performance consultants |
| Content | • Could be planned for an entire year in advance<br>• General<br>• Predefined curricula | • Constant demand for new learning<br>• Personalized<br>• Modular learning objects |
| Learners | • Employees of the company<br><br>• Passive recipients | • Business community: employees, suppliers, customers<br>• Self-serving, active agents |
| Training Systems | • Offline, stand-alone solutions (Lotus, Excel, etc.)<br>• Asynchronous data management | • Networked systems<br><br>• Real-time tracking and analysis |

**Table 1.** How e-business changes the training landscape (© Intellinex Europe 2001)

10 years ago, as does Peter Ungeheuer, Director of Organizational Development with the Berlin branch of Cell Network, an international e-learning specialist.

Nevertheless, it makes sense for the discourse in our profession to adapt a broader definition of e-learning that goes beyond the limits of a strictly technology-focused description. Figure 2 depicts how such an environment, which we refer to as the "e-working landscape," might possibly look.

In this sense, one could perceive e-learning, equivalent to e-business, in its role in the fundamental transformation of learning environments and human performance technology systems into the e-working landscape. Using Web technology, e-learning is shaping collaborative spaces to integrate with other value-enabling systems in an organization, such as competence and content management. Its purpose grows to lifting the performance of individuals in business communities through work-related competence development.

Why does it make sense to define e-learning in this way? Figure 3 provides an answer, as it lists important benefits that can be achieved through e-learning as a performance lift that goes beyond the commonly mentioned bottom-line advantages such as cost and time savings. Paul Campman, e-learning manager for Cisco

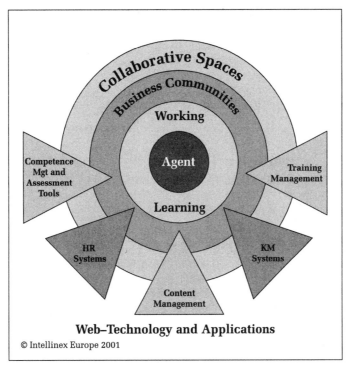

**Figure 2.** The e-working landscape

Benelux, offers an illustrative summary: "The far-reaching benefits of e-learning are achieved once you can track a learner and prescribe the next set of modules based on the job/task requirements in a just-in-time (JIT) manner—ultimately tying it all back to your business objectives."

# Deliberate Adoption: E-Learning Acceptance in European Organizations

Despite the confusion that sometimes surrounds the definition of e-learning, it's probably fair to say that by now organizations in Europe have a solid understanding of e-learning and its benefits. Whereas in the past solution providers had to explain why their offerings would add value to an organization, now the focus is on the "how-to" aspect of e-learning implementations. The "why" question is rarely asked anymore.

## Partnering as a Best Practice

Lufthansa's Dr. Christ points out that one of the reasons for this shift in focus might be that partnering within an organization and beyond its borders has reached a

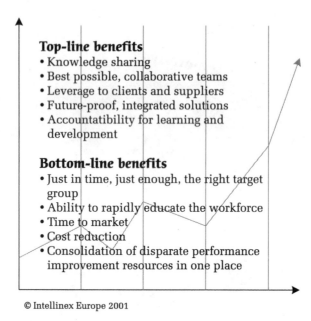

**Top-line benefits**
- Knowledge sharing
- Best possible, collaborative teams
- Leverage to clients and suppliers
- Future-proof, integrated solutions
- Accountatibility for learning and development

**Bottom-line benefits**
- Just in time, just enough, the right target group
- Ability to rapidly educate the workforce
- Time to market
- Cost reduction
- Consolidation of disparate performance improvement resources in one place

© Intellinex Europe 2001

**Figure 3.** E-learning as a carrier for performance lift

new level. He suggests that a new atmosphere of collaboration has started to emerge, partly because of the climate that the e-business culture has created and partly because of the bitter lessons that people learned from past pilot projects. He says that the old "not invented here" resistance that inhibited the implementation of cross-departmental projects seems to have disappeared.

Today, experts such as Dr. Christ and Deutsche Bank's Rautenberg find it easier to secure management's support for massive e-learning infrastructure investments, which are considerably higher than those requested in the past for other forms of training delivery by training and development functions. Sailing in the backwater of other money-intensive B2E initiatives, and of the e-business transformation in general, training and development departments enjoy a general willingness of senior management to approve the requested e-learning projects as long as they can show the potential benefits to them.

## Blended Solutions

This doesn't mean that companies all over Europe are only doing e-learning these days and have forgotten about all other types of training and development. As Martin Delahoussaye writes in the January 2001 issue of *Training* magazine (p. 62), "a mix of traditional and technology-driven training initiatives has surfaced as the best solution for European organizations."

Cisco's Paul Campman argues in the same way when he suggests that "smart companies are blending the best of both worlds, delivering a learning experience that takes advantage of the Internet's capabilities yet maintaining human involvement in the learning process—albeit in most cases, these human roles have changed somewhat."

To further illustrate this point, we can say that professionals in France, Germany, the Netherlands, and the Scandinavian countries closely focus on the architecture and the technology behind an e-learning solution. They see the added value of using a data-driven training administration and learning management system for strategic purposes such as performance and competence management.

On the other hand, they are bound to consider the social aspects of learning, a factor that historically has been of utmost importance in Europe. E-learning solution providers are therefore forced to show how technology can serve as an enabler for such purposes. In this regard, European e-learning buyers are usually pretty receptive to vendors who offer an integration of diverse channels (including traditional means of training delivery) that allows for social exchange such as forums, chat, online coaching, etc.

## Quality as the Show-Stopper

According to Dr. Christ, the very comprehensiveness with which Europeans commonly approach business issues might be one of the reasons that they have been slow to adopt e-learning. Especially in Germany, professionals tend to consider all possible aspects of the e-learning phenomenon (including all hypothetical ones, of course). However, since e-learning has so many facets, the proverbial German engineering mind inevitably approaches its limits when it attempts to account for all theoretical eventualities of this complex subject matter. But instead of implementing a pragmatic but potentially sub-optimal solution (which would be inconsistent with German culture), the logical consequence is inertia—or, to put it in nicer terms, thoughtful deliberation.

A less satirical version of why Europeans have been reluctant to implement e-learning solutions is offered by Jane Massy, a consultant and e-learning specialist with the European Centre for the Development of Vocational Training (Cedefop). She says that Europeans usually want to know whether or not something is working and what the potential outcome might be *before* they engage in it. In contrast, people in the US tend to have more of a "just do it" approach with the intention of improving the quality *later on*. As a consequence, Massy explains, Europeans have been slow to adopt e-learning as long as they perceived a lack of quality. However, since e-learning products and solutions have reached a level of quality that seems to be acceptable to Europeans, adoption rates are increasing now.

Spinning this argument a little further, this actually could turn out to be an advantage for Europe, as Cell Network's Ungeheuer suggests. He says the slowness with which European organizations started to adopt e-learning puts them into the position to avoid many mistakes that are common for the emergence of a new industry. Now that the shortcomings of early e-learning efforts are becoming apparent, Europe would have the chance to enter the stage on a much higher-quality level.

When it comes to quality, Europeans especially want to make sure that e-learning solutions are localized and adapted to their respective cultures. Delahoussaye perfectly captured this point in his article:

> Europeans want more than linear-learning and talking pictures; they also want training in their local language with cultural references to which they can relate and connect. ... Overcoming the localization issue is, therefore, key to the growth of distance learning across the continent. (*Training*, January 2001, p. 65)

Both Rautenberg and Dr. Christ are quick to point out, though, that quality is a relative factor. There is no generally agreed-upon quality standard for e-learning that is valid throughout all of Europe, or anywhere else, for that matter. Another important issue, they say, is that quality is a term that is defined by the client, i.e., the buyer of e-learning products. Since modern training and development departments perceive themselves as service delivery organizations, they can produce only what their customers (internal or external) are willing to pay for. Fortunately, many of these clients are receptive to what research recommends, and therefore request the change from old page-turner CBTs to open-structure and case-based learning environments.

## The Race Is Tight, the Future Is Bright: Trends in the European E-Learning Market

E-learning expenditures in Europe will hit more than $3.9 billion by 2004, up from just $717 million this year, according to a recent IDC study (IDC, 2001). Arm in arm with this growth, experts say, a market consolidation will take place that will cure many of the "children's illnesses" of this young industry.

For customers, this means that they must first develop a sense of trust and confidence for a provider's offerings before they will be willing to take on the heavy investments necessary for large-scale e-learning implementations. The risk that a provider might not survive in the long run or that a technology will not succeed in the market still needs to be a regarded as a major consideration for a company's purchasing decision. However, one can expect this issue to be resolved within the next 24-36 months with further market consolidation and the emergence of technology standards, established processes, and integrated, end-to-end solutions.

The matter of trust, however, has more implications, as Bright Wave's Brown cautions. He argues that the e-learning industry is still supply-driven. US suppliers outnumber home-grown European suppliers, particularly in e-learning technology (LMS, authoring tools, collaboration software, etc.) and generic content. His conclusion is that there is a greater role for trusted "old economy" providers to offer end-to-end solutions. Europeans tend to seek greater academic legitimacy for new ideas and practices than their US counterparts and there is less willingness to support smaller innovative methods. It's going to be interesting to see how this issue will play out in terms of the aforementioned dawning consolidation that is expected for both the European and the US market.

It is probably safe to assume that this consolidation will take place in two directions: a) vertically, i.e., in the direction of integrated solutions, and b) horizontally, i.e., through mergers and acquisitions by which technology and consulting companies will expand their portfolios and the traditional training companies will merge with young e-learning shops (merger of "clicks" and "bricks"). At the same time, consolidation will take place in all of the three e-learning sectors: content, technology, and services.

Therefore, US-based companies that intend to succeed in the European arena will need to consider benchmark dimensions as they are described throughout this article and summarized in the following list:

- Content validity
- Language, culture, and business conduct
- Instructional design and pedagogy
- Workplace regulations and laws
- Technology integration
- Social validity
- Trust
- Comprehensiveness of services and solutions

## Technology

In the technology arena, success will likely come to international providers whose solutions resemble the kind of broad and comprehensive e-learning approaches described above. Standards that guarantee reusability, compatibility, and ease of integration, such as AICC, SCORM, or IMS, will play an important role in widespread acceptance of such solutions.

In this regard, it's helpful to realize that standards are generally seen as a *sine qua non* when it comes to establishing new technologies in Europe, since the European continent includes many countries. For instance, traveling only a few hundred miles from Frankfurt, Germany in either of the four directions, one arrives in another country with a different culture and a different language, be it Denmark, France, Italy, or Poland, just to mention a few. Therefore it's no surprise that European companies are accustomed to thinking in terms of international standards, in order to sell their products beyond the borders of their local markets. Good examples of this are the high-definition television (HDTV) or the wireless technology (UMTS) standards that were developed in joint partnerships between public and private sponsors throughout Europe.

## Content

Although English is the common business language, the acceptance and success of e-learning projects will depend on providing content that reflects both the local language(s) and other idiosyncrasies such as culture, customs, or legal regulations. For instance, vocational training is quite formalized in many European countries, and corporations play an important role as suppliers of this type of training. They are, however, bound to consider the input of the unions and the respective works councils, as Peter Martin cautions. As Senior Vice President for Equity Research for Jefferies & Company, Martin predicted at a panel discussion at the ASTD 2001 conference that "Europe is going to be more difficult [for American organizations to succeed in] due to employment laws." For example, in Germany, unions have to be consulted for any kind of work-related training and companies need to be aware of many, many workplace regulations. Translated to the e-learning market, this means that internationally operating providers will depend on local partners or resources, both for the adoption of globalized standard content and the creation of new and customized training materials.

However, as we said before, when it comes to quality it's not *only* about the localization of content. When, one or two years from now, technology (in the form of an LMS, for instance) will be a commodity and the focus will shift toward quality content, the success of e-learning will highly depend on the provision of engaging, performance-enhancing, value-adding, and targeted learning materials. Research organizations such as IDC, Cedefop, or WR Hambrecht see plenty of room for improvement in this area as shown in a recent survey:

> There is strong demand to improve the value of content with better pedagogical quality and evidence of improved performance impact, demonstrating real cost effectiveness. Large numbers of respondents expressed concerns about quality and re-usability of content. (Cedefop, November 2000)

## Services

Aside from the consulting branches of the "Big Five" companies, professional services providers that are independent and address the entire e-learning value chain are currently not easy to find in the European market. However, the demand for these services seems to be quite large, as evidenced by the increasing number and breadth of topics at e-learning congresses and exhibitions these days.

For instance, an informal Intellinex survey conducted among visitors of Learntec 2001, Germany's preeminent e-learning conference, found that 71% of the respondents agreed with the notion that the following are all prerequisites for the effective integration of e-learning solutions:

- the development of a sound e-learning strategy
- the transformation of an organization's business processes
- a performance management system that matches these new conditions

Not all organizations, however, will be able to do this on their own, which opens the door for companies that can provide both local and international e-learning consulting resources. Vendors that can show proof of their global capabilities will be better positioned to survive the upcoming market consolidation, because transformation lies not in the implementation of software, but in the redesign of entire HRD processes and systems. Such important shifts require sound knowledge of the local flavors of workplace-related laws, regulations, and conduct of business.

## Fraternal Twins: E-Learning in the Old World vs. the New World

Besides all the technology and "e"-euphoria, we shouldn't forget that the same old question still needs to be answered, as pointed out by Stefan Jepsen, leader of the e-learning team at DaimlerChrysler Services Academy: "What's the business problem that e-learning is supposed to solve and, deriving from this, what's the learning philosophy of the organization?" In this regard, there is no difference between the European and the US e-learning market.

What is also fairly similar between the US and Europe is the demand for anywhere, anytime learning and performance support, which is an outcome of the notion that learning is not viewed as an event anymore, but has to be embedded in working and performance, or, as Gloria Gery recommended during a presentation at the Online Learning Conference 2001 in London, "Accommodate the natural way of learning and stop forcing people to change their focus from doing to learning."

While several commonalities exist between Europe and the US, there are also significant differences to be considered, as shown in Table 2. One differentiator, for example, is that although the European e-learning market is potentially bigger than its North American counterpart, it cannot be seen as a single entity, but as a highly granularized cluster of many local sub-markets. Solution providers that intend to be successful here need to address factors such as language, culture, local workplace regulations, differences in infrastructure and attitude, customs, and locally influenced approaches to learning that are not even consistent within

| Similarities with US | Differentiators |
|---|---|
| • Business issues: fast-paced change, skills shortage, etc.<br>• Demand for value-adding learning materials aligned with business goals<br>• Demand for integrative all-in-one e-e-learning solutions<br>• Integrations of e-learning with other HR functions and KM<br>• Demand for technology standards | • Highly granularized market with different workplace laws, languages, cultures, approaches to learning, and differences in infrastructure and attitude<br>• Different conduct of business<br>• Demand for localized e-learning services close to the customer<br>• Demand for localization of technology and learning materials<br>• (Technology) Standards are generally seen as a *conditio sine qua non* |

© Intellinex Europe 2001

**Table 2.** Similarities and differentiators between Europe and the US

Europe, not to mention on a global level.

Elliott Masie's conclusion from this situation is to "train globally [and] learn locally" (*Learning Decisions*, May 2001, p. 6). In other words, the players in this field will succeed only if they realize that they have to compete on local grounds—even in a global village and even though the training industry for the first time has the chance to become a truly global industry, considering the similar business issues, technologies, and solution providers. Learning, after all, is a process of acculturation and socialization, which are by definition local matters.

So who's got it better in the current e-learning market, Europe or North America? It is not up to us to be the judges here and give a final answer to this question—if there is any. With Goethe's help, however, we can say one thing for sure: Europe, you've got it different!

## References

Cedefop. (2001). *E-Learning Taking off in Europe: New Survey Figures Give a Fresh Perspective.* www.trainingvillage.gr/etv/PressRelease/press_rel_elearning1.htm.

Delahoussaye, Martin. (2001). "European Echo." *Training, 1*(38), 61-65.

Gery, Gloria. (2001). *State of the Industry.* Online Learning Europe 2001, London.

IDC. (2001). *European eLearning Market to Grow to $4 Billion by 2004.* emea.idc.com/press/20010105.htm.

Masie, Elliott. (2001). Special Edition: E-Learning Questions and Opinions. *Learning Decisions, 5,* 6.

*The authors would like to acknowledge the following experts for their invaluable con-*

tributions to this article: Karen Boyle, InSite Learning; Robert Hohmann, Intellinex Europe; Heike Pfeifle-Shull, McKinsey; and Andrew Wolff, PricewaterhouseCoopers.

*Christian Völkl is a senior consultant and project manager for Intellinex Europe, the e-learning venture of Ernst & Young. As a Fulbright alumnus and graduate of the San Diego State University Educational Technology Master's program, Chris spent several years in the US working for global companies such as PricewaterhouseCoopers and Internal & External Communications. He has over nine years of experience in multimedia-based technologies as a designer, project manager, and consultant. As a board member for research and development for ISPI Europe, he has considerable international experience in performance consulting, education and learning, e-learning strategy development, and instructional design. Chris can be reached at christian.voelkl@intellinex.de.*

*Folkert Castelein is the Chief Inspiration Officer and Manager of Performance Consulting for Intellinex Europe. Folkert joined Intellinex after 10 years with Cap Gemini Ernst & Young, where he was a manager of Business Consulting Units. Folkert has considerable international experience in management consulting, performance management, program management, implementations, IT solutions, learning and change processes, education, e-learning strategy, and organization development. You can reach Folkert at folkert.castelein@intellinex.nl.*

# Covering Your Assets: 10 Things Trainers Should Know About Copyright Law

## Sarah Fister Gale

*As trainers make greater use of the Web, they face greater risks involving copyright law. How much do you know about copyright law and the legalities of using materials owned by others and protecting the materials that you create?*

Trainers have always been notorious copyright infringers. They think no one will care if they use a copy of a cartoon on an overhead or include a clip from a favorite movie in their opening video. Often, no one will care if they use the materials in-house, on a small scale.

But with the growth of the Web and the proliferation of Web-based training, copyright infringement is becoming a bigger issue—one that you, as an e-learning professional, should know something about. And the concern is not just that you are stealing, but that you are being stolen from. Any content you put online can be easily copied and reused, greatly depreciating the value of all that hard work you invested in the first place.

In effort to protect you from nasty lawsuits and lost profits, we've compiled some advice from experts as to what you should know about copyright law. While some of their suggestions are specific to developers of Web-based training, much of what they have to say applies to anyone who creates training materials and programs. Here are 10 ways you can protect yourself and your work.

**1.** Assume that if a copyrighted work doesn't belong to you, it belongs to someone else. And if it belongs to someone else, assume that you need permission to use it, says Francine Ward, a Mill Valley, Calif., speaker and consultant who specializes in copyright and workforce liability issues.

The material you want to use—articles, photos, cartoons, case studies or anything else found online—may be in the public domain, but you can't be sure unless you do the research. (Although its focus is music and lyrics, the Public Domain Information Project's Web site [www.pdinfo.com] offers good guidelines on copyright law and the public domain.) "Generally, reproducing someone else's copyrighted work for your own commercial purposes infringes on the rights of the owner," says Ward, who is also an attorney. She adds that the fair use doctrine sometimes provides an exception.

If the owner finds out you used even a small part of his or her copyrighted work, say one line from a poem or a 10-second clip from a movie, you could be sued or at least threatened with a lawsuit, adds Patricia Eyres, an attorney and president of Litigation Management and Training Services Inc., a Long Beach, Calif., firm that specializes in proactive legal management in the workplace. So, if you simply must use someone else's material in your training, contact the owner and get permission.

**2.** If you create something that generates income, whether it's a Web-based course or a workbook, register it. "If you take the time and effort to create it, protect it," says Ward.

Registering your work is as simple as filling out the appropriate form (which can be accessed online at lcweb.loc.gov/copyright/) and sending it—along with a copy of the work, its documentation and a small fee—to the copyright registration office.

You can't sue someone for copyright infringement if you don't register your work, warns Eyres. And registering your work after it's been infringed upon won't help your case.

**3.** Never author directly to the Web. Before you publish a course or any other Web-based document, create it in a medium you can store securely on a computer that is not connected to your server, suggests Ann Carter, principal partner of onlyOnline.net Inc., a New York City firm that develops and repurposes multimedia content for e-learning applications. "Have a good security protocol and use it," she says. "If you can, attach a digital signature to the source files for further protection."

**4.** If you are selling Web-based training, ask site visitors to read and accept a copyright agreement electronically before granting them access to the content. Doing this lets users know the material is copyrighted and shows them that you mean business about protecting it, says Carter.

She also encourages training developers to allow users to download and freely distribute some content, as long as they acknowledge and include a link to your site. "If you give something away, you also take some of the thrill out of theft. In the Internet culture, making it difficult to steal challenges some people to make the attempt," she explains.

**5.** Always place the copyright notice symbol © on your copyrighted work, says Ward. In March 1989, copyright laws were enacted that state you no longer need to include the © symbol to prove ownership of your work. However, Ward strongly suggests that you use the symbol. Her reasons? It tells the world that the work belongs to you and discourages theft.

When you put training online, Carter suggests including a statement of copyright ownership on the site and creating a link to it from every page. Along with the statement, consider adding a written policy and a "mailto:" link that lets people seek permission to copy or use certain material from the site.

**6.** When you use other people's copyrighted material in your work, you cannot protect your copyright. By amusing learners with a quip from your favorite movie or by including someone else's research or article in your course material, you lose the opportunity to protect and sell your largely original efforts, says Eyres. If you do sell a product that contains someone else's copyrighted material, that person can sue you for part of the profits. So, if you plan to sell your work and keep all the profits, create everything yourself—from the graphics to the content.

**7.** If you create something as an employee of a company, the copyright in the work that you created within the scope of your employment belongs to the company, unless you have a written agreement that says otherwise. Internal trainers often believe that if they create a video or a course syllabus while on the job, they can take it with them when they quit or use it for outside engagements such as freelance consulting.

Not so, says Ward, unless they have an agreement with their employer that specifically transfers the copyright to the employee. Otherwise, the trainer risks being sued for copyright infringement.

**8.** When hiring independent consultants, photographers or instructional designers, be certain your work-made-for-hire agreements make it crystal clear who owns the copyright. If a contractor creates a Web site or draws a cartoon and you want the copyright, make sure he or she signs a transfer of copyright agreement at the beginning of the relationship. Doing this, Ward says, guarantees that you or your company own the rights to the end product.

**9.** Encourage your organization to draft, communicate and enforce anti-copyright infringement policies. Work with your in-house counsel to draft a policy that clearly spells out what copyright infringement is. Include examples of violations, such as photocopying magazine articles and stealing graphics from the Web. Also, specify how the company will deal with employees who disregard copyright laws. Remember that courts often hold companies liable for the actions of their employees.

**10.** Stay informed. Visits to the following Web sites can help you gain a better understanding of how you can protect yourself and your work. These sites also can help you keep up with changes to current copyright laws.

The U.S. Copyright Office Home Page: **lcweb.loc.gov/copyright/**
When in doubt, go to the source. This site has information about what copyright is, how to get one for your original work, and where to go when you want permission to use others' copyrighted materials.

10 Big Myths about copyright explained: **www.templetons.com/brad/ copymyths.html**
This site attempts to debunk common myths about copyright. The advice is simple, straightforward and makes sense even to those of us who don't have a law degree.

WWW Multimedia Law: **www.batnet.com/oikoumene/index.html**
This site has articles and links to other sites that answer questions about copyright law and the Internet. It also features sample chapters from *The Internet Law and Business Handbook* (Ladera Press, 2000) by J. Dianne Brinson and Mark F. Radcliffe.

*Sarah Fister Gale is a contributing editor to* Online Learning Magazine. *She can be reached at sfister@mn.rr.com.*

# Welcome to Part Two: Developing Great E-Learning

This part assumes that you come with one or both of these interests:

- You must identify vendors and select e-learning software
- You yourself are engaged in developing learning and support software

What you'll find in Part Two has those challenges in mind. In this part, we look at what constitutes quality. Shonn Colbrunn and Darlene Van Tiem provide insights into effective contemporary development and implementation processes. They make it clear that familiarity with instructional systems development (ISD) is not a sufficient guarantee that quality e-learning programs will result. You'll find new approaches that recognize the power of technologies and cognitive science.

Much of the excitement about e-learning centers on interactivity, personalization, content structure, and engagement. And so do concerns. In Part Two we get into nitty-gritty details. William Horton, Pam Northrup, Dean Spitzer, and Marie Jasinski and Sivasailam Thiagarajan focus on content, collaboration, and interactivity. This section offers two articles about learning online through games. Lguide's Le'a Kent provides criteria for thoughtful consideration of potential software purchases. Wise developers should be intrigued with what Zane Berge and Lin Muilenburg, Kent, and Horton say about the elements of quality online instruction. Paul Shotsberger and Ronald Vetter present the possibilities associated with wireless delivery of e-learning.

This section includes two articles about objects and standards. What are they? Why should we care? What can we do if we are intrigued? David Wiley and Richard Clark cover this critical topic.

Here in Part Two, authors help people develop and choose better software and systems. In Part Three the focus is on implementation: what to do after the purchase.

# From Binders to Browsers: Converting Classroom Training to the Web

## Shonn R. Colbrunn and Darlene M. Van Tiem

*Organizations are taking greater advantage of the Web to provide training that is more immediate, convenient, and consistent. But there are challenges in converting classroom courses to Web-based training. This article examines the major challenges and offers some suggestions for overcoming them.*

Organizations are recognizing the value of human knowledge as a resource and the need for employees to update their knowledge and skills periodically. However, helping employees enhance their knowledge and skills presents many challenges (McCormack and Jones, 1998). For one thing, time away from the job for training interrupts productivity. Equally important, the need for information can be immediate, while an appropriate conventional classroom-delivered course may not be scheduled in a timely manner, forcing the employee to wait for the information. Another vexing problem is consistency of the message content. Because traditional classrooms provide unique learning situations based on the experiences, needs, and interests of students, it is difficult for all workers to hear the same message and come away with the same understanding. To resolve the problem, web-based training (WBT) can provide a uniform, technology-based format. In addition, training can be implemented throughout an organization simultaneously. As a result, organizations are increasingly relying on web delivery as a solution to issues of immediacy, convenience, and consistency (Shotsberger, 1996).

As organizations continue to embrace this delivery mode, you can expect to see more and more new courses developed for the web. However, you can also expect requests to convert existing classroom courses to web delivery. Over the past two years, we have been extensively involved in this type of work through research, teaching, and management of course-conversion projects. While the basic elements of web-based instructional design still apply, we have learned that there are a number of unique issues and challenges that arise when converting a classroom course.

# Organizational Readiness

One of the most important considerations when preparing to launch WBT is organizational readiness. For WBT to be successful, it is important to consider the issues related to the organization's culture and technology.

## Culture Changes

Although many employees are ready and eager to take advantage of the convenience that web-delivered training offers, the organization and its existing culture may not be supportive. As a result, WBT courses get completed and offered, and employees register and begin the lessons, but few complete the course modules. People issues get in the way. Distance learning initiatives, including WBT, need to overcome these hurdles (Verduin and Clark, 1991).

Time allocation is the most immediate factor. Employees need to work attentively at their computers, progressing through content explanations and application activities, taking tests or other self-checks to verify learning, and tracking progress through an embedded database structure. This point seems so simple, but reality is far from it! Coworkers can notice WBT trainees working on a module and stop by just to ask a quick question. Supervisors frequently request that WBT trainees postpone their learning to work on pressing departmental needs. Days and weeks go by and trainees learn little. It is plain to see that Sushanna Zuboff's 1988 prediction that learning would become the new form of work is a long way off. In many organizations, work is work, and learning is something extra, a perk.

In fact, in an effort to increase productivity and thus shareholder value, senior management in many organizations encourages employees to learn on their own time. Self-study opportunities are promoted through academic-based tuition assistance, audiocassette, CD-ROM, or web-based lessons. The expectation is that it is the employee's responsibility to maintain necessary and future-oriented skills and competencies. In many organizations there is a definite trend to encourage people to complete learning activities on their own time.

In contrast, many employees believe training ought to be part of on-the-job time. Consensus about whether to and how to encourage WBT on company or personal time needs to occur. It is important to resolve the stalemate. Management, workforce representatives, and training personnel need to determine when and where training will be completed.

Communicating policy and cultural expectations openly and honestly will prepare employees to take advantage of WBT opportunities. To determine cultural readiness, consider the following questions:

- Will special computer locations be set aside for uninterrupted learning? Will some sort of "Do Not Enter" sign be posted? Are employees going to need to commit some personal time to learning?
- Will learning be documented and considered on performance appraisals? Will acquired skills and competencies be included in an organizational database (knowledge management), allowing employees to automatically be considered for advanced assignments or special projects? Will pay-for-knowledge or some skill recognition be implemented?

## Technical Readiness

Another organizational challenge is equipment sufficiency and compatibility. Computers may not have the capacity or cabling bandwidth to support an interesting web-delivered course. It is also likely that equipment purchases have not been to uniform specifications. This could mean that the capacity to choose any one approach may be difficult. However, without consistent platforms or standardized capability, too much variety exists that would require an unreasonable number of course versions.

In addition, it is necessary to ensure that adequate technical staff can be available to support the needs of the system, both at the originating server and also at the learner's location. Dedicated technical staff may not be needed, but sufficient priority should be attached to WBT.

The following questions can be used to assess an organization's technical readiness:

- Does the target audience have ready access to computers? Do those computers have Internet or intranet access? Intranets with high-speed network connections (T1, DSL, ISDN) are critical if the course will be graphic intensive.
- Does the company have a standard browser and version? The more variety there is, the more difficult it will be to design a course. Since the course will need to be designed for the "least common denominator" of browsers, there may be severe limitations in the amount of interaction or functionality that can be used.
- How does the information technology (IT) support department feel about plug-ins? While plug-ins provide opportunities for increased functionality and media types, they create a maintenance issue for the IT support staff—

it is essentially new software that must be installed and updated for every student. In addition, the license fees for plug-ins can be expensive with a large number of students. Many organizations today prefer the "thin-client" approach: Program the entire course using languages (HTML, JavaScript) that function within the browser software alone.

# Course Appropriateness for the Web

If you have determined that your organization is ready for WBT, you then need to determine if your particular course is appropriate for the web. Some courses are ideal for web-based delivery, while others are not optimal for the Internet medium (Harrison, 1999; Forcier, 1999). In most cases, courses that focus on content and information (not requiring experiential learning that closely duplicates job situations) are good candidates for web-based learning.

## Content Rich

Courses ideal for WBT are fact oriented and have a well-defined body of knowledge. The web is a good delivery medium for knowledge and comprehension of facts and principles, and for the application of knowledge. Application can be through simulations, games, case studies, or structured problem solving. Ideally, simulations or application exercises cover situations that can be thought through and resolved independently by an individual learner. It is possible to build opportunities to communicate with an instructor on an asynchronous (not in real time) or as-needed basis.

## Low-Fidelity Job-Performance Outcomes

Web courses should not require a close approximation to job environments (Webb, 1996, p. 24). For example, the web is not the right delivery mode for technical situations where body movement practice is needed relative to assembly operations or where patient medical conditions need to be assessed and inferred through sight, sound, and touch.

## Minimal Interaction Among Students

Interpersonal skills development or courses dependent on extensive person-to-person interaction between the instructor and students or among students are not optimum based on current web technology. In the near future, the technology may be sufficient to support involved interactions. For example, at this point, bandwidth and equipment are inadequate to enable realistic personal desktop video-conference camera shots. In addition, few organizations have audio cards at workers' desktops because it is too distracting in the work environment to have extensive dialogue, even if the learner wears a headset. Most WBT is designed to be asynchronous and not delivered simultaneously; in contrast, real-time human interactivity promotes optimal growth in people skills (Moore and Kearsley, 1996, pp. 128-131).

## Structural and Managerial Considerations

WBT involves thinking through some mundane delivery factors (Mantyla and Gividen, 1997, pp. 103-104). WBT courses need to be organized by modules based on major topic areas. There should be natural segments in the subject matter. In addition, courses should be taught with sufficient frequency and have large enough audiences to warrant the time, effort, and expense of the WBT conversion. Evaluation of learning for computer-based courses can use conventional methods such as pre- and post-tests and structured application exercises. However, it may be judicious to consider audioconferencing as a debriefing and wrap-up strategy.

If your classroom course contains primarily desirable characteristics (see Figure 1), then it will likely make an effective WBT course. However, as bandwidth and technology improvements allow for increased interaction and multimedia, a greater variety of courses will become feasible for web delivery (Hall, 1997).

|  | **Desirable Characteristics** | **Limiting Characteristics** |
|---|---|---|
| **Content** | Rich in information Individual application exercises | Group exercises |
| **Job Fidelity** | Word-based, hypothetical situations | Complex realistic activities needing sensory input |
| **Social Interaction** | Static, observable, simulations | Extensive, dynamic personal dialogue |
| **Structure** | Modules based on natural segments | Highly individualized or unstructured learning |
| **Frequency** | Sufficient to have large learner audience | Limited number of learners |

**Figure 1.** *Desirable and limiting characteristics of potential courses for web development*

# Building the Right Project Team

Once you have determined that your course content is appropriate for web delivery, you must then assemble your design and development team. Whether you go with internal resources or a full-service vendor, make sure you have the appropriate people involved.

You might be thinking that putting an existing course on the web will be quick and easy because the content is the same. All you need is someone who can cut and paste into HTML, right? One thing we learned is that you should always plan for a full-scale development effort. Without a full development team, you will end up with an electronic instructor guide, not a learning intervention.

As with any project, the sponsor plays a critical role in setting direction, allocating resources, and removing barriers. First and foremost, the sponsor should understand the organizational readiness issues and the criteria for determining whether to convert a course to the web. In addition, your sponsor needs to have a realistic picture of the type and number of resources needed. Finally, your sponsor must be able to support deployment and maintenance of the course once it is finished.

At a minimum, your development team should include a project leader, instructional designer, graphic designer, programmer, editor, and subject matter expert (SME). Each of these team members plays an important role in the process. Make sure that you (or your development vendor) have these skills represented and roles defined on your team.

The instructional designer plays a critical role in the process (Willis, 1994). In addition to managing course content, the instructional designer must also be responsible for approving the interface design, functionality of interactions, and page templates. While a technical developer has an eye for technical quality (perhaps asking, Are there any bugs?), an instructional designer brings an eye for quality of instruction (Can someone learn from this?). Another critical competency an instructional designer brings is a familiarity with the content. Knowing the type of information that is to be presented is critical for upfront design decisions related to the interface and navigation.

In addition, do not underestimate the need for SMEs. They are critical team members for design of new course elements, such as graphics and exercises. When beginning the project, make sure that the sponsor can provide experts and ensure they have time free for the project.

## Design Strategies

There are a number of published guidelines for the design of WBT, including Brandon Hall's *Web-Based Training Cookbook* (1997). Guidelines on screen design, navigation, and hyperlinks are very important to understand and apply in any WBT development project. However, through our experience, we have identified a number of unique design strategies specific to the conversion of a classroom course. These strategies should be considered when converting text, converting graphics, and creating exercises.

## Converting Text

When considering course content, it is easy to think that the conversion to WBT is an exercise in cut and paste.

Think again. The text used in an existing instructor-led course was written to facilitate a presentation by an expert. However, the text in a web-based course needs to facilitate self-study learning for a novice (see Figure 2). This distinction is critical in the conversion of the text.

**Instructor Guide for Text**
Refer participants to Form A
- Ask, What functions are recorded on Form A?
- After brainstorming and creating a function diagram to the measurable level, the team would then enter the functions in the Action column of Form B
  - But, not all functions go on Form B
  - Only the measurable function (shown in yellow on the slide)

**WBT Text**
Look at Form A. After brainstorming and creating a function diagram to the measurable level, the team then enters the functions in the Action column of Form B. Remember, not all functions go on Form B--only the measurable functions do.

**Figure 2.** *Example of text conversion*

Essentially, the conversion to WBT is very similar to converting a course to a self-study workbook. Content has to be rechunked and organized for proper pacing and flow. Exercises and checkpoints need to be interspersed appropriately to allow for reflection and interaction. You need to capture the extra stories, explanations, and tidbits that the instructors regularly used to enrich the learning experience. In addition, the wording should be carefully reviewed and enhanced so that it clearly presents the message to a reader, as opposed to a listener.

## Converting Graphics

As with text, conversion of graphics is also a considerable undertaking. The first reaction of some might be that classroom presentation slides will work just fine as graphics in the web-based course. However, the purpose of those slides is to support the instructor's presentation. Many slides are actually textual statements or lists that summarize a chunk of content.

In WBT, graphics are used to visually represent or enhance the content. Therefore, you need to eliminate or reinvent many of the slides to serve as graphics. Replace lists or bulleted text with images or diagrams (see Figure 3). In addition, the original presentation slides may require reformatting to maintain consis-

Classroom Presentation Slide                    WBT Graphic

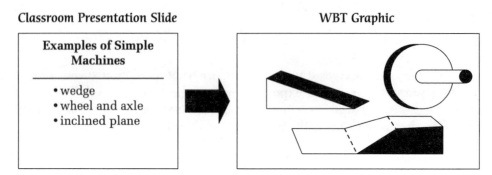

**Figure 3.** *Example of graphic conversion*

tency in graphic colors and styles. Assume that all graphics will need to be created from scratch, using the presentation slides for conceptual purposes only.

## Creating Exercises

One of the keys to successful WBT is interaction. Courses that are just "electronic page-turners" quickly turn off students. In our projects, we faced a number of issues related to the design of exercises and interactions for WBT. Our two main challenges were converting existing classroom exercises and managing the limitations of technology.

***Converting Classroom Exercises.*** One thing we learned is that straight conversion of existing exercises from the classroom course is ineffective. For example, one of the classroom activities involved applying a problem-prevention process. As a team, the students read a case study scenario, brainstormed some potential failure categories, and categorized the information on a chart. We created the online version of this exercise to follow the same format, except that students would not work in teams.

Through our pilots, we learned that this type of exercise was too difficult to do individually. Since traditional classroom exercises often take advantage of group interactions and team synergy to help students learn, simply using the same format will not work. Self-study learning requires much more structured activities with more frequent feedback to help motivate the student.

To solve this problem, we converted the activity to a series of multiple-choice and fill-in-the-blank questions that slowly led the student through the process (see Figure 4). It was simpler than the original activity, but the change greatly helped individual learners. It held their attention and provided structure to an activity that, as originally written, would have required a high level of self-directedness to complete.

Another thing we learned is that "classroom props" should not necessarily be re-created for the web-based course. For example, one of our classroom activities

**Classroom Exercise**
- As a team, brainstorm a list of potential failure categories for an umbrella.
- Choose the 2 or 3 most significant failures and assign hazard levels based on the Hazard Ranking Table on page 32.
- Record your failure categories and hazard levels on a flipchart.
- Present your rankings and rationale to the class.

**WBT Exercise (Directions)**
- Review the list of potential failure categories for an umbrella.
- Choose the 2 or 3 failures you feel are most significant by clicking on the checkbox to the left of the description.
- using the information on the Hazard Ranking Table, assign the appropriate hazard levels by entering the number in the box to the right of the failure description.
- Click on Next to compare your answers with the suggested answers.

**Figure 4.** *Example of exercise conversion*

required students to build and test paper helicopters. Paper helicopters were chosen because they were easy to build in a classroom and effectively illustrated a concept, not because they were similar to the students' actual work projects (automotive systems).

When converting a course to the web, take advantage of the opportunity to simulate objects related to the students' real work projects. Because the medium is entirely electronic, there is no advantage to using the same props or objects as examples. Instead, illustrate the learning concepts with graphics or descriptions of real work objects. For the programmer and graphic artist, it is the same amount of work.

***Limitations of Technology.*** One current frustration with developing WBT is the limitations of technology. Using a basic programming approach (straight HTML and Java Script) for interactions can be very restricting. However, we learned that through creative use of those interactions, it is still possible to create interactive, engaging learning activities.

As we often forget, the key to engaging learners is not always by "wowing" them with flashy actions. Instead, you can pull them into a story or scenario. For example, use suspense and game-like competition. You can create an intriguing, interactive case study in which the students try to "solve the mystery." With simple interactions (that is, select the options, fill in the blank), you can easily illustrate teaching points.

Another strategy that will engage students is to create a simple quiz game in which the user competes against the computer to win points. Adding the element of competition is not difficult from a technical standpoint, and it makes learning fun for the student. Even if the interactions are simply multiple-choice questions, their creative packaging is the key to making an effective exercise.

## Project Time Savers

When embarking on a project to convert a classroom course to the web, there are a few things you can do to save time. First, seek to reuse effective elements from other web courses. On our projects, we reused the interface and navigation framework from a similar course that the same vendor developed. As a result, we did not use formal storyboards to review the initial content—it was just as easy for our designer to present the content on line within the existing interface. This saved us a tremendous amount of design and development time.

Second, review your deliverables and course materials on line. We used this to our advantage by making all project deliverables and course materials available through a project web site. Project plans, agendas, and timelines were posted for team members to download and review, and actual draft versions of the course were presented in their intended delivery format. Not only did this save lots of paper and postage, but it helped to ensure that all reviewers were looking at the correct version of the materials.

Third, plan for a SME to complete a thorough review of the existing course content prior to assembling the development team. You will find that some content will be inaccurate or outdated, particularly if the course has not been well maintained. Taking time for SMEs to revise content during development can significantly delay your progress. By doing this preliminary review, you can establish an agreement with your team that storyboard and production reviews will focus primarily on clarity, flow, and presentation, rather than content accuracy.

As the popularity of the web continues to increase as a tool for corporate training, organizations will continue to convert classroom training to WBT. By taking the correct approach and considering these key issues, your conversion projects can quickly produce high-quality results.

## References

Forcier, R.C. (1999). *The computer as an educational tool: Productivity and problem solving.* Upper Saddle River, NJ: Merrill.

Hall, B. (1997). *Web-based training cookbook.* New York: John Wiley & Sons, Inc.

Harrison, N. (1999). *How to design self-directed and distance learning: A guide for creators of web-based training, computer-based training, and self-study materials.* New York: McGraw-Hill.

Mantyla, K., and Gividen, J.R. (1997). *Distance learning: A step-by-step guide for trainers.* Alexandria, VA: American Society for Training and Development.

McCormack, C., and Jones, D. (1998). *Building a web-based education system.* New York: Wiley Computer Publishing.

Moore, M.G., and Kearsley, G. (1996). *Distance education: A systems view.* Belmont, CA: Wadsworth Publishing.

Shotsberger, P.G. (1996). "Instructional uses of the World Wide Web: Exemplars and precautions." *Educational Technology*, 36(2), 47-50.

Verduin, J.R., and Clark, T.A. (1991). *Distance education: The foundations of effective practice*. San Francisco: Jossey-Bass Publishers.

Webb, W. (1996). *A trainer's guide to the World Wide Web and intranets: Using online technology to create powerful, cost-effective learning in your organization*. Minneapolis: Lakewood Books.

Willis, B. (1994). *Distance education strategies and tools*. Englewood Cliffs, NJ: Educational Technology Publications.

Zuboff, S. (1988). *The age of the small machine: The future of work and power*. New York: Basic Books.

*Shonn R. Colbrunn is an instructional systems designer for MSX International, an engineering and business services provider based in Auburn Hills, Michigan. For the past three years he has worked on site at Ford Motor Company, providing instructional design, project management, and technology-based training expertise. He may be reached at scolbrun@ford.com.*

*Darlene M. Van Tiem, Ph.D., is an Assistant Professor, School of Education, University of Michigan, Dearborn. She received the ASTD National Technical Trainer of the Year, 1992, and the ASTD National Excellence in Leadership award for her work with the automotive industry. She has coauthored two ISPI books—Fundamentals of Performance Technology: A Guide to Improving People, Process, and Performance and Performance Improvement Interventions. She can be reached at dvt@umich.edu.*

# Ten Things to Look for When You're Buying WBT

## Le'a Kent

*Anybody with any experience of Web-based training knows that choices are abundant—and almost as overwhelming as the hype. So, how do you make any decisions? This article offers some suggestions, based on two years of evaluating thousands of courses from more than 200 providers.*

For e-learning customers, the past two years have been a time of promise and confusion. The promise comes from the industry's rapid growth, which brings an unsurpassed variety of vendors and products to choose from. The confusion comes from the same place: with hundreds of companies jockeying for attention, many training professionals feel overwhelmed by an onslaught of hype. Every vendor, it seems, is "the industry leader," offering a "best of breed" solution that is "second to none."

If only it were so. E-learning is no training panacea. Because e-learning is a young industry, few publishers have established reputations based on past performance. How can learning professionals cut through the hype and find solutions that work?

An abstract set of criteria isn't necessarily going to be useful for training professionals trying to navigate this marketplace. We can all imagine the ideal online course, but when you're making purchasing decisions, your ideals need to be based in reality.

Over the past two years, Lguide has evaluated thousands of courses from over 200 publishers. We have a good sense of the marketplace based on actual best practices of courseware publishers. We outline them here to give you some idea of what to look for and what to expect when you're choosing online training.

While there are several factors that customers must consider when choosing appropriate e-learning materials—price, learning management system (LMS) compatibility, and end-user technical platform being but a few—this set of criteria prioritizes content, instructional design, and navigability. In other words, we focus on the quality of the end-user experience.

# Marketplace Overview

## Business Skills Training

The majority of publishers who are successful at hawking their e-learning wares moved quickly to transfer existing training strategies and existing content into a Web-based format. They built large catalogs quickly, gained a foothold among customers, and generated a good deal of visibility, but their courses are not aging gracefully. They often suffer from a highly template-driven design and from inconsistent or mediocre content. In contrast, many smaller publishers offer more focused catalogs of courses and seem to have targeted their development efforts to the needs created by particular subjects. They customize their course design to complement the subject matter, and they address the limitations of those subject areas that do not lend themselves easily to online training. For advanced business skills topics, many stronger publishers such as UNext and Quisic also partner with reputable colleges and universities.

The lesson here? If you want excellent course quality and a vast number of courses on a wide range of subjects, you won't be able to get that from a single publisher. You'll either have to compromise on quality, work with more than one publisher, or work with a company that aggregates multiple publishers.

## Desktop Software Training

In desktop software training, the state of the industry is sound. With a large number of vendors competing to build courses for the same relatively small group of leading desktop applications (notably the Microsoft Office Suite) and a performance environment (the user's workstation "desktop") that lends itself well to replication in a Web-based training course, the courses in this area are very strong. Users can expect high-quality training products from many publishers.

## Professional IT Training

The performance environment for most professional IT skills matches the Web-based training environment, making it possible to devise realistic exercises online. Many IT publishers have been involved with e-learning longer than publishers in other subject areas, so users aren't exposed to first-generation products and the marketplace has had time to assign publishers some fairly accurate reputations. Furthermore, frequent turnover in IT certification exams and in the technology itself drive publishers to update courses frequently. With frequent updates of content come frequent opportunities to update course design. Not surprisingly, many IT publishers keep their course offerings on the leading edge of course design.

# Ten Things to Look For

## Content

### 1. Practicality

Good content must be accurate, practical, and immediately useful to users. While users may benefit by understanding the theories and concepts that underlie effective business practices or computer programming languages, they benefit most from courses that offer specific recommendations for practices they can integrate into their everyday work lives. Offerings like DDI's interpersonal communication and teamwork courses are successful because they focus on concrete techniques that learners can use.

**Buyer Beware.** Content can be impractical in one of two ways: it can be too theoretical, or it can be commonsensical. A minority of business skills and IT courses remain on a theoretical level, offering few concrete points, examples, or exercises. Quite a few business skills courses remain on a commonsensical level, repeating truisms and failing to teach concrete skills. For example, a time management course may say procrastinators need to stop putting things off, but may fail to offer concrete techniques for doing so.

### 2. Conciseness and Organization

We use "conciseness" to indicate the ratio of information to time spent in the course. Users may be willing to spend hours on a course to learn complex skills, but when courses belabor basic points, they waste users' time. Many courses are still largely text-based, so it is also paramount that the text be clear, concise, and well organized. Reading text on a computer screen is tiring, and users have schedules that only get busier. Concise, organized courses "cut to the chase." They present central points first and use diagrams, bulleted lists, or outlines to organize their most important points. Quisic's advanced business skills courses are notable for their clarity, and even complicated IT topics can be explained concisely—the writing in DigitalThink's IT courses is extremely straightforward.

**Buyer Beware.** In business skills courses, common organizational problems include: requiring users to click the mouse repeatedly to display a series of bullet points, presenting central points spread out over several screens, and spending dozens of screens covering simple points. These problems are rare in desktop and IT courses.

### 3. Authentic Examples

Examples, case studies, and scenarios are effective methods of concretizing abstract concepts and turning theory into advice. But even helpful tips and suggestions will fall upon deaf ears if the course material is inauthentic. If a scenario doesn't sound realistic, users won't buy into it or the point it's making. Many publishers turn to audio and video clips to solve the problem of authenticity, but multimedia often only complicates the problem. In a text-based course, you need good writing, but when multimedia is incorporated, you need good acting and production quality as well. In desktop software and professional IT courses, it's easy to find scenarios and examples that realistically present tasks commonly found in the workplace. Some business skills publishers offer highly authentic courses, but they're considerably more rare. Some exceptions to this rule include AchieveGlobal and Harvard Business School Publishing. They offer interactive simulations in which characters respond realistically to the learner's actions.

**Buyer Beware.** Authenticity is a major problem in business skills training. Common problems include badly written dialogue, dialogue that is simplistic, and scenarios that don't really illustrate course concepts. Occasionally, desktop or IT courses will also have laughably simplistic examples.

### 4. Graphics and Multimedia

Graphics can help enliven a course page and add visual variety to the course experience, but they're most effective when they actually illustrate course material. Too many publishers are clearly drawing from the same pool of clip art and stock photographs, sometimes depicting scenes that bear no resemblance to the scenarios described in the course text. The best courses have clear diagrams and outlines of main ideas or central processes.

Many analysts of the Web-based training industry suggest that as levels of Internet bandwidth increase, so will the quality of Web-based training courses. The idea is that bandwidth allows the use of video and audio multimedia components, and that multimedia will automatically make courses better. Unfortunately, this isn't always the case. The difficulty of creating authentic scenarios increases tremendously as course designers incorporate audio or video scenes, because bad acting or production quality can undercut otherwise well-done dialogue and examples. For an example of a very good audio track, check out Harvard Business School Publishing's Online series. The professors and professionals speak naturally, and both their expertise and personality come across to the listener. Ninth House uses professional actors to make video scenarios realistic and engaging.

**Buyer Beware.** Wooden acting and bad production values are common. Less often, you may see multimedia or graphics that are entertaining, but irrelevant to the course topic. Some publishers use audio simply for reading lectures rather than creating compelling examples. Particularly in OSHA and business skills courses, it's common to find overcomplicated diagrams, bad clip art, and graphics unrelated to the course topic.

### 5. Clear Sense of Audience and Prerequisites

In most desktop software and professional IT topics, skills build upon each other, so it's essential to have a clear sense of audience and a clear set of prerequisites. Look for publishers that specify prerequisites clearly and in detail, listing specific skills, tools, or languages that learners are expected to know.

**Buyer Beware.** Many publishers still use vague prerequisites, and even when a clear prerequisite is listed, the course level may not match the prerequisite. Two common complaints about introductory IT courses are that they leave out large chunks of basic information, and are therefore hard to get a handle on, or that they are condescendingly basic and waste your time.

### 6. Meaningful Context

In business courses, context is usually clear. It's obvious why you'd want to manage your time better or learn how to run a meeting. It's also clear when to apply skills. You apply meeting skills at meetings, and you apply communication skills when communicating. The same isn't true in desktop and professional IT courses. Novice Excel users don't know when or why to use a Pivot Table. Once learners move past technical basics, they often encounter features and procedures that aren't particularly intuitive and that are hard to understand unless learners know when and why they might use them. Basic tools and tasks can be taught by rote, but without some kind of context—the "why" that accompanies the "how"— explanations in intermediate or advanced desktop and IT courses will not be particularly effective. DigitalThink, ActiveEducation, and most established desktop software publishers do a good job of teaching programs in context, usually via realistic projects and exercises.

**Buyer Beware.** Some desktop software courses still cover only how to operate the program features, not how to use them in a workplace situation. Often, these courses seem like a tour or demo of the course features. Even the most reputable IT publishers occasionally err with respect to context. In otherwise strong catalogs, some courses may provide too much context, others not enough.

## Navigation

### 7. Custom Learning Paths

Custom learning paths tailor course material to a user's knowledge based on the results of a pre-assessment. Be aware that custom learning paths are only as good as the assessments that drive them. A poorly designed pre-assessment can lead you down a custom path that includes material you don't need while skipping the material you do. If the course allows users to skip around, custom learning paths are not essential. Custom learning paths are offered in business, desktop, and IT courses, but they're most useful in desktop and IT courses where topics are more clearly outlined and more easily tested. Custom learning paths work best when they give a suggested path that the user can follow, but allow the user to navigate flexibly. Educational Multimedia's desktop courses offer accurate custom learning paths—the pre-assessment reliably directs learners to areas they need to brush up on.

**Buyer Beware.** We haven't seen a really good custom learning path in a business skills course. The pre-assessments used to create custom learning paths are rarely sophisticated enough to accurately gauge user knowledge. Often, a highly guessable multiple-choice test is used as a pre-assessment, so the custom path leaves out concepts that the user really does need to learn. In other cases, the pre-assessment tests jargon that is unique to the course, so a learner who knows the course concepts may fail the pre-assessment anyway.

Occasionally, custom learning paths make it difficult for the learner to access units excluded from the custom path.

### 8. Bookmarking

Bookmarking features allow users to leave courses and return automatically to the spot where they left off. Courses without bookmarking force users to remember, hours or days later, where they were when they were interrupted. A bookmarking feature is essential for any course longer than an hour. Since most online learners are taking courses in busy environments that bring inevitable interruption, this is an important feature. Additionally, when learning IT skills, many users need to pause to assimilate information. Good bookmarking should retain quiz and test scores and automatically return the user to the module where he or she left the course. Bookmarking shouldn't prevent the user from reviewing earlier modules. Bookmarking is standard in most online courses.

**Buyer Beware.** In a minority of courses, bookmarking is absent. In courses without flexible navigation, this is a substantial problem. If a course's navigation does not allow users to skip ahead, bookmarking is a must.

## Skills Practice and Assessments

### 9. Valid Assessments

Good assessments challenge you and test your performance of a new skill, not just your reading comprehension. Tests should also give you feedback more extensive than providing a simple score. Users should be able to go back through the test and see exactly which questions they answered correctly, and they should be able to get explanations for questions answered incorrectly.

The best publishers use simulation-based final assessments that challenge learners to put their newly learned skills into practice. While it's undoubtedly difficult to create this kind of performance-based assessment, the results are worth it.

Courses that incorporate these elements are far more effective than their more static counterparts. These kinds of assessments are fairly standard in good IT or desktop software training, and are becoming increasingly common in business skills.

Some courses use post-assessments to prepare review tutorials of chapters that learners should re-examine.

**Buyer Beware.** Many business skills courses have frequent multiple-choice questions that test your recall of something you read on the previous page. This sort of testing gauges short-term recall and memorization of key words, but not actual understanding. Another common testing problem is overly simple questions that can be answered with common sense alone.

### 10. Realistic Practice

Interactivity is only effective when it is thought provoking. Courses that just require users to click the "Next" button engage the hand but not the mind. Guiding learners through realistic practice, on the other hand, will both require and inspire thought.

In desktop and IT courses, learners can usually do exercises either on their own computer or in a simulated environment in the course. In desktop software training, both simulation in the course and exercises on the user's desktop can work well. Look for simulations that closely mimic the look, feel, and functionality of the desktop program. If a course directs learners to do exercises on the desktop, be sure that sufficient support and feedback is provided.

Most reputable IT publishers maintain a very good balance between explanations and hands-on exercises, whether on your computer or in the course.

Realistic practice exercises in business skills courses can be divided into two categories: those that react to users' choices with detailed feedback and branch into different paths based on the answers, and those that progress to the next step regardless of the choice. The latter can become very frustrating, making users feel that any thought that went into their answers was wasted. An increasing number of business publishers offer realistic practice or assessment simulations that accurately respond to the learner's answers. These simulations are especially effective in topics like call center training, where clever use of audio can very easily simulate the emotional atmosphere of a call. Ulysses Learning, for instance, offers very realistic audio clips of calls from upset customers.

**Buyer Beware.** Many publishers still offer "simulations" in which the appearance of the performance atmosphere is duplicated on the screen, but the functionality is not. Some publishers label an activity a "simulation," but the activity really functions more as a lecture or a quiz. In this case, the user isn't applying skills, but merely asking or answering questions. Even the best simulations can become frustrating if coaching or feedback is not available.

IT course developers sometimes attempt to capitalize on an offline brand by simply putting a lengthy, detailed IT book online. Unless they also develop the features seen in sound online courses, the experience can be tedious.

## About this Article

This article was drawn from Lguide's report, *E-Learning Course Publishers: A Comparative Analysis and Industry Directory*, an analysis of 40 major e-learning vendors published in March 2001. The complete report is available at Lguide's Web site: www.lguide.com.

*Le'a Kent is a Senior Consultant at Lguide, an independent provider of e-learning consulting services. Lguide offers unbiased analysis of e-learning products and services. In addition to its consulting services, Lguide offers customers access to its expertise through its subscription site's library of e-learning research and analysis and by publishing in-depth research reports on Web-based training. Leading associations and publications in the e-learning industry, including the American Society for Training and Development (ASTD) and Online Learning Magazine, have relied on Lguide for research and analysis. Recent consulting clients include Cisco Systems, Washington Mutual Bank, the City of Seattle, and the State of Washington. For more information on Lguide products, visit Lguide at www.lguide.com.*

# Putting Learning Standards into Practice: A Primer

**Richard Clark**

*If you're curious or concerned about standards, this is the article to read. It provides an overview of the reason behind standards, an explanation of types of standards, and a report on the activities of standards groups. There's also an interesting interview of Wayne Hodgins, chair of the Learning Objects Metadata group in the IEEE Learning Technology Standards Committee.*

There has literally been no example of a significant change in history where there hasn't been an adoption of common standards.
—*Wayne Hodgins*

Have you been looking to change how you develop and deliver instruction, from monolithic "courses" to smaller re-usable "objects"? If so, you have probably seen many unfamiliar terms—"AICC," "IMS," "SCORM," and "metadata"—tied to "learning standards." As a designer, developer, or training manager, these terms matter if you have an interest in changing the face of training and education.

## Why Do We Need Standards in Training?

The industrialized world runs on standards. From power cords to compact discs, standards guarantee that products from multiple vendors can work together and will continue to work over time. Standards define processes and systems so that competing vendors' products can integrate with each other. Thus, standards encourage *both* competition and cooperation and are of primary benefit to the consumer.

Standards perform a similar role in the training world by enabling interoperability, reusability and scalability. In the case of learning and training examples would include the ability to move content from one management system to another, the ability to reuse content from multiple suppliers and/or created on multiple authoring technologies, or the ability to assess and track a learner across multiple systems.

Standards often come from humble beginnings. A wise designer provides *specifications* to developers and vendors. These can ensure that multiple groups create materials that work together. A department could standardize on distributing training materials in PowerPoint or HTML, for example. The members could agree on how materials would be viewed and reproduced. They could establish shared testing and grading procedures. And finally, they could devise procedures for cataloging, labeling ("tagging"), archiving, and retrieving materials for re-use in new contexts. This work could lead to small self-contained pieces of training that can be mixed and matched in different ways. From these specifications, standards can be made.

Trainers in the commercial aviation industry were concerned about these same issues—how to manage content from multiple vendors, how to administer tests and record scores, and how to label training materials for re-use. In response, they formed the Aviation Industry CBT Committee (AICC). In 1992 the AICC defined both hardware and software specifications: the type of computers used to view training, the operating system used, and the structure of course files. The end result was more modular training. Once vendors adopted the AICC specifications, airlines could link training modules from multiple vendors into one course.

The AICC wanted their specification to have broad popular support so vendors would adopt it. This happened, turning portions of the AICC specification into a *de facto standard.*

The power of standards, synchronization, and re-use was clear to the American military, themselves under pressure to move towards more "joint" efforts. The US Department of Defense formed the Advanced Distributed Learning (ADL) initiative to automate training for the US military; they defined the Sharable Courseware Object Reference Model (SCORM) to combine training materials and delivery tools from multiple vendors. SCORM builds on established specifications, including portions from AICC and IMS.

While American universities continue in their mostly maverick ways, the ARIADNE project helps universities across the more united Europe to combine documents into "knowledge pools." They want to use an array of diverse extant materials as components in individual courses and programs. Today, the ARIADNE project has moved from generating specifications into creating a working repository of materials.

## What Do Standards Mean in This Context?

Wayne Hodgins—the Director of Worldwide Learning Strategies for Autodesk and the chairman of the Learning Objects Metadata group in the international IEEE Learning Technology Standards Committee—believes in the power of consistent and well-defined vocabularies. He provided some quick and simple definitions:

**Specification:** a documented description for the solution of a specific problem. Stated in clear and unambiguous terms such that a solution can be created, developed or implemented. Specifications can literally be developed by any group but are most typically developed by consortiums or collaborative efforts of experts in the subject matter being specified. Examples of groups creating the learning technology specifications include IMS, AICC, and ARIADNE.

**Standard:** A status or state of a given specification. Some specifications become standards, falling into two classes:

- **"de jure" Standards:** *De jure \De` ju"re\ [L.] By right; of right; by law; often opposed to "de facto."* The designation/certification of a specification's status by an accredited body. The standards body ensures that the specification being standardized is free of any proprietary or special interests, is developed in an open and consensus based model, is broadly applicable and useful, and is implement able. There are only a few such accredited standards bodies in the world and they include:
  - **IEEE LTSC:** Institute for Electrical & Electronic Engineers—Learning Technology Standards Committee
  - **ISO/IEC–JTC1/SC36:** International Standards Organization—Joint Technical Committee #1 (Learning Technology)—Sub-Committee #36
  - **CEN/ISSS:** (European) Learning Technology Workshop
- **"de facto" Standards:** *De facto adj: existing in fact, whether with lawful authority or not.* Typically, when a critical mass or majority choose to adopt and use a specification. For example, TCP/IP, HTTP, VHS, etc. are all "de facto" standards.

## How Do I Tell the Difference Between the Groups Involved?

Understanding the different functional roles and responsibilities is the key to making sense of the otherwise confusing acronym "alphabet soup" of the groups involved such as AICC, SCORM, IEEE LTSC, IMS, ALIC, and ARIADNE. To clarify the roles, Hodgins describes four stages a specification goes through on its way to becoming an accredited standard.

These stages may not happen in a strict sequence. Also, a single specification

| Stage | Activities | Representative Groups |
|:-----:|------------|------------------------|
| 1 | Generating potential specifications, research projects, and ideas. | Researchers and practitioners |
| 2 | Refining and extending specifications. | IMS, AICC, ARIADNE |
| 3 | Testing specifications, working out implementation issues. | ADL (SCORM), early adopters, software developers |
| 4 | Verifying and "cleaning up" specifications (e.g. removing vendor-specific content.) Yields an accredited (de jure) standard. | IEEE, ISO |

**Table 1.** Activities and the groups involved

normally contains many sub-specifications that travel through the process at different speeds.

Specifications can become useful even in the first stage, if they are widely accepted and implemented. The AICC specifications are a shining example—they filled a need and were vendor and industry neutral, so found widespread adoption. The SCORM "plugfests" are bringing vendors together to test components built on these specifications and to ensure that the pieces work together. Thus, these specifications are emerging as *de facto* standards.

## How Are Standards Used?

To understand how learning standards work in practice, let's look at the major areas they address: *interoperability, re-use,* and *distribution*.

**Interoperability:** This term refers to independently created parts that work together. Consider the challenges of a corporation that must provide training and performance support to a global audience. If the corporation settles on specifications internally—e.g., the AICC protocols and the IMS packaging specifications—it should be able to assemble disparate tools and content into a working whole. It shouldn't matter which software was used to author courses or which machine runs the LMS.

Interoperability brings several practical advantages. Most organizations will not find a complete off-the shelf solution; interoperable parts make it easier to build a tailored solution. As an organization's needs grow, it can begin with a basic product today and scale up as needs demand without being limited to a single vendor. Finally, having interoperable content and systems will simplify buying or building courseware—developers can use familiar tools to produce the materials before deploying to the organization's specific system.

Learning specifications define interoperability in terms of *protocols* and *file formats*. Each of these protocols may incorporate other common protocols, e.g. the AICC specifications based the *HTTP AICC CMI Protocol* (HACP) on the HTTP protocol used for the World Wide Web. The file formats usually take a generic file format (e.g. text or XML) and put it to a specific use, as in the *IMS Question & Test Interoperability Specification* that uses XML to describe questions and tests.

**Re-use:** Karen, a product training manager, has a typical need: maintaining hundreds of instructional documents while "the engineers change the product monthly." She must search through current training materials to locate and update outdated information. At the same time, her sales training counterparts want to use her materials. How can standards help her?

Karen's first need is to catalog what she has and share that list with others. To do this, she can use learning object *metadata*. Metadata is just a fancy name for a labeling system, a standard way to describe the attributes of content with *metadata tags*. This metadata can be put into their own repositories and linked or shipped alongside the content or embedded as *meta tags*. Web pages can include meta tags to assist search engines; such tags include a brief description of the page, descriptive keywords, and the page's title. (See Figure 1.) Many books also includes metadata. For example, see the "cataloging-in-publication data" on the copyright page of many books.

```
<html><head>
<meta name="KeyWords"
content="Aviation,Training,CBT,CMI,CAI,CBI,TBT,Computer
Managed Instruction,Distance Learning,EPSS,AICC,LMS, con-
tent, Learning, WBT,computer-based training,Learning
Management Systems (LMS),Test Bank Systems,Learning
Objectives,CBT Interchange Language">
<title>AICC - Aviation Industry CBT Committee</title>
</head>
```

**Figure 1.** Example HTML meta tags for the AICC home page

Perhaps Karen could tag her materials with a title, description, and standard keywords, but she will need more information to search effectively. Building on a specification such as the IEEE's Learning Object Metadata specification, she can produce a more finely detailed catalog. She and others, such as the sales group, can then search that catalog to find specific pages. Figure 2 gives an example of learning object metadata for a "page turner" course entered in to a hypothetical corporate training catalog.

```
<RECORD>
  <GENERAL>
  <TITLE>Telephone Billing System Feature Summary</TITLE>
  <CATALOGENTRY>
    <CATALOG>CorporateTraining_v1</CATALOG>
    <ENTRY>(en,TBS-F1)</ENTRY>
    <LANGUAGE>en</LANGUAGE>
    <DESCRIPTION>Features in the July 2001
  release</DESCRIPTION>
    <STRUCTURE>Linear</STRUCTURE>
    <AGGREGATIONLEVEL>3</AGGREGATIONLEVEL>
```

**Figure 2.** *Example learning objective metadata for a simple linear course*

**Distribution:** The last example brings up an interesting problem—how to package and distribute the example course. People often learn from a combination of sources—including instruction, reference documents, job aids, and tests—so there has to be a way to label and package multiple elements. A package could describe each element, the dependencies between the elements (e.g. learning outcomes and prerequisites for each, and which elements must be learned from first), along with the elements themselves.

Standards define *content packaging* or *course exchange* as the information required to ship a course or courses as a single unit. This information can be used to install the course into a LMS or to populate a database with information about each element and the relationships between them.

To find the distribution-related specifications, look at IMS or SCORM for *course sequencing* or *content packaging*.

## Where Are Standards Today? Where Are They Going?

To discover more about the current state of standards and their future directions, the author spoke with Wayne Hodgins.

**Richard Clark:** *So, why should an Instructional Designer care about standards? How about training executives, instructors, and learners?*

**Wayne Hodgins:** Primarily because they enable more effective learning for more people. However the degree of impact depends on whether they want to shift from the old way of building monolithic courses toward using more granular content. From my perspective, there appears to be a strong consensus and growing practice working towards a new content or data model that is based on having repositories of small re-usable content objects, all tagged with rich metadata attributes, and then assembled into "just the right" information and learning objects. This model enables the realization of the dream for truly personalized learning. In my opinion, it's not even possible to have that dream without standards.

**RC:** *What about companies that have been building their own learning object systems?*

**WH:** Some people will do it themselves and be successful. But when you do it all yourself, you're limited by your own time and resources. The specifications out there are the result of many people's work and a very broad consensus. Developing work using these specifications and standards enables the dramatic expansion of the benefits from this collective work and the extended scope and reach achieved through interoperability and reusability. Simply put, you'll get farther, faster; it's enlightened self-interest at work.

**RC:** *So people gain quite a bit from adopting standards.*

**WH:** What's important right now is that we put the emerging accredited specifications and standards into practice and thus make them *de facto* standards by virtue of their widespread adoption. I advise everybody who is designing or building training to push the vendors to adopt the specifications, to talk in terms of functional requirements referencing the appropriate specifications and ask if their products comply. The ideal would be to have the accredited standards become the *de facto* standards. As I caution all the standards and specifications groups I work with, quality needs to be foremost in the opinion of those using our results and success is defined by the degree of popular use.

**RC:** *What if the specifications change during the process of becoming accredited standards?*

**WH:** In one sense I guess this is the risk any of us take if we choose to be "early adopters." However, based on the experience so far, it has been more a process where the early adopters have been an integral part of the specification development process and have thus shaped and guided the specifications themselves. As a result when these specifications emerge as fully accredited standards, such as those from IEEE, LTSC, and ISO, they are not only very ready for mass use, they are the very ones which the early adopters are already using. If you start with standards, you're in a better place to move ahead than if you designed everything on your own.

The good news is that the standards themselves aren't likely to change much. It's really interesting and fortunate that there is no competition between two specifications in the same area, that everyone is working on a different piece. We're not in a "Betamax vs. VHS" situation. There will be competition on implementation, which is good.

**RC:** *How do you go about choosing a standard?*

**WH:** Most people ask that question in the wrong way. They say, "Should I use AICC or IMS? What about SCORM?" Most of the conversation has been focused on the organizations, but we need to focus more on the utility. Training managers need to sit down, identify their needs and requirements, and then match specifications to their requirements.

If you have seen the SCORM overview presentations, they depict SCORM as a bookshelf—a collection of freestanding specifications. Standards are composites of other standards, so implementers only need to care about the parts they're trying to implement. So a company whose main issue is the content would be focused on metadata and sequencing, while a department that needed to track learner progress would care about assessments, progress tracking, profiling, and interfacing to HR systems such as PeopleSoft or SAP.

**RC:** *Identifying the specific parts of the standards and specifications is only the beginning of the process. The real work is in implementing them?*

**WH:** Yes, as always. However, there is a growing amount of help and assistance as more vendors are bringing products and services to the market, and the ADL initiative has done the hard work of collecting the pieces from the various specification and standards groups and making them work. The SCORM plugfests have been incredibly useful in getting vendors to bring their products to the table to work the problems out.

**RC:** *Changing directions, what's the relationship between the standards and current theories of adult learning? Is any one theory emerging as the basis for most of these?*

**WH:** My usual answer, which some people call a "Wayne-ism," is *"very much and not at all."* We have very consciously worked within the adult learning theories, but have not forced the standards to incorporate a specific taxonomy. You can use Merrill, or Bloom, or something you make up yourself. But what we've learned from the work with XML (and other projects) is you can have a universal standard that does not embody a specific theory but which allows you to incorporate whichever taxonomy you want to use. And you *will* need a taxonomy.

**RC:** *Do you have any success stories you can share? Any examples of how this is changing practice?*

**WH:** The one that most people talk about is CISCO. It was literally a survival situation—as fast as they were growing in personnel and acquiring new technologies, they needed to train all their new people on all the new products. This daunting challenge was met through the dramatic transition to do the *majority* of their training via e-learning and the Internet. All of this enabled through their well-published creation of "Reusable Information Objects" or RIO model for all their learning content and the adoption of learning standards within this model. It would also be important to note that at Cisco, as with almost all the success stories I know of, they made training and the integrated use of technology a cultural issue as much as anything else.

The greatest story in my opinion, however, is in the collective groundswell of implementations and success stories that I discover literally daily in my travels around the world. It is not just one company or organization, but many of them, large and small, globally dispersed; and entire communities are coming to common conclusions and successful implementations.

I think the other factor that sometimes obscures the view of the broad adoption and success that I have the privilege to observe is that almost all of our work has become project-based. Almost everything we do is part of a project, so the success stories are also embedded in projects as opposed to being at the organization or corporate level.

If you really want to see where this is going, back up a level and look at the momentum that's building: all of the content management systems, learning content management systems, and learning management systems. That should convince you this isn't a fad, that standards are here to stay.

**RC:** *Thank you, Wayne*

**WH:** You're welcome.

## Conclusion

To summarize, the value of standards lies in their ability to catalyze a fundamental change: a shift from creating and delivering monolithic courses to fine-grained content that can be re-used in many contexts. They do this by leveraging on the work that's being done throughout the world on packaging, cataloging, managing, and delivering instructional content. Standards affect all levels of an organization and all stages of instructional and informational development and learning.

Let's close by showing the standards in action for Karen, the product training manager mentioned earlier:

It's January 4, six months into the new standards-based training project, and her first month using the new Learning Content Management System. The process of cataloging materials is nearly complete, along with breaking the files into smaller pieces and converting them into a few chosen formats. Version 6 of the Telecom Billing System is due out in a month; there's just enough time to get the sales and support people trained.

She begins by skimming the old course to familiarize herself; it's a traditional full-day course that's been quite popular in the past. She notes the pages that need changing and sends the list off to the original contractor

| Role | Activities |
|---|---|
| HR and training executives | Facilitates using standard components for computer-mediated instruction, anytime and anywhere. Facilitates testing and progress tracking. |
| Training managers | Facilitates the development of content by many people at different times. Facilitates "mining" old content as the basis of new instruction. Encourages re-use of objects in many settings. |
| E-learning designer | Facilitates developing focused, objective-based modules. Gives flexibility for combining instruction, job aids, tests, and performance support. Facilitates the development of content databases. |
| Instructor | Facilitates the development of content databases as sources of supplemental course materials. Can enable the use of e-learning tools for individualized instruction, allowing the instructor to take on a more individualized "mentoring" role (either in-person or on-line.) |
| Learner | Facilitates the deployment of fine-grained, "just-in-time" training tailored to individual needs. |

**Table 2.** *Roles and activities*

who worked on the course. Jerry will be able to enter his changes once for distribution across the World Wide Web.

Karen then considers the needs of the sales force. They rarely come into the classroom, or even sit down for long stretches at the computers, so she works out a plan with sales training. They decide to record a brief introductory presentation and add self-study materials. She sets up a new directory, locates the self-study guides and job aids in her database, and saves them as files. The sales trainers will record the video, put it on-line, and burn a CD-ROM for distribution to the field (in addition to making everything available on the Web).

Jean-Pierre, Karen's manager, knocks on her door. "How can we make sure people take the new training?" They consider offering a certificate and decide to implement on-line testing. A call to the HR department gets permission to put the test on the company-wide Learning Management System along with URLs into her new LCMS. The new system has been a long time coming, but this year she'll finally find enough time to take that trip to Hawaii.

## How Do I Learn More?

### The standards

AICC: www.aicc.org

IMS: www.imsproject.org

Microsoft has implemented the LRN ("Learning Resource iNterchange") toolkit for marking up data in the IMS format, http://www.microsoft.com/elearn/

SCORM: www.adlnet.org/ (click on "SCORM")

ARIADNE: http://ariadne.unil.ch/

IEEE LTSC: http://ltsc.ieee.org

Also collaborating with the Dublin Core Metadata Initiative: see
    http://dublincore.org/

CEN/ISSS: www.cenorm.be/isss/Workshop/LT

ISO: http://jtc1sc36.org/

W3C: Basic standards for the World Wide Web forming the basis for virtually all e-learning standards: http://www.w3.orc

## Key Web Sites

Learnativity: www.learnativity.com

'The Instructional Use of Learning Objects": http://reusability.org/read

*Richard Clark, a Learning Technology Manager at Hewlett-Packard, designs and develops training curricula for HP's Software and Solutions Organization. He also consults within the company to groups needing help with training design and e-learning infrastructure. He is working on two Web sites for the instructional technology community: http://et.sdsu.edu/RClark and http://www.nextquestion.net. He can be reached at Richard_clark2@hp.com or rdclark@nextquestion.net.*

# Learning Objects Need Instructional Design Theory

## David Wiley

*"Learning objects seem to be poised to become the instructional technology of online learning." Most of this article explains the concept of learning objects and shows their importance. But the author concludes with a key point—"instructional design theory must be incorporated with any learning object implementation."*

The purpose here is to introduce a concept known commonly as the "learning object." First we will look at the learning objects literature and lay the groundwork for a working definition of the term "learning object." Next we will note that while there are several efforts to cash in on the learning objects idea, very little actual educational research is happening with regard to learning objects. Finally, we will critically examine the LEGO metaphor commonly associated with learning objects and suggest what may be a more appropriate metaphor.

## What Is a Learning Object?

Technology is an agent of change, and major technological innovations can result in entire paradigm shifts. The computer network known as the Internet is one such innovation. After effecting sweeping changes in the way people communicate and do business, the Internet is poised to bring about a paradigm shift in the way people learn. Consequently, a major change may also be coming in the way educational materials are designed, developed, and delivered to those who wish to learn.

"Learning objects" (LTSC, 2001a) currently lead other candidates for the position of technology of choice in the next generation of instructional design, development, and delivery, due to their potential for reusability, generativity, adaptability, and scalability (Hodgins, 2000; Urdan & Weggen, 2000; Gibbons, Nelson, & Richards, 2000).

Learning objects are elements of a new type of computer-based instruction grounded in the object-oriented paradigm of computer science. Object-orientation highly values the creation of components that can be reused in multiple contexts (Dahl & Nygaard, 1966). This is the main idea behind learning objects: instructional designers can build small (relative to the size of an entire course) instructional components that can be reused in different learning contexts. Additionally, learning objects are generally understood to be digital and deliverable over the Internet, meaning that any number of people can access and use them simultaneously (as opposed to traditional instructional media, such as an overhead or video tape, which can be used in only one place at a time). Moreover, those who incorporate learning objects can benefit immediately from new versions. These are significant differences between learning objects and other instructional media that have existed previously.

Supporting the notion of small, reusable chunks of instructional media, Reigeluth and Nelson (1997) suggest that when teachers first gain access to instructional materials, they often break the materials down into their constituent parts. They then reassemble these parts in ways that support their individual instructional goals. This suggests one reason why reusable instructional components, or learning objects, may provide instructional benefits: if instructors received instructional resources as individual components, this initial step of decomposition could be bypassed, potentially increasing the speed and efficiency of instructional development.

To facilitate the widespread adoption of the learning objects approach, the Learning Technology Standards Committee (LTSC) of the Institute of Electrical and Electronics Engineers (IEEE) formed in 1996 to develop and promote instructional technology standards (LTSC, 2001a). Without such standards, universities, corporations, and other organizations around the world would have no way of assuring the interoperability of their learning objects or other instructional technologies. A similar project called the Alliance of Remote Instructional Authoring and Distribution Networks for Europe (ARIADNE) had already started with the financial support of the European Union Commission (ARIADNE, 2001). At the same time, another venture called the Instructional Management Systems (IMS) Project was just beginning in the United States, with funding from Educom (IMS, 2001). Each of these and other organizations (e.g., the Advanced Distributed Learning Initiative, or ADL [2001]) began developing technical standards to support the broad deployment of learning objects. Many of these local standards efforts have representatives on the LTSC group.

The Learning Technology Standards Committee chose the term "learning objects" (probably from Wayne Hodgins' 1994 use of the term in the title of the CedMA working group, "Learning Architectures, API's, and Learning Objects") to describe these small instructional components, established a working group, and provided a working definition:

> Learning Objects are defined here as any entity, digital or non-digital, which can be used, re-used or referenced during technology supported learning. Examples of technology-supported learning include computer-based training systems, interactive learning environments, intelligent computer-aided instruction systems, distance learning systems, and collaborative learning environments. Examples of Learning Objects include multimedia content, instructional content, learning objectives, instructional software and software tools, and persons, organizations, or events referenced during technology supported learning (LOM, 2001).

This definition is obviously broad, and on examination fails to exclude any person, place, thing, or idea that has existed at any time in the history of the universe, since any of these could be "referenced during technology supported learning." Accordingly, different groups outside the Learning Technology Standards Committee have created different terms that generally narrow the scope of the official definition to something more specific. Other groups have refined the definition but continue to use the term "learning object." Confusingly, these additional terms and different definitions of "learning object" are all Learning Technology Standards Committee "learning objects" in the strictest sense.

Having multiple definitions for the term "learning object" makes talking about learning objects confusing and difficult. For example, computer-based training (CBT) vendor NETg, Inc., uses the term "NETg learning object" but applies a three-part definition: a learning objective, a unit of instruction that teaches the objective, and a unit of assessment that measures the objective (L'Allier, 2001). Another CBT vendor, Asymetrix, defines learning objects in terms of programming characteristics. "ToolBook II learning objects—pre-scripted elements that simplify programming ... provide instantaneous programming power" (Asymetrix, 2000). The NSF-funded Educational Objects Economy takes a technical approach, only accepting Java Applets as learning objects (EOE, 2000). It would seem that there are as many definitions of the term as there are people employing it.

In addition to the various definitions of the term "learning object," other terms that generally mean the same thing confuse the issue further. David Merrill has used the term "knowledge objects" (Merrill, Li, & Jones, 1991), and is currently writing a book on the topic of object-oriented instruction design to be called "Components of Instruction" (personal communication, March 21, 2000). This is sure to introduce the term "instructional component" into the instructional design vernacular. The previously mentioned ARIADNE project uses the term "pedagogical documents" (ARIADNE, 2001). The NSF-funded Educational Software Components of Tomorrow (ESCOT) project uses the term "educational software components" (ESCOT, 2001), while the Multimedia Educational Resource for Learning and On-Line Teaching (MERLOT) project refers to them as "online learning materials" (MERLOT, 2001). Finally, the Apple Learning Interchange simply refers to them as "resources" (ALI, 2001). Depressingly, while each of these is something slightly different, they all conform to the Learning Technology Standards Committee's broad "learning object" definition. Obviously, the field is still struggling to come to grips with the question, "What is a learning object?"

This confusion forces any article on the topic to answer the question, "What is a learning object?" The Learning Technology Standards Committee definition seems too broad to be useful, since most instructional technologists would not consider the historical event "the war of 1812" or the historical figure "Joan of Arc" to be learning objects. At the same time, creating another term only seems to add to the confusion. While the creation of a satisfactory definition of the term learning object will probably consume the better part of the author's career, a working definition must be presented before the discussion can proceed. Therefore, the remainder of this article will define learning object as "any digital resource that can be reused to support learning." This definition includes anything that can be delivered across the network on demand, be it large or small. Examples of smaller reusable digital resources include digital images or photos, live data feeds (like stock tickers), live or prerecorded video or audio snippets, small bits of text, animations, and smaller web-delivered applications, like a Java-based calculator. Examples of larger reusable digital resources include entire web pages that combine text, images, and other media or applications to deliver complete experiences, such as a complete instructional event. This definition of learning object, "any digital resource that can be reused to support learning," is proposed for two reasons.

First, the definition is specific enough to define a reasonably small set of things: reusable digital resources. At the same time, the definition is broad enough to include the estimated 33.5 terabytes of information available on the publicly accessible Internet (Internet Archive, 2001).

Second, the definition is based on the LTSC definition (and encloses a proper subset of learning objects as defined by the LTSC), which makes issues of compatibility explicit. The definition captures what the author feels to be the critical attributes of a learning object, "reusable," "digital," "resource," and "learning," as does the LTSC definition. With that compatibility made explicit, the proposed definition differs from the LTSC definition in two important ways.

The definition explicitly rejects non-digital and non-reusable resources. The definition of learning object presented does not include people, historical events, books (in the traditional sense of the term), or other physical objects. The definition also drops the phrase "technology supported" which is now implicit, because all learning objects are digital.

Third, the phrase "to support" has been substituted in place of "during" in the LTSC definition. Use of an object *during* learning doesn't connect its use *to* learning. The LTSC definition implies that a banner advertisement atop an online course web page would be a legitimate learning object. While it may appear at the same time, it doesn't function instructionally. The definition proposed here emphasizes the purposeful use of learning objects to support learning.

Armed with a working definition of the term learning object, the discussion of the instructional use of learning objects can proceed.

## Instructional Design Theory and Learning Objects

Instructional design theories have been overviewed frequently in the literature (Dijkstra, Seel, Schott, & Tennyson, 1997; Reigeluth, 1983, 1999b; Tennyson, Schott, Seel, & Dijkstra, 1997). Reigeluth (1999a) defines instructional design theory as follows:

> [I]nstructional design theories are design oriented; they describe methods of instruction and the situations in which those methods should be used, the methods can be broken into simpler component methods, and the methods are probabilistic. (p. 7)

Instructional design theory, or instructional strategies and criteria for their application, must play a large role in the application of learning objects if they are to succeed in facilitating learning. That is, learning objects can't just be treated as pretty clip art—they have to be used in a principled way to support learning. The natural question, then, is "How do we do this?" Thinking about two of the largest issues in the learning objects area—combination and granularity—in instructional design terms might be a good start.

### Combination

While groups like the Learning Technology Standards Committee exist to promote international discussion around the technology standards necessary to support learning object-based instruction, and many people are talking about the financial opportunities about to come into existence, there is astonishingly little conversation around the instructional design implications of learning objects.

Indicative of this lack of thought about instructional design was item 7(d) of the Learning Objects Metadata Working Group's (a working group of the Learning Technology Standards Committee) Project Authorization Request (PAR) form (LOM, 2001). The PAR is the mechanism by which IEEE projects are officially requested and approved, and must contain statements of the project's scope and purpose. Section 7 of the PAR deals with the purpose of the proposed project, and item (d) in the Learning Objects Metadata Working Group's PAR (LTSC, 2001b) reads as follows:

> To enable computer agents to automatically and dynamically compose personalized lessons for an individual learner.

The LOM group was purportedly designing metadata to support this goal. Metadata, literally "data about data," is descriptive information about a resource. For example, the card catalog in a public library is a collection of metadata. In the case of the card catalog, the metadata are the information stored on the cards about the Author, Title, and Publication Date of the book or resource (recording, etc.) in question. The labels on cans of soup are another example of metadata: they contain a list of Ingredients, the Name of the soup, the Production Facility where the soup was canned, etc. In both the case of the library book and the can of soup, metadata allow you to locate an item very quickly without investigating all the individual items through which you are searching. Imagine trying to locate *Paradise Lost* by sifting through every book in the library, or looking for chicken soup by opening every can of soup in the store and inspecting their contents! The Learning Objects Metadata Working Group is working to create metadata for learning objects (such as Title, Author, Version, Format, etc.) so that people and computers will be able to find objects by searching, as opposed to browsing the entire digital library one object at a time until they find a satisficing one.

The problem with 7(d) in the PAR arose when people began to actually consider what it meant for a computer to "automatically and dynamically compose personalized lessons." This meant taking individual learning objects and combining them in a way that made instructional sense, or in instructional design terminology, "sequencing" the learning objects. It seemed clear to some that in order for a computer to make sequencing or any other instructional design decisions, the computer would need instructional design information to support the decision-making process. The problem was that no instructional design information was included in the metadata specified by the current version of the Learning Objects Metadata Working Group standard.

The lack of instructional design discussion at this standards-setting level of conversation about learning objects is disturbing because it might indicate a trend. One can easily imagine vendors asking, "If the standards bodies haven't worried about sequencing, why should we?" Once technology or software that does not support an instructionally grounded approach to learning object sequencing is completed and shipped to the average teacher, why would he or she respond any differently? This sets the stage for learning objects to be used simply to glorify online instruction, the way clip art and dingbats are used in a frequently unprincipled manner to decorate newsletters. Wiley (1999) called this "the new CAI–'Clip Art Instruction'" (p. 6). Instructionally grounded sequencing decisions are at the heart of the instructionally successful use of learning objects.

## Granularity

Discussion of the problem of combining learning objects in terms of "sequencing" suggests another connection between learning objects and instructional design theory. The most difficult problem facing the designers of learning objects is that of "granularity" (Wiley et al., 1999). How big should a learning object be? As stated above, the Learning Technology Standards Committee's definition leaves room for an entire curriculum to be viewed as a learning object, but such a large object view diminishes the possibility of learning object reuse. Reuse is the core of the learning object notion, as generativity, adaptivity, and other -ivities are all facilitated by this property of reuse. This is why a more restrictive definition has been proposed in this article.

From an "efficiency" point of view, the decision regarding learning object granularity can be viewed as a trade-off between the benefits of reuse (the smaller the object, the more places I can use it) and the expense of cataloging (the more objects, the more metadata I have to create). From an instructional point of view, alternatively, the decision between how much or how little to include in a learning object can be viewed as a problem of "scope." While reality dictates that financial and other factors must be considered, if learning is to have its greatest chance of occurring, decisions regarding the scope of learning objects must also be made in an instructionally principled manner.

From this point of view, the major issues facing would-be employers of learning objects, granularity and combination, turn out to be perhaps the two considerations known best to instructional designers: scope and sequence. Unfortunately, no one seems to be talking about learning objects from this perspective—they're always talking about the technology or the financial opportunities.

## Interest in the Learning Objects Idea

A report released by investment banking firm W. R. Hambrect contained more than the common predictions for the future of online learning (e.g., that the online learning market will reach $11.5 billon by 2003 [Urdan & Weggen, 2000]). As evidenced in the report, even brokers are talking about learning objects and encouraging investors to make sure that the e-learning companies they buy rely on the technology:

> [Online learning content] development cycles are predicted to shorten by 20% every year to two or three weeks by 2004. This imperative will drive more template-based designs and fewer custom graphics. Learning objects

will be created in smaller chunks and reusable formats. As a consequence, the industry will become more efficient and competitive.... We are convinced that the move to defined, open standards is crucial to the continuing successful adoption of e-learning, especially as it begins to transition beyond early adopters into the rapid growth phase of the market. Authoring tools will need to operate across different platforms and communicate with other tools used to build learning systems. Content and courseware must be reusable, interoperable, and easily manageable at many different levels of complexity throughout the online instructional environment. Enterprise learning systems have to accommodate numerous and varied learner requirements, needs, and objectives. Corporate customers need to be able to easily track content created by multiple content providers through one training management system and search vast local or distributed catalogs of content to identify learning objects or modules on a particular topic. The race for education technology standards is on (Urdan & Weggen, 2000, p.16).

Whether or not the learning object paradigm is grounded in the best instructional theory currently available, there can be little doubt that the United States and the world are about to be flooded with learning object-based tools. Microsoft has already released a toolset it touts as "the first commercial application of work being delivered by the Instructional Management System (IMS) Project" (Microsoft, 2001). Recognition, adoption, and the potential for future support for the learning objects idea is significant, and includes some of the biggest players in software, higher education, and even investment. Learning objects seem to be poised to become *the* instructional technology of online learning. However, technical standards and venture capital are not enough to promote learning. In order to promote learning, technology use should be guided by instructional principles.

## Conclusion

Wiley (2000) posited and presented three components of a successful learning object implementation: an instructional design theory, a learning object taxonomy, and "prescriptive linking material" that connects the instructional design theory to the taxonomy, providing guidance of the type "for this type of learning goal, use this type of learning object." In addition to providing a worked example of this process, Wiley (2000) also presents design guidelines for the five learning object types identified in his taxonomy. This three component approach is, however, largely untried. We need empirical trials of this and other approaches. These trials need to be reported and improved on. This is the scientific method, the way we make things better.

The main theme of this article, if you haven't noticed, has been that instructional design theory must be incorporated in any learning object implementation

| Learning Object Characteristic | Fundamental Learning Object | Combined-closed Learning Object | Combined-open Learning Object | Generative-presentation Learning Object | Generative-instructional Learning Object |
|---|---|---|---|---|---|
| Number of elements combined | One | Few | Many | Few-Many | Few-Many |
| Type of objects contained | Single | Single, Combined-closed | All | Single, Combined-closed | Single, Combined-closed, Generative-presentation |
| Reusable component objects | Not applicable | No | Yes | Yes/No | Yes/No |
| Common function | Exhibit, display | Pre-designed instruction or practice | Pre-designed instruction and/or practice | Exhibit, display | Computer-generated instruction and/or practice |
| Extra-object dependence | No | No | Yes | Yes/No | Yes |
| Type of logic contained in object | Not applicable | None, or answer sheet-based item scoring | None, or domain-specific instructional and assessment strategies | Domain-specific presentation strategies | Domain-independent presentation, instructional, and assessment strategies |
| Potential for inter-con-textual reuse | High | Medium | Low | Medium | High |
| Potential for intra-con-textual reuse | Low | Low | Medium | High | High |

**Table 1.** Preliminary taxonomy of learning object types

that aspires to facilitate learning. Like any other instructional technology, learning objects must participate in a principled partnership with instructional design theory if they are to succeed in facilitating learning. Everyone seems to be banking on learning objects' ability to revolutionize learning. This revolution will never occur unless more voices speak out regarding the explicitly *instructional use of learning objects*—the automated or by-hand spatial or temporal juxtaposition of learning objects intended to facilitate learning. These voices will have to be powerful and articulate to penetrate the din of metadata, data interchange protocol, tool/agent communication, and other technical standards conversations. While instructional design theory may not be as "sexy" as bleeding-edge technology, there *must* be concentrated effort made to understand the instructional issues inherent in the learning objects notion. The potential of learning objects as an instructional technology is fabulous, but will never be realized without a balanced effort in technology and instructional design areas.

## References

ADL. (2001). Advanced distributed learning network website. Retrieved February 8, 2001 from the World Wide Web: http://www.adlnet.org/.

ALI. (2001). Apple learning interchange website. Retrieved February 8, 2001 from the World Wide Web: http://ali.apple.com/.

ARIADNE. (2001). Alliance of remote instructional authoring and distribution networks for Europe website. Retrieved February 8, 2001 from the World Wide Web: http://ariadne.unil.ch/.

Asymetrix. (2000). *Customer case study: Venturist, Inc.* Retrieved February 8, 2001 from the World Wide Web: http://www.asymetrix.com/solutions/casestudies/venturist.html.

Dahl, O. J., & Nygaard, K. (1966). SIMULA—An algol based simulation language. *Communications of the ACM, 9* (9), pp. 671-678.

Dijkstra, S., Seel, N., Schott, F., & Tennyson, R. (Eds.) (1997). *Instructional design: International perspectives.* Mahwah, NJ: Lawrence Erlbaum Associates.

EOE. (2001). Educational objects economy website. Retrieved February 8, 2001 from the World Wide Web: http://www.eoe.org/eoe.htm.

ESCOT. (2001). Educational software components of tomorrow website. Retrieved February 8, 2001 from the World Wide Web: http://www.escot.org/.

Gibbons, A.S., Nelson, J., & Richards, R. (2000). The nature and origin of instructional objects. In D.A. Wiley (Ed.), *The instructional use of learning objects.* Bloomington, IN: Association for Educational Communications and Technology.

Hodgins, W. (2000). *Into the future.* Retrieved February 8, 2001 from the World Wide Web: http://www.learnativity.com/download/MP7.PDF.

IMS. (2001). Instructional management systems project website. Retrieved February 8, 2001 from the World Wide Web: http://imsproject.org/.

Internet Archive. (2001). The Internet archive: Building an "Internet library." Retrieved February 8, 2001 from the World Wide Web: http://www.archive.org/.

L'Allier, J.J. (1998). *NETg's precision skilling: The linking of occupational skills descriptors to training interventions.* Retrieved February 8, 2001 from the World Wide Web: http://www.netg.com/research/pskillpaper.htm.

LOM. (2001). *LOM working draft v5*. Retrieved February 8, 2001 from the World Wide Web: http://ltsc.ieee.org/doc/wg12/LOM_WD5.doc.

LTSC. (2001a). Learning technology standards committee website. Retrieved February 8, 2001 from the World Wide Web: http://ltsc.ieee.org/.

LTSC. (2001b). IEEE standards board: Project authorization request (PAR) form [Online]. Available: http://ltsc.ieee.org/par-lo.htm.

MERLOT. (2001). Multimedia educational resource for learning and on-line teaching website. Retrieved February 8, 2001 from the World Wide Web: http://www.merlot.org/.

Merrill, M.D., Li, Z., & Jones, M. (1991). Instructional transaction theory: An introduction. *Educational Technology, 31*(6), pp. 7-12.

Microsoft. (2001). *Resources: Learning resource interchange.* Retrieved February 8, 2001 from the World Wide Web: http://www.microsoft.com/eLearn/resources/LRN/.

Reigeluth, C.M. (1983). Instructional design: What is it and why is it? In C.M. Reigeluth (Ed.), *Instructional design theories and models: An overview of their current status* (pp. 3-36). Hillsdale, NJ: Lawrence Erlbaum Associates.

Reigeluth, C.M., & Nelson, L.M. (1997). A new paradigm of ISD? In R.C. Branch & B. B. Minor (Eds.), *Educational media and technology yearbook* (Vol. 22, pp. 24-35). Englewood, CO: Libraries Unlimited.

Reigeluth, C.M. (1999a). The elaboration theory: Guidance for scope and sequence decisions. In C.M. Reigeluth (Ed.), *Instructional design theories and models: A new paradigm of instructional theory* (pp. 425-454). Hillsdale, NJ: Lawrence Erlbaum Associates.

Reigeluth, C.M. (1999b). What is instructional design theory and how is it changing? In C.M. Reigeluth (Ed.), *Instructional design theories and models: A new paradigm of instructional theory* (pp. 5-29). Hillsdale, NJ: Lawrence Erlbaum Associates.

Tennyson, R., Schott, F., Seel, N., & Dijkstra, S. (Eds.) (1997). *Instructional design: International perspectives*. Mahwah, NJ: Lawrence Erlbaum Associates.

Urdan, T.A., & Weggen, C.C. (2000). *Corporate e-learning: Exploring a new frontier.* Retrieved February 8, 2001 from the World Wide Web: http://wrhambrecht. com/research/coverage/elearning/ir/ir_explore.pdf.

Wiley, D.A. (1999). Learning objects and the new CAI: So what do I do with a learning object? Retrieved February 8, 2001 from the World Wide Web: http://wiley. ed.usu.edu/docs/instruct-arch.pdf.

Wiley, D.A., South, J.B., Bassett, J., Nelson, L.M., Seawright, L.L., Peterson, T., & Monson, D. W. (1999). Three common properties of efficient online instructional support systems. *The ALN Magazine, 3*(2). Retrieved February 8, 2001 from the World Wide Web: http://www.aln.org/alnweb/magazine/Vol3_issue2/wiley.htm.

Wiley, D.A. (2000). *Learning object design and sequencing theory*. Unpublished doctoral dissertation, Brigham Young University. Retrieved February 8, 2001 from the World Wide Web: http://davidwiley.com/papers/dissertation/dissertation.pdf.

*David Wiley teaches instructional technology at Utah State University. He received his Ph.D. in Instructional Psychology and Technology from Brigham Young University in 2000. While there, he founded OpenContent (www.opencontent.org), "to facilitate the prolific creation of freely available, high-quality, well-maintained content." He is the author of* The Instructional Uses of Learning Objects *(2000) and he recently contributed "Learning Objects" to be published in* Educational Technology: An Encyclopedia *(Santa Barbara, CA: ABC-CLIO, 2002). E-mail him at wiley@cc.usu.edu or dw2@opencontent.org.*

# A Framework for Designing Interactivity into Web-Based Instruction

## Pam Northrup

*Interactivity—engagement in learning—is crucial for success in Web-based learning. This article discusses five attributes of interactivity and presents a framework for instructional design to promote those forms of interactivity.*

Interactivity has been defined in several contexts for Web-based learning. Hillman, Willis, and Gunawardena (1994) put it very simply as *engagement in learning.* Most can agree that interactivity is two-way communications among two or more persons. Garrison (1993) further suggests that the purpose of interaction is to promote explanation and challenging perspectives among two or more learners. The interaction itself is categorized within a *learning context* with the purpose of task/instructional completion or social relationship building (Berge, 1999; Gilbert and Moore, 1998), with a mixture of both types of interaction being common.

Moore (1989) classifies interaction as engagement in learning through (1) interaction between participants and learning materials, (2) interaction between participants and tutors/experts, and (3) interaction among participants. Northrup and Rasmussen (2000) take a similar approach in classifying interaction as (1) student to student, (2) student to instructor, (3) student to instructional materials, and (4) student to management [feedback]. The notion of adding management/feedback as one of the interaction strategies arose due to the need to close the communications loop on areas of instructional content, but also on general social communications.

Until students receive a "reply" in some form verifying that what they sent was accurate, they typically are uncomfortable. Additionally, students may not, be conceptualizing concepts in the manner intended. Interestingly, Yacci (2000) defines interaction through the lens of a student. Students must perceive that the message loop is complete, rather than the instructor assuming that it is complete. There must be mutual coherence for the message loop to be closed.

The idea of feedback as the indicator of completed communications is mentioned in several places (Berge, 1999; Liaw and Huang, 2000; Weller, 1988). Weller suggests that feedback occurs when learners actively adapt to the information presented through the technology, which the technology, in turn, adapts to the learner. Kulhavy and Wager (1993) suggest that feedback on incorrect responses assists in furthering individual learners' understanding of specific concepts.

Sorting out the instructional and social interactions that occur in a Web-based course, coupled with the types of interactions (student to student, student to instructor, student to content, and student to management/feedback), presents a challenge to designers of Web-based instruction. This article provides a framework of interaction attributes that can be used to select strategies and tactics to facilitate interaction on the Web. The framework encompasses five interaction attributes: (1) interaction with content, (2) collaboration, (3) conversation, (4) intrapersonal interaction, and (5) performance support. Each will be discussed, and multiple examples of how each fits within both a theoretical and a pedagogical context will be provided.

## Types of Interactions

All interactions should involve complex activity by learners to include engaging and reflecting, annotating, questioning, answering, pacing, elaborating, discussing, inquiring, problem-solving, linking, constructing, analyzing, evaluating, and synthesizing (Liaw and Huang, 2000). The levels of interactivity include  interaction between participants and learning materials, interaction between participants and instructors/experts, interaction among participants; management/ feedback communications (Moore, 1989; Northrup and Rasmussen, 2000) are embedded within both content and social interaction (Gilbert and Moore, 1998). Although content and social interaction are interwoven into highly interactive Web-based courses, each will be discussed independently to further explain the role of both forms of interaction in a Web-based course.

*Content interaction* is based on the theory of learning that is most appropriate to achieve educational outcomes within the course itself. In many Web-based courses, multiple layers of learning outcomes exist, thus suggesting that multiple strategies may be incorporated into the course. Some courses may include an intensive case study, while maintaining a weekly schedule of online lectures and discussion sessions. Other courses may adhere more loosely to a semester-long simulation, with its outcome being an explanation of findings and events. It is difficult to prescribe one "best fit" for content interaction, given the wide range of possibilities available on the World Wide Web. It is important, however, to ground the design of the learning environment in solid theory and pedagogy, as distance learning has been criticized for having very little, if any, theoretical context (Moore, 1993). Hannafin, Hannafin, Land, and Oliver (1997) discuss *grounded design* as a context for dealing with the range of design decisions that best facilitate learning outcomes, Grounded design is defined as "the systematic implementation of processes and procedures that are rooted in established theory and research in human learning" (p. 102). Grounded design does not presume that one belief system is superior over another; it merely suggests alignment among the foundations, assumptions, and methods selected.

*Social interaction* is a key element in online learning. Given that the nature of online learning is *"anytime ... anywhere,"* the potential for isolation and frustration exists. The social interaction of the course must, at least initially, be designed into the course. Through collaboration and communication, the opportunity for learning more about peers and connecting with them in non-task specific conversation is more likely to occur. Although social interaction may have very little to do with a course, it is still valued as the primary vehicle for student communications in a Web-based learning environment. Non-task/content-specific social interaction may include conversation in a chat room, inquiries about used textbook purchases, or questions about using a new version of a piece of software.

Many aspects of social interaction, however, are directly related to the instructional outcomes of a course. For example, when collaborative teams of students work toward project completion, there is still the need for relationship building in the learning community. Relationship building is a necessary component of collaboration and communication and the perceptions of the efficacy of this type of social interaction can impact the learning outcomes of the course. By the very nature of social interaction, learners are directly able to foster content interaction (Liaw and Huang, 2000).

## A Framework for Online Interaction

Interaction doesn't just happen. It must be *designed intentionally* into the Web-based course. Oftentimes, when Web-based instruction fails, it is because it was not designed well, not because the technology itself was inherently "bad."

It can be assumed that the more interaction, the better. However, the overuse or misuse of interaction strategies can lead to boredom, overload, and frustration (Berge, 1999). Additionally, it lessens the likelihood that students will be able to surmise what is "important," and once again, frustration may occur when students perceive interaction as online busywork. Gilbert and Moore (1998) suggest that the more interactive the Web-based course becomes, the more complex it is to use. For novice distance learners, complexity may very well lead to more frustration and isolation. Future Web-based tools hopefully will promote collaboration and interaction online in a much easier to use format (Liaw and Huang, 2000). For now, designers of Web-based courses should weigh the *frequency* and the *quality* of interactions required that best facilitate the learning outcomes to be achieved, where frequency does not always equal quality.

A framework for online interaction is included below that provides five interaction attributes of an online course: (1) interaction with content, (2) collaboration, (3) conversation, (4) intrapersonal interaction, and (5) performance support. Embedded within each attribute are possible strategies and tactics that can be used to facilitate both content and social interactivity. The attributes of Web-based instruction should be filtered through the philosophy and pedagogy that is presumed appropriate for the course, preferably adhering to the grounded design approach suggested by Hannafin *et al.* (1997).

Oftentimes, lists of strategies and tactics are provided as design suggestions for Web-based courses. When suggested out of context, it is difficult to surmise how the online experience may be structured. For example, in a list that suggests threaded discussions be used, there is still little detail as to how they are to be used within the learning experience itself. In a more behaviorist notion, threaded discussion may be used to elicit responses to given questions. In a situated learning environment, threaded discussions may be used to discuss influences on the environment with a scientist in an attempt to determine why native plants are not surviving. Each interaction attribute will be discussed in relation to content and social interaction, bearing in mind that both interaction strategies are woven throughout a successful Web-based course.

## Instructional Content and Interactivity

The instructional content is the central component of a Web-based course, as this is where new knowledge, skills, and abilities are presented. Whether students learn declarative knowledge or participate in a large-scale simulation, the way in which knowledge is shared sets the stage for all interactivity within the Web-based course. When given a choice, instructors many times will select [and design] instructional methods and techniques that are consistent with their theoretical and philosophical views.

Categorically, instruction is presented either through an instructor-centered approach [direct, formal instruction] or through a more student-centered approach. There are times when one style of instruction is better than the other. When the outcomes of instruction are to analyze, synthesize, or evaluate, or when ill-defined authentic problems are the focus, a more student-centered approach would best facilitate the learning outcomes. An instructor-centered approach would work well for instruction that is procedural, declarative, or well-defined in role and definition.

**Instructor-Centered Approach.** Much of what exists online as Web-based courses appears to have a strong instructor-centered influence. In much of the instruction, *information* is presented, *examples* are provided, *practice* exists, and, in many cases, *feedback* is available through mentors and instructors. Examples of instructor-centered instruction include lectures presented via text and graphics online, through PowerPoint, and through audio-narrated PowerPoint lectures with note-taking guides.

**Student-Centered Approach.** Student-centered learning is appropriate for outcomes of instruction that are focused on analysis, synthesis, and evaluation (Berge, 1999). Land and Hannafin (1997) further suggest that student-centered learning provides "interactive, complementary activities that enable individuals to address unique learning interests and needs, study multiple levels of complexity, and deepen understanding" (p. 168). Using open-ended strategies for learning, such as situated learning, learners will actively construct meaning to determine how to proceed. This student-centered approach fosters a greater responsibility for learning and requires students to be more self-regulated in their approaches to learning. In some cases, scaffolding is provided that will facilitate self-regulation, thus providing strategies that students can use to create unique approaches to complex problems (Jonassen and Land, 2000).

Examples of student-centered learning in a Web-based environment include demonstrations, debates, simulations, role-plays, case studies, and discussion groups (Berge, 1999; Liaw and Huang, 2000; Paulsen, 1995). Rasmussen and Northrup (1999) propose that Online Internet Expeditions provide an optimal situated learning experience for students. In *Camp Habitat [http://mentor.coe.uwf.edu/camphabitat/],* side-by-side with experts, students can explore native Florida habitats both virtually and locally to analyze the effects of humans on the environment (see Figure 1). While ongoing guidance is available through multiple sources to promote self-regulation, students actively participate in the expedition by posing problems faced within their environments, conducting investigations using various tools and communications equipment, and solving novel problems posed by their habitat. The Web-based expedition provides a framework that students can use as a model or as a source of comparative data for their own investigations.

In another example of student-centered learning, a Web-based Online Professional Development, *The Making of a Technology-Rich Classroom [http://mentor.coe.uwf.edu/onlinepd/mainpage.html],* provides a context for classroom teachers to use information and site-based examples of "model" teachers using technology effectively in their classrooms while filtering the models and examples according to their own classroom needs (see Figure 2). A framework is

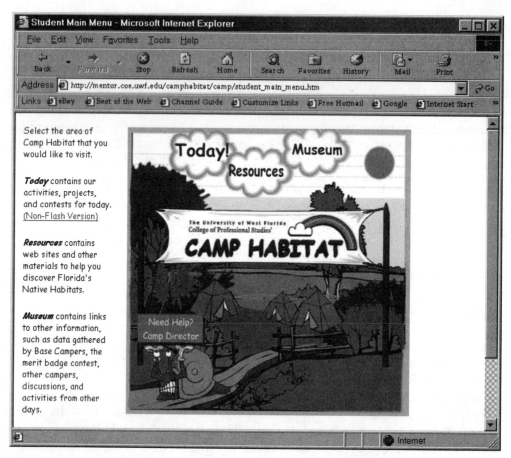

**Figure 1.** Camp Habitat

provided for assessing technology readiness, another framework is provided in planning for a technology-rich classroom, and much opportunity exists for conversation and collaboration with peers and expert technology-users. As a result of the professional development, teachers integrate technologies that are available to them in their classroom.

## Collaboration and Interactivity

Designing collaborative online learning environments is an obvious strategy for promoting interactivity. Many of the same factors that exist for campus-based students in collaborative groups parallel collaboration on the Web. Topics such as group size, group role definition, group assignment, and shared grading all are issues as well on the Web. A collaborative group's members should be committed to the "group goal" and to maximizing each other's learning. Johnson and Johnson (1994) suggest very strongly that groups do not become collaborative just because

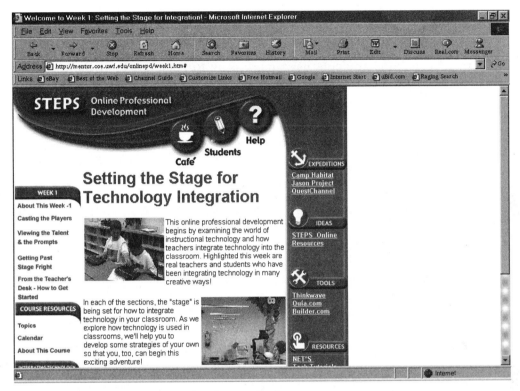

**Figure 2.** The making of a technology-rich classroom

someone assigns them together as a group. An effective collaborative group requires positive interdependence, group and individual accountability, promotive interaction, and interpersonal skills (Johnson and Johnson, 1994; Slavin, 1990, as cited in Frank, 1999).

Trentin (2000) proposes that quality can be obtained through highly interactive courses. Occasionally, however, a strong collaboration component in the course may hinder some students' participation. If, for whatever reason, some students are unable to participate in collaborative, group building exercises, those students may be left to communicate with only the instructor or mentor. Courses relying heavily on collaboration must indicate the collaboration requirement prior to class or alternative accommodations must be made for students unable to participate fully.

## Conversation

Communicating online requires much clarification about the goals and objectives of e-discussion. Otherwise, students may not gain from the experience and the learning community will not form as intended. Many students complain about getting too much information online, not being able to follow concurrent threads in a threaded discussion, and not being about to keep up with multiple conversations occurring in chat sessions. Despite some of the negative student comments, much can be said about conversation and e-discussion. Written communication seems to be more reflective, as students have more time to compose their thoughts and articulate in the manner intended online (Berge, 1997; Sherry, 2000).

To facilitate successful online conversation, Chism (1998, pp. 7-8) suggests six strategies (as cited in Sherry, 2000):

- *Building group coherence* by getting to know one another online. This form of social interaction will go far in establishing a comfortable environment and in establishing the community of learners.
- *Sharing information* by assigning collaborative groups to become resident experts in specific areas—then requiring the collaborative group to share its knowledge with others online.
- *Processing ideas* by elaborating on discussions, sharing cases, and asking questions of one another through listservs.
- *Online tutoring* as a tool for asking peers questions in preparation for an upcoming test.
- *Refining communication skills* by framing arguments and leading e-discussions.
- *Providing feedback to students* through peer critique and instructor critique online.

Engaging in both synchronous and asynchronous forms of conversation can extend learning online while motivating the online learner and extending the social interaction of the course (Sherry, 2000).

### Intrapersonal Interaction

Monitoring one's own learning is essential for survival in a Web-based environment, even more so than in a traditional environment. Oftentimes, this element of Web-based design is not included, yet it is essential that learners work independently and can self-regulate their own learning. Many cognitive strategies can be embedded within a Web-based course, along with tips and ideas for time management and independent learning.

For example, a notetaking guide can be included in Web-based courses to assist learners in determining what is important. The intent of this notetaking guide is to be used as a companion to the RealAudio PowerPoint lectures provided weekly in a graduate instructional technology course. Additional cognitive strategies embedded within the context of this Web-based course are self-questioning, summaries, explanation of to-be-learned content, and standard times for completion of each of the weekly assignments.

## Performance Support

Performance support is recognized as "… an electronic system that provides integrated access to information, advice, learning experiences, and tools to help someone perform a task with the minimum of support by other people" (Gery, 1991; Raybould, 1995). A review of the literature on EPSS suggests a series of goals and benefits of performance support, in prompting day-one performance. The basic premise of this just-in-time tool is to generate performance and learning at the moment of need, while assisting in building the knowledge infrastructure for-work that will be done in the future. Karat (1997) suggests four benefits of performance support: (1) enhanced productivity, (2) reduced training costs, (3) increased worker autonomy, and (4) increased quality due to uniform work practices. EPSS provides *cognitive training wheels* that can be progressively removed, as the performer no longer requires guidance and assistance.

In a Web-based course, retention will suffer if students are not supported throughout the course. Using the framework of EPSS, student support may include tools, information, advice, and learning experiences required to be successful online. When students are engaged in an online program and are truly "distance" students, there will be additional needs of financial aid, registration, library access, and more that must be woven into the Web-based structure. Many online providers encourage students to complete a pre-course tutorial on "How to Be a Distance Learner," while others provide online quizzes to determine if distance learning is "right" for the individual learner. However, in most cases, that is the extent of support provided to students, other than the heroic efforts provided by professors of disciplines like History and Accounting as they attempt to train students how to use chat rooms and reformat their computers. Yet their role should be to provide a rich experience for students in their content area, not to serve as the help desk. Distance learning *support* should be available "anytime … anyplace," just as the advertisements suggest.

Supporting performance for the technical and even motivational components of the course is important and must be considered when a Web-based course is designed and presented. On university campuses, in industry, and in the military, Offices of Distance Learning may have educational materials for students, tutorials on how to use chat rooms, and Distance Learner student guides.

In addition to supporting entire programs at a distance, performance support can also provide in-course assistance. In Figure 3, SID, or Support for Instructional Designers, is included in a Principles of Instructional Design graduate course as a tool to guide first-semester designers in the design and development of their first instructional materials (Northrup and Rasmussen, 2000). SID provides advice in three areas: (1) Teach Me, (2) Show Me, and (3) Guide Me. In *Teach* Me, SID provides brief five- to 10-minute tutorials on each aspect of the Instructional Systems process (at a novice level). *Show Me* provides several completed examples of each

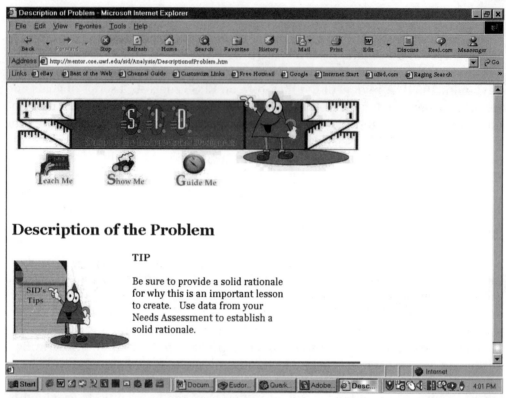

**Figure 3.** Support for instructional designers (SID)

step. *Guide* Me walks students through the process of creating three component objectives or conducting a learner analysis.

## Conclusion

It is a given that interaction is valued as an important variable in Web-based learning environments. The design of interaction into a Web-based learning environment can present challenges, as too much interaction is perceived as busywork, while too little interaction is viewed as isolation. Both are frustrating to the online learner. The trick is to provide levels of interaction appropriate to the learning outcomes of the course, while constantly ensuring that the communications loop is perceived by the online learner to be "complete."

Within the context of social and instructional interaction, this article has presented a framework of interaction attributes that should be considered in the design of Web-based instruction. Attributes include (1) interaction with content, (2) collaboration, (3) conversation, (4) intrapersonal interaction, and (5) performance support. Performance support that provides information, advice, learning experiences, and tools to support learners "just in time" may alleviate many initial fears expressed by online learners. Once the initial fears are lessened, collaboration and conversation will begin to emerge.

Whether the course suggests a student-centered or instructor-centered approach, the quality of online interactions can promote successful learning outcomes. It is the responsibility of the instructor and even the institution to provide a learning environment in which the learner has the opportunity for appropriate interactions with content, the instructor, and other students (Berge, 1999; Moore, 1993). Additional consideration for feedback through interacting with a management/feedback tool should also be given.

## References

Berge, Z.L. (1997, May/June). Characteristics of online teaching in post-secondary, formal education. *Educational Technology,* 37(3), 35-47.

Berge, Z.L. (1999, January/February). Interaction in post-secondary Web-based learning. *Educational Technology*, 39(1), 5-11.

Chism, N. (1998). *Handbook for instructors on the use of electronic class discussion.* Ohio State University, Office of Faculty and TA Development.

Frank, S.B. (1999). *Collaborative learning in a constructivist Web-based environment in principles of financial accounting.* Unpublished doctoral dissertation, University of West Florida, Pensacola.

Garrison, D.R. (1993). Quality and theory in distance education: Theoretical considerations. In D. Keegan (Ed.), *Theoretical principles of distance education.* New York: Routledge.

Gery, G. (1991). *Electronic performance support systems.* Boston: Weingarten Publications.

Gilbert, L., and Moore, D.L. (1998, May/June). Building interactivity into Web courses: Tools for social and instructional interaction. *Educational Technology,* 38(3), 29-35.

Hannafin, M.J., Hannafin, K.M., Land, S.M., and Oliver, K. (1997). Grounded practice and the design of learning systems. *Educational Technology Research and Development,* 45(3), 101-117.

Hillman, D.C., Willis, D.J., and Gunawardena, C.N. (1994). Learner-interface interaction in distance education: An extension of contemporary models and strategies for practitioners. *The American Journal of Distance Education,* 8(2), 30-42.

Johnson, D.W., and Johnson, R.T. (1994). *Learning together and alone: Cooperative, competitive, and individualistic learning* (4th ed). Boston: Allyn and Bacon.

Jonassen, D.H., and Land, S.M. (2000). *Theoretical foundations of learning environments.* Mahwah, NJ: Lawrence Erlbaum Associates.

Karat, J. (1997). Evolving the scope of user-centered design. *Communications of the ACM,* 40(7), 33-38.

Kulhavy, R.W., and Wager, W. (1993). Feedback in programmed instruction: Historical context and implications for practice. In J.V. Dempsey and G.C. Sales (Eds.), *Interactive instruction and feedback.* Englewood Cliffs, NJ: Educational Technology Publications.

Land, S.M., and Hannafin, M.J. (1997). Patterns of understanding with open-ended learning environments: A qualitative study. *Educational Technology Research and Development,* 33(1), 47-73.

Liaw, S., and Huang, H. (2000, January/February). Enhancing interactivity in Web-based instruction: A review of the literature. *Educational Technology,* 39(1), 41-51.

Moore, M.G. (1989). Three types of interaction. *The American Journal of Distance Education,* 3(2), 1-6.

Moore, M.G. (1993). Theory of transactional distance. In D. Keegan (Ed.), *Theoretical principles of distance education.* New York: Routledge.

Northrup, P.T., and Rasmussen, K.L. (2000). *Designing a Web-based program: Theory to design.* Paper presented at the annual conference of the Association for Educational Communications and Technology, Long Beach, CA.

Paulsen, M.F. (1995). *The online report on pedagogical techniques for computer-mediated communication,* http://www.nettskolen.com/forskning/19/cmcped.html.

Rasmussen, K.R., and Northrup, P.T. (1999). Situated learning online: Assessment strategies for online expeditions. *Diagnostique,* 25, 71-82.

Raybould, G. (1995). Performance support engineering: An emerging development methodology for enabling organizational learning. *Innovations in Education and Training International,* 32(1), 65-69.

Sherry, L. (2000). The nature and purpose of online discourse: A brief synthesis of current research as related to the WEB Project. *International Journal of Educational Telecommunications,* 6(1), 19-51.

Sherry, L., and Wilson, B. (1996). Supporting human performance across disciplines: A converging of roles and tools. *Performance Improvement Quarterly,* 9(4), 19-36.

Slavin, R.E. (1990). *Cooperative learning: Theory, research, and practice.* Englewood Cliffs, NJ: Prentice-Hall.

Trentin, G. (2000, January/February). The quality-interactivity relationship in distance education. *Educational Technology,* 39(1), 17-27.

Weller, H.G. (1988, February). Interactivity in micro-computer-based instruction: Its essential components and how it can be enhanced. *Educational Technology,* 28(8), 23-27.

Yacci, M. (2000, August). Interactivity demystified: A structural definition for distance education and intelligent computer-based instruction. *Educational Technology,* 39(4), 5-16.

*Pam Northrup is Director, Educational Research and Development Center, Division of Technology, Research and Development, University of West Florida, Pensacola, Florida (e-mail: pnorthru@uwf.edu).*

# Games That Teach: Simple Computer Games for Adults Who Want to Learn

**William Horton**

*If you've never considered using games to teach, read this article. If you've dismissed the idea for any reason, read this article twice. The author, who has been designing technology-based training since 1971, makes an excellent case for using games and offers guidelines and resources for doing so.*

I hate computer games. Most of them bore me to tears. Anyway, I lack the quick eye-hand coordination needed to excel at games. Let's be honest. I can't even get out of Level 2. I have long regarded computer games and video games as the opiates of the leisure class. But a couple of incidents changed my opinion of them.

Several years back, my sister and her husband came for a visit. In idle conversation, I mentioned that I'd just gotten a copy of the game *Myst*. My brother-in-law's mood perked up when I offered to let him play it. This pragmatic, bright civil engineer played the game with relish—for 30 straight hours! Wow. Something powerful was going on. If only I could get people to devote that much attention, effort, and passion to the books I'd written or courses I'd developed or books I'd written!

The second incident occurred in a toy store in Boston. Two children were examining a game on one of the store's computers. A girl, about eight years old, was explaining the game SimCity to her brother who was about five or so. "You can't just jump in. You have to think. I wanted to be a good mayor, so I built lots of parks and gave all the city workers raises. I didn't have any dirty factories. But my city went broke and things got real bad. And all the people got upset. It's hard to help people sometimes. You can't just do what you think they want." This child had learned an important political and moral lesson—from a computer game.

I decided right then that I had better take another look at computer games. Could we use techniques developed in commercial games to make training more engaging and more effective? Well, since then I have been involved in several projects that have used simple games for training and testing adult learners. Let me share some of the insights I have gained.

## Why Use a Game?

A well-designed game lets us implement many of the principles of effective teaching: interactivity, feedback, multimodal presentation, graduated challenge, and so forth. Games can:

- Make training more appealing to those who consider traditional classroom training and e-learning boring beyond endurance.
- Seduce voluntary learners into taking the dreaded TEST.
- Allow learners to discover patterns, trends, and relationships for themselves. Such incremental, discovery learning takes place naturally—I call it *stealth learning.*
- Teach learners the consequences of negative actions. In fact, games provide an opportunity for learners to get these non-productive or negative behaviors "out of their system."
- Provide extensive practice to hone skills and to modify habitual behavior, especially where correct responses must become "second nature."

Games, however, are not for everyone and they cannot do everything. Games are seldom effective to:

- Teach large amounts of detailed, factual information.
- Make boring information interesting. Games make the form of instruction more interesting but seldom make the subject matter more involving.
- Replace books, classrooms, and traditional e-learning tutorials.

If your goal is to teach large amounts of factual information, a game may prove too expensive. If, though, your goal is to test whether the student has acquired the terminology of a field, a simple word game fits the bill.

So, before you begin developing a game, answer these questions:

1. Is your primary goal to teach? To test? Or just to provide practice?
2. What are you trying to accomplish? Are you trying to teach specific knowledge? Or modify an attitude? Or improve a skill?

3. What form is the information you are trying to convey? Is it verbal or visual? Is it conceptual or perhaps a physical activity?

Your answers to these questions will help you decide what kind of game to develop or whether a game is the best solution. Here are some of the different types of games from which you can choose.

## What Type of Game Should I Use?

There are many types of games—some more suitable than others—that you can use as a metaphor for your own tests, err, I mean games. The ones we're going to discuss are models we have found the easiest to adapt and create. Use our ideas as a starting point.

### Arcade Games

In arcade games the player has to shoot and quickly destroy moving images, before they shoot the player. These are also called "shoot 'em ups" and "twitch and splat" games. An example, should none come readily to mind, is Mortal Kombat.

I saw an example of an arcade-style game used in a business setting. Newly hired employees were required to shoot down the flying logos of competing companies. However, since all the flying logos were of competitors, no learning took place. The game was just a test of hand-eye coordination.

Figure 1 shows the same game after we added the logos of partners and customers. Shooting a customer or partner costs points. Now the game teaches players to quickly recognize and distinguish among competitors (foes) and partners and customers (friends).

We generally *do not recommend using this type of game.* Though good at teaching fast, visual recognition and hand-eye coordination—certainly valuable for gun fighters—it is of questionable use in business and technical training. In an era rife with workplace violence, do you want to be teaching marksmanship?

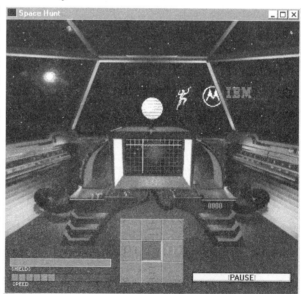

**Figure 1.** Arcade game used to test recognition of partners and competitors (Used with permission of William Horton Consulting, Inc.)

If a job does require quickly recognizing and responding to visual stimuli, such as in quality-control inspections, operating high-speed machinery, and reacting to emergency conditions, consider using a timed, real-speed simulation of the job rather than a metaphorical gunfight.

## Word Games

A lot of examples come to mind when we think of word games: crossword puzzles, Scrabble, word searches, hang man. Figure 2 shows a crossword puzzle used to teach learners the best words and phrases to use when dealing with upset customers. On another project, a very similar puzzle was used to test knowledge of Visual Basic commands.

**Figure 2.** Crossword puzzle used to test verbal knowledge (Used with permission of William Horton Consulting, Inc.) You can try out this puzzle at www.Designing WBT.com/ html/exampleTestsCrossword.htm.

Word games are a great way to exercise and test vocabulary knowledge, such as words in a foreign language, the terminology peculiar to a particular business, or maybe the keywords used in a programming language. Use them as an alternative to the fill-in-the-blank test question.

## Jigsaw Puzzles

Jigsaw puzzles are great at teaching part-to-whole relationships and focusing attention on visual and schematic relationships among the parts of that whole.

**Figure 3.** *Jigsaw puzzle of architectural details* (Used with permission of William Horton Consulting, Inc.) You can try out this game at www.DesigningWBT.com/html/example ActivityLearningGameJigsaw.htm.

Figure 3 shows an example of a jigsaw puzzle used to test visual knowledge. Remodeling contractors are asked to put the scrambled pieces of a house into the correct position. This game tests their ability to correctly recognize architectural details and relationships.

Figure 4 shows an example used for teaching abstract relationships. It teaches network administrators the relationships among network adapters, network protocols, clients, and available cabling. In the stage of the game shown, the learner is trying to hook into Token-ring cabling with an Ethernet adapter. The learner hears a buzzer-like sound indicating there is a problem and an explanation appears in the message window. Upon successful completion the learner hears a short, happy melody plus a message indicating the solution is correct.

## Quiz-Show Games

Popular game shows like *Jeopardy* and *Who Wants to Be a Millionaire?* can provide a basis for a training game. Using a popular game show as a model has the advantage of ensuring the game will be easy to learn, plus you have a ready-made audience. You can modify them to teach and test a variety of skills and knowledge.

Figure 5 shows such a game-show style interaction. Learners are tested on the depth of their knowledge of Microsoft's Visual Basic for Applications.

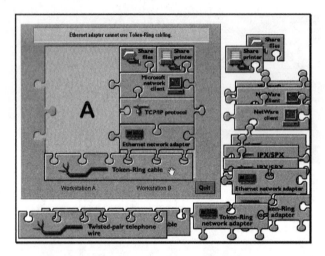

**Figure 4.** Jigsaw puzzle for teaching relationships among the components of a computer network (Used with permission of William Horton Consulting, Inc.) You can try out this game at wwwDesigningWBT.com/html/example ActivityLearningGameJigsaw.htm.

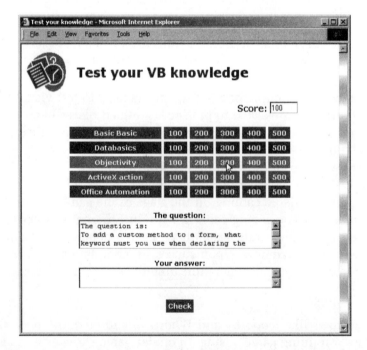

**Figure 5.** Quiz-show game used to test knowledge of a programming language (Used with permission of William Horton Consulting, Inc.) You can try out this game at www. DesigningWBT.com/html/exampleActivityLearningGameGameshow.htm.

## Flash Cards

All right, all right! I know flash cards don't *seem* like a game, but they do provide much of the same kind of challenge—and the same potential for learning. Think of games like *Name that Tune* or *You Don't Know Jack*.

Figure 6 shows an example that tests knowledge of the concept of *inheritance,* important in object-oriented programming. After a short explanation about the rules of inheritance, learners get to practice with a game. In the game learners are presented a series of objects containing certain variables and methods. Their task is to click (as quickly as possible) on the class from which the object is formed. The scoreboard allows learners to track their performance.

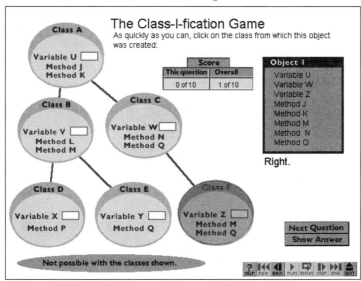

**Figure 6.** Flash-card style game (Used with permission of William Horton Consulting, Inc.)

The essence of the flashcard metaphor is that learners are given a question to answer or a problem to solve. They must answer immediately from memory without consulting any reference materials. Flashcards are good for testing knowledge that learners must memorize thoroughly or skills they must apply automatically.

Flashcards can be used to teach, exercise, and test a range of knowledge such as technical terms for business managers, safety markings for factory workers, or the sounds of various types of heart arrhythmias for cardiac surgeons. The point is, flashcards are very flexible.

## Simulations

Simulations let people practice a difficult activity in a fun, challenging way without the danger posed by real-world failure. They give people a safe, non-judgmental place to practice a skill. Several popular examples of simulation games are

Microsoft's Flight Simulator and SimCity by Electronic Arts, Inc.

Simulations as a training tool are good when it is too expensive or too dangerous for someone to learn on the job—teaching nuclear power plant control room personnel how to manage an emergency shutdown or how to land a 747 at O'Hare in Chicago. Or, how to operate a computer program without erasing your hard disk.

Figure 7 lets learners practice interacting with dialog boxes to define a connection to a database on their computer. After a short lesson walked learners through the steps necessary to create their data source name (DSN), this simulation let them practice what they had learned without the danger of actually causing any problems with their computer system. The purpose of this simulation was not only to reinforce the sequence of steps involved in creating the DSN, but also to help them gain confidence by practicing in a safe environment.

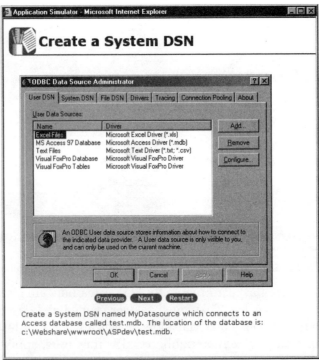

**Figure 7.** Simulation of a computer interaction (Used with permission of William Horton Consulting, Inc.) You can try out this game at www.DesigningWBT.com/html/exampleTestsSimulation.htm.

Simulations can cover more abstract activities and lifetime-long time spans. Figure 8 teaches southern landowners to manage forestland. This activity is difficult because it takes 30 years to grow a tree. One lifetime is not long enough to learn the job, especially considering the effects of weather, variable lumber prices, and insect infestations. In this model, learners can see the results of their actions

**Figure 8.** Simulation of a complex eco-system (Used with permission of William Horton Consulting, Inc.) You can try out this game at www.DesigningWBT.com/html/exampleBeyondSimulationsTreefarm.htm.

and policies over a period of 100 years-something they cannot do easily in real life.

With simulations players learn from their successes and failures—without the risks of fatal exceptions or bankruptcy.

## Adventure Games

Late at night, in the basement labs at MIT in the 1960s, students hovered over Teletype terminals to play some of the first computer games. Ironically, today such games are the best at teaching higher-level skills.

In the classic computer adventure game, players navigated an imaginary world. They would be given a text description of a scene and would type in simple commands to communicate their intentions. The resulting dialog might look something like this, where the player's actions are in UPPER CASE:

To your north is the wall of a castle. You are standing before the door of the castle. Behind you and to your sides is the forest. The castle is quiet

and dark, but from the forest you hear the cries of wolves. Near your feet you see a green rock.
PICK UP ROCK
OK. You are holding the rock.
THROW ROCK AT DOOR
The door opens slowly. Through the door you see a dark corridor...

More recent versions of the adventure genre have included graphical examples like *Myst*, where the user navigates a three-dimensional island by clicking on paths and objects in the scene.

Well, life is an adventure. Business, too. So we should not have much trouble finding uses for the adventure game format to let people learn by navigating a world and discovering its rules for themselves.

Figure 9 shows an example used to teach interviewing skills. In the game, the player must interview a witness to a bank robbery in order to gather information necessary to identify the culprit. Learners are given a number of possible questions to ask. By choosing the most appropriate questions in the right sequence, they can solve this crime in the fewest possible steps. However, if they display inappropriate or counter-productive behavior, they will do poorly in the game and play may be terminated.

Adventure games can include graphics and video segments to illustrate each scene, but the essence of the game is immersing the learner in a story in which they play the pivotal role and their decisions determine the outcome.

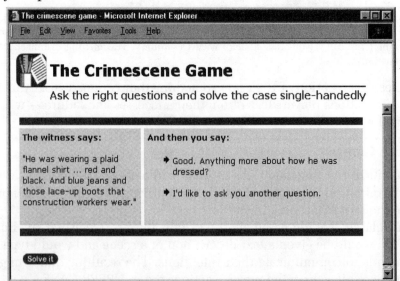

**Figure 9.** *Adventure game used to teach interviewing skills* (Used with permission of William Horton Consulting, Inc.) *You can try out this game at www.DesigningWBT.com/html/exampleActivityLearningGameCrimescene.htm*

Such adventure games can be used to teach, exercise, and measure many kinds of leadership and human-interaction skills. They can also be used to teach problem-solving skills for complex situations that require judgment more than applying a simple set of rules.

# What Makes a Good Learning Game?

A good learning game shares the characteristics of good training and engrossing entertainment. But getting the mix right is the hard part. Here are some characteristics found in most good learning games.

## Winning Requires Learning

In a good learning game, success depends on mastering the material you are trying to teach. Winning proves mastery of the material.

Do not follow the model used in many educational games, where learners are rewarded for surviving a conventional math drill by being allowed to shoot up some aliens. The game is merely a bribe. And all that is learned is that math is boring.

Though luck may play a part, it should never determine the outcome, else the player is gambling, not learning. Luck, in the form of randomly generated events and conditions, can add variety and prevent the game from becoming predictable. In the forestry game (Figure 8), weather, timber prices, and the spread of insect infestations are all influenced by random effects, but not to a degree the learner cannot overcome these variations. In the Leveraged Investment game (Figure 11), movement of the stock market is mostly random. However, a consistent, conservative investment strategy will prove successful over the long run. Luck should never factor more in the outcome than the learner's skill.

## Graduated Challenge

Good games are never too difficult nor too easy. The better you get at the game, the harder the game becomes. Players, even those without any prior practice or knowledge, succeed on their first attempts. And players with extensive practice and experience still find the game challenging.

In the HTML Laboratory, shown in Figure 10, the learner is challenged to create a series of Web-page ingredients using HTML code. The goals are arranged in order of increasing difficulty to keep the activity challenging and to build on prior successes.

In the quiz-show game, shown in Figure 5, questions with higher point values are more difficult than those with lower point values. In the Leveraged Investment game (Figure 11), the graduated challenge is subtler. A very conservative investment strategy will keep the player from going bankrupt. However, to make more money, learners must invest more aggressively. Alas, aggressive investments run greater risk of catastrophic losses. Finding the right balance takes considerable play and honest reflection.

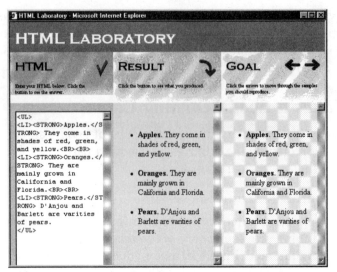

**Figure 10.** Virtual laboratory challenging learners to create various Web-page elements in HTML (Used with permission of William Horton Consulting, Inc.) You can try out this game at www.DesigningWBT.com/html/exampleActivity VirtualLab.htm.

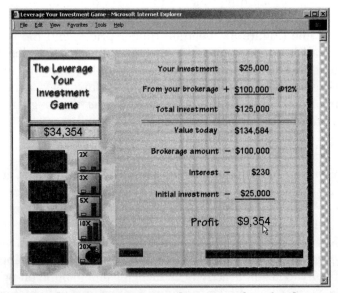

**Figure 11.** Leveraged Investment game shows results of risky investments (Used with permission of William Horton Consulting, Inc.)

## Continual, Intrinsic, Rich Feedback

In a good game you always know how you're doing. Your progress is clear. The consequences of an action are seldom obscure.

In the Leveraged Investment game, shown in Figure 11, learners make risky investments and reap the rewards or suffer the losses that result. After each investment, learners are presented with a detailed accounting of their gains and losses.

In both the Crimescene Game (Figure 9) and the Class-I-fication game (Figure 6), learners receive continual feedback, the first through the reaction of the witness to each question and the second through a scoreboard.

## Easy to Learn and Play

If a game needs an instruction manual or help file, the game is probably too hard to learn. If players must spend more than a few minutes learning the rules of the game, the game is not efficient learning. Think of the time spent learning the game as an overhead cost and keep it low.

In the Nutrition Game, shown in Figure 12, participants are given a series of nutritional goals and asked to order a meal that helps them meet each goal. After ordering the meal, they see how well they met the objective.

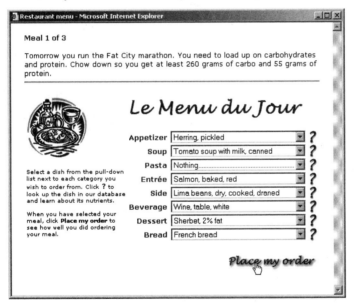

**Figure 12.** Nutrition game (Used with permission of William Horton Consulting, Inc.)

You can try out this game at
www.DesigningWBT.com/html/exampleBeyondSimulationsDietgame.htm.

To make the game easy to play, we used the familiar human situation of ordering a meal as the metaphor, used familiar Web-form selection lists as the user interface, and provided on-screen instructions.

Either devise a game with few rules or base your game on another game whose rules the viewer has already learned, for instance a jigsaw puzzle (Figure 3) or crossword puzzle (Figure 2).

## Modular and Flexible

Good games adapt to your training needs. You can use them for individual players alone, pairs of players competing against each other, and for an entire classroom. They can be readily translated into other languages or moved to another compute platform.

A well-designed game separates the programming from the content, thereby allowing even non-programmers to quickly create additional games. A good game should not be rendered obsolete by a change in technology or subject matter.

# Myths About Games, Adults, and Learning?

If you want to use games in your e-learning efforts, you must confront some of the dangerous half-truths and misunderstandings common about computer games, especially the myths that occupy the heads of those who must approve and fund your efforts. Let's confront the myths one by one.

## Myth: Games Are Just Entertainment

A good learning game successfully balances learning and entertainment. We want learning to be entertaining, but which do we emphasize? Let's consider a spectrum from pure entertainment to pure learning. Figure 13 shows where common entertainment games and e-learning courses fall on this spectrum.

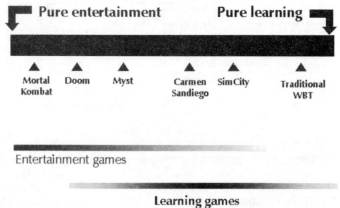

**Figure 13.** Spectrum of games (Used with permission of William Horton Consulting, Inc.)

On the left are games aimed at pure entertainment. To the right are instances of pure learning. The proper role models for e-learning are those games in the middle. But where within that range should you build your game? The table shows a few guidelines:

| Make your game more entertaining if ... | Emphasize learning if ... |
| --- | --- |
| • Learners need more motivation<br>• Learners are not interested in subject matter<br>• Learners see no immediately obvious benefits to learning<br>• Preceding material was dull | • Learners are already motivated by interest in the subject or by the intrinsic rewards of learning<br>• Little time to learn many concepts |
| • Younger students | • Older students |
| • Management is concerned with its "dull" image | • Management is afraid of seeming frivolous |

## Myth: Management Will Never Let Us Do a Game

To many executives "game" connotes frivolity and poor productivity. Here are several strategies to help you overcome management resistance.

Many executives feel that games are just for kids. Point out that kids do play games. Kids like the Joint Chiefs of Staff and the President of the United States. Kids like the senior pilots of most airlines. Show examples of how games (or "simulations," as they are called in business and government) are used by adults to explore complex scenarios, develop decision-making skills, and hone critical skills.

Part of the negative reaction may hinge on the very word *game*. So, call your game something else: activity, exercise, practice, rehearsal, simulation, interactive assessment, or immersive learning environment. Do not call it a "test," though. Managers may like the term, but learners will not.

Prove that your game works. Test it with people who simulate your target learners. Demonstrate in means, medians, and standard deviations that the game effectively teaches or measures learning.

Finally, let executives play the game themselves. Let them see how the game is both entertaining and educational at the same time. Let it seduce them.

## Myth: You Have to Be a Programmer

Rich, complex interactivity does require some programming; but the amount is getting less. Some very effective learning games were created with no programming or coding.

Consider investing in tools that let ordinary folk quickly create a wide variety of games. For example, Gameshow Pro from LearningWare, Inc. (www.learningware.com) helps you create quiz show-style games, Crossword Compiler (www.x-word.com) makes setting crossword puzzles a snap. Computer Game Shells from Thiagi Software let you create different kinds of word games by inserting your own content into premade games.

If you want to develop your own simple games, you can do so with common multimedia and Web-authoring tools. Macromedia (www.macromedia.com) offers a line of products for creating interactive media. Good choices for developers of learning games include Flash, Director, and Dreamweaver (with the CourseBuilder extensions). Such tools provide a good starting point for creating your own games. They require only your creativity, the ability to specify the logic, and access to the necessary graphics.

On some projects, we have created game shells or templates that non-programmers have used to create a series of games. Figure 14 shows an example of using a template to create one of our quiz-show games. Here the author just replaces the placeholder questions and answers with the actual text.

```
//Authors: enter your questions here. Be sure
//to put double quotes around the questions.
//Use single quotes for quotes within questions.
//Use \r to break the question at a particular point.

question_1_100 = "What function creates a new directory?"
answer_1_100 = "MkDir"

question_1_200 = "In the caption for a button, what character
makes the next charater the ALT key shortcut?"
answer_1_200 = "&"

question_1_300 = "What command process pending events?"
answer_1_300 = "DoEvent"

question_1_400 = "What event is triggered when a user tabs
into a field?"
answer_1_400 = "GotFocus"

question_1_500 = "What property of the Err Object contains the
name of the application or object where the error originally
occurred?"
answer_1_500 = "Source"

question_2_100 = "[Type the question for Row 2 Column 1
here.]"
answer_2_100 = "[Type the answer for this question here.]"
question_2_200 = "[Type the question for Row 2 Column 2
here.]"
answer_2_200 = "[Type the answer for this question here.]"
```

**Figure 14.** Filling in a game template (Used with permission of William Horton Consulting, Inc.)

## Myth: Games Are Too Expensive

With development costs of over a million dollars, commercial entertainment games are indeed expensive. However, effective games for learning can cost much less. None of the examples shown in this paper required more than one person-week to create. Once a single game is created, the amount of time to create additional games may drop to hours because the programming and many of the graphics of the first game can be reused.

## Myth: Games Require Lots of Graphics and Animation

Have you ever read a novel and then seen a movie based on that novel? Can you think of cases where the novel was more vivid than the movie? Multimedia plays in the imagination of the player. Screen displays are merely a way to produce an experience. Animation and graphics can certainly effect a strong experience, but so can well-chosen words that trigger memories, as in the Crimescene game (Figure 9). Rich interactivity can more than substitute for heavy media. Notice that the HTML Laboratory (Figure 10) and the Nutrition game (Figure 12) are mostly text but involve ample interaction and feedback.

# How to Use Games in E-Learning

Learning games are quite flexible. You can use them to make small points in a presentation, to let learners practice a low-level skill, or to serve as a single question in an end-of-module test.

Games can also serve as the core of a lesson or an entire course. When used this way, they need to be supplemented with other kinds of materials in order to deliver a complete learning experience. Figure 15 shows a scheme for using games as the core of a lesson or course.

After a brief introduction, the learner has a choice of how to proceed: either by studying a traditional tutorial or by playing the game. Learners who pick the game spend their time interacting with the game. Within the game, they can review the rules at any time. After the game or tutorial, learners are shown a summary to help them lock in the essential concepts they should have learned, whether in the game or tutorial.

Probably the most important pathways are those back and forth between the game and the tutorial. Often the game player's performance will plateau. At this point, the player realized that more knowledge is necessary to reach the next level in the game—and the tutorial might just provide that knowledge. Conversely, the tutorial-taker may pine for an authentic opportunity to try out the knowledge being presented and choose to jump into the game for some meaningful practice. The crossover between tutorial and game may continue until the learner has met the objectives of the course.

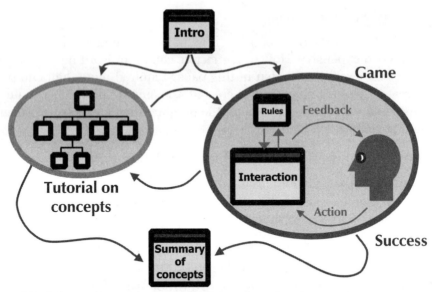

**Figure 15.** *Scheme for using games within e-learning* (Used with permission of William Horton Consulting, Inc.)

If you look closely at the Leveraged Investment game (Figure 11), you will see a tutorial button; and, in the Tree Farming game (Figure 8), you can see a button to display an online book on the subject.

## So, Where Can You Go for Help?

Here are some resources to help you continue learning about games for teaching.

### Books

*Digital Game-Based Learning*, Marc Prensky, McGraw-Hill Higher Education

*Macromedia Flash 5 ActionScript for Fun and Games*, Gary Rosenzweig, Que

*Windows Game Programming for Dummies*, Andre Lamoth, Hungry Minds

*Advanced Lingo for Games*, Gary Rosenzweig, Hayden McNeil

*Sams Teach Yourself Game Programming with Visual Basic in 21 Days*, Clayton Walnum, Sams

*Designing Web-Based Training*, William Horton, John Wiley & Sons

### Journals and Magazines

**Computer Graphics and Applications**
IEEE Computer Society          http://www.computer.org/subscribe/

***Simulation and Gaming***
Sage Publications          http://www.sagepub.co.uk/

***Game Developer Magazine***
CMP Media LLC          http://www.gdmag.com/

## Websites and E-Zines

**Gamasutra**          http://www.gamasutra.com

**Gamespot**          http://www.zdnet.com/gamespot/

**Flash Kit Arcade**          http://www.flashkit.com/arcade/index.shtml

**The JavaScript Source**          http://javascript.internet.com

**Thiagi.com**          http://www.thiagi.com

**Designing Web-Based Training**http://www.designingwbt.com

*William Horton has been designing technology-based training since 1971. A prolific author, Bill's books include* Designing Web-Based Training, Designing and Writing Online Documentation, *and* Secrets of User-Seductive Documents. *He is also co-author of* Getting Started in Online Learning *and* The Web Page Design Cookbook. *His three newest books are being published in ASTD's series on e-learning:* Leading E-Learning, Evaluating E-Learning, *and* Using E-Learning. *You can reach him at william@horton.com.*

# Virtual Games for Real Learning: Learning Online with Serious Fun

## Marie Jasinski and Sivasailam Thiagarajan

*It's easy to become obsessed with technology in training. But this article shows how "unglamorous, low-tech-but-highly-touch communications technology like e-mail, Internet forums, and chat can be used as primary tools to promote and encourage collaborative interactive learning online."*

For the past five years, we have designed, facilitated, and evaluated a series of Web-based games on a range of topics with over one thousand practitioners, mostly within the vocational and corporate training sectors in Australia and the USA. Our observations and feedback from these players reinforce our suspicion that unglamorous, low-tech-but-highly-touch communications technology like e-mail, Internet forums, and chat can be used as primary tools to promote and encourage collaborative interactive learning online. This article documents our observations and experiences in the use of e-mail games.

## Terminology

While we call these activities "training games," they go beyond training into other strategies for performance improvement. In some contexts, "game" seems to be a loaded word and stirs debates that are often tangential to our objective. In such situations, we simply revise the terminology to position our activity more appropriately with labels such as *electronic experiential strategies, modified Delphi technique,* or *interactive learning experiences.*

## Why Virtual Games?

Educational and training organizations have invested significantly in the development, support, and management of online learning environments. Yet as they move into the implementation phase, there are mixed reports about the effectiveness of these environments. While instructional designers are showcasing outstanding successes, many online training products are gathering dust on virtual shelves.

Attracting learners, trainers, and other stakeholders to adopt an online learning environment seems a bit like handing out samples of a new product line in a supermarket. Customers certainly come and taste, and may even buy a trial-size pack, but sampling does not always lead to sustained use.

While enough learners enroll in online courses and successfully complete them, others do not stay or return. Keeping learners from dropping out is a challenge for many online facilitators and trainers. Instructional designers are currently exploring strategies for motivating learners to not only come but also to stay, contribute, and return to the world of online learning. This article focuses on one particular perspective: how to encourage person-to-person interactivity with a games-based methodology that uses e-mail.

## Promoting Person-to-Person Interaction Online

Most people promote interactivity as the most valuable feature of online learning: focused on the screen, hand on the mouse button, leaning toward the screen, learners are poised for interaction! However, a closer look at many instructional offerings online reveals that much of this interactivity merely connects the learner with the content. We do not believe this is enough. Neither does rigorous research.

Most online environments overlook communication technologies like e-mail, forums, and chat as potential learning technologies. Yet we have found that these technologies offer unique opportunities for supporting learner-to-learner and learner-to-facilitator interaction that encourages higher-order cognitive skills, such as application, analysis, and synthesis. Through the use of open-ended and often provocative questions, virtual games are a challenging way to create and process content, check and assess participant understanding, use role play and simulations to solve problems, make decisions, and provide feedback.

## How to Play an E-Mail Game

In an e-mail game, a facilitator and a group of players address a key issue by sending and receiving messages during several rounds of play spread over days or weeks. Unlike fancy Web-based or real-time games that involve sophisticated graphics, programming, and simultaneous play in chat rooms, our e-mail games are limited to low technology and text messages. Typical e-mail games exploit the ability of the Internet to ignore geographic distances and capitalize on the ability of participants to generate and process content. In the early rounds of play, the interaction is between players and the facilitator, while in later rounds, players come together to discuss processed content and to debrief the process.

In addition to training, we use e-mail games for benchmarking and idea-sharing activities. Most of our games have been played in a professional development context in the LearnScope Virtual Learning Community (www.learnscope.anta. gov.au). (LearnScope is an Australian national professional development program aimed to encourage teachers and trainers in the vocational education and training sector to utilize online technologies to achieve more flexible learning.)

Here are three of our e-mail games.

**Depolarizer.** This role-playing game uses e-mail and a bulletin board. Depolarizer is based on the philosophy that many issues that we treat as problems to be solved are actually polarities to be managed. We begin the game with an open-ended question (e.g., *Do lurkers learn?*). During the six rounds of the game, players explore this issue from both a personal perspective and also from a designated role. By informing the players about the range of positions, we increase their awareness of the spread of opinions around the issue. By having players randomly role-play extreme positions, we encourage them to think about the issue from different points of view. By reviewing extremely polarized comments, we help players make more informed decisions. The game typically encourages players at extremes to get closer to the average. Thus, it may not change anyone's opinion, but it increases players' level of awareness of alternative points of view.

**Galactic Wormhole.** In this role-play game, players participate in a time-travel scenario to explore an issue relevant to their context (e.g., the status of online learning for vocational training in the year 2004). Each player is given either a utopian scenario in the form of a newspaper headline *(Australian Vocational Education and Training Sector Leads the World in Online Learning)* or a dystopian scenario *(Australian Vocational Education and Training Sector Rated the Lowest in Online Learning).* Players are randomly assigned one of these two scenarios and given one of five stakeholder roles of trainer, learner, manager, decision-maker, or industry client. Each player is then asked to submit a 150-word news story outlining how his or her stakeholders contributed to either this utopian or dystopian future. These scenarios are submitted anonymously to the facilitator who collates and posts them in a forum. After reviewing all the optimistic and pessimistic scenarios, players submit their five top ideas for ensuring a utopian future. Finally, players vote on critical issues that need to be addressed to ensure the utopian future.

**C3PO.** This acronym C3PO stands for *Challenge, Pool, Poll, Predict, and Outcome.* In Round 1 of C3PO, players receive an open-ended challenge (e.g., How do you increase person-to-person interaction in Internet-based training?). Each player sends three ideas to meet this challenge. In Round 2, the facilitator sends the resulting pool of ideas to the players and asks them to generate a priority list. Players read through the pool of ideas, select the three that personally appeal to them most, and send them to the facilitator. In Round 3, players review the original pool of ideas, make a prediction of how the entire group would have voted, and identify the top set that would have received the most votes. During the selection process in Round 2, the players consider how they personally feel and react to the ideas. During the prediction process in Round 3, the players put themselves in other players' positions and estimate the reaction of the population. As one player put it, "The prediction step forces you to stop thinking wishfully, projecting your preferences, and become absolutely objective." The player with the closest prediction is the winner. After the results are announced, players participate in an online forum to debrief the game.

## Player Reactions

From player comments during and after each e-mail game, we have identified these emerging factors to be explored in greater depth:

**E-mail is familiar, available, cost-effective, and widely used.** User confidence with e-mail means the focus can be on the learning process without players being distracted by unfamiliar technology. E-mail is very inclusive, as online novices and experts can participate on an equal footing.

**E-mail comes to the desktop.** No passwords are needed and there are no download holdups. The game is integrated with the daily work of players, minimizing the effort required for participation.

**E-mail games promote more effective learning.** This person-to-person approach is different from the person-to-computer methods used for many electronic games. In addition, the games require active participation as players must generate and process the content.

**E-mail games transcend space and time constraints.** The distributed asynchronous process permits colleagues anywhere in the world to share their expertise and to address common issues. Several of our games have involved players from the US, Australia, Greece, Canada, France, India, Poland, Israel, Argentina, Mexico, and the United Kingdom. As the deadline for each round contains sufficient number of days, players at different time zones can arrange their participation to suit their personal schedules.

**The process is motivating and engaging but not time-consuming or laborious.** The division of a game into rounds creates anticipation and is not time-demanding. The dropout rate is low. Even if a player misses a round, he or she can join in the next without losing too much of the flow.

**Players can be anonymous.** This aspect of e-mail games attracts participation by many people who normally "lurk." Anonymity allows people to be more candid and extreme in their opinions without fear of reprisal or ridicule. We have also effectively used play names to increase this anonymity.

**E-games achieve productive outcomes.** These games generate ideas, solve problems, and encourage dialogues on topics and issues that are relevant and salient to the participants.

**E-mail games are continuously improved.** The built-in iterative feedback process through structured debriefing provides dynamic formative evaluation for immediate refinements that even better meet user needs.

**E-mail games are versatile and inclusive.** We have different game templates that are suitable for the full range of performance-improvement needs: informing, applying, analyzing, and synthesizing. The games have been used for strategic planning, problem solving, brainstorming, and exploring controversial issues.

## Designing E-mail Games

E-mail games are easy to adopt and adapt. The templates for these games are deliberately designed to permit easy replacement of old content with new: the content changes, but the process stays the same. Once players have participated in a game, they can easily modify it for use in their own context.

However, there is much more to a successful e-mail game than plugging in new content and knowing that the process will work. Besides choosing the right game template, we need to consider different design components when deciding whether an e-mail game is appropriate for a training context.

- *The task.* What to do want your learners to do? Will a game be appropriate strategy to achieve a learning task?
- *The technology.* Do your learners have the appropriate hardware, software, and technical support to enable them to effectively participate in an e-mail game?
- *The media.* Is a text-based medium like e-mail an appropriate way to achieve the learning task? Is this a suitable technology for your user group?
- *Players.* Does the learning context enable players to effectively participate in e-mail games? (Issues to consider include voluntary versus mandatory participation, learning location, computer literacy, and type of support provided.)

- *Facilitation.* Do you have the time, commitment, and skill to facilitate a virtual game?

# Facilitating an E-mail Game

The heart of the matter for a successful virtual game is effective facilitation. Although players generate and process the content, the facilitator orchestrates the game. To provide a seamless virtual game, facilitation requires technical, administrative, interpersonal, and instructional design functions. Here is a quick look at these factors:

**Technical.** Facilitators need a working knowledge of the communication technologies they will be using to play virtual games as well as spreadsheets for data management. If players experience technical difficulties or get confused with the forum software, they will most often turn to the facilitator for assistance. Developing a FAQs file allows the facilitator to be responsive to most queries.

**Administrative.** As responses to e-mail games arrive, they must be processed quickly and accurately in preparation for the next round of play. Accurate and systematic recordkeeping, like player tracking, collation of input, and sending out of next rounds, is critical to the smooth flow of e-mail games.

**Interpersonal.** While the game templates provide the steps needed to play a game, facilitating a game is more than a mechanical process. Setting the scene, sustaining motivation, and debriefing relies on the human factor and a fair degree of interpersonal skill. Facilitators need to monitor the progress of a game and determine when to change the pace, contact individual players, and change the tone of the play. Player participation patterns vary. Some players reply promptly, others leave it to the last minute, some miss rounds, and some register but never contribute.

**Instructional design.** Virtual games require a dynamic instructional process. The facilitator is close to the players and in a position to be responsive to feedback. As the games are played in rounds, it is easy to use a just-in-time instructional design process. If something is not working, it can be readily changed.

# The Game as an Excuse for the Debrief

Players can sometimes have a great time participating in an e-mail game but learn nothing. To ensure that the games have maximum impact on performance improvement, debriefing is perhaps the most important component of an e-mail game. It provides the opportunity for reflection to take place and facilitates the transfer of learning from the game to the work context.

As a follow-up to our e-mail games, we use a threaded-discussion forum for debriefing. This forum provides an opportunity for players to meet and share their experiences.

## Conclusion

Virtual games are serious fun and offer a challenging way to quickly and effectively process open-ended, divergent questions that require application, analysis, and synthesis.

*Marie Jasinski is Principal Lecturer at MindMedia, Douglas Mawson Institute, South Australia (e-mail: mariejas@dmi.tafe.sa.edu.au).*

*Sivasailam Thiagarajan, a Contributing Editor to Educational Technology, is president of Workshops by Thiagi. He also writes the monthly Thiagi GameLetter, published by Jossey-Bass/Pfeiffer (e-mail: thiagi@thiagi.com).*

# Don't Forget the High-Touch with the High-Tech in Distance Learning

**Dean R. Spitzer**

*"At its very heart, learning is a social process." That's the basic point of the first part of this article. The second part outlines 15 keys to facilitating distance learning successfully, based on the author's experience.*

There is both good news and bad news in Distance Learning (a.k.a. Web-based Learning, Online Learning, e-learning). The good news is that the quantity of Distance Learning (subsequently to be referred to in this article as "DL") is growing rapidly and the technology to support it is improving dramatically. According to DL guru Brandon Hall (2000), a majority of U.S. companies (92% of large companies) are offering some form of online learning. Academic institutions at all levels are now offering either fully online courses or classes in which online work plays a role. More good news: there are a tremendous variety of technological alternatives for developing and delivering DL—from do-it-yourself kits to sophisticated commercial packages that have everything built in, from authoring and administration to learning objects and content management, from portals to knowledge management, from virtual classrooms to almost completely virtual institutions.

The bad news is that courseware and facilitation are not keeping pace with technological innovation. The reality of DL is often far removed from the promise.

In fact, users' initial enthusiasm for DL has frequently been undermined by content that is little more than information dumping, confusing navigation, long download times, eyestrain from endless text screens, and so-called "discussions" that are really just monologues posted on online bulletin boards. According to *Training* magazine, "A good deal of online training is simply not that engaging" (Zielinski, 2000, p. 72). Sadly, according to Scheer (2000, p. 32), in many organizations, employees "see DL not as a preferred alternative to classroom training, but as a consolation prize." Unfortunately, most DL learners have no knowledge of what a dynamic, engaging online learning experience could be!

There is no doubt that DL is here to stay. The economics of DL are extremely compelling. One corporate executive boasted, "We can cover ten times the material at one-third the cost!" But is the purpose of DL to just to cover material? Of course, it depends on what kind of learning we are referring to. Knowledge can be acquired through access to information. However, as we progress up the cognitive domain and deal with affective learning, interaction becomes increasingly important. "If all we had to do was read information about a particular skill, then just send the students a book" (Miller, 2000, p. 2). Or, as Ken Wax (2000, p. 136) rhetorically asks, "Is clicking a button to turn a page interactive?" Brown and Duguid (2000, p. 221) feel that this "delivery view of education leads people to think of educational technology as a sort of educational forklift."

The notion of DL as a panacea is leading many of us old-timers in the ed tech field to experience "déjà vu all over again!" According to consultant Ken Wax (2000, p. 136), "We've seen this fascination before. It happened in the mid-'80s, when videos, one of distance learning's earlier incarnations, were going to save vast amounts of money." Now instructional videos are relegated to the scrap heap of educational innovation. The same is true of other educational technology "panaceas." The seductive promise of teaching machines, instructional television, and computer-based training was never able to overcome the reality of lack of good courseware and ineffective human intervention. Although Web-based learning is currently reaching its pinnacle of popularity, it appears to be suffering from exactly the same problems. We shouldn't be surprised, though; history has a way of repeating itself.

Perhaps the most discouraging symptom of the DL problem is the very high dropout rate. There are so many other priorities that get in the way of online learning. Even a DL supporter as strong as Allison Rossett, Professor of Educational Technology at San Diego State University and a Contributing Editor of *Educational Technology*, attempted her first DL course—and dropped out! She explained:

> The things that made me a dropout are the same things that make the Web so compelling .... The beauty of 'anywhere, anytime, whenever you want,' too readily turns into not now, maybe later, and often not at all .... Lacking a dynamic instructor, powerful incentives, links to the job and fixed sched-

ules, Web learning is at a dramatic disadvantage in capturing and holding attention .... Yes, everyone can learn from the Web. But my experience makes me wonder how many will. (Rossett, 2000, p. 99)

The missing link in Rossett's DL experience was not technological, but the lack of a human mediator who could provide the things that technology could not: relevance, personalization, responsiveness, and flexibility.

Zielinski (2000) tells the cautionary tale of another DL course in which a manager "had built roughly eight hours of self-directed multimedia learning content for a course on statistical process control. But as the first week of training progressed, students started dropping out. By the end of week two, not one of the twenty enrollees had completed the training" (p. 72). Zielinski adds: "Training in your own cubicle, amid interruptions and piles of work to be done, is just not as much fun as schmoozing with colleagues at a hotel or at a well-appointed off-site training facility."

In contrast, the DL Master's Degree Program in Instructional and Performance Technology that I designed and led at Boise State University had, during my tenure, a 5 percent dropout rate per year! So, what made the difference? It certainly wasn't the technology. The technology we used was very primitive and cumbersome. It wasn't glitzy courseware. All courses were entirely text-based, and there was no multimedia. The factor that made the difference was the amount of personal attention and online interaction. This admittedly labor-intensive approach was able to overcome all the other weaknesses in the program and meet the human needs of students. I have found that good human facilitation can compensate for most other deficiencies, while state-of-the-art technology and fancy graphics alone cannot sustain student interest and motivation for long.

The American Society for Training & Development (ASTD) has recently launched a study to explore the high dropout rate problem of Web-based training courses. Not surprisingly, preliminary findings indicate that the major reasons relate mostly to human factors, such as lack of incentives, lack of accountability for course completion, and the inability of poorly designed courseware to keep learners' attention (Skipper, 2000).

Almost twenty years ago, in his blockbuster bestseller *Megatrends* (1984), John Naisbitt predicted that one of keys to the success of technology was to marry "high tech" with "high touch." Sure enough, companies who have entered the e-commerce arena during the last few years are finding out the importance of this "megatrend"—often too late. The best-designed and most technologically sophisticated e-commerce Web sites will not substitute for outstanding customer service *by real human beings.* The same is true for DL.

As with any technological innovation, DL depends upon some human interaction to make it work. Although it seems that some people have unlimited tolerance and patience for technology's limitations, most of us do not. Furthermore, this finding has been replicated time and time again. For example, in their study of technological failures, Lister and DeMarco (1987) found that lack of effective human interaction was usually the main culprit.

At its very heart, learning is a *social* process (Brown and Duguid, 2000). Unfortunately, human interaction is often the last thing on the minds of technologists fascinated by the latest delivery system hardware. In fact, hardware has never been the major constraint to instructional innovation. The constraint has always been with software and "peopleware." In the Web-based world, there is no problem finding appropriate hardware or authoring and learning management software. But just try to find a wide range of good highly interactive courseware. Furthermore, the cost of developing and updating good software is astronomical, especially given the rapid obsolescence of knowledge. In the long run, the costs of courseware make the cost of any hardware purchases seem relatively insignificant.

The power of the Web is in providing access to tremendous amounts of information. As a research tool, the Internet is unparalleled. However, as an interactive tool, we have yet to adequately understand its capabilities and limitations. It certainly is not an instructional panacea, anymore than teaching machines, videos, and CBT were. Regardless of its limitation, Web-based learning should have a prominent place in education and training for the foreseeable future. It is simply time that we discovered how to use it more effectively.

So, what is the answer to this dilemma? As for many dilemmas, the answer is compromise. The latest compromise is "hybrid" or "blended" learning approaches—the combination of technology and human intervention. This can include the use of DL to supplement or complement classroom instruction, or the use of a "live" facilitator to enhance technology-based instruction.

## The Keys to Effective Distance Learning Facilitation

Virtual classrooms can be wonderful "places" to learn. However, creating good virtual classrooms and successful DL learning experiences requires a lot of effort and human facilitation. Unfortunately, while DL technical skills are becoming very common, DL facilitator skills are still scarce indeed. What's more, there are very few sources of knowledge or skill on how to be an effective DL facilitator. That is why I felt so compelled to write this article.

In my many years as a DL facilitator and consultant, I have found 15 keys to effective DL course facilitation:

**1. Make sure that you really want to do it!** Are you ready? DL facilitation is difficult and much different from traditional teaching. To be effective, a DL facilitator must be willing to be re-educated in the use of a very unique way of teaching and communicating. DL is causing the faculty role to change from that of a content expert to a combination of content expert, learning designer, and learning process implementator (Phipps and Merisotis, 1999). In addition, good DL requires much more time and effort on the part of the instructor (Palloff and Pratt, 1999). Effective DL facilitation requires a commitment to learning new instructional styles and patterns of behavior that many traditional instructors are not prepared to make.

**2. Ensure that students have the prerequisites to succeed.** There are enough obstacles to DL success, without having students handicapped with the wrong hardware or software, or lacking other essential resources. Convenient access to the right technology is essential to DL success. It has been found that the use of technology is inversely related to one's distance from the technology (Palloff and Pratt, 1999).

Here are some suggestions for creating a solid foundation for a successful DL experience. Before the course starts, make sure that students feel comfortable with the technology that will be used. Give students, especially those who are new to DL, practice using it before the course begins. Be aware that it has been found that DL students have a tendency to often overlook even the most explicit instructions, do the unexpected, unanticipated, and forbidden, and focus on the inconveniences, rather than the conveniences (Harasim *et al.,* 1996). A short pre-course tutorial can also go a long way toward eliminating problems later on. I also usually provide an online guidebook about positive DL learning habits, collected from students in previous courses.

**3. Anticipate and prevent technical problems.** Don't let Murphy's Law sabotage your course! Nothing can undermine online learning like network or server problems, and students who don't know how to cope with them. Who should students contact if they do encounter technical problems? Remember that for students new to DL, anxiety is already very high. Make sure you have discussed contingency plans for potential technical problems. For example, what should they do if they encounter a network interruption? One instructor, who did not have a good contingency plan, had a very unhappy group of students when a network outage occurred just when an assignment was due. It is good idea to set up a "buddy system" so that students will have at least one person who they can call to do some preliminary troubleshooting, or to just ask advice. Even if it doesn't solve the problem, such a peer support system will significantly reduce anxiety.

**4. Make students feel welcome.** When students show up for a traditional class, they immediately know if they are in place at the right time, or not. In the physical classroom, there are ample visual and auditory cues, as well as other students to talk and identify with. In contrast, a virtual classroom can be a very cold and forbidding place, with virtually no communication until the class officially begins. Most instructors in conventional classes are used to just showing up for the first class and getting right down to business. In virtual classes, there is rarely a synchronous kick-off or "first class session." Students log on at different times to begin work. When students log on for the first time, they should receive a public welcome from the instructor/facilitator, and other students should be encouraged to do the same. In addition, courses should have a welcoming portal that makes students feel "at home" and provides access to the course syllabus, links to pre-course preparation, and other useful information about the course.

**5. Take orientation very seriously.** Probably the biggest gap in DL facilitation is in the area of student orientation. Virtual classes need much more orientation than do traditional classes. Without the customary visual and auditory anchors that are present in the normal classroom, DL students are often somewhat *dis*oriented at the beginning of a course. That is why it is so important for DL students to know what to expect—especially for their first DL experience. Make sure everyone knows what's expected and by *when*. Establish norms for course participation. If you want a high level of participation, make sure that the quantity and quality of participation are components of a student's grade. Don't forget to discuss online etiquette ("netiquette") and establish schedule of regular "office hours." Guidelines are essential for effective online interaction; however, rules that are too rigid can constrain participation. Finally, one of the best ways to get students involved early on in a course is to ask them to share *their* expectations.

**6. Keep information presentation to a minimum.** Although the Web is a wonderful method for disseminating information, the real value of DL is not information presentation, but interaction. Unfortunately, too much of what purports to be DL today is just enormous amounts of information posted on a Web site. Certainly, the Internet is great for research, but Web-based learning should be more than automatic page-turning or scrolling down endless pages of text. If you want people to read vast amounts of text material, send them a book!

**7. Develop a sense of community.** A "sense of isolation" can be a real problem in DL. David Passmore, a professor of education at Penn State University, has said, "Few Web-based courses I've seen address the problem of lack of learner connectedness" (Zielinski, 2000, p. 72). In fact, it has been found that "the need for social connection is a goal that almost supersedes the content-oriented goals for the course" (Palloff and Pratt, 1999, p. 11).

Here are some tangible suggestions for building an online community. Distribute a list of participants and their contact information. Better yet, provide each student with a "home page," including contact information, a brief biography, personal interests, and (if possible) a photograph. Do you know why professionals love attending conferences so much? Because of the "networking." The most successful DL courses also promote personal networking. Provide access to an online forum specifically concerned with networking and community building, such as a "virtual coffee lounge." Some of the best learning opportunities are the unintended ones.

**8. Create a congenial, non-threatening environment.** One of the most important things a DL facilitator can do is establish a positive environment for learning. Error tolerance is vitally important. DL students often feel uncomfortable with the new mode of communicating, especially with communicating everything in writing. Furthermore, the expectation of active participation might be intimidating to students who are accustomed to being more vicarious learners. If students evidence discomfort, discuss it openly. Students can benefit vicariously from facilitator encouragement. One of the best ways to create a positive learning environment is to encourage peer-to-peer interaction. Another way is through encouraging humor.

**9. Get everyone involved.** First impressions are important. The patterns of interaction early in a DL course are likely to continue. Therefore, get students interacting immediately. Start the course with a high-momentum activity, like a case study that involves a high degree of participation and a lot of discussion.

**10. Gradually phase out direct involvement.** After the initial start-up, remain in the background. DL leaders—unobtrusive, but always there to help the group succeed. "Faculty must be able to relinquish their role of power within and over the educational process" (Palloff and Pratt, 1999, p. 85). Stay in the background, but the effective facilitator is always available to help, coax, redirect, summarize, and encourage.

**11. Be vigilant.** There is tremendous entropy that can take over in online communication, if it is not carefully managed. Pay attention to who is participating and who is not. In a physical classroom, it is easy to pick up non-verbal cues, but in a virtual classroom, we must depend on the verbal ones. It is vital for an effective facilitator to intervene if there is conflict. When students are exhibiting desirable behaviors, such as insightful comments and students helping each other, make sure that their actions get positively reinforced. Intervene if there is dysfunctional conflict by making a clarifying comment. Sometimes it is necessary to end discussions in order to keep the course on track and on time. If personal issues surface (such as lack of participation or poor-quality interaction), use private e-mails to address them without embarrassing the individual. Summarizing frequently will highlight important points and keep interactions on track. Interspersing questions can help check for understanding.

**12. Be responsive.** Nothing is as discouraging in DL as non-responsiveness. It can be like depositing something in a black hole. Students need to get feedback on their comments and other contributions. Provide prompt feedback on assignments. All students want to know the score, but for distance learners this feedback is most important. Build frequent response opportunities (assignments, self-assessment, quizzes, etc.) into the course, so students can receive frequent feedback. In addition, actively solicit feedback from the students. I recommend regular mini-surveys to see how things are going, or just asking students, "How do you feel about ... ?" The best DL instructors view the course as a dynamic process, rather than a static event.

**13. Keep students interacting.** Online interaction is simply not as natural as face-to-face interaction for most people. Some students simply don't feel as comfortable participating in written discussions; others find that the discussions take too much time. But the benefits of online interaction far outweigh the disadvantages, and it is vital to keep a critical mass of students engaged. Without sufficient participation, the richness of interaction and feedback is lost. As one observer has remarked, "The best distance-based courses are facilitated by instructors who involve all the class participants in the online discussions" (Summers, 2000, p. 2). Do whatever you need to do to keep students interacting. Use creative methods to stimulate discussion, such as stimulating debates. Be controversial. Provide incentives for involvement. Send subtle reminders to students who are not participating as much as they should. Also, give students an opportunity to serve as online discussion or small group leaders.

**14. Keep the course interesting.** Provide a variety of learning experiences. Human beings thrive on variety. Use a variety of instructional activities and media to avoid potential boredom. There is no harm in using books, CD-ROMs, and guest "speakers" to supplement the Web-based content. Use synchronous as well as asynchronous communication. As Henry (2000, p. 33) explains, "The focus should be on multiple-media rather than multimedia." Relevancy is another key to keeping students engaged. One of the greatest benefits of DL is its ability to connect people with so much diverse experience—but this diversity is all too rarely used. Students should be actively encouraged to share their professional experiences with other students and demonstrate how the course concepts relate to it. People are much more engaged in activities if they view the activities as relevant to their lives and interests, and they will learn much more when the experiences of others become part of the curriculum.

**15. Provide follow-up learning opportunities.** No DL course should end abruptly, but, unfortunately, most do. Once the final assignment is turned in, the course tends to vanish into thin air. This leaves students without a real sense of closure or guidance about what to do next. Therefore, I strongly recommend that you provide students with opportunities to continue their exploration of the subject matter, and continued interaction with other students. For example, why not set up a post-course discussion forum and provide links to other information, resources, and follow-up courses?

## Conclusion

Of all the educational technologies that have exhibited great promise, Web-based distance learning appears to be the most promising. However, until those enamored with the hardware and software acknowledge the importance of human intervention, the full promise will not be realized. As Brown and Duguid (2000, p. 225) warn, "The technological reach that conquers distance doesn't necessarily provide the reciprocity that allows people to form, join, or participate in worthwhile learning communities." We need to face up to the fact that, despite the best efforts of some to replace the antiquated, but ageless, relic of the live instructor, education and training will never become entirely instructor-less. In fact, I believe that well-facilitated DL can do everything that classroom instruction can do, and more.

I am encouraged by the amount of concern for the "human dimension" of distance learning that has recently been displayed in the pages of this magazine and in some others. Perhaps distance learning is finally reaching maturity—both technically and instructionally.

## References and Suggested Readings

Brown, J.S., and Duguid, P. (2000). *The social life of information.* Boston: Harvard Business School Press.

Hall, B. (2000, May). The future of online learning. Annual Conference, American Society for Training & Development, Dallas, TX.

Harasim, L., Hiltz, S.R., Telles, L., and Turoff, M. (1996). *Learning networks.* Cambridge, MA: MIT Press.

Henry, R. (2000, May). Letter to the Editor. *Training,* 32-33.

Lister, T., and DeMarco, T. (1987). *Peopleware: Productive projects and teams.* New York: Dorsett House.

Mason, R., and Kaye, A. (1989). *Mindweave: Communication, computers, and distance education,* Oxford: Pergamon Press.

Miller, G.T.W., (2000, March). Can we assume? *Online Learning News,* 1-5.

Naisbitt, J. (1984). *Megatrends: Ten new directions changing our lives.* New York: Warner Books.

Palloff, R., and Pratt, K. (1999). *Building learning communities in cyberspace.* San Francisco: Jossey-Bass.

Phipps, R., and Merisotis, J. (1999, April). *What's the difference? A review of contemporary research on the effectiveness of distance learning in higher education.* Institute for Higher Education Policy, 20-43.

Rossett, A. (2000, August). Confessions of an e-dropout. *Training,* 99-100.

Scheer, T. (2000, May). Letter to the Editor. *Training,* p. 32.

Schifter, C. (2000, March-April). Faculty motivators and inhibitors for participation in distance education. *Educational Technology,* 40(2), 43-46.

Shotsberger, P.G. (2000, Jan.-Feb.). The human touch: Synchronous communication in Web-based learning. *Educational Technology,* 40(l), 53-56.

Skipper, J. (2000, April). Distance learning barriers: ASTD study. *DL News,* IBM Corporation, p. 1.

Spitzer, D. (1998, March-April). Rediscovering the social context of distance learning. *Educational Technology,* 38(2), 52-56.

Summers, A. (2000, March). Can we assume? *Online Learning News,* 1-5.

Wax, K. (2000, May). Old tapes: Distance learning's dirty little secret. *Training,* p. 136.

Zielinski, D. (2000, March) Can you keep learners online? *Training,* 65-72.

*Dean R. Spitzer is Senior Consultant, Learning Services Consulting, with IBM and Contributing Editor for* Educational Technology *(e-mail: spitzer@us.ibm.com).*

# The Handheld Web:
## How Mobile Wireless Technologies Will Change Web-Based Instruction and Training

**Paul G. Shotsberger and Ronald Vetter**

*"The next revolution is right around the corner," the authors of this article proclaim. "This technological transformation has the potential to fundamentally change ... Web-based instruction and training."*

After approximately ten years of innovation and development, the World Wide Web seems to have thoroughly pervaded U.S. society. Most Americans use the Internet daily to stay in touch with family and friends; colleges and universities have included instituting Web-based courses among their mission goals; top business priorities involve establishing and enhancing customer services on the Web; and television and other media are replete with Web addresses and Web enhancements for their programming and advertisements. It is difficult to imagine how the Web could become more integral to our daily lives. Yet, it appears that the next revolution is right around the corner, and this technological transformation has the potential to fundamentally change the way Web-based instruction and training is done.

Mobile wireless technologies are not particularly new. We have had cell phones with us throughout the 1990s, and whereas they might at first have seemed only a luxury or a novelty, in this decade they are viewed as more of an accessory and even a necessity. An important change in mobile communications took place in the late 1990s with the introduction of digital (as opposed to analog) transmission technologies. Though a quiet innovation at first, with only a few companies, such as Nokia, taking advantage of the new capabilities, it is becoming apparent that two-way digital services may be the "next big thing" in wireless communications (AT&T, 2000). This is because digital wireless can transmit not only voice but also data, and it is wireless data that many believe will be the dominant form of Internet communication within the next five to ten years (Lewis, 2000). Already in Japan, where wireless phone-generated e-mail is said to be three years ahead of the U.S., the number of wireless phone subscribers has surpassed the number of fixed-line clients (Schmetzer, 2000).

We now see Fortune 500 corporations positioning themselves to become major players and partners in the wireless data market. The variety of industries represented by these companies, as well as the size of their financial investments, provides a sense of how widespread this phenomenon might be. Microsoft has begun partnering with makers of handheld computing devices to produce the next generation of Pocket PCs, such as the recently released Hewlett-Packard Jornada; Toyota has joined forces with Intel, Hewlett-Packard, and Compaq to produce "My Car Universe"; and AOL is working with Compaq and chip-maker Transmeta on the next generation of Internet appliances that will no longer be based on the traditional Windows/Intel computing platform.

The expectation is that these mobile devices will possess sufficient bandwidth for the average user to have a satisfactory experience sending and receiving e-mail, surfing the Web, and even playing audio and video files. This expectation seems justified. By late 2001, Boeing will be installing a new technology called Connexion that will allow domestic airline passengers 128 kilobits per second (Kbps) Internet access from their seats (Field and Rosato, 2000). It is estimated that by 2005 pedestrians will connect at rates up to 384 Kbps, while car passengers will be able to go online at up to 144 Kbps (Lewis, 1999). An even more optimistic prediction comes from satellite company Teledesic. Teledesic is building a global, broadband "Internet-in-the-Sky" that boasts several megabits per second (Mbps) of network bandwidth with availability expected by 2004 (www.teledesic.com).

With the increasing popularity of small portable computers, many new applications will be enabled.

Whether on foot, on the road, or in the air, we will be capable of connecting to the Web at speeds that today would be attractive for the home desktop user. This article considers the impact of this new technology on one particular application domain, namely Web-based instruction and training, or WBI/T. We provide a discussion of the relevant technological infrastructure issues, content design and development issues, and differing modes of communication as they pertain to mobile wireless WBI/T, followed by a scenario of one possible WBI/T application.

# Wireless WBI/T Issues

Mobile wireless WBI/T issues can be organized around three overarching categories: compatibility, content, and communication.

## Compatibility

Web content in the future will need to be accessible everywhere, from PCs to TVs, to cellular phones to palm-size devices. A primary focus for wireless technologies, therefore, is universal access protocols and languages that are platform independent. The choice of media access control can affect both performance and use of wireless networks. The media access control protocols used in cellular and personal communication services systems differ considerably, even within the U.S. This directly affects the interoperability and roaming of mobile users.

In addition, Internet planners recognize that emerging handheld devices will require changes to existing Internet/Web standards. Leavitt (2000) states that "Wireless technology's bandwidth and latency constraints cannot support such longtime Internet standards as HTML, HTTP, IP, TCP, and TLS (transport layer security), which are inefficient over mobile networks" (p. 17). Work is underway to modify these protocols and standards to make them more suitable and efficient in a mobile environment.

The World Wide Web Consortium (W3C) has developed several open recommendations, extending existing Internet standards, to enable wireless devices full access to the Web and its information base. With the rapid introduction of new kinds of Web browsers (digital TVs and various handheld devices) and new types of Web page input (from microphones, cameras, scanners, pen-based devices, etc.), improved document markup and style sheet support was clearly needed. The W3C devised several recommendations in the interests of Web device independence, content reuse, and network-friendly encoding. These recommendations include the Extensible Markup Language (XML) for richer semantic information; improved Cascading Style Sheets (CSS), and Extensible Style Sheet Language (XSL) to further separate content from presentation; and a Document Object Model (DOM), which defines a language-independent application programming interface that applications can use to access and modify the structure, content, and style of HTML and XML documents. These W3C specifications, along with the Wireless Application Protocol (WAP) specifications, will enable a wide range of wireless networking applications to become a reality.

As stated previously, many different wireless access technologies exist that are not interoperable, making the task of designing and building network applications for each technology unworkable for developers. The additional need for redesigning all Web sites to support downloading by mobile users makes the problem that much more difficult. Even if all of this can be achieved, the information content still has to be adapted for transmission over wireless links and displayed on a hand-held device. WAP is an effort to solve these problems: it allows the development of applications that are independent of the underlying wireless access technology.

WAP is a specification developed by WAP Forum, a consortium of companies interested in developing applications for wireless communications networks (www.wapforum.org). The WAP Forum attempts to use existing standards and technology whenever possible, and introduces new technology to produce industry-wide specifications. The main outcome is the interoperability of different wireless networks, devices, and applications using a common set of application and network protocols. The protocol architecture is similar to that of the World Wide Web; however, it uses a Wireless Markup Language (WML) optimized for mobile devices with power, CPU, input, and display restrictions. (One might say that WML is to WAP as HTML is to HTTP.)

Whereas developers of commercial content specifically targeting mobile devices might opt to begin programming using WML, those involved in educational applications might be better served by employing Extensible Hypertext Markup Language (XHTML). Not only does XHTML provide an intelligent means of media management for the variety of browsers downloading Web content, it also affords a much more effective way for developers to ensure a consistent appearance of Web content across browsers (Holzschlag, 2000).

Though XHTML has stricter syntactical rules than HTML, the commands are essentially the same. Nonetheless, it would still be a daunting proposition to check the HTML code for every Web page to verify, for instance, that no commands are written in upper case. Fortunately, there is assistance available for translating Web pages. The W3C offers a freeware tool called TML Tidy, which will automatically update HTML pages to XHTML (www.w3.org/People/Raggett/tidy/). At this point, Tidy is not Windows compatible and will only run in MS-DOS mode, though this will hopefully change soon. However, there do exist graphical interfaces such as HTML-Kit that allow Tidy to run in a Windows environment (www.chami.com/html-kit).

## Content

One of the appealing aspects of WBI/T is the capability for providing just-in-time support for collaboration and decision-making. The advent of mobile wireless data devices takes the attractiveness of this capability to a new level, allowing the user to be literally anywhere and request information and support from Web site resources. As O'Leary (2000) notes, commenting on college undergraduates, "They no longer want a 'just in time' education. They seek a 'just for you' customized education..." (p. 28). Thus, the WBI/T venture will need to continually become more personalized for participants, Web content must be easily accessible and navigable, and changes made to content since the last visit ought to be readily apparent. In this respect, developers of WBI/T should take note of such recent commercial Web ventures as My Yahoo, myCNN, and so forth. On these sites, interfaces and content are tailored to the user's needs and history, and other material of little interest to the user is filtered out. The need for this kind of filtering is made more evident when one considers the screen space and memory capacity most wireless users are afforded.

Wireless WBI/T participants should be able to take advantage of the relevant content and collaboration available on a site without being overwhelmed by either a media-heavy environment or a lack of organization within and between pages. The solution might be a hybrid system that would cache information on the local handheld device. This system could use a DVD disk containing primary Web content along with a wireless connection that would add the interactivity and real-time updates to the content. Some other helps would be navigation maps and notifications of updates upon arrival at the site. In a more sophisticated environment, one might also consider an intelligent agent that would "push" notification of new content to participants before they log in, prompting a visit to the site at a convenient opportunity.

Anytime/anywhere access will allow WBI/T to infuse more interactivity into the design of content. As a result, there will need to be a large number of small modules and a high degree of user interface with these modules. This will enable more effective human-computer communication as these devices make it possible for users to be always connected and therefore have information pushed to them and be able to respond almost immediately.

Another way in which to enhance interactivity would be through the use of advanced Web forms that allow user input beyond text typed from a keyboard. It is at least likely that users would, of necessity, be restricted to making responses using pen-, voice-, video-, or symbol-input. As an example, Japanese "keitai" mobile phone users can choose from a menu of 125 standard symbols to generate e-mail messages. These devices allow users to avoid having to master two native alphabets containing 3,000 characters, as well as the western alphabet, while providing them with a cost-effective and highly efficient way of communicating with others (Schmetzer, 2000).

## Communication

WBI/T developers and facilitators recognize the importance of communication to the educational enterprise. Facilitator-participant and especially participant-participant communication is the glue that holds WBI/T courses together. Without it, participants feel isolated and WBIFT falls into the old distance education model of students reading the text and taking a test. With it, participants become part of a larger community of learners who are connected with each other both professionally and personally.

The primary mode of communication in WBI/T currently is asynchronous, employing e-mail, listservs, and threaded discussions to engage participants in forums that promote multiple perspectives on and novel applications of course material. Those in WBI/T are also beginning to recognize the positive influence synchronous communication such as chats and role-playing can have on Web-based learning (Pullen, 1998; Shotsberger, 2000).

It remains to be seen what forms of communication will prove most useful for the mobile wireless user, who may or may not have access to a keyboard. WBI/T coordinators will have to think seriously about the best way to support disconnected operations. For those devices that include a keyboard (or some variant) allowing text input, e-mail, listservs, threaded discussions, and text-based chats are all viable options. These tools have proven to be fast and effective for desktop WBI/T participants, and there is every reason to believe they would be adequate for wireless users as well. In fact, recent research has shown that in comparisons of synchronous communication methods, text-based communication is as effective as more media-rich approaches for facilitating coaching and approximating in-person participation in a seminar (Pullen, 1998). Where text-input is difficult or impossible, one option may be to include audio input, either in a seminar format or one-to-one. A text-based chat enhanced with audio would allow a participant using a wireless device to read text entered by classmates, but then offer input audibly into the discussion.

## Sample Scenario for WBI/T Using the Handheld Web

The lead author has trained preservice and inservice mathematics teachers over a five-year period using Web-based professional development (Shotsberger, 1999). Primary advantages of this kind of training are the ability for teachers to access training materials at work or home, the opportunity for collaboration with teachers from different schools and school districts, and the capability for implementing training and receiving feedback on implementation during the school year. Being "wired" has given these teachers access to a world of information and interaction that was unheard of ten years ago, eliminating some, but not all, of the physical isolation barriers common to the profession.

Whereas the term "just-in-time" is used to describe this kind of computer-supported learning, the truth is that even as physical walls are being removed between teachers, time constraints remain a huge barrier to collaboration. The causes of this roadblock range from limited availability of network connections at the schools to the problem of scheduling collaborative meetings within the constraints of a full teaching schedule (even at the same school). The wireless technologies discussed in this article can help overcome these difficulties. For teachers in older school buildings in which classroom wired network connections and telephone lines do not exist, or for teachers who "float" from class to class and do not have a permanent room assignment (which is all too common), the capability of communicating via a handheld device could provide an excellent way for teachers to stay in touch with colleagues and parents. These teachers would not need to wait for access to a typically limited number of computers with Internet connection.

In southeastern North Carolina, the majority of high schools are on a block schedule system consisting of four 90-minute periods. With fewer and longer periods, teachers have greater opportunity to collaborate with colleagues who have the same planning period. Unfortunately for teachers at smaller, rural schools, there may be only one or two teachers from the same discipline available for collaboration at any given time. Participants from different schools who possess wireless devices could notify colleagues of their availability to chat synchronously online, and if the chat is text-based, the transcript could become part of an archive asynchronously accessible by all participants.

The Jornada series of Pocket PCs includes such features as handwriting-recognition software and the capability for recording short voice messages. This would expand a teacher's options for recordkeeping both in and out of class. It has long been lamented by the education community that teachers generally do not produce written or even oral records of the strategies they employ in the classroom. Handheld devices could give teachers a highly portable way of documenting the results of implementation, which could then be shared with colleagues face-to-face, in a chat, on a discussion board, or as a Web page.

We should make clear that we are not just speaking about migrating a few PC functions to a mobile platform or using the mobile device while "out of the office," which is a common business application today. Rather, we envision these devices actually replacing the full functionality of the desktop PC. Therefore we do not have in mind popular technologies such as palmtops (e.g., the Palm VII) or Internet-ready cell phones, primarily because they lack a full-scale Internet browser that can handle a wide variety of Web content. This is not to say that such capabilities may not be added in the future, but it is important to note that the Jornada and other models of Pocket PCs already come with browsers that support HTML 3.2 and Javascript, with the added ability of playing audio and video files. This difference should not be underestimated, given the large volume of existing Web sites that will be of interest to educators as well as developers of educational content.

## Conclusion

A consideration of the full range of implications of the handheld Web for WBI/T would be impossible at this time, primarily because so little is known about adoption and impact of this technology. However, wireless voice devices are already in wide use, and there is every indication that wireless data devices will be welcomed in the U.S. as they have been in Japan and Europe. This will require WBI/T developers and coordinators to carefully consider the implications of this technology for their programs, especially in light of compatibility, content, and communication issues. The authors believe that ultimately WBI/T will be positively transformed as a result of anytime/anywhere educational opportunities that are made possible by this emerging communications and computing infrastructure.

## References

AT&T (2000). *Delivering the Right Stuff.* AT&T 1999 Annual Report.

Field, D., and Rosato, D. (2000, April 27). Boeing Planes Soon Will Boast Net, TV, E-mail. *USA Today.*

Holzschlag, M.E. (2000, May). Squeaky Clean Markup. *WebTechniques,* 26-29.

Leavitt, N. (2000, May). Will WAP Deliver the Wireless Internet? *Computer, 33*(5), 16-20.

Lewis, T. (1999, October). UbiNet: The Ubiquitous Internet Will Be Wireless. *Computer, 32*(10), 126-128.

Lewis, T. (2000, February). Tracking the 'Anywhere, Anytime' Inflection Point. *Computer, 33*(2), 134-136.

O'Leary, A. (2000, Spring/Summer). Get Wired, Go Digital, Build a Web-Based Learning Community. *Educational Technology Review,* No. 13, 28-32.

Pullen, J.M. (1998). Synchronous Distance Education and the Internet. *Proceedings of INET '98 Internet Summit* (http://www.isoc.org/inet98/proceedings/4b/4b_l.htm).

Schmetzer, U. (2000, May 24). Wireless 'I-Mail' Connects in Japan. *Chicago Tribune.*

Shotsberger, P.G. (1999). The INSTRUCT Project: Web Professional Development for Mathematics Teachers. *Journal of Computers in Mathematics and Science Teaching, 18*(1), 49-60.

Shotsberger, P.G. (2000, January-February). The Human Touch: Synchronous Communication in Web-Based Learning. *Educational Technology, 40*(1), 53-56.

Varshney, U., and Vetter, R. (2000, June). Emerging Mobile and Wireless Networks, *Communications of the ACM, 43*(6), 73-81.

*Paul G. Shotsberger is Associate Professor, Department of Mathematics and Statistics, University of North Carolina at Wilmington (e-mail: shotsbergerp@ uncwil.edu).*

*Ronald Vetter is Professor, Computer Science Department, University of North Carolina at Wilmington (e-mail: vetterr@uncwil.edu).*

# Designing Discussion Questions for Online, Adult Learning

## Zane L. Berge and Lin Muilenburg

*In online discussions, whether in workplace training and higher education, can serve as a catalyst, helping participants to better understand. But to be most effective, facilitators must plan their questions. This article offers excellent advice for asking questions, preparing particpants, and managing discussions.*

Increasingly, educators and trainers are asked to design and deliver training for online classrooms. What teaching methods work best? Is discussion the same online as in-person? What questions are most effective for the instructional goals of the course?

Much of what goes on in training within organizations in the workplace and in higher education takes the form of students hearing, seeing, or reading content that was structured by the instructor, followed by the instructor asking a question of the student(s) about that content, with the instructor then reacting to each student's response. In traditional classrooms that are instructor-centered, with lectures and a focus on content, the pattern described above occupies up to 80 percent of the classroom time, with up to 100 questions per classroom hour being asked (Brown & Edmondson, 1984; Gall, 1984). But a higher *frequency* of instructors soliciting response from students is not necessarily what leads to more effective learning. This may be especially true if the goal is to foster *discussion* (Dillon, 1985).

Even in classrooms that do not use such teacher-centered approaches, question-asking is at the heart of understanding. Online learning environments, Web-based or otherwise, are often more learner-centered than traditional, brick-and-mortar classrooms. Online classrooms that use computer conferencing are characterized as being discussion-oriented; authentic, problem- and project-based; inquiry-focused; and collaborative (Berge, 1997). In this type of learning environment, it is usually more important for the instructor to ask the "right questions" than to give the "right answers."

## The Right Questions

The right questions depend greatly on what the instructional goals and objectives are for the training, development, or education that is to take place. The right questions are those that foster learner engagement in the learning process. The emphasis in the workplace is shifting from training to a focus on the learning organization. In a lot of ways, the move to the learning organization is a philosophical shift in which organizations are recognizing that a well-trained and well-educated workforce is an important area in which they must build competitive advantage.

It is also a recognition that learning is not finished after a particular degree or certificate is achieved. Rather, education is life-long and necessary for individuals to gain the competencies needed on the job and in the complex problems of adult life. Questions that simply ask learners to recall facts are not going to be very effective in helping learners solve authentic problems, in their jobs, or in advanced studies. Such problems as found in adult life require higher-level thinking, such as clarifying, expanding, generalizing, making inferences, analysis, synthesis, and evaluating.

## Levels of Questions

The difference between low-level thinking and higher-level thinking has to do with the cognitive complexity for the learner. One of the better-known taxonomies for framing a discussion of cognitive complexity was presented by Bloom and his colleagues (1984). It involves six levels, from simple to more complex: knowledge, comprehension, application, analysis, synthesis, and evaluation. Following are example questions for each level, along with the instructional processes and keywords often used with each category:

**Knowledge (remembering).** The instructional processes are commonly repetition and memorization, with keywords within such questions as *define, list, name, recite, describe,* and *identify.* "What is the definition of constructivism?"

**Comprehension (understanding).** Instructional processes are usually explanation and illustration, with keywords such as *summarize, paraphrase, convert, explain, extend,* and *rephrase.* "Can you tell me, in your own words, what Martin Luther King Jr. said in his 'I have a dream' speech?"

**Application (transferring).** Processes are usually practice and transfer, and keywords are *apply, use, demonstrate, operate, solve,* and *employ.* "Can you post a lesson plan using the criteria listed on page 45 of your textbook?"

**Analysis (relating).** Processes are most often induction and deduction, with keyword indicators including *relate, distinguish, point out, break down, support,* and *differentiate.* "What factors distinguish communism from socialism?"

**Synthesis (creating).** Instructional processes involve divergence and generalization, with keywords such as *formulate, compare, create, predict, devise,* and *produce.* "What would an economic system be like that combines the salient characteristics of capitalism and socialism?"

**Evaluation (judging).** Processes involve discrimination and inference, with keywords being *appraise, decide, assess, defend, judge,* and *justify.* "Using evidence that you select, take a position and defend it regarding whether capitalist or socialist countries have a higher standard of living,"

This and what follows are true of adult online learning, whether in higher education or in the workplace classroom.

There are other taxonomies for categorizing cognitive complexity. Most are structured along the lines of "knowing about something," versus "knowing how to use or apply something," versus "evaluating or synthesizing something." Regardless of the taxonomy used, designing questions for the desired cognitive level is a significant design element, as demonstrated in the types of sample questions above.

## Purposes of Questions

In addition to helping learners engage in higher-order thinking, question-askers have many other purposes for asking their questions. Borich (1996, pp. 343-344) lists the following purposes for questions:

- To arouse interest and curiosity.
- To focus attention on an issue.
- To stimulate learners to ask questions.
- To diagnose specific learning difficulties.
- To encourage reflection and self-evaluation.
- To promote thought and the understanding of ideas.
- To review content already learned.
- To help recall specific information.
- To reinforce recently learned material.
- To manage or remind students of a procedure.
- To teach via student answers.
- To probe deeper after an answer is given.

While there may be some additional purposes for questions, in general, questions for instructional purposes can be grouped into the following categories (with examples):

**Interest-getting and attention-getting.** "If you awakened in the year 2399, what is the first thing you would notice?"

**Diagnosing and checking.** "Does anyone know Senge's five principles of a learning organization?"

**Recall of specific facts or information.** "Who can name the main characters in *Moby Dick*?"

**Managerial.** "Did you request an extension on the assignment due date?"

**Encourage higher-level thought processes.** "Considering what you have read, and what was discussed in the posts this past week, can you summarize all the ways there are to overcome obstacles to effective teamwork?"

**Structure and redirect learning.** "Now that we have discussed the advantages and limitations to formative evaluation, who can do the same for summative evaluation?"

**Allow expression of affect.** "How did you feel about our online guest's list of ten things trainers do to shoot themselves in the foot?"

As you can see, each of these types of questions can be used in designing online instruction, depending upon the instructional purposes(s), goals, or objectives for the course or program.

## Tips for Online Questions

Here are several tips, based on our experience, that may help in designing questions for online discussion:

- Essentially, online questions are the same as offline. However, you must take care in making sure the question is clearly stated. Questions, and just about everything else done online, are more easily misunderstood. Currently, Web-based and computer-based conferencing use text, with little video or audio. Until this changes, question-askers have at their discretion word choice, word emphasis, and the context in which it is raised, but not voice inflection. Voice inflection carries a lot of meaning in in-person classrooms.
- One of the easiest ways to *stifle* discussion is for the instructor to post a long, well-articulated post on the subject at hand. Our experience is that learners tend to think, "that's the last word," and end their contributions to that topic after that, even when topic closure is not the instructor's intent.

- The more diverse the group of learners, and the more complex and divergent the question, the more diverse the responses may be. You should expect unusual answers, either correct or incorrect, and make sure that the instructor or other participants respond in an appropriate and reasoned, ethical manner that matches the cultural norms or expectations for each of the participants.
- Humor and sarcasm often are mistaken online. Similarly, learners should not be embarrassed or punished through the use of questions, or any other methods, for that matter.

## Principles for Designing an Online Discussion

There are several guiding principles for effective online instructional discussions that are germane to this article: (1) design the discussion ahead of time, (2) prepare the learners for the discussion, (3) manage the discussion in process (Eisley, 1999), and (4) summarize the discussion. Eisley recommends that you:

- Tie the discussion to your objectives.
- Make sure the most salient points get made. This helps to guide learners and allows you to efficiently manage the discussion, and you will know the right time to wrap up discussion.
- Structure the discussion (focus the content, specify the format, avoid questions which invite non-responsive communication or redundancy).

Consider the paths of thinking that may be activated by the questions asked to facilitate discussion. Consider the divergent directions that questions might take the discussion and possible learner responses to each question. What follow-up questions should be asked? This is different from an outline of content to be covered. It is not creating a rigid plan. Instead, various possible outcomes are being considered. By taking the time to prepare these follow-up questions ahead of time, the instructor (or designated learners) can be ready with questions that will draw out the discussion and lead to constructive thinking within each participant, while the discussion stays generally focused on the content and goals.

## Prepare Learners for Discussions

We cannot expect learners to automatically know how to constructively participate in an online discussion. Participants must be taught such things as "netiquette," how to write effective e-mail, and how to compose a response, and they must be made aware of the instructor's expectations early in the process.

Nadine Burke (1999) provides a wealth of information on her Web site to teach learners how to respond to her questions and the comments in classmates' posts:

- If a classmate has a lengthy response, cut the parts that are not important to your reply and leave only the part to which you wish to reply.

- If you are going to respond to a number of paragraphs in the original post, consider spacing down to under the paragraph you wish to comment on and type your response there. Placing the comments between paragraphs helps your reader know what you are referring to.
- If you just want to say, "I agree," that does not add anything of real value to the conversation. Instead, try to figure out why you agree, how you can expand upon the point you agree with, or what new information can you add to that to continue the conversation.
- Feel free to disagree with your classmates' opinions, but do so with respect. Cite evidence to be able to support your dissenting opinion.
- Never resort to name-calling or obscenity.

## Manage the Discussion in Process

The discussion has started and participants are beginning to post responses to the question provided. What should be done to facilitate this discussion? Feedback is important, especially individually given feedback. Private e-mail to encourage newcomers to the discussion and to welcome participants is also useful. You may also send private notes explaining how individual participants may be able to respond in a clearer manner, if they need to spell-check, or if they need to watch their tone or attitude (Burke, 1999).

What kinds of questions should you ask to promote ongoing discussion and constructive thinking? Savage (1998) suggests probing question such as:

- What reasons do you have for saying that?
- Why do you agree (or disagree) on that point?
- How are you defining the term that you just used?
- What do you mean by that expression?
- Is what you are saying consistent with what you said before?
- Could you clarify that remark?
- When you said that, just what is implied by your remarks?
- What follows from what you just said?
- Is it possible you and he are contradicting each other?
- Are you sure you're not contradicting yourself?
- What alternatives are there to such a formulation?

How do you know when to jump into the public forum with comments? If things are going well, do not interfere. Resist the temptation, if it exists, to post a public reply until the conversation is waning.

**Summarization.** At the day/time that has been designated, or when the discussion has covered the salient points designed in the instruction, close out the discussion with a summary. A more in-depth analysis would be too long and not within the scope of this article. But suffice it to say that the instructor or designated student(s) should summarize the essential points that have occurred during the online discussion or ask some prompting questions to redirect and recharge a somewhat different discussion.

## Conclusions

Questions, designed to generate and facilitate discussion online for instructional purposes, need to be planned. Since much of online teaching is learner-centered, the methods used emphasize discussion, inquiry, authentic projects or problem-solving, and collaboration. Effective questions, as part and parcel of online discussion, can serve as a catalyst for increased adult learner understanding and meeting the instructional goals in both workplace training and higher education.

## References

Berge, Z.L. (1997). Characteristics of online teaching in post-secondary, formal education. *Educational Technology, 37*(3), 35-47.

Bloom, B., Englehart, M., Hill, W., Furst, E., & Krathwohl, D. (1984). *Taxonomy of educational objectives: The classification of educational goals, Handbook 1: Cognitive domain.* New York: Longman, Green.

Borich, C.D. (1996). *Effective teaching methods* (3rd ed.). Englewood Cliffs, NJ: Merrill.

Brown, C., & Edmondson, R. (1984). Asking questions. In E.C. Wragg (Ed.), *Classroom teaching skills.* New York: Nichols, pp. 97-119.

Burke, A.N. (1999). *Helpful files for online teaching,* www.delta.edu/annader/mentor/.

Dillon, J.T. (1985). Using questions to foil discussion. *Teaching and Teacher Education, 1,* 109-121, 537-538.

Eisley, M.E. (1999). "Guidelines for conducting instructional discussions on a computer conference" [DEOSNEWS Electronic Serial], www.ed.psu.edu/acsde/deos/deosnews/deosnews2_1.asp.

Gall, M. (1984). Synthesis of research on questioning in recitation. *Educational Leadership, 42*(3), 40-49.

Savage, L.B. (1998). Eliciting critical thinking skills through questioning. *The Clearing House, 71*(5), 291-293.

*Zane L. Berge is a Contributing Editor of* Educational Technology *and Director of Graduate Training Systems programs, University of Maryland Baltimore County, Baltimore (e-mail: berge@umbc.edu).*

*Lin Muilenburg is a doctoral candidate in the Department of Behavioral Studies and Educational Technology, University of South Alabama, Mobile (e-mail: LinM@zebra.net).*

# Welcome to Part Three: Managing E-Learning Success:

## Strategies That Turn Promises into Performance

P art Three recognizes that the purchase decision, even with all its challenges, might just be the easiest of them all. What comes after the purchase is where the rubber meets the road.

Marc Rosenberg provides an overview of what's involved in successful implementation of e-learning. Jim Moshinskie discusses engaging employees in e-learning; he provides strategies for before, during, and after e-learning classes. Both Rosenberg and Moshinskie cover strategic and tactical approaches to e-learning management. Brandon Hall provides an overview of the steps necessary to pull off a successful e-learning initiative in any organization.

Nory Jones and James Laffey, Rebecca Vaughan Frazee, and Tom Barron note the importance of garnering broad and firm support and commitment for e-learning. Barron focuses on critical IT relationships. Frazee looks at late adopters and resistance patterns associated with technology. Barry Raybould reminds us that a performance-centered and systems approach is critical here.

Allison Rossett and Kendra Sheldon press for a larger view of e-learning, a view that includes knowledge management. John Jacobs and John Dempsey look at some of the technologies emerging and how they will start affecting the delivery of e-learning, and Jan Greenberg and Gary Dickelman discuss the idea of a performance support environment.

Part Three helps professionals see and treat e-learning as more than an event or library of courses. The focus here is on managing the larger change management process. In Part Four, we examine what authors see on the horizon.

# The Four C's of Success: Culture, Champions, Communication, and Change

**Marc J. Rosenberg**

*The following is a chapter from* E-Learning: Strategies for Delivering Knowledge in the Digital Age. *It looks at the foundation concepts for effectively implementing e-learning in any organization. At a broader level, these ideas apply to any initiative in an organization designed to help it move forward.*

It's not the strongest of the species who survive, nor the most intelligent, but the ones most responsive to change.
—Charles Darwin

One of the most important tenets of e-learning is that it bridges work and learning. While the best classroom experiences bring work into the learning environment, the best e-learning experiences bring learning into the work environment. Whether it's online training or knowledge management, the premise of e-learning is that it can be accessed anytime and anywhere it's needed.

This is a fundamental shift from the time-honored practice of going to school (i.e., the training center). Now school comes to you—at work, at home, and on the road. As practical as it seems, there is often overt and covert resistance to e-learning on the job. Some of this resistance comes from the business's front line (difficulty equating learning with work); other resistance comes from the company's senior leaders (difficulty appreciating the value of e-learning). There can also be resistance within training organizations (difficulty accepting e-learning as a legitimate form of learning). In order for e-learning to prosper in a business—to be sustainable—a strong learning culture is required. It's not just a climate that supports classroom learning or e-learning, but one that embraces learning as a whole—as an important activity of everyone in the firm. Organizations that are truly "learning organizations" quickly move beyond the "where" and the "how" of learning, concentrating instead on ingraining it into the work culture. Bottom line—e-learning cannot thrive without careful attention to the "four C's": a *culture* of learning, *champions* who will lead e-learning efforts, *communications* that position e-learning's value, and an integrated *change* strategy to bring it all together.

## Building a Learning Culture

The failure of e-learning to get any traction in a company is often related to the quality of the initiatives themselves. But even the best programs deployed with the best intentions often create little lasting impact. Although a particular e-learning initiative may prove a success from a learning and performance standpoint, it's often viewed as a unique occurrence, certainly not replicable throughout the organization, and most certainly not something to replace what's always been done! What we see over and over again is "reinventing the wheel"—organizations studying and restudying e-learning and trying yet again to break down the traditional walls of training, often by building "new and better" e-learning solutions rather than tackling the real culprit: the culture.

Too often companies invest in new technology only to find that the existing culture won't support it. For e-learning to be successful, the culture must get beyond lip service to recognize learning as a valued part of what people do—a productive activity and not a waste of time. Building a learning culture is hard work. You have to overcome the perceptions that learning and work are different (and that work is productive while learning isn't), that learning takes place only in the classroom, and that learning and training are one and the same. Clearly, eliminating resistance and changing these beliefs is essential to building a learning culture, but how do you do it?

Think about it this way. From the viewpoint of resistors, e-learning not only doesn't make sense, it constitutes a high risk and a certainty of short-term costs with a vague promise of long-term gain. They may integrate e-learning into their current practice in ways that make sense to them from their *current* perspective (such as seeing e-learning through the "eyes" of the classroom paradigm). But this is missing the point of the innovation or distorting it so badly that the resulting benefits are minimal—and their skepticism about the long-term benefit is confirmed. They have the best intentions, but kill the innovation anyway.

## Culture-Building Strategies That Don't Work

In the past, organizations have tried several approaches to build enthusiasm and support for learning. Some create an air of success when, in fact, the efforts have foundered. This has been most notable when training organizations seek to expand their influence. In their efforts to create enthusiasm for training (not necessarily learning) they tried to:

**Give customers what they want.** Organizations that embarked on a "retail" philosophy have created a customer-supplier model for internal training. They believe that the customer (i.e., employee) knows best and that their responsibility is to do the very best job of meeting the wants or needs of these customers. Many training organizations see the students as the customer. While serving customers is well-meaning, for the most part, the students in the classroom are really not the customers. The customer is the person who pays for the training, and in most businesses that is usually the organizational leader who controls the training budget. Furthermore, giving customers what they want may not necessarily be giving them what they need. For example, a training organization continues to offer project management training when it is clear that the company has enough project managers. Why? Because it's in demand—perhaps some business unit declared project management training as a requirement for promotion. No one was interested in what the business will do with all those surplus project managers, least of all the training organization. Should they offer courses in other areas that are not business related? As one executive said to me: "Do you mean that if employees wanted a course in basket-weaving, we should provide it?" Incredibly, the response from one training organization: "If they're willing to pay, we'll do it."

**Create and distribute a robust course catalog.** If a little training is good, certainly more must be better. That's the philosophy of those who embrace the approach of having something for everyone. Catalogs get fatter and fatter. We take our five-day course and we break it down. You can take a shortened version of the training in three days or two days, and for executives, a one-day briefing if you want. This can result in numerous versions of the same training, only "sliced and diced" differently (a redundancy issue) or the offering of programs that have minimal worth but are in hot demand (a value issue). This is often designed to drive more business to the training center on the false assumption that if your classrooms are filled you might have a learning organization.

**Think of training as just another product and sell it.** A lot of training organizations are getting into the mode that they are an internal business and have to sell everything they do in order to generate the revenue to stay in business. Instead of hiring instructional designers, they hire salespeople. This is a direct result of telling the company: "Look, you don't need to fund us—we'll fund ourselves." At some of these training organizations you'll find half the employees in that organization are involved in some form of selling. Account management, receivables, billing—all kinds of activities that have nothing to do with the mission they're charted to do.

In each of these three scenarios the focus is in increasing training activity. Not only does this fail to create a learning culture in the organization, it is also very risky for the training group. First, all the measures are inwardly focused. How many students, how much tuition, etc.? These are not the cost, quality, service, and speed requirements to which businesses must adhere. Second, it disengages the training function from the workplace by emphasizing the business perform-ance of the training organization in isolation from the rest of the company. No mat-ter how much money an internal training organization makes, it's really money that's transferred from other parts of the company. Somewhere along the line it's not how much business the training department did, but how much value it pro-vided to the firm that will be questioned. To their detriment, many training organ-izations get caught up in their own "results" and forget to whom they are really accountable. As expenditures are more closely scrutinized, some major training organizations in both large and mid-sized firms have been drastically downsized, or shut down completely when they failed to adequately answer the "value" ques-tion: Why should we invest, or continue investing, in e-learning—what benefits will it bring to the company? In the end, training activity, even lots of it, does very little to instill a learning culture in the organization if the value proposition (the response to the "Why" question) is weak.

Here are other attempts to build a learning culture that have been tried with little long-term success.

**Make training "free":** Instead of selling it, how about giving it away? The problem here is not so much the free access to training, but that it is usually accompanied by little in the way of direction on who takes what. In most of these situations, the training budget is exhausted before anyone realizes it. Some people may have taken the training that's right for them, while others may have wasted their time on unnecessary training. Still others may have missed their opportunity altogeth-er. But when the money runs out, don't think for a moment that people will stop demanding their "free" training. Free training can work if it is managed well—through competency models (following), and strong linkage to business needs, career development, and training paths. This will control the "demand" side of the equation.

**Build competency models … but don't actually use them.** Competency models are becoming important in the development of precision learning systems—the type of system that directs the precise information and instruction to each employee based on his/her competency requirements. The problem is that most competen-cy models sit in big binders and never get implemented into the overall assessment system. And since competencies are driven by changing skill requirements and the changing knowledge base, they're always changing themselves. No sooner is a competency model for a job completed than it needs revisions. Saying you have a competency model is pretty worthless unless you are actually using it.

**Call yourself a "corporate university."** While there's a lot to be said for elevating the visibility of learning in the organization as a way to build the right learning culture, just changing your name and adding a more lofty mission statement is not enough. The best corporate universities are fundamentally different from the training organizations they replaced (which begs the question of whether the term "university" is even appropriate). So if selling seats in the training center remains the major driver of your business, calling yourself a corporate university will quickly ring very hollow.

**Move everything to technology.** Decide to end all classroom training. Just close the classrooms, put everything on the Web, declare victory, and move on. We know this is not appropriate, and organizations that believe the use of technology will bring some sort of learning utopia to the business are kidding themselves. It's not even close to being that easy. The classroom, when used appropriately within a comprehensive learning architecture, has a very important role in the learning culture of a company.

**Mandate training.** When everything else fails, organizations think about *requiring* people to attend training. Strategies based on expressions like "If they won't come to training, if they won't take our training, we'll simply force them to and that will build a learning culture" do not work. Sometimes training should be mandated, as in the case of safety, sexual harassment, insider trading, etc. But simply using a mandate to force people into the classroom may create a resentful culture rather than a learning culture.

The problem with all of these efforts is that they are focused on the training function. There is little effort to shape the world outside of the training organization. There's lots of effort to push a message onto the company, but little effort in engaging the company in that effort.

## Culture-Building Strategies That Do Work

There is an emerging set of strategies that can help create a climate for learning. Instead of a training organization "push," these approaches are designed to "pull" the company into a learning mode, and as such, require collaboration outside the training organization and across the firm.

**Make the coach or the direct manager accountable for learning.** We like to say that employees are accountable for their own development. That's fine, but it should not take the responsibility away from the direct manager. Managers have a major role equal to that of the employee. They can meet with people before and after key learning events, helping them integrate new skills, knowledge, and ideas into the workplace. And they can foster their own small learning organization by providing time for sharing and discussion of ways to improve everything from morale to productivity. Build requirements for people development directly into managers' job descriptions and appraisals, and provide training for them on how to make this work.

There is no one in the company more influential than front-line managers—they can make organizational change easy or kill it outright. Robert Brinkerhoff and Stephen Gill[1] point out the problems encountered when trainers and managers are at cross-purposes. The attitude of trainers that "I can teach but I can't make anyone use what is taught—that's the manager's job" and the manager's view that "training is irrelevant if it contradicts my way of doing things" point directly to a culture problem that needs to be addressed up front. Once managers are on board with support for learning, you've cleared a major hurdle.

**Focus at the enterprise level.** Cultures can be modified when there's enough critical mass of people wanting the change to happen. Working culture issues group by group can be frustrating and failure-prone. If the training and development community within the company is fragmented, work first to bring unity to the function; otherwise there will not be enough clout to change much of anything.

**Integrate learning directly into work.** Wherever possible, make e-learning (and other forms of learning) a part of everyone's daily work activities. Simply taking time out to share new insights or problems is a start. Encouraging all employees to spend some time each day accessing information from the Internet and intranet, and providing forums that enable everyone to participate in discussions, helps solidify the learning communities that are the essential building blocks of a learning culture. But more can be done. Institute a process of personal and managerial assessment of each employee—not for appraisal purposes, but for developmental purposes—and then ensure that the resources to close performance gaps are made available to all who need them. Reward knowledge sharing and penalize knowledge hoarding. People who willingly contribute their knowledge and expertise can be recognized through financial incentives. Organizations can also create an environment that allows contributors to be recognized as experts and to "own" the content. When others see that knowledge sharing is a rewarded behavior, more will participate. If the incentives are well-designed, knowledge hoarders will be left behind. Their expertise will be eclipsed by others and they will soon realize that the only way to be recognized as an expert or leveraging what they know is by sharing it with others. If your business has an appraisal or compensation system that doesn't bring out this distinction, you need to improve it so it does.

Creating an atmosphere of learning builds a strong new culture that has the momentum to displace the old.

**Design well and certify where appropriate.** Learning cultures are influenced by quality learning products. This is especially true for e-learning, as it represents something new and untested. So make sure the quality is there. If you have quality programs, based on valid and implemented competency models, certification becomes a possibility. Certification is a performance-based assessment, as opposed to knowledge testing or credit hour models—what you can do rather than what you know or how many classes you've taken—although there are many certification programs based solely on these weaker criteria. Some jobs can benefit from certification because it provides a sense of accomplishment for the learner and a barometer of the capacity of skills for the firm. If done right, certification can be a valid predictor of job performance. And when people see that certification is tightly linked to jobs, performance, pay, and other recognition, they'll take notice and become involved. Many high-tech companies, such as Microsoft, Cisco, Lucent, and Oracle, have developed extensive certification programs, increasingly administered on the Web. Being a Microsoft, Cisco, Lucent, or Oracle "certified" technician or engineer is becoming a general entry-level requirement in the communications, computing, and other technology industries. Certification is impossible if you don't know exactly *what* people are supposed to do and how *well* they are supposed to do it.

**Pay for knowledge.** We often talk about pay for performance, with top performers earning more than poor performers. But why not pay for knowledge as well? This is not simply an incentive for learning *anything* an individual wants to learn; rather, it is motivation for people to learn in areas that the firm believes will be useful in the future. If people take the initiative to learn new skills that can be directly applied to improve performance in a demanding business environment, isn't that effort worth recognition, maybe even monetary recognition? This is where a good certification program can be useful in setting the standards for a pay-for-knowledge strategy. Perhaps the reverse is even more of an issue. If the firm sends a message that building your own intellectual capital—capabilities that can help the company succeed—is not important, the "learning organization" can shut down.

**Everyone's a teacher.** There may be no better way to create a learning culture than to create a teaching culture, where everyone has an obligation to teach others. Whether as a formal classroom instructor, a seminar presenter, an e-learning designer, a knowledge management contributor, or a mentor, the experience of creating and delivering information or instruction is not only rewarding, it can change an entire firm's perspective on learning. Think about it: When was the last time your CEO taught a course at your training center?

**Get rid of the training noise.** Stop using jargon that continues the confusion between learning and training, and between information and instruction. Emphasis on tuition, registration, courses, and objectives can interfere with people opening up to new e-learning approaches.

**Eliminate the ability to pay as a gatekeeper.** The ability to pay for learning can certainly be a roadblock on the way to building a learning culture. How often do we say, "The training is available; here's how much it costs"? In many companies, business units that are doing very well have the money to send their people to training. So training becomes a perk for the parts of the company that actually have the most money and are doing well in the first place. The business units that are not doing well may not have the money to send their people to training. They're the people who need it most, yet they're also the people who can least afford it. A learning culture can be nurtured by eliminating ability to pay as a barrier. Instead, target a more equal share of training opportunities where the business is weak, even if that part of the business can't afford to pay for it. By radically lowering delivery and access costs, e-learning breaks down this barrier.

**Make access as easy as possible.** Enable people to get to e-learning resources easily. This means placing key e-learning access points on the intranet pages people visit most. Don't rely on people remembering a variety of URLs or having to use search engines to find the particular online training or knowledge management site they are interested in. Even more innovative—extend access to learning to the home. This may create concerns about cost and security, but the advantages are often worth it. Delta Airlines and Ford have given computers and Internet access to all of their employees. Besides the obvious employee-benefit aspects of this initiative, these companies now have instant access to everyone in the company for communications and learning—including those employees, such as assembly line workers or flight attendants, who do not regularly work with computers. Furthermore, this will help build a Web-savvy workforce that will be more accepting of change brought on by new technology.

People embrace learning when they see direct relevance and benefit for them and when they sense support from the firm. When you hear, "We can't get our people to take the computer-based training. They don't want to take it... They don't do it... They don't like it," you are hearing more than a simple rejection of an e-learning product. The same is true for comments like "When we bring people to the training center, we take them far enough away from their boss/job so that they'll pay attention to the training. If we do it over the Web, this won't happen. Therefore we need to keep the training center/classroom model." Either way, you are hearing the culture tell you that e-learning, or any learning for that matter, is not important.

## Signs Your Senior Leadership May Not Be Serious About E-Learning

Organizational cultures and their leaders are reflections of each other. Building a culture that will embrace e-learning means building senior management support for that culture. There may be lots of activity, in terms of programs launched and money spent. But without support from the top, these initiatives have no "legs"—they just aren't durable enough to build the momentum and critical mass that's necessary to transform the organization into one that accepts e-learning, and learning in general, as a natural part of the firm's everyday work life.

How can you tell whether senior management is truly behind e-learning? How do you know if they are willing to back these initiatives up so they can be sustainable? How will you know if those at the executive level are committed as *champions* of these initiatives? While many senior managers say they support e-learning, it would be unwise to invest your resources and completely change your direction based just upon a statement of support. There are many cases where executives say they support a new initiative (whether it's e-learning or some other initiative), but their actions tell a different story. The following are telltale signs that what senior management says about e-learning may not be what they believe.

**Work is assigned to people already overloaded or who don't have a clue.** Giving this work to people who, because of their current workload or lack of experience, cannot possibly accomplish the goals of the e-learning initiative can be devastating to any e-learning strategy. Whether the basis for the assignment is a lack of understanding of what it takes to do this work (from a time or expertise point of view) or a failure to prioritize and eliminate work that is no longer necessary (thus freeing up time), this behavior can be disastrous, even if the people assigned are enthusiastic about it. Of course, even if the work is assigned to the right person or group, if leaders don't convey the message that e-learning is everyone's responsibility, there's a chance that those not directly involved will ignore it.

**Support or directives are given without any money.** While e-learning is very cost-effective, the initial work to get it going requires a significant up-front investment. Without the financial resources necessary to get e-learning initiatives going, they often wither on the vine. It's important to determine if this is a true budget issue (i.e., there really isn't any money to spare) or if it's a priority issue (i.e., money is allocated to other projects that might be curtailed to free up funds). Management support for e-learning is questionable at best if they are unwilling to help find the money that's needed.

**During budget cutting activities, the e-learning budget is always cut first.** This is related to the overall issue of money availability. But if you hear something like "I really do believe in this, but the needs of the business come first," you have a problem. And the problem is compounded if most of the training and development budget "sacrifice" comes from e-learning, especially if the cuts are coming from the leadership of the business, and the leaders of the training and development functions cannot or do not intercede.

**Senior managers refuse to learn anything about e-learning.** Sometimes, executives are too busy to devote a considerable amount of time to learning about e-learning, or they don't have a deep enough understanding of the broader perspectives of what e-learning is. Leadership in e-learning doesn't necessarily have to come with e-learning expertise. But if executive disinterest appears less like a time or education issue and more like an obvious signal of lack of real support, or even fear, you may have a problem. This concern is compounded if no one on the executive's staff is interested, or if you can't find *anyone* at the top who wants to learn about e-learning.

> Tech-based learning has been slow to move up the corporate ladder, in part because older managers are less comfortable with computers and the Net than younger ones.
>
> —*Business Week*[2]

**Leaves it to the team to make *all* the decisions.** Compounding a disinterest in e-learning is the abdication of all decision-making to subordinates. This is different from having specialists on staff for advice and decisions of a technical or implementation nature, while strategy decisions remain in the hands of the leader. Together, the refusal to learn about e-learning and the deference of *all* decisions to others often represents a complete and destructive disengagement from the process.

**Refuses to tell his/her boss anything about it.** When leaders express support for e-learning, but then display behaviors that seem to indicate that they don't want anyone to know about it, there's a problem. It's natural for people to be hesitant about fundamental change and the level of risk they've exposed themselves to. But refusal to communicate can mask a much higher level of insecurity about e-learning and a lack of confidence in those who are working on it. The key is to differentiate between cautiousness associated with a new venture and an extreme need for self-preservation should something go wrong.

**Does not assign any deliverables or accountability.** When no actual deliverables are assigned and no consequences are articulated relative to an e-learning initiative, the perception becomes one of a meaningless exercise or "flavor of the month." Saying you're serious without defining the expected results and the rewards and consequences associated with the assignment can lead to insurmountable disbelief and a subsequent unwillingness of senior managers to see the transformation through.

**Believes that going to training is either a perk or a sign of a performance problem.** Sometimes the wrong signals about the role of training can impact an e-learning strategy. If business leaders believe that training programs are a reward for good performance (i.e., "best workers") or only for those who need remedial work (i.e., "worst workers"), they will be less likely to support corporatewide, all-employee initiatives—e-learning or otherwise.

**Approves other learning strategies that undermine e-learning.** Be wary if the leadership says one thing ("I support e-learning!") but does another (e.g., builds more classrooms or purchases a popular but unneeded training program in an effort to generate "student days"). Without a rationale that signifies a broad-based, strategic approach, it's more likely that the decision maker is being influenced by different advisers, factions, or political pressures, and that a coherent, agreed-upon e-learning strategy is not in place.

**Suggests that employee use of the Web at work is disruptive.** When business leaders say they want to restrict employees' Web access at work because they'll engage in unproductive, non-work activities (such as visiting sports or entertainment sites), they are putting up a smoke screen. In almost all situations, employees who are likely to spend time on the Web instead of working are the same employees who would find reasons to "goof off" even if the Web wasn't around. Labeling this as a technology issue masks a probable management or supervisory failure. Concentrate on increasing access to the Web, not restricting it.

## Helping Senior Managers Become True Champions of E-Learning

If we're not careful about these signs, we're likely to think we have management support when we don't. This could lead to questions a few months later by the same managers who now say they never authorized the expense or didn't really understand what you were telling them in the first place. This creates tremendous credibility problems for future endeavors.

But how do you get senior managers to support e-learning? That's probably the number-one question on everyone's list of issues, and with good reason. Without support at the executive level, it is highly doubtful that an e-learning initiative will succeed. The challenge is to move from just words of support to true ownership of the initiative. That means senior management will have to put some "skin in the game." Besides simply supporting e-learning, managers can show ownership through their vigilance—they can personally get involved in helping to lead the initiative, to make sure it goes the way it should. They can involve themselves in the experience, becoming "e-learners" like everyone else. But most important, they can pay for the initiatives. As sponsors, they will put up much of the financial resources to get e-learning off the ground. Like any investor, when you put up some of your own money, you have a vested interest in seeing the investment pay off.

Wishing business leaders would free up funds and support e-learning is not the same as making it happen. Here are seven ways to engage executives so their support will be genuine and long-lasting.

**1. Build a sound business case.** Any good business case must justify the investment in e-learning in three ways. First, that e-learning does in fact meet specific business needs of responsiveness to fast-paced change (speed of deployment, updating), support for front-line workers (availability and access where and when needed), and performance improvement (increased competence). Second, that it is more economical than other forms of delivery. And third, that the company recognizes the need to manage knowledge as an asset, not just a cost (i.e., what is the value of the firm's intellectual property? If it has no value, why do companies try so hard to protect it?). All of these justifications are required.

**2. Use success stories.** Senior managers want evidence that e-learning works. If it represents a new way of thinking for them, they will probably want more evidence than might be thought necessary. This is why finding opportunities for small successes is a good move. Just finding that one manager or one business unit that is willing to try something new can make all the difference. Often, these opportunities are in areas of the business that are in trouble and willing to try some radical new ideas to improve their situation. Or you just might find a risk taker who wants first-mover advantage in e-learning. (He/she wants to get there first to have more control over future direction.) Work carefully but speedily to demonstrate the effectiveness of e-learning in this unique situation, and then, when the positive results are in, showcase your work to a larger audience (always sharing credit with your sponsor/client).

**3. Educate executives.** This doesn't mean sending executives to school; few learn that way (which calls into question the way we do so much management training). What it does mean is letting senior managers learn how other organizations and companies are succeeding with e-learning. Identify those leaders who you feel are most likely to come around and support e-learning, and provide opportunities for them to visit with their peers in other parts of your own business or at other companies (or invite leaders of best practices in other firms to visit your company) to see what e-learning can do. Give them some short business-oriented e-learning publications that address their chief concerns. Provide benchmarking data that indicates the efficacy of e-learning. Recommend a business conference where they can talk to their peers and experts about e-learning. Have them hear positive stories from people who have experienced e-learning themselves.

**4. Coach executives.** This is a little different from education. Here you are an adviser, helping the leader develop policy or strategy around e-learning. Some of the assistance you can provide includes:

- helping reprioritize learning initiatives
- creating the proper messages about e-learning
- preparing recommendations for the discontinuance of training and other programs that are no longer needed (this includes preparing the people associated with these programs for the change)
- developing motivational and incentive strategies that support the change
- helping with the business case

**5. Overcome prior perceptions.** If you're inside the training organization, chances are you're perceived as responsible for classroom training only. Repositioning yourself in an e-learning framework from an online training perspective is challenging enough, but convincing people that you can do knowledge management (and performance support) work is even tougher. Again, having a success story to showcase is a real boost. But you may also have to take people from where they are and help them understand where you're going. So if you get enthusiastic support from a business leader for traditional CBT, don't say no or "We don't do this anymore" so quickly. You may not find such a solid supporter elsewhere. See if you can begin with CBT but move to a more advanced strategy, educating your executive client along the way. It's OK to take one step backward if this will enable you to take many steps forward in the future.

Another useful strategy is to come at the issue from the perspective of the benefits of learning and e-learning. Talk about productivity, lower costs, etc., and deemphasize technology if you feel your audience is not ready for it. You may find more receptivity to a business approach than one centered on learning.

**6. Work the politics.** If you know a leader who's been pleased with the results from e-learning, ask him/her to spread the word for you with his/her peers. If you are a chief learning or knowledge officer, or have access to him/her, use the power of that office to set the tone about e-learning throughout the business. Training directors can also play a critical role by being the link between the operational issues of training (what they do) and the learning and development strategy of the business (what they can become). The key is finding and leveraging an e-learning champion—someone who is at the level of the people you need to convince. Peer-to-peer conversations can be instrumental in opening up the doors you need to get e-learning started and keep it sustained.

**7. Ignore the disbelievers.** Don't waste time trying to sell e-learning to those who don't want it or, worse, are bent on destroying it. Their resistance could be based on good intentions, genuine strategic disagreements, or personal issues such as fear of losing power. Many come around when they see the benefits. When senior management sees something that works and can be replicated, they'll be more likely to jump on board. However, there will always be some people whom you cannot convince of anything. If they are disruptive, you may have to deal with them, probably politically through your champions (although I have seen more direct approaches, such as asking hostile participants to leave a meeting, which almost always adds to the credibility of the meeting for those who remain). But if they simply ignore you, return the favor. There's plenty of work to be done with people who are willing to try something new.

## Leadership and Communication

In the end it all comes down to leadership. Whether you're on the front line or in a support position, in the executive suite or in the training organization, you need to find opportunities for leadership to emerge: leaders who can make a compelling case for e-learning and who can convince some groups to give it a try, leaders who are knowledgeable in the e-learning field but who also place the needs of the business at the center. Finding the right leader, or champion, is a critical step. Leaders must be able to chart a course without seeming dictatorial, and help the organization develop a shared vision about e-learning. They must also have the resources necessary to fund the e-learning initiative *and* the organizational clout to get it applied. The only thing worse than not being able to build a desperately needed e-learning solution is to actually build one only to find the organization for which it is intended is unwilling to use it.

> There is nothing more difficult to take in hand, more perilous to conduct, or more uncertain in its success than to take the lead in the introduction of a new order of things.
>
> —Machiavelli

With a leader in place, you set about evaluating and carefully reworking the organizational climate to create an environment that will support your initiative. Developing an effective communications plan will be an important element in this effort. Here are nine steps to follow to ensure that your communications are well received.

**1. Consolidate your strategy development.** Multiple e-learning strategies within an organization can create confusion and convey a lack of mission. It's best if you can establish an enterprisewide strategy. If not, work to create a seamless linkage between the efforts of each business unit or organization. Communication suffers if your audience perceives that there are multiple groups vying for their attention with virtually the same message. It gives the appearance of chaos, which will not help your efforts to change the learning culture.

**2. Trash old training communication vehicles.** Start fresh. If you're going to focus on e-learning, especially in the broader sense of online training and knowledge management, don't rely solely on your traditional training communication strategies, such as quarterly schedules, catalogs, or your training registration Web site. You don't want to create the perception that this is still the old training organization in a new suit of clothes. Communicate more from a business and learning perspective, and less from a training and course perspective.

**3. Use the Web to communicate.** This would be a good time for a new Web site that focuses on the relationship between learning, community, and business performance, with e-learning as a way to get there. Print, video, and other formats may have a role to play in your communications strategy, but make the Web your *primary* medium and create a seamless link between your Web-based communications and your e-learning portal. Don't just use the Web as an elaborate advertisement—the days of the Web as just "brochureware" are over. Add content and tools that can add immediate performance and business value to the user. And don't forget to use online communities as a way to get your message out.

**4. Avoid selling and focus on value.** People should not equate your communications as a sales pitch, especially if you have previously used the same vehicles to sell training classes and registrations. Clearly articulate your value proposition and demonstrate its worthiness to your clients and stakeholders. But be careful not to confuse the features of e-learning, which describe facts and characteristics (e.g., the technology allows instant updating for greater accuracy) with its benefits, which describe how it meets specific needs (e.g., people will be able to make faster, better, and more informed decisions). When the value of embracing your strategy is clear, usage will follow.

**5. Communicate value from the top down.** Get your sponsors involved in your communications. After all, if you've built management ownership, getting them to communicate your message should be easy (and, if they don't participate, it may be another sign of their marginal support). Communication from the top also lends credibility to your efforts to institute a learning culture. When Dell Computer found that many of its employees didn't have adequate Web experience, it launched a "Know the Net" campaign, championed by Michael Dell himself.

**6. Build support with coaches first.** Create a separate communications strategy for front-line managers, as their support is critical for workplace learning. Begin your work with them early, before the deployment of your e-learning initiatives—it will take some time to win them over. Use knowledge management to build a manager community (which can be more universally beneficial than just supporting a learning culture), and use that community to create heightened awareness of their role in supporting learning.

**7. Build and promote an initial win.** Center your communications around best practices and examples of what e-learning can accomplish. Showcase what you have already done, even if it's a small win, along with endorsements and testimonials of benefits and impact (from senior managers and learners, if possible). It's fine to back this up with more theoretical or conceptual "white papers" about e-learning, but don't lead with them. An "ivory tower" image is not helpful when you are trying to demonstrate your business value.

**8. Control external messages.** This is very important. All the while you are trying to communicate your message, you can be sure that outside vendors and consultants are also communicating to your target audience. These groups will certainly have a role to play in your strategy, but their sales messages must not create additional noise in your communications channel. Create a communications funnel through which all messages will be filtered before passing them through to your audience. You may not be able to stop vendors from sending literature and e-mail to your stakeholders and clients, but you can work with them to be sure that what is said is supportive of where you're headed as a business. This is not an easy task, but it is important for the effectiveness of your overall communications plan.

**9. Encourage Web savvy.** Create messages that tell employees that the Internet/intranet is just as much of a work tool as the telephone or the computer. The more people use a new technology, the more comfortable they become with it—and the more comfortable they'll be with online training and knowledge management. Remove barriers like charging for use or restricting access to only senior departmental managers. If the Web is abused, deal with it as a supervisory and performance issue, not as a technology or a learning issue. For most people, if they're motivated to work, the Internet shouldn't prove any more of a distraction than anything else in the workplace—the technology will become transparent.

## Why a Successful E-Learning Strategy Needs an Effective Change Strategy

Preparing your business for a shift to e-learning requires that you build your learning culture, find and leverage your champions, and create sound, value-based communications. But these efforts cannot be accomplished haphazardly. The best way to approach these important issues is through a systematic change strategy, often referred to as "change management."

Change management focuses on ensuring that an organization and its people are committed and capable of executing a business plan. It involves establishing an environment for change, enabling high performance, and sustaining workforce commitment over the long haul. It is about moving an organization toward its goals by improving the performance, productivity, speed, flexibility, and motivation of the workforce, and about building the capabilities of business leaders to lead sustainable change.

From an e-learning perspective, many change management techniques have already been discussed within the culture, champions, and communications strategies presented. But in order to know precisely where to target your efforts, it's important to determine the readiness of the organization to accept e-learning.

The question of acceptance has three dimensions.

First, there is the issue of motivation. Are people supportive of this change or are they inclined to create roadblocks? Before you introduce your first e-learning communication, and especially before the first e-learning solution is deployed, conduct a readiness assessment. Look at your stakeholders, from executives and front-line managers to your target audience. Listen carefully to what they say about a particular change. Assess their attitudes and willingness to try this new approach.

Understand why people are resistant to e-learning. Look not just at the outward symptoms (e.g., refusal to participate, demands for reinstatement of classroom training), but at the underlying causes as well (e.g., loss of attending training as a reward, fear of technology, supervisor distrust of learning on the job, fear or inability to learn without help). As stated previously, sometimes people appear resistant when in fact they are simply following a different path that seems better for them—you're not even on their radar screen. Use your champions and communications plan to help turn change avoiders into change acceptors. Target specific messages about your value proposition to the specific groups having problems making the transition. Provide extra help along the way, especially peer-to-peer support. Create the right incentives (monetary or otherwise) that will encourage participation. And finally, make the new way easier and more comfortable than the old.

> The problem is not how to get new thoughts into your mind, but how to get the old ones out.
>
> —Nancy Austin, coauthor of
> *A Passion for Excellence:*
> *The Leadership Difference*

Second is the issue of competence. Do people have the skills and knowledge to successfully engage in e-learning initiatives? We've suggested that the learning curve for the Web is pretty quick, but that doesn't mean people won't need some help. This is especially true if computers are new to the work. For example, when computer technology was first introduced into manufacturing, workers resisted because they didn't believe that technology could equal their artisanship. When this was overcome, most workers needed extensive training on how to use the new tools. Once they were comfortable with these new systems, learning additional systems was significantly easier. So don't simply plop computers down in the workplace where they haven't been before and expect everyone to rush to use them. Remember that you are radically changing the work environment as well as the learning environment. Plan for this and take some time. Keep in mind the importance of motivation—involve people in the change as much as possible.

The third issue is one of resources. If you are going to introduce e-learning into the workplace, be sure everyone has access and that the technology is adequate to make the experience worthwhile rather than painful. And be sure there is enough money and other resources to sustain the program over the long haul. You don't want to reorient people to e-learning only to have budgets cut, forcing everyone to go back to the way they used to learn. If this happens, your next try will be far more difficult.

## Four Additional Rules of Change

In addition to culture, champions, and communications, if you're introducing e-learning into the organization, follow these four additional rules to ease the transition.

**1. Don't put change management off until deployment.** The longer you wait to implement effective change management in support of e-learning, the greater the likelihood that the e-learning initiative will fail. Graph A in Figure 1 shows what can happen if the change strategy is implemented simultaneously with an e-learning initiative. In this scenario, the introduction of e-learning causes work disruption, which is natural with any major change. But because the supporting change management intervention was not introduced until deployment, it can take a significant amount of time to turn things around. And, in some cases, a change strategy may be introduced so late in the game that the e-learning initiative will not recover. However, an early focus on the human dimensions of change ensures employee readiness and ability and the highest business impact.

Graph B in Figure 1 shows the beneficial impact of deploying a change strategy in advance of any e-learning initiative. In this scenario, the change strategy is deployed *in advance* of the e-learning intervention. People have the information and especially the time to get ready. There's still a dip in performance and other issues as e-learning is introduced, but it is far less severe. Recovery is quicker and acceptance over the long term is more assured.

**2. One size doesn't fit all.** Don't assume that everybody needs the same approach to helping them accept change. Senior executives will likely respond to a different strategy (perhaps observing best practices or benchmarking their peers in other companies) than rank-and-file workers (who may be more interested in what's in it for them). Front-line managers, who are key "change leaders," will also require special attention.

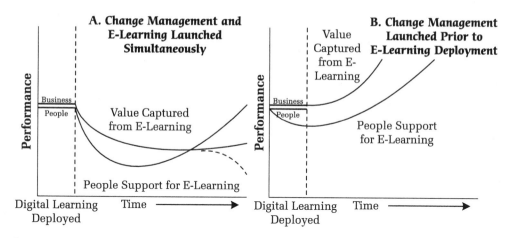

**Figure 1.** *Delaying change management until e-learning is deployed can jeopardize the entire initiative, but launching a change management initiative prior to e-learning implementation can enhance its success.*

**3. Focus on change from start to finish—and beyond.** Acceptance of change cannot be accomplished in one- or two- hour meetings scheduled the day before your e-learning solution is deployed. Not only is starting early important, but to prevent old behaviors from reemerging, the change strategy must be maintained long enough so this new way of learning becomes the *preferred* way of learning.

**4. Be open and don't oversell.** Don't hide critical information from employees or assume they can't be trusted. Don't whitewash the real reasons, probably economic and business related, why classroom training has been replaced with e-learning. Don't portray e-learning unrealistically or create unnecessary hype that employees will recognize as just propaganda. Tout benefits for the company and benefits for employees, and be honest about the increased responsibility e-learning makes on individuals.

## How Dell Creates an E-Learning Culture

Dell Computer Corporation is a high-tech company, full of young, computer-savvy employees. Yet even in this environment, the classroom is still an icon of learning. To create a culture where people will accept e-learning, Dell Learning, the company's training organization, and Dell regional training organizations combine technology with some aspects of the "old school." When a new program or tool is released on the Web, it is sometimes introduced in a nonthreatening classroom situation to help people feel more comfortable with it. This results in higher levels of use on the job.

Dell did a thorough analysis of why many people prefer classroom training and turn away from Web-based CBT. One of the reasons cited most often is the need for, or lack of, feedback—from the instructor and from each other. So the company built a variety of feedback and coaching mechanisms into each e-learning component—both instructional and informational. From simple quizzes and practice exercises to role-playing and extensive simulations in a "safe" environment, getting people engaged is the key. In every product there are opportunities to check understanding. Even more static Web sites use some feedback to create a level of interactivity and "stickiness" (i.e., getting learners to come back to the site as needed). People aren't forced to do exercises, but they can use them if they're concerned about their mastery of the content.

Meeting the requirements of senior management is not enough; often there is a wide chasm between what managers and users think is needed. Basing an e-learning solution on what people say should be done, rather than what is actually done, often dooms the program because it is unauthentic. So Dell brings end-users into the development process in the beginning. By ensuring that both groups are intimately involved in development, the company ensures that each solution bridges any potential "divide" between the company's strategic initiatives and what individual contributors actually do on a daily basis.

Each Dell e-learning solution is prototyped and tested repeatedly. Whereas most companies conduct alpha and beta tests, Dell goes further, putting the program out to the field for users to "try out" and comment on its usability and value. Targeted end-users can provide comments on the program during the user-acceptance testing (UAT) period. By the time the solution is put into production, many end-users have already had some experience with it.

Dell also has deployed a competency assessment system where employees can rate their skills (and be rated by their managers and peers). The results form the basis of an appropriate e-learning solution customized to the user and designed to address specific deficiencies. By linking personal development with e-learning, Dell has found that employees see a direct benefit of each program. Larger deployments are usually preceded by a communications initiative to let people know what's coming. Finally, every effort has been made to help managers create an atmosphere where learning is a legitimate part of the workday. At Dell, many call center representatives, for example, have time set aside for learning—time when they don't have to be on the phones.

None of Dell's techniques for creating e-learning acceptance are a radical departure from its culture. Dell's tagline is to "Be Direct," and most e-learning solutions eliminate unnecessary instructors, processes, and other impediments in the process. Dell uses thorough implementation of good instructional design and user testing to create a quality product and good communication to help everyone understand its benefits. The key is using these techniques systemically, rather than haphazardly, so that they are ingrained in the e-learning development process.

# Knowledge Management as a Facilitator of Change at AT&T

Learning has always been a powerful tool in the facilitation of change, and e-learning can be especially useful in large change situations. Take one of the most disruptive changes that can befall a company—a merger or acquisition. For each partner in a merger, or for the acquirer and the acquired, the ability to handle change can mean the difference between success and failure.

One good example can be seen when AT&T acquired the cable company TCI. While AT&T was a huge, primarily centrally controlled global business, the local cable franchises were much more independent, having themselves been acquired over the years. And while AT&T faces significant competitive challenges, many of these franchises were, for a long time, sole providers in their geographic areas, having signed multiyear contracts with local governments. Each franchisee had its own way of doing business, its own accounting and billing systems as well as divergent methods and procedures for operating its business.

So the task of building a unified, nationwide broadband communications network required the merging of two cultures. Each time a local cable market was "launched," it was critical that any problems experienced were not repeated in the next launch. In addition, it was also important to capitalize on the best practices that were uncovered. Valuable insight and information needed to be shared by subsequent markets. The company wanted a way to share learning so the team would get better and smarter. The result was a *Lessons Learned* knowledge management (KM) system.

While people were always encouraged to post on the intranet what they learned as they went through a conversion, it was mostly a lot of information provided by well-meaning individuals who had no format and no framing to guide them. This clearly wasn't working, as each posting was written differently and at a different level of detail.

The new knowledge management solution did two things. First, it allowed users to submit a lesson learned via a template/input tool that was easy to use and ensured that each contribution would be in the same format and depth. The tool also enabled the filtering of some invalid content, such as gripes and rumors. Each contribution was automatically sent to an SME for validation prior to publication on the site.

The other part of the KM system was a knowledge retrieval tool for searching the Lessons Learned repository to find information of direct value to the user. This helped reduce information overload and helped create a stronger sense of community among the teams moving from market to market.

The results of this project have been invaluable in reducing occurrences of "reinventing the wheel" and in providing everyone with access to best practices.

But there were other findings from this work that have implications for any e-learning deployment. First, don't assume that everyone has access to the Internet. It's important to balance "e-enabling" with reality. In this case, field installers didn't have access on the job, nor did some of the technicians on the cable company side. So the KM system allows people to phone or fax in their contributions. Second, it's important to provide people with the incentives and time to use the system. Just because it's on the server doesn't mean anybody will use it—or value it. When workers are in crisis mode, learning in any form can take a back seat, if you're not careful. Third, identify the project's owner. In the early stages of this project, no one was held accountable for the project, so it was virtually ignored. Now that the project is part of the charter of the national rollout team, people are taking notice.

Like every other effort, this example of e-learning (knowledge management) being used to facilitate positive change could not be successful without the correct incentives, support, and access. But because these issues were identified and leveraged appropriately, the system works.

## What About the Training Organization Itself?

This chapter has dealt primarily with introducing e-learning into an organization and the obstacles that can get in the way or kill it. But one of the major obstacles can be the misguided assumptions, confusion, reticence, or downright anti-e-learning position of the training department itself.

### An E-Learning Journey

#### Leading an Organization Through the Change to E-Learning

When I came to Lucent in 1998 to lead the group responsible for training a global sales and technician force, as well as our external customers, I found the Denver-based organization in pretty good shape, with a solid reputation for quality training. But I also knew that to succeed globally, and to remain competitive, we had to be more nimble, more responsive, and more flexible than ever before. In a nutshell, we had to get faster and get better while at the same time lowering our costs. So I knew that some significant changes were necessary. I think the staff knew it, too, although there was a lot of uncertainty as to how to get there.

With the long tradition of quality classroom training, the organization also had a lot of experience in technology-based learning, most notably in satellite delivery, as well as CD-ROM and traditional CBT. (We're currently using outbound satellite broadcasting to hundreds of downlinks worldwide, with an Internet-based connection back for interactivity; and we intend to move to the Web as broadband capabilities are deployed in our company.) This technology would enable us to be the connecting point for anyone in the business who wanted to reach a worldwide audience of employees, resellers, or customers. We needed to make our messages easy to understand and easy to access. If we were just going to do satellite-based training, the transition would have been easier. After all, we were already doing that—we just needed to do more and make it interactive. But I recognized that we also had an opportunity and an obligation to use learning technology to deliver information—such as product announcements, competitive intelligence, technical briefings and manuals—in addition to training.

I began to talk about the power of moving beyond just training, of using technology to provide a wide range of informational services as well. While many folks on my team understood where we needed to go, others were confused. So were our stakeholders and clients. We not only had to deal with issues of reducing our classroom training offerings, we also had to explain this broader mission. Resistance surfaced and the natural "antibodies" began to form. If our mission was to succeed and if we were to survive, I had to deal with the technological and the people side of change simultaneously.

I took a strategic business approach, not an educational approach, to explain the road ahead. I talked less about training and training issues and more about the state of our business. I repeatedly asked everyone to see beyond their jobs, to understand how we impact the company and what the company expects of us. If there was confusion, we would clear it up. Nobody should be in the dark about the direction we're going, and we set out to address this on day one.

I had prior experience in organizational change (at US WEST and IBM, among other companies) and that experience was invaluable. I worked to understand the culture that I came into. It was very powerful and I had to respect it. I never denigrated training or the training profession. I never led anyone to believe that it was a second-tier job in the company. Once people realized that I was not here to destroy them, they opened up. I was bringing in a new perspective, but I was not just passing through to get my ticket punched. I was in the same profession as they were and I was going to stay around for a while. I began to ask questions like "What could we become?" and "How do we create our future?" In addition to being a practitioner in this field and having good business acumen, I think leaders need a change orientation and an open mind.

I worked to create the context and the frame of reference that would enable people to hear my message. I elevated professional development to an activity of high importance. I asked everyone to focus on the training marketplace as hard as they focused on the telecom marketplace.

We used force field analysis to identify opportunities for initial e-learning and "e-information" wins. We looked for people who wanted to do things differently and partnered with them; we didn't force ourselves on anyone. We'd take small victories if necessary—we knew that a couple of small wins were better than one big disaster. We turned bad news into opportunities. When companies issue the dreaded financial emergency-induced "travel ban," it normally sends waves of panic throughout training organizations. But what if we could respond quickly with e-learning solutions that negated the client's travel problems? We found a few partners that liked this idea, and we worked with them—quietly, until we had the successes we needed.

The results? We've gone from having to sell ourselves to worrying about being able to meet all the demand for our e-learning services. It's no longer a matter of me convincing anyone; it's now a matter of me keeping up with the growing requirements of our clients. Greater needs in shorter time frames. We have to deliver, and we do.

So in turning an organization around to e-learning and expanding its mission and value proposition, I recommend a strategy based on performance. Low-key it in the beginning, but move quickly. There is a window of opportunity between when a need is recognized and when a client will move past you to another solution. Create a sense of urgency and take some risks. There's not a whole lot of this around, but you cannot play it safe and make this transformation. Solutions create opportunities for more work and more solutions. You grow on your reputation. Then you cross the line between hanging by a thread and being invaluable. It's a great feeling and you'll know it when you get there.

As we become more invaluable every day, there are some lessons we've learned along the way. First, quality instructional design is paramount. No matter what technology or business pressures you have, you can't cheat on quality. Second, people want options and choices; there's no single answer. Create multiple opportunities to help end-users enhance their performance. Think about them having many needs. Third, think "no boundaries." From the classroom to being a part of the knowledge supply chain, you can't allow artificial barriers (between training and information) to get in your way. Fourth, develop your people. Seeding is an important tool. Bring in new people who think differently and who have different approaches. They can stimulate change. I think the fact that I was from outside the company was helpful here. Finally, focus on collaboration as a key responsibility of leadership.

When I interviewed for this position, I was told that Lucent had great managers in this business and that any number of them could manage the training function very well. But that wasn't what they were looking for. They wanted a new perspective and new ideas, someone who could help them understand how the resource could be used differently. When I came on board, I was perceived with fear. No one knew what my agenda was. I focused on leading the change effort as my initial and most important objective. I let my performance, and the performance of our organization, speak for itself, and people have changed their point of view. They've come around to a new way of thinking—an appreciation of the progress we've made together.

*—Raymond L. Vigil, Ph.D., Vice President of Avaya, Inc. (formerly part of Lucent Technologies) and leader of Avaya University. Previously at Lucent, Ray ran the Learning Solutions organization in the firm's Enterprise Networks business unit. (rvigil@avaya.com)*

## Notes

1. *The Learning Alliance: Systems Thinking in Human Resource Development.* San Francisco: Jossey-Bass, 1994, p. 57.
2. April 3, 2000, p. 154.

*Dr. Marc J. Rosenberg is a senior principal with DiamondCluster International (www.diamondcluster.com), a premier business strategy and technology solutions firm. He is the author of the best-selling book,* E-Learning: Strategies for Delivering Knowledge in the Digital Age *(McGraw-Hill, 2001). Dr. Rosenberg is a past president of the International Society for Performance Improvement (ISPI) and holds a Ph.D. in instructional design, plus degrees in communications and marketing. He has spoken a the White House, keynoted numerous professional and business conferences, and authored more than 30 articles in the field. He is a frequently quoted expert in major business and trade publications. You can reach him at marc.rosenberg@diamondcluster.com.*

# How to Keep
# E-Learners from
# E-scaping

## Jim Moshinskie

*Success of e-learning using the newest technologies depends on the oldest factor, the root of all learning—motivation. This article reviews research, presents a model for developing motivation, and offers recommendations.*

Corporations implementing e-learning projects are quickly discovering that surprisingly high attrition rates are occurring. Motorola University, one of the first major corporate universities to establish an extensive online curriculum, found that a significant gap existed between employees that had registered for online courses as compared to their actual completion (Good, 2000). Reports such as these have led corporate trainers to rethink their e-learning strategies and revisit the timeless question of how to motivate learners to take a course, learn the material, and then transfer that knowledge back to the worksite.

Motivation to learn can be expressed as the attention and effort required to complete a learning task and then apply the new material to the worksite (Esque and McCausland, 1997). Generally, learners fall into one of two categories when it comes to motivation:

1. **People with an active attitude towards life.** Consciously or unconsciously, they look upon their lives as a process of continuous learning. In general, they are active and enterprising with a strong intrinsic motivation to learn. They hardly need extrinsic motivations and might even feel restricted by certain

aspects of them. Consequently they often have clear-cut ideas about the route of learning and are ready to organize and structure it themselves.

2. **People with a more passive attitude towards life.** They prefer to be guided rather than taking the initiative to learn. Because of an initial lack of intrinsic motivation and consequently a reluctant approach towards learning, extrinsic motivation becomes a key issue for them especially as a "starter" to overcome what often presents itself as an initial barrier.

To apply the appropriate treatment, it is advisable to discover from the beginning (through a questionnaire, for example) to which group a potential learner belongs. Several self-scoring inventories exist for determining a learner's locus of control. (For an online example, see www.rexgatto.com.)

This paper focuses on creating extrinsic motivational techniques to complement the intrinsic needs of your learners. It was developed by members of the eLITE (e-Learning Incites Training Excellence), a weekly web-based training think tank that includes performance improvement technologists from two educational organizations and eight corporations. Based on a review of literature and on lessons learned from their e-learning projects, the eLITE members developed a motivational model for online courses, as shown in Figure 1. Using this model, the group devised a process to improve extrinsic motivation before, during, and after online courses, as summarized in Table 1.

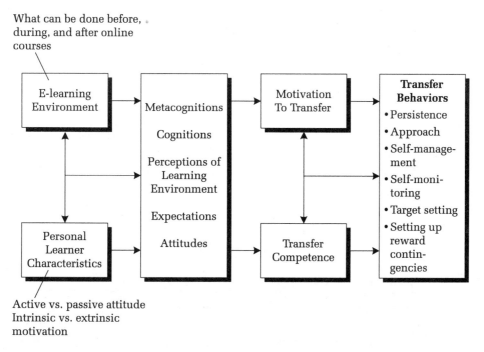

**Figure 1.** The motivational model developed for this paper

| | Before Learning | During Learning | After Learning |
|---|---|---|---|
| **Instructional Designer/ Developer** | Understand learner and environmental needs. | Provide learning opportunities to match specific learner needs. | Evaluate degree of success. Encourage learner reflection on what and how learning addressed needs. |
| **Manager** | Contribute to designer's understanding of content and learner needs. | Support and reinforce learning efforts. | Provide environment conducive to application of new skills. Congratulate learner on completion of the course. Reward efforts at application of skills. |
| **Learner** | Actively participate in development plans. Prepare for learning activity (pre-work, etc). Express learning (value) preferences so they can be addressed. | Actively relate learning to potential work application. | Review what was learned. Find and request ways to apply what was learned. Give input on how lesson can be improved. |

**Table 1.** Process to improve intrinsic motivation

Motivation for job-related e-learning can be influenced through steps taken at different points in time. In addition, it is useful to note that those in the different *roles* of the learning process are in the position to take the steps most appropriate at particular points in time.

These extrinsic events are not just individual elements acting independently, but rather are synergistic, combining to create a dynamic, exciting environment. These elements may alternatively or additionally heighten the perceived relevance of the learning activity or create urgency to complete it. The objective is to create an external instructional environment that enhances the learner's internal interpretation of the environment, and thereby provides the motivation necessary to start, continue, and finish online training (Clark, 1999).

## Before the Online Course

While many managers try to save time—and money—by insisting that the instructional team jump right into instructional design activities, most performance improvement technologists can attest readily to the necessity of a thorough front-end analysis (FEA). During the needs analysis stage for online instructional interventions, focus on these key points:

**Find the real needs.** One emerging message in today's information-rich e-learning environments is that employees must see how the training directly addresses their real needs in the workplace. Therefore, develop instructional objectives that demonstrate the usefulness of instruction matched with authentic exercises and concrete examples directly applicable to their daily struggles within the workplace. The course should contain goals with specific standards of performance that can be completed in a short time. It should match the learner's ability level and blatantly answer: *"What's in it for me?"*

**Involve key stakeholders.** Research shows that a supportive work environment motivates learners to transfer the new knowledge to the workplace (Broad, 1997). Successful organizations know that key stakeholders such as managers, trainers, and peers must closely participate in all phases of instructional design and then support the learners when the online training occurs. Managers and peers will be needed later to help fellow trainees avoid information overload anxiety by becoming active coaches and creating opportunities for practice and feedback by using collaborative technologies such as chat, voice chat, and discussion threads.

**Match the learner's values and motives.** McClelland (1984) suggests that the notions of the need for power, achievement, or affiliation serve as the primary levers in explaining performance variations among individuals. Instruments to measure values, motives, and learning styles have existed for many years and are not usually part of the assessment and design of face-to-face (F2F) learning events, let alone distance learning. In the case of web-based training, it may be critical that an understanding of the general value set mix of learners be established prior to design and delivery.

Both values and motives relate to behavior, but in different ways, as shown in Table 2. Values often influence people's choices about where to invest their energies, while motives reflect how much pleasure people get out of certain activities such as being with people (high need for affiliation), doing better at challenging tasks (high need for achievement), or having impact or influence on others (high need for power). Table 3 presents some possible activities to engage learners' value orientations. While assessing the discrete mix of all learning groups may prove impractical, planning some activities that support different value orientations will increase the energy and enjoyment of the learner and may lead to greater completion rates.

**Prepare the work environment.** Make certain the workplace is prepared to support the completion of training and the application of new knowledge and skills. Tactics include simple housekeeping issues like making sure learners have web

| Values | Motives |
| --- | --- |
| Choose areas of importance | Natural drives |
| Conscious level | Unconscious |
| Help an individual make decisions in current time | Predict types of behaviors a person will gravitate toward over time |
| Adaptive–developed from experiences throughout one's life | Basic–influenced by early emotional experiences and perhaps genetic |
| Less difficult to change | More difficult to change |

**Table 2.** A comparison of values and motives

| Goal | Power | Achievement | Affiliation |
| --- | --- | --- | --- |
| **Tapping into the Value Attribute** | Believe that completing the learning event will make them more successful in influencing others. | Believe that the learning event will contribute to their success in the future. | See the learning group as referent. Should identify with other learners in the event. |
| **Tapping into the Motive Attribute** | May enjoy the learning more if they have the opportunity to direct or support the activities of others within the learning event | May enjoy the learning more if they are given feedback on their progress in attaining goals during learning events. | May enjoy the learning more if they have the opportunity to work with others and develop increased rapport. |

**Table 3.** Matching value and motive attributes to the primary levers of learner motivation

access and a quiet place to work. Ensure it is viewed as acceptable or safe to participate in training during working hours, if this is the case. Supervisors and managers should know the content to be covered (and ideally have completed the online course themselves). Train the supervisors on how to effectively coach and reinforce desired application of new knowledge and skills on the job.

**Consider both push and pull strategies.** Push strategies include requiring and monitoring training completion. An advantage of many learning management systems (LMS) is that they allow real-time tracking and reporting of training participation. Informing learners of this fact and having managers recognize early completers and alert laggards that their absence of participation is visible to management will often promote higher participation and completion rates. The principle here is to set an expectation and to "inspect what you expect."

Pull strategies, on the other hand, attempt to inspire rather than require the learner to complete the e-learning. Communication and promotion of the learning experience are among the most effective pull strategies. Remember, people will not complete training if they do not know it is available. Communications can take place through any medium or combination of media, e.g., emails and newsletters. Conoco University distributed colorful mousepads that advertised the course web address on them.

To be effective, your promotional literature should include one or more of these motivational strategies:

1. **Focus on results.** Tell learners what they will be able to accomplish by completing the e-learning. If possible, share success stories from alumni.

2. **Focus on ensuring success.** Stress that the e-learning was designed around situations and needs of people like them, so it will be immediately applicable to them. Also, inform learners that the e-learning is structured so that successful completion is well within their capabilities. Remember, fear of the unknown and fear of failure are significant barriers to training participation for many people as the Conoco University learned (sidebar, "Conoco's University's 'Business Literacy' Course"). Consider sharing testimonials from other learners who had similar fears or doubts before they attempted the e-learning.

3. **Enhance the importance of the learning process.** Many learners are more motivated if they know a learning experience is endorsed by senior executives or recognized experts, is accredited or earns credit toward a degree or industry credentials, or earns tangible rewards, points or other perks. Cover such facts in e-learning announcements.

4. **Highlight the topics of interest.** Even the most reluctant learners may be more motivated to participate in e-learning when they know a topic that interests them will be covered.

5. **Include non-instructional strategies**. The non-instructional approaches to motivation can be of monetary or non-monetary nature. Monetary compensation includes salary adjustments, perks, differential pay, time off with pay, or gifts. Non-monetary compensation includes improved working conditions, new tools and equipment, awards, and career opportunities (Thiagarajan, Estes, and Kemmerer, 1999).

   If the effort will be tied to a certification system that clearly delineates to the workers what activities they need for advancement, motivation seems to increase. Other motivators to consider include admittance to a follow-up classroom event in a desired location such as a resort, maintenance of current certification, peer pressure, and peer recommendations, that is, respected peers speaking highly of the training.

6. **Provide a learning portal**. The instructional team can create corporate-specific learning portals (or learning management systems) which serve as an entry point for the intended audience. Learning portals can be dynamically generated using a combination of employee profiles, pre-tests, and self-selection of topics of interest. The portal then presents to the employee a customized list of learning opportunities that are relevant to their level, responsibilities, and advancement goals, thereby increasing their motivation to take and complete courses specific to their development needs. These may include relevant company-offered courses, both classroom and distance learning, conferences, university degree programs offered online, virtual discussion groups, virtual presentations, and online clipping services. This site should include not only the courses available, but also list any monetary and non-monetary awards as well.

---

### Conoco University's "Business Literacy" Course

Conoco University learned an important cultural lesson when it implemented its online Business Literacy course to 15,000 employees in 42 countries in 1999.

Sandy Staton, the project leader, discovered that employees in some cultures resisted starting the course if they thought failure was a possibility and they might "lose face." Therefore, how many times the student had to take the course to get a passing score was not recorded. Only when the student passed the course was a certificate printed and put in the employee file. Thus, no employee "lost face."

This project won the 2000 Award of Excellence from the International Society for Performance Improvement.

(Source: Sandy Staton, University of Conoco, 2000)

---

## During the Online Course

As the learner takes the online course, several strategies can be used to create and maintain motivation. These include:

**Maintain a conducive environment.** Increased motivation can be directly related to how the learner is impacted by environmental factors, people support, learning design strategy, and ease of use when it comes to technology infrastructures.

Environmental factors such as a physical location conducive for learning (minimal noise interruptions), access to appropriate materials (library and handouts), time to engage in the activity (think time), and a profile approach to specific content needs are included in the framework. Another aspect of this framework is support from people within and outside of an organization. Online learning with peers, teams, facilitators, and subject matter experts in dynamic synchronous and asynchronous communities also provide a robust and engaging experience to increase learner motivation and retention. Positive support from management through rewards and incentives is also a key enabler to improved learner motivation. David Weekley Homes, a Houston-based homebuilder, distributes miniature, bright orange "Mind at Work" construction cones that employees place on their computer monitors while taking online training. This alerts others not to bother them unnecessarily during the training. David Weekley Homes' first course, which earned a 2001 Award of Excellence from ISPI, garnered a 86% completion rate (http://hsb.baylor.edu/html/mo/portfolio).

**Chunk the information.** When instruction is divided into compact, 20-minute or less learning chunks, also referred to as learning objects or learning bytes, the material can be effectively presented to the learner in a digestible fashion. The instructional design of this learning chunk should focus on the ROPES communications model, which includes a review of prerequisites, an overview of objectives, interactive presentation of new material, job-related exercises, and a brief summary (Moshinskie, 2000). In this process, the "need to know" must be clearly separated from the "nice to know."

**Build on the familiar.** Learners become motivated by lessons that incorporate their beliefs and examples of things they can relate to handily. The online learning should tie the instruction to the learners' prior knowledge and experience so learners can build on what they already know. Learners will accept moderate amounts of unfamiliar content, but the designer should incorporate analogies with familiar content frequently (Gagné and Medsker, 1996).

**Vary the stimulus.** Online learners cannot stay motivated by turning pages on the web. Borrowing from videogame makers and movie directors, you can vary information presentation and stimulations using audio, video, animations, and well-told stories. Courses should include a variety of interactions, such as puzzles, case studies, scenarios, and simulations that directly engage learners (Norman, 1993). While online courses can recommend what path to take, learners should be able to stray from it to pursue their own interests and make their own discoveries (Gibson, 2000).

**Give legitimate feedback.** Letting employees know how well they are learning the content and performing the new task acts as an incentive for greater effort. In other technology-based courses, especially CD-ROM courses, learners ignored praise when it was overstated (e.g., *Great Job!*). Therefore, use the data-gathering capabilities of the web to provide user-specific advice based on analyzing their performances electronically and in real time (Dempsey and Sales, 1993). This information can also be used to provide unrequested help when learners are faltering, especially early in the instruction. The goal should be to focus on their ongoing performance, and not the score alone. Although the web has the ability to present a global classroom with many students, feedback should be on the individual's progress and not comparisons with other learners (Clark, 1999).

**Provide the human touch.** Just as a trainer in the corporate classroom can provide visible extrinsic presence and support, the online environment needs to also encourage and help cyber learners. Chat rooms, email, electronic office hours, audio streaming, and on-line mentoring can supply the human touch—not only from the trainer but also from fellow students as well. Motorola University assigned support staff to first time learners to keep them on track (sidebar, "Motorola University").

---

### Motorola Unversity

How did Motorola improve its e-learning completion rates? Here are some lessons learned:

1. Assign learning guides to first-time learners. As the human contact for e-learners, learning guides provide a social touch to the online experience by answering questions and keeping the e-learners in contact with any support staff for technology or content requirements during the first two to four weeks.  This has greatly improved completion rates of online interventions.

2. Motorola also learned that the actual learning strategy design also contributes to a more positive experience to maintain motivation by ensuring acceptable usability standards, interactivity, and adaptive paths based on learner response.

3. The actual technology infrastructure must be optimized for the e-learner. Installation and access, system throughput, and equipment availability must be readily apparent and easy for the e-learner. The level and degree of integrated and implementation of any one of these components (environment, people support, design strategy, and technology infrastructure) will impact learner motivation.

(Source: Chris Good, Motorola University, 2000)

---

**Provide a social context.** Because web-based training can be presented to globally dispersed employees, the performance improvement technologist will need to pay attention to the cultural demographics of the learners. Use non-cultural metaphors that all learners will understand and do not offend a global audience (Horton, 1999).

**Build opportunities for fun.** Although, according to Maslow, the need to play games or to have fun is probably located more to the end of our hierarchy of motives, there is something about people which requires more than a purely mechanistic approach to learning (O'Connor, Bronner, and Delaney, 1996). Therefore, we should build in opportunities for learners to have fun, but having fun is a rather complex phenomenon. Items involved in including fun within a course include:

- Curiosity and attraction—technical elements, e.g., an animated sequence with sound, to grab the learner's attention and stimulate interest in the course.
- Feeling well—This is the result of a combination of psychological and physical stimuli. Psychologically the players—or learners—need assertion, assurance, and being told that they are doing well.
- Success—Learners need success, but they also need to be challenged. Challenge means competition—either with oneself (facing and solving problems) or with others (finding out who is the best). In either case there are winners and losers. However, the ratio between winning and losing is important. If the challenge is too easy it doesn't provide the "kick." Not enough adrenaline (which is a physical stimulus for feeling well) is produced. Feeling bored could lead to a breakoff. If the challenge is too difficult, the frustration will outscore the initial benefits and might, again, eventually lead to a breakoff. This points to a direct connection between the degree of challenge or the kind of competition and the completion of a game or a course.
- Time passing quickly—The subjective perception of how quickly time passes during a game or a lesson of a study course could serve as an indicator of how well the cocktail of challenges was mixed.

**Make it timely.** Provide learners with easy and immediate access to the content. This aspect of "just-in-time" learning maximizes the motivational aspect of training by providing content at the moment of need. The corporate learning portal should allow quick access to all available course offerings, pre-assessment tools, suggested roadmaps, and search capabilities to other web-based courses that fit the learners' needs. Courses can also be linked to the firm's online knowledge bases, providing access to the latest initiatives, firm publications, news releases, and methodologies.

**Stimulate curiosity.** When we make our learners curious, they exhibit a higher desire to know more about a topic (Gagné and Medsker, 1996). Some of this curiosity can be provided by using today's web-based technology that allows audio and video streaming to stimulate the learner's sensory curiosity. Search engines, hyperlinking, online brainstorming that incorporates instant messaging, and online chat including voice chat can encourage cognitive curiosity. Additionally, when developing interactions, the instructional designer needs to include real people and concrete events rather than abstractions. When the University of Toyota teamed with Baylor University and VuePoint Learning System to create its first online pilot course (Zienstra, 1999), each module began with a realistic scenario that involved employees facing a problem that they would likely see in the workplace (Figure 2).

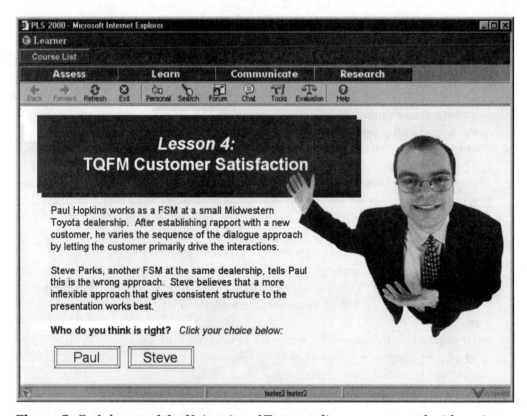

**Figure 2.** Each lesson of the University of Toyota online course opened with an interesting question to motivate the learner to take that lesson
Courtesy of Bob Zienstra, University of Toyota, and VuePoint Performance Learning System (www.vuepoint.com)

## After the Online Course

Even when the learner completes the online course, motivational strategies can also improve the transfer of training back to the workplace. Several key strategies can be particularly effective:

**Celebrate successful completion.** When the learners complete a course, special effort should be taken to congratulate them. A personalized congratulatory email from the instructor helps. Placing their name on the learning portal or in the company online newsletter may make successful graduates pleased and motivate those who have not yet finished. In the University of Toyota course, those who completed the course became eligible to go to Los Angeles for realistic sales-training exercises with fellow graduates. Your company's employee privacy policies may limit how much of this you can do.

**Provide support when the learner returns to the workplace.** The trainer's responsibility does not end when the learner completes the course. Tactics to foster transfer of learning in the workplace include:

- Encourage an environment of continuous learning where new ideas are advocated and welcomed,
- Connect trainees to other successful users,
- Provide clear expectations of how they will implement the new content at their jobsite—and be evaluated later, *and*
- Tag those who complete the training as online learning "experts" who serve as valuable mentors to other employees who are taking the training. Such "flag and tag" procedures motivate both the learner and the employee who now serves as a recognized online coach (Esque and McCausland, 1997).

**Reinforce the learning.** Follow-up to the training ensures that the skills or knowledge learned is not lost. One way is to communicate the key learning achievements to the learner's supervisor. This allows the supervisor to observe the application of this knowledge and reinforce its use. Periodic reinforcement acts as a reward system that acknowledges the effort required to incorporate new skills into your daily activities. Communication with the learner on a regular basis after the course helps the learner to focus on applying the content. This may take the form of a questionnaire exploring how they were able to apply the content or scheduled alumni chat sessions to discuss further courses and application.

**View e-learning as a process not an event.** Most traditional instructor-led training is viewed as an event. After the class ends, the student has a tendency not to think about the material again because the training event is over. Online learning should be viewed as a process. A good e-learning course includes well-designed content for the core modules as well as complementary and supplementary material that aids the learners in their day-to-day tasks at work. Moreover, coaches and virtual mentors can provide support before, during, and after a learner has completed an e-learning course using communications technology available over the web.

In addition, EPSS, or electronic performance support systems, have returned in popularity due to the just-in-time/just enough nature of online learning. These types of systems are very effective in providing learning, assessment, and job support.

## Understanding Metacognition

Enough cannot be said about knowing your audience. Understanding how your particular audience learns (metacognition) and their willingess to apply new knowledge to their job (motivation to transfer) could also provide you with information to create better e-learning experiences for them.

Examine metacognitive strategies. Learners bring their own interpretations of the virtual online environment and how they learn best from it. One way that performance technologists can better understand these interpretations is to examine the metacognitive strategies used by learners during an online course. Metacognition addresses how a person learns, and it varies between people. After your learners finish a course, invite them "to think how they learn." Analyzing their reflections provides important metacognitive insight about their learning process. By collecting data on these processes, you can build an evolving database that can guide the development of future online learning events. For example, perhaps your target population does better in a synchronous environment rather than an asynchronous environment (Campbell, Campbell, and Dickinson, 1996).

Determine environmental favorability. Motivation to transfer what was learned online to the actual workplace depends upon trainees' perceptions of managerial and social support for the use of their new skills, referred to as environmental favorability. The learners can be asked several questions which specifically address their motivation to transfer using both open-ended and closed-end type responses (Machin and Fogarty, 1997). Once the data are collected from the trainees, appropriate statistical tools can analyze the data and perhaps uncover correlations to future performance.

Table 4 provides some open-ended questions that can yield information about both the motivation to transfer and metacognitive strategies used by your learners. Using the information, it will be possible to derive three ratings:

- Rating 1. The degree of motivation to see the course through to a successful end.
- Rating 2. The degree to which the person has effective strategies to be successful.
- Rating 3. The degree that each of the three primary driving levers of power, achievement, and affiliation motivate that particular student.

## Conclusions

Motivation, that is, the drive of the learners to start and finish a course and transfer the knowledge back to the worksite, results from the intrinsic drive within the individual learner and extrinsic efforts externally supplied by the online learning environment. This paper presented numerous extrinsic motivational strategies available to online developers before, during, and after the course. Online instructional designers especially need to understand how their students learn best (metacognition) and then provide a complementary external environment that interacts with those specific needs positively.

It is impossible and inadvisable to incorporate all these strategies in any one course. However, as you monitor and evaluate e-learning courses, you can deter-

| Measuring Motivation |
|---|
| Why are you enrolled in this course? |
| What's in it for you if you are successful in this course? |
| How important is it to you to complete this course? |
| What does 'success' mean to you with respect to this course? |
| Have you set objectives for yourself with respect to this course? If so, what are they? |
| What are the probabilities of you seeing this course through to its very end? |
| Do you foresee any challenges or difficulties that would get in the way or make it more difficult for you to complete this course? |
| Is there anything you know about how to learn that you will take into account in how you approach this course? |
| To what degree do you hope that this course will contribute to your ability to influence others more successfully in the work situations you face or are likely to face? *(power orientation)* |
| To what degree do you hope that this course will increase your ability to meet anticipated job challenges?  *(achievement orientation)* |
| To what degree do you believe that working with others in the course is important to your learning?  *(affiliation orientation)* |

**Table 4.** *Some possible questions to measure motivation to learn, motivation to transfer, and primary drivers of motivation*

mine which motivational strategies work best for your particular target population. Thus, you can slowly move from creating online courses using intuition to having some theoretical basis for design and development. By monitoring the learners' responses to these techniques and developing a metacognitive approach unique to your audience, you can increase the effectiveness of online learning and make it a more effective tool in your performance improvement toolbox.

The foregoing discussion has focused largely on what can be done to increase motivation at different points in time. It is also important to recognize that it is not just instructional designers who can make substantial contributions to the success of learning activities. Many of these ideas can be made more effective through the involvement of those in different roles in the organization. This suggests a collaborative approach to making learning effective. A matrix such as offered in Table 1 could be helpful in identifying how each role could be useful to optimizing the value of training. It may fall upon trainers to take the responsibility for encouraging appropriate contributions by those in other roles.

# References

Broad, M. (1997). Overview of Transfer of Training: From Learning to Performance. *Performance Improvement Quarterly*, 10(2), 7-21.

Campbell, L., Campbell, B., and Dickinson, D. (1996). *Teaching and Learning Through Multiple Intelligences*. Needham Heights, MA: Simon & Schuster.

Clark, R. (1999). *Building Expertise*. Washington, DC: International Society for Performance Improvement.

Dempsey, J., and Sales, G. (1993). *Interactive Instruction and Feedback*. Englewood Cliffs, NJ: Educational Technology Publications.

Esque, T., and McCausland, J. (1997). Taking Ownership for Transfer: A Management Development Case Study. *Performance Improvement Quarterly*, 10(2), 116-133.

Gagné, R., and Medsker, R. (1996). *The Conditions of Learning: Training Applications*. Fort Worth, TX: Harcourt Brace.

Gibson, E.C. (2000). The Viability of Internet Based Training. IBT Technologies, Inc. White Paper. [http://www.ibt-technologies.com].

Good, C. (2000). Motorola University's Response to E-Learning Drop-out Rates. Report made to the eLITE Think Tank, October 15, 2000.

Horton, W. (1999). *Designing Web-Based Training*. New York: Wiley.

Machin, M.A., and Fogarty, G.J. (1997). The Effects of Self-Efficacy, Motivation to Transfer, and Situational Constraints on Transfer Intentions and Transfer of Training. *Performance Improvement Quarterly*, 10(2), 98-115.

McClelland, D. (1984). *Human Motivation*. Cambridge, MA: Cambridge Press.

Moshinskie, J. (1999). Using ROPES to Design Online Instruction. [http://hsb.baylor.edu/html/moshinsk].

Norman, D. (1993). *Things That Make Us Smart*. Reading, MA: Addison-Wesley.

O'Connor, B., Bronner, M., and Delaney, C. (1996). *Training for Organizations*. Cincinnati, OH: South-Western.

Staton, S. (2000). Going Global: Process and Lessons Learned. Paper presented to the Corporate Learning: Transformation to On-Line Conference, New York, NY, December 2000.

Thiagarajan, S., Estes, F., and Kemmerer, F. Designing Compensation Systems to Motivate Performance Improvement. (1999). In Stolovitch, H., and Keeps, E. (Eds), *Handbook of Human Performance Technology* (2nd ed), pp. 411-429. San Francisco: Jossey-Bass.

Zienstra, R. (1999). University of Toyota's Pilot E-Learning Course: Lessons Learned. Presentation made at the annual Corporate University Xchange Conference, Miami, FL.

*Dr. Jim Moshinskie serves as the Accenture Professor of Human Performance at Baylor University, Waco, Texas. Dr. Mo, as he is better known, coordinates the new Performance Improvement Technologies major in the Hankamer School of Business and directs the Center for*

*Corporate E-Learning. The Center conducts e-learning pilots and sponsors one-day boot camps onsite to corporate trainers entitled "E-Learning Made E-Z." Contact him at James_Moshinskie@baylor.edu.*

*This paper was produced with the eLITE (e-Learning Incites Training Excellence) Think Tank. Members include Claude Balthazard, Ph.D., Organizational Studies, Inc.; Larry Carille, Ph.D., A.T. Kearney, Inc.; Chris Good, Motorola University; Ira Kasdan, Carlson Marketing Group; William N. Knapp, Deloitte Consulting, chair; Ara Ohanian, VuePoint Corporation; Bruno Strasser, Werner-Siemens-Schule Training Center, Stuttgart, Germany; Michael VanHoozer, BSI Consulting; Michael Walsh, SynerProject; and John Boyd, VuePoint Corporation.*

# Six Steps to Developing a Successful E-Learning Initiative: Excerpts from the E-Learning Guidebook

**Brandon Hall**

*Wherever you may be in terms of e-learning, this article should provide guidance. Excerpted from the* E-Learning Guidebook, *it outlines six steps, then gives an overview of the pieces required for an e-learning initiative and a glossary of essential terms.*

Amid the economic downturns of the last quarter of 2000 and the recession scares of 2001, some corporations still remain solidly competitive. A key differentiator of these survivors is their unique vision of learning. Rather than thinking of learning as a cost center, these organizations recognize that learning is key to promoting and harnessing the innovation so critical to their strategic advantage. The typical "negative" issues associated with training—loss of productivity and company revenue due to travel time and mileage reimbursement—are fast decreasing, thanks to e-learning.

The following six steps will help you understand what lies ahead and get you on the road to e-learning success.

# An Introduction: Benefits of E-Learning

Organizations around the world are witnessing the benefits of e-learning—cost savings/avoidance, flexibility, and increased productivity. Virtually all of the organizations featured in *E-Learning Across the Enterprise: The Benchmarking Study of Best Practices* (available at www.brandon-hall.com) are far enough along to be measuring costs savings/avoidance and ROI. IBM alone reports saving nearly $200 million in only one year as a result of implementing an e-learning strategy.

Some additional detail on the benefits of e-learning include:

**No Need for Travel**
- Alternative training mode for offsite personnel.
- Instructors are not held by geographic boundaries.
- More students can view the presentation at once.

**Shorter Development Cycles**
- Faster delivery of appropriate training to applicable staff members.
- Higher rates of student completion than found in self-paced training.
- A more efficient mode of offering penetrating data.
- Flexibility to modify or change content and to make it accessible on demand.

**Cost Savings for the Corporation**
- Reduction of internal training costs.
- Reduced time out of workplace for participants.
- Students retain learned knowledge easier.
- Learning Management System (LMS) software that is integral to the implementation of e-learning in the enterprise provides a tool for optimum intercommunication and data compilation.
- No travel costs.
- Flat fee pricing structures give organizations unlimited access to training for one year.

This article is based on the *E-Learning Guidebook: Six Steps to Implementing E-Learning*, available at www.brandon-hall.com. The *Guidebook* was designed as a quasi "Cliff Notes" for those of you just beginning to stake out e-learning and for those of you who are already fully engaged. If you are new to the subject, read through step by step to become familiar with the decisions and planning that lie ahead. For those of you who have already begun, check out the step that you are currently at for tips and ideas. Best wishes in your journey!

# Step 1: Prepare for E-Learning

No matter how good these benefits look, they can be obtained only through careful analysis and planning. Before conducting a detailed readiness assessment, consider performing a strategic assessment to determine the major barriers your organization needs to overcome to successfully implement an e-learning initiative. Start out by conducting a readiness assessment, using a three-step approach:

## 1. Select the relevant dimensions to consider, for example:
- Business Drivers
- Stakeholders
- Content
- Technology
- Learners
- Tracking

## 2. Identify your major assets and barriers for each, for example:
### Business Drivers
- Customer satisfaction is flat or declining.
- Skilled workforce is difficult to attract and retain.
### Stakeholders
- The training department is eager to introduce e-learning.
- Managers view training as an investment rather than a cost.
### Content
- Few cultural and language adaptations are required.
- Current content is well documented and structured.
### Technology
- There is sufficient time to put in place the hardware/software required.
- Security issues (firewalls) have been resolved.
### Learners
- Learners are geographically dispersed.
- Learners welcome new initiatives and innovations in training.
### Tracking
- Metrics for participant progress have been defined.
- Participants' progress in curricula must be better managed.

## 3. Consider implementation strategies.
Once you've determined your organization's readiness for e-learning, consider how you are going to build the business case for e-learning, developing a strategy that aligns the learning vision to key business goals and drivers, to secure necessary upper-level support and funding.

- How will you define e-learning in your organization?
- Will it include asynchronous and synchronous web-based course, CD-ROMS, videos, electronic performance supports systems, and knowledge management systems?
- How will you make sure that e-learning is aligned to the needs of the business?
- Who will champion and maintain the initiative?

- How will you communicate and market your e-learning initiative internally?
- How will you measure training effectiveness?

# Step 2: Develop a Strategy

As is true with most enterprise-wide change initiatives, mapping a strategy and securing executive sponsorship are the critical first steps. Given the very substantial business imperative and business impact of e-learning, it is not surprising that those organizations featured in *E-Learning Across the Enterprise: The Benchmarking Study of Best Practices* (available at www.brandon-hall.com) have very high levels of executive support. One organization states it simply: "Senior management supports e-learning because it delivers what is needed when it is needed." Another claims: "Without it, our project would have been lost in the shuffle of changing priorities and other commitments for capital."

Here are three approaches to developing an e-learning strategy that correlate to an organization's experience with e-learning.

## Level 1: Little or No E-Learning Experience

If your organization has had little or no e-learning experience, the business case should be built around either an off-the-shelf generic product approach or a "narrow and tall," problem-focused approach. The main benefits should be focused on access to information—more efficient and flexible delivery.

For example, Dell Computer Corporation, a pioneer of the direct business model, instituted a "narrow and tall" approach to e-learning. When John Coné, Vice President of Dell Learning, joined the company over five years ago, he did not ask for a major financial commitment for an e-learning initiative. Instead, he targeted one part of the organization, realizing that e-learning would later migrate to other areas of the company. His approach has been to change the financial model so that Dell Learning operates on a tuition-based, pay-as-you-go model, rather than an overhead model. Coné makes the business case for specific programs and solutions.

## Level 2: Two or More Successful Basic E-Learning Projects

If your organization has implemented two or more successful e-learning projects, consider building the business case around a problem-focused approach, where content is more customized and offers problem-based skills practice through the use of simulations.

For example, there were a couple of factors that drove Domino's Pizza, Inc. to look at e-learning, beginning around 1995: inconsistency in training tools and variations in training delivery experience across its franchises. Due to high turnover, the cost of training was high, especially if travel was involved. Out of this, Domino's has developed CD-ROM-based training on a variety of topics for employees at the franchises, such as basic informational training (e.g., how to make a pizza), customer service, and some soft skills procedures (such as money drop and making change). They also provide a variety of management development topics to the franchises on marketing, profitability, and hiring. Harrison Withers, Training Manager at Domino's, says this particular e-learning scenario has worked well for Domino's because "it addressed the business gaps we were having at the time."

Since each franchise owns its own computer system, they have not yet tackled web-based training for the franchise group. There are still too many platform compatibility and Internet access issues for web-based training to be realistic—although that could change in the future.

## Level 3: Two or More Successful Intermediate or Advanced E-Learning Projects

Finally, if your organization has implemented two or more successful e-learning projects where learning is problem-centered and simulation-based, your organization may be ready to build a business case around an enterprise-wide solution. The focus of this level is collaboration through virtual group workspaces, providing the opportunity to engage face to face with other learners in real work.

For example, IBM decided on a bold e-learning concept, implemented as a company-wide, core initiative. The company needed to provide leadership development and build the management competencies of 30,000 IBM managers worldwide. IBM's Director of Management Development, Nancy Lewis, decided to "just do it" and develop her program accordingly. Lewis wanted to focus on the effectiveness of e-learning, rather than efficiency, and her effort paid off in both areas. Participants in the Basic Blue e-learning program learned nearly five times more material than via previous interventions. And Basic Blue delivers five times as much content at one-third the price of a traditional classroom-based approach.

Now, let's talk about the main strategies for building your business case.

## Aligning E-Learning with Business Goals

Adopters of e-learning report an additional benefit of this mode of training: at last training is seen as having an integral role to play in overall organizational strategy. E-learning not only enables e-culture within the organization, it also creates synergy among knowledge management, performance support, and high-commitment management practices. Those featured in our best practices study used three basic strategies. First, they developed a clear and purposeful vision of learning, knowledge, and performance and they illustrated how e-learning technology could activate that vision. Second, they made that vision compelling enough to increase all stakeholders' openness to change, which is especially important in selling the concept to employees. Finally, they recommended the use of various vehicles to communicate targeted and compelling reasons for e-learning to line managers, instructors, employees, and other stakeholders prior to and during the implementation.

## Speaking C-ese

When you're trying to sell the benefits of e-learning to your C-level executives (you know: CEOs, CFOs, CIOs, et al.), speaking their "language" can be crucial to building your business case. Knowing how to speak "C-ese" will dramatically improve your chances of getting your e-learning proposals and initiatives approved. So let's brush up on some words, phrases, and tactics that will help prepare you to make presentations or to create e-learning proposals for any of your C-level executives.

- **Get to the point.** The C-level crowd need not hear all the minute details of your training methods. Instead, get right to the point. Shorten your presentation to just the salient points that will help you make your business case for e-learning.
- **Focus on the bottom line.** When writing your proposal, always choose words that focus on the bottom line. Find out what business issues matter the most, and show how e-learning will effectively solve those issues. For example, C-level execs are intrigued by phrases such as:
   "Improve our customer satisfaction"
   "Increase our market share"
   "Decrease our operating expenses"
   "Improve employee performance"
- **Use real figures.** Avoid using information that is too general or vague. C-level executives respond best to examples that are "by the numbers." Project how much money will be saved and how many more employees will benefit by launching new e-learning programs.
- **Focus on the "how."** Demonstrate how the e-learning intervention leads to desired outcomes. For example, key messages that may help you strengthen your case for e-learning can include the following:
   "E-learning will help us to train our employees as much as 50-60% faster."
   "It will reduce operating costs by eliminating travel expenses associated with large instructor-led workshops."
   "It will allow employees to learn more skills and thereby reduce turnover."
   "It will allow our training department to evolve into a constant, always available outfit."
- **Focus on delivery.** When making a C-level presentation, put your primary emphasis on making improvements to the training delivery.
- **Look at the big picture.** Stay focused on the bigger picture, use company relevant demos, acknowledge any potential downside, demonstrate a workable plan, and be prepared to answer questions.

### Determine Who's Going to Pay

Moral support from senior management is great for the e-learning implementation, but, based on our best practices study, organizations that remember to treat executives as their bankers will have greater success. Regardless of where the money will come from, making the e-learning business case to management is key to getting funding and protecting it from cuts.

In order to reduce the financial load on the training department and make the e-learning implementation less vulnerable to budget cutting, some organizations have shared the costs of their e-learning infrastructure across several departments. For example, at one of the organizations featured in our best practices study, IT owns the LMS, Sales owns another component, and Management Development owns yet another component.

Communicating the need for continual reinvestment in learning is essential to ensure the ongoing sustainability of the implementation. Best practice organizations suggest drawing a parallel with the investment in R&D.

## Step 3: Select Technology and Content

Fundamentally, there are two major parts to an e-learning program: a Learning Management System (the software to register and track learners) and content (the material your employees will learn).

### Selecting a Learning Management System (LMS)

An LMS is software that automates the administration of training events—the foundation for most corporate e-learning programs. The system can be used to register users, track courses, record data from learners, and provide appropriate reports to management. These basic capabilities are just the starting point. LMSs also provide company management, assessments, personalization, and other resources in both online and classroom-based settings.

Careful evaluation of potential systems is critical because of the high investment cost and long-term impact of selecting the right LMS for specific organizational needs. There are several considerations when selecting a LMS.

- Identify business requirements and the features your company may or may not need.
- Understand the e-learning industry standards your LMS product should adhere to and what standards are evolving and influencing future refinements to the product.
- Use and understand the terms and acronyms associated with this industry.
- Discern who the major players are in the industry and the level of satisfaction their customers have experienced. (See our customer satisfaction study, *Learning Management Systems: Voice of the Customer.*)

- Find a method for comparing key features of differing products. There are hundreds on the market with varying benefits and features.
- Know the best way to write a Request for Proposal (RFP), using guidelines and templates that get the best responses. (See www.brandon-hall.com—the LMS report section—for a sample RFP template.)
- Develop questions you need to ask your LMS vendor to get at information beyond that found in the vendor proposal.

## Choosing Content: Build or Buy?

Next is determining whether to build or buy content. You will probably need to find a happy medium, but a good rule of thumb is to use off-the-shelf courses whenever possible to reduce costs. There are a number of choices that offer the usual trade-offs of time, effort, cost and effectiveness.

Will online courses replace all classroom training? Let's hope not. There are unique advantages to meeting face to face with peers in a classroom and having an instructor lead you through the content while answering questions. Perhaps 50% will be the max for online learning, with the balance being classroom-based.

For example, many organizations, including IBM, Ernst & Young, and Verizon Communications, use a "blended" approach, combining online courses with classroom-based activities. This allows you to take the best of each approach to maximize value for both the learner and the organization.

| | **Cost** | **Risk** | **Effort** |
|---|---|---|---|
| Buying off-the-shelf courses | Low to medium. | Low, in terms of the greater likelihood of getting well-designed courses, created by outside professionals. | Easiest solution, especially when hosted by a learning portal, versus having to install it on your intranet. |
| Building your own custom courses | High. Requires new skills among staff. | Medium. Less expensive than custom courses developed by an external source, but more expensive than off-the-shelf courses. | High, if they will be high-visibility courses. |
| Building custom courses, using an outside developer | Low. No need to retrain your own staff. | High. | Low, in terms of the greater likelihood of getting well-designed courses, created by outside professionals. |

**Figure 1.** Cost, risk, and effort of building versus buying

### Learning from the Best: Insights About Building Courses

If you decide to build, here are some course-building tips shared by participants in our benchmarking study.

- **Content from here, there, and everywhere.** Organizations such as Shell and the U.S. Navy acquire their e-learning content from a broad variety of sources, making systematic "build-versus-buy" decisions and finding ways to manage the high cost of content. Facing up to culture issues in global organizations is also essential.
- **Learning objects and templates.** Learning object strategies (learning in bite-size nuggets that can be reused) are well in place and still evolving at Cisco, Ernst & Young, and Verizon Communications and are in development at Air Canada.
- **My own time, my own place.** Confirming the trend toward online self-instruction, eight of the 10 best-practice organizations studied are using self-paced courses to allow anytime, anywhere e-learning.

## Step 4: Sell E-Learning to Everyone in the Organization

### Leading the Charge

In some organizations, a single champion or evangelist is primarily responsible for kick-starting the e-learning implementation. However, most participants in the best practices study suggest that the impact of e-learning on the organization is widespread, forcing changes in accounting processes, IT, training staff assignments, skills, etc. Therefore it will be important to monitor and continuously improve implementation using a team, such as a learning council or steering committee consisting mostly of business managers and training representatives who are sponsored by the executives of their specific business functions.

### Assembling a Team

As mentioned above, e-learning sometimes results in major shifts in needed skills for a variety of staff. There are several strategies for providing a smooth transition to e-learning:

- Involve instructors early and throughout the implementation process.
- Start small to build confidence.
- Choose team members with skill sets that complement your own.
- Make training and trial e-learning project teams open to those who wish to advance their skills in those areas.
- Use an internal competitive bid process to find required skills.

E-learning teams are generally highly leveraged and need to integrate strategic, learning design, technological, and product skills. Once e-learning is truly operational and efficient strategies have been employed, staff requirements generally decrease.

## Partnering with IT

Whether the IT function is internal or outsourced, its key role in the e-learning implementation process cannot be overstated. To effectively partner with IT, it is suggested by best practices companies that you do the following:

- Understand the challenges of e-learning for your IT department—there are many!
- Know and exploit IT's key initiatives and dates for software and network upgrades, annual equipment purchases, ERP implementation, and other investments that impact e-learning.
- Get IT staff on your selection committees or at least in the room when vendors come to present.
- Leverage e-commerce expertise in the IT function to help with the distribution of e-learning.

## Marketing E-Learning Internally

We've already talked about presenting your vision for e-learning to business leadership. Here, we're focused on communicating to the front line in order to gain acceptance from both employees and their managers. Since e-learning may be a new phenomenon to your organization, both groups are likely to raise concerns that you must be able to address head-on.

For employees, the issue is usually one of unfamiliarity—learning at the desktop instead of in the classroom. How will you provide a quiet, non-distracting environment where desktop learning can take place, particularly if employees are in cubicles or shared workspaces? Rockwell Collins addressed this issue by building geographically dispersed learning centers where people could go to learn.

How do you make e-learning something that people want to do? Dell Computers offers a unique approach to this issue. They develop "e-magnets"—content that people want that is only made available on-line. One of their first on-line courses, the "Dell Business Model," was authored and approved by CEO Michael Dell and has been tremendously popular. That course has helped create user acceptance of e-learning at Dell.

Line managers and supervisors can potentially pose the biggest hurdle to a successful e-learning implementation. As some companies like American General have found, if managers don't buy in, they won't let their employees take the time to use e-learning during the workday. Even though e-learning at the desktop often requires only half to two-thirds as much time as classroom-based training, there can be the misperception that it is taking employees "away from the job." How do you counter this? In the case of American General, they countered with face-to-face meetings with managers to address their issues and explain how e-learning works. For instance, for American General's customer service representatives, it was a matter of accommodating e-learning to the needs of the business and scheduling e-learning sessions during non-peak work hours.

## Step 5: Implement Enterprise-Wide

It's tempting, when first encountering e-learning, for a trainer to focus on issues related to "my course." Is e-learning appropriate for my course? How do I get my course online? What authoring program should I use? How do I learn to author? This is natural because this is how we adopted previous classroom technologies. We thought about: How can I use videotapes in my course? How can I use PowerPoint in the classroom?

It's worthwhile, however, to put aside one's course for a moment and think about the big opportunity of e-learning: *enterprise-wide e-learning*. Enterprise-wide e-learning is a significant, system-wide implementation of e-learning aimed at making a significant business impact.

Enterprise-wide e-learning is typically aimed at one or more of these benefits:

- *Access:* Making training more available to learners.
- *Costs:* Reducing training costs.
- *Content:* Increasing the scope of offerings.
- *Reinvention:* Reengineering how training happens.
- *Relevance:* Making training more meaningful to people's work.
- *Speed:* Responding to constant change and rapid product innovations.
- *Efficiency:* Avoiding the lockstepped scheduling of classroom training.
- *Empowerment:* Putting the responsibility for learning in the hands of learners.
- *Business:* Using fast, effective learning as a competitive weapon.
- *Globalization:* Making training both consistent and available across the world.
- *Convenience:* Letting time-pressured students learn at the best time and place.
- *Connection:* Connecting learning data to other systems, such as HRIS.

Enterprise-wide e-learning typically involves a lot of courses. There's usually an online catalog and maybe even competency maps. And because it involves so many people and so many courses, an LMS is a necessity. Finally, an enterprise-wide e-learning commitment will probably include a blend of learning that integrates live e-learning, classroom training, online courses, and a variety of other methods.

## Step 6: Measure the Business Benefit

### Results That Speak to Stakeholders

Several best practice organizations are choosing measure e-learning based on growth in performance, competencies, and intellectual capital. These critical measures are naturally linked to business impact and help to maintain the case for the e-learning initiative. We have synthesized several helpful tips from early adopters of e-learning in a wide variety of industries. Specific examples of the trends and statistics mentioned can be found in our two reports, *Building the Business Case for E-Learning* and *E-Learning Across the Enterprise: The Benchmarking Study of Best Practices* (available at www.brandon-hall.com).

When developing a strategy for monitoring and reporting results to your senior team, remember to do the following:

- Underscore that the deployment of e-learning must be focused on people.
- Maximize success by focusing less on numbers and more on the nature of learning.
- Focus on benefits, not features.
- Communicate the obvious returns from e-learning: reduced training time, delivery of training to the learners' workplace.
- Cite examples from research showing instruction delivered via computers requires 35-45% less learning time.
- Estimate the cost savings accrued because of the elimination of training facilities and printing.

When reporting on the learning gains associated with e-learning, focus on:

- Evidence demonstrating that e-learning secures better worker retention of what is learned and better application to real work situations.
- Statistics that underscore that e-learners typically achieve higher test scores and have improved attitudes toward e-learning format.
- Numbers that prove a higher number of e-learners achieving "mastery" level.

When addressing performance gains associated with e-learning, try to:

- Provide specific examples (e.g., statistics that show major improvement in "hit ratio" on sales calls).
- Describe anecdotal evidence (e.g., trainees reporting higher confidence in making calls).
- Show numbers (e.g., an increase in outbound sales call volume).
- Cite results from research (e.g., e-learning pilot banks achieved nearly 50% of yearly sales goals in the quarter immediately after training).
- Reinforce the common performance drivers that great e-learning implementation can impact (e.g., sales or related issues, number of customers, marketing and awareness, production, personnel).

Illustrate how e-learning is helping to build or maintain a competitive position:

- Provide examples that demonstrate how e-learning results link to your and other organizations' enhanced competitive position.
- Share specific incidents that demonstrate how e-learning has helped organizations capitalize on increasing diversity in the workforce.
- Reinforce to your senior team that e-learning rapidly and consistently provides workers with skills, knowledge, and attitudes to innovate and help them make sound decisions individually and in teams.
- Remind them that innovative organizations fare better in tough competitive environments.

For additional ammunition, calculate and present real cost savings:

- Cite statistics that show a reduction in training time.
- Point out the resulting reduction in travel and entertainment expense and facilities.
- Add that e-learning also reduces the cost of creating or purchasing the training and/or delivery systems.

## E-Learning Market Map: An Overview of the Pieces

The following is an overview of some of the basic pieces required for a successful e-learning initiative, adapted from the Market Guide for E-Learning, available at www.brandon-hall.com under "More Resources."

| Architecture and Tools | Sample Vendors |
|---|---|
| Learning Management Systems | • Docent<br>• Isopia<br>• Learnframe<br>• Saba<br>• TEDS<br>• THINQ TrainingServer |
| Authoring Tools | • Macromedia Dreamweaver with Coursebuilder<br>• TrainerSoft |
| Live (synchronous) E-Learning Tools | • Centra Symposium<br>• Interwise |
| Collaboration Tools | • CommuniSpace<br>• LearningCommunities |

| Architecture and Tools | Sample Vendors |
|---|---|
| Content Management Systems | • Avaltus<br>• Generation21<br>• Intelliprep<br>• Knowledge Mechanics<br>• Mindlever<br>• Peer3 |
| Simulation Tools | • Extreme Software<br>• Paragon Solutions<br>• Rapid |
| Digital Video/Audio Tools | • Flash<br>• Quicktime<br>• Real Player |
| Testing/Assessment Tools | • Pedagogue Solutions<br>• Questionmark<br>• Quiz Studio |
| **Services** | **Sample Vendors** |
| Custom Course Development | • Allen Interactions<br>• Cognitive Arts<br>• Quisic |
| System Integrators | • Accenture<br>• Deloitte & Touche<br>• PricewaterhouseCoopers |
| Large-Scale Course Conversion | • LeadingWay<br>• LearningByte International |
| **Content** | **Sample Vendors** |
| Learning Portals (course aggregators) | • GeoLearning<br>• Headlight<br>• THINQ |
| Online Degree Programs | • UNext-Cardean University<br>• University of Phoenix<br>• Western Governor's University |
| Online Course Publishers | • DigitalThink<br>• ElementK<br>• KnowledgeNet<br>• NETg<br>• SkillSoft<br>• SmartForce<br>• Syntrio |

| End-to-End Solutions | Sample Vendors |
|---|---|
| These sample vendors provide a mix of products and services from nearly all of the above categories. | • Click2learn<br>• Global Learning Systems<br>• IBM Mindspan<br>• Mentergy |

# E-Learning Glossary

**AICC**  The Aviation Industry CBT Committee (AICC) is an international association of technology-based training professionals that develops training guidelines for the aviation industry. These guidelines apply to the *development*, *delivery*, and *evaluation* of training courses that are delivered via technologies. We recommend choosing vendors who meet this standard.

**Application Service Provider (ASP)**  An application service provider is a company that offers individuals or enterprises access, over the Internet, to software applications and related services that would otherwise have to be located on their own computers.

**Asynchronous E-Learning**  E-learning that does not occur simultaneously. Some examples of asynchronous e-learning include taking a *self-paced course*, exchanging e-mail messages with a mentor, and posting messages to a discussion group about a course topic.

**Classroom-Based Training**  This term for traditional training replaces the term "instructor-led training," which confused those using online instructors.

**Collaborative Tools**  Tools that allow learners to work with others via email, threaded discussions, or chat. In some cases, collaboration is used in team-based projects.

**Competency Management**  Used to identify skills, knowledge, and performance within an organization. Such a system lets an organization spot gaps and introduce appropriate training, compensation, and recruiting programs based on current or future needs.

**Content Management System**  This is an application that stores and distributes the right content to the right learner at the right time. It allows a programmer to modify a course in minutes rather than over weeks of authoring and testing.

**ERP/HRIS**  Enterprise Resource Planning (ERP) is an industry term for large, often multi-module software applications that manage many facets of a company's operations, including product planning, parts purchasing, maintaining inventories, interacting with suppliers, providing customer service, tracking orders, and managing resources and financials. SAP, Peoplesoft, and J.D. Edwards are some well-known ERP providers. Human Resource Information Systems (HRIS) are similar to ERP applications, but are aimed specifically at the management of a company's human resources.

**IMS Standard** The Instructional Management Systems (IMS) Standard is a set of technical specifications defining how learning materials will be exchanged over the Internet and how organizations and individual learners will use these materials. Initiated by Educom and developed through a partnership of academic, commercial, and government organizations, the goal of these specifications is the adoption of a set of open standards for Internet-based education.

**Knowledge Management System** This is software that collects, stores, and makes information available among individuals in an organization. It includes information about such resources as people with a certain expertise. It can correlate what people have learned from doing their jobs and it is designed to facilitate the exchange of these understandings among employees.

**Learning Environment** A learning environment is software designed as an all-in-one solution that can facilitate online learning for an organization. It includes the functions of a Learning Management System for those courses within the learning environment, but it may not be able to track online courses that were not created within this particular learning environment.

A learning environment is characterized by an interface that allows students to register and take courses, staying within that environment for the duration of the course. The program will usually include some self-instructional portions, along with an academic model of a multi-week course. This model is often facilitated by an instructor, where a group can proceed week to week with seminar assignments. Most learning environments also include an authoring capability for creation of additional courses for the instructor.

**Learning Management System (LMS)** Software that automates the administration of training events. The LMS registers users, tracks courses in a catalog, and records data from learners; it also provides appropriate reports to management. The database capabilities of the LMS extend to additional functions such as company management, online assessments, personalization, and other resources.

Learning management systems administer and track both online and classroom-based learning events, as well as other training processes (these would need to be manually entered into the system for tracking purposes). An LMS is typically designed for *multiple* publishers and providers. It usually does not include its own authoring capabilities; instead, it focuses on managing courses created from a variety of other sources.

**Open Database Connectivity (ODBC)**   This is an application program interface to access information from numerous different types of databases, including Access, dBase, DB2, etc. Although Microsoft Windows was the first to provide an ODBC product, versions now exist for UNIX, OS/2, and Macintosh platforms as well.

**SCORM**   The Sharable Courseware Object Reference Model (SCORM) is a set of standards that, when applied to course content, produces small, reusable learning objects. A result of the Department of Defense's Advanced Distributed Learning (ADL) initiative, SCORM-compliant courseware elements can be easily merged with other compliant elements to produce a highly modular repository of training materials. We recommend choosing vendors that meet this standard.

**Skill Gap Analysis**   Compares an employee's skills with the skills required for the job to which he or she has been or will be assigned. The purpose is to identify clearly the skills employees need in order to succeed in their current or planned positions and to compare employee skills against those requirements. The result is an improved understanding of exactly which skills employees need to develop further.

A simple skill gap analysis consists of the list of skills required for a specific job along with a rating of the employee's level for each skill. Ratings below a certain predetermined level identify a skill gap.

**Synchronous E-Learning**   Synchronous, or live e-learning, means that communication occurs at the same time between individuals and information is accessed instantly. Examples of synchronous e-learning include real-time chat and video or audio conferencing.

*Brandon Hall, Ph.D., is a leading independent e-learning analyst and lead researcher of brandon-hall.com, helping organizations make the right decisions about technology through his writing, advising, and presenting. With more than 20 years as a training professional, he is the author of nearly 20 widely cited e-learning research reports and the groundbreaking Web-Based Training Cookbook. He also consults with Fortune 500 companies such as Microsoft, Cisco, Johnson & Johnson, and others to help develop their e-learning strategy and select complementary tools. Brandon can be reached at info@brandon-hall.com or 408-736-2335 or by visiting www.brandon-hall.com.*

# How to Facilitate E-Collaboration and E-Learning in Organizations

## Nory B. Jones and James Laffey

*E-learning and e-collaboration, as "interrelated mechanisms for sharing valuable knowledge throughout the organization," can constitute an important competitive advantage. This article outlines what the authors have found "to help positively influence employees to adopt and use technologies effectively."*

## Introduction and Significance

In an era that is becoming predominantly digital, many organizations are struggling to keep up with the rapidly changing technologies flooding the market. Two related trends that are gaining momentum involving new technologies in organizations are e-collaboration and e-learning.

E-collaboration involves the use of collaborative technologies to allow people throughout the organization to easily share their data, information, or knowledge/expertise via a digital archive or repository, often called an organizational memory. Ideally, this allows people who are located anywhere in the company, whether they are in the same office or halfway around the world, to access relevant information when and where they need it. For example, an executive would have access to the latest financial projections from her managers around the world to make decisions no matter where she happened to be—in her home office or in another country entrenched in merger negotiations. A service representative would be able to research how other service reps successfully solved similar customer problems. A marketing manager could share successful marketing strategies in reaching different target market customers with his counterparts throughout the company. While precise data on how many companies are using e-collaboration is scant, many articles documenting its uses and successes point to a growing trend in use.

The essence of this knowledge sharing is summed up by Pan and Scarbrough (1999), who said that "Knowledge management is the way organizations build, supplement, and organize knowledge and routines around their activities and within their cultures and develop organizational efficiency by improving the use of employee skills. It is the capacity within the organization to maintain or improve organizational performance based on experience and knowledge. Organizational knowledge is knowledge that is available to organizational decision-makers and which is relevant to organizational activities." Beckman (1999) summed up the importance of KM by stating: "Knowledge management is considered a key part of the strategy to use expertise to create a sustainable competitive advantage in today's business environment." E-collaboration extends the capacity of an organization and increases the potential range of strategies available for implementing knowledge management.

Implicit in the statements above is the idea that successful organizations must continually learn and adapt to changing environments, essentially becoming "learning organizations." Bassi et al. (1998) stated: "The inextricable link between rapid technological change and the emergence of the global economy has created the necessity for profound change in the way people and organizations work. As a result, workplace learning is arguably more strategic to the competitive advantage of both individuals and employers than at any point in all of recorded history." And because of the increasing demands on workers to become more productive and efficient, e-learning becomes a valuable way for companies to provide learning channels in a convenient and cost-effective manner. E-learning involves the use of technologies to allow associates to gain new knowledge and skills at their convenience in terms of time and location. Examples of demands for changing skills and knowledge include continually changing computer applications, knowledge about customers, suppliers, or the industry, marketing or service techniques, or new technical skills. Thus, e-learning, which involves the same basic technologies as e-collaboration, represents an opportunity for companies to provide a wide array of training to meet the needs of employees when and where they can easily access it. However, e-learning does not simply mean access to training materials and courses through distance learning systems, but also includes "learning by doing" that is supported by access to support while engaged in work. Knowledge management systems become dynamic performance support systems and help employees learn new competencies as they take on challenging tasks (Laffey, 1995).

What is the relationship between e-collaboration and e-learning and why are they important to managers? As time-to-market and innovation pressures for competitive advantage increase, companies are continually seeking new ways to learn and innovate. Berry (2000) contends that innovation and time represent the driving forces behind competitive advantage. "The sooner employees grasp the new knowledge, the sooner the new expertise can be applied to revenue growth strategy." Cohen and Levinthal (1995) suggest that a firm's competitive advantage may be linked to its "absorptive capacity": its ability to acquire and retain valuable knowledge from outside the firm. Thus, the learning component becomes an important way for associates to bring valuable knowledge into the company. However, once inside the organization, this knowledge must be shared with those associates who can readily use that new knowledge. E-learning and e-collaboration systems thus represent related mechanisms for facilitating and enabling this process as shown in Figure 1.

E-learning essentially represents the more formal mechanisms for disseminating knowledge throughout the organization, whereas e-collaboration represents a less structured approach, though with its own formal and informal rules. E-learning and e-collaboration thus represent interrelated mechanisms for sharing valuable knowledge throughout the organization. Once someone learns something via e-learning, he or she can share the knowledge and new ideas via the e-collabora-

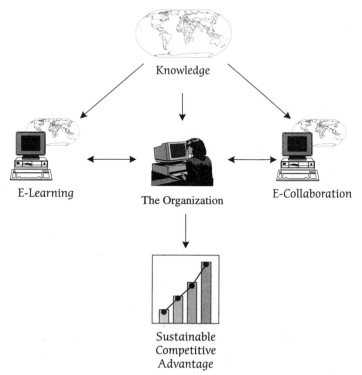

**Figure 1.** A model of e-learning and e-collaboration in the organization

tion systems. This can similarly motivate associates to continually enhance their own knowledge base through continued e-learning.

While both concepts sound great in theory, it is not as easy as simply investing and installing the technology and telling associates to "go at it." Wise companies will do their homework to learn what factors will influence employees to use these technologies for either e-collaboration or e-learning. Therefore, the purpose of this article is to outline what we have found to help positively influence employees to adopt and use technologies effectively.

## Findings from the Literature

Based on our review of prior research from the academic literature, we found many factors that influence people to either embrace or reject new technologies. Pan and Scarbrough (1999) developed a framework of factors that appear to strongly influence the successful adoption and use of collaborative technologies. The cumulative effect of these factors is to create an environment that motivates, facilitates, and enables the successful adoption and diffusion of innovations such as e-collaboration or e-learning technologies. Within this framework, they suggest that there are three broad groups of influencing factors. They coined these terms as:

1. **Infrastructure:** "The hardware/software that enables the physical/communicational contact between network members; provides the means to share knowledge," e.g. the technology.
2. **Infostructure:** "The formal rules which govern the exchange between the actors in the network, providing a set of cognitive resources (metaphors, common language) whereby people make sense of events on the network." We also perceive this as the rules or norms that govern the systems.
3. **Infoculture:** "The stock of background knowledge which actors take for granted and which is embedded in the social relations surrounding work group processes; core values and attitudes, reflected in employees and managers' willingness to exchange knowledge to solve company problems." This would also be known as the organizational culture.

Within the framework of these broad factors, we take research findings as subelements within them to explain which factors other researchers found that contribute to e-collaboration or, by extension, e-learning.

**Infrastructure:**

- Relative advantage: Clearly perceived value and benefits of new system, especially over pre-existing substitute tools.
- Adequate training on the new system.
- Reasonable expectations of the new system.
- The digital collaboration system should be user-centered/user-friendly.

- The new system should match/be compatible with pre-existing work processes.
- Time for experimentation with and adaptation to new system.

**Infostructure:**

- Ownership and filtering of the collaboration system, particularly in a database type knowledge repository to maintain the recency and relevancy of the information/knowledge contained in the e-collaboration or e-learning system.

**Infoculture:**

- Good leadership; championship of the new system. The commitment and support of top leadership has been suggested as vital to the success of a new venture such as e-collaboration or e-learning. Leadership commitment and support may strongly influence all of the other factors involved with infoculture.
- Need for a strong collaborative/cooperative organizational culture. This often stems from the leadership influence on the organization.
- Involvement, motivation, and commitment by users and top managers.
- Organizational rewards/incentives to effectively use system.
- Need for good working relationships: trust and communication among associates and managers.

## Our Research Findings

We conducted an empirical study to examine attitudes and perceptions towards a newly adopted collaborative technology in a scientific Contract Research Organization. A web-based CSCW (computer-supported collaborative work) technology that allowed individuals to share data, information, or knowledge any time, any place was introduced into this company in January 2000. Initially it was used by the leadership team. However, over the course of the year, it was slowly adopted by employees throughout the organization. By the end of the year, approximately 45-50 employees were using this system.

After interviewing 30 users on their perceptions relating to prior research findings, followed by a web-based survey, the following trends emerged.

The greatest reason why most individuals used this CSCW technology was the perceived relative advantage in using it. These users saw a clear benefit to themselves or to their departments or the company from using this new technology. It provided benefits that other, existing tools could not. The following quotes serve to demonstrate this point as well as emphasizing the benefits derived including time savings, access to information, and the ability to interact and share information with multiple people irrespective of time or place.

I can be in any location, as long as you're on the net and it's loaded up, you can go out and deal with it on my terms, my time, rather than somebody else's.

The real benefit of using BSCW is that it allows the client to have access to it 24 hours a day. It's important to us in some respects because we work with clients that are spread out all over the United States and even in Europe. So, if someone can access that without any special mechanisms, like having to dial long distance across the ocean or worry about a time zone difference. If they log on, and get on the web, they can access that document, download it themselves, make changes in the document when they're at work and you may not be and then upload it, when you come in the next day, the thing is freshly uploaded and you've got something where changes have been made.

I like the version piece that keeps track of a historical version because there's been times that I want to go back and look at something and compare month to month, quarter to quarter, year to year and I don't have to keep track of that. I can look at it by date.

It cuts down on the number of meetings that we need to have a great deal because we can take care of a lot of business just over the network instead of having everyone come in and meet and go over stuff. It saves a lot of time. You can do that at your convenience rather than ... "Oh, I've got a meeting at 10:00 o'clock!"

From introducing it to where other people are advocating it as a high value solution, to a genuine need. Well actually, no other mechanism offered us a solution.

Success breeds success. There wouldn't be too many people using it if they heard horror stories about it. And it's so that somebody can go in—one of the most advantageous things of having a site like that is that—you can go into it whenever—you don't have to wait for somebody to respond to you with a document, with an e-mail or with whatever, but you can go in and see as far as your privileges extend and see what's been done. It really facilitates anything when you can do things at your convenience rather than ... with the meetings or like I know some people were working on a report—they'll get the draft ready—they'll put the draft report on the site while they turn it into QA, the sponsor can go ahead and look at it. If they have changes they want to make, they can do that almost simultaneously.

The quantitative surveys reinforced the interview results where relative advantage was cited by 87% of the respondents as either exerting an influence or a strong influence on their use of this technology.

The second major finding involved who exerted the greatest influence on the adoption and continued, effective use of the new technology. From our research, it was clear that the most profound influences came from top leadership and managers.

In most organizations, new technologies often represent a forced adoption. In this situation, the president/CEO of the company championed the purchase and execution of this CSCW technology to fill a need in the company. In the interviews, approximately 39% of the respondents indicated that the president/CEO exerted the greatest influence on their motivation to use the system. Another 17% indicated that their managers exerted the greatest influence on their motivation to use the system. The following quotes serve to reinforce this.

Oh absolutely—our CEO. He initiated that that was what we would use. Based on his experience, he picked the product that we would use.

Oh yeah—Dr. A! He goes in there and looks—who's been reading it, who's been revising it, yeah. It was the greatest motivation to begin with, and actually, I don't get into it that often; maybe once or twice a month because my billings don't change that much—whereas somebody like John probably's in there every week, every day, because he's got a lot of flux in his group.

Dr. A. Then the managers. Not yet (been influenced by anyone else), but my door's open. If you can give me the opportunity to do my job better or faster, I'm ready. Because no matter how fast computers get, they're never fast enough.

(President) I pretty much had to hold people's feet to the fire to make them use it, where we had to help them because they naturally assumed that this was more difficult than it was, and with anything that's new, there are some impediments initially. But we've gone from helping people over those thresholds of resistance to where we're getting people complaining—"How come I'm not on BSCW?"

Those representative statements demonstrate that, while executives and managers exert a strong influence initially, the perceived need or relative advantage then continues to exert an influence as associates see the benefits in using the system. The quantitative survey results similarly show that approximately 70% of the respondents believed that executives or managers exerted an influence or a strong influence on their motivation to use this new technology.

The literature discusses the need for an organizational culture that promotes knowledge sharing. Our results showed that approximately 97% of the respondents agree that information should be shared within their own departments while about 63% believed information should be shared throughout the entire company.

Thus, there does appear to be a need to good communication and knowledge sharing. Similarly, the literature discusses a need to tie reward and compensation systems to the effective use of a new technology and sharing information and knowledge. In our qualitative results from the interviews, there was support for this idea, as demonstrated by the following quotes.

> You know, incentives usually mean monetary or time when you're talking about a company and just about anybody is attracted, especially when its encourage you to do something that you already need to do or want to do. It's especially attractive—it allows you to find the time that you may not have had before.

> I think that an incentive system would help. I'm one for rewards or incentives and any time you say reward or incentive, dollar signs automatically pop up in the minds of many people. And I take money—I'm not shy—I take money. But to me, I think this is probably worldwide, as far as the behaviors in companies if you do something wrong you hear about it, but if you do something right, you never hear a word. And I'm a big proponent to stopping and saying, "You did a really good job by getting all that taken care of."

> Any time—anybody will take a bribe or a hint if there's money involved. I think that would help. You're always going to have people who are computer phobic. Or people say, "I don't have time for this," and a lot of people resist change. That might be just the motivator for them to get in and actually play around with it and once they get over the uncomfortable and the unfamiliar, things that we all go through when we go through something new, that might be just the motivator to get them past that hump and realize, "Hey—this is not so bad."

> I think the performance evaluation would motivate people to use it. That's what motivated me to use it. I don't think cash or bonuses or incentives like that would be appropriate. I mean, that's ... it should be part of their performance, part of their job.

> Make no bones about it, people are motivated differently. But most people are motivated by the almighty dollar. Maybe an extra day of vacation, some people may value their free time more than dollars, whatever it is. I think actually what they did was they had a list of things you could choose from; roughly the same dollar value. So the company didn't care which one you picked, but it depended on which one was more rewarding to you. And it was absolutely tied to their performance appraisal.

> I think that people are inclined to share if they are that type of person. Rewards don't always work.

Interestingly, despite the interest in this concept when people were interviewed, only 53% of respondents indicated that ties to their performance appraisal would motivate their use of this system and sharing knowledge, while 60% indicated that it was simply an expected part of their job.

Finally, the issue of prior technology experience was explored as well as the influence of individual attitudes. The results from the interviews appeared to lend strong support to the contention that the more technology experience people have, the easier it is for them to adapt to and effectively use a new technology. This is demonstrated by the following quotes.

> The more computer skills you have, the more you'll be willing to try new technologies.

> In the beginning, I used to be reluctant because you spend time learning something—I was Mr. WordPerfect years ago and then someone said, "Why aren't you working in Word and why aren't you working in Microsoft?" And I said, "Well, I don't want to leave something I've learned." But actually, through all the jobs I've had, and the different experiences within research, I've learned so many different programs that now it's simple to change.

> I'm kind of the guy who always wished he knew more. I'm always the guy asking all about how do you do this, how do you do that because of my limited knowledge. I know the basics. I know how to get around. I know what I want to do. I either don't have the time or haven't taken the time to learn all the specifics that an intimate user would have. But to me, in the work that we do, computers are invaluable and things keep getting ... becoming better communicated, easier, and there's good and bad.

> When I first started using BSCW, it was probably a little intimidating because I had never been in it, but that intimidation didn't last long because I've been through so many software changes—I've been through 3 different software systems in the accounting department. I've used multiple spreadsheet programs and so I think I was fortunate enough to come into the computer technology at an age that it didn't scare me.

Again, it was interesting to see the theme of relative advantage emerge in respondents' discussions of prior computer experience. The emerging theme was that after using this new technology, the benefits of the system became apparent to them, increasing their motivation to continue using it. However, in the survey responses, only 47% of the respondents indicated that their experience with computers exerted an influence on their current use of the new technology.

In terms of attitudes and personalities, the interview responses showed that 45% of responses related to an eagerness with and enjoyment of new technologies, as demonstrated by the following quotes:

I'm a computer-oriented person. I'm no genius with the computer, but things are a lot easier with the computer. There's a lot of other things that we do around here that I'd like to do by the same method. If I had my way, we will get to that point.

I think technology is great. We've come a long way. I took my first computer class in grad school, so I went all the way through high school and college—we did have computer accounts in college, but we just played Star Trek and other games. I think it's been a boon in the respect that you can, if things are working right, get a lot of things done.

Some days! I kind of like going out and looking at new stuff because I just need extra stimulation. I'm not one of those "stick with what we know" people because I get bored. Maybe it's just a short attention span! I don't think it hurts a person to be aware of what's going on because otherwise, your knowledge gets out of date so quickly.

There's one thing I like about it—I love computers. I get tired of changing. I do get tired of software changing so often, but in general, I really do like to manipulate it. In my job, I virtually sit there and other than my filing, everything I do is on that computer.

I like getting new stuff. I love learning it. I'm not the most expert by no means. But I'm always willing and eager to learn new things.

It was interesting that in the survey results, only about 47% of the respondents said that their enjoyment of technology influences their use of this new system.

## Conclusions and Recommendations

What have we learned from this research and how does this relate to the successful implementation of e-collaboration and e-learning? Based on the findings of other researchers as well as our own findings, we would make the following recommendations to managers who are interested in introducing e-collaboration and/or e-learning systems into your companies.

**1. Relative advantage of the e-collaboration or e-learning system.** The perceived relative advantage has been shown to exert the greatest influence on user motivation to initially adopt and then effectively use an innovation such as e-learning or e-collaboration efficiently and effectively. Therefore, management and the system champion should first clearly identify and communicate the specific benefits that will create relative advantage for the users: i.e., what's in it for them? The concrete reasons of why and how e-learning or e-collaboration will make the users' jobs easier, better, more efficient, improve quality, save time, etc. This recommendation also assumes that e-collaboration or e-learning is truly consistent with the goals of the company and the users. In addition, there is an assumption that the specific systems associated with e-collaboration or e-learning have had all the bugs worked out and potential problems solved. These would include issues such as developing a user-friendly interface and easy data entry mechanisms or solving system compatibility issues.

**2. Top leadership commitment, involvement, and support.** Because top leadership have the authority to allocate resources and the power to execute reward systems, we recommend that there be at least one top leader in the company who acts as the champion for your e-collaboration or e-learning initiative.

**3. Extensive communication.** The top leader who champions this new system should then actively communicate the clear benefits or relative advantage of this system over existing tools in the company. When the message is communicated clearly so that potential users can see the benefits they can derive from it and the message is communicated from a credible and powerful source such as a top executive, it will enhance buy-in and credibility.

**4. Reward structures or incentives.** For an e-collaboration system, a direct link to associates' performance appraisals will send a clear signal on the importance of using this technology to share knowledge. Again, if associates understand the importance of sharing their knowledge (#2) and they recognize that they will be evaluated and rewarded for valuable contributions, this adds to the motivation. For an e-learning system, if associates understand the benefits of additional skills in terms of their career potential as well as enhancing company performance, they will be similarly motivated. In our research, many respondents indicated that reluctant or apprehensive participants would benefit from incentives to motivate them to try the system and overcome their fear of using it or sharing their knowledge. This may be an option if your workforce is resistant to adopting new technologies, fears sharing information or knowledge, or feels pressured by time demands that inhibit them from participating in e-learning experiences.

**5. A culture that supports and encourages continual learning and collaboration.** While it is difficult to change an entrenched organizational culture, with the support of top executives, it is desirable to promote a culture of collaboration and sharing. This ties into the reward structures and performance appraisals where people are rewarded for learning and sharing.

In conclusion, each organization is different with its own culture and norms. While these recommendations are based on our own findings as well as those from the literature, we believe they may be generalizable to most situations as they are grounded in classic management and technology theories. More research is needed to support and refine our ideas, but in an increasingly dynamic and competitive era, it may be worthwhile attempting to use these methods to promote e-collaboration and e-learning in your organization.

## References

Bassi, L., Cheney, S., and Lewis, E. (1998). Trends in Workplace Learning: Supply and Demand in Interesting Times. *Training & Development*, 52(11), 51-75.

Beckman, T.J. (1999). The Current State of Knowledge Management. In J. Liebowitz (Ed.), *Knowledge Management Handbook*. Boca Raton, FL: CRC Press, 1-22.

Berry, J. (2000). Corporate Training—The E-Learning Factor. *InternetWeek*, 836 (Nov. 6), 61-64.

Cohen, W.M., and Levinthal, D.A. (1990). Absorptive Capacity: A New Perspective on Learning and Innovation. *Administrative Science Quarterly*, 35(1): 128-152.

Laffey, J. (1995). Dynamism in Electronic Support Systems. *Performance Improvement Quarterly*, 8(1), 31-46.

Pan, S.L., and Scarbrough, H. (1999). Knowledge Management in Practice: An Exploratory Case Study. *Technology Analysis & Strategic Management*, 11(3), 359-374.

*Nory B. Jones is an adjunct assistant professor in the Department of Marketing, School of Business and Public Administration at the University of Missouri-Columbia. Her major research interest focuses on knowledge management and the improvement of human performance using technology. You can reach her at (573) 882-2588 or jonesnb@missouri.edu.*

*James Laffey is an associate professor in the School of Information Science and Learning Technologies at the University of Missouri-Columbia. His research interests involve using technology to facilitate learning and performance. He is currently the co-director of the Center for Technology Innovations in Education, where he leads several NSF projects involving how technology can be used to enable learning communities. You can reach him at (573) 882-5399 or laffey@missouri.edu.*

# Technology Adoption: Bringing Along the Latecomers

**Rebecca Vaughan Frazee**

*As organizations rely more and more on technology, it becomes increasingly impor-
tant to know how to work with people who are slow to adopt technology or who
resist it. That's the focus of this article: to understand the reasons and to find ways
to overcome them.*

New technologies are increasingly becoming integrated into our daily routines, changing the ways we conduct our personal and work lives.
Organizations are now adopting technology, such as an e-retailer who
chooses to use an online chat feature to connect with customers or a nonprofit
organization that begins to incorporate Web-based reporting. Another example is a
financial services firm that moves a quarter of its training courses to the Web.
Individuals, too, are adopting technology, such as the teacher who finds that his
classroom has been outfitted with five new computers and must now figure out
how to use them for teaching and learning, the grandmother who wants to start
viewing digital photos from her children and grandchildren, or the salesman who
switches from his old paper-based day planner to a new personal digital assistant.
At home or at work, technology adoption is affecting nearly everybody.

According to research by The Media Audit regarding individuals, Internet use
continues to rise, especially among senior citizens, homemakers, and minorities.
For instance, today 37% of senior citizens are online (a 51% increase since 1998)
and more than 43% of homemakers are now on the Web (an 80% increase since
1998) (Pastore, May 2001b). A report by the Association for Financial Professionals

shows that 63% of financial professionals are using the Web for communication, decision-making, and doing business, as compared with 36% in 1999 (almost a 200% increase). SES Research found that 76% of Canadian small businesses surveyed were online at the end of 2000 (Pastore, May 2001a).

Though Internet use continues to rise, the data above also suggests that 63% of seniors, 57% of homemakers, 37% of financial professionals, and 24% of Canadian small businesses have *not* yet adopted the Internet. In June 2001, Michael Pastore of the INT Media Group wrote, "More than 400 million people use the Web on a daily basis, but there are billions of people who have neither heard of the Internet nor have any intention of going online anytime soon. According to research by Ipsos-Reid, even among the most developed Internet markets in the world, such as the United States, Canada, Sweden and the Netherlands, about one-third of the people who could use the Internet choose not to. In fact, the research found that only 6 percent of the world's 6 billion citizens are online" (Pastore, June 2001).

## Resistance to Change

As the data above indicates, more and more people and organizations are increasing their reliance upon technologies. While some individuals and organizations readily accept change, others have a low tolerance and may proceed a bit more cautiously, especially when it comes to technology. In describing response to change and innovation, you may hear individuals and organizations labeled as *innovators, early* or *late* adopters, or even *laggards*, terms introduced by Everett Rogers and popularized in describing the challenges of marketing high technology to consumers. Pastore (2001) labels those who aren't choosing to go online *non-intenders*. Interestingly, in the United States, "those deciding or being forced to use a computer for the first time, after reaching full maturity, is the fastest growing segment of the computer and technology training market" (Redding, Eisenman, and Rugolo, 1998). Because these older Americans likely have little computer experience, the introduction of new technologies, such as the Internet, can present considerable challenges and change. Any kind of change can at first seem like more work than it's worth and will undoubtedly be met by some form of resistance (Cravens, 2000). Here we turn out attention to these "late adopters," "laggards," or "resistors."

## Why Do We Care About the Resistors?

Training and performance professionals often serve as agents of change, supporting and moving an organization and its people towards the introduction of new concepts, procedures, or tools that increasingly rely more on technology. "Whether technological solutions work or fail basically depends on the people involved, with the biggest obstacle to successful technological innovation being the inability to get people to adopt the automated tools" (Occhiuto and Dickes, 1999). The most difficult hurdle, then, will be overcoming resistance from those who are reluctant to accept the change—the late adopters.

# Late Adopters

## Who Are They?

Technology's *late adopters* are often characterized as reluctant, resistant, skeptical, and pragmatic; with their eyes on the bottom-line, they have no patience for unproven ideas. They are bound by tradition and have a low tolerance for change. Most want a user-friendly, complete, and well-supported product (Redding et al., 1998; McKenzie, 1999). They expect the new technology to provide a big payoff and they require compelling evidence to switch their time-tested, comfortable behaviors. Table 1 compares early and late adopters.

|  | **Early Adopters** | **Late Adopters** |
|---|---|---|
| Response to change | Respond to change as it occurs. Perceive opportunities enthusiastically. | Initially, they wait. |
| The learning task | Early adopters learn along the way, incrementally. | For late adopters, the learning task is that of "catching up." |
| Appreciation for technology | In keeping pace with change, early adopters experience the technology "in the trenches" as it evolves with plenty of war stories to tell. Thus, they appreciate the advantage of today's technology versus that of days gone by. Furthermore, they share a common understanding and appreciation for technology with other early adopters. They value technology. | Coming into the game late, late adopters lack experience with older versions of the technology as it evolved and, therefore, have difficulty sharing the early adopters' enthusiasm. With high expectations and no historical perspective, they don't value technology that much and are less willing to put up with the troublesome nature of getting up to speed on technology. |

**Table 1.** Comparison of the characteristics of early and late technology adopters

## Why Do They Resist?

As cited by Wolski and Jackson (1999), the Technology Acceptance Model suggests that technology resistance depends on the users' perceptions related to their "beliefs and norms regarding the technology." Executives at EarthLink.com suggest at least three factors that keep people from adopting Internet technology: lack of money, a fear of technology, and a lack of understanding of the technology's value (Borland, 2000). Here are some examples of why individuals and managers resist technology adoption.

Ipsos-Reid surveyed people in 30 countries who aren't on the Internet and who claim they have no plans to go online. The most frequently mentioned reasons for staying offline are "have no need for the Internet" (40%), "no computer" (33%), "no interest" (25%), "don't know how to use it" (16%), "cost" (12%), or "no time" (10%).

## Individual Resistance

**It will cost too much.** The Ipsos-Reid survey of people in 30 countries who don't plan on going online, 12% reported that it costs too much and 10% reported that there was no time . The perception that making the change will cost too much, including concerns about how much time will be required, is compounded by the fact that during the transition period there is often decreased productivity (Glynn and Koenig, 1995). This can lead to major hesitation to move forward with the technological innovation.

**Fear.** Many people feel insecure about using an unknown technology. They may have low confidence in their abilities, or they may actually lack the necessary skills. Therefore, they feel little sense of control, at the mercy of system failures and busy technicians. 16% of those surveyed by Ipsos-Reid said they didn't use the Internet because they didn't know how (Pastore, June 2001). For example, a sales associate who is forced to use a new laptop with clients may be afraid to use it because something may go wrong or the client will know more than he does.

**Peer pressure.** Especially for people who closely affiliate within communities of practice, such as accountants, lawyers, sales agents, or other knowledge workers, the decision to use technology is strongly influenced by what others think, or the "subjective norm" of the peer group and the larger organization. Are the majority of people in the group using technology? Is there status associated with the use of technology? If the group norm does not encourage technology use, look to peers as a source of resistance.

**Lack of perceived value.** According to Brian Cruikshank of market research company Ipsos-Reid, "In the developed world, a substantial number of people who could very easily go online have decided not to. They see no compelling reason to be on the Web. The hype and the promise of the Internet clearly hasn't impressed them—not yet, at least" (Pastore, June 2001). In fact, the Ipsos-Reid survey found that two of the most common reasons people said they stayed off the Interent are that they had no need for it (40%) or they had no interest in it (25%).

## Resistance from Management

According to Glynn and Koenig (1995), the underutilization of information technology is often rooted in management resistance. Why would managers resist?

**Tyranny of the urgent.** In addition to the ever-present complaint of insufficient funding, managers often suffer from what some call the "tyranny of the urgent," or today's constant and immediate demands for day-to-day business results. The common perception is that there is simply no time to ramp up with some new innovation. However, this "lack of time" excuse often stems from a lack of perceived value regarding the technology change—we make time for the things we value most.

**Misconceptions about technology.** Glynn and Koenig (1995) cite the research of Kirby and Turner (1993), who found that "adoption of IT by small business is influenced primarily by the computer expertise of the owner-manager." Often, there is a lack of understanding or a misconception of the capabilities and necessary effort associated with computer hardware and software. Many underutilize existing systems because they don't understand what it can really do for them. In turn, they also resist new systems because they have a misunderstanding of what it will really take (i.e., money, tools, time) to adopt any new technologies.

**Anticipating resistance from others.** Managers often anticipate resistance from their own people—those who will have to adopt the new technology. For instance, McWilliams (1994) found that the two main concerns business owners have regarding technology adoption are staff training and planning (Glynn and Koenig, 1995, p. 264).

## Why Are They Adopting Now?

Those individuals and organizations that adopt technology early in the process perceive that they are doing so by choice. On the other hand, late adopters may perceive that there is no choice at all. Rogers says that late adopters "often adopt an innovation only out of economic necessity or strong peer pressure" (Harris, 1997). In organizations, leadership may call attention to a new, desirable technology, but more likely, they are forced to change under pressures from customer demands, the media, or advances in professional practice (Wilson, Dobrovolny, and Lowry, 1999). For individuals, the story is much the same. For example, faculty, teachers, and trainers are finding themselves pressed by their leaders to use new software and hardware in the classroom (McKenzie, 1999; Noble, 1997). GE's Jack Welch has pressed for the shift of training out of classrooms to online delivery. Call center reps, sales agents, and volunteer directors are expected to use the technology on their desktops.

## Critical Success Factors That Facilitate Technology Adoption

### Don't Underestimate the Effects of Change

Rogers says that an innovation is truly adopted only when users tailor and "reinvent" it to meet their professional or personal needs. Ely (1999) suggests that trainers and educators move beyond the focus on technology adoption and diffusion to a focus on *implementation.* "Implementation is the payload. What does adoption mean if it is not followed by implementation?" (p. 24).

When we encourage people to adopt a new technology at work, we are asking them to change in two ways: 1) learn a new "tool" that is vastly different from other tools they've used in the past, and 2) change the way they do their jobs, which could include rearranging their physical space, their schedules, and their relationships with others. For example, when we encourage sales agents to start using laptops, or we ask trainers to add an online component to their workshops, or when we ask volunteer coordinators to use the Internet to recruit and manage their volunteer pool, share resources with other volunteer agencies, and submit online reports to the federal funding agency, not only are we asking them to learn a new technology, we are suggesting that they change the way they conduct their business on a daily basis and that they reinvent their relationships with colleagues and clients. "How your organization will access and use technology will affect just about every function of your agency" (Cravens, 2000).

How can we anticipate the force of change and face it head on? Cravens (2000) says, "The successful integration of a new technology ... requires good and ongoing communication, long-term commitment by the entire staff, monitoring, support, intervention and patience." The critical thing to remember is that while change may be inevitable, "true change in perspective, and, therefore, in practice, comes only as a result of a conscious, self-initiated, willing decision within each practitioner. That kind of change cannot be mandated, but it certainly can be catalyzed, energized, and supported" (Harris, 1997, p. 55).

How do we "catalyze" change and convert reluctance into enthusiasm? Based on Ely's (1999) eight conditions for the successful implementation of educational technology innovations, and further review of the literature, the following suggestions can help facilitate technology adoption and integration. Table 2 summarizes these suggestions.

### Clearly Articulate the Benefits of the New Technology

This is by far the most important element of successful technology adoption and integration. If people are going to expend the effort to adopt new technologies, not only must they perceive the innovation as useful, but they must see the relative

| Action | Procedure |
|---|---|
| Clearly articulate the benefits of the new technology | Clearly identify the benefits of the new system to those who will use it.<br><br>Address skepticism.<br>• Describe some possible uses that might "sell" the idea of adopting new technology to a late adopter. What potential downfalls might there be? How would you counter those?<br>• Show possibilities, but don't devalue prior experiences. Use their language, not "new age" rhetoric that is perceived as fad or fashion.<br>• Address fear. Many late adopters are frightened of "breaking" the machine. How could you make them more comfortable with the technology?<br><br>Tap into their pragmatic side, answering "What's in it for me?" Many late adopters don't see or know what the technology can do for them like tech-enthusiasts do.<br>• Clarify bottom line. Demonstrate outcomes that they value, such as return on investment and the relative advantage of new way vs. current.<br>• Give concrete, personally relevant examples of benefits.<br>• Highlight dissatisfaction with the status quo. |
| Provide strong leadership | Establish clear vision and goals.<br><br>Make certain that the support extends beyond one leader who might be transferred or depart.  What ensures long-term support?<br><br>Go beyond using technology as a tool. Link it to strategic goals. Provide examples.<br><br>Introduce technology where it can have the most impact only after you have a clear understanding of current processes.<br><br>Encourage participation and shared decision-making, including communication among all parties involved in the process, collaboration and participation among participants, and local decision-making autonomy.<br><br>Target "opinion leaders." |
| Demonstrate management commitment and support | Ensure access to proper equipment and resources.<br><br>Provide timely, adequate internal and external personnel and systems to support the new technology.<br><br>Concentrate support on late adopters.<br><br>Allow time to get up to speed.<br><br>Collect continuous feedback throughout the process for mid-course, dynamic correction. |

**Table 2.** Critical success factors that facilitate technology adoption

| Action | Procedure |
|---|---|
| Ensure the necessary skills and knowledge | Define specific needs and support the training effort with other elements of the larger organizational system. |
| | Provide active, problem-based learning environments so they can work on real-world challenges and needs. |
| | Provide a solid framework that explains the logic behind the effort and establishes a common language and paradigm. Try to get in their shoes. What do you remember about your initial use of a new technology such as driving a car, using a fax machine, or getting cash from an ATM? |
| | Rely on peers and teams. Use groups of mixed abilities and styles. |
| | Use peers for follow-up to influence, coach, and support colleagues. |
| | Provide training and job aids to support development and provide coaching. |
| Emphasize rewards and results | Encourage people to reflect on personal, intrinsic rewards that come with seeing personal growth and visible results. |
| | Provide extrinsic rewards for their extra effort. |

**Table 2.** Continued

advantage of the new system over the status quo (Ely, 1999). "It is clear from the literature that small businesses will adopt IT only when they are forced to in order to gain or maintain a competitive advantage" (Glynn and Koenig, 1995, p. 265). However, we must find a way to demonstrate the possibilities that they value without devaluing past experience or current practices.

**Demonstrate outcomes that they value.** There can be many different reasons why someone might begin to value and care about adopting technology. Do they wish to work better or faster? Do they want to look smart among their colleagues? Are they trying to keep up with or move ahead of their competitors? Rogers says that in order to encourage adoption, the perceived benefits must be compatible with cultural factors such as shared experiences and social norms. For instance, people care about winning the admiration of friends and colleagues. Therefore, raising the status of the new technological innovation will help facilitate its adoption.

**Highlight dissatisfaction with the status quo.** R. Buckminster Fuller said, "You never change anything by fighting it. You change things by making them obsolete." The perception that "things could be better" is what Ely (1999) calls the *dissatisfaction with the status quo*. "Whether the dissatisfaction is an innate feeling or an induced state (as brought about by marketing campaigns, for example) it is an emotion that calls for change" (p. 24). For training professionals, this creates an opportunity for us to influence, in essence, by creating or encouraging a perceived dissatisfaction and subsequent appreciation.

## Provide Strong Leadership

There must be evidence of support for the new system in the way of strong, strategic leadership and sufficient sponsorship from the executive level. On a more tactical level, strong project leadership is necessary to manage the day-to-day implementation of the new system. Most importantly, all parties who will be affected by the new technology must be encouraged to participate in the process, and they must be a part of the discussion about how the technology can be used. In many cases, the technology innovation is best introduced at the grassroots level.

**Establish clear vision and goals.** Establish a clear vision of how the organization will operate with the new system and provide clear goals and expectations for how staff will use it. For instance, clarify what you mean by "integration" or "adoption." We say we want people to adopt technology and integrate it into their work, but oftentimes we don't have a clear understanding of what that means or what that may look like, and neither does the end user.

Furthermore, this vision must go beyond simply "using technology as a tool." Integration is not merely about using a desktop publishing template or an electronic spreadsheet. Such oversimplification can actually cause frustration by creating false expectations, implying that the new technology should be easy to learn and easy to use, like a hammer, for instance. Technology is truly integrated when it is used seamlessly to support and extend work. "It is not something one does separately; it is part of the daily activities ..." of the user (Dias, 1999, p. 11). Technology must engage users in meaningful activities that enable them to reach the goals they already care about in ways that are easier, faster, and smarter.

**Introduce technology where it can have the most impact.** If your organization is unsure about exactly where to begin, start by introducing technologies that will provide the most benefit to the organization *and* to its clients. Cravens (2000) cites a contribution to the CUSSNET (Computer Use in Social Services Network Internet discussion group) by David Arons of Tufts University, who suggests that the challenge may be to identify "technologies that both increase efficiencies within the organization ... and can be made accessible to the organization's clients. Basically multi-use technologies to help the organization better serve their clients and lower their overhead."

Before integrating technology into the organization, make sure you have a good understanding of current processes, that is, how information and work flows with current systems and technologies. Cravens recommends that the organization should identify formal and informal process structures, value-adding tasks that can and cannot be automated, non-value-adding tasks that can and cannot be automated, and political and social agendas.

**Encourage participation and shared decision-making.** Create an environment that fosters communication and collaboration, encourages shared decision-making, and balances local autonomy with standards (Ely, 1999; Wilson et al., 1999). Harris (1997) says, "Offer them, rather than require them." As training and performance professionals, our job is to encourage, assist, and facilitate rather than mandate, coerce, and deliver. Consider how issues and concerns are shared and expressed within the organization, whose opinions count in defining the issues, who and what is behind the innovation, and how the organization generally deals with change (Harris, 1997).

**Target opinion leaders.** Grassroots efforts, though seemingly slower, are oftentimes more effective than top-down approaches because they "complement the natural ways in which new tools are adopted by members of social systems" (Harris, 1997, p. 25). At the grassroots level, Rogers suggests targeting a group's *opinion leaders.* Not to be confused with early adopters or innovators who may be perceived by the group as being odd or on the fringe of the group, opinion leaders are those individuals whose perspectives are sought out by others most frequently, who conform more closely to a group's norms than *early* adopters or innovators do, and who are "at the hubs of the system's interpersonal webs" (Harris, 1997, p. 25).

Cravens (2000) cites contributions to a nonprofit listserv that support grassroots efforts. "What I have found is that if you can get one person using a program and it really helps them do a better job, others will get interested…. [In our case, use of the new system] spread from unit to unit after we saw its benefits. Now counties all over the State are using it in one fashion or another to suit their needs. This was done without forcing the technology on anyone. It is a much slower process, but seems to be more acceptable to staff."

## Demonstrate Management Commitment and Support

Management must provide visible evidence that the new technology is part of a complete system and that there is adequate and ongoing support for the technology and for staff during and beyond the learning curve process. Here are some ways to provide visible evidence of management support.

**Ensure proper access to equipment, resources, and technical support.** In addition to providing the necessary hardware and software, ensure that everyone has access to sufficient resources such as documentation, references, job aids and training materials. Make every effort to ensure that the new equipment is compatible with existing systems (Dias, 1999; Ely, 1999). Provide the necessary financial resources, technical assistance, and administrative support (Dias, 1999; Ely, 1999; Wilson et al., 1999). Providing access to proper resources will reduce the perceived risk associated with the new technology, what Rogers calls "trialability" (Harris, 1997).

**Concentrate support on late adopters.** A common marketing strategy has been to target early adopters and hope that they will entice the late adopters to come around. McKenzie (1999) cites Moore (1991) and suggests, "The assumption that late adopters follow the lead of early adopters has proven to be wrong-minded and dangerous." When considering where to target your support resources, don't assume that early adopters will shepherd or sympathize with the reluctant late adopters. These two groups are vastly different, have different needs, and typically don't understand each other.

Instead, identify those individuals or groups within an organization that could potentially require a higher level of assistance. Give them extra support during the initial phase of implementation to ensure early success with the new system. As the manager from a nonprofit organization shared on a listserv, "we had line supervisors do a simple inventory of staff skill and have tentatively identified several 'soft spots' (staff who may need a higher level of support)—we plan on shifting a portion of our support resource to these areas during the initial phase of rollout hoping to facilitate early success experiences" (CUSSNET contribution in Cravens, 2000). Remember: while you may need basic support in the beginning to ensure early successes, as people become more comfortable and advanced in their abilities, the need for more advanced and in-depth technical support will increase (Rogers, 1999).

**Allow time to get up to speed.** Even when they are willing to change, staff will have to spend extra time learning the new system, and the initial perception may be that the system has made things worse, not better. This is especially the case for those who may have had unrealistic expectations, thinking that the new technology would miraculously and immediately make their jobs easier. As we said earlier, until they are fully skilled with the new system, users may also experience a sense of vulnerability. People need time to learn, plan, and collaborate (Wilson, 1999).

**Collect continuous feedback throughout the process.** Technology adoption and integration is a dynamic process, not a static event. The technology and the environment into which we introduce it will continue to change. Once again, this is change that we must embrace. We can do so by closely watching the innovation as it evolves. "If things change, we like to know about it, and know how those changes relate to conditions within the organization" (Wilson, 1999, p. 27). That means we must create feedback mechanisms that allow for mid-course correction and that include those closest to the work so they can give their input and "co-design the solution at all stages in the local setting" (p. 28).

## Ensure the Necessary Skills and Knowledge

Another way that management must show its support is by making professional development a priority to ensure that everyone is able to use the new system. Cravens (2000) cites Ferrante-Rosenberry (1999), who recommends a 30/70 rule for supporting the effort: for every dollar budgeted for the new system, 30 cents should go to hardware and software and 70 cents should be used for training and support. After first ensuring that the new system is as user-friendly as possible (what Rogers calls *complexity*), we must make sure that people *perceive* it as useful. Do this by providing staff with ample opportunities for training and hands-on practice. Give them job aids, information, and reference materials to encourage self-reliance with the new system (Ely, 1999, Dias, 1999). While they admit that it is a slow process, executives at Earthlink.com are trying to address the fear factor by making their software easier for customers to use, and they're spending millions on advertising to educate people about the Internet (Borland, 2000).

**What might training look like?** Training efforts will be successful only if they respond to defined needs and are supported by other elements in the system. Training can be used to bring about new skills and knowledge, change attitudes about the benefits and difficulties of using new technology, and increase confidence and motivation.

Dias (1999), citing Jonassen (1995) and others, suggests that in order "to construct an environment ripe for [technology] integration, we must think differently about teaching and learning" (p. 11). One such learning environment might involve a problem-based approach in which people learn new technologies by accomplishing meaningful, contextualized, work-related goals. In this case, the role of the trainer would be one of "facilitating more that delivering, encouraging rather than mandating, assisting rather than coercing" (Harris, 1997, p. 55). The trainer would encourage colleagues to work together on teams and learn from each other, pairing someone who is a little more tech-savvy with a peer or colleague who is more familiar with the business. The box on the next page provides a checklist for ensuring that late adopters have the necessary skills and knowledge.

**Rely on peers for follow-up.** One-time training "inoculation" isn't going to transfer new skills to the workplace. True technology adoption and integration requires support and follow-up in the form of systems and informal learning. Peers can be tapped to do the following:

- **Influence.** Peers are often seen and emulated as role models and opinion leaders. As more of their peers start using a new technology regularly, late adopters will feel the pressure to come on board. As we said earlier, focus initial efforts on the opinion leaders who will naturally spread the word (Harris, 1997). Then, use these peer success stories as examples of the possibilities and benefits of using the new technologies.

---

### Checklist for Training and Supporting Late Adopters

❏ Provide a solid framework that establishes clear needs, goals, requirements, and the logic behind the technology.

❏ Establish a common language and vocabulary that will facilitate communication, reduce frustration, and enhance learning.

❏ Provide ongoing, incremental practice and feedback mechanisms so learners see their progress.

❏ Address different learning styles. Ask them how they like to learn best.

❏ Create active, problem-based learning environments so they can work to achieve real-world challenges and needs.

❏ Promote collaboration that encourages learners to work together, exchange ideas, and examine what and how others have done things similarly, including examples and success stories to boost confidence.

❏ Rely on peers and teams to influence, support, and coach.

❏ Use groups of mixed abilities and styles. If the training is to be self-directed, make sure to include support, because late adopters by nature may not be experienced self-directed learners.

❏ Support any training efforts with job aids, coaching, and systems that will support performance on the job.

---

- **Provide community.** "Communities of practice," strategies often used in corporations, can help here. The web provides a friendly place for late adopters to converse and share concerns and successes (Rossett and Sheldon, 2001).

- **Coach.** Peer coaching allows colleagues to observe and help each other throughout implementation. Address skepticism by coaching late adopters in the potential application of the new technology (McCray, Hoppe, and Greenwood, 1997).

- **Support.** For instance, peer study groups provide opportunities for ongoing dialogue that can facilitate collaborative planning and problem solving.

### Reward Desired Performance

People will be required to invest time and energy to adopt a new system, so give them incentives and reward their efforts. Encourage people to reflect on their own personal, intrinsic rewards that come from seeing visible results, what Rogers call "observability," such as pride in their new accomplishments, increased efficiency, or new transferable skills. Also, provide extrinsic rewards for their extra effort, such as peer recognition, monetary rewards, or a new computer for attending a series of workshops (Ely, 1999). One way this can be done is through the use of "activity reporting" related to technology use. The reporting of their own technology use gets people to reflect on their own use, establishes technology use as important in their peer community and within the organization, and exploits the "peer pressure" component that can be a powerful facilitator of change (Wolski and Jackson, 1999).

# In Conclusion

Henry David Thoreau said, "Things do not change, we do." When introducing a change such as the roll-out of a new technology, we must remember to focus on those individuals who must change the most. That change will be difficult for them, and we should not take their task lightly. We must include them in the development of a clear vision of what is to be, and provide them with visible, authentic support and reinforcement as they move in desired directions. Most importantly, we must gain a clear understanding of that which concerns them and motivates them before ever asking them to adopt a new order of things (Rossett, 1999).

## Bibliography

Borland, John. (2000, May 4). Rivals Battle AOL for Net's Dawdlers. CNET News.com. http://www.canada.cnet.com/news/0-1004-200-1814711.html.

Cravens, Jayne. (2000). Introducing New Technology Successfully into an Agency and Why Your Organization Needs a Technology Plan. Coyote Communications, May 17, 2000. http://www.coyotecom.com/database/techbuy.html.

Dias, Laurie B. (1999). Integrating Technology—Some Things You Should Know. *Learning and Leading with Technology, 27*(3), 10.

Ely, Donald P. (1999). Conditions That Facilitate the Implementation of Educational Technology Innovations. *Educational Technology,* 39.

Ferrante-Roseberry, Phil. (1999). Presentation, Philanthropy News Network, "Nonprofits and Technology" conference, Seattle, January 26-27, 1999.

Glynn, Karen, and Koenig, Michael E.D. (1995). Small Business and Information Technology. *Annual Review of Information Science and Technology,* 30, 251-273.

Harris, Judi. (1997). Who to Hook and How: Advice for Teacher Trainers. *Learning and Leading with Technology, 24*(7), 54-57.

Jonassen, David H. (1995). Supporting Communities of Learners with Technology: A Vision for Integrating Technology in Learning in Schools. *Educational Technology, 35*(4), 60–63.

Kirby, David A., and Turner, M. (1993). IT and the Small Retail Business. *International Journal of Retail and Distribution Management, 21*(7), 20-27.

McCray, Gordon E., Hoppe, Betsy, and Greenwood, Tamara. (1997). Strategies for Supporting User Populations with Divergent Capabilities in a Technology-Intensive Learning Environment. http://hsb.baylor.edu/ramsower/ais.ac.97/papers/mccray.htm.

McKenzie, Jamie. (1999). Reaching the Reluctant Teacher. *From Now On: The Educational Technology Journal,* Summer 1999. Available: http://fno.org/sum99/reluctant.html.

McWilliams, Gary. (1994). Mom and Pop Go High Tech. *Business Week*, November 21, No. 3400, 82-86, 90.

Moore, Geoffrey A. (1991). *Crossing the Chasm: Marketing and Selling Technology Products to Mainstream Customers.* New York: Harper Business.

Noble, David F. (1997). Digital Diploma Mills: The Automation of Higher Education. http://www.firstmonday.dk/issues/issue3_1/noble.

Occhiuto, Mick, and Dickes, Bruce. (1999). People Are Key to Technology Adoption. *The National Underwriter.* http://www.acord.org/software/Peoplearticle.html.

Pastore, Michael. (June 2001). Why the Offline Are Offline. INT Media Group. http://cyberatlas.internet.com/big_picture/demographics/article/0,,5901_784691,00. html.

Pastore, Michael. (May 2001a). Canadian Small Businesses Increase E-Commerce. INT Media Group. http://cyberatlas.internet.com/markets/smallbiz/article/0,,10098_760121,00.html.

Pastore, Michael. (May 2001b). Internet Use Continues to Pervade U.S. Life. INT Media Group. http://cyberatlas.internet.com/big_picture/demographics/article/0,,5901_775401,00.html.

Redding, Terrence R., Eisenman, Gordon, and Rugolo, John. (1998). Training in Technology for Late Adopters: Learning in Retirement, Computers for Seniors. *Journal of Instruction Delivery Systems, 12*(3).

Rogers, Everett M. (1995). *Diffusion of Innovations.* 4th edition. New York: Free Press.

Rogers, Patricia L. (1999). Barriers to Adopting Emerging Technologies in Education. *Journal of Educational Computing Research, 22*(4), 455-472.

Rossett, Allison, and Sheldon, Kendra. (2001). *Beyond the Podium: Delivering Training and Performance to a Digital World.* San Francisco: Jossey-Bass/Pfeiffer.

Wilson, Brent, Dobrovolny, Jackie, and Lowry, May. (1999). A Critique of How Technology Adoption Models Are Utilized. *Performance Improvement, 38*(5), 24-29.

Wilson, Carol W. (1999). Portrait of the Early-Adopter: Survey of Instructors of WWW Courses. Presentation, Mid-South Instructional Technology Conference, Murfreesboro, TN, March 28-30, 1999. http://www.mtsu.edu/~itconf/proceed99/wilson.htm.

Wolski, Stacy L., and Jackson, Sally. (1999). Technological Diffusion Within Educational Institutions: Applying the Technology Acceptance Model. Presentation, SITE 99—Society for Information Technology and Teacher Education annual conference, San Antonio, TX, February 28-March 4, 1999.

*Rebecca Vaughan Frazee is an instructional designer and performance consultant in San Diego, California. Most of her work centers on the development of training and education profession- als, helping them expand their focus from training to more systemic performance solutions. Rebecca is currently pursuing a doctorate in educational technology at San Diego State University and the University of San Diego. She worked as assistant to the editor on this ASTD E-Learning Handbook. Rebecca can be reached at rebvaughan@att.net.*

# How Can We Use Knowledge Management?

## Allison Rossett and Kendra Sheldon

*Why does an article on knowledge management belong in a book on e-learning? The authors put the case succinctly: "Training professionals have typically focused on developing brainpower more than managing it. ... Training professionals must claim a leadership role in managing the wealth of intellectual resources extant in the organization." This article is excerpted from* Beyond the Podium: Delivering Training and Performance to a Digital World.

*Astrid:* Just got an e-mail from a sales guy who told me he flat out wasn't going to contribute any of his sales proposals to the knowledge base.

*Brock:* You'd think he'd want to, with all the applause they're getting for putting customer materials, presentations, and proposals into the system. All you need is one good experience using the sales knowledge base and they turn around fast. I saw it with one of the senior reps from Sweden. He needed a presentation for a higher education group in Eastern Europe. He found one that had been done for Chile. He read the commentary from the sales leader and was able to edit it to work for his own needs. He said he saved five hours.

*Astrid:* Recently, I've been redesigning classes so that each includes introductions to our knowledge bases and related on-line communities.

*Brock:* I should do that too. I've been putting some of the training examples and tools into the bases, but I hadn't thought about pointing to the repositories in class.

# Defining Knowledge Management

*Knowledge management (KM) is about delivering the right knowledge to the right people at the right time.* That, however, takes some doing. As Astrid complained above, not everybody is eager to pitch their ideas and work products into the collective knowledge base. As Brock will soon see, there's still a strong preference for personal and unique inventions.

A famous quote attributed to the Hewlett-Packard founders goes something like this: "If HP only knew what HP knows. ..." That sentiment rings bells in every kind of organization, from a school to a government agency to a corporation. Knowledge management (KM) is represented by large and small efforts to address that issue, to collect lessons learned in the organization in a way that facilitates continuous updates and wide distribution. Getting a grip on this knowledge, accumulating it, nurturing it, updating it, and making it vital are at the heart of KM. More than a decade ago, Prahalad and Hamel (1990) concluded that the core competencies—or the collective expertise—of an organization are the essence of competitive advantage. Knowledge management codifies that critical advantage, suggesting both content and interactions.

Schwen, Kalman, Hara, and Kisling (1998) and Horton (1999) noted two perspectives on knowledge management. The first views knowledge as content that can be captured and transferred. The second views knowledge as a social process that brings people into fruitful conversations across borders and boundaries. Of course, when suitably stirred, the content can serve as grist for the conversations and the conversations can transform into archival aspects of the knowledge repository.

The "knowledge as content" perspective leads to the development of systems that encourage the efficient gathering, using, and disseminating of knowledge through, for example, knowledge repositories for business intelligence, anecdotes, presentations, and commentaries. A few years back, a global computer company asked its learning and education unit to establish an on-line place for sharing "smarts" across sales units, countries, and product groups. The envisioned purpose was to house sales presentations, product specifications, work sheets, proposals, and commentary about presentations and proposals. In addition, the hope was to provide a conduit to information about place-bound training and on-line classes related to generic sales skills and specific products. Imagine, for example, that a salesperson is scheduled to present to a utility company in Hanover, Germany. In preparation, she might access the database to see what others around the world have said and done in similar situations. She could look for information about this customer and this industry in the European Union and for others who have found themselves with a similar task, no matter the geography. She could rework prior presentations, duplicate FAQs and customer support materials, and even communicate with the originator of materials or approaches that interest her.

The "knowledge as an interactive and social process" provides her with other kinds of options. This perspective encourages the creation of "communities of practice," groups of individuals who communicate because they share opportunities, problems, customers, or other interests. The saleswoman might post a query to an on-line sales community, for example.

On-line communities exist outside organizations as well as within them. A favorite example is www.babycenter.com, an on-line community for pregnant women and related others. Babycenter transcends any one family, country, or organization, instead linking women and related others by the baby's due date. The government of the United States offers another instance. The United States Corporation for National Service supports listservs for agencies providing services to seniors volunteering in their communities. These listservs bring together the people who share that important mission.

There is obvious value in interactions within organizations too. The technology sales organization described above supports parallel conversations for people who sell products into higher education, telecommunications, insurance, energy, and government, for example. They also launch on-line connections to talk about new and extant product groups. Although the purposes of these particular interactions are conventional, internal connections happen for other reasons too, just as they would at the water cooler.

Friends within large corporations report participation in on-line communities that focus on such things as corporate child care centers or gay and lesbian issues. Another example is a Website called egroups (wwwegroups.com), which concentrates on the challenges confronted by on-line community moderators (www.egroups.com/group/eModerators).

## Why Knowledge Management Matters

Knowledge management is attracting attention everywhere. The World Bank has labeled knowledge management an "urgent necessity" for global development and is spearheading knowledge management initiatives in Third World countries. IBM's corporate strategy is replete with KM perspectives, emphasizing shared lessons, repurposed efforts, and collaboration across geographies.

Studies by KPMG and the Conference Board found that 80 percent of the world's biggest companies have KM initiatives in progress (Barth, 2000). The nonprofit Knowledge Management Consortium, founded in 1997, promotes practical, measurable applications of KM to business and other organizations. Their magazine, *Knowledge Management,* distributed in print and on the Web (www.kmmag.com), covers KM initiatives, pioneers, and software options.

A study done by Rossett and Marshall (1999) found that consulting companies were leading the way with knowledge management, both through support of their internal efforts and through services for clients. Marshall and Rossett found that people in consulting firms were four times more likely to have a formal KM system comprising dedicated staff and technology than were other kinds of organizations. The consulting firms distinguished themselves in many ways, including greater unrestricted access to information and reduction in command-and-control management policies.

Even school-based educators are intrigued with KM. They are establishing knowledge bases and communities of practice on-line, such as www.21ct.org, www.eduhound.com, www.parentsoup.com, wwwpar-inst.com, and www.kn. pacbell.com/wired/bluewebn. These useful, non-commercial sites model the possibilities for commercial organizations, whose KM efforts are often shrouded behind intranet firewalls.

Not surprisingly, the Web that has spurred the growth of KM also provides extensive coverage of it. A KM Website, www.brint.com, has grown like Topsy, evoking oohs and ahhs from a group of students impressed and overwhelmed by the profusion of resources. Joe Katzman, a KPMG senior consultant, links to many KM resources at www.pathcom.com/~kat/k-windows/knowledge/links.htm. A favorite on-line KM site of ours is www.knowledge-nurture.com. Sponsored by Buckman Laboratories, it is a free, rich source of information about knowledge management. Figure 1 shows some of what Buckman Labs is doing.

One company that started as a training and development consulting firm has altered its strategy to emphasize knowledge management. LeadingWay, headquartered in Irvine, California, developed a technology to integrate knowledge management and learning. Jill Funderburg-Donello, chief knowledge officer, put it this way:

> While many of our clients still choose to deliver their knowledge in the form of training, especially in an on-line format, what differentiates us is that we don't limit them to delivering knowledge only in a learning environment. The content is held inside the knowledge system, so the format for delivery is flexible. The efforts that previously went into developing training, one delivery method, now can be leveraged to many formats, such as job aids and audio coaching. That same content that was used in sales training is also available as just-in-time performance support, sales presentations, product specification sheets, and other marketing materials.... Update the knowledge once, it's automatically updated everywhere. We treat knowledge as something that needs to be accessible in many different places—not just the training room.

Why so much attention to KM? What attracts LeadingWay, teachers, and consulting companies to the concept? Why does KM intrigue executives, when a conversation about training has traditionally produced MEGO (my eyes glaze over)?

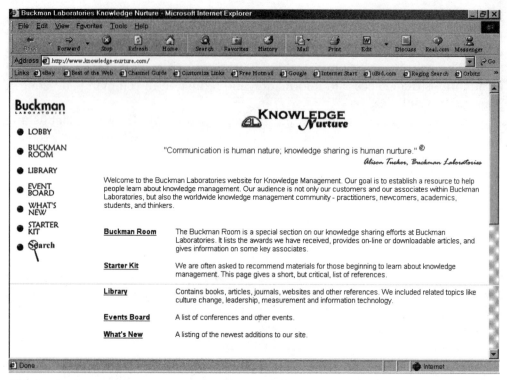

**Figure 1.** The Buckman Laboratories knowledge management site
*Source:* Copyright © 2000, Buckman Laboratories. Used by permission.

We think the answer hearkens back to that quote attributed to Hewlett-Packard at the beginning of this chapter. There is a widespread realization that value is being frittered away through carelessness and attrition. Research conducted by Szulanski (1996) for the American Productivity and Quality Center (APQC) revealed that successful practices typically linger in a company for years, often unrecognized and unshared. When they were recognized, he found that it took over two years before other entities within a company began to adopt best practices actively, if at all. Knowledge management is an attempt to do far better with the "smarts" within people and organizations.

## Knowledge Management and Training

Training professionals have typically focused on *developing* brainpower more than *managing* it. Neuhaser, Bender, and Stromberg (2000), in a book that focuses on the culture of knowledge work, defined knowledge management as "managing people's brain power and the company's collective memory." That is exactly the point here. Training professionals must claim a leadership role in *managing the wealth of intel-*

*lectual resources* extant in the organization. Although that endeavor includes training events, of course, it is also much more than any event or product.

As Rossett and Funderburg-Donello (2001) wrote, "KM distinguishes itself from traditional methods in its emphases and the ways it takes advantage of new technologies *to shift the wealth of individual knowledge into organizational resources.* KM boosts performance by shifting from structured, targeted learning events to the creation of dynamic databases that capture knowledge and connect people without the limits of time and space." They continued, "Where training builds capacity to help people respond IF a need emerges, KM creates resources that are there WHEN they are needed."

The San Diego Sandbox helped Rossett and Funderburg-Donello transfer their passion for the link between KM and training into a tangible resource; they devel-

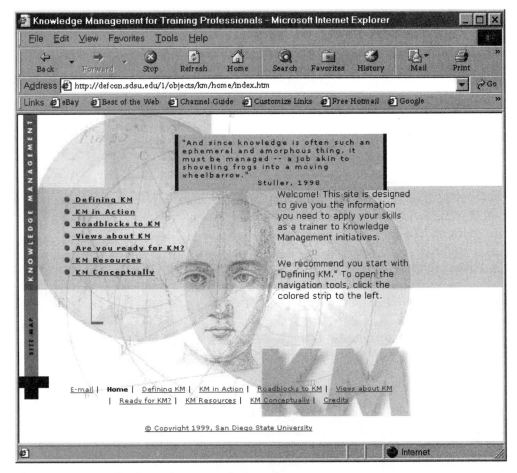

**Figure 2.** SDSU'S KM *and training home page*
*Source:* Copyright © 1999, San Diego State University. Used by permission.

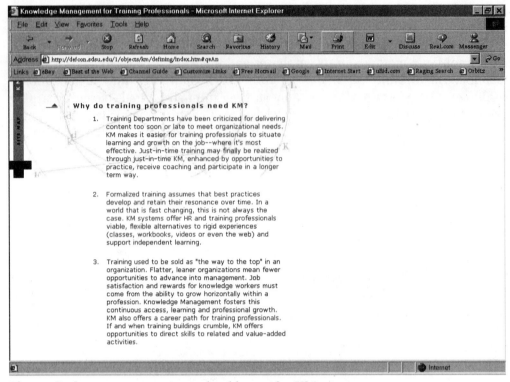

**Figure 3.** Some reasons trainers should consider KM

*Source:* Copyright © 1999, San Diego State University. Used by permission.

oped a Website (defcon.sdsu.edu/1/objects/km/home/index.htm) devoted to this fertile ground. Figure 2 is an example of how this site welcomes training professionals to the topic of KM. Figure 3, also from that site, highlights three ways that KM matters to the individual training professional.

Table 1 highlights the distinctions between training and KM. The right-hand column, associated with KM, is generous. It doesn't preclude conventional training activities, but encourages new and broader ways for the professional to contribute to people and organizations.

As Rossett and Funderburg-Donello (2001) argued, there is much in KM that feels familiar:

- Devotion to human development and performance improvement
- Interest in capturing facts, information, knowledge, and expertise and in making all of it more readily available
- Connections among individuals for the purpose of deepening and distributing expertise, relationships, and work products
- Recognition that training alone cannot provide certain performance improvement

| Training Typically | Knowledge-Management Perspectives |
|---|---|
| The goal is development of individual capacity and memory. | The goal is creating, nurturing, and refreshing organizational resources and interactions. |
| The focus is on building up what's inside the individual. | The focus is on constructing a robust environment to surround people and enrich the organization. |
| A customer might say, "When can we schedule a class to introduce sales reps to the product?" | The customer will not typically come to us for KM. How can we change that? |
| Our responsibility is products and services that teach. | Responsibility expands to content development and social interactions. |
| We develop individual brainpower. | We collaborate to manage the organization's brainpower. |
| We communicate the right way to do it. | We attempt to show many ways to handle it, with commentary that illuminates standards and customization. |
| We work to build events, classes, and programs that will stand the test of time. | We contribute to materials and systems that enrich the organization and are updated readily, regularly. |
| Interventions must be of sufficient length and magnitude to justify travel costs. | The system is salient for problems and opportunities that are great and small, important and mundane. |

**Table 1.** KM and training

- Dedication to making certain that what is learned in class or on-line contributes to practice at work

The solution is cognitive distribution. Gery (1989), Rossett and Gautier-Downes (1991), and Pea (1993) encouraged others in the field to accept the concept of distributing performance-enhancing materials into learning experiences, such as training, *as well as into other means,* such as job aids, on-line help systems, and documentation. Trainers know that take-away materials extend the influence of the classroom. Knowledge management is a supercharged and systemic manifestation of that realization. Responsiveness to this concern is part of the strong case for KM, as wraparound knowledge bases and conversations accompany participants back to where the work gets done.

## What Trainers with KM Perspectives Do

It is hard to argue about the potential for fruitful interplay between training and KM. Stamps (1997), however, reported that a review of seventy knowledge management projects by the American Productivity and Quality Center (APQC) found that only two projects involved training staff or human resource managers. Has time improved the situation? Are training and human resource professionals now capitalizing on the possibilities presented by KM?

Perhaps. Some signs of progress are provided as examples in this chapter. Look at LeadingWay. Consider Saba Systems. Visit Mindlever and Generation 21. We cannot yet point to a groundswell of change, but there are optimistic and tangible changes.

We're attempting here to encourage movement toward a definition of training that includes knowledge management perspectives, services, and products. Figure 4 presents an expanded view of the possibilities for the training and development professional. Note the parallel and linked work and the way that people, services, and materials move freely from one aspect of the work to the other.

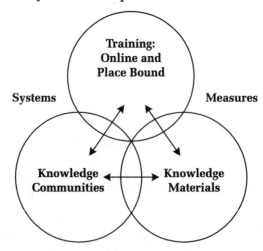

**Figure 4.** *An expansive professional role for trainers*

A discussion of some of the new opportunities for you as a trainer presented by KM perspectives follows.

### Create a Rich Environment

Where once trainers attended to the richness of rooms, lessons, and classroom interactions, KM prompts us to see, manage, and shape the learning and support possibilities within a larger environment. Consider two aspects of KM, the content and the social.

How can you contribute on both sides of the coin? What can you add to the knowledge bases? How can you salt on-line communities with cases, commentary, and examples? How might instructors and training professionals increase their influence by participating in on-line communities? Can you provide opportunities for individuals to self-assess in light of changes in services, products, and markets? Can you launch communities that target training and HR initiatives, such as safety or the rollout of a new operating system? Which aspects of classes create the most interest? For what materials do you receive requests? Those are the objects that should find their way into the organizational knowledge bases.

## Bust the Boundaries of Classrooms

Knowledge management does not signal an end to classroom instruction. Instead, it means *sharing the best of the classroom with the rest of the organization.* The arms of the instructor are extended when training and KM come closer together. The instructor's "war stories" can be distributed across the organization. His examples can be posted on-line, along with commentary and caveats. His genius can now be coded in various kinds of support at the employee's fingertips. Other perspectives on the topic can accompany his and provide intriguing contrasts.

Visit on-line communities to solicit emergent problems so that classes are directed at pressing issues. Use the time in the classroom to test drive the rich KM resources to which participants may refer later after the class, when problems and opportunities are pressing.

Knowledge management transports relationships and ideas beyond four walls and into the organization (Barron, 2000). A pharmaceutical company provides an example. One of the key goals for their KM investment is to bring scientists from diverse fields and geographies together, on-line. Boundaries, especially disciplinary ones, are often viewed as stifling innovation. They believe that moderated KM communities tweak ingrained preferences.

## Establish Broader Access to Information

Marshall and Rossett (2000) found that access to information did not occur with regularity in their respondents' organizations. Most managers were expected to justify *sharing* information, not *restricting* it. When the default is restricted access, it presents a barrier to KM. What can you do as a trainer? How can you draw attention to the problem? How can you serve as a voice for a freer flow of information?

## Nurture Relationships

Most trainers are devoted to nurturing warm and supportive relationships in the classroom. Their careers often started because of those very talents, now extending to mentoring and coaching relationships. There is no need to abandon these inclinations. Instead, bring caring from the training center into the field. Help people with similar interests find one another. Provide a place where people can go to examine alternative approaches to selling X or repairing Y. Create a way for relationships commenced in classes to continue electronically. Tend to concerns about employment security and intellectual property.

## Ask Familiar and New Questions

Here we go from instructional designer to knowledge engineer, a leap that is not so great as many perceive it to be. One on-line resource from the Netherlands about concept mapping offers a list of software tools for representing content: www.to.utwente.nl/user/ism/lanzinLy/cm_home.htm.

Resources associated with knowledge engineering and data mining are available at www.kdnuggets.com/companies. The box on the next page presents questions that are at the heart of the KM effort. Notice that they are similar to those we've asked when trying to get at the essence of expertise.

## Ask Different Things of Instructors

Two organizations, one associated with government and the other with manufacturing, bemoaned the many ways that their instructors have been dragging their heels regarding learning technologies and knowledge management. The instructors preferred the podium. They enjoyed engaging their students in classrooms. Many liked to travel to teach. Although some of that will continue, of course, the time has come for moving many critical lessons from the training center to the knowledge mainstream of the organization. As a trainer, you can help instructors to think of themselves as content sources. Assist them in transferring examples, commentary, and tools into knowledge repositories. Work to allay their concerns about doing so.

Instructors share our frustrations with failures associated with transfer. Through KM, instructors extend their influence, reaching beyond the classroom and into on-line communities and knowledge bases. In a KM world, instructors are valued most for what they know and the economic worth it brings to the organization, rather than for their ability to deliver in a classroom.

Not to be overlooked is concern about the employment security of experts and instructors. If what they know is captured and accessible, some are concerned about whether they continue to add value. Imagine that an instructor thinks, "If I give it to the knowledge base, how do I maintain importance in the organization?" It's a fair question.

The response involves a two-part role for instructors: (1) assuming new roles, including coaching, tailoring, participating on-line, and assessment, and (2) taking responsibility for continuing refreshment of the classes and resources so that they reflect emergent concepts, best practices, and line priorities.

## Questions for KM Success

### Anticipate Potential Obstacles

Has the organization attended to both sides of the equation, both the people and the technology?

How will the organization create a sharing and secure culture? How will it recognize and honor contributions?

How will you counter cultural resistance to putting favorite ideas where others might use, adapt, or even criticize them? Wim J. Nijhof, from the University of Twente in the Netherlands, described a European KM project that foundered because of inattention to culture and work preferences.

Do employees have the research and reference skills necessary for using the KM system?

Are they curious about their work, eager to find appropriate resources?

How will the system refresh itself?

How will it maintain quality and meaningfulness?

What kinds of approaches will be used to solicit feedback from users and potential users? How will this information inform the system? How will it help users assess contributions?

How can we slice and dice documentation and training materials to increase their use within the KM system? How can we infuse KM resources into classes and coaching sessions?

### Ask Questions

What is keeping our people up at night? Where are they most proud?

What decisions are most difficult? To what might people refer for support and guidance?

What URLs are people pointing to? What strategic goals are related?

What examples and stories are repeated to new folks?

What know-how would have the most value if captured and archived?

What stories will provide critical lessons?

Where can other perspectives and approaches deepen knowledge? Save time?

How can we take the approaches of experts and bring several of their approaches together to look at core problems and opportunities?

What aspects of classes deserve wider distribution? Are there any checklists, cases, problems, tools, or war stories that deserve more eyeballs?

What elements from on-line conversations would enrich the system?

## Establish Alliances

As a trainer, you must seek new allies to educate about this expanded view of training. What is your relationship with information technology (IT)? Are you familiar with the databases used in the organization? Do you have access to them? When was the last time you contributed? When was the last time you worked with the line to update entries and add materials related to a growing concern or opportunity? Are you at the table when KM discussions are held? Do colleagues across the organization know of your interest? Can colleagues describe the fertile ground between training and KM? Find ways to *demonstrate* the rich possibilities inherent in this relationship. Mount pilot programs that illustrate those possibilities.

## Repurpose Nearly Everything

Why is there a distinction between training materials and other materials? Why are the examples and work products housed within knowledge bases, rather than typically and generously sprinkled throughout classes? Why are the examples and war stories that enrich training not yet populating knowledge bases? The most valuable aspects of classes and knowledge bases should be starring on both stages. You must focus on building and encouraging materials that are actionable and on giving them featured roles via KM systems and learning opportunities.

## Structure Materials and Conversations to Enhance Meaningfulness and Quality

Marshall and Rossett (2000) found that *information overload* is an issue for training and performance professionals. Information overload is antithetical to KM. This has led some organizations to employ "cybrarians" or content managers to rationalize resources, refresh content, and then assure that it matches contemporary work and priorities. Jakob Nielsen's Website reiterates the importance of good information design with far-reaching commentary, ideas, and examples (www.useit.com).

Junk, and torrents of it, should worry us. In Barth's article, IBM's Scott Smith admitted just such a concern. According to Smith, in the past, the IBM Global Knowledge Management Consulting and Solutions organization encouraged contributions to the knowledge base with bonuses. What did they get? They got many, many contributions; most just beating the deadline set for the end of the year. Smith was quoted as saying, "Not only did they all come in at one time, they were incredibly long and unintelligible." Learning leaders must play a role in establishing systems to encourage, honor, and authenticate useful contributions.

## Attend to the Social and Tacit Aspects

Knowledge management focuses on capturing that which is both critical and subtle. A 1997 Ernst and Young study of KM in 431 firms, reported by Pfeffer and

Sutton (2000), found that firms were investing in knowledge repositories, such as intranets and data warehouses, building networks to identify internal resources, and implementing technologies to facilitate collaboration. Pfeffer and Sutton complained that this snapshot of KM reflected a limited view of the possibilities, one that showed a preference for codified information, such as statistics, canned presentations, and written reports, over stories, gossip, and insight into the way things *really work.*

Many teachers, for example, have said that what they heard in the teachers' lounge encouraged success during their first years of teaching. Sales professionals often talk in similar fond ways about their informal social learning networks. Knowledge bases should be populated with anecdotal lessons just like those that once were shared in the lounge or local restaurant. It also points to the importance of communities of practice, where social networks are established and nurtured. An on-line paper by Hill and Raven (itech1.coe.uga.edu/itforum/paper46/paper46.htm) discussed factors contributing to on-line community successes.

## Contribute to a Sharing, Positive Culture

It is almost trite to urge attention to establishing a sharing culture. Barth's article about KM horror stones reiterates that point (Barth, 2000). After an initial gush of enthusiasm for the topic, how is the organization telling its people that sharing, rather than hoarding, is expected and honored? If organizations fail to encourage sharing, knowledge bases and communities will languish, no matter the investment in technology.

What role can training and human resources play here? How can you as a trainer and performance professional help the organization anticipate stumbling blocks? How can you collaborate with colleagues to grapple with these issues? Pfeffer and Sutton (2000) cite a study by Teresa Amabile in which she showed that people who gave negative book reviews were perceived by others as more competent, leading to her conclusion that pessimism tends to be honored more than optimism. Would you toss your work products into a system where people are likely to criticize them? How can you protect willing participants in ways not so different than those employed in classrooms to nurture effort and bravery? There's a role for training professionals in fostering a culture that encourages people to risk and share, not hesitate, fear, and hoard.

## Use Classes and Orientations to Create KM Habits

Examine classes. Look at on-line instruction. Are you showing off the knowledge bases in both venues? Are you talking up the communities of practice? Are you presenting real problems and then showing students how existing materials from the knowledge bases will help solve them? When you orient new people, do you talk about the organization's on-line communities and knowledge repositories? Do you provide information about those rich resources, just as you would connect new people to the on-line catalogues of classes? Establish habits that encourage seamless movement between classes and organizational knowledge resources.

## Attend to Individuals Not Yet Ready to Be Self-Reliant

Are potential participants ready, willing, and able to engage with knowledge bases and communities of practice? Some are not. Many lack the meta-cognitive skills to search, find, adapt, and use the nuggets they do find. This creates a growing and critical role for training and development professionals.

## Concentrate on Strategy, Management, and Integration

Conventional metrics typically incline training professionals toward staffing classes and boosting attendance. Knowledge management has the potential to change that, at least in part, as success depends on management and integration of a rich knowledge environment. Why move in this direction? There are many reasons, of course. One that appeals to executives is that brick-and-mortar classes have limits on enrollment. The resource can be used up; this happens when the seats are filled or the instructor is jet-lagged. Knowledge management bases cannot be exhausted.

How will you manage a steady and productive stream of knowledge assets? How will you distribute those resources through many delivery channels? How will you integrate them into mundane work? What communications systems will you wrap around them? How will you tailor the systems to meet the needs of diverse constituencies?

Dabbling in KM is futile. KM, much like training, must be an integrated aspect of the organization. Marshall and Rossett (2000) found that when resources are allocated to *both* KM technology *and* personnel, representing a significant commitment, those organizations reported strong evidence of KM.

## Strengthen the Organization Afterward

A knowledge base offers rich resources to individuals. For example, it might help a salesman generate a sales proposal; it also might show him alternative ways to compare his company's product to competitors' goods. And after the salesman made his case to the customer, that same repository can welcome his labor. The system that coached and prompted his efforts now turns into a home for his contributions. When and if he chooses to leave the company, some ideas and artifacts will remain behind, enriching the organization. This seems fair and, not surprisingly, it appeals to organizational leaders.

## Live the Expanded Role

Brook Manville, profiled by Stuart Silverstone (2000), has a career that reflects the possibilities inherent in bringing KM and learning together. Manville was a

McKinsey and Company leader in global knowledge management. In early 2000 he joined Saba Software, a learning management systems company that has recently moved into end-to-end e-learning services. Now, Manville is Saba's chief learning officer and "customer evangelist." When asked by Silverstone about how KM is changing, he said (as we've been saying too), "First is the convergence of training—learning and learning programs—with knowledge management. Second, the Internet and markets on the Internet will play an increasing role in the distribution of knowledge and learning assets."

## Why KM Falters

Our excitement about KM should be tempered with caution. The success rate is not yet what it ought to be. Knowledge management will not deliver unless we can anticipate the obstacles and make a concerted effort.

Johanna Ambrosio (2000) reported that at least half of all KM initiatives fail; some peg the failure rate as high as 70 percent. Why? Ambrosio offered several reasons, especially when HR and IT aren't involved together in the KM effort. She pointed to the failure of organizations to tailor compensation systems to support the unselfish values inherent in KM.

In the article, Viant's Chris Newell describes a better way: "We have eight different ways to earn stock, and five are directly related to growth and learning." Ambrosio also highlighted the importance of sponsorship for KM initiatives.

KPMG's Knowledge Management Report 2000 (Barth, 2000) found that the benefits of KM did not live up to expectations. They cited the following reasons for those frustrating results: lack of updates, failure to integrate KM into normal working practices, complicated systems, lack of training, and the fact that users did not perceive personal benefits.

Here are some key questions we should bring to the table when discussing KM initiatives in our organizations:

- What elements in the culture will encourage sharing rather than hoarding?
- In what substantive ways can the organization counter resistance to putting favorite ideas where others might use, adapt, or even criticize them?
- How will the organization deal with the issue of ownership, identity, and security?
- How will the organization recognize and honor contributions?
- How can we assure both quantity and quality of contributions? (See epinions [www.epinions.com] and fathom [www.fathom.com] for two different approaches to this issue.)
- How will we direct our system and top priority issues?
- What are people most concerned about? Where do they spend time? How do the systems address concerns and save time?

- Is the sponsor able to rivet attention across the organization? To maintain interest and commitment?
- Are the sponsor's interest and attention dependable or will they shift capriciously?
- Is the purpose of sufficient weight in the view of organizational leaders to attract and hold interest and resources?
- How will contributors be afforded the security and status that come from being the unique ones with knowledge about the topic at hand? (Marshall and Rossett found that only one-third of respondents' organizations offered incentives for contributions to a knowledge base and that not just any incentives would do.)
- How does the organization discourage restricting access to information?
- What makes the content in the repositories worthy? What is good stuff? What has meaning? (Because you can't guarantee perfection in a system that typically favors *rich options* over *one right answer,* you must seek customer and user reactions.)
- Do the knowledge bases reflect user priorities? (Although one salesperson might be compelled by product templates, fact sheets, and FAQS, others might crave commentary and war stories.)
- Where else might the systems founder?

Examine the questions listed above, in the literature, and in *Knowledge Management.* Even though the idea of separating knowledge from owners and sharing widely has immediate appeal to most executives, recognize that some individuals and constituents will be put off by the concept. How are you protecting intellectual property and answering employees' concerns that KM will capture their ideas in order to replace their labor? Although there are no easy answers here, these are issues that can bring the best of systems to a halt.

## Questions and Answers

*You're in training. Why are you talking to me about knowledge management?*
I am in training. Most important is that I am focused on learning and performance for the organization. That brings me to want to extend the reach of our classrooms and instructors and create a more learning-oriented environment throughout the organization.

*What does training bring to KM?*
We know the kinds of issues, questions, and problems that are plaguing people in the organization. We can help focus knowledge bases on what really matters. We also have many wonderful examples and tools in training that should be featured in the KM system. And the KM repositories and communities must be introduced in classes and encouraged. It's an opportunity to build good habits.

---

*Any hesitations about KM for training?*

Yes. In fact, an on-line interview with Dave Jonassen in Elearning Post (www. elearningpost.com/elthemes/jonassen.asp) raised important questions about KM and training. His main point: knowledge and learning cannot be managed— they depend on generative activities by learners. What do you think?

*What about IT?*

What about IT? They must be front and center in KM efforts, of course. No argument there. Our intention is to work with them to keep the efforts fresh and focused.

*I love training. KM sounds like something that a database person or a librarian ought to be doing. How does a training person fit in?*

Training events will endure, just be more carefully selected, and often supported by knowledge objects now available wherever and whenever needed. Rather than looking at KM as threatening training, see it as a way to extend the arms of the instructor. By the way, database and library reference skills are of great value too.

*IT won't let us into the action.*

Have you shown them reasons to invite you in? What knowledge objects are you contributing? In what ways are you adding value to the communities of practice? How are you creating knowledge and reference habits in the organization? What's the history of your relationship to their training efforts? This is a critical relationship, for many reasons. Why not use KM to forge closer ties?

---

## Questions and Answers

The box below presents typical questions that might be raised by sponsors and executives—and by you—as you examine the possibilities inherent in KM. We also offer some possible responses.

## Spotlight on People

### Dr. James Z. Li

Li's adult life has been dedicated to the "science" of knowledge. In 1991 Dr. Li had a vision, which he described thus: "If you could manufacture cars, you can manufacture knowledge." Li is the founder and chief executive officer of LeadingWay Corporation.

**Training and Knowledge Management.** Discussing the importance of knowledge management for trainers, Li was direct: "It's time for training professionals to think about this question: 'What business are you in?'

## Knowledge Management in a Hurry

"I have an hour."
Visit http://www.kmmag.com.
Visit http://www.buckmanlabs.com and http://home.att.net/~nickols/~articles.htm.

"I have a day."
Read Tom Stewart's *Intellectual Capital.*
Read Horton (see Resources).
Visit http://wwwbrint.com.

"I've got a week."
Visit http://defcon.sdsu.edu/1/objects/km/home/index.htm.
Read Tiwana (see Resources).
Read Leonard (see Resources).
Attend a conference. They are listed at wwwkmmag.com.

"A lot of people in the training business are a bunch of dodos. They don't know it but they are about to become extinct. You may think it's a result of the Internet and e-learning, but it's not. It's because of the way they think and the mind-set they have. They are like the people aboard the Titanic who believed that the ship was unsinkable. They are like railroad companies who thought they were in the railroad business. They forgot about the passengers and did not realize they were in the business of transporting people. For organizations to survive in the 21st Century, they really have to take a global view of how to move people from beginners to experts and how to move knowledge from the ones who have it to the ones who need it faster and cheaper. Training professionals are in a good position to help their companies produce, distribute, and manage knowledge for peak performance."

**Organizations and Knowledge Management.** Li commented, when asked about the future of organizations and knowledge management: "Ten years ago, both IT and training organizations were facing the same question: 'How can we be strategic to our organization?' Ten years later, if a CEO does not have an IT or Internet strategy, he/she gets fired. Did you ever know a CEO who got fired because he/she did not have a training strategy?"

Li believes that, in the future, "The companies who will flourish are the ones who can create distribute, and manage knowledge the fastest and cheapest. Training is the first step on the journey to expertise. Performance support lets you perform like an expert along the way, and knowledge management accelerates the pace of those who follow and learn from your experiences. The combining of all three into a single knowledge system offers a powerful tool for companies to compete in the knowledge economy."

Li concluded, "It's time for training organizations to become knowledge organizations and integrate KM into training and performance support practices to form a knowledge system that will change the way people learn, work, and share expertise."

**Example of a KM Initiative.** Li gave us an example of a KM initiative at his own company, LeadingWay. He said, "We help our customers manufacture, distribute, and manage knowledge. We believe in the principle of 'eat our own dog food' so we have implemented a knowledge system for our own employees that covers finance, sales, operations, and development in the form of LeadingWay University. KM is our competitive weapon in growing our organization and making LeadingWay a star in the emerging e-learning industry."

Li described the initiative thus: "Each group and individual has a set of core performance measures, and a knowledge system is built for each functional group. A knowledge system is an integration of training, performance support, and a knowledge management system. When new employees are hired, they go to LeadingWay University to take just enough training to get them started doing simple tasks on their jobs. They can access the knowledge systems 'just in time' on the job through the performance support system. If they still cannot do their job with the help of the reference materials, they have access to training on that task, either through e-learning or direct learning help."

He explained, "Any time a knowledge gap is identified or a best practice is found, we update the knowledge system immediately so that new knowledge is immediately available through both training and performance support systems. Because we use our 'Create Once, Knowledge Everywhere' [COKE] technology, we can update the knowledge once and distribute it in training, support, and knowledge management systems without the duplication of effort. Over time, the knowledge system gets smarter and smarter and will become a critical component of our business."

**Contributions of the System.** Li shared that the initiative improved morale, boosted productivity, and reduced training costs. Revenue also doubled, and so did the number of employees. Li said that the company also "achieved the highest customer satisfaction in corporate history."

**Advice for Training and HR Professionals.** Li offered the following advice: "KM is not about technology. It is about out-of-the-box thinking. Every training initiative can be transformed into an integrated learning and KM initiative, if you are willing to refocus your attention from training to knowledge."

**Recommended Resources.** Li recommended APQC and their series on KM best practices, as well as LeadingWay's own white paper, "The Promise of E-Learning and the Practice of Knowledge System Design," at wwwleadingwaycom.

## Jim McGee

McGee is one of the founding partners of DiamondCluster International. He described his background as follows: "We started DiamondCluster in 1994 with the idea of integrating technology, strategy, and implementation skills into a single, coherent organization. Before coming to DiamondCluster, I was one of the initial research fellows at Ernst and Young's Center for Business Innovation in Boston. At the Center, Tom Davenport, Larry Prusak, and I did some of the early research in the KM arena. Before that I was at the Harvard Business School, where I was doing research and getting a doctorate in electronic commerce.

"At DiamondCluster, I've been in charge of both our learning and KM efforts. I don't like the titles of 'chief learning officer' or 'chief knowledge officer.' I think they're seriously misleading. Periodically, I've described myself as Diamond Cluster's 'chief knowledge architect.'"

**Training Professionals and Knowledge Management.** McGee described why training professionals must cultivate an interest in knowledge management in this way: "I think these are fundamentally the same question. The only reason *not* to be interested [in knowledge management] is if you think you're in an organization where all the relevant knowledge is already well-understood and codified. Then you can ignore KM. You can probably also forget about your job or your organization in due course.

"In most of the organizations I see, the half-life of the knowledge base is getting shorter and shorter. If the knowledge base is turning over more rapidly, the learning organization (I prefer learning to training for a lot of reasons) has to get itself involved in how to help connect that knowledge to the mission of the learning organization. In other words, if you don't get yourself embedded in the knowledge that matters (that is, what's most relevant as tested in the marketplace), you're left doing compliance training or otherwise becoming marginalized in the organization."

McGee continued, "What I'd like to see more of from training organizations are efforts to improve the learning capacities of the organization and the individuals in it. That's more a disappointed commentary on how poor the learning skills are of even some of our brightest college graduates than anything else. Most of them know how to get A's, but few of them remember how to learn (if, in fact, they really ever knew much about how that happens)."

**KM at DiamondCluster International.** We asked McGee to tell us about a KM initiative that contributed in his organization. He said, "We've tried a number of things. Some worked well. Others were largely failures, in retrospect. As a rapidly growing organization, we've been willing to try lots of things and kill the bad ideas pretty quickly.

"Overall, one of the things we have done in our early years is to focus on establishing elements of our cultural norms to foster knowledge sharing and use. Our cultural efforts have been more impactful in our early years than have our technology-centered efforts. That's beginning to shift as we get bigger, although I'm willing to bet that the cultural norms we've established will continue to pay off.

"For example, we had the notion early on of designating a number of our people as 'knowledge leaders,' who we expect to develop younger staffs knowledge expertise and to contribute to client projects on the basis of their specific expertise, rather than their client relationship management skills or project management skills."

McGee continued, "We've been a high communications culture from the first days—voice mail and e-mail as part of the tech base. On a cultural note, knowledge leaders are always expected to get back to people quickly with answers to questions. Further, everyone is pretty comfortable sending queries out into the 'ether' and expecting to get help from somewhere. We've used mailing lists, intranets, and a variety of other technology tools to help that process and to help keep some more permanent resource of answers to questions handy. Recently, we've been having pretty good luck using instant messaging tools as another element in the mix."

McGee described what he believes is the most interesting effort/experiment that DiamondCluster has done, something they affectionately call the "Bizarre Bazaar." He explained, "The bazaar is something we tried first in the summer of 1997. One of our culture-building and sustaining practices are regular 'all-hands' meetings, where we bring everyone in the firm together for a face-to-face meeting.

"Early on, these meetings were monthly; then we shifted to bimonthly, and now we hold them quarterly but have expanded them to a two-and-a-half-day session. For the July '97 meeting, we decided to devote half the agenda to a mini-trade show/bazaar. Any project team that wanted to could volunteer to set up a booth about their project. People could then move from booth to booth to see what was going on among their peers. We handed out awards for the best displays and teams got seriously into showing off their projects. We called it the 'Bizarre Bazaar' to encourage a bit of playfulness and have succeeded on that score."

McGee said, "The bazaar has now become an annual event. We hold it now in January at an all-hands meeting where the various MBAs and undergraduates with outstanding job offers also attend. Obviously, the bazaar provides a venue for projects to show off their stuff and for our people to interact with one another in a very high-energy, high-intensity setting. The trade-show setting also gives us an opportunity to showcase the breadth and diversity of our client work. One of the side effects is that it lets teams see how interesting their work is to others."

He continued, "It's not unusual for a team to get bored with its work and feel that other teams are doing more interesting work. The bazaar setting offsets that effect quite nicely. There are other things I think are important about the bazaar. One, it shows the power of culture in leveraging knowledge—far more powerful than technology if you can focus on making it work. Two, it shows the role and limits of central management/authority. We set up the circumstances and venue for the bazaar, but we let the teams choose how and what to do about it. In an organization like ours, with a very wide scope of practice, it's very important to allow for a great deal of latitude and judgment on the part of the field."

**Advice for Training and HR Professionals.** McGee gave the following advice for training and HR professionals:

- "Don't look for or expect silver bullet solutions.
- Focus on understanding organizational dynamics.
- Don't restrict your perspective to inside the boundaries of your organization.
- Don't let the IT group get hung up on technology nits.
- Take advantage of early encounters/contact with new employees to set them along good paths of practice—help them connect to the 'hidden' aspects of the organization faster.
- Focus KM efforts on the real problems of ~K-workers in the field-don't get distracted by KM systems designed to appeal to the egos/distorted perspectives of senior management."

**Recommended Resources.** For people who want to learn more about knowledge management, McGee recommended Drucker (1999), Davenport and Prusak (1998), and Wenger (1998).

## Resources

Ambrosio, J. (2000, July 3). Knowledge management mistakes. *Computer World.* www.computerworld.com/cwi/story/0,119,NAV47_ST046693,00.html.

Barron, T. (2000). A smarter Frankenstein: The merging of e-learning and knowledge management. *Learning Circuits.* Retrieved December 15, 2000 from the World Wide Web: www.learningcircuits.org/aug2000/barron.html.

Barth, S. (2000, October). KM horror stories. *KM Magazine, 3*(8), 37-40.

Davenport, T. H., and Prusak, L. (1998). *Working knowledge: How organizations manage what they know.* Boston: Harvard Business School Press.

Drucker, P. E. (1999, Winter). Knowledge worker productivity: The biggest challenge. *California Management Review, 41*(2).

Eisenhart, M. (2000, October). Around the virtual water cooler. *Knowledge Management, 3*(10), 49-52.

Gery, G. (1989). The quest for electronic performance support. *CBT Directions, 2*(7), 21-23.

Hackos, J.T., and Stevens, D.M. (1997). *Standards for online communication.* New York: John Wiley & Sons.

Hill, J.R., and Raven, A. (2000). Online learning communities: If you build them, will they stay? On-line at http://itech1.coe.uga.edu/itforum/paper46/paper46.htm.

Horton, W. (1999). WBT and knowledge management, allies or arch-enemies. Paper presented at the WBT Conference, San Diego, California, April 1999.

Hutchins, E., and Hollan, J. (1999). *COGSCI: Distributed cognition syllabus.* (www.hci.ucsd.edu/131/syllabus/index).

Lakewood Publications. (1998). Third world KM: The best place to start? *Online Learning News, 1*(39). www.ollo98.com/resource/newsletters/content.htm.

Leonard, D. (1995). *Wellsprings of knowledge: Building and sustaining the sources of innovation.* Boston: Harvard Business School Press.

Marshall, J., and Rossett, A. (2000). An exploratory study of the relationship between knowledge management and performance professionals. *Performance Improvement Quarterly, 13*(3), 23-40.

Martinez, M.N. (1998, February). The collective power of employee knowledge. *HR Magazine, 43,* 88-92.

Neuhauser, P.C., Bender, R., and Stromberg, K.L. (2000). *Culture.com.* Toronto, Ontario: John Wiley & Sons.

Nickols, F. (2001). Knowledge management. On-line at http://home.att.net/~nickols/articles.htm.

O'Dell, C., and Grayson, C.J., Jr. (1998). *If only we knew what we know.* New York: The Free Press.

Pea, R. (1993). Practices of distributed intelligence and designs for education. In G. Salomon (Ed.), *Distributed cognitions* (pp. 88-110). London: Cambridge University Press.

Pfeffer, J., and Sutton, R.I. (2000). *The knowing-doing gap.* Boston: Harvard Business School Press.

Prahalad, C.K., and Hamel, G. (1990, May/June). The core competence of the corporation. *Harvard Business Review, 68,* 79-87.

Prusak, L. (Ed.). (1997). *Knowledge in organizations.* Newton, MA: Butterworth-Heinemann.

Rossett, A. (1999). *First things fast: A handbook for performance analysis.* San Francisco: Jossey-Bass/Pfeiffer.

Rossett, A., and Funderburg-Donello, J. (2001, July). Encouraging performance professionals to welcome knowledge management. *Performance Improvement Journal, 40*(6).

Rossett, A., and Gautier-Downes, J. (1991). *A handbook of job aids.* San Francisco: Jossey-Bass/ Pfeiffer.

Rossett, A., and Marshall, J. (1999). Signposts on the road to knowledge management. In K.P. Kuchinke (Ed.), *Proceedings of the 1999 AHRD Conference* (Vol. 1) (pp. 496-503). Baton Rouge, LA: Academy of Human Resource Development.

Rossett, A., and Tobias, C. (1999). A study of the journey from training to performance. *Performance Improvement Quarterly, 12*(3), 30-42.

Schwen, T.M., Kalman, H.K., Hara, N., and Kisling, E.L. (1998). Potential knowledge management contributors to human performance technology research and practice. *Educational Technology Research and Development, 46*(4), 73-89.

Silverstone, S. (2000, August). A conversation with knowledge management pioneer Brook Manville. *Knowledge Management, 3*(8), 45-48.

Stamps, D. (1997, August). Managing corporate smarts. *Training, 34,* 40-44.

Stewart, T.A. (1997). *Intellectual capital: The new wealth of organizations.* New York: Doubleday.

Szulanski, G. (1996, Winter). Exploring internal stickiness: Impediments to the transfer of best practices within the firm. *Strategic Management Journal, 17,* 27-43.

Tiwana, A. (2000). *The Knowledge Management Toolkit.* Englewood Cliffs, NJ: Prentice Hall.

Ulrich, D. (1997). *Human resource champions: The next agenda for adding value and delivering results.* Boston: Harvard Business School Press.

Wenger, E. (1998). *Communities of practice: Learning, meaning, and identity.* New York: Cambridge University Press.

*Dr. Allison Rossett, Professor of Educational Technology at San Diego State University, was the Year 2000 inductee into the* Training *magazine HRD Hall of Fame. She has authored three award-winning books:* First Things Fast: A Handbook for Performance Analysis *(1999),* Training Needs Assessment *(1989), and* A Handbook of Job Aids *(1991). In 2001, she co-authored* Beyond the Podium: Delivering Training and Performance to a Digital World. *Rossett has Web sites that provide tools associated with recent books and projects: www.jbp.com/rossett.html and edweb.sdsu.edu/people/ARossett/Arossett.html. Rossett is the editor of this yearbook and can be contacted at arossett@mail.sdsu.edu.*

*Kendra Sheldon is a writer and performance consultant living in San Diego. With a master's degree in telecommunications and a background in media, technology, and education, her work has appeared in local television, radio, and new media publications. She is a freelance writer/editor who has worked in San Diego media for more than 15 years. She is currently employed by Pacific Bell Education First, working with the Applications Design Team to develop and maintain Web-based resources and applications for educators and librarians, and completing a Master's of Education degree.*

# Distributed Cognition: A Foundation for Performance Support

## Jan D. Greenberg and Gary J. Dickelman

*This article tackles a question crucial to e-learning: How do we think, learn, and perform? The authors discuss the origins of the theory of distributed cognition and conclude that the theory would lead to the development of "systems that ease the cognitive burden and enable performance."*

How do humans think, learn, and perform? Where does cognition lie? The traditional view has been that cognition exists solely inside one's head (Salomon, 1993)—that it is a "localized phenomenon that is best explained in terms of information processing at the level of the individual" (Rogers, 1997). However, an alternate, perhaps radical, view of cognition has been developing over the past 15 years or so: distributed cognition. This approach, formally developed by Ed Hutchins and his colleagues at the University of California, San Diego, provides a new paradigm for rethinking all domains of cognitive phenomena. Hutchins proposes that, rather than thinking of cognition as an isolated event that takes place inside one's head, cognition should be looked at as a *distributed* phenomenon—one that goes beyond the boundaries of a person to include environment, artifacts, social interactions, and culture (Rogers, 1997; Hutchins and Hollan, 1999). At the same time Hutchins et al. were developing these theories, we saw the emergence of performance support systems. These are environments that enable people to complete work with a minimum of training or learning in advance of doing a task. A performance support environment also transcends the boundaries of the person and includes a variety of enabling artifacts, environmental factors, and social/virtual interactions (Gery, 1991).

## Roots of Distributed Cognition Theory

Salomon (1993) generally identifies the modern studies/fields of cognition, anthropology, and cultural psychology as the roots of distributed cognition. Cole and Engström (1993) take a more focused look at the roots, tracing them back to the origins of psychology as a distinct discipline and its further development by the cultural-historical school of psychology earlier in this century (this includes the works and contributions of Vygotsky, Leont'ev, and Luria). Cole and Engström (1993, p. 9) identify a number of points that summarize the cultural-historical concept of human activity, examples of which bear repeating here because they are at the foundation of the current understanding of distributed cognition:

- "Cultural mediation has a recursive, bidirectional effect; mediated activity simultaneously modifies both the environment and the subject."
- "Cultural artifacts are both material and symbolic; they regulate interaction with one's environment and one's self. In this respect, they are 'tools,' broadly conceived, and the master tool is language."
- "The cultural environment into which children are born contains the accumulated knowledge of prior generations. In mediating their behavior through these objects, human beings benefit not only from their own experience, but from that of their forebears."
- "A natural unit of analysis for the study of human behavior is activity systems, historically conditioned systems of relations among individuals and their proximal, culturally organized environments."

This last point helps lead into a more in-depth discussion of distributed cognition. It is with the growing acceptance of the constructivist view of human cognition that a more serious look is being taken at the possibility that "cognitions are situated and distributed rather than decontextualized tools and products of the mind" (Salomon, 1993, p. xiv). This is coupled with the idea that not only do social and other situational factors have an impact on cognitions that occur in one's mind, but that the social processes *themselves* should be considered cognitions (Resnick, 1991). Salomon (1993) describes three sources for the growing interest in distributed cognition: the increasingly important role that technology is playing to handle intellectual tasks that ease an individual's cognitive load; the re-emphasis on Vygotsky's sociocultural (or cultural-historical) theory (individuals' cognitions are situated within, rather than just interacting with, social and cultural contexts of activity and interaction); and a seemingly growing dissatisfaction with the notion of cognitions as only in one's mind, coupled with a shifting attention on cognitions that are situated, context-dependent, and potentially distributed in nature. Interestingly, these same three notions form the basis for supporting performance on the job in a computer-mediated environment versus "training" individuals to do things in advance of doing them. Organizations are learning that they can foster knowledge acquisition and turn knowledge into action by such application; that billions of dollars poured into many training and education programs does not turn knowledge into action (Pfeffer and Sutton, 1999).

## Principles of Distributed Cognition

Flor and Hutchins (1991) said that distributed cognition is a new branch of cognitive science that is devoted to the study of how knowledge is represented both inside the heads of individuals and in the world (environment, culture, social interactions), the transmission of knowledge between different individuals and artifacts, and the transformations through which external structures go when acted on by individuals and artifacts. They hoped that, by studying cognition in this way, an understanding of how intelligence is exhibited at the systems level (rather than the individual cognitive level) would be achieved. In this paradigm, systems have goals.

Nardi (1996) notes that distributed cognition is concerned with structure—representations inside and outside the mind—and the transformations these structures go through. Because of this focus on internal and external representations, much attention is paid to studying these representations. This may take the form of finely detailed analyses of particular artifacts (Norman, 1988; Hutchins, 1995) and finding stable design principles that are widely applicable across design problems (Norman, 1988, 1991). Another main emphasis of distributed cognition is on understanding the coordination among individuals and artifacts, for example, how two programmers coordinate the task of software maintenance among themselves (Flor and Hutchins, 1991).

In his seminal work *Cognition in the Wild*, Hutchins (1995) carefully observed and detailed the functioning of navigation aboard a U.S. Navy amphibious transport helicopter. In particular, he studied how the sailors used human communication and tools to navigate the ship. He documented and described the sailors' use of nautical tools as well as the social arrangements through which the cognition involved in navigation was accomplished. From this work, a number of principles emerge: cognition is mediated by tools; the critical role of tool mediation in cognition means that cognition is rooted in the artificial; cognition is a social affair that involves delicate variations and shades of communication, learning, and interpersonal interactions. A fourth principle that Nardi (1998) draws from Hutchins' work is the importance of "functional systems"—systems that are made up of a person or group in interaction with a tool. She explains that functional systems mean that "what a person can do with a tool is profoundly different than what a person can do without the tool" (p. 39). In this case, tools could be anything from computer simulations to counting on fingers, hugs from a teacher that help a student stay on task, or closing one's eyes when trying to remember something. In fact, she goes on to say that "to talk about the person without the tool—

cognition without tools—is to make a huge mistake" (p. 39). Thus, the functional system becomes an important unit of analysis.

Distributed cognition looks for cognitive processes, wherever they may happen, on the basis of the functional relationship of elements that participate in this process (Hutchins and Hollan, 1999). A process is not cognitive just because it happens in a brain; conversely, a process isn't deemed noncognitive because it happens in the interactions among many brains. The second distinguishing principle concerns the range of media assumed to participate in cognitive processes. Hutchins and Hollan note that traditional information-processing theories look for cognitive events in the manipulation of symbols inside an individual's head. Distributed cognition looks for a broader class of cognitive events; it does not expect these events to be encompassed within an individual's head. Hutchins and Hollan state that if these principles were applied to the observations of human activity in its natural state (e.g., how people go about their jobs on a daily basis), at least three kinds of cognitive process distributions would become clear: first, cognitive processes may be distributed among members of a social group; second, cognitive processes may involve coordination between internal and external (environmental and/or material) structure; and third, cognitive processes may be distributed through time in a way that the end results (products) of earlier events can change the nature of events that come later.

Performance support takes advantage of the second process as coordination between internal and external structures is supplied by the performance-centered interface that manipulates the artifacts. It takes advantage of the third process, whereby the cognitive processes necessary to reach end results (attain goals, create products) are facilitated through time by the dynamics inherent in the performance-based interface.

Observing distributed cognition environments uses a number of methods for data gathering and analysis. Rogers (1997) notes that cognitive systems being described and analyzed at the work setting require extensive field work and familiarity with the work practice. This typically involves observing the work being done, taking comprehensive field notes, recording work events, and transcribing and encoding them. An important part of this type of analysis is re-representing the raw data collected at different levels of abstraction and detail and focusing on the changes in representational states (the various resources of knowledge and information that are changed in doing an activity) in the cognitive system.

These are precisely the activities of performance support analysis and design, where practitioners engage in the observations of the work being done, take comprehensive field notes, record work events, and transcribe and encode them. The ultimate goal is to abstract the artifacts and process elements of the native human activity system and replace them with new representations that are computer based. If successful, the distributed cognition system will be re-represented in the performance-based system, such that a human being engaged in the system will be able to achieve goals without support or "training events" that are external to the system.

According to Don Norman—

> The sciences of cognition have tended to examine a disembodied intelligence, a pure intelligence isolated from the world. It is time to question this approach.... Humans operate within the physical world. We use the physical world and one another as sources of information, as reminders, and in general as extensions of our own knowledge and reasoning.... With a disembodied intellect, isolated from the work, intelligent behavior requires a tremendous amount of knowledge, lots of deep planning and decisionmaking, and efficient memory storage and retrieval. When the intellect is tightly coupled to the world, decisionmaking and action can take place within the context established by the physical environment, where the structures can often act as a distributed intelligence, taking some of the memory and computational burden off the human (Norman, 1993, pp. 146-147).

We see, therefore, that it is the goal of performance-centered systems to establish a representation of an optimal environment for decisionmaking and action, where many of the burdens of memory and computation are alleviated. Conventional systems (e.g., enterprisewide, transaction-based, data-centered systems)—as opposed to performance-centered systems—add to the burdens of memory and computation.

Pea (1993) believes that intelligence is not a quality of the mind alone, but a product of the relationship between mental structures and the tools of the intellect provided by culture. He sees intelligence as accomplished rather than possessed. Distributed intelligence is always present in tools, modes of representation, and other artifacts that are created to "offload" what would otherwise be a heavy and error-prone cognitive burden. In Pea's view, the phenomenon of distributed cognition clearly shows how external resources change the nature and functional system from which activities emerge. This, in turn, can powerfully affect our concept of what, how, and why one needs to know. Following this, one might place greater emphasis on cognition with tools rather than cognition alone without tools. Thus, performance-centered computer tools and programs designed to accentuate distributed cognition, emphasizing partnership and access, are very different than tools aimed at fostering solo abilities. They have led to a change from educational goals and activities that are designed to—but fail to—foster competent performance to distributed cognition systems aimed at mastery and accomplished performance.

Perkins (1993) proposes that distributed cognition is a system that involves both person and physical environment/social resources (surround), an idea he calls "person-plus." This person-plus is a unit of analysis that jointly participates in thinking as well as learning and—we can infer—performing. This model is analogous to the model of performance support of a human activity system, consisting of human performer, tools system, and task system (Banerji, 1999).

# Applications in Learning and Performance Support

It is instructive to look at how the distributed cognition theory plays out in enabling performance by looking at what it has to say about the design of a performance support system. If one believes that cognition is basically distributed (rather than residing solely in one's head), then one would agree that the individuals, tools and artifacts (e.g., data, electronic tools, wizards, knowledge bases, and so on), values, rules, social and communication interactions, and even the arrangement of space in a work environment would constitute a very complex, interacting system. Furthermore, all of these elements would bear intelligence in them (Pea, 1993). The goal of cultivating partnership as well as solo capabilities, as Salomon (1993) indicates, would suggest a performance environment that is designed to foster a community of performers—a place where workers are able to perform—where expertise becomes distributed in ways that provide the impetus for mutual appropriation (Brown et al., 1993). Examples follow that help illustrate how the theory of distributed cognition informs both learning and performance.

## Engineering a Community of Learners

Brown et al. (1993) designed and implemented innovative classroom practices with students in grades 5-7 from inner-city schools to "support multiple, overlapping zones of proximal development that foster growth through mutual appropriation and negotiated meaning":

> "Mutual appropriation" refers to the bidirectional nature of appropriation ... learners of all ages and levels of expertise "seed" the environment with ideas and knowledge that are appropriated by different learners at different rates, according to their needs and to the current state of the zones of proximal development in which they are engaged (p. 192).

The learners provide a detailed description of a classroom design (including basic classroom activity structures, the classroom "ethos," the roles of students, teachers, curriculum, technology, and assessment) that would foster intentional learning and distributed expertise in the classroom setting.

Two forms of collaborative learning—reciprocal teaching and the jigsaw method—are used as methods for sharing expertise throughout the classroom environment.

In reciprocal teaching (a method for enhancing reading comprehension), an adult teacher and a group of students take turns leading a discussion. The leader begins by asking a question and ends by summarizing the main point of what has been read. The group then rereads the text and discusses any questions about meaning or interpretation if needed. The activities of questioning, summarizing, clarifying, and predicting within and between the group members not only support reading comprehension skills, but enable students with varying levels of skill and expertise to participate to the extent they are able and to benefit from the variety of expertise exhibited from the group members. Brown et al. chose this particular method because it would "evoke zones of proximal development within which novices could take on increasing responsibility for more expert roles" (p. 196). In addition, skills, knowledge, and expertise are developed in the context of an authentic task (reading comprehension).

In the jigsaw method, students are assigned part of a classroom topic to learn and then to teach the information to others using the reciprocal teaching approach. Students form research groups and prepare teaching materials using computer technology. The jigsaw part comes into play when the students come back together in learning groups, in which each student is an "expert" in one part of the topic. The expert in each part of the topic is responsible for guiding reciprocal teaching groups in his or her area. All students in a learning group are experts in one part of the topic, teach it to others, and develop questions for a test that everyone will take on the complete topic.

## Literacy Explorer

It is interesting to note the similarity between the distributed cognition environment described above that fosters reading competency and the goals of the performance-based Literacy Explorer under development at George Mason University (GMU) (Bannan-Ritland and Egerton, 2000). The performance-centered system provides support for a dyad consisting of both a lay reading/literacy facilitator and a child/reader with disabilities. The system provides guidance, resources, and information for lay literacy or reading facilitators to integrate best practices into their reading sessions with the children. At the same time, the system helps the facilitator choose appropriate reading material, prepare the child/reader for a reading session, and conduct the session interactively.

Many of the artifacts of collaborative learning, reciprocal teaching, and jigsaw are reflected in the process support, reading strategy support, and decisionmaking artifacts of the performance-centered interface. For example, many elements are based on the guided reading process (Fountas and Pinnell, 1996), which recognizes that reading skill and strategy instruction should not be taught in isolation, but should be taught in relation to that which is relevant to the child. Children decode words semantically, syntactically, and graphophonetically, which requires performance support from both computer-based sources and from the facilitator. The lay facilitator, on the other hand, needs artifacts that enable him or her to encourage these forms of cuing until the reader finds them intuitive. From a distributed cognition perspective, it is no surprise that the GMU design team concluded that Literacy Explorer needed to support both the facilitator and the reader simultaneously to be successful (Bannan-Ritland and Egerton, 2000).

## CSILE

Computer technology holds much promise for the application of distributed cognition theory to instruction. Local-area and wide-area networks now enable large numbers of individuals to work at the same time in a common environment on common problems (Hewitt and Scardamalia, 1998). This form of communication gets around many of the logistical limitations associated with large-group, face-to-face interactions (e.g., time, energy, and expertise to design and implement a distributed learning classroom environment). Computers also offer a medium for storing knowledge artifacts and searching through libraries of similar artifacts created by others.

One such instructional computer application of distributed cognition is the Computer-Supported Intentional Learning Environment (CSILE) (Oshima et al., 1995; Hewitt and Scardamalia, 1998). Essentially, CSILE is a networked database system that encourages learners' intentional learning through ongoing and progressive conversations. Learners are encouraged to express their thoughts in the database through text or graphics, then to "manipulate their represented knowledge in building further knowledge" (Oshima et al., 1995). Learners share their represented knowledge with others; thus, anyone can build on his or her own knowledge using the knowledge of others. Knowledge-building occurs through dynamic interaction among learners and the knowledge base they construct together. Hewitt and Scardamalia (1998) relate their work on CSILE with the development of an alternative classroom model called "knowledge-building community." Both the classroom design and technology support the notion of a group of individuals dedicated to sharing and advancing the knowledge of the collective (community). The goal promoted here is that of a decentralized learning environment where learners' ideas become the objects of inquiry, the collective's knowledge is primary, and learners assume responsibility for activities typically done by the teacher (e.g., planning, organizing, posing questions).

CSILE and the knowledge-building community provide models for numerous performance-support efforts designed for knowledge workers, such as bank relationship managers, high-end sales people, and brokerage branch managers (see Christensen's remarks in Dickelman, 2000). This highly generative work requires performance support to embrace the notions of knowledge management per CSILE: continuous capture, maintenance, validation of knowledge in the distributed cognition framework. The nature of distributed cognition in such a performance-centered context lends itself precisely to bridging the gaps between learning and knowledge and between knowledge and performance.

Some distributed cognition models gather and present knowledge workers with blended solutions of training/learning, performance support, and knowledge management, creating a *knowledge community* similar to CSILE. They plant the seeds of knowledge sharing and management into training and performance support through team activities, making them a natural part of doing work. In these corporate settings, *workers'* ideas become the objects of inquiry, the *organization's* knowledge is primary, and *workers* assume responsibility for activities that management typically does. According to performance support practitioner Barry Raybould, "A performance support system is the infrastructure for knowledge management. Performance-centered design transforms knowledge into performance by creating an interface to the knowledge base" (Dickelman, 2000).

## Conclusion

Distributed cognition is really a commonsense notion when we think about the things that help us perform. Artifacts—the contrived elements of a computer interface that represent the optimal environments in which we perform—aid cognition. For example, objects that suggest what should be done with them (Norman [1988] calls this "affordance"), such as a horizontal door handle, lighten my cognitive load in that I don't have to consult a manual or an expert to figure out what to do with it (push it!). The door handle exhibits no cognition of its own (Pea, 1993, would disagree) because of its shape and configuration, but in combination with a human activity system, it enables cognition and, ultimately, performance.

The distributed cognition approach is a viable framework and methodology for examining interactions between individuals and artifacts, and therefore particularly possesses profound implications for how we live, work, learn, and perform (Brown et al., 1993; Hewitt and Scardamalia, 1998). Individuals and artifacts are the characteristics of today's computer-mediated work processes. In building the computer systems, we must study the environments of excellent work performance—where business goals are met through human activity systems—then abstract and replicate the essential artifacts in the interface. Instead of data- or transaction-centric systems that, for example, overload memory, we would have distributed cognition-centric systems that ease the cognitive burden and enable performance. Distributed cognition is therefore a foundation for performance support.

## References

Banerji, A. (1999). "Performance support in perspective." *Performance Improvement,* 38 (7).

Bannan-Ritland, B., and Egerton, E. (2000). "Literacy explorer: A performance support tool for novice reading facilitators." *Performance Improvement,* 39(6), 47-54.

Brown, A.L., Ash, D., Rutherford, M., Nakagawa, K., Gordon, A., and Campione, J. (1993). "Distributed expertise in the classroom." In G. Salomon (Ed.), *Distributed cognitions* (pp. 188-228). New York: Cambridge University Press.

Cole, M., and Engström, Y. (1993). "A cultural-historical approach to distributed cognition." In G. Salomon (Ed.), *Distributed cognitions* (pp. 88-110). New York: Cambridge University Press.

Dickelman, G. (2000). "Performance support in Internet time: The state of the practice." *Performance Improvement,* 39(6), 7-17.

Flor, N., and Hutchins, E. (1991). "Analyzing distributed cognition in software teams: A case study of team programming during perfective software maintenance." In J. Koenemann-Belliveau et al. (Eds.), *Proceedings of the fourth annual workshop on empirical studies of programmers* (pp. 36-59). Norwood, NJ: Ablex Publishing.

Fountas, I.C., and Pinnell, G.S. (1996). *Guided reading: Good first teaching for all children.* Portsmith, NH: Heinemann.

Gery, G. (1991). *Electronic performance support systems.* Tolland, MA: Gery Associates.

Hewitt, J., and Scardamalia, M. (1998). "Design principles for the support of distributed processes." *Education Psychology Review, 10.* Available: http://csile.oise.utoronto.ca/abstracts/distributed.

Hutchins, E. (1995). *Cognition in the wild.* Cambridge: MIT Press.

Hutchins, E., and Hollan, J. (1999). "COGSCI: Distributed cognition syllabus." Available: http://hci.ucsd.edu/131/syllabus/index.html.

Nardi, B.A. (1998). "Concepts of cognition and consciousness: Four voices." *Journal of Computer Documentation, 22,* 31-48.

Nardi, B.A. (1996). "Studying context: A comparison of activity theory, situated action models, and distributed cognition." In B.A. Nardi (Ed.), *Context and consciousness: Activity theory and human-computer interaction.* Cambridge: MIT Press.

Norman, D. (1988). *The psychology of everyday things.* New York: Basic Books.

Norman, D. (1991). "Cognitive artifacts." In J. Carroll (Ed.), *Designing interaction: Psychology at the human-computer interface.* New York: Cambridge University Press.

Norman, D. (1993). *Things that make us smart: Defending human attributes in the age of the machine.* Reading, MA: Addison-Wesley.

Oshima, J., Bereiter, C., and Scardamalia, M. (1995). "Information-access characteristics for high conceptual progress in a computer-networked learning environment." Available: http://www-cscl95.indiana.edu/cscl95/oshima.html.

Pea, R. (1993). "Practices of distributed intelligence and designs for education." In G. Salomon (Ed.), *Distributed cognitions* (pp. 47-87). New York: Cambridge University Press.

Perkins, R. (1993). "Person-plus: A distributed view of thinking and learning." In G. Salomon (Ed.), *Distributed cognitions* (pp. 88-110). New York: Cambridge University Press.

Pfeffer, J., and Sutton, R.I. (1999). *The knowing-doing gap: How smart companies turn knowledge into action.* Boston, MA: Harvard Business School Press.

Resnick, L.B. (1991). "Shared cognition: Thinking as social practice." In L. Resnick, J. Levine, and S. Behrend (Eds.), *Socially shared cognitions* (pp. 1-9). Hillsdale, NJ: Erlbaum.

Rogers, Y. (1997). *A brief introduction to distributed cognition.* Available: http://www.cogs.susx.ac.uk/users/yvon-ner/dcog.html.

Salomon, G. (1993). *Distributed cognitions: Psychological and educational consideration.* New York: Cambridge University Press.

Salomon, G. (1993). "No distribution without individuals' cognition: a dynamic, interactional view." In G. Salomon (Ed.), *Distributed cognitions* (pp. 111-138). New York: Cambridge University Press.

Vygotsky, L.S. (1978). *Mind in society.* Cambridge, MA: MIT Press.

*Jan D. Greenberg is Training and Development Associate for East Coast Migrant Head Start Project in Arlington, Virginia, where she has been employed for more than 12 years. She is a graduate of the University of Maryland and an M.S. candidate in Instructional Technology at George Mason University. Jan may be reached at greenberg@ecmhsp.org.*

*Gary J. Dickelman is Vice President of the Consulting Division for GURU, Inc. He specializes in the application of human factors engineering, learning technology, information technology, and business process engineering to business systems analysis through implementation. He is a contributing author to* Using Computers in Human Resources *(Jossey-Bass, 1992) and* The Instructional Technology Handbook *(McGraw-Hill, 1993). Gary may be reached at gdickelman@pcd-innovations.com.*

# Getting IT Support for E-Learning

## Tom Barron

*IT can be a vital ally in the push for e-learning—but it usually takes some support for trainers to develop a healthy relationship with IT. Here are four cases that show how in-house trainers are dealing with their colleagues in IT.*

Getting the attention of information technology executives these days isn't easy. They're neck deep in e-business initiatives and face a daily onslaught of requests from various departments, line managers, and CEOs for new services and capabilities. Unless e-learning excites the top brass—or IT executives themselves—training managers are often told to take a number and get in line.

Even if the top decision makers are tempted by e-learning's various promises, they may not see their own training departments as key players in leveraging those promises. In some cases, executives turn to IT—not the training staff—to pursue e-learning.

What are training professionals doing about that affront? Many are realizing the value of developing a relationship with in-house IT staff that synchronizes their desire for scalable e-learning with the capabilities—and clout—that their IT people can provide. In some cases, it's a matter of building on a solid foundation of past collaboration and positive initial uses of e-learning to train IT staff; in others, it's more about extending an olive branch or rebounding from earlier e-learning disappointments. Working with IT staff, trainers can knock on executive suite doors, armed with arguments around scalability, consistency, and efficiency (three words executives are particularly fond of) together with IT's input on the feasibility and impact of e-learning on an organization's IT infrastructure.

Of course, many trainers who have witnessed the field's migration to electronic delivery have taken the initiative to learn the technology ropes firsthand. A growing number have moved from standup instruction roles to become e-learning-content developers and to boast skill sets and titles that reflect their growing IT savvy. With their combination of education and e-learning development skills, these folks are uniquely suited to make the case for e-learning investments, say some industry consultants.

Another option for shifting to e-learning has become increasingly popular, particularly among mid-size and smaller businesses: external hosting of e-learning through vendors or third-party ASPs. For training managers who win support from the top for e-learning and have either a mandate for fast implementation or an IT department that is overwhelmed with other projects, external hosting is a viable answer. It's also a way around irreconcilable differences.

One obvious reason to woo IT executives toward e-learning is that they have significant sway in corporate technology decisions.

"While trainers were busy checking out all the possibilities for e-learning in the past year, IT people were being promoted," says Ed Mayberry, a training and e-learning consultant. Mayberry, author of a *Learning Circuits* article in January 2000 on strategies for partnering with IT, says IT staff has reasons of its own to pursue partnering. "Failure to do so will most likely lead to wholesale outsourcing of both departments," he writes in a companion to this article that provides pointers for partnering. (See sidebar, "Pointers on Partnering with IT.")

Another reason to tighten the bond with IT is that IT people are among the most seasoned and enthusiastic of e-learners, with the majority of e-learning offerings still centered on IT skills. Capitalizing on technical staff's desire for e-learning, while demonstrating the growing opportunities for broader business skills e-learning for the rest of the organization, can make a powerful argument, particularly given the technology's low recurring costs once an infrastructure is in place.

Following are vignettes on how in-house trainers in four separate organizations are grappling with their "significant others" in IT.

## Long-Term Commitment

Chuck Kater has been in the training field long enough to remember tinkering with Plato, among the earliest commercial CBT authoring tools. As such, he has a wizened perspective on training's migration to technology-delivered approaches and the sometimes stormy relationship with IT staff it has spawned. His 1980s-era dabblings with early CBT iterations convinced Kater, now the director of educational technology for a subsidiary of a *Fortune* 500 consumer products manufacturer, that a new era was at hand. But by the early 1990s, Kater recalls, conflict between training and IT departments were frequent and inevitable.

"Back then, network infrastructures were projected out five or 10 years without any knowledge that the training department would want to use any of those resources. We just sort of sprung up in front of IT—not just in my company, but across the industry."

Kater believed even then that IT experts were necessary partners in the drive toward e-learning and sought to build a relationship with IT staff. That included learning about the infrastructure needed to support the technologies of the day, which evolved from text-based CBT to multimedia content stored on CD-ROM. But each new technology brought new conflicts. When CD-ROMs took hold, for instance, his IT department—and many others—raised hell over the prospect of employees loading their own software on company computers, which could foul network settings. The solution brokered by Kater was to design training's CD-based content to run without installing any components.

"It was our way of doing what we wanted to do without adversely affecting their world," he says. It was also part of a pattern of accommodation and conciliation that would later prove to have merits.

By the mid-1990s, Kater had a familiar and steady rapport with colleagues in IT. As he supervised custom content development, Kater would meet with IT staff quarterly to update them on his department's activities and to discuss future IT needs. When the company decided to launch an intranet in 1996, the two departments worked closely to coordinate content and infrastructure capabilities. Two years later, when they began developing Web-based training, Kater and the IT staffers followed a now-familiar pattern.

"The difference between the early 1990s and late 1990s could be described as the difference between our saying *Here's what we want to do, can you support us?* and *Here's what we want to do, what do you think and how could it be improved?*" he says. "We used to approach them as customers, and now we approach them as partners."

Kater's most recent e-learning initiative has involved using synchronous or virtual classroom technology to train sales reps across the United States. An earlier implementation, managed internally over the company's intranet, led more recently to a decision to use an externally hosted offering. Consulting with IT staff, it became clear that the bandwidth demands of the technology would be too much for the already strapped internal network infrastructure, says Kater. So, his organization's IT staff endorsed the recommendation to seek external hosting.

"This was a case of our taking something off IT's plate—with their blessing," he says. Similar thinking went into a recent decision to explore externally hosted LMS offerings, he says. But those decisions don't end the need to continue courting and collaborating with IT, he adds. "There's always going to be a need to discuss with them what we're doing, even if we're having things hosted externally. We're getting into using streaming technologies that require significant bandwidth on the user's end, which taxes the network.

"To not have IT involved in the decision making would be the IT equivalent of taxation without representation," says Kater.

## Conflict Yields Cooperation

Though Chuck Kater's experience represents a model of forethought and diplomacy, Barb Lesniak's is probably more common, at least among small companies. A self-taught Web-based training developer and primary e-learning content developer for a 3,000-employee electronics manufacturer, Lesniak has had to push for e-learning with little cooperation—and much confrontation—with in-house IT staff. Along the way, she has become something of an IT expert in her own right, though her title—human resource specialist—doesn't reflect that expertise.

Until the end of 1998, Lesniak says she pursued custom e-learning development for employees, distributors, and end users—with little support from the company's IT director. In part, that was due to other pressures facing the small IT department as it grappled with networking separate facilities. But, she adds, the lack of support was aggravated by the IT director's inexperience and distrust of training. "We were viewed more as a threat than an ally," she says.

As a result, Lesniak resorted to back-door tactics to put her e-learning online. She found some free space on a company server and uploaded her custom content for a pilot project, complete with reporting capabilities that would provide test results for a simple LMS system she designed using Microsoft Access.

"I admit I was a bit of a renegade," she says of her darkest days in the push toward e-learning. Encouragement from higher up the corporate ladder kept Lesniak hoping that the conflict with IT would eventually be ironed out.

When the IT director told Lesniak that her methodology for the system's test reporting capability was unworkable, she was skeptical. "They changed the coding in a way they said they had to, but the way they did it made the results useless," she says. As she later gained more knowledge of the company's IT architecture, she learned that the coding changes were unnecessary.

Fortunately for Lesniak, upper management got wise to the IT director's shortcomings and a new director was hired in late 1998. It took six months to gain the new director's confidence, she says, undoing an impression left by the outgoing director. But a working relationship has since blossomed where confrontation once reigned.

"When he saw my JavaScript coding, he knew I knew what I was doing, and that helped gain his trust," she says.

The e-learning content Lesniak developed has proven particularly popular among outside distributors whose understanding of the firm's electronics components is vital to sales. Its popularity "has boosted our role tremendously," she says.

And something of a mentoring relationship has developed between Lesniak and IT as they work toward expanding Lesniak's earlier e-learning creations. "The only conflicts we tend to have now are over what programming languages to use, and bandwidth is always an issue," she says. The IT director advises Lesniak on programming languages that would be beneficial for future content she develops.

"Now I have a dual role: I'm sort of an IT person devoted to the HR department. My supervisor in HR doesn't understand as much about what I do as does the IT director," she says.

## Trainer as IT Expert

As he reflects on a background that is equal parts training, consulting, and e-learning development and management, Rick Reichenbach says there is no secret to maintaining a relationship between training and IT.

"All the commonsense wisdom you hear about partnering is true," says Reichenbach, who recently left a top e-learning management post with McDonald's to join K-12 e-learning technology developer Broadform.

Reichenbach says earlier stints with consulting firms Arthur Andersen and Omniplan, where he worked with clients to implement multimedia CBT and e-learning, provided valuable practice in just that sort of relationship building.

"As a contract provider, it's important to get with IT people early on," says Reichenbach, who started out with a bachelor of arts degree before gradually morphing into an e-learning expert. "If the IT department is uncomfortable with what you're doing, you stand a difficult chance of succeeding."

Fortunately, Reichenbach began learning the language of IT early through work as a multimedia content author and saw the importance of partnering with IT in numerous client rollouts of CD-ROM-based training. In some of those implementations, wrong assumptions by training staff about computer hardware—attributable to a lack of coordination with IT staff—thwarted best-laid plans. Later work developing an e-learning infrastructure for McDonald's made those earlier-era problems seem like a cakewalk, he says.

At McDonald's, where he worked for three years in charge of front- and back-office systems training, Reichenbach's dual knowledge of training and learning technologies was tapped and tested. Though he headed an "operations technology" department more closely aligned with IT management, he worked with the training department to develop a curriculum review that analyzed opportunities to leverage technology for training. He and his staff used that review as the basis for learning technology development.

"One thing that's critical is to draft a really detailed set of functional requirements that you can provide to IT," he says. Functional requirements include things such as audio, clickable image maps, text-entry options, and other interactive features. "Then someone on the IT side can drill down from those functional requirements to determine the specific hardware and software requirements for the system," he says.

In his unique role as a trainer with IT expertise, Reichenbach led an effort by McDonald's earlier this year to investigate LMS systems. In that role, he worked with the training staff to develop functional requirements, then helped review systems for his IT department as a judge in an analysis of LMS systems sponsored by an IT industry magazine.

One area in which Reichenbach says IT staff can be of great value to training professionals is assessing the quality of e-learning software from a "code quality" perspective. "Training people are typically more concerned with content quality, not code integrity," he says—such as whether software will run over different hardware or browsers. "It's an area where IT has a lot of experience and where they can provide a major benefit."

## Anonymous and Aggrieved

Kim Smith (not her real name) says she's learning the hard way the importance of coordinating closely with IT in pursuit of e-learning. One of two people in a year-old training department for the U.S. division of a European-based manufacturer, Smith and her colleague sought development of custom content at the CEO's behest to help employees understand the company's diverse activities. They vetted custom developers, selected one, told them what they wanted, and put the developer in touch with internal IT staffers to coordinate on issues such as bandwidth and hardware and software needs. That's when the problems started.

"When the vendor came in and showed us a demo of their work, it was very interactive, with lots of video clips," says Smith, who asked for full anonymity in exchange for describing her woes. But when a close-to-final version of the content was presented, it was more along the lines of e-reading than an interactive experience. The vendor explained that, after talking with IT, it became clear that the bandwidth for video was unavailable. Smith says that IT denies that it placed bandwidth limits on the content and that enough bandwidth was available. She's still sorting through the finger pointing, while acknowledging she should have taken a more active role in overseeing the project.

"One thing we've learned is you can't rely on the outside vendor to drive the project," says Smith, who adds that because of her lack of knowledge about IT issues, she put too much faith in direct communication between the vendor and IT. "Now, we know we have to work more closely with our IT department and stay on top of the project."

Smith, who has an education background and is now cutting her teeth in a training role, says the project is being resuscitated and that the company CEO is keen on developing e-learning. "Luckily, we have strong support on top," she says.

## Beware the Curmudgeon Role

Consultants say many of the hurdles faced by trainers in pursuing e-learning revolve around coordinating with IT and other internal advocates of the technology.

## Pointers on Partnering with IT

The environment for training professionals is changing in ways that seem hard to believe. As a wake-up call, I pose the following question: Why should organizations have training departments when ASPs offer employees top-quality, low-cost, end-to-end training solutions that record learner performance and personalize content and curriculum to individual career paths?

If you can answer that question, your job is safe—for now. But I suggest that IT and training departments get beyond basic communication skills, team up, and start formulating business plans. Failure to do so will most likely lead to wholesale outsourcing of both departments.

To get started:

- Start subscribing to technical journals.
- Visit techie Websites, such as webmonkey.com.
- When you hear an unfamiliar acronym, look it up in the *Free On-Line Dictionary of Computing* at foldoc.doc.ic.ac.uk/foldoc/index.html.
- Communicate with the IT department whenever you get an opportunity. If the terminology they use sounds foreign, listen more and talk less.
- Purchase some simulation-based computer games and play them.
- Build your technical vocabulary.
- Keep up-to-date on key industry trends.

To do your homework, develop a critique sheet for e-learning by finding five e-learning sites and critiquing them. For each of the following, provide a definition that you understand and find one vendor that provides related services:

- Application service provider (ASP)
- Virtual private network (VPN)
- Co-location
- Server
- Hub
- Ethernet
- Learning management system (LMS)
- Content management system (CMS)
- Dynamic Website
- Bandwidth
- Firewall
- Personalization.

E-learning is the future of training departments, so you need to decide where you plan to go when learning environments become server-based. Training departments can address these changes proactively through strategic partnering.

Your new goal is to work with your IT department to develop practical e-learning solutions that suit your company's needs. If the IT department requires labor and hardware to implement new training solutions, the training department could shoulder some of the costs.

Training and IT departments have incredible amounts of knowledge, skills, and abilities. Each department must combine its efforts and develop new learning solutions to benefit their organizations—or else!

—Ed Mayberry

Ed Mayberry is an e-learning strategist with Wilweb.com, the Web-based training arm of Wilson Learning; ed_mayberry@wlcmail.com.

"IT people have something to learn from trainers and vice versa," says Lillian Swider, principal of LPS Associates, who specializes in consulting on the use of virtual classroom technology. "We understand instruction, they understand technology—and those are two important pieces of the puzzle."

Swider continues: "It's amazing how often it's *ready, fire, aim* when it comes to implementing e-learning. People are in a hurry and strategy gets lost in the rush." She points out that trainers can play a crucial role as brokers who synchronize the needs of various departments as part of their effort to investigate and invest in e-learning technologies.

GartnerGroup e-learning consultant Clark Aldrich strikes a more dire tone in discussing the impact of e-learning on training departments:

"Traditional training groups are being marginalized," Aldrich told attendees of the ASTD TechKnowledge 2000 Conference in September. "Business leaders are not looking to training people for a lot of these skills they need to roll out e-learning."

According to Aldrich, trainers can fight the trend by aggressively promoting use of the technology and partnering with other in-house e-learning believers, including IT folks who often have the most firsthand experience with e-learning.

Trainers should avoid the trap that IT departments fell into in the past decade of being professional curmudgeons over new technologies that capture executives' attention. "Knowledge management, data warehouses, ERPs—every single one was fought by the IT department, and every single one was forced on them by business units that argued they had to adopt them for competitive reasons," says Aldrich.

Aldrich forewarns, "It's critical for traditional training people not to play that same role. It didn't work for them, and it's not going to work for you."

*Tom Barron is a consulting editor for* Training & Development *and* Learning Circuits. *Contact him at tbarron@lightlink.com.*

# Emerging Instructional Technologies: The Near Future

## John W. Jacobs and John V. Dempsey

*E-learning technologies continue to evolve as technology itself evolves. This article looks at three specific technological trends that are likely to have strong influence over instructional design: object-oriented distributed learning environments, the use of artificial intelligence environments, and the expanded effect of cognitive science and neuroscience.*

*What is the use of a book, thought Alice, without pictures or conversations?*
*—Lewis Carroll*

As in most professions, better tools make for better products. This also applies to the design of instructional systems. The past 15 years have witnessed the development and continual upgrading of sophisticated computer-based programs that have revolutionized the way instruction is developed and implemented. Embedding any of a wide variety of media into the instructional environment can be done almost effortlessly. Similarly, course management functions at the individual and group levels can be implemented quickly and efficiently as can sophisticated assessment, feedback and branching capabilities. All in all it has never been easier to design, develop, and implement effective instructional courseware. And yet a core element of developing effective instructional systems continues to involve activities completed before the development process begins, including requirements analysis, task/skill analysis, matching learning demands to instructional technologies, and so on. Technology-enhanced tools continue to pave the way for improvements in how instructional courseware is developed and implemented. It is the adherence to sound instructional theory throughout the entire design and development process, however, that will ensure the achievement of high impact learning outcomes.

This article reviews and discusses three emerging instructional design and technology areas that we believe will have a profound influence on the field of instructional design and technology, at least within the foreseeable future. This article also provides a glimpse of tools and trends that are likely to affect learning and instruction during the next 10 to 20 years and forge an enduring relationship between distributed cognition and the craft of instructional design.

## Three Emerging Influences

Three technology influences or forces that we believe will make a conspicuous contribution to the field are (a) the proliferation of object-oriented distributed learning environments, (b) the use of artificial intelligence applications, and (c) the expanded effect of cognitive science and neuroscience.

### Object-Oriented Distributed Learning Environments

Object-oriented programming languages, such as C++ and JAVA, have been in use for several years and SmallTalk, the precursor to these languages, has been in use since 1970. Object-oriented programming currently has a dominant role in guiding the future of software application development, including those for designing and delivering instruction. Among the primary benefits of using an object-oriented programming language is the ability to separate programming function from associated data elements. This separation, in conjunction with a hierarchical layering of functional attributes, allows programmers to more easily reuse programming code and in many cases reduces the time and resources needed during software verification and validation (i.e., debugging). Object-oriented programming is being used increasingly to develop Internet applications because of its potential integration with HTML and XML. In the parlance of object-oriented programming language, program elements are linked rather than embedded. Conceptually and in practice, the notion of "linked objects" is creating a revolution in the way instruction is designed, developed, and delivered.

**Linked Objects.** The conceptual underpinnings of distributed learning environments are relatively straightforward. The devil, as always, is in the details. For starters, take a typical stand-alone, technology-based training (TBT) program that can be generated using one of the many commercially available software applications. Now engineer it so that instructional materials (including text passages, graphic images, video, and audio files) are integrated into the program as linked objects. In the near future, organizations will develop a repository of instructional content materials (i.e., learning objects), to include specific elements (e.g., text passages, photos, etc.) as well as more complex instructional chunks, that can be reused via programming links as needed by one or more instructional platforms. Information content can be easily updated on an as-needed basis to ensure that the information is accurate, up-to-date, and tailored to the specific needs of individual learners.

For example, say your organization developed instructional courseware using an off-the-shelf, TBT development platform. The courseware involved training newly hired employees to operate an existing piece of equipment. One module of the instruction involved completing maintenance-tracking paperwork used to schedule ongoing preventative maintenance activities. Suppose also that the equipment is scheduled to be upgraded with new operating capabilities and that this will affect, among other things, the way equipment usage is reported. Using an object-oriented architecture, changes to the instructional modules involving the new equipment capabilities can be completed using resources developed by one group, while changes to the maintenance-tracking module can be completed by a separate group. The distributed nature of the instructional environment allows changes to be made to the central TBT program, which is then accessed by individual employees using a personal computer (PC) via a local- or wide-area networked communication link.

You can now begin to see the potential for such a centralized control, decentralized application instructional environment. To enhance learning effectiveness, a TBT program needs to measure and keep track of key learning events and activities at both the individual and group levels. This is where a distributed instructional environment can have a significant advantage over a stand-alone system. Within a distributed instructional environment, learning activities and events can be tracked within and across lessons or entire courses of instruction, making it possible to detect and address learning trends in a highly specific manner. It will be possible for distributed learning systems to integrate information about an individual's aptitude, learning preferences, goal orientation, and so forth within a tailored instructional program that matches learning needs to instructional technologies and activities.

**Training Jackets.** Storing information pertaining to individual learners is a key component of any TBT program. However, storing such information in a central location is problematic due to privacy issues and the need to establish secure data transmission channels. The military aviation community (among others) has developed a conceptual model, referred to as an "electronic training jacket," to describe this capability (Kribs & Mark, 1999). A trainee's electronic training jacket incorporates a host of information related to the five "W" questions illustrated in Table 1.

The electronic training jacket is considered a key component within a comprehensive instructional management system (IMS). For the training jacket concept to work, it needs to be transportable and to have an embedded capability for

| Query | Examples of Data |
|---|---|
| Who is the trainee? | key biographical information such as name, identification number, position, aptitude, and learning styles |
| What is the trainee's personal history? | key work experiences to include formal and informal education and training history |
| Where is the trainee headed? | types of operational assignments the trainee is likely to encounter; overall career path goals/options |
| When will the trainee be expected to apply the training? | immediately versus sometime in the future, operate with or without job aids, work independently or with others |
| Why is this training being completed? | initial, remedial, or maintenance training; expected level of competence as a result of training (expert, journeyman, basic) |

**Table 1.** Five W's applied to a training jacket

positively identifying individual trainees. One potential application being researched by the military and industry (and more recently higher education) for accomplishing this task involves what is referred to as "smartcard" technology. These identification cards/units contain embedded microchips that provide positive identification using one or more of the following: thumbprint, voiceprint, retinal scan, DNA scan, or some other as yet undeveloped identification technique. If needed, the smartcard also can hold in its local memory the individual's training jacket information, making it readily transportable. Once the smartcard is activated using the positive identification technique, it could be inserted into a PC via a card scanner or other device, thereby allowing the trainee to access the IMS and initiate a training session. Interestingly, some relatively inexpensive and commonplace technologies such as WebTV, which provides Internet access via television, have smartcard capabilities.

The Advanced Distributed Learning (ADL) initiative (Department of Defense, 1999; see also www.adlnet.org/) is currently the source of funding being used to develop the electronic training jacket and associated IMS capability. At present, the ADL initiative is in the prototype development phase. This initiative is aligned with an instructional technology standards initiative seeking to develop electronic "data tags" that will facilitate the development of an object-oriented, distributed training architecture that would support military, industry, and academia (Graves, 1994). Such an instructional development environment, if developed correctly, would establish an open architecture within which individual (proprietary) solutions could be implemented, but that allow information and resources to pass between proprietary instructional development and delivery platforms.

**Meta-Data Tags.** Meta-data tags refer to "data about data" (see www.imsproject.org/metadata.html) and are used to label the wide variety of learning resources needed to manage and deliver instruction within a distributed learning environment. Meta-data tags can index an individual learning resource (object) using multiple attributes. Consider the following example: an animated graphic depicting the integration of various systems (i.e., hydraulic, electrical, mechanical, etc.) within an aircraft landing gear. This learning object can be represented within a single meta-data tag using hierarchically derived indices or attributes covering nine areas: general, life cycle, meta data, technical, educational, rights, relation, annotation, classification. Within the educational area, sub-level attributes can specify a variety of information concerning the nature and use of the instructional resource or object. For this example, the sub-level attributes might include the following:

- Interactivity Type: student controlled
- Learning Resource Type: graphic, animated
- Interactivity Level: medium
- Intended End User Role: example, demonstration
- Learning Context: maintenance, troubleshooting, systems
- Typical Age Range: adult
- Difficulty: low

The meta-data tag and associated sub-level attributes facilitate reuse of this learning object across various courseware boundaries. Thus, this same learning object can be used in other lessons within the same curriculum that deal with aircraft maintenance, troubleshooting, system integration, hydraulic systems, electrical systems, mechanical systems, and so on. Similarly, other course developers involved in developing courseware supporting an entirely new curriculum can use this same learning object. The IMS standards will promote an open, distributed-learning architecture supporting a wide variety of instructional development platforms. Based on the rapid, and sometimes unpredictable, advances driving the information technology fields, the IMS standards development process will be ongoing and will at times take a back seat to technology innovations and subsequent market share acceptance rather than establishing a smooth, pre-determined path of change.

From an educational research perspective, meta-data tags will allow the field of instructional design and technology to develop theoretically based, empirically validated courseware design principles at a level of specificity as yet unimagined. For example, by collecting data across various instructional platforms and information content areas, it will be possible to determine what instructional features (e.g., media type, level of interactivity, etc.) interact with specific learning styles or preferences to produce above-average gains in learning and knowledge transfer. The key to making this a reality is to establish research-reporting guidelines to ensure that individual study results can be integrated within a larger body of knowledge and that support analysis using meta-analytic or other useful quantitative and qualitative review procedures (Hays, Jacobs, Prince, & Salas, 1992; Johnston, 1995).

## The Application of Artificial Intelligence

Instructional systems of the future will be able to perform a number of high-level activities involved in monitoring and regulating the instructional environment at individual and group levels. At the individual level, future instructional systems will diagnose learning needs, aptitudes, and styles; develop instruction tailored to pre-identified needs and aptitudes; modify the level and type of feedback and instructional strategy based on learner responses and progress; and implement best practices guidelines based on up-to-date research findings. At the group level, future instructional systems will monitor and allocate instructional resources (e.g., schedule team activities or computer simulator time); collect and analyze data across individuals, tasks, and settings; and generate lessons learned, best practices guidelines, etc., for use by instructional design and technology researchers and practitioners.

These high-level functions can only be accomplished by integrating some form of artificial intelligence (AI) within the course management component of instructional systems architecture. There are several approaches that have been used by AI researchers to embed "intelligence" within computers (Gardner, 1985; Pew & Mavor, 1998). What follows is a brief description of two basic instructional approaches that we believe will integrate AI functionality and in so doing open up new vistas in development of future instructional systems.

Instructional systems of the future will combine information content with automated teaching and learning principles (i.e., pedagogy) to create combination push-pull learning environments. Information push (I-PUSH) learning environments will be based on an expanded use of intelligent tutoring system (ITS) applications. Information pull (I-PULL) learning environments will be based on intelligent interfaces allowing learners to construct their own learning experiences using integrated tool sets. These tool sets will include the capability to conduct concurrent information search and analysis operations and to rapidly develop simulated environments for testing ideas or fostering knowledge transfer to real-world settings.

ITS applications have been effectively employed in a variety of content areas and have been shown to produce results approaching those attributed to one-on-one tutoring (Merrill, Reiser, Ranney, & Tafton, 1992). At their heart, ITS frameworks are viewed as highly interactive, computer-based instructional environments whose goal is to actively guide (i.e., push) learners toward achieving expertise within a given content area. Within an ITS framework, two contrasting models are generated and used to guide the instructional process: one depicting how an expert would perform and the other depicting how a novice would perform (Ohlsson, 1986). The expert model reflects an ideal solution path that is generated by conducting an in-depth analysis of the cognitive process steps a typical subject-matter expert performs when faced with the same problem or problem type. The novice model may encompass several sub-models, each of which depicts an erroneous solution path that a novice learner may explore when faced with a given problem or problem type. The key elements of ITS that set it apart from conventional computer-based instruction are an ability to accurately diagnose learning errors by matching error patterns to pre-defined models of novice performance and tailoring subsequent instructional activities (e.g., via feedback, branching, etc.) so that learner performance more closely matches that of the expert model.

Within a typical ITS framework the tutor provides information, examples, feedback, and so forth, necessary for learning to take place. McArthur, Lewis, and Bishay (1993) contrast instruction-led approaches engendered by the ITS framework with learner-centered approaches (in their words "interactive learning environments" or ILEs) that in our view can be characterized as an I-PULL learning environment. Within ILEs, the learner takes on the primary responsibility of managing the learning process, typically by employing tools that allow information to be collected, manipulated, and represented.

Our vision of I-PULL learning environments expands the concept of ILEs on several fronts. For example, I-PULL intelligent interfaces will be off-the-shelf platforms that can be trained to work closely with an individual user/learner. Initially, an intelligent interface will gather information about an individual's learning style and information-processing strengths and weaknesses based on the results of an extensive questionnaire coupled with the results from a series of pre-programmed learning assessment exercises. As individuals interact with the software tools to locate, store, and use information for ongoing work and leisure pursuits, the intelligent interface will provide suggestions on how to improve learning efficiency and effectiveness based on validated learning-to-learn principles and personal usage characteristics.

Among the more valuable tools increasingly available to instructional designers are simulations and simulation games (Jacobs & Dempsey, 1993; Dempsey, Lucassen, Gilley, & Rasmussen, 1993). Simulations and simulation games will be used within both I-PUSH and I-PULL learning environments. A wide variety of simulation techniques, such as 2-D and 3-D modeling, role playing, video, and case studies will increasingly be used to create realistic environments for developing and testing new ideas or practicing specific tasks and associated skill sets. Once created, simulation environments will be capable of being exported so others can use them for individual training or as part of a distributed simulation activity involving two or more participants. Intelligent computer-generated agents will also be included within the simulation environment to allow realistic collaborative interaction.

Whenever artificial intelligence learning systems are discussed one question invariably materializes. When will AI systems truly demonstrate human-like "intelligence" in the form of learning (i.e., the ability to change behavior based on past experience) and flexible problem solving? It is our belief these momentous achievements will occur at a modest level within the next decade due to developments in related fields. First, AI researchers have used a variety of cognitive modeling approaches that more closely mimic the functioning of human information processing to investigate such critical performance issues as situational awareness, decision making, and knowledge acquisition (Pew & Mavor, 1998). Second, recent advances in parallel processing offer a possible breakthrough in raw computing power, which have impeded the ability of AI researchers to write programs performing relatively simple cognitive tasks (e.g., object recognition) under real-time constraints. In addition, there are alternative technologies offering great promise. One such technology is field-programmable gate array (FPGA), a relatively new type of integrated circuit that can be thought of as intelligent hardware (Faggin, 1999). Using FPGA, future computing systems can not only be the size of the current micro-chip, they can have inherent hardware architectures incorporating properties that are found only in biological neural networks. Learning systems using FPGA technology may be capable of displaying such key intelligent functions as real-time learning and self-repairing. When used in combination with increasingly sophisticated and powerful cognitive processing software approaches, these hardware advances will usher in the beginning of a revolutionary era in intelligent computing that will greatly influence the field of instructional design and technology.

## Cognitive Science and Neuroscience Contributions

Advances in the related fields of cognitive science and neuroscience have been based, in part, on the ability of researchers to monitor electro-chemical activity within the brain and to more accurately match brain structure and associated neural activity to overt actions, such as psychomotor behavior, recall of information, and decision making (Davidson & Irwin, 1999; Tononi, Edelman, & Sporns, 1998). Technology improvements in this area continue to enhance the level of precision with which neural activity can be monitored. Innovations will likely include the ability to influence brain activities affecting learning and these innovations will be incorporated into advanced instructional systems.

What we shall refer to as "brain mapping" will open up a new vista for instructional design and technology research that will have direct application to the design of instructional systems. For example, it will be possible to monitor the level of knowledge acquisition and retention by monitoring the relative amount of brain activity as well as the specific neural pathways being activated. This may even give rise to a new class of learning objectives that describe this new learning event. For instance, "The learner will demonstrate understanding of the concept of 'network interoperability' by exhibiting neural activity in .04% of his/her superior temporal gyrus mass and by exhibiting cross modal activation starting in the temporal lobe and moving to the pre-frontal lobe."

In the area of interdependent learning, where two or more individuals must collaborate their efforts to enhance team or group performance, much has been written about the need for establishing a shared mental model across team members (Stout, Cannon-Bowers, Salas, & Milanovich, 1999). By monitoring the timing and extent of neural activities across the various team members, it may be possible to determine what activities enhance team collaboration, cohesiveness, and overall performance effectiveness.

What if a learner is having difficulty assimilating new information? Can a gentle electrical impulse focused on a specific brain region spur acquisition and recall of to-be-learned information? If a learner is temporarily unable to focus on the task at hand or is experiencing a more general sense of low motivation, can focused neural stimulation assist the learner to refocus his/her attention or generate a more general sense of purpose and self-efficacy? These questions focus attention on much bigger issues that need to be addressed as research in this area expands. Certainly, as one crosses the line between passive monitoring of neural activities and into active manipulation of these activities, there is the need to pay heed to ethical and legal issues related to free will and mind control.

For researchers and practitioners in the area of instructional design and technology, monitoring neural activity associated with learning is intriguing because of the opportunity for obtaining direct feedback related to mental processes. Tracking internal activities at the neural level is important, but provides only a partial solution for advancing the field of instructional design and technology. Another important component involves the ability to track learner performance and provide effective feedback. The following section discusses advances in these two key areas.

**Advanced Performance Tracking.** Imagine your goal is to improve your serve in tennis. Now imagine slipping into a tight fitting leotard-type outfit that fully covers your body from head to feet. This "body glove" incorporates an intricate electrical grid that transmits precise body position and relative movement information to a personal computer (PC) located several feet away.

The PC has attached to it a large, flat panel display system that visually simulates your movements in real-time using a realistic three-dimensional model that matches your body type, weight, and so on. Next, you begin practicing your serve. After three or four tries, the system provides a verbal and visual (using the flat-panel display) critique of key elements that make up an effective serve, such as initial stance, ball toss, and arm and racket motion. Your 3-D image is superimposed upon an ideal image modeled after a highly proficient service motion of someone your age and with your ability level. The program then provides you with verbal and visual instructions on each service element individually, and then gradually combines two or more elements until you are now practicing the entire serve as one fluid motion.

After several much-improved practice serves, you check your progress on the computer by reviewing your three most recent service motions superimposed on top of the ideal image. In addition, you request an analysis and progress report from the program. Alas, your forward arm motion and wrist snap just prior to striking the ball needs additional work because it produces a slower than expected serve that has too much side spin. After several more attempts at self-correction (with verbal and visual prompts and feedback generated by the program), you decide you need more direct help. You now slip your arm into a device that looks like a long glove that reaches to your shoulder. This device is slightly thicker than your body glove performance tracking system and has embedded into it what the manufacturer refers to as micro-hydraulic capabilities. Responding to the verbal directions from the program, you set your body position to a point where your forward arm motion is to begin. You now feel a warm sensation in your arm, wrist, and hand as the micro-hydraulic arm gently shows you the correct arm and wrist motion. During the next 20 or so practice swings, you feel less and less influence from the micro-hydraulic device and, in fact, the program confirms that your muscle memory has now been altered slightly to incorporate the newly corrected arm motion and wrist snap. This result is confirmed by the program's analysis indicating key elements of your service motion more closely match those of the ideal model and your serve is now 5-10 miles per hour faster than before.

The previous example provides a vision of what an advanced performance tracking and feedback system can offer in the way of enhanced training processes and outcomes. Note also the system's ability to diagnose training needs prior to prescribing remedial training. Future instructional systems will have embedded in them the ability to conduct performance assessment at the whole-task or part-task level.

## A Little Farther Down the Road: Cybernetics and Nanotechnology

For nine days in August of 1998, Kevin Warwick, a professor of cybernetics at the University of Reading, wore a tiny capsule measuring 23mm by 3mm surgically implanted in his left arm. The capsule contained a power source and microprocessors. Warwick, an expert on intelligent buildings, programmed the implant to open doors, have his computer speak to him about his e-mail, run baths, and chill wine (Witt, 1999). Although it may be a while before we can control computers directly from our nervous system, it is something that even the middle-aged authors of this chapter are likely to see in their lifetime. Highly miniaturized, powerful computer implants will be available (at least for those who can afford them) and will likely be a more common elective operation than cosmetic surgery.

There are many implications of Warwick's implant. For instructional designers, the question is an old one: "Would a job aid be more practical or effective than an instructional program?" Many well-known performance-technology authors (e.g., Mager & Pipe, 1970) have been asking that question for decades. If there is something too cumbersome to remember, why shouldn't we cart the knowledge as an external memory source, perhaps even one that can be inserted and removed as we now do with removable storage on a personal compute? Recall that a few years ago the idea of 100mb of data on something the size of a floppy disk was incredible! Just as Moore's law, which originally stated that the amount of data storage that a microchip can hold doubles every 18 months (Raymond, 1994), is now outdated, looking at computer-based electronic performance support systems (EPSS) as static is unrealistic. We will learn more and more, yes. But we will also carry our knowledge with us. Although less invasive "wearable technology" will be more commonplace than implants, humans and technology will interact in ways that we are just beginning to envision.

Just as H.G. Wells was a leading visionary for many of the inventions that took place in the mid-twentieth century, Neal Stephenson (1992; 1995) is emerging as a prophet for the future of learning technologies. Stephenson's novels contain many plausible future technologies that impact learning. In Stephenson's novel, *The Diamond Age, or a Young Lady's Illustrated Primer*, for example, hundreds of new technologies are made available through nanotechnology, based on the manipulation of individual atoms and molecules to build structures to complex, atomic specifications (Drexler, 1986). In Stephenson's future, the age of what "could" be done is replaced with the age of what "should" be done, much more so than the 20th century, when, at times, we have initiated irreversible error. Regardless of how we attain them, we will unquestionably have available to us many new technology-generated tools in the very near future. For instance, in *The Diamond Age*, the "primer" from which the protagonist learns is made of "smart paper," which is very thin sheets consisting of infinitesimal computers sandwiched between "media-trons" that project necessary images. At the time this chapter is being written, both Xerox Parc and MIT have developed commercially viable electronic paper technologies that is lightweight and as flexible as newsprint. This electronic paper stores images viewable in reflective light, has a wide viewing angle, is relatively inexpensive, and is electrically writable and erasable. Like many of the newer innovations, by the time you read this, electronic paper could be available through local or on-line vendors and fast on its way to becoming a commonplace fact of life.

## Distributed Cognition and Instructional Design

The last decade has brought some dissatisfaction and, in certain cases, caustic criticism of the traditional ADDIE (analyze, design, develop, implement, and evaluate) approach to instructional design (e.g., Gordon & Zemke, 2000). These critics charge that ISD is too slow and clumsy to meet today's challenges and (ironically) is too process-driven, especially for use by less experienced designers who look at the instructional design models more linearly. Related criticisms contend that ISD is not a real "science." Although, as with most arguments, there are contrasting views (e.g., Merrill, Drake, & Pratt, 1996), these criticisms attract notice to the changing nature of instructional design. The exciting developments in the area of instructional design and technology that we have discussed will no doubt shape the way future instructional programs are developed and implemented. Even so, advanced technology applications will not make up for a lack of sound instructional theory and educated instructional design professionals.

What is needed in our view are instructional design strategies and research aimed at identifying how best to implement emerging instructional technologies so that they increase learning outcomes while ensuring individual privacy and promoting the highest possible ethical standards. We are not advocating letting the technology drive the instructional design process. Rather, it appears evident that distributed learning environments will increasingly blend I-PUSH and I-PULL instructional technologies, and in so doing move toward what has been referred to as a "constructivist" approach (Driskell, Olsen, Hays, & Mullen, 1995). To aid learners in their attempts to "construct" meaning from information/knowledge, instructional designers will rely more and more on emerging educational technology. This not so subtle shift toward a learner-centered instructional environment will, in our view, usher in a new instructional systems paradigm that has an increased emphasis on developing new technology-based tools for aiding learning processes.

Much of what we have discussed in this chapter has been centered in instructional technologies that we believe to be viable in the foreseeable future. Many of these technologies employ what Salomon (1996) and others refer to as distributed cognition. In essence, distributed cognition recognizes that a person solves a problem or performs a task with the aid of other resources. The knowledge brought to bear on the task is distributed among the individual and other resources (e.g., computers or other people). Perkins (1996) refers to this as "person-plus." The theory of distributed cognition hypothesizes that information is processed between individuals and the tools and artifacts provided by the environment or culture. A primary force causing us to move toward distributed cognition is the limitation of the individual, unaided human mind. Professionals in most fields have jobs that are increasingly more complex, more specialized, and require access to exponentially increasing domain knowledge. Distributed cognition is a compelling response to this limitation (Norman, 1988).

During the next few years, we see the accelerated effect of distributed cognition affecting both learning and the field of instructional design and technology. Distributed cognition and efficacious instructional design approaches (and cybernetics, for that matter) are all about humans and technology interacting as complementary infrastructures. Things (often sophisticated computer technologies) that can store, retrieve, and analyze information are becoming an integral part of our learning opportunities. Humans (teachers, coaches, other specialized professionals) have shared understandings and experiences that are unavailable in things. Even in the near future, instructional design certainly must become more facilitative in creating environments in which the learner interacts smoothly with these two infrastructures. The traditional instructional systems approach that seeks to engineer learning through a more or less linear approach is giving way to a new instructional paradigm that places a premium on learner control and the emergence of educational technologies that facilitate the learner's ability to construct meaning out of a rich pool of available information.

## Summing Up

An acquaintance of ours shared a story of a vacation trip that she took with her young daughter to an historical settlement such as Williamsburg, Virginia or Plymouth, Massachusetts where past technologies are actively recreated. The mother spent the day explaining to the child the different functions of the various tools and furnishings within the aged buildings. We imagine the conversation went something like...

"What's this place, Mother?"

"Well, this is a bakery, dear. Where they made bread."

Entering another building, the girl asked, "What did they do here, Mother?"

"Well, here is where they used this big spinning wheel to make clothes."

Their tour progressed in a similar fashion until they came to a place where the technology seemed very familiar to the suddenly excited child. "I know what this is, Mother," she cried out with absolute assurance. "This is a school! It's set up just like my classroom!"

As the story suggests, education (and training) has for years been the most conservative of fields. Our use of technology has largely been pedestrian, isolated, and uninspired. In this chapter we discuss learning tools and technologies that we believe are likely to make a conspicuous impact. At least two implicit themes emerge. First, it is clear that learning in many environments will take place in much different ways in the future than it has in the past. Research in the effective use of these new technologies of learning is sorely needed.

Second, the accelerated rate of technological change is forcing instructional design and technology, comfortable in its traditional models, to move to address these astounding changes. Our impact as a professional field will increasingly be linked with our ability to do so.

## References

Davidson, R.J., & Irwin, W. (1999). The Functional Neuroanatomy of Emotion and Affective Style. *Trends in Cognitive Sciences, 3* (1), pp. 11-21.

Dempsey, J.V., Lucassen, B., Gilleý, W., & Rasmussen, K. (1993). Since Malone's Theory of Intrinsically Motivating Instruction: What's the Score in Gaming Literature? *Journal of Educational Technology Systems, 22* (2), pp. 173-183.

Department of Defense (1999). *Strategic Plan for Advanced Distributed Learning.* Report to the 106th Congress by the Office of the Under Secretary of Defense for Personnel and Readiness (online: http://train.galaxyscientific.com/dodadl.htm, accessed 4/29/00).

Drexler, K.E. (1986). *Engines of Creation.* New York: Doubleday.

Driskell, J.E., Olsen, D.W., Hays, R.T., & Mullen, B. (1995). *Training Decision-Intensive Tasks: A Constructivist Approach.* Report submitted to the Naval Air Warfare Center, Training Systems Division (N61339-95-C-0006 / NAWCTSD TR 95-007), Orlando, FL.

Faggin, F. (1999). Hardware/SoftWhere? *Forbes ASAP*, Big Issue IV: The Great Convergence, pp. 61-62.

Gardner, H. (1985). *The Mind's New Science: A History of the Cognitive Revolution.* New York: Basic Books.

Gordon, J., & Zemke, R. (2000, April). The Attack on ISD. *Training*, pp. 42-53.

Graves, W.H. (March/April, 1994). Toward a National Learning Infrastructure. *Educom Review, 29* (2) (online: http://www.educause.edu/pub/er/review/ reviewArticles/ 29232.html, accessed 5/10/00).

Hays, R.T., Jacobs, J.W., Prince, C., & Salas, E. (1992). Requirements for Future Research in Flight Simulation Training: Guidance Based on a Meta-Analytic Review. *The International Journal of Aviation Psychology, 2* (2), pp. 143-158.

Jacobs, J.W., & Dempsey, J.V. (1993). Simulation and Gaming: Fidelity, Feedback, and Motivation. In J.V. Dempsey & G. Sales (Eds.), *Interactive Instruction and Feedback*, (pp. 197-227). New York: Educational Technology Publications.

Johnston, R. (1995). The Effectiveness of Instructional Technology: A Review of Research. In *Proceedings of the Virtual Reality in Medicine and Developers' Exposition*, Cambridge, MA: Virtual Reality Solutions (online: http://www. vetl.uh.edu/surgery/effect.html).

Kribs, H.D., & Mark, L.J. (1999). *Interactive Multimedia Instruction Trade-Offs Tool (IMITT): Interim Scientific and Technical Report.* Report submitted to the Naval Air Warfare Center, Training Systems Division (NAWC-TSD) by Instructional Science and Development, Inc. (N61339-98-C-0054), Pensacola, FL (online: http://www.isd-net.org/p_ph2aoo2.html, accessed 5/13/00).

Mager, R.F., & Pipe, P. (1970). *Analyzing Performance Problems; or, You Really Oughta Wanna*. Belmont, CA, Fearon Publishers.

McArthur, D., Lewis, M., & Bishay, M. (1993). *The Roles of Artificial Intelligence in Education: Current Progress and Future Prospects*. Rand Corporation (MDR-8751515 & MDR-9055573), Santa Monica, CA (online: http://www.rand.org/hot/mcarthur/Papers/role.html, accessed 11/22/99).

Merrill, M.D., Drake, M.J., & Pratt, J. (1996). Reclaiming Instructional Design. *Educational Technology, 36* (5), pp. 5-7.

Merrill, D.C., Reiser, B.J., Ranney, M., and Tafton, J.G. (1992). Effective Tutoring Techniques: A Comparison of Human Tutors and Intelligent Tutoring Systems. *The Journal of the Learning Sciences, 2* (3), pp. 277-306.

Molegash, P. (1999). Technology and Education: Current and Future Trends. *IT Journal* (online: http://etext.virginia.edu/journals/itjournal/1999/molebash.html, accessed 5/16/00).

Norman, D.A. (1988). *The Psychology of Everyday Things*. New York: Basic Books.

Ohlsson, S. (1986). Some Principles of Intelligent Tutoring. *Instructional Science, 14*, pp. 293-326.

Perkins, D.N. (1996). Person-Plus: A Distributed View of Thinking and Learning. In G. Salomon (Ed.), *Distributed Cognition: Psychological and Educational Considerations* (pp. 89-110). New York: Cambridge University Press.

Pew, R.W., & Mavor, A.S. (1998). *Modeling Human and Organizational Behavior: Applications to Military Simulations*. National Research Council, Panel on Modeling Human Behavior and Command Decision Making: Representations for Military Simulations. Washington, DC: National Academy Press.

Raymond, E.S. (1994). *The New Hacker's Dictionary*. (2nd Ed.). Cambridge, MA: MIT Press.

Salomon, G. (1996). *Distributed Cognition: Psychological and Educational Considerations*. New York: Cambridge University Press.

Stephenson, N. (1992). *Snow Crash*. New York: Bantam Books.

Stephenson, N. (1995). *The Diamond Age, or a Young Lady's Illustrated Primer*. New York: Bantam Books.

Stout, R.J., Cannon-Bowers, J.A., Salas, E., & Milanovich, D.M. (1999). Planning, Shared Mental Models, and Coordinated Performance: An Empirical Link Is Established. *Human Factors, 41* (1), pp. 61-71.

Tononi, G., Edelman, G.M., & Sporns, O. (1998). Complexity and Coherency: Integrating Information in the Brain. *Trends in Cognitive Sciences, 2* (12), pp. 474-484.

Witt, S. (1999). Is Human Chip Implant Wave of the Future? CNN on-line news story posted 1 January 1999 (on-line: http://cnn.com/TECH/computing/9901/14/chip-man.idg/index.html, accessed 12/23/99).

*John W. Jacobs is on the Human Systems Staff in the Institute for Simulation and Training, University of Central Florida, where he was honored as "Researcher of the Year" in 2000 for his work in distributed interactive learning technology. You can e-mail him at jjacobs@ist.ucf.edu.*

*John V. Dempsey is chair of the Department of Behavioral Studies and Educational Technology, in the College of Education, University of South Alabama. You can e-mail him at jdempsey@ usamail.usouthal.edu.*

# Building Performance-Centered Web-Based Systems, Information Systems, and Knowledge Management Systems in the 21st Century

**Barry Raybould**

*Performance support has made a lot of progress in recent years. This article sums up converging developments in related professional disciplines in analysis and design methodologies and describes seven key elements of performance support engineering development methodology.*

With the meteoric rise of the Internet and e-business, web-based systems (both the Internet and intranets) are becoming a major focus of software engineers and human performance technologists. Typical compensatory mechanisms for poor system design such as training and human support systems are becoming unacceptable from a business perspective. Competitive pressures to provide superior customer service and better products mean that workers must achieve competency in much shorter time frames. When software is used directly by consumers via the web, these compensatory mechanisms are no longer an option. While it is possible to compensate for the poor design of a customer service application by providing training and/or levels of more experienced human support, neither option is available to the end user on the web. Therefore, the ability to design software systems from a performance-centered viewpoint is a critical success factor in e-business.

The same principles hold for knowledge management systems: just making knowledge available electronically is not sufficient. Only by having a performance-centered interface built onto the knowledge base is the knowledge rendered useful to achieving business goals. The major question facing organizations today is not whether to do performance-centered design, which was adequately addressed in the 1990s (Gery, 1991; Winslow and Bramer, 1994), but how to get it done.

The body of experience in developing performance-centered systems has grown significantly in the past five years, and practitioners have made considerable progress in elaborating the methodology. This article summarizes the convergence of thinking among various professional disciplines in analysis and design methodologies. It also describes seven key elements of the now-emerged performance support engineering development methodology. This or similar methods will be the foundation for designing performance-centered systems at the beginning of the 21st century, including consumer web applications, intranets, knowledge management systems, business information systems, or any other systems designed to support work.

## Hybrid Process

Over the past 10 years performance support development has progressed from something of an art to a much more structured and documented methodology (Raybould, 1995; Des Jardins and Davis, 1996; Marion, 1997). In parallel, the Human Computer Interaction community has been moving its methods closer to performance support concepts and away from user-centered design toward usage-centered design (Constantine, 1995) and contextual design (Beyer and Holtzblatt, 1998). Figure 1 shows the relationship between performance support engineering and various other professional disciplines.

Key characteristics of the emerged methodologies reveal the following patterns:

All processes start with knowledge acquisition, talking directly to job performers and subject matter experts about the work and identifying goals and barriers to performance. The design process is therefore data-driven according to the work and the performers rather than suppositions by the design team. The rule of three actuals applies: observe actual work (not simulated work); observe actual job performers (not ex-job performers); and observe the actual work place (not an interview room). Observing this rule ensures that barriers to performance are exposed; it also prevents designers from making erroneous assumptions about the

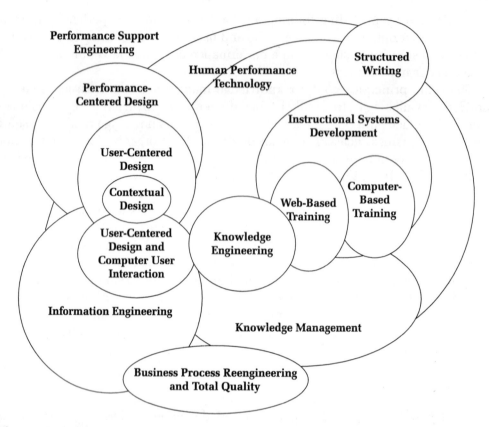

**Figure 1.** Relationship between performance support engineering and other professional disciplines

nature of the work that might lead to inadequate design.

The processes center more on deliverables rather than on a pre-established sequence of activities (see Figure 2). They revolve around a set of models, maps, and representations of the work and the design that are continually refined in an iterative process as the project team learns more about the work and the emerging design.

An example is the Performance Support Mapping® methodology (Raybould, 2000) shown in Figure 3. It comprises elements of information engineering, business process re-engineering, instructional systems design and computer-based training, human performance technology, interface design (usage-centered design and contextual design), knowledge engineering, and structured documentation.

The key phases in this process revolve around a set of deliverables that evolve raw data from job performers and subject matter experts into representations of the work and of the emerging design. There are four phases of activities.

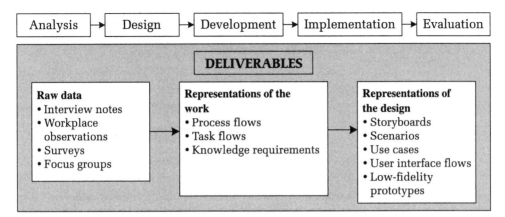

**Figure 2.** *Generalized methodology*

## Phase One: Look and Listen

- Observe current working environments and gather data from job performers and their managers to hear their view of the work, its goals, and barriers.
- Talk to the management of the organization to understand those goals and what is driving the business.
- Conduct surveys to gain more statistically significant data on important aspects of the work.
- Conduct focus groups to explore particularly important aspects of the work or barriers to performance.

Techniques for performing the above activities are derived from various sources, such as the front-end analysis processes for performance technology projects (Robinson and Robinson, 1995; Swanson, 1994), knowledge acquisition techniques from the expert systems fields (McGraw and Harbison-Briggs, 1989; Kelly, 1991; Tansley and Hayball, 1993; Dutta, 1993), techniques from the knowledge management field (Wiig, 1995), and various statistical and survey techniques for performance support projects (Raybould, 2000).

## Phase Two: Understand the Work

- Develop detailed understanding of the work as it exists today.
- Create models and maps that represent the work at the individual, organizational, and process levels.
- Identify key barriers and roadblocks to peak performance.
- Align understanding of key business goals.
- Identify factors that differentiate high and low performers.
- Link goals and barriers to the various models and maps to determine where to concentrate design and analysis efforts.

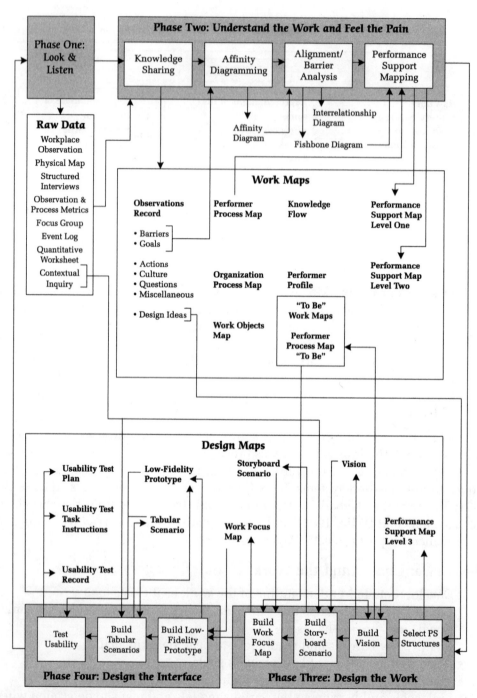

**Figure 3.** Performance Support Mapping® methodology

- Analyze knowledge flows in the organization (Hupp, Polak, and Westgaard, 1995; Raybould, 2000; Horn, 1999; Beyer and Holtzblatt, 1998; Wiig, 1995).

## Phase Three: Design the Work

- Redesign work to remove barriers and roadblocks and to take advantage of technology to provide on-the-job support.
- Build various models and maps to represent the work as it should be and to serve as a blueprint for designing a system interface that will support the performer.
- Create abstract representations of the design, such as user interface flows.
- Envision alternative solutions to work problems and select the most viable solutions (Hupp et al., 1995; Johann, 1995; Raybould, 2000).

These models and maps include adaptations of the Phase Two models. The only difference is that in this phase we are developing "to be" versions versus "as is" versions. In addition, there are some high-level abstractions of the design, such as interface design flows. These facilitate discussions of navigation in the system being designed without getting into the minutiae of the interface design, such as which type of text box to use or where to place buttons on the screen.

## Phase Four: Design the Interface

- Design the interface of the new system using low-fidelity (paper-based) or high-fidelity (computer-based) prototyping techniques.
- Evaluate the design using an expanded set of performance-centered design heuristics.
- Test the new interface with job performers to prove that the new system meets performance improvement goals.

The basic techniques for interface design and testing are described in the Human Computer Interaction (HCI) literature (Wiklund, 1994). The key difference is in the use of expanded heuristics, which is used during design and testing (Raybould, 2000). In the design process the heuristics are used in a cognitive walkthrough of the interface and in screen-by-screen heuristic evaluation to predict usability problems in advance. The same heuristics are applied during usability testing.

# Performance Support Continuum

A consequence of integrating disciplines is integrating what were previously separate interventions. Not all support can be embedded within a tool or system, and it is not always possible to make products obvious (Horton, 1994; Norman, 1992). Support needs to be provided in a continuum (Raybould, 1998b). These include support embedded in the tool or software interface (intrinsic) to support that is linked to the tool (extrinsic, such as wizards, cue cards, coaches, advisors, and help) to support that is separate from the tool (external, such as tutorials, computer-based training, peer support, and telephone hotlines). As support moves further from the tool and requires more time off the job, it becomes less powerful and more expensive to use. As support moves closer to the tool and in the process becomes more granular, it becomes more powerful to use and less expensive in terms of lost time on the job. With reference to Figure 4, the most efficient way to develop a support strategy is to start by building those structures on the right of the continuum and progressively move to the left when a particular structure proves infeasible. This is the performance-centered design approach. This is in direct conflict with traditional approaches that start with interventions at the left and move towards the right (e.g., if there is sufficient budget and time). E-commerce companies are also learning that not all transactions can be completed via the Internet alone. In some cases, human intervention is required at a certain point in the transaction. For cost reasons, these organizations are selecting structures from the continuum from right to left.

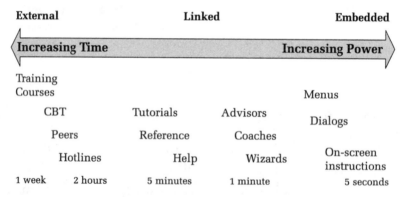

**Figure 4.** *Performance support structure continuum*

## Group Processes

Another consequence of integrating disciplines is increasingly commingling people with very different skills on a single project team. Performance support engineering experience emphasizes the critical importance of group processes during design. There are multiple phases in the development methodology in which group processes are important.

A key problem in many projects is misalignment of organizational goals, which results in considerable project delays as various factions emphasize their own version of the project's goals and evaluate the emerging design from their own perspective. Therefore, a key element of the performance support engineering process is to align the goals of all stakeholders. Group processes such as brainstorming, affinity diagramming, interrelationship digraphs, and fishbone analyses have proved particularly useful in gaining this alignment.

Alignment within as well as external to the project team is also critical to success. Many design projects have gone astray because the design team has splintered into factions, each with its own version of the design. As the design process proceeds, these multiple versions become more and more difficult to reconcile, leading to duplication of effort and unnecessary shifts in design direction. There are several techniques for avoiding these obstacles—for example, ensuring all design options are fully explored and evaluated at the very early design stages and group commitment obtained before proceeding with any single option.

Another aspect to alignment is alignment of understanding of the work as the early knowledge acquisition processes are under way. This is a particular problem on larger projects in which there are multiple teams interviewing workers, job performers, subject matter experts, and management. As all team members cannot go on all the interviews, problems can arise when each team starts to get a different perspective on problems. This situation results in each team developing and supporting a different solution. The only solution to this problem has been effective knowledge sharing during the design process by the separate analysis teams using group processes.

Another more difficult problem is how to involve management and job performers in the design process. In practice it is impossible for performance support engineers to gain a full understanding of the knowledge domain of a business and of management concerns during a project. But without this full understanding, how does an engineer move the analysis and design forward?

The answer lies in the role taken by the engineer. The role needs to shift from that of a person who does all the analysis and design work individually to that of a facilitator. The performance support engineer needs to create a group environment in which the whole team—including the subject matter experts and job performers—comes up with a clear understanding of the work and develops the design together.

This means a trend away from producing multiple revisions of long documents that specify requirements and more toward the concept of a design room, in which representations of work and of the design are posted on the walls of a room in a format that can be easily seen and discussed by all team members simultaneously and that can be easily modified. Another way to think of this is as a design space rather than a design document. Of course, documents are required during the process, but only where appropriate and not in those situations in which group interaction is necessary. To make this process successful, it is important to make representations simple and easily taught.

## Systems Approach

One of the most significant and defining characteristics of performance support engineering has always been its systems focus, where the system comprises both computer and human components. Systems thinking has been applied by several related disciplines, for example, in the performance technology community (Robinson and Robinson, 1995), in business process reengineering (Davenport, 1993), and in learning organizations (Senge, 1990). Taking this viewpoint has two key benefits.

First, it focuses on measurement of actual results against goals and on providing a feedback loop (Figure 5). In this way the combined human/computer system becomes self-regulating. In many cases it is possible to build feedback into a performance-centered tool or system used on the job. For example, a sales system might provide feedback on individual and group sales performance, or a customer service system might provide feedback on customer satisfaction.

Second, this systems viewpoint focuses on finding all potential causes for failing to meet goals, not just those related to the computer system. The other causes might include problems and barriers with the business processes, the organization and its structure, the incentive and motivation systems, or bottlenecks in feedback loops. By identifying these factors, solutions can be found and the barriers overcome.

Another systems viewpoint is the performance/learning cycle model (Figure 6) (Raybould, 1995), which relates performance-centered design concepts to those

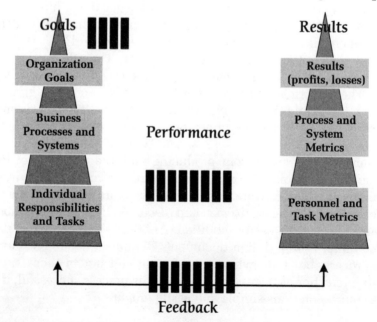

**Figure 5.** Systems model with barriers to performance

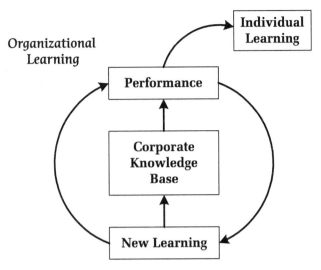

**Figure 6.** *The organizational performance/learning cycle*

of the learning organization (Senge, 1990). Both the generic systems model and the organizational performance/learning cycle model influence the raw data gathered during the analysis phase of the generic performance support engineering development cycle shown in Figure 2 and the Performance Support Mapping® development cycle shown in Figure 3.

## Focus on Goals

A key part of this systems model is the focus on goals during all phases of the process. Recent trends in the HCI community—such as contextual design (Beyer and Holtzblatt, 1998), usage-centered design (Constantine, 1995), and essential modeling (McMenamin and Palmer, 1984)—have also moved in the same direction. These approaches look at the intents or goals of the job performer rather than just the tasks or actions he or she performs.

Performance Support Mapping® from the performance-centered design community goes one step further by identifying a linkage to organizational goals, and it includes various team alignment activities in its development process. This mapping process (Figure 7) also creates a linkage between goals and performance barriers, the tasks and decisions involved in work, and the knowledge, information, and tools needed to support those tasks and decisions. This process makes sure all the factors that might negatively impact the successful completion of work are identified, so that they can be addressed. It also directs further knowledge acquisition efforts (tasks and decisions) that have the most impact on the business

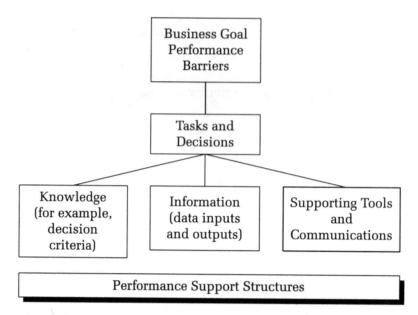

**Figure 7.** *Performance Support Mapping®*

because they relate either to the major goals of the organization or to the major barriers the organization is trying to overcome. Finally, this process focuses on the differences between traditional data analysis and the type of knowledge analysis required in performance support engineering. It is particularly important to focus on these differences for those people who have been trained from the perspective of data structures, who do not have training in knowledge structures.

## Integration of Knowledge with Tools

A distinct convergence toward the concepts of electronic performance support systems and performance-centered design emerged at the beginning of the 1990s in the human performance technology community. The human-computer interaction field, expert systems field, and technical documentation fields have all been moving closer to those approaches advocated by the performance support community (see Figure 8). Technical books have become interactive electronic manuals, stand-alone expert systems have been embedded in information systems, and instructor-led training courses have become web-based training modules integrated with hyperlinked background reference information.

The pattern clearly shows an increasingly close integration of knowledge and support resources into the tools that people use. Information systems are moving from the data management age into the knowledge management age, in which the

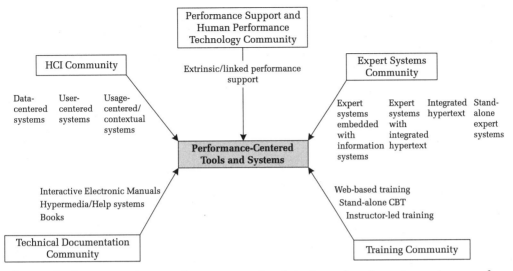

**Figure 8.** *Convergence to performance-centered tools and systems in various professional communities*

foundation of most information systems—the database—is being augmented by a knowledge base accessible via a performance-centered interface. The knowledge base is maintained and enhanced via a knowledge-management system (see Figure 9). A simplistic way of differentiating between these concepts is as follows: "66" is data; "Pat is 66 years old" is information; "Persons older than 65 are eligible for benefits" is knowledge. This trend is still in the embryonic phase, and we are only just learning the issues involved in structuring and managing knowledge bases. The focus for deciding which tools and which specific areas and domains of knowledge to integrate into the performance-centered tool or system is determined through a thorough understanding of business and individual goals described earlier.

## Expanded Heuristics List

Finally, many of the above characteristics of performance-centered systems are repeated in a set of design heuristics or rules of thumb. Traditional user-centered design typically uses the order of eight to ten major heuristics (Molich and Nielsen, 1990). The performance-centered approach employs a larger number of design principles, for example, the 22 design principles in Figure 10 or Gloria Gery's Attributes and Behaviors of Performance-Centered Systems (Gery, 1991). This larger set of principles takes into account principles involved in systems thinking, such as goal establishment and feedback. Another key set of principles derives from question-answering theories in cognitive science (Graesser and Franklin, 1990; Lauer, Peacock, and Graesser, 1992). A key difference between the

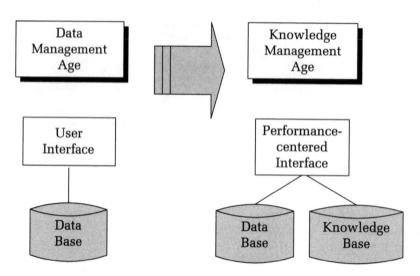

**Figure 9.** Evolution to integrated data and knowledge management

traditional user-centered design principles and the performance-centered design principles is that the latter applies both to the work and to the computer-human interaction, not just to the computer-human interaction alone. For example, the heuristic "provides feedback" when applied to the work would require the designer to give a salesperson feedback on weekly sales results. When applied to the design of the human-computer interface, this principle would result in a confirmation message when an order button was pressed stating, "Order has been sent to warehouse."

## Summary

Over the past ten years there has been a gradual convergence of thinking among practitioners in the performance support community on how to develop performance-centered systems. Other professional disciplines have also been moving toward the performance-support approach. This analysis and design process, refined over many performance support projects, is a hybrid of techniques from multiple disciplines and results in a series of integrated interventions in a performance-support continuum. Since the project team draws together skills from multiple disciplines and integrates job performers and subject matter experts into the analysis and design process, group processes are particularly important. Performance-support engineering takes a systems viewpoint in which the system comprises both computer and human elements. Compared with traditional user-centered design processes, performance-centered design uses a wider range of design heuristics that take into account both this systems viewpoint and the needs of knowledge manage-

| Principle | Description |
|---|---|
| Advance warning | Provides advance warning of consequences. |
| Affordance | Visual appearance suggests use. |
| Answers descriptive questions | Answers: "What is this?" "What are the differences?" |
| Answers functional questions | Answers: "What does this do?" |
| Answers procedural questions | Answers: "How do I?" |
| Automates tasks | Automates tasks whenever possible. |
| Captures best practice | Captures the best practice of the experts. |
| Consistent | Is consistent. |
| Feedback | Gives feedback on what you've done or where you've been. |
| Forgiving | Lets you make a mistake and go back to a previous state. |
| Goal establishment | Helps establish what you can or want to do, or where to go. |
| Interprets | Answers: "Why did that happen?" "How did that happen?" |
| Layered | Provides increasing levels of detail to suit diverse audiences. |
| Matches flow of work | Matches how work presents itself to you. |
| Minimizes translation | Minimizes interpretation of special terms. |
| Proactive support | Proactively monitors and evaluates to provide support when needed. |
| Recognition | Relies on ability to recognize, rather than recall, knowledge. |
| Relevant | Omits irrelevant information. |
| Resources | Provides access and links to all resources and tools needed. |
| Search | Lets you search for answers to questions. |
| Stimulus response path | Provides an unbroken path from stimulus to response. |
| Task or process focused | Directly shows the structure of the task or process. |

**Figure 10.** *Performance-centered design heuristics*

ment. This process, or processes very similar to this, will be the foundation for designing performance-centered systems at the beginning of the 21st century and will be critical to developing successful e-commerce systems and to providing the means for a knowledge management system to improve business results.

## References

Beyer, H., and Holtzblatt, K. (1998). *Contextual design.* San Francisco: Morgan Kaufmann Publishers, Inc.

Constantine, L. (December 1995). "What do users want? Engineering usability into software." *Windows Tech Journal, 4* (12), 30-39.

Davenport, T.H. (1993). "Enablers of process innovation." *Process Innovation: Reengineering Work Through Information Technology.* Harvard Business School Press.

Des Jardins, S., and Davis, H., Jr. (1996). "Electronic performance support systems (EPSS): Making the transition." *Eyes on the Future: Converging Images, Ideas and Instructions,* edited by Robert E. Griffin, Darrell G. Beauchamp, J. Mark Hunter, and Carole B. Schiffman (selected readings of the International Visual Literacy Association Conference, 1995).

Dutta, S. (1993). *Knowledge processing and applied artificial intelligence.* Oxford, England: Butterworth-Heinemann Ltd.

Gery, G. (1991). *Electronic performance support systems.* Tolland, MA: Gery Associates.

Graesser, A.C., and Franklin, S.P. (1990). "QUEST: A cognitive model of question answering." *Discourse Processes 13,* 279-303.

Horn, R. (1999). *Participant's manual for developing procedures, policies and documentation.* Waltham, MA: Information Mapping, Inc.

Horton, W. (1994). *The icon book: Visual symbols for computer systems and documentation.* New York: John Wiley & Sons.

Hupp, T., Polak, C., and Westgaard, O. (1995). *Designing work groups, jobs, and work flow.* San Francisco: Jossey-Bass Publishers.

Johann, B. (1995). *Designing cross-functional business processes.* San Francisco: Jossey-Bass Publishers.

Kelly, R. (1991). *Practical knowledge engineering.* Bedford, MA: Digital Press.

Lauer, W.T., Peacock, E., and Graesser, A.C. (1992). *Questions and information systems.* Hillsdale, NJ: Lawrence Erlbaum Associates.

Marion, C. (May 1997). "Implementing performance-centered design." *News & Views,* Society for Technical Communications.

McGraw, K.L., and Harbison-Briggs, K. (1989). *Knowledge acquisition: Principles and guidelines.* Englewood Cliffs, NJ: Prentice-Hall, Inc.

McMenamin, S.M., and Palmer, J. (1984). *Essential systems analysis.* Englewood Cliffs, NJ: Prentice-Hall Yourdon Press.

Molich, R., and Nielsen, J. (1990). "Improving a human-computer dialogue." *Communications of the ACM, 33* (3), 338-348.

Norman, D.A. (1992). *Turn signals are the facial expressions of automobiles.* Reading, MA: Addison-Wesley Publishing Company.

Raybould, B. (1995). "Performance support engineering: An emerging development methodology for performance technologists and enabler of organizational learning." *Electronic Performance Support Systems: Information Kit.* Washington, DC: International Society for Performance Improvement.

Raybould, B. (1998a). "EPSS and your organization." *Practical Guidelines for Training and Development Professionals,* Info-Line Issue 9806. Alexandria, VA: American Society for Training and Development.

Raybould, B. (1998b). "Performance support structures." *Practical Guidelines for Training and Development Professionals,* Info-Line Issue 9806. Alexandria, VA: American Society for Training and Development.

Raybould, B. (2000). *Performance Support Mapping® workshop participant's handbook.* Ariel PSE Technology (www.arielpse.com).

Robinson, D., and Robinson, J. (1995). *Performance consulting.* San Francisco: Berrett-Koehler Publishers, Inc.

Senge, P.M. (1990). *The fifth discipline. The art and practice of the learning organization.* New York: Doubleday/Currency.

Swanson, R. (1994). *Analysis for improving performance.* San Francisco: Berrett-Koehler Publishers, Inc.

Tansley, D., and Hayball, C. (1993). *Knowledge-based systems analysis and design.* Hertfordshire, England: Prentice Hall International (UK) Ltd.

Wiig, K. (1995). *Knowledge management methods.* Arlington, TX: Schema Press.

Wiklund, M. (1994). *Usability in practice. How companies develop user-friendly products.* Cambridge, MA: AP Professional.

Winslow, C., and Bramer, J. (1994). *FutureWork.* New York: Free Press.

## Related Readings

Gery, G. (1995). "Attributes and behaviors of performance-centered systems." *Electronic Performance Support Systems: Information Kit.* Washington, DC: International Society for Performance Improvement.

*Barry Raybould is a pioneer in electronic performance support systems and performance-centered design. He founded one of the leading consulting companies in this field and recently completed a two-year effort to document and create a new Performance Support Mapping® training program. Reach him at BRaybould @arielpse.com or www.arielpse.com.*

# Welcome to Part Four:
# Is E-Learning Too Good to Be True?

Part Four is all about the best of what is emerging in e-learning. Kevin Dobbs looks at the need for quality in online learning. And Rob Foshay and Coarrie Bergeron ask us to step back and take a reality check on the use of the Web in training.

Is there a digital backlash? That's a question Karl Albrecht and Ronald Gunn address. There are myths about e-learning that are commonly held in the training community. John Moran and David Mager and Warren Karlenzig explore those and provide a needed examination of their validity.

Jack Phillips and colleagues provide a methodology for measuring the return on investment in e-learning and this part concludes with a look at the costs and benefits of e-learning with an emphasis on value by David Forman.

In Part Five we look at the development of the people who will lead the field.

# The State of Online Learning—What the Online World Needs Now: Quality

**Kevin Dobbs**

*Online learning is full of possibilities and promises. But there are numerous obstacles that limit its potential. This article takes on four of these obstacles and presents "a four-point agenda for how to begin the real training revolution."*

In theory, online training is the answer to every company's dreams, a revolutionary approach to learning, heaven-sent in the nick of time. Job descriptions and business models change so quickly in the New Economy that today's workers need just enough training, just in time to complete the project at hand. Planning and coordinating traditional classroom sessions is too time-consuming and costly. Therefore, the Internet, with its promises of speed, efficiency, interaction and collaboration, becomes the obvious medium of choice.

In reality, though, training on the Web, or e-learning as it is often labeled, falls far short of its promises. And it may be years away from living up to its hype. Like most innovations in their early stages, e-learning is still struggling to define and distinguish itself from what came before. Most of the courses or training curricula you'll find on the Web today amount to little more than text or video on a computer screen, merely digitized versions of what's already been done.

There is more to come, right?

"The industry is at a vulnerable stage. It has to get past repackaging dull programs and trying to convince people that they're something else," says Trace Urdan, an online-training analyst with WR Hambrecht & Co. in San Francisco. "But it can make the leap. The potential does exist."

Question is, How to realize it? We spoke to a number of analysts and industry insiders about what it will take for Web-based training to legitimize its still-premature label as a revolutionary educational tool. Their thinking boils down to a four-point agenda for how to begin the real training revolution.

## 1. Quit Pretending that Reading Is Training

Online learning's deficiencies are a touchy subject. Nobody wants to look like a Luddite.

Sunnyvale, CA, consultant Brandon Hall, an ardent e-learning promoter and editor of *Technology for Learning* newsletter, a sister publication to *Training*, illustrated the problem at a conference this spring. Speaking to an audience eager for insight, he mentioned that online training sorely lacks social interaction and quality instruction. He quickly backpedaled, however, and emphasized that it can dispense five times as much "content" at one-third the cost of classroom courses.

The obvious question came from the crowd: "But is anyone absorbing all that content?"

The obvious response: "That's a good question."

What's hazardous about such exchanges, say industry insiders, is that they open the door to critical thought but shut it before any progress is made. This discourages people who are just beginning to explore the potential of Web-based training.

Among the experts who are willing to be blunt in their assessments of online learning's shortcomings, nobody is more outspoken than Roger Schank, professor of education and computer science at Northwestern University and head of a Chicago training company called Cognitive Arts. "Right now, e-learning is a disaster," says Schank. "All you're getting is somebody's classroom notes on the Web. And we call that training. That's frightening to people who know better."

Genuine progress, Schank says, will require genuine risk. It's a matter of someone stepping out of the pack and setting a new standard. Think of television. The vast majority of early TV programming amounted to little more than repackaged radio shows with pictures. Eventually, though, producers started experimenting, and that experimentation paved the way for a medium for which most of the "content" now is fundamentally different from a visual version of Jack Benny's 1940s radio program.

The problem today is that very few e-learning outfits want to take a big step beyond the status quo. To do so would be to risk failing miserably and flushing away millions in start-up capital. It's much safer to package some PowerPoint slides from an existing classroom session and call the result a bold innovation. Hey, the market is buying it.

There are exceptions, of course. Corporate giants such as Bank of America and IBM are working on in-house initiatives aimed at simulating human interaction. In one Bank of America program, for instance, streaming video and audio allow a loan officer trainee to interact with a prospective client. The student asks a series of questions to ascertain the would-be patron's eligibility for a loan. If he makes any illegal inquiries, a lawyer appears in a video segment to scold him for straying into prohibited territory. The direction of the course is determined by the trainee's interaction with the simulated client.

Then there is Ninth House Network, the darling of recent trade shows. For lack of competition, if nothing else, the company is leading the effort to sell advanced Internet programming to general audiences. It's combining content from training stalwarts such as Tom Peters and Peter Senge with the handiwork of Hollywood producers.

Ninth House, headquartered in San Francisco, calls the resulting product an "e-series." The company's offerings are essentially interactive sequences of TV-like episodes, each covering a different business skill: recruiting talent, marketing a new product, situational leadership and so on. In each episode, the trainee exchanges dialogue with a variety of human actors, and the show's plot is directed by that give-and-take. At the end of a show, the decisions the user makes are evaluated and he's instructed on how he could have handled situations in which he erred. "This is not pushing text online," says Ninth House president Jeff Snipes. "It's about something totally different."

It's about making the most of the latest technology, turning an online-training session into a true-to-life situation that is determined by the trainee's decisions and actions—"bona fide interaction," to borrow a phrase often used loosely in the online-training world. "You can't just digitize something and expect it to impress. You have to intrigue people, draw them into activities where they're at the center of everything that's happening," says Larraine Segil, a California Institute of Technology instructor and Ninth House contributor. "The technology is there for this."

In fact, the technology has been here since the advent of CD-ROM, and the new direction suggested by these programs from Bank of America and Ninth House actually can be seen as a kind of backing up. CD-ROM's storage capacity offered instructional designers a new chance to build programs with genuine interaction, and some promising experimentation was taking place when Internet fever came along to rewrite the rules and the goals of computer-assisted learning. The old goal was to build programs with rich and realistic forms of interaction. The new one was simply to dispense "information" widely and cheaply. The pendulum is only beginning to swing back.

The problem for Ninth House and others waiting in the wings is twofold: 1) it costs about $200,000 to produce a single Ninth House episode; 2) the broad bandwidth and high-speed Web service needed to operate such programs via computer networks remain luxuries for most companies. So even if they were sold on the value of the company's high-end programming, most couldn't afford it or manage it on their internal computer systems. Consequently, while Ninth House has some large customers such as First Union National Bank and Empire BlueCross, its client list remains pretty short.

To be sure, the challenges are daunting. But at least a few gamblers are emerging from the scrambling field of would-be e-learning contenders.

## 2. Bring on the Bandwidth

You've heard the mantra a thousand times, but here it is again: bandwidth, bandwidth, bandwidth.

If you take the techies' word for it—and in this grand age of electronic commerce, you pretty much have to since everyone else does—your company won't be satisfied until its bandwidth is sufficiently broad. Contentedness can only be found in stout electronic pipes capable of inhaling mass quantities of everything from Web pages and e-mail to music and video files in a nanosecond. A system that is never busy, that never stalls, that never gives you even a moment to remember what life was like before personal computers.

Anything else and all your rapturous online learners will quickly grow bored and disillusioned while waiting for files to download.

"Internet browsers were created simply to display documents," says Pete Weaver, chief technology officer for Development Dimensions International, a Pittsburgh training and consulting firm. "Now we're trying to turn that on its head and make logging on some kind of rich learning experience. Right away, you have the [bandwidth] problem."

In case you've been on an extended vacation, bandwidth is a measure of capacity. It has to do with the amount of data that can funnel through a computer network in a given time period. Think of a garden hose: the wider the hose, the greater the flow of water. Text and simple graphics don't require much bandwidth. Audio and, especially, video, demand a lot.

Though statistics are scattered and change daily, it's safe to say that the majority of working stiffs—even the ones who log onto computers every morning—lack a reliable high-bandwidth connection. Some major corporations and smaller Web-reliant firms have cleared this hurdle, but thousands of small and mid-sized businesses have not. This is partly because, until recently, such connections were exorbitantly priced, sometimes costing hundreds of dollars a month per user.

Consequently, many people are still using dial-up modems, which are up to 25 times slower than broad-bandwidth services. Others have high-speed access, bolstered by T1 lines, but have unreliable tech support or must share access with coworkers and are left frustrated by the inconvenience, and, in some cases, only marginally improved throughput rates.

Fortunately, competition from new quarters is starting to change all that. More television and phone companies are now jumping into the fray with cable modems and digital subscriber lines. And looking to double up the uses of their existing technologies, the Internet-provider industry is in the midst of a battle to sell high-speed data services. Rates are rapidly declining.

Now it's a matter of time. More businesses are acquiring greater bandwidth. How quickly? Unfortunately, that depends upon whom you ask; estimates vary widely. Meanwhile, the e-learning industry anxiously awaits. In companies without the necessary bandwidth, efforts such as Ninth House's will go unseen.

## 3. Tame the "Standards" Monster

It's next to impossible to get excited about technical standards—tedious stuff that makes most people's eyes glaze over. And yet, for online-learning crusaders this acronym-saturated topic is a red-hot issue.

Wayne Hodgins, a fervent standards advocate, insists that a voluntary set of "interoperability" guidelines would allow companies to more rapidly adopt and improve upon new technology. If ever a subject was worth risking boredom to educate yourself about, this is it, says the director of worldwide learning for software developer Autodesk Inc. in San Rafael, CA.

Let's try it minus "metadata," "scalability," and some other enemies of wakefulness.

To understand what the standards issue means for Web-based training, think "learning objects." Standards would allow us to move pieces of digitized training—in big hunks or small chunks—across various computer platforms, regardless of the authoring systems used to create those various "objects." You could retrieve from online databases just the amount or combination of instructional material you need, when needed.

To do that, you need a universal language for describing when and by whom a particular set of data was collected and how it was formatted. Then, using that standard vocabulary, developers could create templates that make it simple for content providers to include data necessary to make their online courses searchable. Think of a library card catalog system.

If the planned scheme works as predicted, a company could add, subtract or rearrange any amount of content from any developer regardless of the platform on which its original training program was created. "For the kind of continuous learning the Web is supposed to foster, you have to be able to mix and match," says

Michael Pich, training director at Saba Software, an online-training firm in Redwood Shores, CA.

Such commingling not only promises greater efficiency but also reduces costs. Corporate America is often slow to upgrade online courses because, without inter-operability, revisions too often require expensive and time-consuming overhauls. A standards system, proponents say, will allow organizations to instead refine courseware piece by piece, saving money and keeping them abreast of continual-ly advancing technology.

Corporate powerhouses such as Microsoft, Sun Microsystems, and Oracle, as well as some 1,600 colleges and universities, are currently pushing vendors that create and sell software for online-training courses to adhere to these standards.

Headway has been encumbered consistently, however, by one obstacle: lan-guage. All the technoblather that swirls around any standards conversation breeds confusion, even among those closely tied to the movement's core. And that's before you even get to Internet programming languages. Most companies are still working with HTML. But new online-training programs, the ones that are sup-posed to be truly interactive, are based on XML, or Extensible Markup Language, a muscle-bound version of HTML. In a few cases, programmers are working with even newer, more experimental coding.

"It always comes down to language; we're saddled with it," Hodgins says. "At what point, with what language do you start?"

Hodgins does know this much: "The future of e-learning relies on good con-tent, and drawing the best from a number of sources is how you get it. Interoper-ability is crucial for that even to be possible."

## 4. Who's Rating This Stuff?

Different critics put it different ways, but the complaint amounts to this: the Internet is a mechanism used to quickly and widely circulate bad ideas.

They are right, of course, though only partly; good ideas and programs float about cyberspace too. But the challenge is obvious: if you're seeking good training programs developed by outside sources, you need someone to sift through the glut of information and services that is the Web. Someone who knows your company's development plans. Someone with an abundance of time. Someone patient and not prone to fits of rage when confronted by a barrage of nonsensical sales pitches.

You're probably looking for an experienced trainer who also happens to be computer-savvy. Find that person and pay her well.

The problem is, people with those skills are scarce. Moreover, reliable third-party rating or accrediting services for e-learning courseware are either few or non-existent, depending on whom you listen to.

"There aren't *any* independent, unbiased sources out there who can tell you what's working and what's not," says Jay Cross of Internet Time Group, an online-training firm in Berkeley, CA. "Everyone involved is either trying to sell something—like me—or they're an academic who's immediately against it because they're out to defend the classroom."

Such autonomous and reliable sources probably will surface in the months and years ahead. Various groups have already established awards programs in attempts to highlight innovative courses and the creative ways some companies have used them. But at best, such efforts can only complement your own internal evaluations.

"You have to have people in-house who are linked to your company's mission and who can research the market to determine what will work for you," says Urdan, the analyst with WR Hambrecht.

Consider that the alternative is blunted training, the kind your company's best and brightest will regard as a waste of their time—and your money.

## Get Over It and Move On

The pitch is relentless. Training demands evolve faster than ever before. You need a way to keep up. Behold the mighty Internet, complete with an army of "total solutions providers" ready to win every battle with a single Web portal.

You are impressed. Maybe you have to be. Maybe your company has set a mandate to get X percent of all corporate education online within the next 18 months. It's happened at places such as Motorola and Cisco Systems.

Eventually, no matter what the needs of your fast-changing work force, you're left shaking your head, mumbling something about the foolishness of corporate mandates. Your company doesn't get it.

Or gradually, perhaps with the help of an insightful executive, you pick and choose the times and situations when the Web will complement other components of your training initiatives. You pick up on the subtleties and frailties of the new medium; you realize it's not a panacea but just one tool in your bag.

Your company still may not get it, but your students will. Good trainers have always taken into account myriad learning styles, formal and informal settings, classroom and on-the-job instruction. The Internet is just one more element to consider.

"It's still about understanding your company's needs and finding the best way to address them," says Darryl Sink, an instructional design consultant in Monterey, CA.

And don't overlook this: the average worker already spends an increasingly larger chunk of his day staring at a computer monitor. Even if the Web were the universal remedy that the e-learning providers claim, do you think he wants to spend even more time chained to his computer?

"The fact is, people like to be together. We're social," says Rick Corry, vice president of alliances for Pensare Corp., a training firm in Appleton, WI. "The more you use the latest technology, whatever it is, the more you want to interact with people. We can't ignore that."

Indeed, Corry adds, corporate America should embrace that. And, as our fascination with the Internet dissipates, more companies are. But don't expect to wake up one morning to a world enlightened by common sense.

The business world is still spinning very fast. The New Economy is at once ripe with mass mergers and rampant new-business failures, with downsizing and labor shortages, with an insecure and transient labor force. Often the wrong questions are asked and answers are hurried.

This is especially true in the e-learning market. It is, after all, an industry with dozens of organizations offering "solutions" for problems they haven't yet heard of. But if it is to be a profitable and sustainable industry, like everything else Internet, e-learning eventually must provide substance.

*Kevin Dobbs is an associate editor of* Training, *kdobbs@trainingmagcom.*

# Web-Based Education: A Reality Check

## Rob Foshay and Corrie Bergeron

*The Web offers a world of possibilities for education and training, but the visionaries "often fail to address two basic facts of importance to educators and trainers," according to the authors of this article. They discuss here the use of an Internet-based instructional system.*

The first feature films were simply filmed stage plays. The then-new medium was used not to do new things, but rather to do the same old things in a different way. Today, of course, moviemakers use zooms, pans, and special effects to communicate in ways that a stage play cannot. With the Web today, we are still coming to terms with what is truly new about the technology. We talk about this astonishing new communications technology using words from earlier technologies, such as "broadcast" and "publish" and "network." Many (often self-described) visionaries have a big problem with that. They fulminate endlessly about new paradigms and how the Web will transform the world. This is good—we *should* be talking about new ways to use this new medium. But the visionaries' visions often fail to address two basic facts of importance to educators and trainers. First, the network infrastructure we have in the real world of schools and training today is only beginning to be able to support the massive-bandwidth, high-reliability applications they describe in their blue-sky visions of a cyber future. Second, the new medium does not render untrue everything we know about teaching and learning.

## Model T's on the InfoBahn

Except for highly specialized, internal applications, Web applications today and in the near future must work at 28.8 Kbps. Let's face facts. It's a 28.8 world, and it is going to stay that way for the next several years, especially in homes. Yes, you can buy faster modems, but users of 33.6 and 56K modems are often surprised to find that their modem is faster than their local telephone service. There is a limit to how much data a regular telephone line can carry, and a Net connection is only as fast as its slowest component.

Companies, schools, libraries, and state agencies might have high-bandwidth Internet connections and intranets, but chances are that teachers planning lessons at home, outlying regional offices, and traveling personnel dial in via modem. Modem connect time must compete with other telephone needs over the same phone line used for voice and fax. Most homes and hotel rooms don't have ISDN, DSL, or T1 lines or satellite links or cable modems. Widespread, low-cost adoption of these technologies is, unfortunately, still years away, once you get away from the campuses of major corporate or school facilities. Developers of Net-based applications must keep this in mind, or limit their audience to those for whom throughput and persistent connections—and their costs—are not an issue.

## Information or Instruction?

But let's put aside all that gloom and doom and focus on happy thoughts! To what nobler use can we put a new technology than to harness it in the service of education and training? Deliver high-quality instructional materials on demand, enable information-rich and meaningful communication among learners of all ages across the globe, and do it for free! We will all save the world, right?

Here's another bucket of cold water, team. Putting content on a Web page is no guarantee of learning. The Web may be a great way to distribute information, but can you really *teach* with it? There's a big difference between information and instruction, and this basic principle is as true on the Web as anywhere. Since the work of E.L. Thorndike at the beginning of the 20th century, we've known that learners learn what they do, not what you tell them. In a recent conference discussion, Dave Merrill made the same point by arguing that instruction requires *practice and feedback*. Without those two key ingredients, there is no instruction—simply the delivery of information. There may indeed be incidental learning, but you can't really be sure what—if anything—will be learned. And if you cannot say what will be learned, you cannot call it instruction. Now, some would argue that simply connecting learners to the Internet is valuable in and of itself. Maybe. But for the people footing the bill, that's probably not enough assurance of a positive return on investment.

The Web is full of information, but it is amazingly light on instruction. What is needed now is not just presentation but *courseware*—structured, managed content specifically designed to elicit performance, enable practice, and provide feedback. When classroom teachers have avoided the temptation to lecture, they have been delivering courseware for millennia. The principles that apply in classroom teaching and learning still apply to the Web.

## CBE Versus Instructor-Led Distance Ed

The classroom instructors who are adopting the Net as an instructional technology are rather like those early filmmakers. There are a great many applications using the Net as a communications medium to expand the traditional instructor-led classroom beyond the campus walls. Technology-savvy teachers have spent the last several years setting up e-mail, HTML lecture notes, chat sessions, listserves, newsgroups, and other asynchronous communications tools. But in most cases, these teachers are using the Internet to replicate what they would do in ordinary classroom activities: lecture, assign readings and research reports, facilitate learner discussions, and so forth. That's roughly analogous to the early films that simply recorded stage plays from the audience's point of view.

Technology enables many alternatives. Consider, for example, computer-based education (CBE). CBE allows courseware to be delivered without a great deal of real-time instructor intervention, but with lots of practice and feedback. CBE also is private, delivers training and education on demand, and lets learners progress at their own pace. For a generation, research has demonstrated what CBE can do. To be sure, there are limitations to CBE. For example, it is very difficult for a computer to provide meaningful feedback on written responses longer than a few words—not to mention a five-paragraph theme. Nevertheless, a great deal of knowledge and skill is quite amenable to automated delivery.

The point is not that classroom-emulating distance education is bad and CBE is good. The point is that the strengths of CBE and classroom instruction can offset each other nicely. Some classroom instructors use CBE to provide a consistent set of foundation skills, freeing the instructor to do those things that humans do better than machines. The same could be true in a distance-education model, by combining CBE with the technologies for asynchronous group discussion. More generally, we need to get better at combining the instructional formats the technology enables.

## Necessary Components of a Web-Based CBT Instructional Solution

We believe three components are needed to have an effective Internet-based instructional delivery system: management, courseware, and groupware. Let's look at each one. As a case study, we will use *PLATO® on the Internet,* an Internet-based instructional system that PLATO® Learning created in 1995.

*Management* is essential. Any system that claims to *instruct* (as opposed to *inform*) must be capable of placing learners in a managed learning environment that includes the basic functions of curriculum structure, assessment, prescription, enrollment, progress monitoring, record keeping, and reporting. Curriculum structure is a necessary feature of instruction. Implementation of the structure, at the "macro" level at least, is a management function. Assessment is needed because learning is inherently private. Without some facility for assessment and reporting, there is no way for a learner, an instructor, or an administrator to tell how a particular learner is doing. Progress monitoring, record keeping, and reporting are important to provide accountability data for instructors, administrators, and the folks paying the bill. In addition, the records help administrators who want to manage access to resources, so they can be sure that the people who need the training or education are getting it. So, any Net-based CBE system must provide a robust set of learner-management tools, including performance reporting.

In *PLATO on the Internet*, learner enrollment, class assignments, and other management tasks are handled through a special administrator's Web site, using a browser-based interface with a series of databases in the *PLATO*® *Pathways* system. The system contains curriculum structures in "instructional paths," which can be assigned to any individual learner or group, in any way the instructor desires. Assessment is provided through an on-line system of placement and mastery tests. The system makes individual prescriptions and assigns resources according to each learner's path. The system stores records centrally, so learners can log in from any workstations and resume work where they left off. The degree of learner control and access to resources is controlled by the instructor. Reports for management and accountability purposes can be generated for individual learners and instructors in a wide variety of formats.

*Courseware*, of course, is the heart and soul of any Internet-based instructional system. The PLATO® courseware delivered over the Net is identical to the PLATO courseware delivered on standalone workstations. The PLATO library contains approximately 3,000 hours of courseware in math, language arts, and life and job skills. The offerings are deep as well as broad; for example, the math series covers everything from how to count, through calculus and statistical process control.

*Groupware* is the final feature needed to complete a Web-based CBE system. Years before the predecessor of the Internet, the original mainframe PLATO system incorporated synchronous and asynchronous communication features such as TermTalk, TermComment, g-notes, and p-notes. Years before creation of the predecessor to the Internet, these features anticipated the e-mail, chat rooms, and threaded discussion groups Net users are so familiar with today. In an instructional environment, all these facilities serve the valuable purpose of facilitating creation of a community of learners. They also allow skilled instructors to implement instructional activities that are complementary to CBE courseware.

In *PLATO on the Internet,* we saw the need to provide asynchronous communication. We are now evaluating a number of new technologies to upgrade this part of the system.

## Anatomy of *PLATO on the Internet*

In 1995 and 1996, PLATO Learning began incorporating these ideas into *PLATO®on the Internet.* The pilot implementation was in partnership with Tennessee Tomorrow, Inc., a publicly chartered corporation for statewide workforce training. The system saw its 2.1 release in the summer of 1997. Schools, companies, and individual users pay a low monthly per-learner fee for unlimited access to the entire library of PLATO courseware. Clients avoid having to purchase software and pay only for what they actually use.

The system has several components: The PLATO Learning Folder, a Gatekeeper server, a Records server, a Courseware server, and a Web server. These components are illustrated in Figure 1.

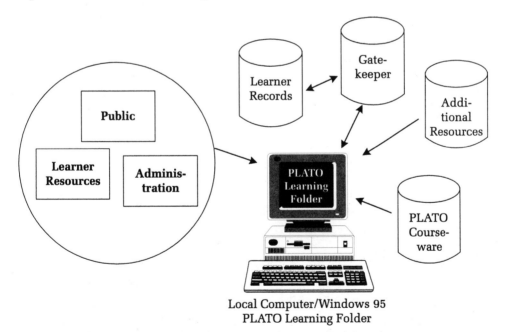

**Figure 1.** Components of the PLATO® on the Internet system

## Components of *PLATO on the Internet*

A set of system files, called the PLATO Learning Folder (PLF), is installed on a local workstation's browser. The system must have Internet access via either a direct connection to a local router or a dial-up connection to a commercial Internet Service Provider (ISP).

When the learner logs on, PLF establishes an Internet connection with a "Gatekeeper" server. The Gatekeeper validates the user's ID, then instructs the Records server to push the user's individual learner record down to the worksta- tion. The learner then selects a lesson, and the PLF streams the files using Macromedia's Flash, Citrix, or proprietary software. When the learner finishes and logs off, the Net connection is re-established and in a few seconds the updated learner record is pushed up to the Records server.

*PLATO on the Internet* is more than just software. Clients such as such as com- munity colleges and schools can use *PLATO* as the foundation for their own courseware offerings, while adding local instructional components as appropriate. Partners purchase *PLATO* account logins in quantity, then can resell them to their local "customers" as part of their own course offerings. For example, a communi- ty college might have a contract with a local manufacturer to provide training in ISO 9000 statistical process control methods. The college could use *PLATO* to assess employees' math skills and assign individualized review where necessary. The college's instructors then would create additional customized classroom and distance-education activities for the manufacturer. Employees could access their assigned *PLATO* lessons at the college, from home, from the local library, from a PC on the factory floor—anywhere a computer can be set up with a browser and Internet access.

## Lessons Learned

To date, thousands of student-years of use have been purchased. Our experience has taught us a number of important lessons.

### Seamless Solution

The need is for a turnkey system that requires a minimum of support. As a result, we spent a great deal of time refining the install and setup procedures and build- ing a robust set of online helps and FAQs.

### Feasibility of 28.8

Although many of our customers have installed the system on intranets, with all the servers behind a firewall, some of their outlying offices—and employees at home—use modems to connect. In addition, many schools still rely exclusively on modems. Our experience has shown that the system does indeed work with a 28.8 connection. However, quality of service from Internet service providers has been quite variable, and we often have worked with our customers to improve their Internet access.

## Instructor's Role

We have found a wide variation among instructors in their comprehension of the learning environment created by *PLATO on the Internet*, and their motivation and skill in using the "community of learners" features of the system. Instructors often begin by viewing the CBE components as a one-for-one replacement for their own classroom teaching and do not grasp the essentially complementary nature of CBE and what an instructor can do. We are finding that, with some instructors, the quality of interaction with their learners goes up as they gain experience with the system. On the other hand, particularly in training environments, we have encountered instructors who expect the computer system to require no instructional support. While the system can function that way, our experience is consistent with research showing that the combination of CBE and instructor participation is the most powerful. A study of the use of *PLATO* to teach developmental studies math in a distance learning environment was recently undertaken with the League for Innovation in the Community College. The study verified the range of instructional options available and confirmed the importance of active instructor involvement. (A monograph reporting the study is currently in preparation and will be available from the League, *www.league.org.*)

## Management

Instructional management is such an implicit part of the conventional classroom teaching environment that instructors may not even be aware of its important role. We have found that, when placed in the environment of *PLATO on the Internet*, instructors often tend to underestimate the importance of instructional management and how the assumptions of the classroom no longer hold.

To meet the needs for instructor and manager training, we have developed an implementation guide and we offer training workshops. We believe instructor and manager training is essential to any innovation and is certainly critical to any client's success with *PLATO on the Internet*.

## Placement

Since *PLATO on the Internet* is designed for adults and young adults and is largely self-instructional, we have found that it is critical to place learners in the correct module. If a new learner is placed in too hard a module, he or she is likely to conclude that learning by computer is "too hard" and become discouraged. If the learner is placed in too easy a module, he or she is likely to conclude that learning by computer is "too easy" and rapidly become bored. It's rare for learners to realize that their feelings are the result of misplacement and rarer still for the new learner to use the learner control built into the system to overcome the problem.

These experiences have created the need for additional teacher training and have emphasized the need for an excellent placement and prescription system as a "front end" to the instructional software. The first version of that system is in use now, and an upgraded system is being designed.

## Conclusion

Developing an easy-to-use, complete, practical, reliable, and cost-effective solution for delivering training and education on the Internet has required considerable research and development. We have found that off-the-shelf technologies offer only partial solutions, at best. Even when the software problems were solved, however, we found that our work was just beginning. An effective solution requires software technology, but expertise in instructional design has been equally important. The learning environments our clients create on the Internet have the potential for both "high tech" and "high touch." These clients are finding ways to reach beyond the physical limitations of the classroom, but—perhaps more significantly—they are using the system to reach beyond the limiting assumptions of the classroom as well. As they—and we—do so, we will begin to understand the ways in which the Net really is a new medium.

*Rob Foshay, Ph.D., is Vice President of Cognitive Learning and Instructional Design at PLATO Learning, Inc., www.plato.com.*

*Corrie Bergeron is the Learning Systems Architect at Walden University, www.waldenu.edu, and president and CEO of Intra-Active Designs, a firm specializing in "information engineering for interactive multimedia." He can be reached at corrie@itasca.net or corrie@waldenu.edu.*

# Digital Backlash

## Karl Albrecht and Ronald Gunn

*This article goes beyond the scope of the two that precede it, to question the rampant optimism surrounding the Digital Millennium. Although the article covers a much broader area than e-learning, it concludes with a question of concern to all interested in e-learning: "What are the consequences of not forging a balance between humans and technology?"*

Something strange happened on January 1, 2000: all across America and the rest of the developed world, nothing strange happened. Virtually everybody was keyed up for the dreaded Y2K event (which meant little more to most people than the turnover of computer clocks), but what we got was a non-event. No economic meltdown, no financial disasters, no planes falling from the sky, no food riots. The anarchists and doomsday cults also came up empty. It was, by any measure, a Big Letdown.

Many people seemed disappointed when nothing happened. It was as if a long-awaited party had been canceled, without explanation.

The arrival of the Digital Millennium seems to have depressed many of us. What otherwise should have been a time for each person to celebrate, ruminate, appreciate, take stock, reflect, dream, and enjoy turned out to be a botched exercise in Digital Mania.

We assert that many people, perhaps a sizable majority, felt vaguely cheated. Yes, there were parties; yes, the ball dropped in Times Square; yes, the news magazines conducted the obligatory review of the century. But, for many people, it all added up to a hollow exercise without the deep personal meaning they had expected (perhaps unconsciously) to feel. We were robbed of a personal milestone and left vaguely dissatisfied.

Many people are still experiencing Digital Angst. If the economy is booming, why doesn't business seem to be fun anymore? Could it be that the triumph of digital process over imaginative substance is wearing thin? Could there be nascent discomfort with the increasingly apparent power imbalance between humans and technology? Why do so many of us feel that we're on a treadmill to nowhere? Who—or what—are we supposed to be keeping up with? And aren't we all just a little tired of hearing about the Internet?

Instant, mostly young, dot.com millionaires are the new heroes of American culture. News reports of their huge success seem to be from another world—the world across the Digital Divide. The dramatic stories on CNN and from other business media contribute to a win-lose, heroes-failures psychosis. As in the Roman gladiator contests, you're either a winner or you're dead.

The big surprise of the Digital Divide may be that it's rapidly becoming more ideological and psychosocial than economic and technical.

In recent years, the Internet and all things digital have outranked almost every other story in news broadcasts, books, and magazine articles. Journalists (wittingly or not) have united with makers of computers and software and with Internet service providers in a half-conscious collusion to popularize the Net phenomenon. The gee-whiz technocracy, with the popular press waving the banner, has an al most messianic obsession with selling the benefits of digital technology to T.C. Mits and T.C.Wits (the celebrated man and woman in the street). We feel it's proper to ask whether the fascination with digital gadgetry, especially in America, is the subject of or result of the unprecedented media treatment.

In its earliest days, Internet devotees hailed it as "the great democratizer." It would level the effects of social status, economic conditions, and political clout. It would put even the tiniest businesses on the same footing with the mighty giants. Now, even the Internet's most rabid promoters concede that it is having the opposite effect. It exaggerates the disparity between the haves and the have-nots. Notwithstanding politically correct ads showing adorable black children somewhere in Africa logging on to the Web, poor people won't be lifted out of their dire economic circumstances by computers or the Internet.

An unvoiced assumption seems to be that all human beings have an equal appetite for consuming and processing information. That seems questionable, judging by the low sales of nonfiction books, for example. The lack of convergence (as predicted) of television and the Internet also casts doubt on a universal insatiability for information.

Listening to its more vocal and determined advocates, one gets the feeling that the Digital Doctrine takes on an almost Fascist overtone, eerily reminiscent of the political environment in pre-war Germany. That may seem extreme, but many well-educated adults have confided to us that they feel intellectually intimidated by what they call the "techno-Nazi" ideology and are reluctant to speak their misgivings. More people, including those who use computers and the Internet regularly, say they are feeling caught in an ideological stampede of sorts.

To read the subtext of the Digital Drama, there's a clearly defined Digital Doctrine—a set of Orwellian ideological premises that must be embraced. What are the key propositions, spoken and unspoken, that define the Digital Doctrine and shape its energy?

## The Digital Doctrine

We seem to be expected to believe the following tenets:

- Technology is a thing unto itself, an all-pervasive agent that governs our lives—as opposed to something that people choose to do with gadgets.
- If a thing can be done, then it will be done and, indeed, must be done—for example, connecting your refrigerator to the Internet.
- The Wired World is our destiny. You must learn to love (or at least live with) the Big Brother aspect. Otherwise, you will certainly be left out (of something) and left behind (somebody).
- Some of us get it, and the ones who don't must either be helped to get it or be driven like sheep to their ultimate destiny to love it in the end.

Vocabulary signals ideology. One of the clearest signs of a developing new ideology is the special lingo its devotees use to signal their allegiance to new truths. Characteristically, the Digital World has cyber-speak, a notably impersonal patois of processes and things. The New Economy-Old Economy shibboleth signals an attitude, a narcissistic in-group psychology that says, "We're the enlightened ones; we get it. Anybody who doesn't agree with the cyber-ideology doesn't get it and will be left behind."

Internet language reflects a pecking order: a *newbie* is a freshman who is expected to be properly humble and respectful toward those who got there first. Classifications according to technology affinity, such as *late adopters* and *resisters,* apply labels to anyone who doesn't enthusiastically embrace a particular new technology.

As management consultants, we've watched with considerable amusement as the "geeks" have suddenly discovered business. In no other dimension of practice have we seen such a rush of idealistic, narcissistic, and ill-informed zealots who have no interest in learning from the experience of others. In record time, the invading cyber-Vikings have created their own business ideology and vocabulary, which, they say, taking great pains to emphasize, owe nothing to the traditional thinking processes of commerce. They characterize established enterprises as "old economy" or "bricks and mortar" to authorize themselves to "reinvent" business. "After all," they pronounce, "the Internet changes everything. The old rules no longer apply"—implying, so why bother to learn them?

Here's a peculiar fact: many of the Netizens who are promoting the Net and all forms of e-business are the same people who screamed bloody murder in the mid-1990s when America Online announced it would give its customers access to the Internet at no extra charge. They lamented that allowing hordes of civilians onto the Internet would clutter up the place with a bunch of newbies and nuisances.

Actually, the Internet will evolutionize business, but not revolutionize it. In fact, companies that take best advantage of online technology are turning out to be the established leaders in the so-called old economy—retailers, publishers, catalogue marketers, banks, and all the rest. Consider that as early as 1989, Hewlett-Packard decided to wire the entire company, putting more than 90,000 employees in contact with each other. Procter & Gamble and Wal-Mart have linked their computer systems—b2b in the current jargon—for well over a decade.

Ironically, many of the old rules still apply, to the consternation of new-economy entrepreneurs. Mark Twain, arguably one of the best marketing consultants in history, lived during the time of the California gold rush. He advised, "When everybody is out digging for gold, the business to be in is selling shovels." Few independent miners made fortunes digging for gold; most went broke. Selling shovels was indeed more profitable than digging with them. One of the few millionaires to emerge from the gold rush period was a Jewish immigrant named Levi Strauss, who made heavy-duty work clothes out of denim and sold them to miners. The ones going broke on the Internet are those digging for gold; the ones making profits are selling them the shovels.

In the business sector, Dot.Com Delusion has spawned a whole new set of ethical dilemmas. Entrepreneurs team up with venture capitalists and stock underwriters to launch businesses that have no hope of long-term viability. Investors rush in like eager sheep, part with their fleece, and are left with worthless hides (at least for the purposes of this metaphor) while the insiders walk away with their cash. Almost all of the so-called Internet millionaires are actually stock market millionaires. It has been about market valuation, not value in the marketplace.

The new message to young people thinking about starting a business is "Forget built to last and learn built to flip." More companies are being created with the sole purpose of taking them public and then flipping them. The quaint idea of building a going concern that will deliver long-term shareholder value is nowhere in the equation. The new cyber-hero isn't the entrepreneur who works hard to build a viable firm, but the one clever enough to promote it and flip it, moving on to the next one before the bills come due. Established firms are, in many cases, at a disadvantage vis-à-vis unprofitable digital-mania firms that can use hyper-inflated share prices to acquire other firms without putting up cash. That puts enormous pressure on executives of all firms to use PR gimmicks and accounting tricks to try to boost share prices to unsustainable levels. Unabated, snake oil begets more snake oil.

## A Few Predictions

E-commerce will be the big failure story of the decade. Successful companies will, of course, continue to use online technology to simplify and integrate their operations, interlocking their systems more with those of suppliers and partners. And most established companies will extend their market reach through Web technology. However, the heart of the e-commerce story as promoted by the press, namely the Internet-only company, will eventually be seen as a total failure.

Internet-only companies doomed themselves to unprofitability early by adopting a fanatical give-away mentality. The idea was to forget about actually selling anything on your Website (at least not for a profit margin) and just get as many people as you can to visit your site—in other words, to aggregate eyeballs. When people visit your site, you can sell their names to other e-merchants that want to advertise their products. Only a few firms have made that portal approach work, and they get most of their revenue from the many smaller Web wannabes that spend their investors' capital trying to build attention share. Few Internet-only companies actually sell enough of anything to cover their advertising and operating costs. As they go out of business and stop buying advertising, even the major portals may go out with them.

Internet companies have been burning through investor capital at an alarming rate, and few have shown enough sales productivity to justify further investment. Despite the breathless press stories about the phenomenal growth rate of online commerce—in percentage terms, of course—the fact is that online sales account for only a small fraction of total retail sales, even in America. The enormous promotional investment fueling the current level of attention to, interest in, and economic activity surrounding everything digital can't be sustained indefinitely. As Internet businesses fail in droves and the investments fail to perform as hoped, digital capital will be scarcer and the artificially sustained energy will wane. Once the Net-bubble has deflated, there will be a massive sag in energy and money for all things digital. Internet Fatigue, as we call it, will be signaled by the widely expressed attitude: "We're tired of hearing about the Internet."

## The S-Curve Rules

Fundamental to the Digital Doctrine is the sacred principle that the number of Internet users will grow without bounds, eventually including all but about three people on the planet. MIT's director of media technology, Nicholas Negroponte, predicted in 1997 that "there will be 1 billion people on the Internet by the year 2000." Many "by the year 2000" predictions are becoming an embarrassment now that 2000 has arrived. Nothing rises to the sky, and pundits who don't understand the principle of the S-curve get to learn about it in a practical way.

The S-curve is a natural principle, almost on a par with gravity, that dictates patterns of growth for everything from bacteria colonies to human populations to stock prices to market demand for new products. Any fast-rising variable goes through an early "getting started" phase, followed by a sharp upward acceleration and then a slower rate of growth that may level off. Plotted on a chart, the pattern looks like a stretched letter S, with its overall shape determined by the rate of growth and distance from the foot to the shoulder. There's every reason to believe that the number of Internet users will also follow the S-curve.

As for 1 billion people on the Internet, we ask, Really? All with more than $10 dollars to spend per year? What if the eventual Internet population isn't 99 percent of the developed world? Suppose it turns out to be less than half, regardless of economics or education, because of people's individual mental proclivity? It seems clear that, even in a highly educated population, some people are more information-oriented than others. What if not everyone is yearning to be a cyber-citizen?

Where might we be on the S-curve now? Most dot.com business models, and much of the economic ideology of the Digital Agenda, assume we're on the early rising part of the S. A frightening thought: What if we're much farther up the S-curve than most people think? What if the hard core of addictive users is mostly committed to the Internet and the rest of us can take it or leave it? How many ventures hang on the assumption of continued exponential growth?

Consider that two-thirds of the world population has never heard a dial tone. Nearly half has no reliable access to electricity or running water. In all likelihood, not more than 10 percent will be eligible economically for the Internet within the next 20 years. The idea that all we have to do is give people computers is a projection of a distinctly American, upper-middle-class worldview and smacks of the Great Society. It's the cyber-equivalent of "Let them eat cake."

In America, home of the first and most wired population on the planet, it seems likely that more than half of the people who will use the Internet in anything more than an occasional way are already doing so. Will every new gadget and killer application grow the population of Internet users, eventually recruiting everyone? That seems more and more unlikely.

Internet Fatigue is already in evidence. The scenario, as we see it: as the Dot.Com Death March continues, more investors will lose faith in the Internet Fantasy. The Digital Dream will become the Digital Nightmare. The same herd of investors who rushed in will rush out of Internet-based stocks—and possibly the whole category, but certainly away from the gee-whiz sectors. Venture capitalists will become choosier and will gravitate toward the shovel makers. At the same time, established "old economy" firms will become ever more competent and aggressive at extending their businesses with online technology.

Profit margins and earnings growth rates of even the most worshipped online companies, such as America Online, will remain appallingly low, and their share prices will be brutally repriced to normal levels. We will likely see one or more major icons of e-commerce such as Amazon.com fail or have to be acquired to continue operating. Advertising expenditures will fall precipitously as venture capital dries up and dot.bomb companies trying to survive cut budgets and promote themselves with Internet banner ads, merely prolonging their agony. Few portals, if any, will stay profitable.

Ironically, there will be a dramatic return of attention in business (and by CNN) to the so-called old-economy companies—you remember, the ones with actual profits. CNN and other media will, of course, claim that they knew all along that the dot.com boom couldn't last.

The ultimate expression of Internet Fatigue will be a loss of interest—a Digital Depression. It won't be possible for the media to keep up the drama indefinitely. Even people who use PC-Net technology every day will be saying, "Enough, already. I get it. The Internet is here. Now, let's get on with our lives." The hardcore addicted population of about 15 to 20 million people worldwide will continue to live in the Wired World. Meanwhile, the digital middle class will continue to take it or leave it.

## Digital Deliverance

Once we've wired the world, we can't unwire it. Is that what we want? If we assume that the wiring will continue at breakneck speed, what are the consequences of not forging a balance between humans and technology? The sci-fi-like scenarios of artificial intelligence surpassing human intelligence take on a meaning with greater gravitas: if we don't insist on substance first, served by process second, and we fail to re-emphasize that technology exists to serve the aims of human community, then a quiet new elite may emerge: people who can turn off the TV and the PC and think.

After one of our recent talks, a senior executive mused, "You know, there'll come a day when people will pay a lot of money to go where they can't be connected."

*Karl Albrecht is chairman of Karl Albrecht International, San Diego, and author of more than 20 books on management and organizational effectiveness. His latest book, published by the American Management Association, is* Corporate Radar: Tracking the Forces That Are Shaping Your Business. *You can contact Albrecht at karl@albrechtintl.com.*

*Ronald Gunn is managing director of Strategic Futures Consulting Group, Alexandria, Virginia, and has been published by* The Futurist, *the American Management Association, and trade associations. You can contact Gunn at rgunn@strategicfutures.com.*

# Top Ten E-Learning Myths

**John V. Moran**
**interviewed by Haidee E. Allerton**

*With all of the hopes and hype for e-learning, it's only natural that myths have been developing in the industry. It can be easy to believe these myths—and make some costly mistakes. Here's a short list from the president of an e-learning provider.*

We talked with John V. Moran, president of GP e-Learning Technologies, and he shared what he and his company have determined about e-learning: it's worth it, it's doable, but don't expect a walk in the park. Here are Moran's top 10 e-learning myths:

**10. There is substantial knowledge base and loads of experts in the e-learning field.** "We're just now building on the knowledge base," says Moran. "It's best to be wary of people who say they've been doing this for 20 years." Only 2 percent of training was Web-based in 1999; 75 percent of that was in information technology. Of $63 billion spent on training, only $1.14 billion of that was over the Web.

**9. Web-enabled learning management systems are easy to integrate. Employee data flows seamlessly from your legacy HR systems into the LMS database.** In reality, this is the hardest aspect to achieve, especially in multinational organizations. In order to track learners for training registration, progress, and so forth, the most fundamental function is a learner's name and address. One size doesn't fit all; not all letters of every person's name fit into the spaces allotted on forms. That will lead to more problems using this LMS platform.

**8. Loads of Web-enabled content exists, and it works on all LMS platforms.** There's little existing content that can be migrated easily from one LMS platform to another. Even when migration is accomplished effectively, course functionality can be lost. "That's a problem with most Web-enabled providers," cautions Moran.

**7. Your information systems department is happy and supportive of your plan to deploy e-learning over its systems.** In most organizations, the IT systems are already taxed, and most IS departments don't want to deploy e-learning through their pipelines, using up their bandwidth. "You need to get IS on board early, or it can be costly," says Moran.

**6. Your IS department welcomes the use of desktop plug-ins.** No, and that's no surprise. Moran says that you can "spend a lot of money on generic content and then find out it won't work without plug-ins."

**5. Most of your employees know what a mouse is.** In fact, 50 percent of the U.S. workforce still doesn't know how to use a computer. Computer literacy is as rampant in the boardroom as on the shop floor. "Most employees have poor navigation skills. You need to prepare the workforce through selling, cajoling, and knowledge—or else even a good learning event will fail," says Moran.

**4. Most adults enjoy looking at the hourglass waiting for downloads of meaningless video clips.** "In fact," says Moran, "too much of most e-learning is what learners don't need to know." Studies show that the average adult learner loses attention after 15 seconds. At one company when a simulation took too long to download, employees lost interest in online learning. It took the company two years to recover. People don't want extraneous video and audio. One reason is that they don't want strange noises coming form their computers, lest other employees or their boss think they're playing games. Says Moran; "Video and audio are fine, as long as they add to the learning objectives."

**3. Employees love to learn on their own time.** Increasingly, employees are expected to take online learning either during work hours or after hours. Both options can present a problem: employees don't like interrupting job tasks, and they don't want to feel they're working for their employers 24/7 by learning job skills after hours. The lesson: employees need to be prepared in order for them to take advantage of online learning.

**2. Adults like learning on a computer, particularly when their navigation skills are challenged.** Moran says GP has found that "the number 1 reason adults don't finish online courses is because they can't navigate."

**1. E-learning is "click and easy."** "We hear that all the time, but e-learning is a difficult journey, though well worth it," says Moran. There's a big up-front cost for setting up a Web-enabled MLS, for repurposing existing content, and for the training (hosting, serving). But in the long-term, the expense can be from one-third to one-tenth of that for traditional training. E-learning implementation will be challenged by employees and IS. Bottom line: "Classroom training will remain. But in five years, there'll be no distinction between e-learning and Web-based training," says Moran. "All e-learning will be delivered over the Web; CD-ROMs won't exist."

*John V. Moran is president of GP e-Learning Technologies, GP Corporation, based in Columbia, Maryland, www.gpelearning.com. You can reach him at jmoran@gpelearning.com.*

*Haidee E. Allerton is editor of* Training & Development. *You can reach her at hallerton @astd.org.*

# Challenging E-Community Myths

## David Mager and Warren Karlenzig

*Because of the ad hoc nature of many online communities, confusion exists regarding how, when, and why to implement these important business knowledge tools. This article outlines the nine most prevalent myths concerning communities and discusses the truths behind them.*

As companies seek to evolve beyond transaction-based e-business to better meet their business objectives, online community efforts are trying to embrace the "extraprise," which includes an organization's customers, suppliers and partners. But the organic roots of online communities have created strong e-community myths. Basing business practices on these myths can detract from the desired experience and may even weaken valuable existing relationships. By challenging these myths and adopting a constructive model, a company can determine the appropriate level of community and meet its goals with realistic, phased community-building efforts.

The following are the nine most common myths we hear when speaking to clients about their community issues.

**Myth 1: *It's not important to determine the cost and benefits of community. We just have to do it.*** The days of the dot-com threat are waning. Potential customer satisfaction and financial benefit need to be weighed against the operating costs of initial and future development. Potential business benefits for pursuing community include brand enhancement; knowledge creation; strengthening customer, partner, supplier, and employee relationships; capturing member preferences and issues; improving cross-selling and up-selling techniques; increasing efficiency by transferring business process functions to members; and responding to competitive threats.

**Myth 2:** *If you build a community site, users will find and gather on it on their own.* Actually, communities need both online and offline member acquisition and retention. And that's just to get them to check out the community. On the Web are many examples of quickly launched message boards populated with many topics but no responses. There may even be some of these lonely message boards on your own site.

**Myth 3:** *Community is just message boards and chat.* Communities are about people, identity, and common interests, not technologies. We define "community" as a group of people who identify and interact around common, purposeful, and mutually beneficial interests. By plotting the value of interactivity along a spectrum, companies can choose whatever level of community is appropriate for their situation. This way they can avoid blindly choosing features and implementing technologies.

Community services are relatively easy to implement in terms of both organizational support and user adoption. EBay Inc. and Amazon.com Inc. use ratings as an effective (if limited) interactivity tool that creates some bonding and identity with the site. E-mail newsletters with links directly into both content and community are commonly used within a variety of vertical communities, such as developer communities at Sun Microsystems Inc.

Community space is probably the most widely misused community experience on the Web. It is best done by Yahoo Clubs and some intranet communities of practice. In addition, companies such as Morgan Stanley Dean Witter & Co. implement user-driven calendaring to support offline community-building.

Community space can provide value through monitoring of interactions, both good and not so good. We ask, Would you rather customers rant on your site, where you can take note, respond, and act, or rant somewhere else? The community space realm can be a risky place to start community—its long gestation period (typically nine to 12 months) is resource-intensive to support and can eventually shift power from the host to the members. As members gain power, censorship becomes impossible without destroying the community. So a company's brand risk profile often determines what degree of community space can be safely implemented.

From a community symbiosis perspective, the lines between owner, host, and community blur. Adobe Systems Inc. and Mattel Inc. both use community symbiosis to develop products as well as to guide community direction. Amazon.com's community provides its Web site with everything from content to infrastructure (hot links to related Web sites).

**Myth 4:** *It's too important to start communities now to take the time to do it right.* Community implementation needs careful consideration because it's one of the few e-business undertakings that can be irreversible. User interfaces are notoriously difficult to change once community regulars become accustomed to a certain way of allowing interactivity. For example, when Apple Computer Inc. attempted to switch its Macintosh communities from a quick yet difficult-to-master Unix platform to a user-friendly GUI platform, the regulars revolted and forced a dual-platform system that delayed new development. In addition, because of the emotional commitment needed to interact with members, a poor initial showing within a community is much more difficult to overcome than an unsatisfactory transaction.

**Myth 5:** *Communities basically manage themselves.* All communities need leadership, guidance, and support. Decisions on the next webcast, the newest community area, or the reeling in of wayward discussion topics must be made for the community to operate efficiently. Because lurkers (who read posted messages but don't contribute) typically make up 85 percent of community members and most initial members are lurkers, companies need to provide initial leadership in starting and continuing conversations. Whether the host company or its members lead is determined by the degree of member identity with the community. The stronger the degree of identity, the greater the likelihood that members will contribute to the community. Technology companies such as Microsoft Corp. and Cisco Systems Inc. require certification, and their members often have the greatest identity with the company. This sense of identity translates into the highest rates of contribution both on the company sites and in traditional Usenet communities.

**Myth 6:** *Communities organize themselves just like the company organizes itself.* Companies often base their organization on marketing segments, not self-identification. For online communities, the opposite is true. Because identity is critical to community participation, starting with the right interest areas can make or break a community's success. Common areas of identification include topics, tasks, geographies, and industries. Recently, member-selective identification has become more common as an organizing force. Angel investors, executives, and thought leaders are using community to extend their networks rather than join or begin e-communities. Online community services and symbiosis facilitate and enrich offline networking.

**Myth 7:** *A community can be started and be fully functional within a month.* Community services can be implemented fairly quickly, but real self-sustaining community takes time to develop. For example, when a site for car enthusiasts needed to help its Web-inexperienced users adopt online community, it used familiar metaphors, such as an online car show and an "ask the mechanic" department, to make clear the value of online interaction. Only after six months of building experiential knowledge did users begin contributing to and using other functions.

**Myth 8:** *If you have a great online community, offline community isn't important.* Communities need a degree of offline interactivity and reinforcement. The Well LLC, the oldest e-community, discovered that intimate online interactivity was stunted without face-to-face interactions. Trust becomes a larger factor as communities develop across the community spectrum. Currently, online deal-making is a supporting function where commodity transactions are facilitated but little real negotiation occurs. As technology improves to include ubiquitous streaming video, this might change, but probably nothing will replace the need for direct human interaction.

**Myth 9:** *All organizations must create their own communities to be successful.* Many options are available to companies today, ranging from application service providers to outsourcing of critical functions and community management to alliances and sponsorship of other communities. Companies potentially can save millions of dollars by understanding these choices and choosing the best options for them.

As the e-business environment evolves, views of community must also change. By challenging these myths, your company can increase its chances of creating a successful e-community. You then can construct and execute a community plan by considering the expected business value and risk profile, community members' identities and needs, and the mix of community and company competencies.

*David Mager and Warren Karlenzig are strategy director and senior strategist, respectively, at Proxicom Inc., an e-business consulting and development company in Reston, VA (www.proxicom.com).*

# Evaluating the Return on Investment of E-Learning

## Jack J. Phillips, Patricia P. Phillips, Lizette Z. Duresky, and Cyndi Gaudet

*Are the results of e-learning worth the cost? This article examines means of answering that big question. The authors review the basics of evaluating training, stress the importance of building support for evaluation, outline the essentials for evaluating ROI, and offer some significant findings from research.*

New technologies are revolutionizing the way industries approach work. Technologically powered systems have replaced traditional work, decreasing the presence of manual labor. Today's workforce places more demands on employees to possess computer skills to execute job-related tasks. Several factors have contributed to e-learning's significant place in the training industry, including corporations employing global representatives, telecommuting, increased technologies, and lack of time to spend in traditional classrooms. Many experts predict that the traditional classroom model will represent less than 30 percent of all formal corporate learning programs by as early as 2003.

The literature suggests that the definition of e-learning is varied and inconclusive for the training industry. For the context of this article, e-learning is defined as the computerization of the educational process. E-learning may include virtual classrooms for call center representatives, corporate-wide learning management systems, synchronous learning events for managers, CD-ROM-based new employee training, and interactive, asynchronous learning interventions for salespersons.

## Key Evaluation Issues

The reasons for evaluating e-learning coincide with those for evaluating any type of learning solution. Some of the most common reasons for evaluating e-learning include:

- Determining if an e-learning solution is accomplishing its objectives
- Identifying the strengths and weaknesses in the e-learning process
- Determining the return on investment of an e-learning solution
- Deciding who should participate in future e-learning solutions
- Identifying who benefited the most or the least from the e-learning solution
- Reinforcing major points made to the target group
- Collecting data to assist in marketing future initiatives (Phillips, Phillips, and Duresky, 2000)

Within the training industry, champions of new e-learning initiatives have experienced roadblocks during the implementation phases of a project. According to the 2001 ASTD *State of the Industry Report*, one reason organizations postpone many e-learning initiatives is to overcome significant up-front development and implementation costs (Van Buren, 2001). One strategic way to build momentum for new e-learning initiatives is to develop comprehensive evaluation processes that demonstrate the value these initiatives bring to key stakeholders and the organization as a whole.

## Evaluating E-Learning versus Traditional Learning

By realizing that some of the same processes used to evaluate other types of learning solutions work with e-learning, the task of evaluation becomes easier. It becomes a matter of expanding the current evaluation techniques and processes to include e-learning as a method of delivery. Evaluating e-learning is both a similar and dissimilar process to evaluating other solutions. Similarities include applying Kirkpatrick's four levels of evaluation (Kirkpatrick, 1994) as well as converting the benefits to monetary value and comparing them to the total costs in order to calculate the ROI (Phillips, 1997). Methods to isolate the effects of an e-learning solution are also similar to those used in evaluating traditional learning solutions (Hodges, 1997). Differences include gathering data as a part of e-learning. Data collection can often be built into the process much easier than with traditional methods. The impact of eliminating time spent on distributing, collecting, scanning, and analyzing the data typically yields a positive cost-benefit ratio. Because e-learners can be remote, some methods for data collection may take a different approach. Instead of traditional focus groups, collaboration tools and conference calls may be utilized to gather data from a group of individuals.

## Evaluation Framework

Evaluation of e-learning is a complex issue and several types of data should be collected. The type of data needed often depends on the purposes of evaluation and particular individuals who need to see the data. While e-learning does not necessarily add to the complexities of the data mix, it will usually influence the way the data is collected.

Different types of data collected can be classified into five levels. (The first four were developed by Kirkpatrick in the 1950s.)

**Level 1, Reaction,** measures participant reaction with the program and captures planned actions during the actual learning activity.

**Level 2, Learning,** measures change in knowledge skills or attitude.

**Level 3, Application,** measures change in on-the-job behavior and specific application actions.

**Level 4, Impact,** measures changes in business impact measures, either individual or in the work unit.

**Level 5, ROI,** compares the monetary benefits of the program with the actual cost of the program.

Sometimes it is also helpful to capture intangible data that purposely is not converted to monetary values, but represents important data. This category can overlap with application and impact measures listed above. When this category is combined with the five levels above, a balanced set of six different types of data are collected, representing a comprehensive measurement and evaluation process. In addition, certain indicators should be measured or monitored. These include:

- The actual utilization statistics
- The retention rates throughout synchronous learning
- Repeat users
- The cost of the program
- The other volume statistics indicating the level of activity

### Case Study

Technology-mediated communication has often been the focus in analyzing the effectiveness of on-line learning. Learners interact differently using technology versus traditional face-to-face methods. While face-to-face participants report a higher level of satisfaction with the interaction experience, technology provides a sense of anonymity, which may facilitate more openness and communication. In a study conducted by Lewis, Geroy, and Griego, it was found that the perceptions of accountability and contribution from the face-to-face learners are higher than those of the technology-mediated learners. It was also found that boldness, conflicts, confrontation, frankness, and frustration were mediums of communication more often used by the technology-mediated learners. Also, trainees may be uncomfortable with the interaction level and may be challenged to try new types of interactions (Lewis, Geroy, and Griego, 2000).

What does this mean with regard to evaluating e-learning? First, consider evaluating the effectiveness of e-learning programs by measuring enrollment, no-shows, and retention rates of participants. Be prepared to mediate interactions among learners within a virtual team. Also, evaluate the intangible data, such as reduced conflict over the course of time. Finally, evaluate the initial comfort level (Level 1) of the participant in an online learning program and implement sequential measurements of participant's comfort level. (Phillips et al., 2000)

# Building Support

As in any other major initiative, evaluation will require commitment and support to be effective. Evaluation is an add-on activity in most situations and represents additional cost. Various stakeholders need to understand the rationale for evaluation and their role in making evaluation work. They must know what type of data is needed, when it is needed, and who needs it.

Support for evaluation rests on six key elements. First, there must be a commitment from the top of the organization to support the evaluation initiative. Second, managers in the organization provide support for evaluation by allocating time, becoming involved in the activities, and insisting that evaluation data be developed. Third, policies, procedures, and guidelines must be developed for consistency so that the evaluation data can be compared across programs. Fourth, skills and knowledge must be improved for evaluation and with technology. Fifth, appropriate technology support must be available to evaluate e-learning. Sixthly, there must be an action orientation to utilize evaluation data for process improvement.

## Case Study

The American Petroleum Company measured the effectiveness of a new technology program. The goal of the training program was to increase job performance in a sales environment. Two needs emerged which provided the impetus for change. One was the need to compete within the industry. The other was a lack of skills and knowledge among the sales consultants in the organization. The training department was determined to conduct an ROI study based on the visibility of the program within the organization. Senior management had agreed to invest in the e-learning program and the training department wanted to be able to provide information on whether there was a return on investment. The ROI showed a 97% return on investment because of implementing the new technology program. (Whalen, 1999)

# Implementation and Integration of ROI in E-Learning

Given the interest in ROI, it is imperative to have a comprehensive measurement and evaluation system that improves the actual calculation of ROI. However, for the process to work effectively, several elements must be present to build a comprehensive system. Connections of frameworks and process models along with implementation and communication issues will be needed to develop a defensible system that can meet the needs of various target audiences.

The implementation of a comprehensive measurement and evaluation system requires five key elements.

1. There must be a framework to collect data that categorizes data into different types and dictates particular time frames to predict data. This could be in the form of a balanced scorecard (Kaplan and Norton, 1996), the Kirkpatrick four-level framework, or the five levels of evaluation described earlier.
2. A process model is needed to show how data is actually collected, how the effects of e-learning are isolated from other factors, and a mechanism to convert data to monetary value and to capture the full cost of the program. Data needs to be properly collected, integrated, processed, and reported.
3. Operating standards and guidelines are necessary to ensure that each step of the ROI process model is consistent. Applying these operating standards ensure that a study can be replicated and is credible in its process.
4. A methodical approach to implementation must be present to ensure that proper support and resources are in place to fully implement the ROI process.
5. Initially, it may be helpful to use many of the published studies around ROI, but eventually, case studies will have to be developed internally to show strong track record.

## Case Study

Acme Incorporated used CD-ROM technology to train its field service engineers throughout the country with the objective of increasing customer satisfaction and increasing the amount of sales. Each of the field service engineers already possessed a laptop computer. The costs for the traditional program were weighed against the benefits of the e-learning experience. Compensation for the instructors was $65,000 per year plus benefits, bringing the cost to $78,000. Compensation for the learner was done on the field service engineers, yielding $164 per day. Delivery costs were assessed, including travel, overhead, equipment, and materials in an instructor-led workshop. After calculating the benefits, the ROI analysis showed a return of 129%. (Kruse and Keil, 2000)

## Selecting Programs for ROI Evaluation

A comprehensive evaluation process is impractical for every e-learning project. When determining which programs to evaluate at levels 4 and 5, consider the following criteria:

- The life cycle of the e-learning program (A long-term implementation and duration would demand an ROI evaluation at some point during the program.)
- The linkage of the e-learning program to operational goals and measures (A direct linkage should be subjected to ROI evaluation.)
- The importance of the program to strategic objectives (E-learning programs focused directly on strategy should be subjected to business impact and ROI calculations.)
- The cost of the e-learning program (The more expensive the program, the more likely it is a candidate for an ROI calculation.)
- The visibility of the e-learning program (Highly visible programs should be subjected to impact and ROI evaluation.)
- The size of the target audience (Larger audiences demand higher levels of evaluation, at least for a sample of participants.)
- The investment of time (High commitments of time demand high levels of evaluation.)
- Interest of top executives in the evaluation (If executives are interested in business impact and ROI evaluation, then it must be developed.)

## ROI and E-Learning

The term "return on investment" (ROI) has been one of the most misused and misunderstood terms in our industry. The classical definition of return on investment, from finance and accounting, is earnings divided by investment. In the context of an e-learning evaluation, ROI becomes net monetary benefits from a program divided by the cost of the program.

ROI needs to be utilized consistently so that comparisons can be made from one program evaluation to another. Return on assets (ROA), return on equity (ROE), and return on capital employed (ROCE) are inappropriate for this evaluation because they focus on issues unrelated to the actual investment in e-learning. Other uses of the word "return" should be avoided unless it actually is a monetary value. For example, the return on expectations (ROE) is often utilized to reflect success related to what the customer expected.

The actual accounting-related definition for ROI for e-learning is net monetary benefits from the program divided by the actual cost of the e-learning program. To build credibility with the target audience for this type of calculation, a conservative approach is needed in the analysis. This approach requires that costs are fully loaded and that monetary benefits are included only if they are directly linked to the program. The development of the ROI requires three steps in a process model:

1. There must be a mechanism to isolate the effects of the e-learning program.
2. There must be some method for converting data to monetary values to use directly in the numerator of the ROI formula.
3. The fully loaded cost of the e-learning program should be tabulated.

## Resources for Evaluation

Because evaluation will require additional steps in the process and cost additional money, it is very important to indicate how many resources are required and to plan and allocate for those resources. Given the affordable cost for the process, it is then possible to profile the appropriate evaluation mix. In this arrangement, expensive evaluations can be conducted for some programs, while leaving more expensive evaluations to those e-learning programs meeting the criteria previously outlined. Best-practice organizations assign 4-5% of their total learning solution budget to measurement and evaluation.

Integrating evaluation into the training process saves time, money, and staff. In order to maximize the evaluation process, it is important to share responsibilities for evaluation. Responsibilities include data collection, analysis of data, interpreting results, consolidating information into report format, and technical support.

Several cost-saving approaches are available that can be taken to keep the commitments of time and cost to a minimum:

- Plan for evaluation early in the process.
- Build evaluation into the e-learning process.
- Share the responsibilities for evaluation.
- Require participants to conduct major steps.
- Use short-cut methods for major steps.
- Use sampling to select the most appropriate e-learning programs for ROI analysis.
- Use estimates in the collection and analysis of data.
- Develop internal capability to implement the ROI process.
- Utilize technology to collect and analyze data.
- Streamline the reporting process. (Phillips and Burkett, In Press)

## The Toughest Issue: Isolating Influence of Other Factors

The implementation of an e-learning program with subsequent skill improvement and knowledge enhancement is only one of many influences that can drive behavior change and business impact data. One of the toughest challenges for evaluation of e-learning is to isolate the effects of the e-learning from other influences. Fortunately, many approaches are available and this issue can be addressed in most, if not all, settings. The important point is to deliberately attack the issue, plan for the method of isolation, and follow through so that only the portion of the output data directly linked to e-learning is actually credited to the e-learning program.

Without some method to isolate the effects of the e-learning from other influences, there is a high probability that the study is inaccurate because of the potential influence of other factors. Consequently, some method to isolate must be planned into the process. Several methods are accurate for isolating the effects of the process. These include the use of control group arrangements, trend line analysis, and sophisticated forecasting models. Unfortunately, in many settings it is not possible or practical to use these methods. Practical methods can be used to allocate the actual improvement connected to an e-learning program. These include the following (Phillips, 1996a):

- Participant's estimate of the e-learning program impact (percent)
- Supervisor's estimate of program impact (percent)
- Management's estimate of program impact (percent)
- Use of previous studies or expert input
- Calculating/estimating the impact of other factors
- Use of customer input

## Second Toughest Issue: Converting Data to Monetary Value

To calculate the return on investment, data collected at level 4 is converted to monetary values to compare with program costs. This requires a value to be placed on each unit of data connected with the program. Ten approaches are available to convert data to monetary values where the specific techniques selected usually depend on the type of data and situation (Phillips, 1996b):

- Output data is converted to profit contribution or cost savings.
- The cost of quality is calculated and quality improvements are directly converted to cost savings.
- For programs where employee time is saved, the participant wages and benefits are used for the value of time.
- Historical costs and current records are used when they are available for a specific variable.
- When available, internal and external experts may be used to estimate a value for an improvement.
- External databases are sometimes available to estimate the value or cost of industry-related data items.

- Participants estimate the value of the data item.
- Soft measures are linked mathematically to other measures that are easier to measure.
- Supervisors and managers provide estimates for the values of the improvement.
- Education and training staff estimate the value of an output data item.

## Case Study

The cost to design the program may be prorated over the expected life of the program. One company developed a computer-based training program to teach maintenance administrators and repair service clerks a specific system technology. An ROI analysis revealed a return of 319% in year 1 and 366% return in years 2 and 3. There was no recurring cost of the initial training design and development, so the cost was spread over a three-year period (the time cycle of the CBT program). Repeat calls were reduced by 22%. (Hodges, 1997)

## The ROI Forecast

In many e-learning projects, the client wants to know the projected payback from the project. E-learning projects often require significant investment and many clients do not desire to venture into the expensive development process without having some sense of the payback. Consequently, there is tremendous pressure to forecast ROI even if it is not very accurate.

Some e-learning project justifications are based on cost savings alone, where the fully loaded cost of the traditional learning is compared with the cost of e-learning. The earnings or net monetary benefits from both approaches are consistent. The evaluation of an e-learning project should include a mechanism for forecasting the actual expected benefits, converting the benefits to monetary values, and then comparing the benefits with the projected cost. The difficulty in the process is to estimate the actual change in business measures linked directly to the e-learning program. The actual change in business measures can be predicted with input from a variety of groups, including designers and developers, vendors, contractors, or suppliers, results from other programs, managers and teams involved in the planned implementation, actual participants in the e-learning program, and subject matter experts.

While the literature is limited in answering all of our questions about e-learning, there are a few significant findings. First, most of the current evaluation at the business impact or ROI level has been driven by those who fund the project. The designers, developers, and implementers are not driving this level of evaluation. Second, available evidence thus far suggests that traditional classroom instruction yields more favorable responses than e-learning solutions (Level 1—Reaction). This issue represents a perplexing problem for proponents of e-learning. Third, e-learning is as effective as traditional face-to-face learning. While recipients of face-to-face instruction have expressed more satisfaction (Level 1) with traditional learning solutions, the learning outcomes for participants of e-learning programs are similar (Level 2—Learning). Fourth, the same evaluation strategies (Levels 1-5) and processes utilized in other types of evaluations can be applied to e-learning programs. Fifth, the return on investment (ROI) studies indicate a positive return for companies implementing e-learning programs. Sixth, creating direct links to evaluation in the computerized training process can significantly save time and money.

## References

Hodges, T.K. (1997). Computer-Based Training for Maintenance Employees. In J.J. Phillips (Ed.), *Measuring Return on Investment,* Volume 2. In Action. Alexandria, VA: American Society for Training and Development.

Kaplan, R.S., and Norton, D.P. (1996). *The Balanced Scorecard.* Boston, MA: Harvard Business School Press.

Kirkpatrick, D.L. (1994). *Evaluating Training Programs: The Four Levels.* San Francisco, CA: Berrett-Koehler Publishers.

Kruse, K., and Keil, J. (2000). *Technology-Based Training: The Art and Science of Design, Development, and Delivery.* San Francisco, CA: Jossey-Bass/Pfeiffer.

Lewis, J., Geroy, G., and Griego, O. (2000). Strategies for Facilitating Interaction When Using Technology-Mediated Training Methods. In *Academy of Human Resource Development Conference Proceedings.* Academy of Human Resouce Development.

Phillips, J.J. (1996a, March). Was It the Training? *Training and Development,* pp. 28-32.

Phillips, J.J. (1996b, April). How Much Is the Training Worth? *Training and Development,* pp. 20-24.

Phillips, J.J. (1997). *Return on Investment in Training and Performance Improvement Programs.* Houston, TX: Gulf Publishing.

Phillips, J.J., Phillips, P.P., and Duresky, L.Z. (2000). Evaluating the Effectiveness and the Return on Investment of E-Learning. In M.E. Van Buren (Ed.), *What Works Online.* Alexandria, VA: American Society for Training and Development.

Phillips, P.P., and Burkett, H. (In Press). *ROI on a Shoestring.* Info-line. Alexandria, VA: American Society for Training and Development.

Van Buren, M. (2001). *State of the Industry Report 2001.* Alexandria, VA: American Society for Training and Development (51).

Whalen, J.P. (1999). The ROI of Implementing an Integrated Learning System to Enhance Sales Performance. In J. Hite Jr. (Ed.), *Implementing HRD Technology.* In Action. Alexandria, VA: American Society for Training and Development.

*Jack J. Phillips, Ph.D., is a world-renowned expert on measurement and evaluation, providing consulting services for Fortune 500 companies and workshops for major conference providers throughout the world. Phillips is the author or editor of more than 30 books—10 about measurement and evaluation—and more than 100 articles.*

*Patricia P. Phillips is chair and CEO of the Chelsea Group, a consulting and research organization that focuses on accountability issues in organizations. She is certified in ROI evaluation and works with professionals around the globe to implement measurement and evaluation processes within their organizations.*

*Lizette Z. Duresky, Ph.D., is the Director of Measurement and Evaluation for First Data Corporation, a Fortune 500 Company that helps move the world's money as leader of electronic commerce and payment services. She is responsible for guiding the Training and Development group in measurement and evaluation processes.*

*Cyndi Gaudet, Ph.D., is Coordinator of Workforce Training and Development in the School of Engineering Technology at the University of Southern Mississippi. She is the founder of the NASA-sponsored GeoSpatial Workforce Development Center. Dr. Gaudet has served as principal investigator for workforce training and development research projects.*

# Benefits, Costs, and the Value of E-Learning Programs

## David C Forman

*This paper examines accountability in e-learning programs and measuring their results. The author provides practical guidance on what, when, and how to measure and presents a five-year financial case study. He proposes a comprehensive evaluation model, the Value Creation Model.*

A great deal has been written about the new business e-environment and the unprecedented compression of time, constant churn, and unlimited choice that now confronts all of us. The softening economy and the dot bombs have reminded us that while these times are different and unique, there are important business lessons—such as the value of customers, revenue, and profits— that still pertain. Accountability still matters.

E-learning is part of this wired new world and it has rather dramatically increased the visibility and credibility of the training industry. There is a confluence of factors that can be attributed to this rise:

1) The accepted recognition that human capital is the cornerstone of the new economy and central to the value of a company and its capacity to innovate.
2) The influx of capital, investment partners, and external players in the e-learning marketplace.
3) The reach, consistency, and growing sophistication of the Internet as a platform and vehicle for training.
4) The realization that education and learning methods are based on past models and practices.

Alvin Toffler captured this final point very succinctly: "Now that we are moving from factory work to anytime, anyplace work, we need an anytime, anyplace educational parallel."

E-learning has not just impacted the image of our industry; it has helped to change some basic tenets. Through training delivered via the web or through blended solutions that use aspects of the web, e-learning solutions have

- instant access
- universal access
- virtual collaboration
- learner control

There are other characteristics of e-learning solutions, many of which exist for any self-paced program (Setaro, 2001). But these four are particularly important in the e-world of compressed time and unlimited choice. John Coné, the Chief Learning Officer of Dell, believes that the most fundamental shift is that "the learner is now in charge." This change rocks the foundation of the training industry and challenges many of our past assumptions (Coné, 2001).

E-learning is more than just a name change for training. It impacts external perceptions of what we do, the valuation of companies, and our internal processes and methods. But this will occur only if e-learning programs and solutions are successful. Moving beyond the hype and the "grace period" allowed any new technology, e-learning has to work in the near future. Currently, most people would agree that 80% or more of the e-learning programs are rudimentary and ineffective. Accountability still matters.

This paper is about accountability and measuring results of e-learning programs. It provides practical guidance on what, when, and how to measure results and it presents a five-year financial case study. The phrase "return on investment" or ROI is intentionally not used to describe the frameworks and activities on the following pages. There are three reasons for this explicit decision. First, there is a long and established literature on ROI, led by the distinguished work of Jack Philips, Scott Parry, and others. It would be difficult to improve on their insights in this or any other forum. Second, ROI almost always focuses on just cost reduction and avoidance. ROI models do include other benefits relating to productivity and revenue gain, but usually the analysis stops with cost reduction. Just as business process reengineering initiatives a decade ago fell out of favor with executives because they chiefly tried to control costs but did not spur innovation or create unique value, ROI must move beyond cost control. But can it? And third, ROI—just like training—perhaps needs a name change and a new orientation. To this end, a Value Creation Model is proposed.

There are three major sections of this paper. The first presents a comprehensive evaluation model that shows the relationship between training effectiveness and business results. Many treatments of costs and ROI are described in isolation, without knowledge of, for example, how many learners completed the program, if learning objectives were achieved, or if improvements occurred on the job. These are all vital to understanding the true impact and value of e-learning programs. The second section is a financial case study. Despite admonitions that business analyses must go beyond just cost reduction, this does not mean that costs should be ignored. In fact, they are fundamental and essential. This in-depth case study provides step-by-step procedures for completing a financial business case. The third section presents a Value Creation Model as the new paradigm for measuring e-learning business impact. A framework is discussed and is illustrated with practical examples.

## Comprehensive Evaluation Model

The financial model is the critical analysis that compares dollars invested in a project to dollars returned. The Value Creation Model links e-learning programs to business growth and strategic initiatives. With training, however, it's essential to place both of these models in a larger context—that of training effectiveness—so the numbers will be meaningful. For example, a financial business case may look great when data on cost reduction or avoidance are presented; but what if learning did not occur and people believed that the training itself was irrelevant to their job? Similarly, it might be useful to know that, for example, only 50% of learners actually completed an e-learning program and this could contribute to lower than anticipated business benefits. Any treatment of financial outcomes, results, and value creation must be placed within the fuller context of an evaluation model.

Figure 1 presents an example of a comprehensive evaluation model that concludes with business results and value creation. The criteria are roughly analogous to Kirkpatrick's 4 levels, although additions have been made based on practical experience and specific characteristics of e-learning programs. In general, the criteria are arranged hierarchically so that the meaning of one criterion can often be explained by examining the criteria that precede it.

**Use.** Before results can be evaluated, it is imperative to determine if the training program was used and if it was used as intended. These measures are particularly important for e-learning, because there is growing evidence that the completion rates for e-learning courses are disturbingly low. There may be several reasons for this finding, including poor quality of courses, lack of incentives, and inadequate time to complete training. But a system must be established to track overall and individual usage rates so that this important baseline factor can be monitored.

**Course Reactions.** Most course evaluations are not systematically developed, do not have a balance between open-ended and forced-response questions, and do not have a set of core questions used for all courses. If rigorously used, course reac-

| Criterion | Method | Measure |
|---|---|---|
| 1. Use | Observation Sign-Up Sheets | Process |
| 2. Course Reactions | Questionnaire | Process |
| 3. Relevance/Attitudes | Attitude Survey | Outcome |
| 4. Knowledge: Facts | Criterion Tests (multiple choice) | Outcome |
| 5. Knowledge: Intellectual Skills | Criterion Tests (simulation) | Outcome |
| 6. Performance | Observation | Outcome |
| 7. Transfer to Job | All of the Above: Attitudes, Knowledge, Intellectual Skills, Performance | Impact |
| 8. Business Results | Systems that Track Time, Cost Savings, Productivity Increase, Revenue Increase | Impact, Money, and Quantity |
| 9. Value Creation | Executive Contract; Corporate Systems | Business Growth |

**Figure 1.** Evaluation model for e-learning

tion questionnaires provide insight into the effectiveness of the structure and content of the course.

**Relevance/Attitudes.** Affective outcomes are frequently overlooked and deemed to be less important than their cognitive counterparts. Not true. Wouldn't it be important to know if a course was thought to be a "joke" and largely irrelevant to everyday tasks, even if learning outcomes were achieved? Or conversely, the transfer of key concepts and processes would likely be significantly impacted if learners were highly motivated and "excited" to apply these new ideas to their jobs. It is very conceivable that attitudes and relevance are *the most important* Level-2 outcomes in the Kirkpatrick model.

**Knowledge: Facts.** Testing done in multimedia and e-learning courses focuses, almost exclusively, on facts. Factual knowledge is easy to measure and the results can be recorded automatically. The important point, however, is that test questions be tied to specific learning objectives. Presumably, these learning objectives will include more varied and diverse behaviors than just recall of factual information. If this is so, then assessment and testing items must include more than just factual items.

**Knowledge: Intellectual Skills.** Increasingly, how much you know is less important than how you solve problems. Higher-level skills involving critical thinking, analysis, and problem solving often separate excellent performers from average ones. Simulations are the preferred way to measure intellectual skills, and they are characterized by multiple, interrelated events that present real-world problems to solve. Based on the specific response of a learner, different paths and decisions are presented. These dynamic learning and testing tools are becoming more prominently featured in contemporary e-learning products.

**Performance.** Training should result in changed behavior; it's not what people know that is important, but what they do. Until recently, it has been difficult or impossible to measure performance—as opposed to knowledge—with multimedia or other self-paced media. E-learning tools have made this outcome more attainable. Virtual labs are now part of many technical skills e-learning programs. Collaboration tools also enable "real-time" monitoring of work products and performance.

**Transfer to the Job.** Training is simply a means to an end. The end is on-the-job behavior change that leads (directly or indirectly) to business results and value creation. For this to happen, training must "stick." Motivation, incentives, reinforcement, and "buy-in" are vital to the success of any training initiative, including e-learning programs. Measurements for transfer impact are usually taken three and six months after the completion of the training program.

**Business Results.** The next criterion deals with the impact on the business. There are three types of levels of business impact: *cost reduction, productivity increase,* and *revenue gain.*

The sidebar presents specific measure of business results taken from published ROI studies (Setaro, 2001; Hall, 1995). These results are compatible with Kirkpatrick's fourth level of evaluation (Kirkpatrick, 1994). But it is important to remember that traditional return on investment (ROI) analysis tended to focus on cost savings only, because costs were the easiest and most direct to measure.

---

### E-Learning's Impact on the Business: Level-4 Business Results

**Cost Reduction by Decrease in Expenses (easiest to quantify)**
- Reduces training expenses by decreasing delivery costs (instructors, facilities, equipment, etc.). Reduces travel expenses (including time) by providing onsite training. Typical ILT cost guideline is $400 per day.
- Reduces outside contractor services by training salaried staff to perform new tasks.
- Provides more cost-effective employee ratios (e.g., more employees per supervisor) by having e-learning provide tutoring traditionally done by supervisors.

---

**Cost Reduction by Increase in Productivity**
- Reduces learning curves so that employees reach full productivity sooner. This is also known as the "time-to-competency" measure that is very important in the e-world.
- Reduces duplication of work so that employees spend less time completing a task, whether this is producing a product, making a repair, or handling a customer's inquiry.
- Increases speed of service so that each employee handles a higher volume and the backlog of tasks is reduced.
- Improves safety, reducing time lost and compensation paid because of accidents.
- Improves compliance with legal and workplace policies, thereby avoiding lawsuits.

**Revenue Gain (hardest to quantify)**
- Increases sales through better prospecting, increased efficiency during the sales process, and higher closing ratios.
- Increases quality of service leading to fewer cancelled sales, better customer retention, and an increase in referral opportunities.

---

Examples of these cost savings measures are included in the sidebar.

**Value Creation.** CEOs care about value creation. They like to reduce costs, but the enlightened ones know that cost reductions only go so far and last so long (usually one year). They think about: improving the top line, beating competitors, and having the capacity to innovate and respond fast. These are the seeds of growth and improved shareholder value, and they need to be included in future business cases and justifications for e-learning programs.

These, then, are the nine evaluation criteria that comprise the Comprehensive Evaluation Model. It is easy to highlight the latter criteria in the model. These are the high-interest, high-visibility criteria. But without an understanding and awareness of how the program is used and perceived and its learning effectiveness, the impact, cost, and value creation criteria have little if any meaning. The whole picture needs to be portrayed.

# Multilevel Financial Model

The next important model is the financial model itself. As previously discussed, it must always be presented within the fuller context of educational effectiveness. The financial model is vital to any successful training operation. It is imperative that e-learning costs and benefits be quantified in a clear and rational business case. All other departments within a company are subject to this discipline.

Should training be treated differently? The CEO doesn't think so. Training professionals must sharpen their business and financial skills to be more effective with executives and to better serve their own colleagues, employees, and programs.

A financial model must be easy to understand. To be successful, all financial analyses must be *implemented in close partnership* with those who make the funding decisions. Different organizations use different financial terminology and have different financial priorities at different times. For example, how does your organization define and use the following: Internal rate of return? Hurdle rate? Payback period? Is cash flow an important consideration? How many years are capital goods depreciated? These are not only important terms; they help to define how a company operates. They form the business lexicon of top management, which should also include training, talent, and human resource professionals.

## Determining Benefits

The first step in building a financial model is to list all the possible benefits from the proposed e-learning program. Place each benefit in one of the categories of business impacts as illustrated in the sidebar—*cost reduction, productivity increase,* or *revenue gain*—and decide how they might be quantified. Rank these quantifiable benefits, starting with those that most closely support the objectives of the decision makers and are most easily attributed to training. Verify your prioritization by having the decision makers "sign off" on the ordered rankings.

Next, select the top-ranked benefits to see if their return can support the training program. Create an initial model to demonstrate the return using only data from the top-ranked benefits. Add additional benefits from the list if the initial list does not provide a reasonable and compelling business case.

It is not useful at the justification stage to demonstrate a financial return too large to be believed, even if the numbers indicate such results. It is more useful to justify the program with a solid return using only a few, easily attributed benefits, such as reduced travel costs or increased span of control. Most decision makers look for a break-even point in two to three years for cash flow and like to see a positive profit-and-loss in the first or second year. At least a 50% return on investment is desirable; anything over 500% becomes questionable unless solid evidence is in place.

It is also valuable to point out to the decision makers *all the benefits not included* in the model. Then track information on all the quantifiable benefits—both those in the justification and ones not originally quantified—as the training program is implemented. This provides a complete picture of the actual return on investment as part of the program evaluation.

# Determining Costs

The other side of the financial model is determining training costs; they deserve careful consideration. With e-learning, it is important to consider all costs, including hardware maintenance, courseware support, and updates. There are two important types of costs: recurring costs, which arise every time a program is offered, and nonrecurring costs, which are one-time expenses, such as hardware purchases.

Compared with instructor-led approaches, e-learning programs generally have higher nonrecurring costs and lower recurring costs. There will usually be a breakeven point in terms of student population, where fewer students suggest an instructor-led approach and more students suggest an e-learning approach. While there are many variables to consider, the breakeven point is often in the 200- to 300-learner range for custom-developed e-learning courses. For existing e-learning products, this number is significantly lower, often below 10 learners.

The other important distinction when determining costs is operating versus capital expenses. Operating expenses typically are variable, recurring costs reported for accounting and tax purposes in the year they occur. Capital expenses typically are fixed, nonrecurring costs that can be depreciated over time. E-learning programs usually result in hardware purchases and software development that can be depreciated. This has an important impact on financial models, as we shall soon see.

# Constructing the Financial Model: A Case Study

Having assembled the appropriate benefits and costs, you can now construct the financial model to illustrate the potential or actual return on investment for the training program. The following is an example taken from actual experience to demonstrate the process. (The actual numbers have been modified to preserve confidentiality.)

A major financial services company was considering the use of e-learning to replace current workshops to train its customer service representatives. There were many potential benefits, but only two were necessary to quantify to support the implementation of the multimedia program. Those selected were in line with the company's objective of extensive growth, while limiting expenses and new hires.

First, it was determined that e-learning would reduce training time: the new program was designed to take 30% less time for new hires and 50% less time for existing employees than the current instructor-led programs. The reduction in training time gave employees more time to perform customer service tasks, so the company could expand with fewer new employees.

Second, the training program provided automated practice on customer service skills, so supervisors spent less time observing and critiquing employees.

Employees became more self-sufficient and more self-reliant. As a result, the employee-to-supervisor ratio could be increased from 10:1 to 12:1. This allowed the company to grow with fewer new supervisors.

The amount of salaries, benefits and support for employees and supervisors not hired, and the amount spent on the workshops that were to be replaced, determined the financial benefits. The cost of the e-learning courseware, the hardware to deliver it, hardware installation and maintenance, other implementation expenses, and annual course updates provided the program costs. It would have been possible to quantify other benefits, but these were not necessary to justify the program.

Figure 2 represents the projected six-year cash flow for the project. A detailed cash inflow chart follows (Figure 3), providing the source of each cash inflow or benefit figure. The program would take time to develop and implement, so the benefits were calculated at a 25% utilization rate for the first year and a 50% rate for the second year. In the third year, the program would be in full use, so 100% of the projected benefits could be counted.

Against the total of $411,000 in benefits in the first year, we can see a cost of

| | Year | | | | | | Total |
| Cash Inflow | 1 | 2 | 3 | 4 | 5 | 6 | |
|---|---|---|---|---|---|---|---|
| **Reduced Training Time** | | | | | | | |
| Headcount Reduction | 539 | 547 | 756 | 865 | 973 | 1082 | 4862 |
| Training Cost Reduction | 30 | 35 | 40 | 45 | 51 | 56 | 256 |
| Better Employee/ Supervisor Ratio | 1076 | 1347 | 1618 | 1889 | 2161 | 2432 | 10522 |
| Utilization Factor (%) | 25% | 50% | 100% | 100% | 100% | 100% | |
| Projected Cash Inflow | 411 | 1015 | 2414 | 2799 | 3185 | 3570 | 13393 |
| **Cash Outflow** | | | | | | | |
| Hardware | 200 | 300 | 0 | 0 | 0 | 0 | 500 |
| Basic Courseware | 863 | 1147 | 0 | 0 | 0 | 0 | 2010 |
| Recurrency Courseware | 0 | 0 | 350 | 350 | 350 | 0 | 1050 |
| Maintenance | 0 | 50 | 50 | 50 | 50 | 50 | 250 |
| Updates | 0 | 0 | 149 | 149 | 149 | 149 | 596 |
| Implementation | 50 | 100 | 50 | 0 | 0 | 0 | 200 |
| Cash Outflow | 1113 | 1598 | 599 | 549 | 549 | 198 | 4606 |
| **Net Cash Flow** | (702) | (583) | 1815 | 2250 | 2636 | 3372 | 8787 |
| **Cumulative Cash Flow** | (702) | (1286) | 530 | 2780 | 5416 | 8787 | |

All figures in $1000s

**Figure 2.** Case study: cash flow at a financial services company

| | Year | | | | | | |
|---|---|---|---|---|---|---|---|
| | **1** | **2** | **3** | **4** | **5** | **6** | **Total** |
| **New Hire Training** | | | | | | | |
| New Hires per Year | 916 | 1048 | 1180 | 1311 | 1443 | 1575 | |
| Total Training Weeks | 2043 | 2337 | 2631 | 2925 | 3219 | 3513 | |
| Reduced Weeks (-30)% | 613 | 701 | 789 | 878 | 966 | 1054 | |
| Headcount Reduction | 13 | 15 | 16 | 18 | 20 | 22 | |
| **Recurring Training** | | | | | | | |
| Employee Base | 1560 | 1953 | 2347 | 2740 | 3134 | 3527 | |
| Total Training Weeks | 1404 | 1758 | 2112 | 2466 | 2820 | 3174 | |
| Reduced Weeks (-50%) | 702 | 879 | 1056 | 1233 | 1410 | 1587 | |
| Headcount Reduction | 14 | 18 | 22 | 26 | 30 | 33 | |
| Total Headcount Reduction | 27 | 33 | 38 | 44 | 50 | 55 | |
| Average Employee Cost (20,000) | | | | | | | |
| Total Savings (in $1000s) | 539 | 647 | 756 | 865 | 973 | 1082 | 4862 |
| **Improved Employee/ Supervisor Ratio** | | | | | | | |
| Current Supervisors | 156 | 195 | 235 | 274 | 313 | 353 | |
| Reduction (-16.7%) | 26 | 33 | 39 | 46 | 52 | 59 | |
| Costs per Supervisor | 41,368 | | | | | | |
| Total Savings (in $1000s) | 1076 | 1347 | 1618 | 1889 | 2161 | 2432 | 10522 |

**Figure 3.** Case study: cash inflow (benefits) in detail

$1,113,000. Because much of this figure can be depreciated, however, the profit-and-loss impact and the ROI is positive, as we can see in the following ROI chart.

Figure 3 shows that $539,000 in headcount reduction savings for the first year is determined by taking the new hires per year (916) and current employee base (1,560) and determining the weeks they spent in training. The person-weeks saved by the multimedia program is then calculated (613—or 30% of 2,043—for new hire training and 702—or 50% of 1,404—for recurring training). These figures are divided by the 48 weeks an individual works each year.

Thirteen fewer people are needed because new employee training takes less time and 14 percent fewer people are needed because recurring training takes less time. This results in a savings of $539,000 in salary costs for the first year of the program.

| Capital Expenses Depreciated (Hardware, Courseware) | | | | | | | |
|---|---|---|---|---|---|---|---|
| Year 1 | (1063) | 213 | 213 | 213 | 213 | 213 | 0 |
| Year 2 | (1047) | | 289 | 289 | 289 | 289 | 289 |
| Year 3 | (350) | | | 70 | 70 | 70 | 70 |
| Year 4 | (350) | | | | 70 | 70 | 70 |
| Year 5 | (350) | | | | | 70 | 70 |
| Year 6 | | | | | | | 0 |
| **Other Expenses Not Depreciated (Maintenance, Updates, Implementation)** | | | | | | | |
| | | 50 | 150 | 249 | 199 | 199 | 199 |
| **Total Cost (Depreciated)** | | 263 | 652 | 821 | 841 | 911 | 698 |

Note: All figures are in $1000s

**Figure 4.** *Case study: depreciated costs in detail*

The reduction in supervisor costs for the first year ($1,076,000) is determined by multiplying the current supervisor count (156) by the reduction in the supervisor/employee ratio (16.7%) and multiplying this figure (26) by the annual costs for a supervisor ($41,368 including support).

Because much of the e-learning costs can be considered capital expenses and depreciated, the cost can be spread out over years—five years in this sample case. Different companies have different policies on time periods for depreciation. The effect of depreciation is seen in Figure 4. The costs in parentheses are those incurred for the year, which are spread out over five years. From a balance sheet viewpoint, this depreciation makes the costs in the first year only $263,000 instead of $1,113,000.

The return on investment is calculated as follows. The annual profit-and-loss impact of $148,000 in the first year is determined by subtracting the depreciated cost of $263,000 from the benefits of $411,000. The 57% return on investment in the first year is determined by dividing the first year's profit-and-loss impact of $148,000 by the first-year cost of $263,000.

In this sample case, the return on investment on e-learning for the first year is 57%, and the cumulative return on investment is 220% over six years (Figure 5).

These impressive figures are pre-tax. They are also very conservative; they assume no salary growth and no consideration for the time value of money (or what could happen to the savings if invested). They also use only two of the many benefits from the training program.

The financial model's assumptions were all developed through discussions

| | Year | | | | | | |
|---|---|---|---|---|---|---|---|
| | **1** | **2** | **3** | **4** | **5** | **6** | **Total** |
| Projected Cash Flow | 411 | 1015 | 2414 | 2799 | 3185 | 3570 | 13393 |
| Projected Cost (Depreciated) | 263 | 652 | 821 | 841 | 911 | 911 | 4186 |
| Annual P&L Impact | 148 | 362 | 1594 | 1959 | 2274 | 2872 | 9208 |
| Cumulative P&L Impact | 148 | 510 | 2104 | 4063 | 6337 | 9208 | |
| **Cumulative ROI (%) (P&L Cost)** | 57 | 56 | 121 | 157 | 181 | 220 | |

Note: All figures in $1000s

**Figure 5.** Case study: return on investment

with the decision makers. Company field sources were used to document all the assumptions, and agreement was reached at each stage. Conservative assumptions were made to reduce any doubt about the accuracy of the figures. The most important considerations in developing any financial model are: keep it simple, flexible and believable; make sure it addresses actual profit-and-loss figures; and gain decision maker support at all stages.

## Value Creation Model

The third model presented in this paper is the Value Creation Model. Perhaps it is somewhat presumptuous to give this name to the following treatment because it is so new and evolving. But it is important to contrast the important tenets of value creation to the financial model or traditional ROI treatments. Value creation is a different way to think about results, impact, and the value of e-learning programs.

Purists will rightly argue that traditional ROI models use Kirkpatrick's Level 4 for business results and that effective Level-4 measures encompass value creation measures. So why do we need another model? The answer is that ROI analyses almost always focus on cost savings. The harder to identify and quantify results are typically ignored. Jay Cross (2000) believes that ROI approaches are best suited to stable times and consistent programs. He further states:

> The traditional conception of ROI is obsolete. The Internet has changed everything. Managers of business units value time more than ROI. Senior executives are more interested in the top line (dramatic growth from new markets and innovation) than the bottom line (the accounting fiction of "profits").

While fictional profits and inflated business cases are not very credible, the economy of 2001 has emphasized the importance of actual profits. But Cross believes that new models and approaches are needed for new times, and his emphasis on the top line, value-creating measures is both relevant and appropriate.

The Value Creation Model depends on the definition and delineation of the term "value." This term will have different meanings for different companies at different times. It is important to understand that it is the *CEO's and top management's perception* of value that is being defined, not the training department's definition. While the definition of value is relative, there are categories or types of value measures that can be identified. These measures are not exhaustive or independent, but they are suggestive of the types of issues that are priorities for executive management.

**Business Strategy Measures**
- Improved Shareholder Return
- Sales and Revenue Growth
- Enhanced Competitive Advantage
- Market Share Expansion
- Entry into New Markets
- Bringing Merged Companies Together
- Reaching Different Audiences, Partners, and Vendors

**Time Measures**
- Time to Respond
- Time to Market
- Time to Hire
- Time to Competency
- Cycle Time

**Human Capital Measures**
- Talent Acquisition
- Talent Retention
- Talent Development
- Enhanced Capacity to Innovate

**Customer Measures**
- Customer Satisfaction
- Customer Retention
- Customer Referral
- Lifetime Value of a Customer

Given this value creation framework, there are three basic operating principles that should be emphasized. These are vital to the success of any evaluation activity, but especially for one as meaningful as value creation. These principles are:

1. **Make a Business Contract with Executives.** Every book, article, and white paper on e-learning and training initiatives states the importance of getting management "buy-in," commitment, alignment, and support. But "buy-in" can mean many different things and is subject to many interpretations. Formalize the process. Develop a two- to three-page contract that defines the e-learning project and its measures of success. Use the three models presented in this paper as a foundation. Get sign-offs from the project team and the executive sponsors.

2. **Gather the Best Data Possible.** Almost every discussion on evaluation and business impact gets bogged down in debates about, for example, "how training can really impact sales because there are so many intervening variables." There is certainly a place for carefully controlled studies, but the business arena is not it. Decisions are made with imperfect and partial data because time is of the essence. It is better to have the best information available than none at all. Laurie Bassi (2001), an esteemed research expert with ASTD and now Saba, offers the following advice on this matter: "Don't let the perfect be the enemy of the good."

3. **Use Company Measures for Value Creation.** The whole point of the Value Creation Model is that it is based on what is real and vital to the organization. If the company has existing metrics for the specific value being addressed, then use these measures. If not, work with a cross-functional team to develop measures that everyone can support. These measures should be stipulated in the e-learning project contract.

A brief examination of two different initiatives highlights how the Value Creation Model can be used.

Cisco Systems is a leader in the field of e-learning. Its technology provides a strong foundation for e-learning solutions, and John Chambers, CEO of Cisco Systems, is a big supporter of anytime, anywhere training via the Internet. Cisco has developed an extensive array of e-learning programs that includes video on demand, interactive web-based learning supported by mentoring, live blended e-learning, live broadcasts, hands-on labs and simulations, and assessments. The two major programs are targeted to 10,000 Cisco field engineers and account managers and 40,000 channel partners (Galagan, 2001; Baumert, 2001). In additions to cost savings, four of the key business impact measures that Cisco tracks are Customer Satisfaction, Time to Competency, Time to Market, and Increased Reach. Their partner program alone increased the reach and access from 5% to over 80% of the 40,000 Cisco channel partners. All four of these measures are contained within the Value Creation Model.

The second example is taken from the work of Laurie Bassi (2001) on the Human Capital Advantage Value Chain. The key elements of the value chain are:

- Satisfied employees are more likely to stay with an organization.
- Retention of key employees drives customer satisfaction.
- Satisfied customers are more likely to remain customers.
- Customer retention drives profitability.

These are important to her research and are part of the Value Creation Model. There are other similar value chains that show the relationship among key business measures. ASTD has pioneered work in this area, and a recent study by Watson Wyatt (2000) has yielded similar results.

The Value Creation Model is an evolving and developing idea. And it is always specific to a certain company during a certain time period. It is an attempt to define "what keeps the CEO up at night" and to directly tie e-learning programs to legitimate and meaningful business issues.

## Conclusion

The benefits, costs, and value of e-learning programs can be addressed with three different evaluation models. The first is a comprehensive model that places business results and value creation within the fuller context of educational effectiveness. Business impacts or cost reductions by themselves do not provide the complete picture. The second model is the financial business case that targets cost reductions and avoidance. It is necessary and meaningful not only to complete the financial model but to become familiar with the financial concepts and terms that are the foundation of business. But cost reductions only go so far. Many executives acknowledge the first-year cost reductions but then reset the baseline for the next year. The third model expressly examines value creation, ways in which the organization grows, improves, innovates, and dominates competitors. Each of these models serves a unique purpose and all three are necessary to completely understand the benefits, costs, and value of e-learning programs.

## References

Bassi, Laurie (2001). "Human Capital Advantage: Measures that Matter." Presentation at The Conference Board E-Learning Conference, San Diego, June 21, 2001.

Baumert, Lisa (2001). "The E-Learning Transformation at Cisco." Presentation at The Conference Board E-Learning Conference, San Diego, June 21, 2001.

Coné, John (2001). "Building Your E-Learning Strategy Today and Tomorrow." Presentation at The Conference Board E-Learning Conference, San Diego, June 21, 2001.

Cross, Jay (2000). *A Fresh Look at Return on Investment*. Smartforce White Paper. Redwood City, CA, 2000.

Galagan, Patricia (2001). "The Cisco E-Learning Story." *Training and Development*. ASTD, February 2001.

Hall, Brandon (1995). "Return-on-Investment and Multimedia Training." Sunnyvale, CA: Multimedia Training newsletter, 1995.

Kirkpatrick, Donald (1994). *Evaluating Training Programs.* San Francisco, CA: Berrett-Koehler Publishers, 1994.

Phillips, Jack J. (1997). *Return on Investment in Training and Performance Improvement Programs.* Houston: Gulf Publishing, 1997.

Setaro, John (2001). *How E-Learning Can Increase ROI for Training.* Thinq White Paper, 2001.

Toffler, Alvin (2001). "E-Learning." *The Wall Street Journal*, March 12, 2001.

Watson Wyatt (2000). "Human Capital Index," www.watsonwyatt.com.

*David C Forman is President of Sage Learning Systems (www.sagelearning.com). His career in the training and technology industry spans 20 years, in which he has held executive positions with Spectrum Interactive, NETg, and Wave Technologies. He is widely published and his Web site contains copies of recent papers, presentations, and e-learning resources.*

# Welcome to Part Five: E-learning for the E-Learning Professional:
## Developing the People Who Will Lead the Field

Part Five is short but important and all about e-learning professionals. First George Lorenzo and Patti Shank tour options for learning about e-learning, both in balmy places like San Diego, and online, such as at Capella and Jones International Universities. They also expand on goals for the development of e-learning professionals.

Shank and also Bob Hoffman in his article press readers to identify developmental needs. We conclude with Albert Ingram's focus on the Web learning developer; he describes four levels of Web site development expertise.

In Part Five, we note that whatever education you have in hand today is probably not a perfect match for emergent challenges. What are you going to do about it? How will you develop yourself to make better decisions about technology and performance? What do you need to know to participate in guiding your organization in its use of e-learning?

When I want to know more about anything, vivid examples prove most helpful. In the concluding Part Six, we provide several and varied e-learning case studies.

# Professional Development to Go?

**George Lorenzo**

*To keep up with developments in e-learning, training professionals are going back to the classroom—often virtually. This article reviews the choices available to trainers who want to update their knowledge and skills.*

There's no question about it: the technologic revolution has changed the way many people think about corporate training. We no longer consider a stand-up presentation to a group of 25 employees the only way to train. It might be more cost-effective, for example, to schedule a synchronous, Web-based class for a group of 250—or 25,000. Follow-up could be done via CD-ROM or e-mail, or even through a learning management system. The potential cost savings of this new approach is fueling the demand for training professionals with the high-tech skills to design and implement these courses.

It's no surprise, then, that even the most experienced trainers are scrambling to keep up with the new digital age of training. For some, this will mean going back to college to seek the latest and the greatest high-tech skills. But these may not be the halls of learning you remember.

## Virtual Higher Education

If commuting to a college campus and spending three hours sitting at a desk in an uncomfortable classroom isn't your idea of fun, take heart: advanced training for training professionals, including graduate-level degrees and certification programs, is now available online.

Be prepared, however, for slightly less glamour than you'll find in the typical corporate training program. The vast majority of online higher education courses are instructor-led, asynchronous and heavily laden with text-based readings. Support materials are provided through both the Web and traditional, class-aligned textbooks, and only a few classes are augmented with videotaped or CD-ROM lectures (sent via snail-mail, of course). Any interactive learning elements are typically facilitated through e-mail and threaded discussions with colleagues and instructors.

The technology is expanding, though. Some courses include synchronous tele-conferencing and text-based chats that are recorded and posted at a secure site; students unable to participate at specific times can review such live discussions later, at their leisure. Quizzes, tests and writing assignments can easily be conducted via e-mail, and library and bookstore resources can often be accessed online. Some courses even take advantage of streaming video and audio components, but make sure you have adequate bandwidth before you get started.

## School for the 21st Century Training Professional

One of the largest providers of online, accredited higher education is the University of Maryland University College (UMUC). Long known as a provider of continuing, part-time education, UMUC has now taken its mission one step further. The school's 24 online-degree programs include a master's degree in distance education. They also offer graduate-level certificates in distance education and technology, foundations of distance education, and training at a distance.

Although UMUC's programs have been "live" for less than a year, about 300 students have already enrolled, says Associate Dean Eugene Rubin, "without any significant advertising."

"The master's degree in distance education program is aimed at a broad cross section of the education and training population," he continues. "It's aimed at people in higher education, the K-12 sector, the nonprofits and government. And it's certainly aimed at the corporate and military communities."

One of these corporate community members is Tracy McLean, a trainer and instructional designer for Zurich Insurance's small business division in Baltimore. When the division began converting, creating and migrating most of its classroom and computer-based corporate training programs over to its new virtual university intranet, McLean decided to expand her skill set. She's now enrolled in UMUC's online master's degree program in distance education.

A married mother of two young children, McLean claims that she would never have been able to pursue a master's degree that wasn't online. "There's no way that I can participate in classroom instruction with the schedule that I have," she says, admitting that she tried the traditional bricks and mortar route at the University of Baltimore but had to withdraw because of "a problem with baby-sitting."

## Professional Development Quick Fix

In this fast-paced, work-'til-you-drop business world, a small educational fix can do a lot of good. For lifelong learners, short-term, squeeze-it-into-my-busy-life professional-development courses can be just the ticket. But busy professionals want—and demand—courses that actually do what they should: boost personal and professional growth while providing new knowledge or skills for employers.

With that in mind, the University of St. Thomas Graduate School of Business in Minneapolis created a unique offering called the Mini MBA. This series of professional development programs includes coursework in franchise management, e-commerce and international management, among other areas, and classes are designed for technical professionals, government managers and other working adults.

Every Mini MBA is different: one meets for one three-hour session (6 p.m. to 9 p.m.) each week for 14 weeks; another consists of two modules in which students meet for two days from 8:30 a.m. to 4:30 p.m., with each module held during a different month; and the Leading Growing Companies program consists of five modules in which students meet for two days from 8 a.m. to 4 p.m. every month for five months. Tuition, depending on the program, ranges from $1,500 to $2,700.

"These programs are designed around the idea of engaging the professions," says George Heenan, executive fellow and director of the St. Thomas School of Business Institute for Strategic Management.

"The idea is for people to take ideas and implement them. It's a way of taking people who are currently in business and have a particular need and bringing them rapidly up to date."

The Mini MBA program was implemented in 1974 with one general MBA covering the core elements of business administration. The program now includes more than 14 Mini MBAs.

"They are all geared toward the practitioner, the person in either business or an organization," says George Meyer, director of professional development centers. "We draw a lot of people from the 'nonprofit sector' who want to be in our programs to mix with the for-profit sector. They come to sharpen their skills. Many come with an eye toward deciding whether or not to take a traditional MBA program."

Mini MBA programs will be offered in an online learning mode in the future, according to Meyers. For now, however, students have to travel to the St. Thomas campus to participate. Some of the Mini MBA programs, such as the one for international management and another for environmental professionals, have been compressed into one-week programs to accommodate international business people who come to Minneapolis to learn from St. Thomas faculty.

> The St. Thomas Graduate School of Business is recognized as offering the fourth-largest MBA program in the United States, according to Heenan. "It really has been developed because of a strong faculty with good ties to the business community, along with focused programs and classes that people find helpful."

McLean enrolled in her first two online classes last fall: Foundations in Distance Education and Technology in Distance Education.

"I have two classes and 12 books," she says. "And we also have to go to external links to get additional information." In addition, online schoolwork includes mandatory participation in threaded discussions with her instructors and classmates. "We have 22 people in the class, so on any particular day or time someone may go in and comment on a thread that's been developed, or they may develop new threads," says McLean. "You have to sign on every day just to stay current with what's going on."

After accommodating her job and family responsibilities, McLean allocates time for studying during the late evening hours and weekends, as well as during her lunch breaks. "I make it fit into my life," she says. Nonetheless, it's a demanding schedule, and next year she plans to enroll in one course instead of two to lighten the load.

In the end, McLean believes that the work will pay off. "I'll be taking classes that will make me aware of problems or issues we may run into trying to get Web-based training programs in place," she says. "I want to get as much out of this as I can, so I can assist my division in moving forward."

## A Capella Education

Now one year into her master's degree in education program, Kris Ginley is a virtual student at Capella University, an exclusively online higher education institution. Ginley, an independent corporate trainer, enrolled in an online program to "become more marketable in the training arena."

Ginley is currently working on a knowledge management system development project for Lucent Technologies; she believes that the training and development coursework offered by Capella will help keep her "current."

In addition to Ginley's master's degree program, Capella University offers an M.S. in education with various other specialization choices, including instructional design for online learning, teaching and training online, and distance education. All of the M.S. in education programs have related graduate-level certificate programs, and Capella also offers an online Ph.D. in education with an emphasis in instructional design for online learning.

"I would recommend someone come in at the certificate level," says Stan

Trollip, Capella's director of learning strategies. He suggests that corporate trainers begin slowly, with a core course like Introduction to Multimedia and Web-Based Instruction class, to see if they are "cut out" for online learning.

"We've designed all these offerings so that people can put their feet in the water," says Trollip. "If they want to go on, they can keep adding courses and apply those credits toward a master's degree. If they still want to keep going, they can apply those credits toward a Ph.D."

Unlike UMUC's 15-week classes, Capella's courses are 12 weeks long. Both programs typically require 10 hours of schoolwork per class per week.

## High-Tech Instruction for High-Tech Skills

For another 15-week graduate certificate program—this one in instructional technology—check out San Diego State University (SDSU). According to program director Donn Ritchie, the program helps students "find ways to increase the effectiveness or efficiencies of performances in the workplace"—a marketable skill for most training professionals.

As with all of the programs featured in this article, this program's broad mix of students includes training professionals from health care, telecommunications, education, and both small and large businesses. There are an equal number of male and female students, and the average age is about 33. "These are folks who already have knowledge and are already competent," says Ritchie, "but they want to increase their skills and become better at what they are doing."

One such student is Janet Jubran, academic relations coordinator for the Environmental Systems Research Institute's (ESRI) virtual campus. The company, which creates geographic information system (GIS) software, provides product support training to customers worldwide. Jubran works with ESRI content developers and IT staff to help design that training, which includes online self-study courses for a variety of GIS applications. She's hoping that SDSU can help her supplement her instructional design background.

"We're trying to make our courses at ESRI a little more interactive," says Jubran. "We've been thinking about using Flash software to have some video and some animation, which is very timely. In Advanced Multimedia Development, the course I'm taking right now, we are making little documentary videos in Flash, and then we are going to put them up on the Web. It will be very helpful when I finish."

The SDSU online classes are "very demanding," Jubran says. "They move along very vigorously. They really emphasize going back to the drawing board, going to the user and getting feedback and then taking that back to work it into your design." And unlike many other online courses, this one requires each student to evaluate whether or not his or her training program will actually achieve its goal: learning.

## Words of Wisdom

What do trainers and designers really need to know about building e-learning environments?

**Dr. Stan Trollip, Director of Learning Strategies, Capella University**
"There are three big buckets that need to be addressed. One is if you are going to be doing instructor-led training, you need to learn how to design courses that are interactive and get people to be really engaged. Second, you need to provide really good and adequate training to the people who are going to be teaching the online courses. Third, if you're going to have instructor-less courses, such as CBT courses, you need a different set of skills to design and develop them."

**Dr. Paula Noonan, Professor, Jones International University**
- Have a basic understanding of HTML and how to use an HTML composer.
- Know how to shift content from a trainer-focus delivery to a content-focus delivery.
- Know what the various application solution providers (ASPs) can do for you if you decide to use their platforms and/or learning management systems for your e-learning. For example, does the platform have all the features you want? How much will it cost per student to use that platform?
- Know what kind of design team you need. Assess your expertise and decide what you have to bring to the table to make things work. Do you need a Web developer, a content expert, a graphic artist?

**Dr. Donn Ritchie, Director, Online Instructional Technology Certificate Program, San Diego State University**
"There are a lot of corporate trainers who have never gone through an educational technology program. So I don't think not having it precludes someone from doing a job well. But those who are new in the field, or those who may be floundering somewhat, or may want to increase their professional competence, or feel there's more out there that they want to learn, can benefit a lot from a graduate program."

**Dr. Chris Olgren, Program Director, Distance Education Certificate Program, University of Wisconsin-Madison**
"As trainers and designers look to develop and deliver training programs through e-learning, they need to find out how that learning is going to differ by using technology. They need to learn what key components have to be incorporated into the program in order to have an effective instructional design—good learner support and instructor services—and how to choose the appropriate technology for the application."

**Dr. Eugene Rubin, Associate Dean of the Graduate School, Master's of Distance Education Program, University of Maryland University College**

"The transport mechanism, the technology, is only half of the formula. The other half is understanding learning and teaching. Traditional training people don't necessarily have the IT background. IT people don't have what the training people have, which is a pretty good knowledge base about how to teach people and how people learn. So, what's emerging right now are some newer credentials that sort of marry those two. There are two things now that may move you up the management ladder. One is a degree in a field that marries the two. The other is, of course, job experience. The problem is that this stuff is expanding fast, and there's not a large pool of people with a lot of experience. Therefore, the credentials are becoming more important."

## Distance Learning ... the Abridged Version

For training professionals seeking something less vigorous than the SDSU, Capella or UMUC courses of study, Jones International University offers a slightly abbreviated option.

Like Capella, Jones is a completely virtual higher education institution. But Jones' courses, such as Using the Internet in Corporate Training, taught by Paula Noonan, are all only four weeks long.

According to Noonan, Jones' classes can achieve real results more quickly by providing students with a means to see online training from both the learner and class-facilitator perspective. "What are the kinds of learning processes that people go through?" Noonan asks rhetorically. "What do trainers need to know in order to create learning that's going to be really dynamic for the learners?"

To complete the class, students must create a Web-based training module of a larger training program. Eventually, these students can build that larger training program themselves.

Laura Isabella, an instructional designer for Ernst & Young in New Jersey, is a huge fan of Jones' four-week program. "The class let me practice creating a sense of community," says Isabella. "One of my biggest challenges now is really getting Ernst & Young people engaged and willing to interact."

Isabella's statement is indicative of the one thing these online higher education providers have yet to prove: that trainers will be able to implement what they've learned when they go back to work in the corporate world. Finding this proof, of course, is an already familiar challenge.

For a more detailed listing of distance education programs, certificates and degrees for training professionals, visit the *Training* Web site at wwwtrainingmag.com.

*George Lorenzo is a freelance writer in Amherst, N.Y., glorenzo@adelphia.net.*

# Not Too Cool for School

## Patti Shank

*If you want to learn more about e-learning, the author of this article contends, "it's extraordinarily helpful to use, struggle with, and fully experience technology-based learning." But, she adds, "I'm dismayed that more of the instructional technology graduate programs aren't online or at least partly online. In this field, practicing what you preach is critical."*

This is a pop quiz! Get out your Number 2 pencil and keep your eyes on your own paper. Here's the question—and it's worth 100 percent, so I hope you studied: What's the one question I get asked the most when I talk to trainers about e-learning?

a. Who owns the intellectual property rights to the content and programming on an educational Web site?
b. Is Dreamweaver better than FrontPage as an authoring tool?
c. How can I learn all the stuff I need to know about designing and developing online learning for my organization?
d. Will the Broncos be Super Bowl champs this year?
e. What's the best site for finding cheap airfares?

If you answered a or b, you get 50 percent credit for realizing these are good questions. If you answered d or e, you're in the wrong class. Pack up your belongings and head to Ms. Pennyfinch's room down the hall. If you answered c, congratulations!

You're right if you think there's an awful lot to learn before you can become a crackerjack designer/developer of learning sites. You have to know something about instructional design for the Web, authoring tools, facilitation in a virtual environment, graphic design, programming, interface design, usability—just to name a few potential areas of study.

In this article, I'll look at some of the formal online certificate, master's and doctorate programs that can help you gain knowledge, skills and credentials in the e-learning field. I'll describe a few of them in detail, and I'll provide links to many others.

## Back to School? Moi?

Vicky Phillips, CEO of geteducated.com (www.geteducated.com), says there's a tremendous need for good instruction about the e-learning field. "There is an especially strong demand for instructional designers to develop online learning programs, and for online instructors who can mentor and motivate students using virtual classroom tools and techniques," she says.

And these are not easy skills to learn. Many classroom instructors, for instance, know how to develop and deliver lectures, but that's not nearly the same as knowing how to mentor folks at a distance.

Learning how to "do" e-learning means different things to different people. Some training professionals want to design content and activities. In other words, they want to do traditional instructional design for the digital world instead of the classroom. Others want to learn how to manage the design and development process.

There are people who simply want to teach online, and need to learn how to use online tools and techniques to facilitate learning. Others see themselves building learning sites with authoring tools such as Dreamweaver and programming languages such as JavaScript.

You need to know what your goals are before determining which program is right for you, says Ann Yakimovicz, principal instructional designer and technology implementation planner for Aprendío Inc. (www.aprendio.com). "The first issue is whether you're looking for education or training," she says. "Do you need specific marketable skills, or do you need theories and concepts? Or both?" Some people just want skills that will take their careers to the next level, she explains. Others want certificate programs that will serve as a springboard into graduate school.

If the route looks too easy, it probably is. Mastering online learning skills requires commitment and an intense investment of time. "Programs are sometimes 'dumbed down' to make learners happy with the ease of learning," warns Yakimovicz.

## Why Online?

In my mind, it's extraordinarily helpful to use, struggle with, and fully experience technology-based learning if your goal is to harness it. And frankly, I'm dismayed that more of the instructional technology graduate programs aren't online or at least partly online. In this field, practicing what you preach is critical.

A while back, when I was the manager of training and health education for a large health care organization, we needed to find alternatives to classroom training to meet the needs of our clinical staff and patients. Taking doctors, nurses and other caregivers away from their day-to-day work was not always possible. And only a few patients came to our classroom-based programs. We had to find other ways to reach out. I saw that I needed additional skills and enrolled in the educational technology leadership master's program at George Washington University.

I chose the distance-based program because I work full-time, have kids, and lead a life full of obligations and activities. (Sound familiar? It's one of the main reasons working adults gravitate toward distance programs.) Soon, though, I began to see that my experiences as a distance student were invaluable to my career goals. In comparing notes with people enrolled in classroom programs, I quickly realized I was better off using technology-based learning to study technology-based learning.

Joan Goloboy, faculty member at the Walden Institute, says her students agree. "I'm teaching seasoned instructors who have a high level of skill and confidence in a traditional classroom," she says. "The most consistent comment I hear from them is how eye-opening it is to put themselves in the students' shoes—to experience the challenges, frustrations and rewards of participating in online education. They soon learn that designing and facilitating an online course is so much more than transferring classroom lectures to the Web."

## Where to Go

The following are three Web sites that can help you learn more about certificate, master's and doctorate programs that relate to the online learning field. You may want to use them as a starting point to find the program that best meets your needs and career goals.

At **www.geteducated.com/articles/teach2000.htm**, you'll find information about many certificate, master's and doctorate programs.

The distance education section of Gradschools.com (**www.gradschools. com/listings/distance/edu_tech_distance.html**) presents good information about the degrees offered by each institution. One of the problems, though, is that many of the listings do not have links to a URL. I would be suspicious of any instructional technology program that doesn't have a Web site—overhead projectors and eight-track players, anyone? Since I know that many of them do, in fact, have Web sites, I wonder how well this site is being maintained. But check it out anyway, because some of the programs listed are not listed on the geteducated.com site.

At **adulted.about.com/education/adulted/msub125.htm**, you'll find links to all sorts of professional development programs for adult educators. Not all are online or related to educational technology or online learning. Programs from non-academic institutions are included. You won't find much information about each program, but links to Web sites are included.

Two programs that I personally know of are missing from these resources' lists: The University of Colorado at Denver's certificate program for designing and implementing Web-based learning environments (**ceo.cudenver.edu/~joni_dunlap/certificate/index.html**) and the Indiana State University Consortium's doctorate in technology management (**web.indstate.edu/consortphd/**).

## Thumbs Up? Thumbs Down? My Take...

Time for full disclosure: I got my master's from the distance program at George Washington University. I teach for the University of Colorado at Denver's certificate program for designing and implementing Web-based learning environments. So I'm not unbiased about these two. I can, however, tell you that I have high expectations and a low tolerance for stuff that doesn't work, as you might have guessed already.

George Washington University's master's in education and human development, educational technology leadership (**www.gwu.edu/~etl/**) is a 36-credit program for folks who want to learn both theory and skills. Courses cover a wide range of topics, including educational hardware systems (where I learned how to install memory and change my power supply!), instructional design, research methods, and multimedia production for education and training. There's an emphasis on leadership of ed tech projects. One minus at George Washington: class size is a bit bigger than what I think is ideal. Overall, it's a solid program, has been in existence a long while, and turns out great grads (you can tell I'm unbiased).

The University of Colorado at Denver's certificate program for designing and implementing Web-based learning environments is a 12- to 16-credit graduate-level program that includes courses on developing educational Web sites, online instructional strategies and multimedia enhancements for educational Web sites.

In these courses, students use standard authoring tools such as Dreamweaver, Fireworks and Flash. Plus and minus: it's pretty intense, very hands-on, and there's lots of work. Students are expected to collaborate and work on authentic projects. My students frequently ask if I think they have nothing else going on their lives. I grin and bear the abuse because I know it'll be worth it for them in the end.

I checked out other programs, and here are some of my impressions, based on their Web sites. Your mileage may vary from mine, so do your own research. Also check out *U.S. News and World Report*, which ranks grad schools each year (**www.usnews.com/usnews/edu/beyond/bced.htm**). There aren't specific rankings for instructional technology or online programs, but it's a good starting place to evaluate a school's reputation.

**University of Maryland University College**
**Online master of distance education**
**www.umuc.edu/mde**
This is a new program that started this past spring. Course descriptions show a good mix of theory and skills that would appeal to a manager of distance ed projects, and it appears to have an international emphasis. Certificate programs are offered as well.

**Penn State**
**Educational technology integration certificate**
**www.worldcampus.psu.edu/pub/programs/edtech/index.shtml**
This is a 15-credit program. It looks to me like it's aimed primarily at educators who need the basics and who want to learn theory that will help them adopt educational technology. It doesn't appear to be for folks who are looking primarily for techie skills. Penn State has a good reputation for quality in distance education.

**San Diego State University**
**Instructional technology certificate**
**edweb.sdsu.edu/itcertificate/home.html**
I like the fact that students in this program learn solid Web development skills as well as theory. Plus, as long as you apply for and transfer to the master's degree program before completing the certificate, you can apply all the courses from the certificate program toward your master's (which is not online, for some reason). SDSU has a very good reputation in this field.

**Capella University**
**Certificate in teaching and training online**
**www.capellauniversity.edu/prgms/ed**
Capella has a number of certificate, master's and Ph.D. programs in this field. The certificate program in teaching and training online consists of four courses (or 16 quarter hours). All quarter-credit hours can be applied to a master's or doctoral degree through Capella University. The courses look like they'd be great for someone wanting to expand his or her skills in this area. The master's in education, with a specialization in teaching and training online, expands upon the certificate with additional theory and project-based courses.

**Walden Institute**
**Certified online instructor program**
**www.waldeninstitute.com/coi/community/COIprog/coiprog.html**
This program is 12 weeks long. I'm guessing, by the amount of content covered, that this is geared toward managers and administrators who need to understand the big picture.

## Students' Take

Now it's time to hear from some of the folks who have attended or are attending some of these programs. I asked them why they decided to go to a certain school and what they think of it. Here's what they had to say:

**Debra B. Sol**
**Title:** Training chief (senior instructional designer/developer)
**Employer:** ManTech Telecommunications Information Systems Corp.
**Program:** George Washington University master's in education and human development, educational technology leadership
**Reasons:** "The program was ideal for me, as I could continue to work while attending school. I hoped to focus on WBT and online instructional development. The program curriculum met my personal and professional requirements, especially the elective classes in needs assessment, human/computer interaction and instructional Web development."
**Comments:** "I have often suggested this program to others who are working in the adult education, technical training and online instructional development field. It is a superior example of applied learning and doing."

**Indira Harper**
**Title:** Graphic design coordinator
**Employer:** Northern Kentucky University
**Program:** University of Maryland University College master's in distance education
**Reasons:** "My employer is in the process of developing a distance learning department, and I'll have a graphic design and development role within it."
**Comments:** "It's convenient. I've tried the traditional way, but never followed through because of the time constraints of in-person learning. The only problem I experience is with technology. I'm proficient in both PC and Macintosh platforms, but the program is more PC friendly. When I am on the Mac (which is most of the time), the conference area is jumbled, so I have to sign off and log back on using a PC. I would recommend this program to people who are disciplined enough to set their own deadlines and stick to them."

**Richard Clark**
**Title:** Training program manager
**Employer:** VeriFone, a subsidiary of Hewlett-Packard
**Program:** San Diego State University certificate in instructional technology
**Reasons:** "I'm responsible for designing, delivering and managing training at my company but didn't have formal training in this area."
**Comments:** "Going through the certificate courses has helped me a great deal. I'm now able to advise and mentor other people in my division to prepare their own online classes."

**Alexander J. Bolla**
**Title:** Professor of law
**Employer:** Cumberland School of Law, Samford University, Birmingham, Ala.
**Program:** University of Colorado at Denver's certificate in designing and implementing Web-based learning environments
**Reasons:** "I became interested in the possibilities of online delivery of law courses, but was pretty much self-taught. I did a respectable job but wanted to know how to make my courses better. Since I really didn't need another degree, I looked for a program that was online and tailored to my specific needs. I considered several but selected this one because it was broad but skill-specific. I wanted a focus on 'interaction learning' strategies and design."
**Comments:** "I'm almost done with the program, and I certainly gained the experience and skills I expected. I'd like to see them put more consideration into the amount of coverage for each of the courses. Some of the time and skill requirements were daunting. I would recommend the program to others without hesitation. It goes beyond typical WBT or CBT."

**Betty J. Whitesell**
**Title:** Assistant professor
**Employer:** Regis University, Denver
**Program:** Capella University, Ph.D
**Reasons:** "I have been an online facilitator for Regis University in the MBA program for more than three years, which influenced my decision to seek an online program for my Ph.D. Traditional programs offered in my geographic area were not geared to the nontraditional student."
**Comments:** "Capella has an intro course that helps students get into the online environment and back into being a student. Courses are offered in an online classroom or by directed study. There is a lot of support and responsiveness by Capella staff and the required residency sessions are offered in a variety of cities and on weekends. Student interaction is marvelous! I've experienced some minor challenges, including needing more information about picking a mentor and the completion of directed study plans. I would recommend Capella to others."

**Nancy Karr**
**Title:** Technical writer and instructional designer
**Employer:** WennSoft Inc., New Berlin, Wis.
**Program:** UCLA, certificate in online teaching (www.onlinelearning.net)
**Reasons:** "I wanted to upgrade my professional skills and gain practical experience, but I already have a master's in adult education. There has been substantial research in learning theory since I finished my degree and I needed to get caught up."
**Comments:** "I gained considerable insight into the online teaching and learning process, as well as some experience in Web page design and using simple multi-

media tools. This program provided a good starting point, but there is much more to learn. The program moderators were good to excellent. To get the most out of the program, you have to be willing to do a fair amount of work. I completed most of the program last spring and summer while I was doing contract technical writing, which gave me the freedom to work from home part of the summer. That gave me the opportunity to spend more time on school. It would be hard to be in a full-time professional position and be able to do the work."

**Deb Tacker**
**Title:** Employee development specialist
**Employer:** Remedy Corp., Pleasanton, Calif.
**Program:** Certified online instructor program from Walden Institute
**Reasons:** "My company is growing rapidly. As a one-person training department, it's getting increasingly difficult to keep up with training needs. I was looking for techniques to help me design courses for effective online learning. I needed to know the differences in designing for a classroom vs. designing for a Web site."
**Comments:** "I gained more than the specific how-to skills I was looking for. The course covered a broad spectrum of objectives, from basic elements of online courses to examining online authoring and management tools. Most of the course participants agreed that the course required much more of a time commitment than we expected. There was a lot of interaction and collaboration with other members of the class, and many realizations about the nature of online discussion."

## See You in School?

So what do you think? Any of these sound like just the ticket? Be sure to evaluate what you're looking for and match programs and schools against your true requirements. And remember that sometimes the toughest programs are the best in the long run.

"A good program needs to be rigorous, if it is to establish or maintain credibility," says Walden's Goloboy. "A major misconception about distance-ed programs is that they will be easy to manage along with a busy work schedule. Distance ed provides an opportunity for flexibility in scheduling, but it still demands time, organization and effort."

She suggests contacting former or current students and faculty—not only for general information, but also to get an idea of the "online personality" of the program and a feel for the legitimacy of the certification or degree.

*Patti Shank is a learning technologies consultant, reviews editor for Online Learning, and faculty member for the University of Colorado at Denver. She can be reached through her Web site at www.insighted.com.*

# Preparing E-Learning Professionals

## Bob Hoffman

*This article reports on what the Department of Educational Technology at San Diego State University is doing to prepare students to design, develop, staff, and manage e-learning projects. It describes the strategies and materials used to help students learn theory and acquire practical experience.*

## E-Learning Is Still Learning, But...

As increasing resources pour into e-learning projects in business, government, and academic organizations, more professionals with e-learning savvy are needed to design, develop, staff, and manage them. Here at San Diego State University's Department of Educational Technology, we are working with learning professionals who are retooling their skill sets and we are incubating the next generation of e-learning designers, developers, and managers. In the process, we're learning to recycle old strategies, adapt proven tools, and invent new ways of helping folks learn via computer networks.

Through its master's degree and two doctoral programs (Ph.D. and Ed.D.), the department strives to nurture balanced professionals with a solid grasp of theory and the ability to apply it in real life. The regimen includes a diet of instructional design (from a variety of perspectives), performance technology, project management, analysis and evaluation, as well as hands-on development work.

Hands-on work is vital, since e-learning professionals must experience first-hand the various development processes that take online training or knowledge management programs from drawing board to implementation and follow-up. They need to be able to communicate on their own terms with Web programmers, TV directors, and database developers and administrators. Students who flourish in the hands-on arena often find employers who prize their ability to whip together prototypes or swiftly deploy low-end, online solutions to problems and opportunities.

Theory provides the foundation. Hands-on practice builds the edifice. This article describes a sequence of courses that constitutes the basic core of the development thread of our master's degree program. The Multimedia Development and Advanced Multimedia Development courses, in parallel with a sequence of instructional design and performance technology courses, are prerequisite to most of the department's other offerings.

## The CASE for Multiple Personalities

Our graduate students, like many adults, seem to learn best when they are engaged in real-world projects, modulated to one degree or another in scope, complexity, and the severity of consequences, suitable to a safe learning environment. We use projects to draw out the "multiple personalities" that make up a good e-learning professional.

Through carefully designed projects we encourage students to develop as craftspeople, artists, scientists, and engineers (see the CASE system, Figure 1). As scientists, we're interested in identifying principles, such as those that describe perception and memory. As artists we "just get a feeling" that one approach is going to work better than another. As craftspeople we have an extensive, tried and proven tool chest of methods to draw on, reaching back to Socrates, Confucious, and a legion of skillful teachers, ancient and modern. And, of course, we are engineers, building and testing our designs to see what works with *these* learners and *this* content, *here* and *now*.

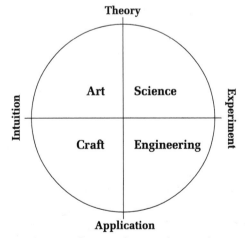

**Figure 1.** CASE: How we know what we know about educational technology. An e-learning professional must be a *craftsperson*, a bit of an *artist*, a *scientist*, and an *engineer*. We apply theory and test our hunches to create learning environments that work for real learners with real learning needs.

We've also found that our advanced students respond positively to problem-based learning—PBL—situations in which they must determine their own learning objectives, figure out how they're going to accomplish them, carry out their plan, and evaluate their own success (Bridges, 1992).

## From Lockstep to Lockout

Multimedia Development (http://edweb.sdsu.edu/courses/edtec541/) is a hands-on course that is prerequisite to the master's degree program. Students get their hands dirty applying audience and content analysis to multimedia navigation design and testing. They put principles of information design to work laying out online information pages.

The course is a study in contrasts. The first half is highly structured, tutorial-driven, as the class moves lockstep through the development of a model project with little variation. During this period, they are also studying basic principles of information design and using an instructional design process to plan their course project. The second half of the course is in modified PBL format, "locked-out" from instructor-centered directives, for the most part, setting their own project goals and organizing themselves (with some guidance) to achieve them.

The tutorial is in eight sessions that take students from hand-coding html (so they'll know how to read and troubleshoot it later on) to creating a multi-page informational Web site using a WSYWYG Web-page editor, processing digital images, video, and sound to integrate with text.

The tutorial itself has evolved through several iterations based on different multimedia authoring tools, beginning with Apple's HyperCard in the early 1990s, through Macromedia Director in the mid-90s, to Web-page editors in the late 90s, and the current Macromedia Dreamweaver authoring system. The Web development iteration of the tutorial is called Homer, with vague, whimsical allusions to "home pages," epic journeys, and post-modern TV cartoons. In Homer, students create a personal Web portfolio that they can adapt to suit their own needs and tastes.

Course instructors present Homer in a unique and effective way. In face-to-face sections of the course, students turn off their computers and watch while the instructor 1) shows them where they're headed—what their work should look like by the end of the session—and then 2) demonstrates all or part of the process of getting there, step by step. Earlier iterations of the tutorial provided videotapes of the demonstration for online or other self-paced learners.

Then students 3) work from a liberally illustrated, meticulously detailed step-by-step print tutorial that guides them through the creation of the product, while the instructor 4) walks around and coaches individuals through difficult spots. Print is ideal in this instance, since students find it difficult to switch back and forth from one window to another in most computer-based tutorials.

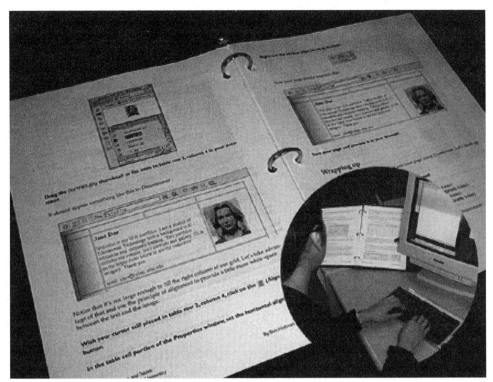

**Figure 2.** A graduate student (inset) works from the Homer print tutorial to develop her Web portfolio

This four-layer method of teaching application software skills has been consistently effective (Bintliff, 1997) and avoids many of the problems and frustrations associated with the "everyone do it along with me" method. In online sections of the course, the process is a bit different, but the materials are essentially the same. The department screens online learners for their ability to organize themselves and for self-reliance.

While they are struggling through Homer, students are also studying principles of Web navigation design and page layout using a mix of methods, including online experimental studies, online instructional modules, and a conventional textbook.

## You Are the Most Interesting Thing You Can Study

The latest addition to our e-learning instructional tool chest is online experiments. While these are still largely in development, early pilot testing indicates these may be powerful learning tools.

Imagine our Multimedia Development course a few semesters ago. The instructor stands (or sits, in the case of online sections) before a group of learners already preoccupied with the difficulties of mastering alien software applications. Now he or she wants them to internalize a long list of principles related to designing text, laying out Web pages, choosing color schemes, devising navigation systems, and so forth. In past semesters, you listened, you watched, you read.

Now, instead of lecturing you on which type fonts are most readable, the instructor points you to an online experiment. Following instructions, you come to a page with two identical text passages, displayed in different type faces. You click on the one that seems most readable to you, and two more samples present themselves. In all, 10 screens in rapid succession present all possible paired combinations of five common Web type faces.

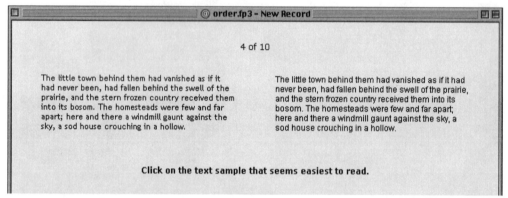

**Figure 3.** *A page from an online experiment for type design*

When you finish the series, a final screen presents the results. You get feedback not only on how you ranked the fonts for readability, but how everyone else did as well. Students appear to be very interested in their own preferences, tested in this way, as well as the likes and dislikes of others, presumably representative of the audience for which they are attempting to design their own sites.

Not only do online experiments such as this provide a motivating, memorable learning experience for trainees, the activity itself also models the science and, to some extent, the engineering sides of our ideal e-learning professional "personality."

Other learning experiments currently being implemented and tested include one on principles of page layout and the learning effects of animation, interactivity, text, narration, and sound effects. A growing battery of these experiments is available online. (For information, please email the author, Bob.Hoffman @sdsu.edu.)

## I CARE

Students further process design principles using online course modules. These modules are distinctive because they are organized using the I CARE system

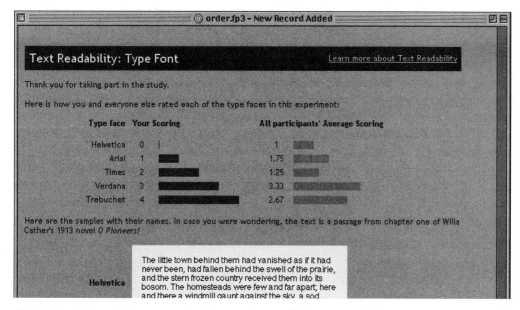

**Figure 4.** The results page from an online experiment for type design

(Hoffman and Ritchie, 2000) developed several years ago by department faculty for the California State University system. I CARE stands for Introduction, Connect, Apply, Reflect, and Extend.

As you might guess, I CARE organizes content into sections closely paralleling a simple instructional design or "lesson plan" system. The Introduction describes the context for the module and presents the module objectives. The Connect section presents new information to the learner. The Apply section provides opportunity for learners to practice what they picked up in the Connect section. Examples include work on projects or participation in online experiments such as those mentioned above. The Reflect section prompts learners to articulate what they've learned, either to themselves in a design notebook, or to their peers through a course listserv or other discussion mode. The Extend section provides remediation, enrichment, self- or teacher-evaluation, and/or course evaluation.

The I CARE system helps students be aware of their own learning process, prompts module developers to appropriately select and sequence material, and models some of the craft aspects of e-learning for our students.

## But Does It Work?

So students begin internalizing design principles through online I CARE modules, online experiments, group discussions, and a conventional textbook (currently Williams and Tollett, *The Non-Designer's Web Book*). After the first few sessions

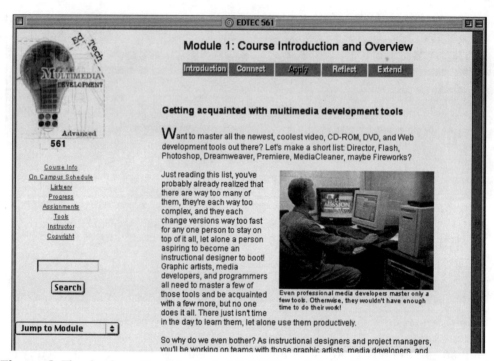

**Figure 6.** The Apply section of a typical I CARE module in the Advanced Multimedia Development course

they start using those principles to design individual final projects. They conduct a small audience analysis, analyze subject matter, and draft a proposal, flow diagrams, and storyboards, exposing them yet again to the craft of information design.

By the end of eight or nine class sessions (eight to nine weeks in a regular academic semester), students have acquired sufficient software application skills and drafted a detailed, principled design, complete with flow diagrams and storyboards, and are ready to launch the development of their own final project.

The PBL-style development of individual course projects takes up most of the second half of the course—about eight sessions. An interesting feature of this development period is two formal user testing events. The first, after only the bare skeleton of their project is complete, lets the novice developers obtain feedback from users on navigation design and, to the extent they are ready for it, page layout. Several weeks later a second session gives them more feedback on page layout, readability, and other issues.

These intervals of development and testing, revision and re-testing, and more revision help students internalize the process of usability engineering and iterative development. This fosters the "inner engineer" in the CASE model.

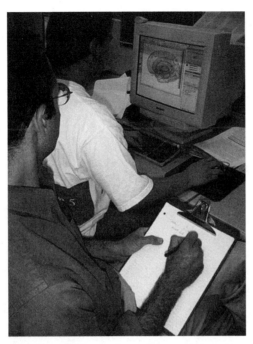

**Figure 6.** *Students conduct usability and quality assurance testing on their prototype e-learning products*

## What's Your Problem?

The follow-up course in the sequence, Advanced Multimedia Development (http://edweb.sdsu.edu/courses/edtec561/), features some of the same elements, including the combination of highly structured tutorials and problem-based learning.

The course combines two workshops, the Educational Video Workshop (EVW) and the Educational Multimedia Workshop (EMW).

The EVW involves a highly structured tutorial, similar in design to that used in Homer (Figure 6), but this time guiding teams of students through the design and development of an educational video project. Teams of about four students are responsible for producing a two- to three-minute educational video that is one of a series of (usually) five or six videos produced by the workshop on a single theme.

The instructor provides the theme and a subject matter expert (SME) with whom participants can work and the Workshop provides most of the information resources participants will need. The EVW provides guidance on how to work with the SME, how to outline the content and develop a treatment, how to write a script and draw storyboards, how to plan a shoot, block the script, draw set plans, schedule talent, crew, and equipment, and, finally, how to shoot, edit, and deliver the final product.

**Figure 7.** The CD-ROM interface for a recent EVW project featuring six short videos about sources of needs assessment information

This scenario gives students a start-to-finish, hands-on acquaintance with the art and craft of educational video development.

Since each team's video is one in a series, some of the problems the teams must address—independently and collectively—is how to devise and conform to a style guide, provide conceptual and visual continuity, and coordinate scheduling. The EVW takes about nine sessions, or weeks in a typical academic semester.

Perhaps more interesting, from the point of view of training e-learning professionals, is the second half of the Advanced Multimedia Development course, which consists largely of the Educational Multimedia Workshop.

For the EMW we chose a project that provides a great deal of structure with respect to overall methods and outcomes, but broad leeway in making decisions about content and how to represent it effectively. The project is the department's Web-based *Encyclopedia of Educational Technology* (http://coe.sdsu.edu/eet/).

The *EET* was first hatched in 1994 as a database for a course on educational television. Students and faculty quickly saw its potential and ported it to the Web the next year. In 1998 we adopted it as the vehicle for the Educational Multimedia

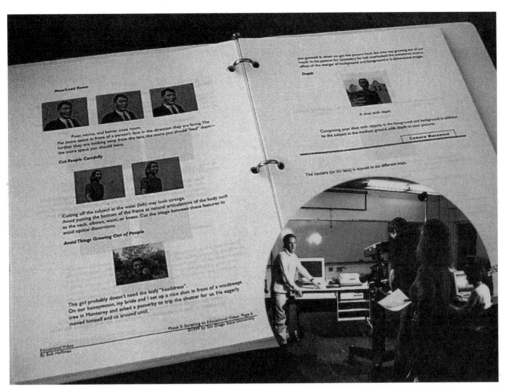

**Figure 8.** The EVW print material and (inset) participants shooting their team's instructional video

Workshop. The EET currently has several hundred short articles on a variety of topics ranging from knowledge management to virtual learning environments.

In the Workshop, each participant designs and develops an online article for the *EET*. Good e-learning depends on effective visuals and sound, in addition to careful use of text, so students spend much time and effort thinking about how people learn with multimedia representations.

The Workshop fosters scientific thinking by inviting students to read and write about the research in our field, as they gather content for their *EET* article. It prompts creativity as they learn to conceptualize and realize effective visual and aural displays. The Workshop encourages them to draw on crafts related to page layout, text design, and information design. And iterative development and user testing cycles give them the hands-on engineering skills they'll need as e-learning designers, developers, and managers.

In some respects, the EMW is highly structured. Participants follow a prescribed instructional design model and work within the constraints of a pre-established style guide typical for a large project such as this one. They even use a template for developing their articles so that they can spend their time worrying about

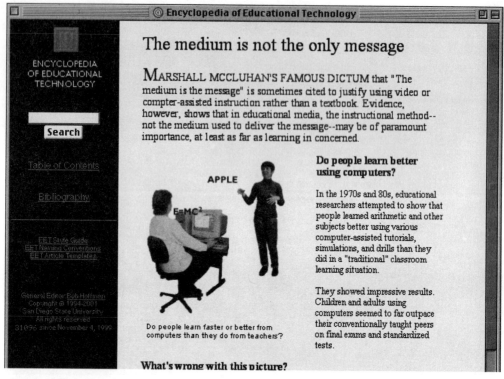

**Figure 9.** A typical article from the EET, on the relative importance of message design versus delivery media. The article gives a brief overview of the issue and uses visuals to help learners grasp important concepts.

content and visualization rather than html and Javascript.

An evaluation of the EMW (Meyer, 2000) found that students felt that six features of the workshop were particularly relevant to on-the-job and other instructional design tasks: 1) Web page development, 2) selection of visuals, 3) Web page design, 4) storyboard creation, 5) prototyping, and 6) use of discount usability engineering techniques.

## What's the (Learning) Object?

We've recently extended our use of project-based and problem-based learning in the development of e-learning professionals to another course, called Instructional Multimedia. One of two major projects in this course involves participants developing reusable learning objects in the context of a simple, database-driven learning management system.

According to Hoffman and Grossman (1999), a learning object is a unit of instruction that is self-contained (independent of other learning material), is scalable for use in a variety of situations, and features well-defined prerequisites. Reusable learning objects are of great interest to most organizations attempting to develop some form of e-learning capacity and/or knowledge management system to conserve and leverage legacy information.

In this project, student teams design, develop, and test learning objects to meet objectives clustered under an overarching goal or set of goals. This project gives students first-hand understanding of learning objects, fosters teamwork and the use of unifying style guides within the context of a large project, and provides an opportunity to review fundamental ideas in our field, as these serve as content for the project.

Craft, art, science, and engineering all come together in the EMW, as learners analyze, research, design, develop, test, and revise their team's object.

## Conclusion

The project—and problem-based learning activities described here—serve several purposes for our students, in addition to helping them learn the hands-on technologies they may need to succeed as e-learning professionals.

First, these activities give them opportunities to exercise their inner e-learning craftsperson, artist, scientist, and engineer, as they prepare to use these in the real world. Second, the activities model a variety of pedagogical approaches they may find useful for their own e-learning tool kits, such as online experiments, reusable learning objects, tutorials, I CARE, and others.

Modeling the strategies is particularly useful for participants in our online certificate program (http://edweb.sdsu.edu/edtec and click on Instructional Technology Certificate Online), since they are getting firsthand experience at the "other end" of the e-learning process.

As a result of these and other strategies we see many participants emerge as well-rounded e-learning professionals, ready to hit the ground running in a variety of roles for a wide range of organizations.

## References

Bintliff, R. (1997). *Is HyperTown an effective teaching tool?* Unpublished report, San Diego State University.

Bridges, E. (1992). *Problem-based learning for administrators.* University of Oregon: ERIC Clearinghouse on Educational Management.

Hoffman, B., & Grossman, S. (1999, October). Object learning on the World Wide Web. Paper presented at the AACE WebNet '99 Conference, Honolulu, HI.

Hoffman, B., & Ritchie, D. (2001) An instructional design-based approach for developing online learning environments. In Kahn, B. (Ed.), *Web-Based Training.* Englewood Cliffs, NJ: Educational Technology Publications.

Meyer, M. (2000). Evaluation report: Educational Multimedia Workshop. Unpublished report, San Diego State University.

Williams, R., & Tollett, J. (2000). *The Non-Designer's Web Book*. 2nd edition. Berkeley, CA: Peachpit Press.

*Dr. Bob Hoffman is an associate professor of educational technology at San Diego State University, where he teaches courses in educational multimedia design and development, both on campus and online. His research interests revolve around how people use interactive multimedia and virtual reality learning environments, as well as how students learn by participating in research projects. You can reach him at Bob.Hoffman@sdsu.edu.*

# The Four Levels of Web Site Development Expertise

## Albert L. Ingram

*This article proposes a four-level model of Web development expertise and describes six major dimensions of expertise that may differ from level to level and that represent "the types of things one must know in order to develop Web sites successfully."*

Just a few years ago, when educators were just beginning to use the World Wide Web, it was much simpler than it is now. HyperText Markup Language (HTML) was the only technology available for developing Web sites, and its capabilities were limited. Because of that, the Web was essentially a way to send and display static pages of simple text and graphics from a server to a browser. Multimedia, interactivity, two-way communications, and page customization were not yet available. Two consequences were that (1) there was less to learn in order to become an expert at Web development, and (2) those of us who taught Web development had much less to teach on the subject.

Today, the situation is far different. Many more technologies are available. HTML itself has expanded, and Dynamic HTML (DHTML) takes us beyond even those changes. Forms have been added to allow information to move in both directions on the Web, and a variety of languages and technologies are available to process incoming information at the server end. JavaScript (and to a lesser extent VBScript) have provided simple programming languages to increase responsiveness and interactivity on the client side. Java (not to be confused with JavaScript) offers a full-fledged programming language designed for more complex tasks on the Web. Pages can now connect to databases so that they are no longer static; instead, they can present information and activities specific to those who are viewing them. They can change on the fly according to such variables as specific users, time of day, location of the user, particular requests and histories, and many others.

New technologies now coming online promise to continue these trends. Active Server Pages (ASP) from Microsoft are making it easier to present customized information. Extensible Markup Language (XML) may broaden the possibilities even further. Other more specific programs from many different companies are providing an incredible variety of options. These by no means exhaust the possibilities, and by the time this article is published there will undoubtedly be many others.

The types of information that we can present on the Web also have changed drastically. While text and GIF and JPG images are still the mainstay of most Web sites, we have many other choices. Animated GIFs were the first step away from stationary images. It is relatively easy to insert sounds and video clips now. Streaming audio and video are possible so that we can receive broadcasts over the Internet. Special plug-in programs allow Web surfers to view Flash animations, Director movies, Authorware programs, virtual reality (VR) environments, and many others.

At the same time, our understanding of how to design Web pages and sites has also grown, although perhaps not as quickly as the technologies available. Key questions about visual design, site organization, usability design, file and database structure, and many other issues are becoming increasingly central to how we design and use the Web. For educators, questions of instructional design and integrating the Web into our instructional systems are also important. Finally, a key concept for educators is interactivity, which most agree is vital to good instruction on the Web (e.g., Gilbert & Moore, 1998).

In sum, there is a great deal to learn when one begins to produce Web sites. It is impossible to "cover" all the technologies, knowledge, and skills one needs in a single course or even in two or three. No one starts out knowing all there is to know, and we all must move through a series of steps or stages in order to develop expertise. Beyond that, everyone who develops Web sites must continually learn more, upgrading his or her skills to keep up with the technology—hardware, software, and development processes. Ultimately, none of us will be able to keep up completely or hope to do all the tasks in a complex Web development project.

How should we organize our understanding of Web development and how to teach it? There are many people, especially in education, who are just beginning to learn to design and develop pages and sites. There are others who are gaining knowledge and skills in all or parts of the process. If we are to design curricula or course sequences that take students from novice abilities to higher levels of expertise, then we must look at the kinds of things that must be learned and the order in which they can or should be taught. Here we make a first attempt at doing so.

The purpose of this article is to propose a four-level model of Web development expertise. These four levels can serve as a curriculum overview or as a plan for an individual's professional development. Although the four levels do seem to capture the current state of the technology (at the time of writing), there is no expectation that these levels will remain static. As new technologies come along and old ones are supplanted, this scheme will have to be revisited. In addition, as one progresses through the levels, it is likely that one will begin to specialize. Undoubtedly, the levels will have to be changed and updated regularly.

The four levels described here are labeled the Basic, Intermediate, Advanced, and Expert levels. They are not meant to be definitive, but they do represent a reasonable progression of skills that one could learn in becoming conversant with Web site development. In addition, we describe six major dimensions of expertise that may differ from level to level. As with the levels, the dimensions are not necessarily completely mutually exclusive. They do represent, however, a reasonable description of the types of things one must know in order to develop Web sites successfully. The six dimensions are as follows:

- Page Design
- Media Use
- Client-Side Processing
- Server-Side Processing
- Site Structure
- Development Processes

First, we describe the six dimensions, and then we explain what someone should be able to do at each level in all of them. Obviously, it is possible for an individual to have skills at different levels within different dimensions. This is especially true at the upper levels; at the lower levels a good developer will probably have skills in all dimensions. Again, the levels should be viewed more as a framework than as a set of mutually exclusive categories. However, people who are significantly more advanced along one dimension than along the others are unlikely to have a complete grasp of the Web or of its possibilities.

## Six Dimensions

### Page Design

Page design is the most basic dimension of expertise in Web development. It has been central to the process since the beginning of the Web. At first, people developing Web pages had to know HTML to develop even simple Web pages. The only way to make a page was to use a text editor or word processor to write the HTML code directly, complete with tags, paired brackets, and all the other paraphernalia involved. However, it didn't take long for more capable Web page editing software to be developed. The first ones helped ease the process by inserting fully formed tags when the user made corresponding menu choices. All the user had to do was insert text, graphics filenames, and hyperlink Uniform Resource Locators (URLs). The first WYSIWYG (What You See Is What You Get) page editor was PageMill for the Macintosh, although, given the differences among computers, screens, and browsers, no editing software can be entirely WYSIWYG. Currently there are any number of editors that make the technical process of developing individual Web pages little different from word processing. Any of them will suffice for making basic and intermediate level pages. To move beyond such basic formatting, more complex (and usually more expensive) editors can produce DHTML, Active Server Pages, and other advanced technologies.

## Media Use

The workhorses of media on the Web are GIF (Graphics Interchange Format) and JPG (or JPEG—Joint Photographic Experts Group) graphics. At the Basic and Intermediate Levels of Web development, one should be able to insert such images into a page as well as use them as backgrounds. More advanced media choices, which may require extra steps or coding in development, include inserting sounds and video clips, animations, and streaming media. To use such media effectively on the Web, one must have both the skills to produce and edit them and the ability to put them on the Web and integrate them with other Web elements. One should also be able to use graphics as hyperlinks.

## Client-Side Processing

The Web (and the Internet in general) works on a *client-server model.* The core of most Internet-based services consists of *server* computers and software, which offer information, processing, and transmission abilities. People access the servers through *clients,* which again are specific software programs running on individual computers. For example, we may send and receive e-mail through specific e-mail client programs such as Eudora, Outlook, or Pegasus on our personal computers. To do so, however, we must connect to email servers, which handle such chores as transmitting our messages to the destination servers and holding incoming messages until our client programs request them. The Web itself consists of a huge number of WWW servers scattered around the world. These range in size from the author's server software running on his office computer to the massive computer banks that serve the Netscape, Microsoft, or Yahoo Web sites. We all access those servers through the client software we have come to call *browsers.* Here the key point is that, with computers and software on both sides of each Web transaction, we have the ability to process information in various ways on either end. This allows a skilled Web developer the choice of deciding where the processing will be most effective and efficient. For example, frequently the servers are much busier than the clients, since the latter spend a great deal of time waiting for a single user to enter commands. Thus, often it can be more efficient and responsive to have the server downloading processing tasks to the client. In other situations, where key information is stored on large databases on the server side, the processing must take place there.

With the advent of Web scripting languages, especially JavaScript and VBScript, the Web developer has gained the ability to create pages that are more interactive and responsive to users without changing the essential nature of the Web and its browsers. Scripts are snippets of programming code that are embedded, much like HTML, in the Web pages that are sent to the client's browser. The last several browser versions from both Netscape and Microsoft have included the ability to interpret and execute these scripts from within the page. The advantage to this scheme is that it minimizes both server load (no extra processing takes place on the server side) and the bandwidth needed to transmit the code (scripts are simply ASCII text that is interpreted on the client side, just like HTML itself). More complex scripts can be used to communicate with the originating server as well, allowing even more flexibility, interactivity, and responsiveness. The ability to use and write scripts is an increasing part of good Web page development, especially in instruction, where scripting can allow more meaningful interactivity. There are large numbers of scripts available for downloading from the Web, so one does not have to become a highly skilled programmer in order to make good use of this technology. Other programs are available to write scripts for you, for example, to produce the code needed to present simple tests and quizzes. Another client-side processing technology is the programming language *Java,* which increases the bandwidth requirements but does put complex processing tasks on the client side. Some have suggested that Java, or something like it, will provide a way to run large-scale applications over the Web.

## Server-Side Processing

For more complex interactivity, the client side of the Web (the browser) and the server side must work together. Whenever one searches a database for information, submits personal or professional information to an organization, or participates in an online Web-based conference, there is likely to be processing taking place on both ends. The first innovation to allow the two-way exchange of information on the Web (rather than just one way from the server to the client) was the online *form.* Forms consist of the text boxes, radio buttons, checkboxes, and, especially, "Submit" buttons that we are all familiar with. Forms are remarkably easy to develop on the client side, as part of a basic Web page. However, the key question in using them effectively concerns what happens when the user clicks the Submit button. Some of the basic things that can happen are:

1. the form results can be e-mailed to someone;
2. the form results can be posted to a Web page automatically (this occurs in online asynchronous discussions, for example);
3. the form results can be sent to a text file or database file on the server, where it can be stored and used to aid subsequent decisions; and
4. the server can have other special programs to deal with form results or almost anything else.

In order to take any of these actions, the server must have programs installed to handle them. Often these programs are CGI (Common Gateway Interface) programs. The programs themselves may be written in a variety of languages, since CGI is not itself a programming language but instead a standard interface among programs on Web servers. PERL has been the most popular CGI language, especially on Unix servers, but many others, such as Visual Basic and C, are used as well. Server-side scripting with JavaScript is also an option now. No matter which language is used, a CGI program allows the server to process form results and do other tasks that can increase the interactivity and responsiveness of the Web to the users. The ability to use existing programs (such as those that e-mail form results) effectively as well as to write programs to perform more complex processing is an important part of being a good Web developer.

## Site Structure

Small Web sites often have little or no structure, and they may not need any. With only a few pages, a small Web site can be linked on an *ad hoc* basis, with little regard to consistency and navigation issues. After all, how lost can one get in a few pages? With larger sites, the need for a planned structure becomes evident in at least two ways. First, in order to maintain and update the site, those working on it need to have a clear idea of where things are, where new material should be entered, and so on. As we move toward more database-driven sites, the structure of the site and the database must be specified early in the development process. At the same time, site users probably will find it easier to navigate and use the site if there is a clear structure to it. Any complex Web site might be organized in many different ways, so the emphasis through the four levels is on ensuring that structure exists, rather than on adhering to any particular structure. There are also several prototypical Web structures that can provide rough templates for a site, such as linear, hierarchical, or Web-like. At the same time, there is evidence that the structure and navigation of a site is intimately bound up with the information that is presented (Spool, Scanlon, Schroeder, Snyder, & DeAngelo, 1999).

## Development Processes

Finally, it is not enough just to have good technical skills in order to do Web development. As sites expand to dozens, hundreds, and thousands of pages, they are taking on the characteristics of large-scale instructional development or software engineering projects rather than smaller, craft-style designs (Powell, Jones, & Cutts, 1998). Nowadays, teams of people develop good sites, since it is unlikely that any individual will have all the skills, let alone the time, to do all parts of a project. Therefore, one of the key skills in Web development is the ability to plan and follow a systematic development process. Such a process is the best way to ensure a high quality site that is developed on time and on budget. Expertise in this area can help us define Web development expertise more generally. A variety of areas can contribute to the processes used, including project management, instructional development, usability engineering, software engineering, and many others (see Figure 1).

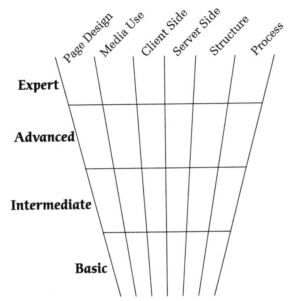

**Figure 1.** The four levels of Web site development expertise

## Levels of Web Development Expertise

Now we describe the four levels of Web development expertise with reference to the six dimensions. The levels are summarized in Tables 1 through 4. Here we will discuss the levels from the point of view of someone learning (or being taught) the skills necessary to progress from one to the next.

### Basic Level

The Basic Level is the first step for someone just starting out in Web development and is characterized by beginner-level skills (at best) in all dimensions. The pages and sites developed by those at the Basic Level tend to be personal sites, practices, and perhaps hobbyist ones. Little information is given, and little attention is paid to who will want to receive it. Someone at the Basic Level is able to enter text, perform basic formatting tasks, use graphics, and so forth. A relatively small number of guidelines can improve these pages immensely (e.g., Maddux, 1998). The media he or she uses are primarily GIF and JPG files for backgrounds and inline graphics. A person at the Basic Level is unlikely to have any expertise whatsoever in either client-side or server-side processing, so the pages and sites developed will consist of static pages served individually with no information returned to or acted upon by the server. The site structure, from my experience in teaching beginners in Web development, is likely to be nonexistent unless individuals are forced to consider the issue. Most sites produced by those at the Basic Level are likely to be very small, however, so the structure is not critical. Finally, individuals at the Basic Level are unlikely to use any systematic development processes, since they are probably more concerned with merely completing the pages reasonably well and linking them together.

| Page Design | • Text entry and formatting (at least these options: fonts, sizes, styles, colors, alignment, headers<br>• Background colors and graphics<br>• Inline graphics<br>• Internal and external text links |
|---|---|
| Media | • GIFs and JPEGs |
| Client-Side Processing | • None |
| Server-Side Processing | • Page serving only |
| Site Structure | • *Ad hoc* structure based on small number of pages |
| Development Processes | • *Ad hoc*, organic, evolutionary, rapid prototyping |

**Table 1.** Basic Level

## Intermediate Level

The Intermediate Level takes people a step beyond the basics in several areas. People at this level are more likely to produce sites that are actually useful to others. The sites probably look better and are at least somewhat interactive, compared to those produced by those at the Basic Level. People at this level, perhaps from experience, start paying attention to the site structure, to navigation, to the file structure on the server, and to other issues. They have probably discovered the need for some planning and development processes, although they may not be skilled in them as yet.

| Page Design | • Text formating (options: lists, special html formats, indentations) • Tables for more complex page formatting • Graphics as links • Links to anchors (same page, other pages) • Image maps for links |
|---|---|
| Media | • Background sounds • PNG files • Animated GIFs |
| Client-Side Processing | • Copy and use (preferably legally!) scripts from other pages with changes • Write own scripts |
| Server-Side Processing | • Forms processing using canned programs (e.g., e-mail and storing in text files) |
| Site Structure | • Planned and deliberate: hierarchical, linear, Web, combination • File structure taken into account |
| Development Processes | • Basic planning, analysis, and design processes. Structure/flow charts and storyboards |

**Table 2.** Intermediate Level

At the Intermediate Level, page design skills are more or less complete. Developers are skilled at using most or all of the standard HTML features. Nowadays, of course, they probably access those features through one or more of the available WYSIWYG editors, not through learning and editing HTML directly. In an HTML page, the most common means of gaining control over the format of a Web page is through the use of tables (DHTML is changing that, however). Therefore, at the Intermediate Level, one key skill is to use tables effectively for page layout. Image maps are another element that can be quite useful in instruction (for identifying the parts of an object being studied, for example), so they appear at this level as well. These technologies can be especially important for developing Web-based learning materials (El-Tigi & Branch, 1997). Among the media used, going beyond GIFs and JPGs, are PNG files (a relatively new graphic format for the Web), animated GIFs (popular, but difficult to use effectively), and background or embedded sounds.

An intermediate Web developer is at least starting to learn about client-side scripting, most likely using JavaScript. The first step in learning Web scripting is usually to download and modify scripts from other pages or from sites offering large numbers of free scripts. Given the availability of scripts to do almost anything, this is a useful strategy for bringing some instructional interactivity to a site without too much effort. Even so, doing this may entail learning a significant amount about the language. On the server side, someone at the Intermediate Level can likewise use canned programs to engage in simple forms handling. Many servers have CGI program libraries available with the ability to perform common server-side tasks. In addition, some Web editors, notably FrontPage, include server extensions that provide such functions.

The site structure is likely to be planned more carefully at the Intermediate Level, with choices made about overall organization (for example linear, hierarchical, or Weblike). The file structure also starts becoming important at this level, because the size of the sites developed is increasing, and the developer needs to be able to find pages and information quickly and easily. In order to produce a coherent structure, a consistent navigational plan, and a useful file structure, the developer must do some serious initial planning and design. Thus, the need to analyze the requirements of the site, design it, and follow that design becomes evident. Some of the tools that he or she might use include charts like structure charts or flow diagrams as well as storyboards for planning the visual look of the site. Often, the most useful design process is to develop a quick prototype of a few pages before committing to the final look and feel of the site. The relative ease of producing and changing Web pages makes this course especially viable.

In summary, the Intermediate Level represents the current state of Web development for large numbers of people who are not professional developers but who develop small to medium-size sites for personal, educational, or professional use. Much useful information has been placed on the Web at this level. However, to be a more advanced Web developer, one must go beyond these two levels. The Advanced and Expert Levels represent much more complex Web development, which approaches the state of the art at the time of this writing.

## Advanced Level

The Advanced Level of Web development moves us into some of the latest technologies on the Web. More important, especially for education, this level includes a significantly greater level of interactivity. Not only is this the level at which one must operate to be a professional Web developer, but to get here it is much more likely that most will require formal training rather than purely self-instructional efforts.

In page design, there are several important elements that are more advanced. Frames have been a part of HTML for several browser generations, but are difficult to use effectively. Done poorly, they can be confusing and disruptive to users; done well, they can help people find their way around a site. DHTML, mentioned earlier, is still a young technology and not standard across browsers. Even so, it now allows precise placement of graphics, text, and other elements in layers that normal HTML does not allow. In addition, the elements can be moved, changed, and made to appear and disappear under user or script control. All of these features make possible much more dynamic, interactive, and responsive Web pages. In addition, Cascading Style Sheets allow the developer to have greater control over fonts, sizes, colors, and styles than that allowed by HTML alone. At the Advanced Level, developers are likely to be able to make good use of video and audio clips to convey information and tone, as well as a variety of specialized media that might require "plug-ins"—small programs that are added to the browser to increase its functionality.

Both client-side and server-side processing take on increased importance at the Advanced Level. On the client side, an advanced developer should be able to write significant scripts as well as begin to use Java programs in various ways. On the server side, the developer might design and program CGI programs. In addition, he or she should begin to connect Web pages to databases to make the sites more individually responsive. These connections can be used for a variety of tasks, from delivering the results of simple information searches to creating all the pages on a site on the fly. While this strategy takes more planning, design, and programming, it can also make updating and maintaining a site much easier.

At this level the advanced Web developer should pay close attention to the structure of both the site and the file system that stores it. It is likely to be a much larger site and the addition of such complex technologies makes it difficult to keep track of what is going on from both the user's and the developer's points of view. Haphazard linking and development will likely ensure that visitors to the site will come away confused and frustrated. When the time comes, as it will almost immediately, for the site to be maintained and upgraded, early attention to structure will pay off handsomely.

Perhaps one of the more important ways that an Advanced developer can differ from those at the earlier levels is in her/his use of more systematic analysis, design, and development procedures. Whether from software engineering, instructional design, or other disciplines, the procedures allow the designer to be sure that he or she is solving the right problems and to design a site to solve them well. These relatively well-established processes also allow better project management, enabling the developers to estimate time and budget more accurately and to meet project goals more reliably. Other disciplines that start to become important at this level as well as the Expert level include information architecture (Rosenfeld &

| Page Design | • Frames<br>• Dynamic HTML<br>• Cascading Style Sheets<br>• More complex tables (e.g., tables within tables) |
|---|---|
| Media | • Audio and video clips<br>• Files requiring plug-ins |
| Client-Side Processing | • Write complex scripts from scratch<br>• Use and modify Java programs |
| Server-Side Processing | • Supplying intermediate CGI to do customized tasks<br>• Connecting to databases for publishing and possible updating |
| Site Structure | • Complex<br>• Fully designed up front<br>• Information architecture and usability considerations<br>• File structure planned and specified |
| Development Processes | • Good analysis and design process drawing on instructional design and incorporating some other elements from other disciplines |

**Table 3.** Advanced Level

Morville, 1998), usability engineering (Nielson, 1993), software engineering (Powell, Jones, & Cutts, 1998), and many others.

## Expert Level

At the Expert Level of Web site development, practitioners are fully capable of using the latest and most effective Web technologies. However, at this level it is unlikely that any individual will be expert in all the technologies. Usually, development at this level demands a team of people, making it even more imperative that the site structure be well-specified early and that good development processes be used.

In page design, Expert Level Web development involves dynamically generated pages that are based on database-driven information, instantiated into page layout templates. This allows a high degree of customization, interactivity, and responsiveness in the Web site (Garrison & Fenton, 1999). Active Server Pages, a Microsoft technology, allow one to produce such pages, and there are other possible technologies as well. Although such sites are currently most likely to be produced for e-commerce sites, as education begins to use them, we should see more sites that adapt to the needs and wants of individual users and students. As far as media go, at this level, sites may include any media that might be transmitted on the Web, including streaming audio and video.

An individual who is expert at client-side processing will have full scripting skills and/or full programming skills in a language like Java. These allow her or him to create highly interactive and capable pages that do far more than simply present static information. On the server side, Expert Level developers are able to produce sites with full database connectivity with complex server-side processing using scripts and programs.

At this level, the structure of a Web site has probably moved beyond one based on linking individual pages in various ways. Instead, there is most likely an abstract model of the site which is instantiated on the fly from databases. This is

| Page Design | • Dynamically generated pages based on database-driven information, page layout, etc.<br>• Very complex interactive elements<br>• Active Server Pages |
| --- | --- |
| Media | • Streaming audio and video |
| Client-Side Processing | • Full scripting skills |
| Server-Side Processing | • Full database interconnectivity, complex server-side processing, programming |
| Site Structure | • Based on abstract model that is instantiated on the fly |
| Development Processes | • Fully planning, analysis and design process combining instructional design and development with relevant concepts from software engineering, usability engineering, and project management, etc. |

**Table 4.** Expert Level

an efficient, effective strategy for producing, upgrading, and maintaining a site but requires a great deal of front-end analysis, planning, and design before any programs are developed or information entered. The development processes used at this level thus include full processes to plan and manage the project, procedures for analyzing such things as the systems and requirements, the instructional needs, and the learners or audiences, and design methods that allow the team to specify exactly the structure and processes on the site. These last may include such techniques as data flow diagrams from software engineering, as well as Rapid Application Development processes that can result in prototypes that can be tried out with members of the target audience. This moves us far beyond the rudimentary Web pages of the Basic Level.

## Conclusions

Just a few years ago, when the author began teaching Web site development to graduate students in instructional technology, students learned how to produce simple pages and link them together. For many, that in itself was a significant step forward and had potential educational advantages. Even though many people still have to learn the rudiments of Web page development to have a significant effect on education and training, instructional Web sites need to go beyond that. Intermediate Level development skills are now necessary to produce sites with even minimal importance for education. If mere information presentation is the goal, there are likely to be no end of sites that one can find and link to where students can find information on almost any topic. The small ones produced by teachers and others at the Basic Level and even at the Intermediate Level are increasingly less likely to add much to that cacophony. To be genuinely useful, instructional sites must go beyond those levels. They should be interactive and present significant learning challenges to students. They should be responsive, adapting the information and activities to the actions and inputs of the students. And they should be customizable, presenting an interface and the content needed by the individual students.

To accomplish these goals, educational Web developers will need to move up through the levels outlined here. Most people in the field can readily move beyond the Basic Level to the Intermediate Level quite quickly. To help people move beyond these, we will need to offer advanced training in a variety of Web technologies, which are fast replacing more traditional computer-assisted instruction development technologies. Clearly these technologies include scripting, programming tools, and database systems. The levels outlined here provide a framework for organizing and approaching that training. As Web technologies advance, the four levels will have to be modified, but the overall structure might remain useful for a longer period of time. In addition, it is important to stress that the levels involve more than just technical skills. Understanding, using, and producing complex site structures is increasingly important as our sites grow in size and complexity. The use of good development processes is one thing that will distinguish professional and effective Web developers from those who merely produce pages.

This need for technical skills in developing Web sites is certainly changing. Already there is less pressure to learn HTML than there was just a few years ago. Although some still argue that direct HTML coding is necessary to produce the best, most efficient, and most customized pages, fewer people see the tradeoff in time and effort to be worth it. We can expect to see other aspects of Web page development automated as well, including education-specific elements. For example, it is now possible to add testing or online discussions to educational Web sites without any significant knowledge of scripting or programming.

Increasingly, instructors and others who develop sites are using pre-packaged systems, such as WebCT (http://www.webct.com/), TopClass (http://www.wbtsystems.com), Web Course in a Box (http://www.madduck.com/) [acquired by Blackboard Inc., http://www.blackboard.com, in spring 2000], and many others to organize and enter the information and other elements in their classes. These systems offer page and site templates into which an instructor can insert the content of a course. In addition, they may include such things as quiz and test systems, synchronous and asynchronous communications, and other elements that would be difficult for most educators to program on their own. One tradeoff in using these systems is likely to be a less customized course. An implication for this article is that these systems lessen the need for expertise in the page design and scripting dimensions, while perhaps increasing the need for good media design and development, site structures, and development processes, especially some form of instructional design.

Another potential trend for the development of educational Web sites is to contract with outside agencies and companies for such services. Such groups could bring to the project a varied set of skills that individuals, small schools and colleges, and others may not have. At the same time, however, the sites produced would still have to be maintained and upgraded, a process that can be more time-consuming and expensive than the initial development, so either the contract must be an ongoing one or in-house skills are still needed.

## References

El-Tigi, M., & Branch, R.B. (1997, May-June). Designing for interaction, learner control, and feedback during Web-based learning. *Educational Technology, 37*(3), 23-29.

Garrison, S., & Fenton, R. (1999, July-August). Database driven Web systems for education. *Educational Technology, 39*(4), 31-38.

Gilbert, L., & Moore, D.R. (1998, May-June). Building interactivity into Web courses:

Tools for social and instructional interaction. *Educational Technology, 38*(3), 29-35.

Maddux, C.D. (1998, September-October). The World Wide Web: Some simple solutions to common design problems. *Educational Technology, 38*(5), 24-28.

Nielson, J. (1993). *Usability Engineering.* New York: Academic Press.

Powell, T.A., with Jones, D.I., & Cutts, D.C. (1998). *Web Site Engineering: Beyond Web Page Design.* Upper Saddle River, NJ: Prentice Hall.

Rosenfeld, L., & Morville, P. (1998). *Information Architecture for the World Wide Web.* Sebastopol, CA: O'Reilly and Associates.

Spool, J.M., Scanlon, T., Schroeder, W., Snyder, C., & DeAngelo, T. (1999). *Web Site Usability: A Designer's Guide.* San Francisco: Morgan Kaufmann Publishers.

*Albert L. Ingram is with the Instructional Technology Program, College of Education, Kent State University, Kent, Ohio (e-mail: aingram@kent.edu).*

# Welcome to Part Six:
# E-Learning at Work:
# Case Studies

Part Six presents a grab bag of e-learning cases. Interested in big companies? We've got them. See Patricia Galagan on Cisco and Kim Kiser on Oracle. Interested in particular training challenges? Kiser's other piece in this section looks at sales training via technology. Warren Longmire, Dan Hughes, and Karen Jost treat project management training online through the use of an object oriented approach. Jennifer Hofmann covers the shift of a soft skills vendor, long known for classroom offerings, to a more blended and technology inclusive approach.

Do you favor a particular kind of organization? Technology companies are, not surprisingly, well represented here. So are insurance companies (see Kiser). Alan Howard describes an interdisciplinary program at the University of Virginia. Even the U. S. government appears here, in the piece by Mary Eisenhart, with examples of knowledge management at work in the GSA, the FCC, and the Navy.

There you have it. E-learning as it is today.

# E-Learning Evangelism

## Kim Kiser

*This article recounts how one person converted managers, course developers, and 1200 instructors to believe in the power of e-learning. It also outlines ways to help instructors make the transition to e-learning.*

Chris Pirie is an unlikely evangelist. As he prepares to deliver his message to a small group of coffee-swilling e-learning conference attendees early one Monday morning, he stands perfectly still, hands clasped as if in prayer. Occasionally looking toward the heavens, he begins to speak. As he does, his passion for e-learning starts to shine.

Pirie, who managed curriculum development for Redwood Shores, Calif.-based Oracle Corp.'s database administrator track before beginning this crusade, speaks about how the Internet can remove barriers to education. No fire, no brimstone, just sincerity.

"In the old world, an instructor could influence the lives of about 24 people a week. On the Internet, you can help thousands," he explains, his English accent diluted by a decade in the United States. This is not about saving souls; it's about saving time and money.

As a member of the team that would move the $10 billion Internet software company into the e-learning age, it was Pirie's job to first convert Oracle's managers, course developers and 1,200 instructors into believers. Now he's taking his message about faster, better, cheaper training to those who buy, sell and use the company's technology.

Pirie's words weren't always welcome at Oracle. "Everyone's knee-jerk reaction was that online education wasn't as good as being in class," he says. "But the

Internet brings amazing possibilities we never had in the classroom."

The Internet also brings amazing possibilities to the way companies do business, which is why Pirie found himself in the e-learning pulpit in the first place. Several years ago, Oracle CEO Larry Ellison became frustrated when he couldn't figure out how many people worked for his company. As he tried to come up with a number, he discovered the firm had 154 human resources databases around the world—just one example of the information silos that had sprung up across Oracle's corporate landscape.

Ellison knew that a company known for its database software needed a better system for managing and connecting information, and the Internet was just the ribbon that could tie such data together.

That epiphany was the impetus for Ellison's crusade to make Oracle the very model of an Internet-driven business. He insisted that the company retool its products to run on the Net and that Oracle employees do unto others by using products themselves before putting them on the market. In addition, Ellison issued a company-wide challenge in the spring of 1999: use the efficiencies garnered by the Internet—and Oracle technology whenever possible—to save $1 billion from the company's bottom line by May of the following year.

Training wasn't exempt from that challenge. In addition to being one of the largest software companies, Oracle had grown into the world's second-largest provider of IT training, posting revenues of $480 million in 1999 from teaching people outside the company to use its products, according to Framingham, Mass., research firm International Data Corporation (IDC).

But the company's education business was fragmented. One group was responsible for customer training, another for employee education, and the company's support, consulting and alliances divisions also had their own training programs. Each group had its own registration system, accounting practices, classrooms and road-warrior instructors who traveled from city to city teaching the same classes from week to week. Not exactly the strongest foundation for a company that wants to run on Internet time. "You could see Larry's programmer-logic brain going crazy with this," Pirie recalls.

Ellison also issued one more challenge to the training groups: move 100 percent of the company's internal training to the Web. The plan had two benefits: it would allow Oracle to train more employees in a short amount of time, while also allowing the company to test-market its online learning offerings. Once perfected, they could then sell many of those courses to customers in an effort to capture a larger share of the worldwide IT training market—a market IDC predicts will grow to $34 billion by 2004.

Back in 1999, however, Oracle instructors and employees were wedded to the classroom, with approximately 85 percent of the company's training business taking place there. Pirie admits he, too, was very much part of the old school.

An opportunity to work with the company's alliances division changed his view of how the Internet could transform teaching and learning. The division, which works with independent software vendors, had created an information portal called the Oracle Technology Network. Developers from vendor companies could go to the site to find software, white papers, and online chats and discussions about Oracle products.

The popularity of the network, which is used by some 1.2 million people, gave Pirie an idea. "I said, 'Wait a minute. These are people who really need to be educated. They're Web savvy; they're hungry for information. Our education units ought to be rising to that challenge.' That's where I first saw the possibilities of what the Web could do for education."

Meanwhile, Ellison had tapped John Hall, then senior vice president for alliances, to consolidate the training organizations. Hall's first job was to create a single Oracle University in a mere 60 days and develop a strategy for using the Internet for training. Hall turned to Pirie to help sell the concept of e-learning to people within the organization.

As Hall's team explored ways to use the Web to develop and deploy curriculum, they looked at how the Internet had changed business and considered how those models might apply to learning.

They decided that if people could buy books from Amazon.com at 1 a.m., why shouldn't they be able to take classes whenever they wanted? If the Internet could allow companies to sell directly to customers, why not use it to connect students with the people who developed the technology they're learning to use? And in the fast world of software development, why spend four to six months developing training material and training the people who would teach it?

"By the time we produced a course or a polished CD-ROM with training on it, many times the product had moved onto another rev," says Bill Dwight, who heads up Java tool development for Oracle.

Hall's group laid out its plans, and Pirie took to the road, spreading the gospel according to e-learning. "I had a lot of convincing to do," he recalls, with a weary note in his voice. "We had to make this change happen. We kind of suspected we could do it, but we were as skeptical as everyone else. Business people, instructors, customers all had their doubts about e-learning." (See the sidebar, "Converting the Classroom Corps.")

As a member of the team that developed Oracle's first blended classroom/Web-based courses for database administrators, longtime instructor and training manager Tony Holbrook liked the idea of using the Internet to teach. However, he admits he had his doubts about whether it would work. "We were trying to put a tremendous amount of training into an online model. We weren't sure how well accepted it would be," he explains.

In addition to the blended courses, Oracle's e-learning team tested three other models for delivering content: e-study, a blend of text, graphics and on-screen interactions; e-seminars, which use recorded streaming video of experts talking about new technology; and Web-based e-classes.

"Initially, we were in the mindset that these things ought to be live," Pirie says of the Web-based classes. "We thought they should be one- to two-hour events with someone talking to you and streaming PowerPoint slides and demonstrations at you."

But when members of the education team sat down to take such courses, they didn't like what they saw. "They were dull. It was hard to keep our attention," Pirie says. The fact was, no one wanted to hang out online for an hour or two. So they broke the courses down into segments—demos, hands-on exercises, quizzes and prerecorded streaming video lectures—that learners could complete in 10 or 15 minutes.

They also found that, given a choice of taking the online courses live or in a prerecorded format, two-thirds of Oracle employees who piloted the courses opted for the asynchronous version, where they could do the work whenever they wanted, skip topics they already understood, and converse with fellow students and instructors through threaded discussions. "All our anxiety about trying to create a live classroom was a holdover from our own perception that training should be live and in the classroom," Pirie says.

But the desire to keep learners connected wasn't the only challenge. When the education team first tested the online courses, the company didn't have a learning management system on which to house them. Oracle had made two false starts at trying to create such technology before perfecting its iLearning hosted system. "If you spend a lot of time building beautiful online course material that's really effective and no one can find it, you're wasting your time," Pirie explains.

Since the company began piloting its online courses, Oracle has saved both time and money—and educated a growing number of employees. Between June and August 1999, when virtually all courses were taught in the classroom, the company had 32,000 internal enrollments. The training cost Oracle more than $9.2 million.

During that same quarter the following year, Oracle had 12,700 internal enrollments in classroom courses and 43,500 in online courses. Despite the increase in enrollments, the company spent $5.5 million for training that quarter, which went a long way toward helping Ellison meet his goal of saving $1 billion.

In October, Pirie took his brand of e-learning evangelism to a different audience: the people who use Oracle technology. The e-learning team unveiled the Oracle Learning Network, an education portal that's the gateway to the company's online courses, at Oracle's OpenWorld users' conference. By the end of that month, more than 3,000 of the 30,000 attendees had signed up for a trial subscription.

Hall says the company hopes the addition of online courses will help Oracle University increase its number of external students from 600,000 to more than 1 mil-

## Converting the Classroom Corps

When Oracle launched its crusade to move learning from the classroom to the Internet, the movement's evangelist, Chris Pirie, wasn't surprised to encounter resistance from instructors.

Trainers were afraid they would lose their jobs. And they were worried that after a career spent in the classroom, they wouldn't be able to teach effectively online.

Turns out, instructors didn't lose their jobs. And the company didn't (nor does it plan to) close down its classroom training business. "We want to grow our business through e-learning. It's a brand new market for us," says Pirie, who is vice president of Oracle Learning Network, the company's online education portal.

To do that, the leaders of the e-learning initiative needed to figure out ways to get instructors excited about teaching online and help them make the transition. Here's what they learned:

**Start spreadin' the news.** Oracle recruited a group of its best instructors, including Tony Holbrook, who is now senior Web content producer, to create some of its initial online courses. Once those instructors saw the benefits, they spread the word to others.

**Teach them to build for the Web.** Oracle encourages instructors to first create content for the Web. To help instructors do that, the education team gave them templates to create pieces of courses and a studio to record video clips. "With 200 products coming out a year, every product manager can have training on a product and have it on the Web in less than two weeks. Then if it makes sense, they can turn it into a classroom course," says Dennis Bonilla, an Oracle University vice president.

**Let them Take 2.** "Some of the best instructors in the classroom are the biggest hams," says Holbrook. "But if you stick a camera in front of them, they're rarely at home." When developing some of the early online courses that used streaming video clips, Holbrook noticed that it took a few false starts before instructors became comfortable talking to the lens. Now instructors get ample opportunity to practice before recording video.

**Cut the small talk.** Holbrook found it works best for instructors to keep lectures and explanations short—to five or 10 minutes. "If they had to talk with no feedback for longer than that, they would begin to bore themselves," he says.

**Tell them to unpack their suitcases.** Holbrook, who started his career at Oracle as a classroom instructor, knows that the life of an instructor means a lot of time on the road. "Some travel 100 percent of the time," he says. E-learning allows them to conduct classes and office hours from their home office—and spend more time with their families.

lion and grow training revenues to more than $1 billion during the next three years.

Cushing Anderson, program manager for learning services and research at IDC, is optimistic about the company's plan. "Oracle is making a strong play to 'e-enable'—that is, to create learning content out of instructor-led classes. That will provide them with greater opportunity to reach deeper into customer companies so those companies will be able to send more people to class," he says. "Also, they're allowing for individual students to track their learning history, and that will endear them to some clients."

In the short term, however, the education team hopes to have 100,000 subscribers to the Oracle Learning Network by December 2001. So far, they're on track to exceed that. By mid-November, some 1,300 new subscribers were coming online each day—a rate much higher than the education group ever anticipated. "That's kind of scary," Pirie, who is now vice president of Oracle Learning Network, confesses nervously.

He pauses, then amends his words. "No, that's very scary."

*Kim Kiser is managing editor of* Online Learning. *Contact her at kkiser@ onlinelearningmag.com.*

# Using Objects for Online Learning: E-Learning for Project Managers

**Warren Longmire, Dan Hughes, and Karen Jost**

*This case study describes the creation of a Web-based product—IPS Associates' e-Planning and Managing Projects—that provides project management instruction and performance support. The article concludes with project outcomes and possible future directions for learning object implementations.*

## Background

Learning objects continue to offer immense promise to producers of e-learning. Objects have the potential to personalize online learning, to cut development time and costs, and to "play" on any platform. Though specifications for creating objects currently vary, a number of object initiatives are moving towards convergence. In the meantime, many e-learning providers have created their own object-based approaches.

This case study describes one such solution. IPS Associates' *e-Planning and Managing Projects* is an online learning and performance support environment based on a three-day classroom course. The online solution is founded on an object paradigm that parallels industry initiatives underway at the time of the project's design phase (in the year 2000). This study presents the process of translating IPS's business requirements into an object-based design in partnership with Viviance new education.

## The Business Case

### IPS Focus

IPS Associates is focused on providing project management techniques that ensure ongoing client success on mission-critical projects. The discipline of project management is carved into three distinct areas: processes, people, and tools. IPS provides project management training, workshops, and consulting that address these key elements for organizational success. Specific to process, IPS teaches a method for organizing, planning, and managing a project through its lifecycle. IPS calls this course *Planning and Managing Projects*. Performance measures include delivering higher-quality projects in a shorter timeframe with decreasing budgets. These three parameters—scope, schedule, resources—logically work against each other in most projects.

Businesses usually follow an "SIO" model: they start with a sound *S*trategy, delivered in an *I*mplementation phase, which is maintained in an *O*perational mode. Applying effective project management technique focuses on and enables successful implementation. Success in the implementation phase is key to turning strategy into action and achieving desired business results.

### The Original "Planning and Managing Projects" Course

IPS is in its 13th year offering project management training and consulting solutions to high-tech companies. The company's foundational course, *Planning and Managing Projects*, has been delivered to over 57,000 students globally via classroom-based, instructor-led training (ILT). The classroom experience uses innovative labs based on real projects that the students bring with them, while targeted lectures and creative energizers support best-practice application.

Students progress through the ILT experience as a working team. The team chooses a real project brought into the class, defines, organizes and plans the project, and follows up with management and closeout activities. Although this experience is primarily focused on training, students exit the three-day experience with initial project planning in hand and the ability to perform on the job the next day.

### Evaluating an E-Learning Solution

The impetus for moving online was driven by client demand for shorter class schedules and lower training costs. Yet converting a successful ILT course to an online environment was, and is still, a challenging prospect. Offering a "me-too solution" would not provide enough customer value to justify the development cost. IPS did not want to simply recreate lectures and workbooks or substitute catchy animations for effective instruction and practice.

An additional challenge was to create a solution that could serve both as a complete course for first-time learners and as a performance support tool throughout the class and afterwards. Given the dual purposes of instruction and performance support, the evolving vision included ongoing online support and access to a range of project management tools, resources, and communities of practice.

IPS proposed that initially most of its students would use the online experience to augment their ILT event, while a smaller number would pursue the experience entirely online.

## Solution Through Partnership

IPS made the decision to partner with a company that had a set of core competencies in creating e-learning solutions. As IPS and Informania (now Viviance) came together, they crafted a shared vision that included:

- personalized learning
- online mentoring to actively support students' learning and performance
- a knowledge base of templates, best practices, and support documents
- interactive, performance-based labs offering results similar to those in the classroom
- flexibility to customize the solution
- the overarching goal of helping students perform better and helping their organizations realize business results.

The business case for the product was completed and approved in January 2000.

# Design and Implementation

## Integrated Performance and Learning Environment

The partner companies began by creating a high-level product concept: "Integrated Performance and Learning Environment" (IPLE). The IPLE concept was visualized as a grid offering multiple types of learning and performance support (Figure 1).

In this diagram, different methods of online learning are shown as "levels" of IPLE. There are many possible routes through the environment and its tools and content.

## Design Requirements

To realize the IPLE concept, the design model was expected to include:

- modular content
- ways to tie lesson content to corresponding IPLE levels
- a self-assessment that creates a personalized learning path

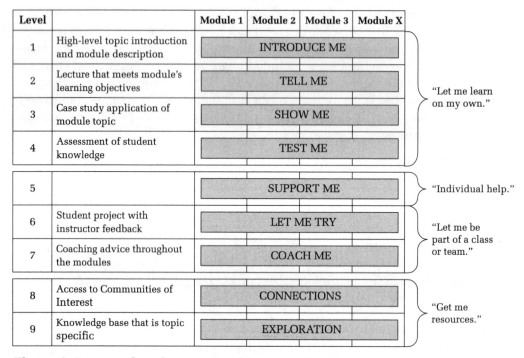

| Level | | Module 1 | Module 2 | Module 3 | Module X | |
|---|---|---|---|---|---|---|
| 1 | High-level topic introduction and module description | INTRODUCE ME | | | | "Let me learn on my own." |
| 2 | Lecture that meets module's learning objectives | TELL ME | | | | |
| 3 | Case study application of module topic | SHOW ME | | | | |
| 4 | Assessment of student knowledge | TEST ME | | | | |
| 5 | | SUPPORT ME | | | | "Individual help." |
| 6 | Student project with instructor feedback | LET ME TRY | | | | "Let me be part of a class or team." |
| 7 | Coaching advice throughout the modules | COACH ME | | | | |
| 8 | Access to Communities of Interest | CONNECTIONS | | | | "Get me resources." |
| 9 | Knowledge base that is topic specific | EXPLORATION | | | | |

**Figure 1.** Integrated Performance and Learning Environment grid

- assessments measuring performance on actual project tasks
- offerings for both individual learners and teams

## Learning Object Paradigm

The team decided to use a learning object paradigm for managing and delivering content. A learning object is a stand-alone unit of digital learning content that is potentially reusable in multiple contexts. Two key learning object specifications were being developed (but were incomplete): IMS Global Learning Consortium's Content Packaging Specification and Advanced Distributed Learning's SCORM (Shareable Content Object Reference Model). Also under way was Cisco System's Reusable Learning Object (RLO) implementation.

Given time limitations, the team needed a model that could be implemented quickly, yet none of the industry object initiatives were ready and/or appropriate for the process-oriented P&MP course. The team realized the project management process could be effectively delivered using small objects only if each chunk were richly contextualized, an attribute not typically associated with more independent and neutral learning objects. Here, each object should provide opportunities for the learner to relate a given project management task to the larger process model by engaging with a lesson, reviewing a case study, performing the task, and applying it to a real project.

Therefore the designers created an object model with similarities to other prominent object initiatives, and some unique aspects. This model can be adapted to specifications in the future. As shown in Figure 2, the model is based on the "levels" of IPLE.

Following a taxonomy that Cisco Systems and others were using, the levels of

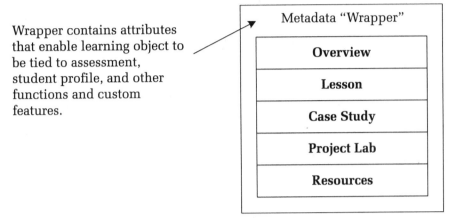

Wrapper contains attributes that enable learning object to be tied to assessment, student profile, and other functions and custom features.

**Figure 2.** *Object model based on levels of IPLE*

IPLE are "information objects" and the collection of information objects that support a single performance objective is a "learning object." Information objects can be seen as a variety of learning events that, as a whole, facilitate the transfer of knowledge into performance and application. This object model was used to break the ILT course into 40 chunks, each organized around one performance objective.

For example, one performance objective from the course is "Identify the Project Team." The corresponding learning object contains the following information objects:

- an Overview with enabling objectives
- a Lesson introducing strategies for identifying a project team
- a Case Study showing how the team was defined for a specific project (including a sample project roster)
- a Project Lab in which learners construct a project roster for a real project
- Resources that support application of the learning material (for instance, one Resource is a link to a short article called "The Challenge of Using Shared Personnel")

## Learning Environments for Object-Based Content

Learning objects are highly structured, with component information objects classified by type and purpose. In creating a delivery environment, one can either highlight the content structure or obscure it (to create the feel of a seamless course). In *e-Planning and Managing Projects*, the environment explicitly mirrors the content structure to add navigational richness, increase learner control, and provide a clear breakdown of the personal learning path components.

In the IPLE interface, within each learning object the information objects are dynamically synchronized to enable navigation up and down the "levels" of the object. In Figure 3 (the home page), note how the left navigation bar displays links to the information objects found in each learning object.

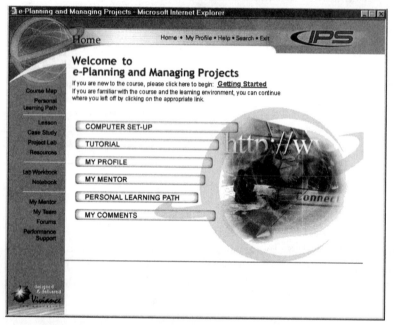

**Figure 3.** IPLE home page

Figure 4 shows the Overview for a learning object (accessible via the Course Map). Each learning object is defined by a high-level performance objective (in this case "Break the Project Down").

Figure 5 shows a Lesson page within the same object.

Figure 6 shows a corresponding Case Study page. Because this is a free-standing, template-based object, a customized version can easily be added (for example, to show how the process is applied on a specific company project).

Figure 7 shows a corresponding Project Lab page.

Figure 8 shows the Resources that support the performance objective.

## Assessment Approach

Since the course is performance-based, assessments were designed to support

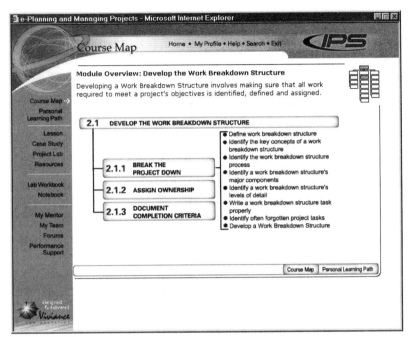

**Figure 4.** Overview for learning object

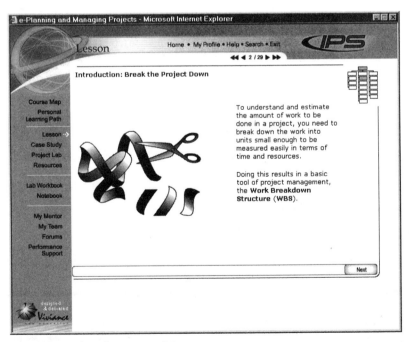

**Figure 5.** Lesson tied to learning object

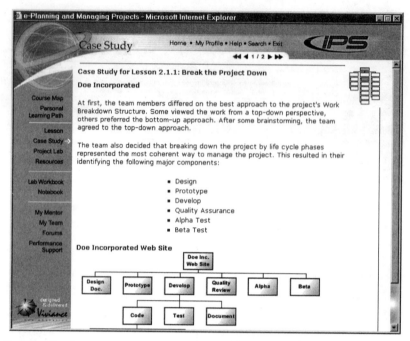

**Figure 6.** Case Study page for learning object

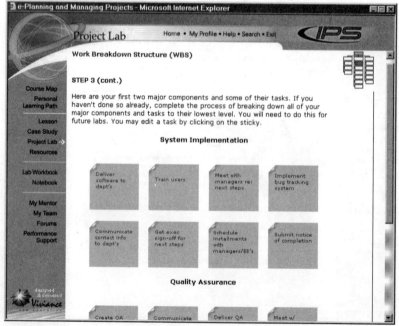

**Figure 7.** Lab Project page for learning object

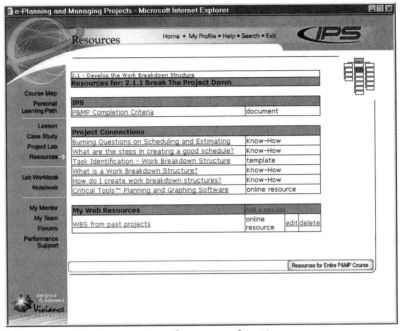

**Figure 8.** Resources that support performance objective

learning at the high level of application. Assessment items may test enabling knowledge and skills, but if an objective is the performance of a skill, the learner must actually perform it in as authentic a context as possible. For this course, this means performance of actual project planning and management tasks on a real project, using the tools and templates project managers actually use.

## Pretest and the Personal Learning Path (PLP)

The pretest is a self-assessment of what the learner already knows or can do. In database applications, pretest data can be used to individualize learning either through system control (the system chooses content and activities) or through guided learner control (the system suggests learning strategies, but the learner retains control). A guided learner control approach was chosen for this product.

The pretest was designed to help learners identify their needs through reflection on the knowledge and skills they already possess. Figure 9 shows part of the assessment for the module "Develop the Work Breakdown Structure."

Based on learner responses in the pretest, the database suggests a learning path. The Personal Learning Path (PLP) is based on the structure of the learning object: the smallest unit of PLP content is the information object. The path suggests areas where learners need to concentrate on lesson content and/or areas where they may only need a refresher, either in the form of a case study or work-

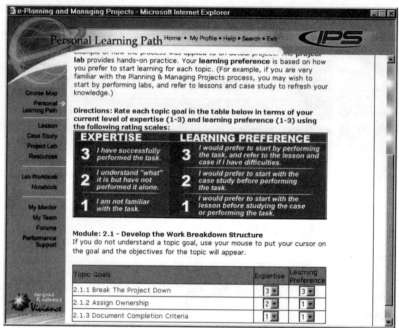

**Figure 9.** *Part of the assessment*

ing through a project lab. The PLP may vary the order of information objects based on learner preference or skill level (e.g. the lesson for a certain topic may be labeled "optional" for an expert performer).

Figure 10 shows a segment of a student's Personal Learning Path.

## Embedded Assessment Items

Assessment items are also embedded in the lessons to encourage engagement with the content and reinforce learning. These "spot checks" include true/false, multiple choice, fill-in-the-blank, matching, clickable graphics, and drag and drop. The different question types are important for assessing different types of knowledge and levels of learning and for keeping learners' attention. Javascript feedback provides immediate, informative answers. The system tracks learner performance on spot checks for each learning object.

## Lab Performance Assessment

The labs provide a final performance assessment. When the learner completes each lab, it is submitted to the mentor for review. The live human mentor uses an online assessment rubric with fields for personalized commentary on the student's performance of each step. Lab data and mentor comments are collected in a Lab Workbook.

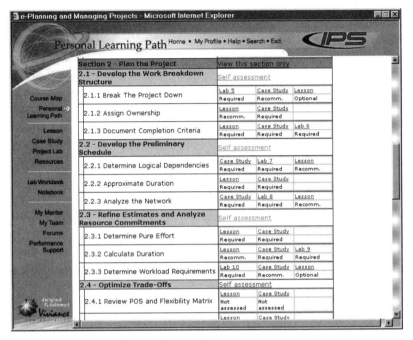

**Figure 10.** *Segment of student's personal learning path*

## Additional Learning and Performance Tools

Community interactions on the site (chat, forums, email) and the use of online mentors additionally support learners by providing other perspectives, answering questions, and providing forms of coaching or scaffolding. The Performance Support section of the site provides quick access to information to be used either during a learning activity or while applying the P&MP process on the job. Registration enables continuous access to these tools for up to a year or more.

# Project Outcomes

## Outcomes for Learners

This description of learner outcomes is based primarily on data from beta tests involving participants from companies that also enroll students in IPS's classroom offerings. Key outcomes follow:

- Learners identified the benefit of flexibility of time, pace, and place.
- Compared with all-day workshops, chunked object content allows learners to digest small sections of the content at a time and to learn parts of the project management process on an as-needed or "just in time" basis.
- Some learners treated the site as a "course" by completing activities in their

Personal Learning Path but not accessing Resources, Forums, or Performance Support. Others made full use of the performance support tools on the site. This suggests that the site does meet the dual goals of learning and performance support.

Additional beta outcomes are discussed below under "Lessons Learned."

## Outcomes for IPS

Key outcomes for IPS included:

- Supporting clients as they fundamentally change the way they conduct business through technology
- Extending the reach of IPS professionals by optimizing the use of their time in the field
- Leveraging intellectual property through an integrated knowledge base
- Offering quickly and easily customizable solutions in support of client needs (customized case studies, resources, terminology and mentor approach).

## Outcomes for Viviance

Key outcomes for Viviance included:

- Improvement of template-based design and development
- Creation of standards and approaches for building learning objects (modularity requirements, structural rules, delivery strategies, editorial standards)
- Addition of new object-based functionality to Viviance's proprietary Thinktanx platform.

# Lessons Learned

This project taught the team a number of valuable lessons from the standpoints of learner needs, site design, and production process.

## Many Learners Crave Structure (Others Do Not)

This product is intended to provide both instruction and "just-in-time" performance support on a self-directed basis. Therefore, the mentor approach during the beta was to act as a resource for learners with questions and provide feedback on Project Labs. Some learners sought the mentor's help rarely if at all. However, a majority of beta participants commented that they would have liked the mentor to take a much more active role in guiding their learning. As a result of this feedback, the mentor approach now includes more frequent mentor-initiated communication with the students, more specific Lab feedback, and regular checking in on learner progress.

Similarly, many students commented that they liked having a schedule for completing course material. (The beta was conducted using a schedule.) Several wanted their schedule to be listed next to their Personal Learning Path. Others did not feel the need for a schedule for e-learning. One way to address this issue is to offer students the option of creating a proposed schedule with their manager and/or mentor.

## Actively Orient Learners to the Environment

Some learners understood the environment quickly, while others needed more guidance. When students first log in, they are given a set of activities for "Getting Started," including taking a tutorial about the site. It is interesting to note that a minority of students actually completed the tutorial—many online learners want to start "doing" immediately and have little patience for a tutorial. This issue was addressed by increasing mentor engagement with learners' first activities on the site.

Learners understood the performance orientation of the site to varying degrees. Many learners cited the Labs and performance support tools as extremely valuable—one participant stated a strong preference for "e-doing rather than e-learning." Others perceived the Lessons as much more important than the Labs and tools. These learners equated information—not application—with online learning. This suggests that learners who are new to performance-based environments may need additional guidance in understanding the learning process and what is expected of them.

## Learners Need Dedicated Time and Manager Support

Learners most often cited "lack of time" as a condition that made it difficult to take the course. The requirement to address "other business needs" was another problem learners faced. A majority of the beta participants said they needed dedicated time and the support of their managers to be able to focus on e-learning. Per some participants, it is advisable to obtain functional manager support at the start of the learning process—preferably via a face-to-face meeting or a phone call, not just an email.

## Some E-Learners Want Paper-Based Material

A small but articulate minority of beta participants had trouble with the fact that all of the content and activities are delivered and performed online. These learners would have preferred a paper-based manual to go along with the online course. They especially wanted to perform Lab activities such as brainstorming on paper. As a result, the Labs were modified to provide the option of performing some work offline and entering the results online. As e-learning becomes more common, it will be interesting to see how paper-based supplements are perceived.

## Planning and Communication Up Front Always Save Time

As with many complex technology-based projects, there were unexpected problems and delays in production. One of the greatest challenges occurred when

Viviance underwent a merger in the midst of production. The team suddenly had several new members and a new technical lead. The existing team wanted to maintain its momentum, but new team members did not understand the vision behind the project. It soon became clear that functional and technical specifications are not enough to convey a product vision. When the project leads took the time to break from production and re-articulate a shared vision with a revised project plan, production efficiency was restored.

# Future Directions

There are a number of possibilities for future developments in object-based e-learning.

## Competency Modeling

Competency-based learning focuses on the intersection of skills, knowledge, and attitudes within the rubric of a competency model rather than a course model. A perennial challenge in implementing competency-based systems is the lack of appropriate learning content that is sufficiently modular to address individual competency gaps. Learning objects can help by matching object metadata with individual competency gaps. As the project management object repository grows, there will be more opportunities for overlaying individual with organizational competencies.

## Combining Objects from Multiple Courses

Effective object tagging will enable delivery of learning objects from multiple courses within one learning environment. This approach would allow a methodology course to be supplemented with objects beyond the scope of the course (such as soft skills training).

## Knowledge Commerce

Currently, most e-learning revenue models are based on a per-student fee or an organizational license. Is the market ready for just-in-time/just-for-me access to learning objects? How will the industry track and charge for access to small chunks of learning? How much is a three-page template, one five-minute lesson, or two questions to a mentor worth? These concerns fit into what Viviance terms "knowledge commerce"—the intersection of e-learning and e-commerce.

The business driver for succeeding in knowledge commerce must be based upon content providers' ability to create appropriate returns on their intellectual property investment. Is this model scalable, sustainable, and provable? How long will it take to promote this model before clients are ready for pay-per-use?

## Conclusion

This project has taught both companies (IPS and Viviance) many lessons about delivering innovative solutions in a competitive environment. Although the focus on learners' performance outcomes has remained primary, technology limitations, incomplete object specifications, and market hesitancy to pursue pure just-in-time solutions has required some compromises on the original IPLE concept. Nonetheless, the result is a real step forward. The next step will be placed successfully only if current wins and failures are appropriately evaluated and lessons learned are applied to future efforts.

*Warren Longmire designs and develops e-learning programs at Viviance new education in San Francisco. He has published several articles and co-authored* Managing Web-Based Training *(ASTD, 1999). He is completing his Ph.D. from the University of Massachusetts, Amherst, and welcomes robust dialogue at wrlongmire@aol.com.*

*Dan Hughes has spent 15 years in the high-tech arena focusing on digital media projects, of which four years were with US WEST in development of video-on-demand and cable modem solutions. His more recent focus has been producing instructional media projects, including the development of technology-based training for NATO troops in Eastern Europe and leading the e-learning initiative for IPS Associates. He holds B.B.A. and Master's of Technology Management degrees. You can reach him at hughes@ipspm.com.*

*Dr. Karen Jost is the Chief Learning Officer of Triage Training group, designers of performance and learning systems and specializing in e-learning. She has taught in Instructional Technology programs at California State University-Chico, Georgia State University, and Northern Illinois University; conducted research in instructional methods such as problem-based learning, uses of technology in learning, and educational change; and published several articles. You can reach her at kjost@triagetraining.com.*

# Interdisciplinary Studies and New Technologies: A Case Study

## Alan B. Howard

*What do employers want? That question led the author of this article to create a terminal master's program that would prepare students for the workplace by adding to "the traditional objectives and methods of the humanities ... active, collaborative, and reality-based work."*

The initial impetus for the American Studies M.A. program at the University of Virginia was threefold. First, in 1994 the English Department had reached a critical juncture in its graduate program: it had passed from unwittingly accumulating the world's largest stock of unemployed Ph.D.s and ABDs and had become a knowing producer of unemployable graduate students in English. Unable to accept the existence of what one of my colleagues termed the "recreational Ph.D.," I determined to create a terminal M.A. that would retool bright and capable students for productive work outside the academy.

Second, I saw a larger trend in which "education" was leaking out of colleges and universities, being taken up by a mix of traditional (libraries and museums) and non-traditional institutions (centers, proprietary universities, amateur historians). This was happening because the new technologies permitted it, because the humanities had—by their resistance to public accountability and their inability to articulate the social value of their enterprise through presenting the undergraduate and graduate curricula as anything more than the means to produce even more unemployable aca-

This article was originally published in *The Technology Source* (http://horizon.unc.edu/TS/) as: Alan B. Howard "Interdisciplinary Studies and New Technologies: A Case Study." *The Technology Source*, November/December 2000. Available online at http://horizon.unc.edu/TS/default.asp?show=article&id=818. The article is reprinted here with permission of the publisher.

demics, and by their inability to engage in meaningful examination and reform of themselves—defaulted on their traditional obligations and filed for bankruptcy.

Third, the new technologies just coming online in 1994 held remarkable promise for interdisciplinary fields and especially for American Studies. In their scale/complexity and in their multimedia capacity, they offered the means by which genuine multidisciplinary work could be pursued. They offered tools for constructing the more sophisticated models of cultural process that were emerging. They suggested a way past the post-structural theory and identity politics that had come to dominate interdisciplinary studies. And, in their ability to integrate various and dissimilar kinds of "cultural texts," not only the print that is our traditional subject and medium but also the images, objects, and events about which Americanists often attempt to speak, they seemed to provide a platform through which genuinely sophisticated cross-disciplinary work could be done.

Since my objective was to prepare students for work outside the university—at best along its periphery—I looked into what people in higher education, corporations, and the public sector were saying about their needs. I found a remarkable degree of agreement. They wanted employees who had all the things that a classic liberal arts curriculum claims to provide: the ability to think critically and analytically, the ability to be articulate in writing and in speech, and the ability to make informed and subtle judgments. They also wanted people who could work in groups, who could carry out projects efficiently and on schedule, who could "think outside the boxes," and who could bring imagination and intellectual daring to an enterprise. And they wanted people who were literate in the new technologies, who had both practical experience and a theoretical understanding of the technologies that were transforming the workplace and the culture as a whole.

## Curriculum Design

The initial program design, then, was an attempt to create a curriculum that would build on the traditional objectives and methods of the humanities but add to them active, collaborative, and reality-based work. The intention was to transform students from passive consumers of information into active producers of knowledge. At the very beginning, I informed the first group of students that they had not actually enrolled in a program—the program did not yet exist—but had instead signed on to build that program. They would certainly hear and read about American Studies, but more importantly, they were going to "do" American Studies. I wanted to collapse the distinctions between teaching and learning, research and teaching. I wanted them to have a sense that their work mattered in the larger public sphere, to challenge them to do work that would not end up in someone's wastebasket at the end of the term but would be pushed out into the street to be tested and used by a wider audience.

On its face, the curriculum was not significantly different from any master's level program in the country—core seminars and seven courses inside and outside the English department. What was different was the approach: I asked the students three simple questions: Where do you think you're going next? What knowledge and skills do you need to acquire before you get there? What synergies are available between this course and what you already know, between this course and the courses you're going to take at the same time, between this course and the work you're doing in the American Studies seminar for the term? American Studies students explore art history and architectural history, sociology and economics and history, government, and even education and law. What holds this universe of individual choices together is the American Studies seminar sequence and the thesis seminar. These seminars are designed to provide students with the opportunity and means to weld a variety of subjects into some sort of whole, to share their new-found expertise with others in the class (learning by teaching others), and to apply that expertise to electronic projects that are then published on the Web.

The curriculum, then, aspires to be, more than an accumulation of credit hours, an integrated and integrative educational process. The program begins with an introduction to research methods course that trains students to work in the library and to do electronic research, which I initiate by assigning each student to be the editor of one segment of the Yellow Pages. Next, students are introduced to scanning, optical character recognition systems, and basic HTML tagging and are assigned short texts—articles, short stories, pieces of longer works that are in production—to put online; in the process, they internalize the above-mentioned skills by applying them. Over time, this has yielded much of the reading material done in both graduate and undergraduate American Studies courses; at this point, about 40-50% of any syllabus is accessible online. Next, students are trained in Photoshop and given instruction on the use of images on the Web. Improving visual literacy is a major challenge that is developed gradually through the program.

This year's class was given the task of mounting an exhibit on *Fortune* magazine covers from the 1930s, an exercise in image manipulation and visual literacy as well as a study of the ways in which the Depression was inflected and refracted by this publication. By the second half of the semester, students were asked to create a small hypertext project that integrated all that they had learned to that point. Initially, the projects focused on Smith's *Virgin Land* and aimed to elaborate on his argument by providing extended information and analysis that Smith's publisher could not afford to include in the printed text, or by providing material that Smith did not see, consider important, or understand. This year's class has begun building a similar site based on Alan Trachtenberg's *The Incorporation of America*; they've digitized the full text, written a synoptic version for distribution outside the UVA campus, and created the first generation of satellite projects for the core text.

The second semester seminar, ENAM 803, is given over to designing, constructing, or amplifying a much larger group project. The first of these was The Capitol Project, begun in 1995; currently we are working on The 1930s, a site begun last year, which is being extended by this year's class. The first task last year was to focus the site conceptually, to design its gross architecture, and to create the first generation of projects. The task for this year was to extend the site by looking at the mass mediation of culture in the period by film, radio, photography, and mass circulation print. To do this, we had to add audio and video to our skills base and acquire some models for interpreting the cultural effects of mass media. Students were asked to select "iconic moments" from comics and cartoons, radio programs, films, and documentary photography from the period and to learn how to create sound and video files for their distribution. The result was an exhibition tentatively called "seascapes/soundscapes," a display space where, over time, we will try to create a kind of taxonomy of mediated culture in the period.

At this point in the semester, students are in the initial design phase of their larger projects for the semester. Last semester, the projects included analyses of Hoover Dam, the invention of country music, *Vanity Fair* magazine, the Chrysler Building, Charlie Chaplin, *Gone With the Wind*, and *Absalom, Absalom*; a comparison of the Depression in the United States and that in Europe; and a comparison of two of Pare Lorenz's documentary films, *The Plow That Broke the Plains* and *The River*. As part of this year's process, students are being asked to critique last year's projects and to offer re-designs for them. At the same time, they're forming their own projects, which include "Amos 'n' Andy go to Market," "The 1933 Chicago Century of Progress Exposition," "Graphic Design in the 30s," "The National Park Service and the Reconstruction of American Landscape," and "Woody Guthrie and the Folk." Also in the spring term, I organized the students as a virtual Web design and development firm. Each student has assumed the role and responsibilities of a particular job area: technical support, project management, professional development, marketing, editing, or placement. They will have those jobs throughout the semester, then assume different ones the next.

The third semester is devoted to the master's thesis. This is a summative exercise, a full demonstration of the knowledge and skills acquired in the program. I compare the students' task to that of 18th century cabinetmakers who built scale models of their work to show around the countryside. Their job is to create in miniature a comprehensive demonstration of actual competencies. After the project has been built, each student will sit for an examination by two professors, myself and someone from English or another department. I've shamelessly used this as an opportunity to educate my colleagues about humanities computing and to seek out alliances around the university as well as to provide students the challenge of explaining their work to people who are not computer literate.

Throughout their tenure in the program, students are encouraged to work part-time at relevant jobs, on campus at places like the Electronic Text Center and The

Institute for Advanced Technology in the Humanities or off campus at private firms. Periodically, work-study students build sites for non-profit organizations and for my colleagues. In short, wherever possible, I find ways to integrate the mundane business of paying the bills with experiences that enhance their training and fatten their portfolios.

# Results

The results produced by the program can, in one sense, be measured by a thoughtful exploration of AS@UVA, the Web site for the program. After four years of work, the site presents four major components. First, The Yellow Pages for American Studies, a selective, annotated directory of the best electronic resources for students and teachers in the field. Second, The Museum for American Studies, a series of museum-like multimedia exhibitions on topics ranging from the art of Grant Wood to the New York World's Fair of 1939-40 to the nature illustrations of Alexander Wilson's American Ornithology. Third, the largest and most fully developed section of the site, Hypertexts, a collection of some 50 electronic texts in American Studies, either "classics" like De Tocqueville's *Democracy in America* and Henry Nash Smith's *Virgin Land: The West as Symbol and Myth*, or "lost" texts, once powerful works like Gilbert Seldes' *The Seven Lively Arts* or Herman Melville's *The Confidence Man*, books that, for various reasons, have disappeared from view and consideration. Fourth, The Capitol, introduced as "an infinitely extensible exploration of the National Capitol as an American icon—cathedral of our national faith, the map of our public memory, and the monument to our official culture." What will be the fifth major component is The 1930s, an effort begun last year to explore and represent the most academically unfashionable decade in American Studies circles—and arguably the most important one for an understanding of modern America.

All of this is, in a superficial sense, what the American Studies Master's Program has accomplished in its short history. The site has won numerous awards; it is linked to by more than 10,000 other sites; it now attracts about 80,000 hits per day, primarily from teachers and students. And all of this at minimal cost to the University. But, as I've already said, this is really no more than the by-product of the more important educational process. To assess the value of that process, you will have to speak with the students themselves. In general, they've gone to places they could not otherwise have gone to, they've taken jobs that are more responsible and interesting—at better pay—than they could have otherwise, and they're moving up in their organizations. Some few have gone on to graduate programs in American Studies or English, but the majority have gone to work for public or corporate information providers, including PBS, Microsoft, Educorp, Maryland Public Television, the Kennedy Center, the Smithsonian Institute, Washington and

Lee University, the University of Alabama, Teach for America, Sacred Places, and NetBeans.

## The Future

We have begun to implement many of the curricular structures and objectives described here in our two-year undergraduate program and, with some modest tweaking, they promise to work just as well at that level. In addition, we are, in effect, exporting this model to other interdisciplinary programs here, particularly a new Media Studies Program that will come online in 2002-03. Finally, we are actively looking for partners at other institutions in American Studies or other interdisciplinary programs with whom we might design collaborative, trans-institutional courses.

*Alan B. Howard is currently the Daniels Family Distinguished Teaching Professor and director of American Studies Programs at the University of Virginia. His attention has most recently been directed at integrating the new technologies into teaching and learning in the humanities. You can e-mail him at abh9h@virginia.edu.*

# Washington's Need to Know

**Mary Eisenhart**

*The importance of e-learning increases greatly when an organization takes on new projects and loses many of its employees. That's the challenge faced by the U.S. General Services Administration—which is why the GSA is investing heavily in knowledge management.*

With the confusion of an electoral gridlock so fresh in our memories, it is easy to overlook the fact that the United States government is one of the nation's largest implementers of knowledge management. In fact, the KM programs in place in many government installations are equivalent in scope to those in business enterprises. The U.S. Navy, for example, has spent $30 billion to transform itself into a knowledge-centric organization. Yet while many business leaders are aware of the military's use of KM for competitive intelligence and knowledge-based warfare, civilian agencies also are reaping the benefits of KM initiatives.

A major case in point was the logistics for the 2000 census, handled by the U.S. General Services Administration (GSA). Tasks included organizing transportation, contracting for telecommunications services, setting up more than 1,000 offices, wiring the facilities and acquiring mass quantities of furniture. Predictably, by the end of the process the GSA had accumulated vast amounts of knowledge on subjects ranging from reliable shippers to the relative merits of renting versus buying furniture.

This was the first time the GSA had managed the census, says Shereen Remez, the GSA's chief knowledge officer. When the next one comes along in nine years, most of the people who acquired that knowledge will be gone from their current posts and perhaps from the agency as well. To preserve their experience—both the tacit knowledge in their minds and the explicit knowledge in their formal reports—for future reuse, it had to be extracted, archived and made accessible to others.

Remez's staff shot hours of videotape while managers talked about what they had learned and the best practices they had devised. Using video allowed the GSA to capture not only the solutions themselves but the contexts of their creation. The tapes will be made available online to GSA staff in text transcriptions and short video clips arranged by subject.

Finding new ways to transfer knowledge from individuals in an organization to their present and future colleagues has become a pressing concern for the government as it copes with the demand to do more with less. Over the second half of the 1990s, the loudly touted "reinvention of government" led to cutting back many operations and downsizing staffs. Meanwhile, a public grown used to the round-the-clock accessibility of e-commerce sites is demanding better, faster service from government agencies.

At the same time, the impending retirement of millions of Baby Boomers adds a sense of urgency for the federal government. Although not yet ready to collect Social Security payments, many government workers of this generation will soon reach 25 years of service, when they are eligible for pensions. When that wave starts to break, the federal workforce (estimated at 2,922,291 civilians in July 2000 by the Office of Personnel Management [OPM]) stands to lose half its members. Although it is not clear how many eligible workers will actually retire, the booming private sector economy is a major lure, and their skills are often in demand.

"In the GSA, we have downsized 25 percent in the last eight years. Our average age is 47, and about half our workforce will become eligible for retirement in the next five years," Remez says. "That's about the same as you'll see across all of government. In many places there's only one person who knows how to manage a system, do a certain process, develop a certain kind of program or be a certain kind of project manager. When those people leave, they leave with their knowledge and expertise between their two ears. Unless you can capture that knowledge before they leave, you lose it."

## First Steps Toward Knowledge

Last May, the Gartner Group estimated that U.S. government spending on technology to enhance electronic government programs will grow from $1.5 billion in 2000 to $6.2 billion by 2005. However, Remez does not expect technology alone to meet the impending challenges. "We see knowledge management as the foundation for electronic government," she says. "If you look at electronic government as the wires and systems that allow you to access services and information, knowledge management is the organizing of that information and knowledge so that it's easy to use and easy to leverage."

The government has no single, overarching KM strategy. Agencies are learning through experimentation. For example, the Federal Communications Commission is developing a knowledge strategy to map its future. The National Aeronautics and Space Administration's Intelligent Synthesis Environment initiative is designed to change the agency's culture to a more collaborative workplace for scientists and engineers. The Federal Highway Administration has saved time and money by incorporating communities of practice that help specialists to share expertise. Remez, who had served as GSA's chief information officer, became in June 1999 the first CKO in the federal government. She has since been joined by counterparts in a growing number of other agencies, all of whom are working to capture knowledge and share resources in their respective organizations. Her move from information officer to knowledge officer indicates a refinement of policy.

In 1996 President Clinton created the CIO Council to serve as a focal point where CIOs and their deputies from the top 28 federal agencies could coordinate on IT challenges that cross agency boundaries. These agencies found themselves grappling more and more with the interrelation of culture, process and technology, so the council's committee on enterprise, interoperability and emerging information technology established a knowledge management working group. Cochaired by Remez and Alex Bennet, deputy CIO of the Department of Navy, the working group functions as a community of practice, offering meetings, archived resources and collaborative facilities to special interest groups (SIGs) formed under its auspices. These SIGs include more specialized communities of practice, KM strategies and best practices, KM training and program planning. The group also developed and maintains the KM.gov Web site, which provides information about knowledge management to the federal government and facilitates communication among the council's members.

While top management collaborates in the CIO Council, technologists often turn to another resource. The Knowledge Management Learning-Consulting Network, hosted by the Federal Aviation Administration and sponsored by the OPM's Human Resource Development Council, is an interagency KM community of interest. Bob Turner, director of the FAA Team Technology Center, cochairs this interagency group, which also holds monthly meetings and invites speakers with expertise in KM issues from both the public and the private sectors. According to Turner, there's some overlap of membership with the CIO Council's KM working group, and the two groups often collaborate and support each other. When his group started, Turner says, they got inquiries mostly from pioneering individuals who wanted information about using knowledge management in their agencies; now teams working on initial implementations are interested. As more members of the group work together, the resource pool and learning in the community grow.

Impressed by Bennet's success in incorporating KM into the Navy's strategic plan, Turner hopes to be part of an FAA team dispatched to learn more from the

Navy. "I believe communities are the primary resource for transfer of tacit knowledge to explicit knowledge," he says.

Along these lines, Turner is developing a project called ShareNets, an informal knowledge hub for technical subjects. "The purpose is to create a network of professionals with shared technical interests and then to create a knowledge bank together," he explains. Less structured than communities of practice, ShareNets are intended to be useful not only to regular participants but to drop-in members who need particular information. In addition to allowing members to submit ad hoc problems to their counterparts, ShareNets will contain contact information, a glossary of terms, an events calendar, forums offering various interaction capabilities and a knowledge bank of documents, links and other resources. Turner is helping to evaluate technology platforms to support the project.

## Transforming Culture

As in the private sector, the most serious obstacles to knowledge sharing in government are not mechanical, according to Susan Hanley, consulting director of Plural Inc., an e-business consultancy in Bethesda, Md. "To make a knowledge management initiative successful, you have to focus not just on technology but on culture and process as well," she says. "If you're asking people to do something differently, you're going to have to create appropriate rewards and incentives so that they will do what you want them to do."

Doing this across constituencies within the federal government is a formidable undertaking, at both the agency and the employee levels. "Each agency was founded with its own specific piece of legislation and has a specific committee it reports to [in Congress], so we're organized in a completely stovepipe way," says Remez. "All of our appropriations are given to a particular agency. It's hard to come across money that people want to share."

Individually, the problem is similar. "Historically, we don't have a culture of sharing," she adds. "To change our system so you couldn't get promoted unless you could show that you'd shared knowledge would be overly prescriptive at this point."

D.C.'s politically polarized culture is itself an obstacle to knowledge sharing, according to Patrick Plunkett, a business strategist in the GSA's Office of Governmentwide Policy. With agency-bashing a favorite congressional practice, many federal workers avoid risk. Even so, Plunkett maintains, more learning occurs when mistakes are made than when everything goes right. If an organization is to learn from its mistakes, a culture based upon trust is necessary and finger-pointing is counterproductive.

"There are far more benefits to political people for being critical than there are for being supportive," says Barry White, director of government performance projects at the Council for Excellence in Government in Washington, a nonpartisan, nonprofit organization dedicated to innovation and reform in the public sector. White, himself a recent government retiree, contrasts this climate with that of business, which generally expects its people to evaluate their course of action periodically and make necessary changes. "In government, the very notion of changing your direction is considered a sign of weakness, and you have to be nervous about it," he says. "The reaction to performance failures is not something that makes people want to go out and put themselves on the line."

Hoarding knowledge has been especially common among technical professionals, says Ron Raborg, director of software process improvement at the Social Security Administration. When the agency's PRIDE Web site first offered a storytelling feature (see the sidebar, "Building a Culture of Sharing"), it was indifferently received because the users saw no reason to share knowledge. However, after several respected project managers participated, the concept caught on and people vied to get their stories and their pictures displayed on the Web site. "Subject matter experts are beginning to share best practices pretty readily," Raborg says.

Within the GSA Remez is sponsoring several pilot programs to find ways to reward knowledge sharing. One success was a best-practices pilot in the agency's Public Building Service. Participants received small awards for sharing best practices, with the possibility of greater reward. "If you try a best practice and it works, and it helps you meet one of the financial measures that we have, you can get a larger monetary reward as a result of doing your work better," she explains.

Downsizing is another motivator for collaboration and sharing. "As you have fewer people left to do what is—at least in our agency—a growing job, you are forced to share," Remez notes.

As making the same mistake twice becomes an unaffordable luxury, storytelling projects such as the GSA's video archive of the census provide repositories of knowledge not only of success stories but also of painfully learned lessons.

Remez says that while entities such as the CIO Council are helping to foster interagency cooperation and current projects in particular agencies are candidates for deployment elsewhere, the government's development of knowledge management strategies is still at a relatively early stage. She recommends to her colleagues that they explore KM options but also urges them to follow good business practice by staying focused on the needs of their constituents and employees. "When you start a knowledge management program, think globally but act locally," she says. "It's not a good idea to start with a top-down order and develop an enterprise solution in the hope that people will come and use it, because they won't."

Instead, Remez declares, "You have to start with a business purpose and try to apply knowledge management and knowledge sharing principles to the areas where you're hurting the most. Come up with a solution that fits your business or your agency's mission."

## Building a Culture of Sharing

The Social Security Administration has been around for more than 70 years and plans to endure for centuries. As one of the more self-aware agencies of the federal government, it has been quicker than many others to explore and adopt knowledge management techniques.

In 1995, SSA launched PolicyNet, a groupware pilot project that now runs on the agency intranet and serves 80,000 users at more than 1,000 offices throughout the U.S. It receives thousands of visits per day and includes more than 130 distinct areas of collaboration. Its objective is to speed up the agency's ability to respond to changes in the law. Because policies to implement a new law often take effect immediately upon passage of that law, agency employees must have access to all materials they need to understand the new policy and be able to explain its impact to clients. Therefore, the agency must create and distribute these materials well in advance.

Subject area experts are responsible for creating the materials; if the relevant expert isn't available at the proper time, that's a problem, says Barbara Laricos, PolicyNet's project manager. In one case she mentions, a highly publicized and sensitive bill passed just as the resident expert went on an extended leave, so the task fell to a policy analyst unfamiliar with the subject. "All of a sudden, he not only had the lead for the project but had to write a 200-page instruction in a heartbeat, to get it out to folks on the front line who had customers coming in the door," she recalls.

Traditionally, Laricos says, the analyst would have written the document quickly in relative isolation; then it would go through an extensive review process. This analyst knew about PolicyNet, however, and took what within the agency's culture were the radical steps of admitting he didn't know enough about the subject matter and asking for help. Using available collaboration tools, he built an informal workgroup of people who had expertise in the area or ties to the legislation, who could review sections of the document as he went on to write others. As a result of this collaborative approach, a process that normally takes 13 weeks took only nine, and participants agreed that the document was of higher quality than if it had been created in the old way.

### PRIDE in Their Work

A new section of the SSA intranet, PRIDE (a loose acronym for Project Resource GuIDE) has been running since last July. Originally it was intended to be a resource for project management best practices and process improvement for the 2,800 IT professionals in SSA's main complex, but now application development communities throughout the country also access it. "Our mission is to build software disciplines in the IT community, capture and deliver organizational knowledge and develop a shared vision of where we're going with SSA systems," says Ron Raborg, director of software process improvement at SSA. "I think we're having that effect."

In creating materials for PRIDE, Raborg and his colleagues brought together experts in the agency"s systems communities in collaborative sessions to codify best practices they'd developed, then archived the resulting information. "Instead of telling them what the best practices are, we're gleaning their knowledge and delivering it to the rest of the IT community," says Lisa Markowski, project leader.

To kick off the site's storytelling feature, the team had the agency's most successful project managers explain their experiences with a particular software process methodology and how it had helped them. Expecting the users to be reticent about sharing knowledge, Raborg and Markowski were surprised at what happened. "We thought it was just going to be a small part of the Web site with a couple pictures and stories, but it turned out to be more popular than we expected," Markowski says. "Starting with three stories, we've had recent requests to add over 100. We've got people coming out of the woodwork wanting to tell their story about how the practices have helped them go home on time and made their lives easier."

PolicyNet is a more mature project than PRIDE, but both are evolving in response to technological advances and the needs of their users. The respective teams collaborate in an ad hoc workgroup and share ideas. One ongoing goal is to make both sites more automated and responsive to the users. Laricos' wish list includes enabling PolicyNet users to set up their own collaboration areas rather than requiring IT staff to do it.

Raborg says that while PRIDE currently is a "passive" site on which users can find information, he'd like to incorporate technology that would ask users questions and guide them to the best answers. "IT project managers don't have time to look around for things on a Web site," he notes.

*Mary Eisenhart is a freelance writer, editor, and owner of You Own Your Own Words Publishing in Oakland, Calif. She has recently contributed articles on business and technology to publications including Knowledge Management and M-Business. For 14 years she was Editor of MicroTimes, California's Computer Magazine. Contact her at marye@yoyow.com.*

# Mission E-Possible: The Cisco E-Learning Story

### Patricia A. Galagan

*John Chambers, CEO of Cisco Systems, Inc., has declared publicly that learning is a strategic priority for his company and important to the world economy. He's a strong proponent of e-learning—and trainers at Cisco are working hard to keep up with his vision.*

Cisco CEO John Chambers has done for training what trainers have long said they most wanted: Chambers declared publicly that learning is a strategic priority for his company and important to the world economy. But there's a catch. He's not talking about the kind of training that most practitioners have in mind when they seek top-level corporate support. Chambers is endorsing the fast-moving, results-oriented learning that is only possible with e-learning.

But why e-learning rather than another thriving Internet application such as e-commerce or e-health? Either one would drive network traffic and thus help Cisco sell more routers and switches.

"I love e-learning because it makes employees more productive, and it's available anytime, anywhere," says Chambers. "Although I think it will take three to four years for e-learning to make as much of an impact as e-commerce or virtual close (closing a company's financial books online), I truly believe that it will change the way schools and universities teach, the way students learn, and the way businesses keep employees up-to-date with the skills and information for this fast-changing Internet economy.

"Not only that, e-learning increases network traffic. And as the CEO of a networking company, I can only be happy about that."

So, what's it like to be a trainer in a company whose chairman has become spokesperson-in-chief for e-learning, declaring far and wide that it's the "next killer app for the Internet" and that its use will "make email look like a rounding error"? Chambers has planted a flag. What about the people who must supply the wind to make it fly at Cisco?

The epicenter for e-learning at Cisco is the Internet Learning Solutions Group. Although it's one of almost 30 training groups in the company (and not the first or the only one to introduce e-learning), it's the proving ground for e-learning as a business strategy that can be applied across the company—in business-speak, "an integrated solution."

"There are solid reasons that Cisco cares deeply about e-learning," says Mike Metz, director of marketing for the Internet Learning Solutions Group.

The first is obvious: the more people learning online, the more networking gear Cisco can sell. The second is that Cisco has big plans for growth and, consequently, has big learning needs. In 12 years, it has become an $18 billion company; in the next four years, it intends to grow to a $50 billion company.

That kind of growth will require Cisco to have a workforce of more than 50,000 employees, a 40 percent jump from today. Data from IDC, a firm that tracks and predicts information technology trends, shows that by 2003, the demand for IT networking professionals will exceed the supply, a shortfall that could leave Cisco and other Internet-related companies ambushed at the skills gap.

"We really believe that our e-learning programs are a more effective way to grow skills in high volume in a shorter time than in the past," says Metz. "It's a fundamental strategic imperative for us to train more people to plan, design, and install the Internet infrastructure that we're building."

## Making It Happen

It's one thing to strategize, another to implement, and nowhere is that more true than with e-learning. The technology is expensive, the pace is fast, and the required mind shifts can be daunting. When training is pushed to a companywide strategic level, the key decision makers are not likely to be training traditionalists.

Enter Tom Kelly, the Harley-riding, poetry-writing, bonsai-growing ex-Marine in charge of the Internet Learning Solutions Group. Kelly has 20-plus years in the training trenches. But, when it comes to e-learning, he's not afraid to attack some sacred cows. "Putting trainers in charge of e-learning is like putting postal workers in charge of email," he says.

When Chambers declared that Cisco would be the leader in e-learning, its own training operations were, to be blunt, a bit of a mess.

"Three years ago, when I joined Cisco, training was an irrelevant backwater," says Kelly. "Training was fragmented, unsupported, and unsuccessful. The gag

## Q&A with John Chambers

**Q:** By being the first CEO of a major company to publicly predict the future of e-learning, you've influenced many other business leaders to think of it in a new light. How did you come to the position you hold? Who or what persuaded you to take such a bold public stand on a relatively untried phenomenon?

**A:** There are two global equalizers in life—the Internet and education. Although the United States has one of the best university programs in the world, education at the K-12 level is broken. I believe that if we don't fix that for our children, the competitive advantage that the United States enjoys today could change. The jobs of the future are going to go to the best-educated workforce, no matter where that workforce is. Leaders around the world get that and that the Internet is going to be key to survival, including Tony Blair of the United Kingdom, Jiang Zemin of China, and Lee Tung-hui of Taiwan.

Given that, I think we need to do what's best for the next generation. E-learning helps eliminate barriers of time, distance, and socioeconomic status, so individuals are empowered to take charge of their own lifelong learning.

**Q:** What's your view of the contribution of e-learning to Cisco's success as a business?

**A:** How many times have you sat in a 40-hour class waiting for the two hours of information you wanted to hear? E-learning is a productivity tool that not only gives students personalized learning or the information to meet their needs, but also allows for assessment and accountability.

was, 'Friends don't let friends work at Cisco training.'"

"It was an interesting dynamic," says Metz, who wasn't on board at the time but who has heard stories. "There were e-learning skunk works around the company, but nothing was coordinated. And then comes this top-down directive."

"Chambers fired the gun," says Kelly. "The mission facing us was 'Make it exemplary and make it serve thousands.'"

The Internet Learning Solutions Group is the largest and most centralized training organization within Cisco, with about 165 staff supplemented by contractors as needed. To answer Chambers's challenge, the ILSG and other e-learning stakeholders across the company came together to form the Cisco E-Learning Business Council, sponsored by HR executive Barbara Beck, head of corporate marketing Keith Fox, and Doug Allred, the executive in charge of customer advocacy. The mission of the council, and therefore of the ILSG, is "to implement an integrated e-learning solution across Cisco."

The council's first task was to uncover all of the e-learning activities in the training underground and then to create processes and standards they could share. Simultaneously, IT began to provide tools for integrating e-learning across Cisco—everything from virtual classrooms to video server technology to templates for content development.

"By no means is everything integrated yet," says Metz, "but at least we're headed in that direction."

In addition to its mission to integrate e-learning across Cisco, the Internet Learning Solutions Group provides e-learning to three audiences: the 10,000 systems engineers and account managers who make up Cisco's field salesforce, the employees of the 40,000 channel partners who resell Cisco products, and hundreds of thousands of end-user customers. Rapid learning for those audiences is considered key to Cisco's growth strategy.

The ILSG's first move was to create a learning portal containing all of the learning resources that the company had for systems engineers and account managers in the field.

"The head of worldwide sales challenged us not to create more training," says Metz, "but first to aggregate, organize, and rationalize the resources that already existed but that nobody could find."

Called the Field E-Learning Connection, the portal puts learners in touch with more than 8,000 learning resources, including online learning, live class schedules, white papers, PowerPoint presentations, recommended books and videos, and more. It's organized around a set of learning roadmaps covering the jobs of every person in the field organization. About 95 percent of Cisco's 10,000 salespeople have logged on since the Field E-Learning Connection was launched in August 1999.

Diane Bauer is senior manager for e-learning marketing in the Internet Learning Solutions Group. With a beeper, a phone, and a security card clipped to her belt, Bauer accessorizes like a California dot.commie. Her outfit the day of our interview is navy pinstripes, but it's about three generations from being a suit. Over the back of her chair is a baseball jacket.

A veteran of two and a half years at Cisco, Bauer was brought in to manage field training when it was still staunchly instructor-led. "At that time, the field executive team wasn't convinced that anyone could learn anything over the Internet," she says.

Bauer arrived at the peak of the training problem. Salespeople and systems engineers were struggling to keep up with new products and technologies. The salesforce, a group of product sellers who "knew their feeds and speeds," were being groomed as solutions providers. And the systems engineers were making the transition from generalists to specialists. Their learning needs were huge.

"There was no standardized way to develop engineers. It was typical to start writing a course for them, only to find there were nine other courses just like it in other parts of the company. Everything we were doing was not meeting their needs," says Bauer.

The field executives were clear about what they wanted from training, says Bauer. They wanted to solve the problems that had plagued classroom training regarding timeliness, relevance, worldwide accessibility, and learner accountability for results. The field executives also wanted to endorse the content and design of all of the training created for their groups.

"And did I mention that they wanted 12 new curriculums rolled out in seven months?" adds Bauer.

"Some people said it was impossible, but that didn't stop us," she says. Following a common Cisco practice when given a mandate but little staff or funds, the ILSG built a virtual e-learning organization made up of people from all over the company. Once they got organized, the group built and rolled out the Field E-Learning Connection in less than five months.

"To make the training relevant and timely, we knew it had to be modular," says Bauer. "That, plus the requirement that it had to be accessible around the world, meant our solution had to be built on the Internet." Subject matter experts and curriculum designers created roadmaps outlining the competencies for each job in the field—everything from sales to systems engineering to account management.

To help the systems engineers become specialists, the number of learning tracks went from three to 29. "We were having trouble scaling the curriculum model to meet the number of new job requirements. Moving to the concept of roadmaps aligned with job skills and then plugging in resources or building them led naturally to the use of reusable learning objects," says Bauer.

Once the field executives endorsed the curriculum plan, the ILSG started building the infrastructure for a learning portal. But then they had to decide what learning resources to put into the portal, and a small war broke out among the trainers over the question, *What is training and what isn't?*

That a purely philosophical quibble could nearly derail a major training initiative lies at the heart of why trainers are often not asked to develop e-learning. Imagine the irony of spending 18 months demonstrating to top management that an e-learning orientation is a huge strategic advantage and having your CEO publicly endorse e-learning, only to have your training staff dig in their heels over conceptual purity. As Cisco trainers debated the "What is training?" issue with the zeal of theologians arguing over what's necessary for salvation, Tom Kelly came to a quick decision: he shut down the strict constructionists.

"Our message was 'That's caca.' E-learning is about information, communication, education, *and* training. That's a huge message that people don't hear often or well," says Kelly.

"Regardless of how trainers categorize training and education," Kelly adds, "the learner only wants the skill and knowledge to do a better job or answer the next question from a customer. So here at Cisco, we view it all as content.

"The important thing is to have good content out there. Does it have to be instructionally sound? Some of it should be. Does *all* of it have to be? No. Does that diminish its value? No, not to the learner. Only to those of us who wander around with our master's or Ph.D.s in instructional design."

Predictably, some trainers moved on to other business units. The team that remained forged ahead with a new kind of training unit. They spent little time designing and delivering training and more time putting training and communication tools in front of subject matter experts. They also worked hard to market e-learning and its benefits, and to develop processes for getting the learning out as fast as possible. Instead of building learning tools and systems, they bought them readymade and worked with IT to integrate them into Cisco networks and systems.

## Measuring Success

The Internet Learning Solutions Group found that the shift to e-learning changed their measures of success. "Reaching competency quickly is what counts now—not the thickness of the book, the length of the class, or the number of people in the seats," says Bauer. On the road to competency, a person may have formal training, do private study, read a white paper, listen to a seminar, or attend an event. Bauer continues, "The point is, did they come out competent, sooner rather than later?"

Once the team had built the Web-enabled roadmaps and started to add learning resources, it could figure out what else the site needed, such as security or search capability.

"If it existed, we said paint it blue and call it *available;* if it didn't exist, paint it white and call it *not built.* That let the user community see that even if we hadn't built everything, we had a plan. A person could mouse over the white boxes on the site to see when something was coming."

One of the requirements set for the e-learning program was accessibility. It had to be easy and quick to use. Putting it on the Cisco intranet helped solve the accessibility problem; introducing choice helped shorten learning time. If a learning objective was to be able to explain the function of firewalls, list the types of firewalls, and demonstrate firewall configurations, the site could give users the choice of viewing a video, attending a class, reading the firewall primer, or taking part in a collaborative event. At the end, the system tested the user's knowledge of firewalls as prescribed in the learning objective.

The site contains an assessment engine that is built into the competency roadmaps. At first, it provided only pre- and post-learning assessments, but now assessment questions appear throughout a module. The assessment software can direct a user back to certain material if necessary, making the assessment more of a learning aid and less of a smart-o-meter.

Some of the e-learning is assessed with the help of live mentors who observe learners' new skills in action, for example on a sales call. The goal is to have online mentors—experts around the globe—available 24 hours a day. The site also offers a storehouse of CBT and interactive multimedia instruction that the e-learning team broke into modules, tagged, and put into an LMS. The LMS tracks their use and wraps in assessment as needed.

The site also provides online access to Cisco's equipment labs so that a learner can connect from a browser to a rack of Cisco equipment, open an interactive training session, and try configuring a switch or a router before doing it at a customer's site. The company saves the cost of sending systems engineers to remote classroom labs, and the systems people gain control over when and where they test out on live equipment.

All of those options for learners—round-the-clock access, lots of choice in how to reach a learning objective, and plenty of feedback—promote a state of continual learning for which the learner, not the instructor, takes responsibility.

"We're breaking down the notion that learning is an event-only model," says Bauer. The flip side is a whole new way of working for the trainer. "When you move from static, event-based learning to e-learning, you're never done. You have to keep your content fresh and continually improve your site. You're just like a dot.com."

E-learning startups tend to follow a learning curve, Bauer notes. The first phase is about Web-enabling your content: just get some courses on the Web, organize them by communities, and offer them through a portal. Next, modularize the content into database objects. Then put content development tools in front of subject matter experts and have the system alert them when their content is aging.

The second phase is about performance. That's where e-learning begins to tie content to performance and measure results more explicitly. Some questions to ask: Are we mapping learning objects to competencies? Are we measuring learners' competency before, during, and after learning?

The next step for the site is a state called learner-centricity. "Instead of having to follow learning roadmaps, users will have customized learning pushed to them as needed," explains Bauer. In addition, the system will be smart enough to know a user's connectivity requirements (how much bandwidth is available), performance needs, and preferred learning style. Indeed, the system will grow smarter about a user with each subsequent log-on, enabling the site to dish up ever more relevant learning snippets.

"We want to be there within three years," says Bauer.

For now, the ISLG is working on more dynamic roadmaps, better search capabilities, improved assessment, and stronger reporting capabilities. That last improvement will enable the site software to report to managers the skill and knowledge levels of the technical salesforce, relative to new strategies. Indirectly, it is a predictor of hiring and training needs.

"One of the most challenging things we face on the road to customization is mobilizing thousands of content contributors without creating chaos," says Bauer. "We're requiring content providers to tag their data by such categories as type, form, audience, origin, language, author's ID, start and end dates, and so forth."

## Again, but Faster

The Field E-Learning Connection had barely launched when the Internet Learning Solutions Group turned its attention to its second customer segment—the 40,000 companies that resell Cisco networking gear. Spread over 132 countries, this audience numbers more than 200,000 people who need to keep up with Cisco products and obtain certification in their use.

The Field E-Learning Connection was all built internally and took seven months from concept to launch. John Chambers didn't think that was fast enough, so for the Partner E-Learning Connection, the ISLG leaned heavily on vendors and got it running in three months—just in time for the worldwide Cisco partner summit in Las Vegas, at which Chambers made his now-famous prediction about e-learning.

Lessons and shortcuts from the field program helped ISLG produce a learning portal that was more personalized than its first one. "When you sign on," says Metz, "it knows who you are, what company you're with, what market you serve, and what geography your company works in. Already, it can push information to users."

The partner site builders, numbering about 100 people, worked in teams covering site development, technology, marketing, content, and prototypes. "We were on such a short timeline that turf wars never had time to develop," says Lisa Baumert, senior manager of the partner site.

As with the field site, the partner connection team made sure it had leadership and stakeholder support from the start, says Baumert. "Cisco people and channel partners from many countries were part of our extended development and pilot teams." Weekly conference calls and access to the site prototype kept them involved. "Getting their buy-in along the way meant that at launch time we had global support."

The portal offers many kinds of learning opportunities, including Web-based courses, interactive multimedia, streaming video, video-on-demand, simulations, audio-on-demand, and more. "We can offer users choices in how to access content depending on how they learn best," says Baumert.

"Our goal," she continues, "is to provide very personalized learning tailored to each user's experience and learning objectives. Eventually, the site will be able to prescribe just those parts of a curriculum that would benefit someone most,

## Switched On

Glen Tapley is a trainer who made the switch to e-learning. One month after he was hired by Cisco as an instructor, the word went out that his training unit "was no longer in the instruction business." Tapley had joined Cisco just as it was getting serious about e-learning.

Burned out by a previous instructor job that kept him on the road 80 percent of the time, he was ready for a change. "My kids would cry on the way to the airport when I headed out for another week away from home."

Now, Tapley is a technical education consultant in Cisco's Internet Learning Solutions Group, a job he sees as having advantages over his previous role as a fulltime classroom instructor.

"E-learning doesn't require skills I didn't already have, but it takes more flexibility of thought to apply the things I used to do to this new arena," says Tapley. It's also easier to get set up to do on-line instruction. "Instead of going to a hotel meeting room with tons of equipment, I just need a couple of PCs and an Internet connection."

Tapley admits that for an instructor, there are downsides to e-learning in its current state. "A lot of old-time trainers moved on to other business units (when e-learning became a priority) because they wanted more platform time. I understand their choice. There's a satisfaction you get from seeing the light go on in someone's eyes when they understand a complex topic. The instructor doesn't get that satisfaction from e-learning."

But Tapley is confident that e-learning will change and improve so that the excitement of the classroom becomes part of the e-learning experience. "In the meantime," he says, "there's plenty of encouragement at Cisco to figure out how to make e-learning better."

---

given their experience. In our decisions about features, functionality, and content, we kept coming back to the user."

Since the Partner E-Learning Connection launched in March 2000, about 30 percent of Cisco's partner companies have logged on. So far, the top countries accessing the site include the United States, the United Kingdom, China, Germany, and Australia. However, reports have tracked individuals from 132 different countries logging on, adds Baumert, "indicating its global appeal."

For the moment, the site language is English, "but we're working with our local offices to translate some courses into Chinese, Korean, Spanish, and Portuguese," says Baumert. "In Asia, localization is more important for the sales content than for the technical content. We're still figuring out how to prioritize the localization effort."

The Partner E-Learning Connection resides outside of the Cisco firewall and thus presents some unique technical challenges. Its users around the globe have varying types of Internet access and unequal amounts of bandwidth. "Access speed is an issue for countries outside the United States," says Baumert, "but also for people in the United States who are logging on to the site from a slow modem at home."

Because e-learning is a relatively new phenomenon for many of Cisco's channel partners, there is a need to market its benefits and promote its use. Baumert advises having a marketing plan to drive awareness and send people to the site.

Baumert is clearly jazzed about working on an e-learning project of this scale. "It's an Internet application that will grow. It's an exciting mix of technology and content, and it can help solve business problems. So, I'm excited to come to work every day."

## Rocky Road

All is not smooth on the road to e-learning, even at Cisco, where conditions make it likely to prosper. The ILSG must continually prove that e-learning works and why. "Everyone wants to know how much you save with e-learning," says Metz, "but the important discussion is what are the things you can do once you have the infrastructure installed that you simply couldn't do in the old model."

Cisco acquires a new partner company on average once every two-and-a-half weeks. Before the Field E-learning Connection established a primary source for learning, account managers had to consult hundreds of internal Websites and wade through piles of email to keep up with acquisitions information. Now the acquisitions page on the Field E-Learning Connection has one of the highest hit rates of any page on the portal.

Before the Field E-Learning Connection existed, salespeople spent days in training away from their customers, peers, and managers, so online learning was a pretty obvious benefit from a time standpoint. But to test how e-learning would work compared to classroom training, the field e-learning team studied 200 resellers taking a certification course. Half attended live classes and labs and took part in study groups. The other half took their training online and used remote labs and online discussion groups. All were tested at the end: the e-learners had a 10 percent better pass rate than the classroom learners.

"The real benefit," adds Metz, "came in the opportunity savings. The classroom learners were out of pocket for a week, away from customers and co-workers. The online learners fit their learning into the valleys of their schedules and experienced little or no hit to business productivity."

There have been substantial savings from e-learning programs at Cisco, especially in manufacturing, the site of one of the most aggressive skunk works. Assembly line workers haven't seen a classroom since 1999; they have access to e-learning right on the factory floor. The result was savings of $1 million per quarter in improved process, and an 80 percent increase in speed to competence.

Another e-learning coup for that unit involved training for ISO 9000 registration. For its initial registration three years earlier, Cisco budgeted $1.4 million for classroom training. In late 1999, it spent less than $20,000 for the training delivered online, with better results measured as fewer inconsistencies with ISO standards. And while the ISO readiness program achieved 100 percent participation across a user community of 6,000 manufacturing and customer service employees, internal e-learning implementation took only four weeks from concept to global execution.

"People like to argue that e-learning isn't as effective as the classroom," says Tom Kelly, "but how effective *is* the classroom? Most of us know that classroom teaching produces about a 25 percent retention rate in the first 10 days, with a decline in skill if you don't use it.

"Tests we've done show equal or better retention with e-learning, mostly because it's targeted at what a person needs to know when they need to know it. Spend 40 hours in a classroom and how many hours of good content will there be that are applicable to you? Not many."

Classroom training's biggest benefit is human interaction, says Kelly, "and none of that happens while the instructor is talking. The benefits of informal learning through interaction give us a way to talk about how to improve e-learning. The big question is how to get human interaction in the e-learning process.

"Cost is the only argument managers will listen to. But it's not right to do e-learning if it's cost-effective but not learning-effective."

Kelly likes to argue that training and its costs should be part of product development, not an afterthought. "Until we make products that don't require any training, training is a product cost just like documentation or packaging the product in a box." To make his point, Kelly ended the practice of having ILSG develop product training.

As a result, more business units budgeted training dollars in 2000 than in past years. Some hired additional professional staff, anticipating that they'd have to pull people out periodically to do training or to create training materials. "It's a recognition that dollars have to be spent on training," says Kelly.

Proving that e-learning saves money and delivers real learning is almost easy compared to another challenge that crops up in companies making major shifts from the classroom to the Internet: making learning time a respected part of a job.

"If you're sitting at your desk going through an interactive exercise or watching a video or, God forbid, reading a book, people think you're not really working," says Kelly. "You're open to Anyone Who Comes Along With a Problem."

At Cisco, a land of cubicles, people who are taking part in an online class can put up yellow police tape to signal that they're busy learning. "We're trying to get

e

## Lessons from a Leader

Presuming top-level support and a good technology infrastructure, here's how to launch an e-learning program.

- Select a target audience whose learning has obvious strategic value to the company. Sales and service employees are a good bet. So are customers.
- If your e-learning mandate comes without a big staff and a budget, build a virtual e-learning team from all across the company. You'll need this anyway to install your e-learning on existing IT systems and to get the bosses of your target audience to support e-learning.
- Take yourself off the stage. Be prepared to let others (nontrainers) have the final say on training design. Give subject matter experts the tools to create good content. Make them accountable for content timeliness and learners responsible for becoming competent.
- To whatever results you are measuring, be sure to add time to competence. E-learning is about nothing so much as it's about speed.
- Start fast and get faster. Use such timesavers as templates and reusable learning objects to make subsequent versions of e-learning happen faster. Remember that e-learning is not an event but a continuous process.
- Don't build everything yourself. That's what vendors and partners are for.
- Market your e-learning effort inside and outside of the company. Anything as new as e-learning needs to be explained early and often.
- Don't get sucked into public debates about whether e-learning is real learning or whether information is a learning resource. Although those topics may keep you up at night, airing them at work makes you seem out of touch with real business issues.

across that learning is a valued part of a job," says Kelly.

Another significant problem facing e-learning, says Kelly, is that there are no widely used industry standards for the tools on the market, and so the tools don't work together—no matter what their creators claim. "Eight years ago, you couldn't send email between different systems even if you were in the same company. That's about where we are in e-learning today."

Kelly doesn't believe that e-learning will change the way people learn. "People will always learn through their senses and by using their bodies, their hands, and their feet. What e-learning changes is the way people teach. I see that trainers have a choice about e-learning: take a risk and try something new, or go somewhere else where their old skills still have value and there's no need to change."

Kelly's personal hope for e-learning is that it will serve a higher purpose than just training the next salesperson or the next customer in a cheaper way. He hopes it becomes the tool that brings the best teachers in the world, the best lesson plans, and the most enthusiasm for learning to the students who want it, anywhere in the world.

"My hope is that e-learning expands their horizons and gives them the skills to achieve a brighter future."

*Patricia A. Galagan is editor-in-chief of the ASTD Magazine Group and ASTD's e-learning spokesperson. You can e-mail her at pgalagan@astd.org.*

# Ready for Liftoff

## Kim Kiser

*Insurance agents haven't been at the forefront of the technology revolution. Prudential Insurance decided several years ago to promote technology, with its LaunchPad program. This article describes this initiative and reports on the results and lessons learned.*

B arbara Burke is racing a deadline. It's mid-December and in order to maintain her certified financial planner designation, the San Rafael, Calif., sales representative for Prudential Insurance has to complete a two-hour ethics course by the end of the month.

Several years ago, Burke would have found herself in a predicament. She would have had to send away for written materials, take the course and submit proof that she'd passed the exam. If she missed the deadline, the Certified Financial Planner Board of Standards could rescind her title. Today, however, she is able to call up The American College in Bryn Mawr, Pa., which offers an approved course, give them her credit card number and within hours receive the online course via Lotus Notes. The college automatically tells the board whether she's successfully completed the training.

Several years ago, taking a course online wouldn't have been possible for another reason: Burke didn't have much experience with computers or the Internet. In fact, she didn't really enter the electronic age until Prudential's LaunchPad program lifted off in 1997. That year, the company began a $100 million initiative to issue IBM ThinkPad laptops to 12,000 salespeople, managers and support staff and to train them how to use technology to improve their productivity. The laptops came equipped with Lotus Notes, a client data system, a client management system, a desktop marketing system and other software.

The project, which was completed in 1999, earned the Newark, N.J., company recognition from *Beyond Computing* and *Network World* magazines for its effort to create a wired work force in an industry that's not known for being on the front lines of the technology revolution.

"Our industry is very slow to change," says Bill Wilson, director of the Independent Insurance Agents of America's (IIAA) virtual university. "When you think about the levels of automation at banks and airlines, the insurance industry runs decades behind them."

## The Countdown Begins

When Prudential introduced LaunchPad, employees' response to the idea of working and training on computers was lukewarm. "Fifty percent of the people we rolled LaunchPad out to—the agent population—were 45-plus and relatively successful in their businesses. Not only were they not comfortable with the technology, but they saw no compelling reason why this would make them more successful," says Jody Doele, vice president of learning and leadership development for the company.

But the strong arm of the Internet and ecommerce couldn't be ignored. For one thing, Web-savvy customers were beginning to shop online for the best insurance rates, and they expected immediate email responses to their queries 24 hours a day, seven days a week.

In addition, the industry itself had changed. When Burke joined Prudential in 1986, her job was selling life and homeowners' policies. Since then, the lines between insurance companies, banks and financial services firms have blurred. If agents who once sold home and auto coverage wanted to get ahead, they would have to able to analyze their clients' financial needs, advise them on how to save for their children's education, counsel them in regard to changing tax laws and, if they owned a business, help them determine what kind of retirement or health plan might be best for their employees.

"It's evolved from a product sale to looking at the full client," says Burke, who is a certified financial planner as well as a registered investment advisor and licensed salesperson.

The need for new skills meant the need for more training. Not only would agents have to go back to school to earn designations such as certified financial planner, but they'd also have to continue taking state-mandated education in order to keep their insurance licenses up to date. On top of that, they would have to take classes required by their employers to learn about new and changing products.

The need for all this training has made the move to e-learning a logical but not necessarily fast one for the industry. Although figures on the number of insurance agents who take their training online don't exist, WebCE.com, a Richardson, Texas, e-learning company that serves the insurance industry, found that 44 states plus the District of Columbia allow insurance salespeople to take online courses to renew their licenses. In addition, PIA Management Services in Glenmont, N.Y., which serves insurance agents in Connecticut, New Hampshire, New Jersey and New York, opened an e-training center for members last June. And the IIAA, a national trade association in Alexandria, Va., has been beta-testing its virtual university with plans to roll it out later this spring.

"Our marketing division did an informal survey to get an idea of what people are doing now and what they're interested in. They found there's not a whole lot of online learning going on in our industry yet, but that it absolutely will grow," says the IIAA's Wilson.

## Exploring a New Universe

Prudential made its move into e-learning after the introduction of LaunchPad. Up until then, the majority of product training was done in the classroom. Burke recalls traveling to places such as San Francisco, Berkeley and Santa Rosa five or six times a year for product launches and other training. "It was a lot of travel and a lot of time away from the office," she recalls. And a lot of time away from potential and existing clients.

Then there was the chore of keeping track of the courses she had completed and those she still needed to take. Looking back, Burke laughs about the technologically advanced monitoring tool she used: a checklist on a yellow legal pad.

In 1997, as salespeople and managers were going through classroom and CD-ROM training to learn to use their new laptops, staff from Prudential's professional development and marketing technology departments began working with KnowledgePlanet. The Reston, Va., e-learning vendor would help them create a Web-based system on which salespeople could launch courses, take exams and track both online and classroom training from any computer that could connect to the company's intranet.

As they built the Prudential Learning Network (PLN), staff from KnowledgePlanet and Prudential needed to put information on the Web quickly, so they converted some of the books and white papers used for product training to HTML-based courses. "The first phase was straightforward page-turning; it was boring," says Randy Eckels, a KnowledgePlanet vice president, who was involved in converting the courses and integrating them into the learning management system (LMS).

They also had to fit several courses created by outside vendors into the system. In order to work with the LMS, the courses needed to comply with the Aviation Industry CBT Committee (AICC) standards. Eckels says they had to test each one to make sure KnowledgePlanet's platform could indeed track progress and results.

"Typically when someone says they're AICC-compliant, there are various versions of the standard. You can never be certain of what they mean when they say that," he says. So far, they haven't had compatibility problems between the LMS and the courses.

As developers from KnowledgePlanet began customizing their hosted LMS for Prudential, they discovered a unique requirement: the system would have to be able to handle a wave of users coming online at the 11th hour to complete courses before a deadline. "We would see incredible peak use at midnight before the time was up," Eckels says. "A lot of planning had to go into making sure that when that peak capacity hit, performance was acceptable and users had a good experience."

But that's not what happened the first time they tested the system. Eckels recalls how the network "dragged to a screeching halt" the first time they encountered a crunch. Before rolling out the system companywide, KnowledgePlanet had to pump up the bandwidth. "We started with a 256-kilobit line and had to go to a fractional T1," Eckels says.

Since December 1998, when the Web-based version of PLN went live, Prudential has been using it to deliver training on its own products as well as on topics such as business insurance, estate planning, 401(k) plans, disability, long-term care and Medicare supplement insurance. Eight of those courses are approved for continuing education credit in most states.

Eckels says KnowledgePlanet has been gathering data in an effort to improve some of the homegrown modules. He hopes to work with the Prudential team to make the text-based page-turners more interactive—and more compelling—by using learning objects (small chunks of content that can be swapped among courses) to deliver individualized content to people with different needs and learning styles.

## All Systems "Go"

So far, some 7,000 agents are tapping into PLN daily to get notifications about new product training, take Web-based courses and assessments, and access their transcripts so they can track which company- and state-mandated courses they've completed, according to Doele.

The system, which logs more than 20,000 completed assessments each month and has had a record high of 33,000, has also saved the company more than $3 million. Such savings have prompted Prudential to look for other ways to use technology to deliver training.

"Starting a year ago, we made a very concerted effort to reduce the amount of face-to-face time necessary," says Anne Starobin, vice president of professional development for retail distribution, the department that oversees sales staff training. During that time, Starobin's group has been experimenting with a blended approach that combines videoconferencing, synchronous online courses and classroom time to train the managers who run Prudential's agencies. They also have been testing different delivery methods to teach newly hired financial services managers about products, policies and procedures.

According to Starobin, approximately 75 percent of management training and nearly 90 percent of the training for established agents is now technology-delivered.

The success of PLN has encouraged other parts of the organization to launch their own e-learning initiatives. Doele says her group has been piloting a system similar to PLN and hopes to someday have a learning network that will serve all of the company's 58,000 employees. She ultimately wants to use technology to create "living personnel files" that will detail employees' job competencies and point them toward training to help with their professional development.

"Computer-based training, video streaming, anything you use technology to do presents us with tons of opportunities to change the paradigm of how people think about education and learning," she says. "It moves it more toward: How do I gain knowledge when I need it to enhance my performance?"

## Enjoying the Ride

Online classes aren't the only part of Prudential's e-learning initiative that helps improve performance. Burke says LaunchPad's capabilities have helped her be more productive and, for the past three years, be named to the Million Dollar Round Table. The Round Table, an association for professionals in the life insurance-based financial services business, recognizes agents who earn a certain amount in commissions each year.

Burke has been using LaunchPad to teach as well as learn, creating PowerPoint presentations to help educate her clients. "If you can present something from a multimedia approach, all of a sudden understanding goes up. When people understand something and it has meaning for them, they get motivated to proceed," she says.

She also uses reference software to get immediate, up-to-date information on taxes and other topics. And using a program that analyzes cash flow and savings, she can show clients how much money they'd have available at retirement if they increased their savings by $300 a month, for example.

In addition, LaunchPad's client data system has helped the confessed Post-it Note queen keep tabs on her 2,000-plus clients. "I know who had a baby, where they went on vacation, what question they asked last week and whether it was followed up on," she says.

But what's helped Burke the most is the ability to do business anytime, anyplace. Last year, when her mother was terminally ill, Burke went online from a hospital room in Knoxville, Tenn., and communicated with her assistant and colleagues. "LaunchPad allowed me to run my business across the country for almost two months," she says.

## Ensuring Learning

Training managers from Prudential have learned several lessons about designing technology-based courses:

**Stick to the subject.** "If content is directly related to the problems agents face in a sales situation or trying to fill out an application, they relish the opportunity to utilize the technology," says Jody Doele, vice president of learning and leadership development for the company. If not, it will be a hard sell.

**Let learners help with the design.** When developing courses, Anne Starobin, vice president of professional development for retail distribution, says she pulls together a team that includes representatives from Prudential's training department, subject matter experts and trainees. "By the time we roll something out, we have a good understanding of who the audience is and what their learning preferences seem to be, and we have buy-in and advocacy from field management and sales professionals because they have been involved from the beginning," she says.

**Don't ask for smiles.** When looking for feedback about online courses, Starobin prefers to use online surveys rather than smile sheets. "We ask specific questions about the knowledge they gained, three things they learned that they'll do differently, and how they felt about the methodology," she explains.

It also allowed Burke, who has been working toward her charter life underwriting and charter financial consultant licenses, to continue her studies by logging on to the Internet or popping in a CD-ROM whenever she had the time. "I don't lug books anymore, anywhere," she says.

*Kim Kiser (kkiser@onlinelearningmag.com) is managing editor of* Online Learning Magazine.

# Blended Learning Case Study

## Jennifer Hofmann

*Recipe for blended learning: start with a few online tutorials, add one synchronous event and a pinch of discussion forums for flavor, and stir. And, the author concludes, "Most imperative, bring together the right team ... and be willing to fail a few times in order to get the right blend."*

Every few months a new trend hits the training industry. One of the latest trends revolves around the application of blended learning solutions. The idea behind blended learning is that instructional designers review a learning program, chunk it into modules, and determine the best medium to deliver those modules to the learner. Various media include, but are not limited to, technologies such as

- traditional classroom or lab settings
- reading assignments
- CD-ROM
- performance support tools
- teletraining
- stand-alone Web-based training
- asynchronous Web-based training
- synchronous Web-based training.

During the past year I worked on a project that epitomized the concept of blended training. The client, which we'll refer to as ACME Training Solutions, was a soft-skills training provider that was recognized for its high-quality traditional classroom courses. The company was feeling pressure from clients to deliver content via alternative, preferably Web-based, methods. ACME needed to develop quality—and marketable—training products based on their existing proven content.

That seemingly monumental task was assigned to a product development team. To start, the development team needed to decide whether soft-skills could be taught using online learning tools. Generally, soft-skills training, such as management development, focuses on skills that people must exhibit through interaction. The questions facing the team were *Can you teach soft skills online?* and *Are synchronous practice sessions realistic?*

The answer was a resounding *Yes*. The team's research also revealed that synchronous practice is more realistic than traditional face-to-face methods for certain audiences because they use those skills over email and the telephone more than in face-to-face environments.

The team's second order of business was to conduct a needs analysis that identified the following critical success factors:

- Asynchronous Web modules needed to be developed to deliver the course's core content.
- Follow-up courses using a live, synchronous medium were necessary to provide learners an opportunity to practice skills.

## Tools

Early on, the product development team recognized that developing Web-based training was a far reach from their core competency of developing traditional classroom training. Therefore, the team enlisted vendors with specific areas of expertise to support each critical success factor.

To challenge and engage learners, the development team needed to produce courses that offered more than the average page-turner tutorials. After reviewing several authoring packages, the team decided to use Macromedia Flash to create asynchronous learning modules. Flash gives developers the capability and tools to build interactive and visually effective programs that can be delivered over low bandwidth.

The asynchronous modules the developers built included read-only content for learners new to the subject matter and more interactive and complicated tools for learners who had participated in other learning events and needed refresher materials. Audio was incorporated throughout the modules.

Likewise, the team's research and participation in several live demos led them to select Centra's Symposium as the synchronous classroom tool based on its capability to create breakout rooms.

# The Blend

The team spent a year designing and testing the new program. Its final instructional concoction was a blend of training technologies that answered market needs while remaining true to the content's quality. Basic course features included the following.

**Tech checks.** Learners can't be successful if the technology doesn't work. The first step in the learning process was to download the required software—Centra Symposium and, if necessary, the Flash plug-in. Next, learners had to test the software plug-ins for functionality. Technical support assistance was available.

**"Learn How to Learn Online" program.** In many organizations, the first part of a synchronous program is spent teaching first-time learners the point-and-click classroom's system and features. The team found that 10 to 15 minutes was ample time to learn navigation basics, but more time was needed to master learning in this type of environment.

Based on that feedback, the team created a "Learn How To Learn Online" program, which consisted of introductions, a tools overview, ground rules, and tips for creating an effective learning environment. It also focused on the curriculum's blended qualities and explained policies for using the asynchronous module, such as attendance and participation.

That type of instruction may be tedious for participants who have participated in synchronous events previously. Be sure to offer learners the option to opt out of this feature.

**Participant guides.** Although participant guides are often absent in Web-based training, a well-designed participant guide can be a critical success factor for synchronous programs. The team took pains to ensure that the guide wasn't a simple book containing copies of the same screens used online. The participant guide contained prework exercises and module instructions.

**Asynchronous Web modules.** Asynchronous modules present content that's essential to the learning process and can be accessed at a learner's individual pace. Throughout the course, the modules challenge users to make crucial decisions that reinforce the skills being presented. Requiring one to two hours to complete, the asynchronous features offer additional information on key concepts, examples, interactive exercises, and assessments. The modules also contain tools—in this instance, forms—that learners are required to complete, print, and bring with them to the synchronous event. The team found that learners who didn't complete the asynchronous modules were less likely to be successful in the live event.

**Live, instructor-led events.** Synchronous events are key to the learning design because they give learners the opportunity to ask questions, interact with peers, and practice skills in a more realistic environment. Because the instructional design for the original classroom initiatives was based on small group interactions and practice, breakout rooms were a natural online tool.

**Just-in-time tools.** To help facilitate lifelong learning, participants were directed back to the reinforcement tools in the asynchronous Web modules, including examples, refresher exercises, tip sheets, and so forth.

## Lessons Learned

During the year of design and testing, the development team spent a great deal of time learning. The first difficult lesson was that not all participants will follow directions or do prework. The development team had to find creative ways to ensure that the asynchronous modules and other pre-class assignments were completed, such as the forms that learners had to complete to understand the synchronous class discussion.

Next, because many things were happening at the same time during the complicated synchronous design, the team added a producer role to help facilitate the learning process. The producer was responsible for the following tasks:

- Warm up learners before class begins.
- Assist facilitation, especially in breakout rooms.
- Scribe on the whiteboard.
- Respond to chat notes.
- Launch surveys and breakout rooms.
- Resolve technical questions and problems.
- Handle late arrivals and disruptive participants.

Perhaps the biggest lesson learned by the entire team was that re-creating learning online and determining the right blend isn't easy or to be taken lightly. To create interactions that meet the same standards as traditional programs, invest the time to research the audience and the technology tools. Most imperative, bring together the right team, either internal or external, and be willing to fail a few times in order to get the right blend.

*Jennifer Hofmann is president of InSync Training Synergy, a company specializing in synchronous learning. She can be reached at jennifer@insynctraining.com.*

# E-Learning Resources

ere is a list of resources associated with e-learning and training and development. We've gathered relevant Web sites, discussion lists, articles, and books, along with some handy Web development tools. Since we encourage continuing professional development and participation in communities of practice, we've also included a list of magazines, journals, and professional organizations that target training and performance professionals.

## Learning, Training, and Technology

About.com (www.about.com/)

ASTD Learning Communities (www.astd.org)

Brandon-hall.com (www.brandon-hall.com)

Brandon Hall's Discussion Group About Online Learning Management Systems (groups.yahoo.com/group/brandonhall-ils)

Brandon Hall's Discussion Group for E-Learning Authoring Tools (groups.yahoo.com/group/brandonhall)

Brint.com (www.brint.com/)

CEO Forum (STaR Charts and Reports) (www.ceoforum.org)

DEOS-L—Distance Education (www.ed.psu.edu/acsde/deos/deos-l/deosl.asp)

Distance Education Clearinghouse (www.uwex.edu/disted/home.html)

Distance Educator (www.distance-educator.com)

Education Network Australia (www.edna.edu.au)

Education Queensland (New Basics) (www.education.qld.gov.au)

elearningpost (www.elearningpost.com)

Explorations in Learning & Instruction: The Theory Into Practice Database (home.sprynet.com/~gkearsley/tip/)

Influent Technology Group (www.influent.com)

ITFORUM (itech1.coe.uga.edu/itfForum/home.html)

League for Innovation in the Community College (www.league.org)

Learnativity (www.learnativity.com)

The MASIE Center, the Technology and Learning ThinkTank (www.masie.com)

Minnesota ODNetwork—General training and development information (www.mnodn.org/about_OD/od_defn.htm)

NETTRAIN—Teaching online (listserv.acsu.buffalo.edu/archives/nettrain.html)

North Central Regional Technology in Education Consortium (2000) *Plugging In* (www.ncrtec.org/capacity/plug/plug.htm)

Online Learning Reviews (mailto: OLReviews@vnulearning.com)

Quality Training (www.qualitymag.com/training99.html).

ROInet—evaluation and measurement of HRD and training (groups.yahoo.com/group/ROInet)

SmartForce (www.smartforce.com)

Stanford University Learning Lab (learninglab.stanford.edu/)

TCM Internet Services: Training & Development Community Center (www.tcm.com/trdev)

Techies.com (www.techies.com/)

TechLearn (www.techlearn.com)

TechLearn Trends (mailto: techlearn-trends@lister.masie.com)

Teleport Internet Services (www.teleport.com)

Training and Development Discussion Forum (groups.yahoo.com/group/trdev/)

Training Business E-Visory (mailto: esfusion@sellmoretraining.com)

Training Registry (www.trainingregistry.com)

Training Super Site (www.trainingsupersite.com)

TrainingZONE (www.trainingzone.co.uk/)

UK-HRD (www.ukhrd.com)

WBTOLL-L—Web-Based Training/Online Learning Listserv (www.training-place.com/source/thelist.html)

Web-Based Instruction Resource Site (www.stockton.edu/~harveyd/WBI/main.htm)

Web-Based Training Information Center (www.filename.com/wbt/index.html)

# Knowledge Management

Brint on Knowledge Management (www.brint.com/km/)

International Center for Applied Studies in Information Technology, Knowledge
 Management Central (www.icasit.org/km/)

The KNOW Network—A community of knowledge-based organizations
 (www.knowledgebusiness.com/home/index.asp)

*Knowledge Management* (magazine)
 (www.destinationcrm.com/km/dcrm_km_index.asp)

Knowledge Management for Training Professionals—San Diego Sandbox (defcon.
 sdsu.edu/1/objects/km/welcome/)

Knowledge Nurture—Buckman Laboratories (www.knowledge-nurture.com/)

KnowledgeOne.com (www.knowledgeone.com/Mkm/lwko/index.asp)

# Learning Objects and Standards

Advanced Distributed Learning (ADL) Network (www.adlnet.org)

Aviation Industry CBT Committee (AICC) (www.aicc.org)

IEEE Learning Technology Standards Committee (LTSC) (ltsc.ieee.org)

IMS Global Learning Consortium (www.imsproject.org)

Learnativity: All About Learning Technology Standards
 (www.learnativity.com/standards.html)

# Performance

American Productivity & Quality Center (www.apqc.org)

Bad Human Factors Designs (www.baddesigns.com)

EPSScentral (www.epssinfosite.com)

*First Things Fast: A Handbook for Performance Analysis* and free web tool
 (www.josseybass.com/legacy/rossett/rossett.html)

Zigon Performance Group (www.zigonperf.com/resources/links.html)

# Tools for Developing Quizzes and Surveys

CASTLE—Computer Assisted Teaching and Learning (www.le.ac.uk/castle/)

Create A Quiz (pc-shareware.com/quiz.htm)

Dazzler Deluxe (www.intelamedia.com/visitors_index.htm)

Hot Potatoes (web.uvic.ca/hrd/halfbaked/mactutor/index.htm)

Question Mark (www.questionmark.com/us/home.htm)

Quiz Factory (www.learningware.com/quizfactory/)

QuizPlease (quizplease.com/)

Test Generator (www.testshop.com/)

Xenu's Link Sleuth (checks Web sites for broken links)
   (home.snafu.de/tilman/xenulink.html)

Zoomerang (zoomerang.com/)

## Reference Tools

Educational Resources Information Center (ERIC) Database (askeric.org/Eric/)

E-Learning Glossary (www.learningcircuits.org/glossary.html)

MeansBusiness (database of extracts from business books, periodicals, and Web
   sites) (www.meansbusiness.com/)

National Training and Seminar Portal (Training and Seminar Locators)
   (www.tasl.com/)

RefDesk.com (www.refdesk.com/)

TechEncyclopedia (www.techweb.com/encyclopedia/)

Technology Grant News (www.technologygrantnews.com)

## Suggested Books and Articles

About.com. Digital Divide. (racerelations.about.com/msubdigdivide.htm?
   once=true&iam=ask&terms="digital+divide")

American Association of University Women. (2000). *Tech-Savvy: Educating girls
   in the New Computer Age.* New York: Marlowe. (www.aauw.org/2000/tech-
   savvy.html).

Benton Foundation. Digital Divide Network. (www.digitaldividenetwork.org/).

Bridges, William. (1991). *Managing Transitions: Making the Most of Change.*
   Reading, MA: Addison Wesley.

Brown, John Seely, and Duguid, Paul. (2001). *The Social Life of Information.*
   Boston: Harvard Business School Press.

Brunner, Cornelia, and Tally, William. (1999). *The New Media Literacy
   Handbook: An Educator's Guide to Bringing New Media into the Classroom.*
   New York: Anchor.

Burnside, Robert M. (July/August 2001). E-Learning for Adults: Who Has the
   Goods? *The Technology Source* (http://horizon.unc.edu/TS/default.
   asp?show=article&id=882).

Cairncross, Frances. (1997). *The Death of Distance: How the Communications Revolution Will Change Our Lives*. Boston: Harvard Business Press.

Clark, Ruth E. (1998). *Building Expertise: Cognitive Methods for Training and Performance Improvement*. Washington, DC: International Society for Performance Improvement.

Driscoll, Margaret, and Alexander, Larry. (1998). *Web-Based Training: Using Technology to Design Adult Learning Experiences*. San Francisco: Jossey-Bass.

Drucker, Peter. (1999). *Management Challenges for the 21st Century*. New York: Harper Business.

Ertmer, Peggy A., and Quinn, James. (1999). *The ID Casebook: Case Studies in Instructional Design*. Columbus, OH: Merrill-Prentice Hall.

Fister, Sarah. (July 2001). Use It or Lose it: Ten Ways to Improve Your WBT with Usability. *OnlineLearning Magazine* (www.onlinelearningmag.com/new/jul01/feature3.htm).

Gery, Gloria J. (1991). *Electronic Performance Support Systems*. Boston: Weingarten Publications.

Gilbert, Thomas F. (1978) *Human Competence: Engineering Worthy Performance*. New York: McGraw-Hill.

Hale, Judith A. (1998). *The Performance Consultant's Fieldbook*. San Francisco: Jossey-Bass.

Hall, Brandon. (1997). *Web-Based Training Cookbook*. New York: John Wiley & Sons.

Hammer, Michael, and Champy, James. (1993). *Reengineering the Corporation: A Manifesto for Business Revolution*. New York: Harper.

Hodgins, Wayne, and Connor, Marcia. (2000). Everything You Ever Wanted to Know About Learning Standards but Were Afraid to Ask, LiNE Zine (www.linezine.com/2.1/features/wheyewtkls.htm).

Horton, William K. (200). *Designing Web-Based Training: How to Teach Anyone Anything Anywhere Anytime*. New York: John Wiley & Sons.

Levine, Linda. (2001). *Integrating Knowledge and Processes in a Learning Organization* (www.brint.com/members/20120418/organizationallearning/).

Longmire, Warren. (March 2000). A Primer on Learning Objects, *Learning Circuits* (www.learningcircuits.org/mar2000/primer.html).

Mager, Robert M., and Pipe, Peter. (1985) *Analyzing Performance Problems*. Belmont, CA: Fearon.

Mager, Robert M. (1984). *Measuring Instructional Results*. Belmont, CA: Fearon.

Mager, Robert M. (1984). *Goal Analysis*. Belmont, CA: Fearon.

Morrison, James L., and Meister, Jeanne C. (July/August 2001). E-Learning in the Corporate University: An Interview with Jeanne Meister. *The Technology Source* (horizon.unc.edu/TS/default.asp?show=article&id=888).

Noble, David F. (1998). Digital Diploma Mills, Part II: The Coming Battle over Online Instruction (communication.ucsd.edu/dl/ddm2.html).

O'Gorman, Adam. (2001). The Application of Evolutionary Learning Theory in the Transition from Training to Performance Support (www.geocities.com/adamopolis/index.htm).

Pennsylvania State University. Web-Enhanced Learning Environment Strategies (www.ed.psu.edu/nasa/weletxt.html).

Reeves, Byron, and Nass, Clifford. (1999). *The Media Equation: How People Treat Computers, Television, and New Media Like Real People and Places.* Stanford, CA: CSLI Publications.

Robinson, Dana Gaines, and Robinson, James C. (1995). *Performance Consulting: Moving Beyond Training.* San Francisco: Berrett-Koehler.

Rosenberg, Marc J. (2001). *E-Learning: Strategies for Delivering Knowledge in the Digital Age.* New York: McGraw-Hill.

Rossett, Allison, and Gautier-Downes, Jeannette. H. (1991). *A Handbook of Job Aids.* San Francisco: Jossey-Bass/Pfeiffer.

Rossett, Allison, and Sheldon, Kendra. (2001). *Beyond the Podium: Delivering Training and Performance to a Digital World.* San Francisco: Jossey-Bass/Pfeiffer.

Rossett, Allison. (July 1997). That Was a Great Class, but..., *Training & Development* (www.astd.org/CMS/templates/index.html?template_id=1&articleid=10988).

Rossett, Allison. (1999). *First Things Fast: A Handbook for Performance Analysis.* San Francisco: Jossey-Bass.

Rossett, Allison (August 2000). Confessions of a Web Dropout. *Training, 37*(8), 100-99.

Rummler, Geary A., and Brache, Alan P. (1991). *Improving Performance: How to Manage the White Space in the Organizational Chart.* San Francisco: Jossey-Bass.

Ruyle, Kim E. (May/June 1998). The "Three Rs" of ROI, *Technical Training* (www.astd.org/virtual_community/comm_evaluation/ROI.pdf).

Schank, Roger C. (1997). *Virtual Learning: A Revolutionary Approach to Building a Highly Skilled Workforce.* New York: McGraw-Hill.

Senge, Peter M., Kleiner, Art, Roberts, Charlotte, Ross, Richard, Roth, George, and Smith, Bryan. (1999). *The Dance of Change: The Challenges to Sustaining Momentum in Learning Organizations.* New York: Doubleday.

Silberman, M. (Ed.). (2000). *The Consultant's Tool Kit.* San Francisco: Jossey-Bass.

Stewart, Thomas A. (1997). *Intellectual Capital: The New Wealth of Organizations.* New York: Doubleday/Currency.

Stolovitch, Harold D., and Keeps, Erica J. (Eds.). (1999). *Handbook of Performance Technology*, 2nd edition. San Francisco: Jossey-Bass.

Tiwana, Amrit. (2000). *The Knowledge Management Toolkit.* Upper Saddle River, NJ: Prentice Hall.

Twigg, Carol A. (2000). *Who Owns Online Courses and Course Materials? Intellectual Property Policies for a New Learning Environment* (www.center.rpi.edu/PewSym/mono2.html).

University of Texas System. (2000). Copyright Crash Course (www.utsystem.edu/OGC/IntellectualProperty/cprtindx.htm).

Urdan, Trace A., and Weggan, Cornelia C. (2000) *Corporate E-Learning: Exploring a New Frontier* (www.wrhambrecht.com/research/coverage/elearning/ir/ir_explore_a.pdf).

U.S. Commerce Department, National Telecommunications and Information Administration, Office of Policy Coordination and Management. Falling Through the Net (www.digitaldivide.gov).

## Related Journals and Magazines

*American Journal of Distance Education* (www.ed.psu.edu/acsde/ajde/jour.asp)

*American Journal of Education* (www.journals.uchicago.edu/AJE/home.html)

*Aspects of Educational Technology*—Yearly Series

*Canadian Journal of Educational Communication*

*Chronicle of Higher Education* (chronicle.merit.edu/)

*CIO Magazine* (www.cio.com)

*Computers and Education* (www.elsevier.nl/inca/publications/store/3/4/7/)

*Computers in Human Behavior* (www.elsevier.nl/inca/publications/store/7/5/9/)

*Computers in the Schools*

*Computing Teacher*

*The Distance Educator* (www.distance-educator.com)

*Education Policy Analysis* (olam.ed.asu.edu/epaa/)

*Education Week* (www.edweek.org/)

*Educational Computer Magazine*

*Educational Media International*

*Educational Technology* (www.bookstoread.com/etp/default.htm)

*Educational Technology and Society* (ifets.ieee.org/periodical/)

*Educational Technology Research and Development* (Association for Educational Communication and Technology) (www.aect.org)

*EDUCAUSE Review* (www.educause.edu/pub/er/erm.html)

*Elearningmag.com* (elearningmag.com/)

*Elearningpost* (www.elearningpost.com)

*EPSS Newsletter* (www.epssinfosite.com/)

*Exchanges: The On-Line Journal of Teaching and Learning in the CSU* (www.exchangesjournal.org/)

*HR Magazine* (www.shrm.org/hrmagazine/)

*HRD Quarterly* (www.hrdq.com/)

*Innovations in Education and Teaching International* (Staff and Educational Development Association) (www.journals.tandf.co.uk/journals/routledge/14703297.html)

*Journal of Asynchronous Learning Networks* (www.aln.org/alnweb/journal/jaln.htm)

*Journal of Computers in Mathematics and Science Teaching* (Association for the Advancement of Computing in Education) (www.aace.org/pubs/jcmst/index.html)

*Journal of Computing in Teacher Education* (International Society for Technology in Education) (www.iste.org/jcte/index.html)

*Journal of Continuing Higher Education* (www-unix.oit.umass.edu/~carolm/jche/)

*Journal of Educational Computing Research* (baywood.com)

*Journal of Educational Multimedia and Hypermedia* (Association for the Advancement of Computing in Education) (www.aace.org/pubs/jemh/index.html)

*Journal of Educational Technology Systems* (baywood.com)

*Journal of Research on Technology in Education* (International Society for Technology in Education) (www.iste.org/jrte/)

*Learning & Leading with Technology* (International Society for Technology in Education) (www.iste.org/L&L/index.html)

*Learning Circuits* (American Society for Training & Development) (www.learningcircuits.org)

*Lguide* (www.lguide.com)

*Online Learning Magazine* (formerly *Inside Technology Training*) (onlinelearningmag.com)

*Performance Improvement Journal* (International Society for Performance Improvement) (www.ispi.org/)

*Performance Improvement Quarterly* (International Society for Performance Improvement) (www.ispi.org/)

San Diego State University library listing of electronic journals and magazines (infodome.sdsu.edu/research/ejournals/ejournals.shtml)

*Syllabus* (www.syllabus.com/)

*T+D* (formerly *Training and Development*) (American Society for Training & Development) (www.astd.org/virtual_community/td_magazine/)

*Tech Trends* (Association for Educational Communications and Technology)

*Technological Horizons in Education (T.H.E. Journal)* (www.thejournal.com/)

*The Technology Source* (horizon.unc.edu/TS/)

*Training* (www.trainingmag.com/)

*Training Business E-Visory* (mailto: esfusion@sellmoretraining.com)

*Training Research Journal* (www.bookstoread.com/etp/default-d.htm)

*Webnet Journal* (Association for the Advancement of Computing in Education) (www.aace.org/pubs/webnet/)

## Professional Organizations

American Center for the Study of Distance Education (www.ed.psu.edu/ACSDE/)

American Educational Research Association (www.aera.net/)

American Society for Training and Development (www.astd.org/)

Association for Educational Communications and Technology (www.aect.org/)

Association for the Advancement of Computing in Education (www.aace.org)

Canadian Association for Distance Education (www.cade-aced.ca/)

Distance Education and Training Council (www.detc.org/)

EProacte (European Union, Information Society Programme) (www.proacte.com)

Instructional Telecommunications Council (www.itcnetwork.org/)

International Council for Educational Media (www.educa.ch/icem/index.html)

International Council for Open and Distance Education (www.icde.org/)
International Society for Performance Improvement (www.ispi.org/)
Organization Development Network (www.odnetwork.org/)
Society for Human Resource Management (www.shrm.org/)
United States Distance Learning Association (www.usdla.org/)

# Index